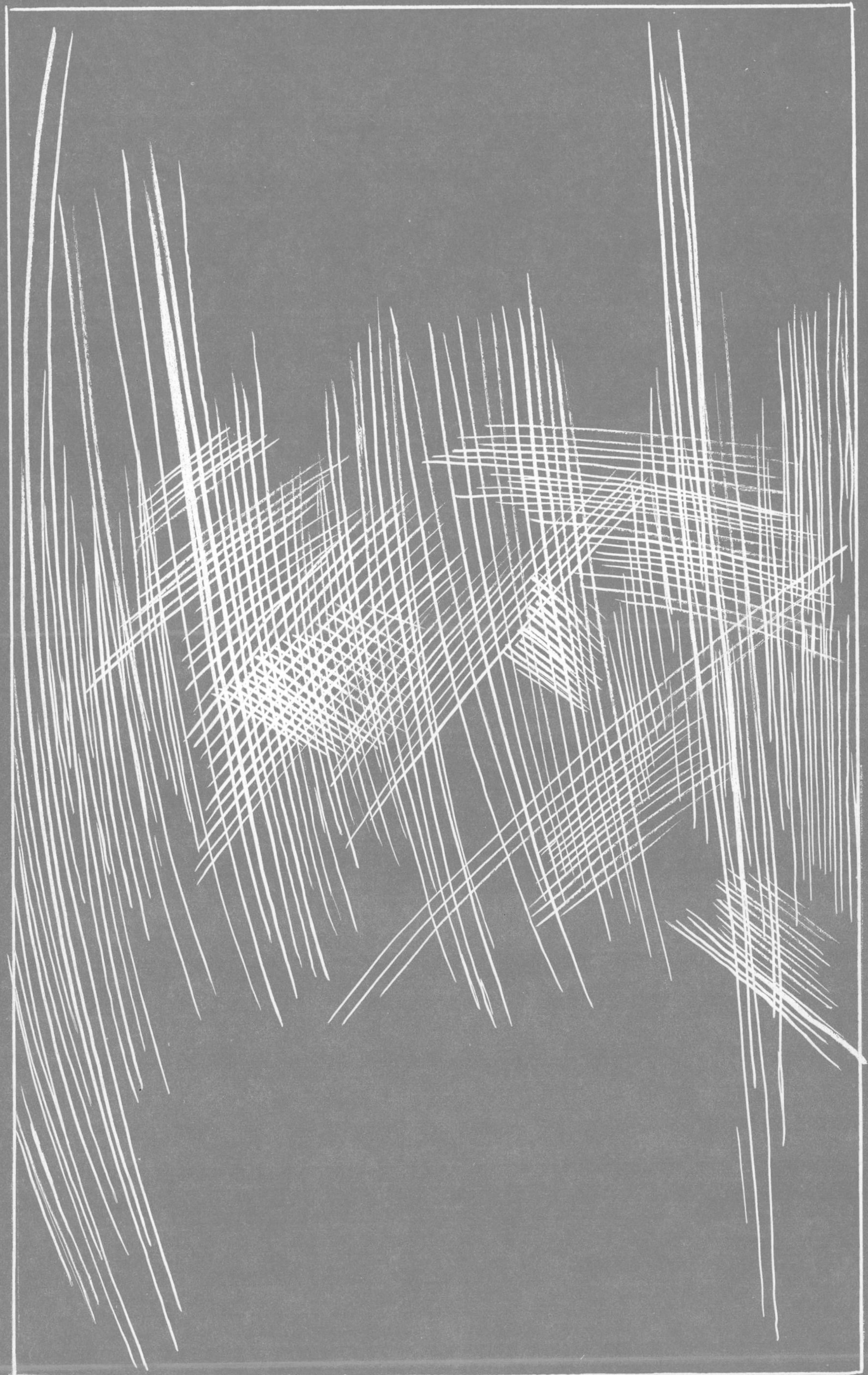

# the STRANGE DEATH of ALEX RAYMOND

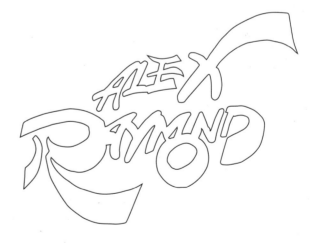

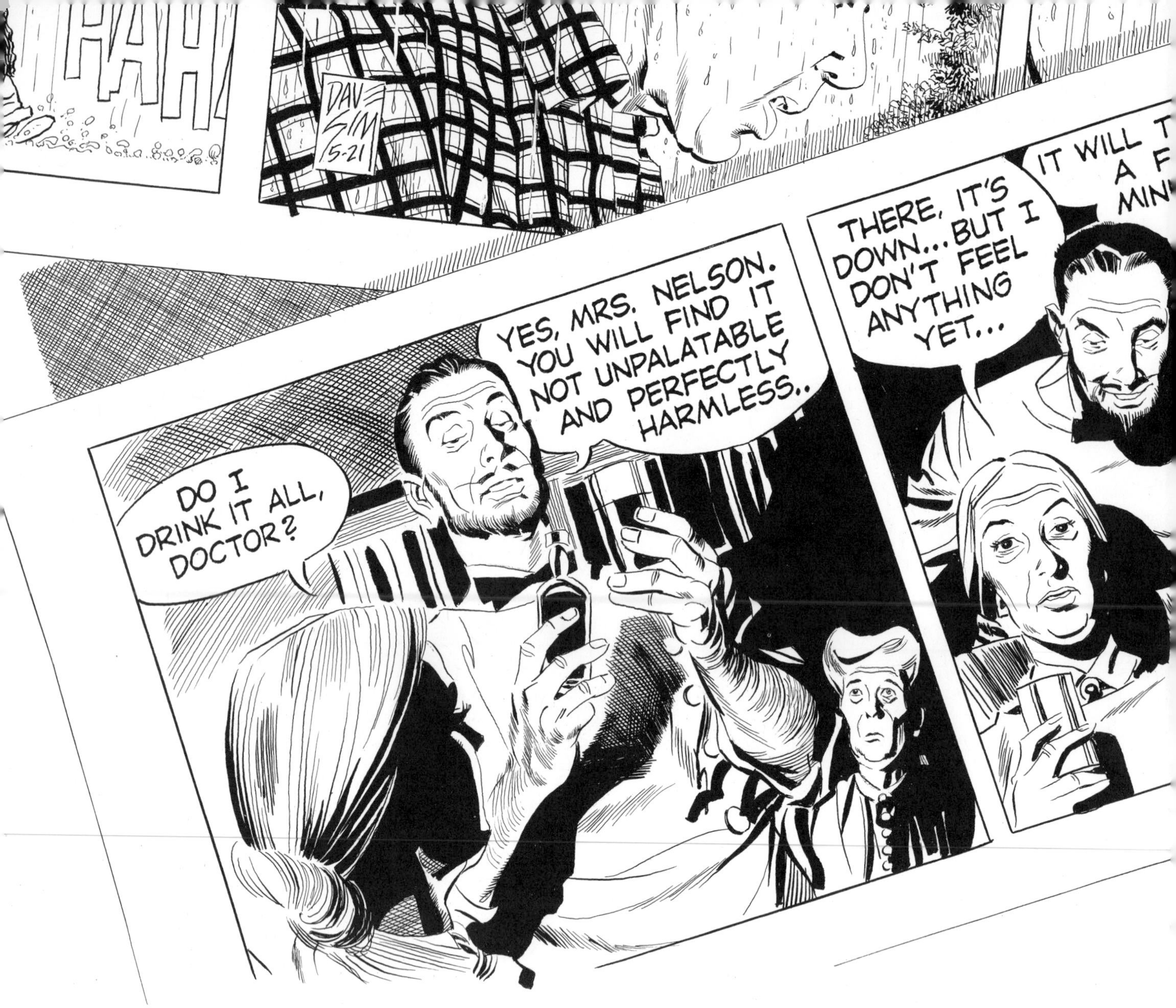
DAVE SIM 5-21
DO I DRINK IT ALL, DOCTOR?
YES, MRS. NELSON. YOU WILL FIND IT NOT UNPALATABLE AND PERFECTLY HARMLESS..
THERE, IT'S DOWN... BUT I DON'T FEEL ANYTHING YET...

**THE STRANGE DEATH OF ALEX RAYMOND**
AUGUST 2021. FIRST PRINTING.

**Written by Dave Sim and Carson Grubaugh.**
**Drawn by Dave Sim and Carson Grubaugh.**

**Research and proofreading by Eddie Khanna.**
**Digital production, book design, digital lettering, and additional art and hand lettering by Sean Michael Robinson for Living the Line.**
**Proofreading by Alma García.**
**Photo reference of Jack VanDyke provided by Devon Avant.**
**Additional lettering by David Birdsong and Benjamin Hobbs.**



ISBN- 13: 9781736860502

PRINTED IN CANADA by Marquis Imprimeur, Montmagny, Quebec.

Special Thanks to:
Jack VanDyke, manager
LOCAL HEROES
COMIC BOOKS &
GRAPHIC NOVELS
Billy Ireland Research Library
OHIO STATE UNIVERSITY
Bird Library
SYRACUSE UNIVERSITY
Arlen Schumer

## foreword by

# eddie CAMPBELL

## (author/illustrator of *From Hell, Alec, Bacchus, The Lovely Horrible Stuff*)

As a ten-year-old, from the first time I saw Jack Kirby's signature on a comic, I was more interested in what the artist was doing than in the actions of Thor or any of the characters. Which is not unlike saying that a normally intelligent person would be more interested in what the Beatles were doing than in what Sgt. Pepper was up to. I followed Kirby's lines and shapes and figures around the page, and off the page. In later years my own comics have often been about artists and what they do and so I am drawn immediately to this one by Dave Sim.

Sim's subjects were the artists of what we call the photorealist style. The comics orthodoxy has tried to sideline it, but there has been a small revival of interest in the style. A history of it exists, but not all in one place, or in a book. Sim marks out the parameters for us, drawing himself as a cold case curmudgeon in a gallery, giving us an open-ended shaggy dog story that outlines a mystery, unsolvable at this late date. He circles around it in ever constricting maneuvers into a subatomic world of artist feuds and jealousies and affairs and brushed inklines, taking apart the panels of old comics, copying them and delving into them for meaning. It's like the great English novel *Tristram Shandy*, in which every manner of digression keeps the narrator from arriving at the moment of his own birth. In this one life is at its other end, with the artists Alex Raymond and Stan Drake suspended in midair in a doomed sports car, a microsecond from catastrophe while Dave Sim ponders matters metaphysical, mechanical, conspiratorial, and art-historical. To say that it is all about the traveling and not the arriving could be a bad taste joke.

Sim was not content to evaluate this peculiar corner of art until he himself had mastered its technique, so he has thrown out all of his material prior to the instant of mastery, those situations and ruminations that we are certain we saw in the published part-issues and wonder why they've been ruthlessly culled. He was a pen guy in the 1990s when he and I crossed each other's paths several times, and now he masters the brush, like some ancient philosopher-calligrapher. And if he doesn't like me putting the thoughts in his balloon, I can only say that's what he's been doing with Alex Ramond, Stan Drake, and the rest. All of them late, very. The obsession kills the obsessor. The book must not end.

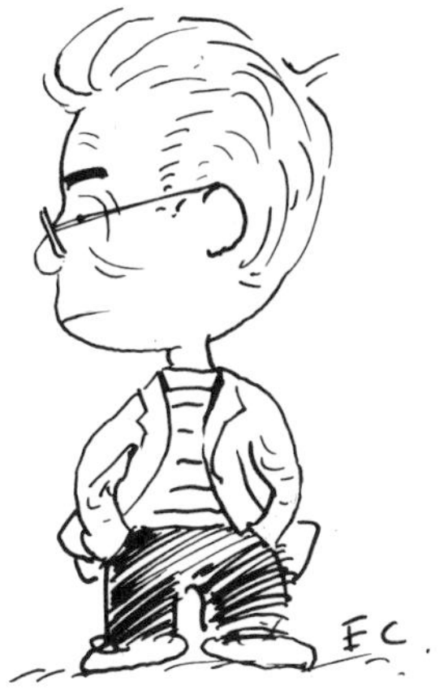
EC.

— Eddie Campbell, March 2021

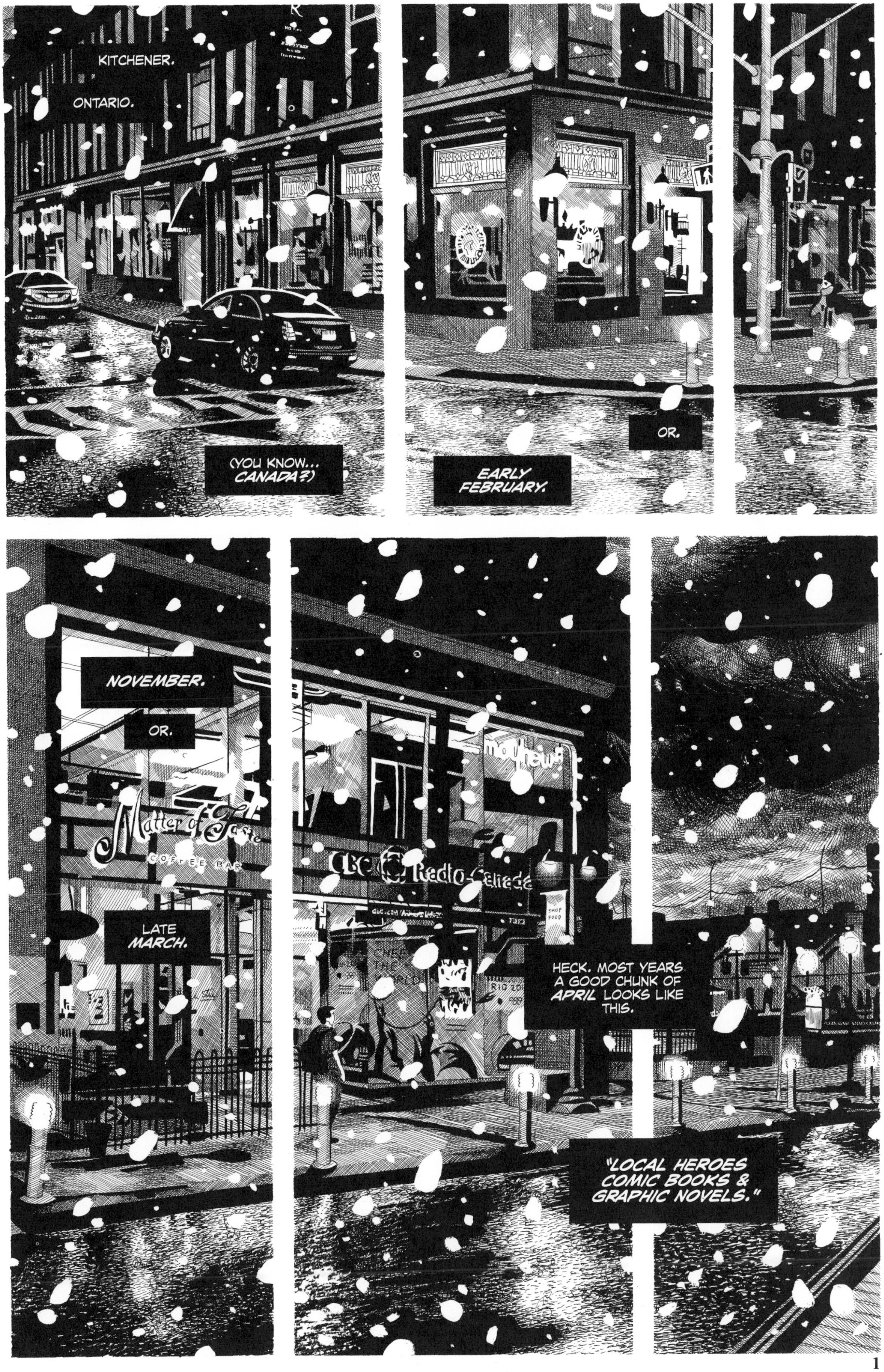
KITCHENER.
ONTARIO.
(YOU KNOW... CANADA?)
EARLY FEBRUARY.
OR.
NOVEMBER.
OR.
Matter of Taste
COFFEE BAR
LATE MARCH.
CBC Radio-Canada
mayhew
HECK. MOST YEARS A GOOD CHUNK OF APRIL LOOKS LIKE THIS.
"LOCAL HEROES COMIC BOOKS & GRAPHIC NOVELS."

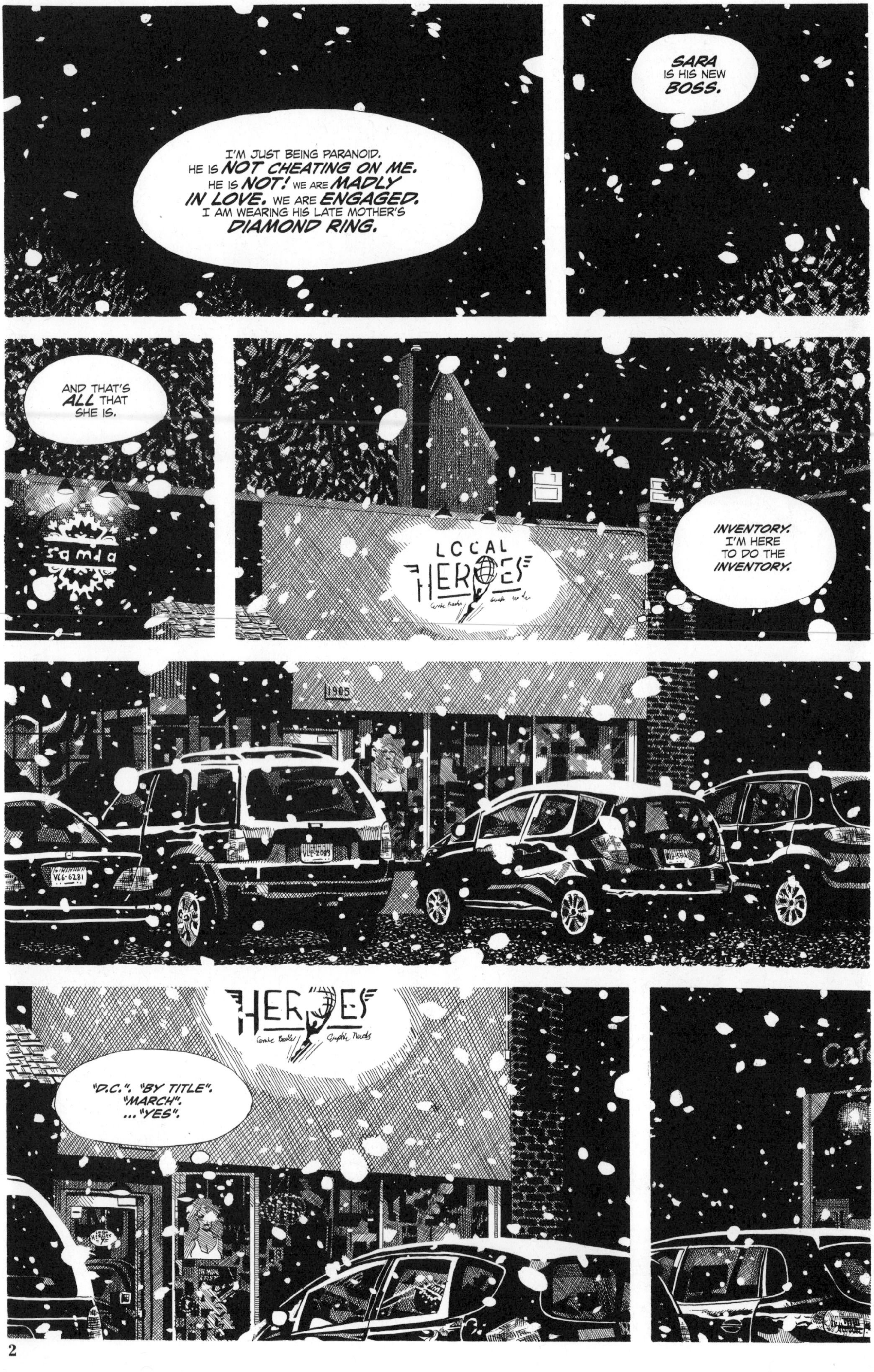
I'M JUST BEING PARANOID. HE IS NOT CHEATING ON ME. HE IS NOT! WE ARE MADLY IN LOVE. WE ARE ENGAGED. I AM WEARING HIS LATE MOTHER'S DIAMOND RING.
SARA IS HIS NEW BOSS.
AND THAT'S ALL THAT SHE IS.
LOCAL HEROES
INVENTORY. I'M HERE TO DO THE INVENTORY.
1905
HEROES
"D.C.". "BY TITLE". "MARCH". ..."YES".

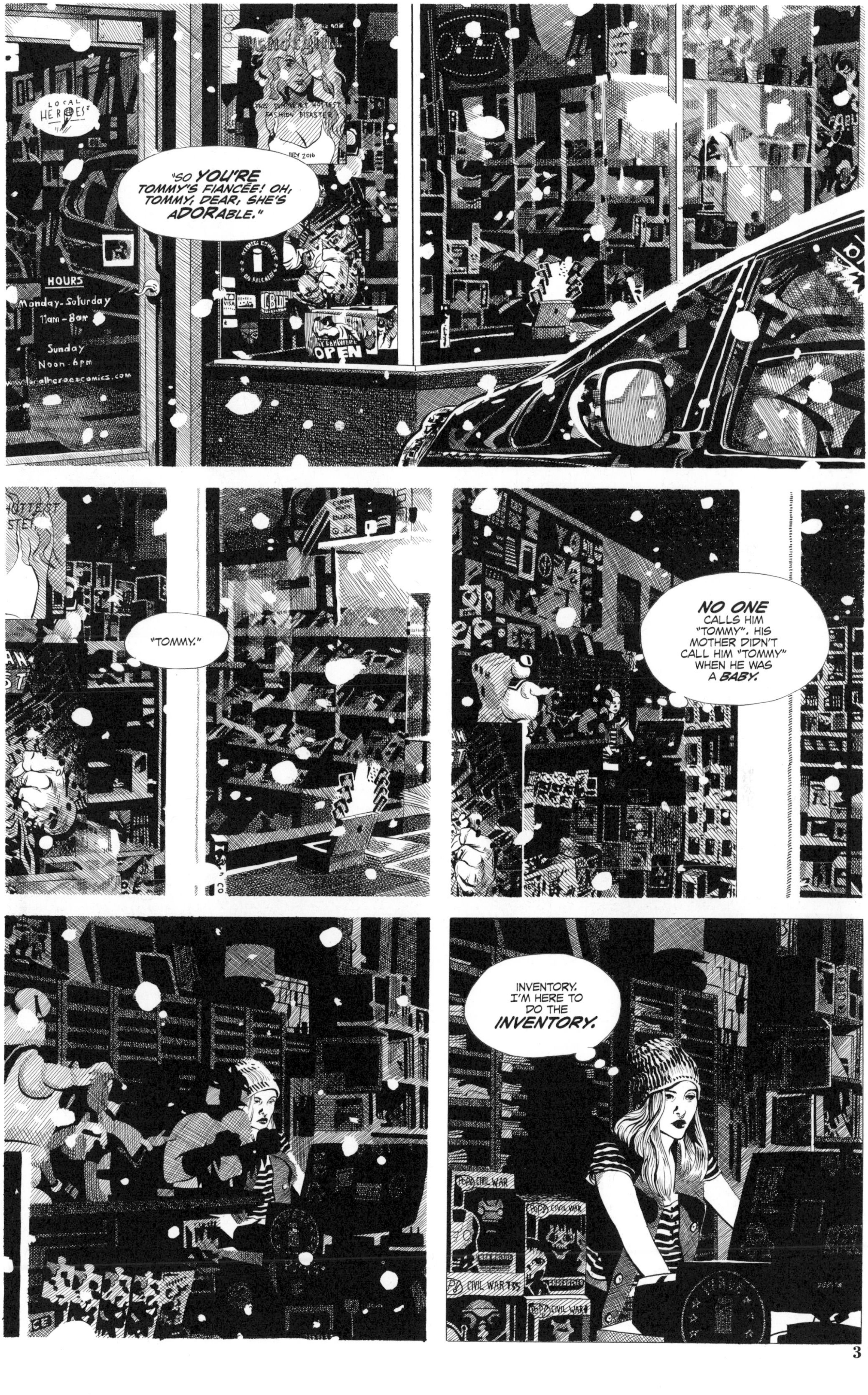
LOCAL HEROES
HOURS
Monday-Saturday
11am-8pm
Sunday
Noon-6pm
"SO YOU'RE TOMMY'S FIANCÉE! OH, TOMMY, DEAR, SHE'S ADORABLE."
OPEN
"TOMMY."
NO ONE CALLS HIM "TOMMY". HIS MOTHER DIDN'T CALL HIM "TOMMY" WHEN HE WAS A BABY.
INVENTORY. I'M HERE TO DO THE INVENTORY.
CIVIL WAR

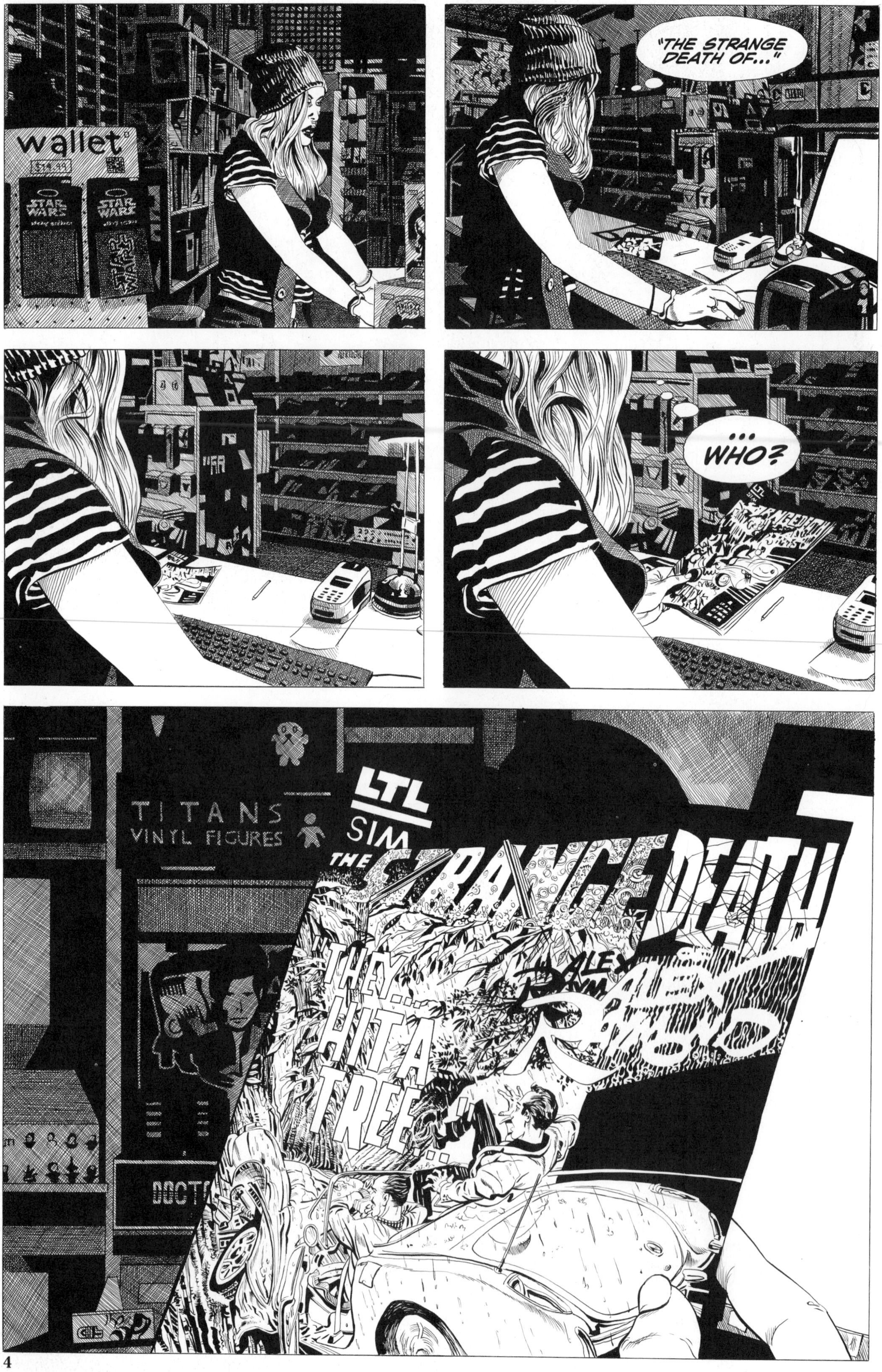
wallet
STAR WARS
STAR WARS
"THE STRANGE DEATH OF..."
... WHO?
TITANS
VINYL FIGURES
LTL
SIM
THE
DOCTO

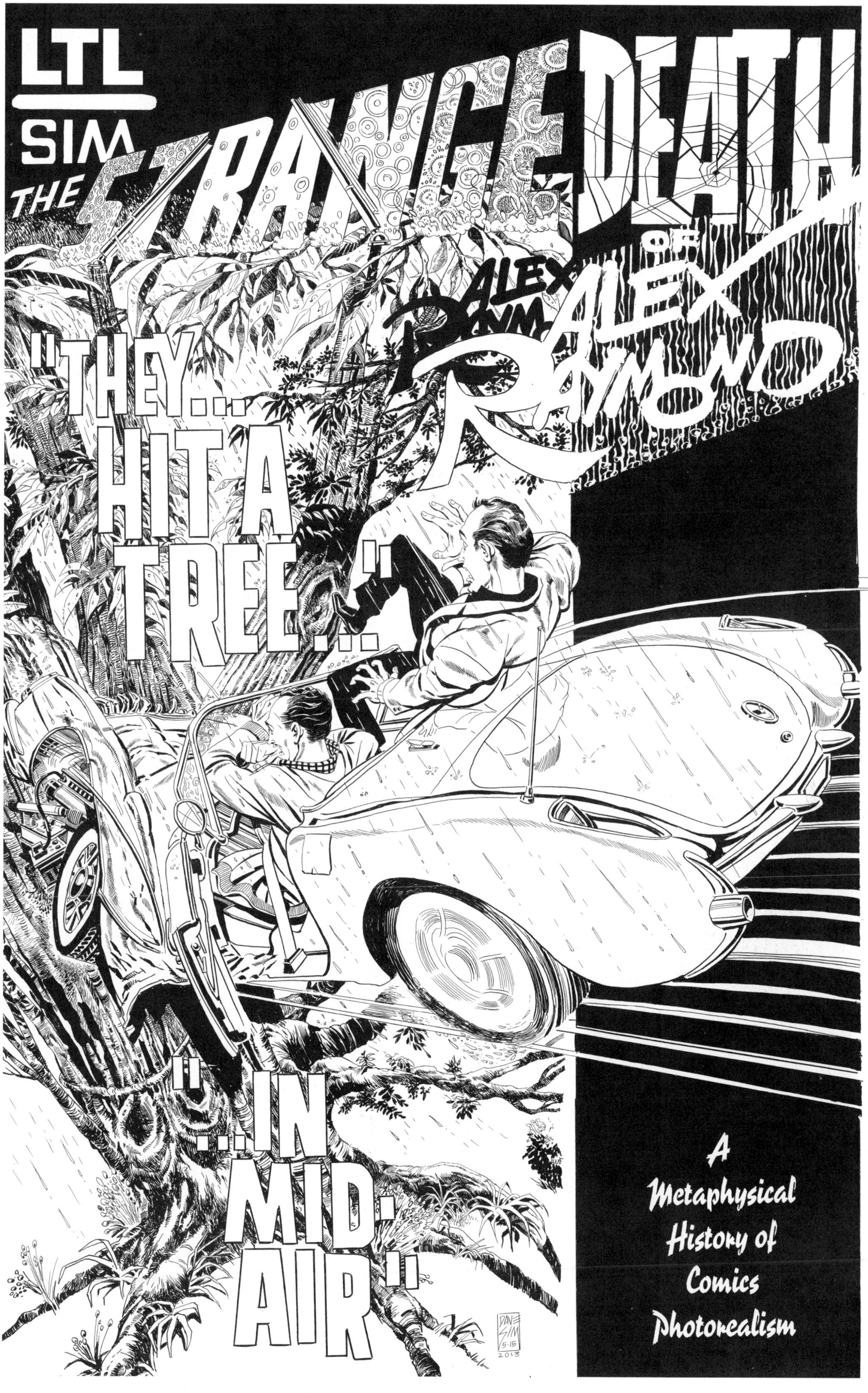
LTL
SIM
THE STRANGE DEATH
OF
ALEX RAYMOND
"THEY... HIT A TREE..."
"...IN MID-AIR"
A Metaphysical History of Comics Photorealism
DAVE SIM 5-15 2013

# THE STRANGE DEATH OF ALEX RAYMOND

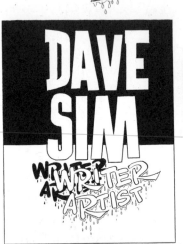

**DAVE SIM** WRITER & ARTIST

ROY THOMAS' INDISPENSABLE MAGAZINE *ALTER EGO* NO. 113 OCTOBER 2012... PART FOUR OF JIM AMASH'S EPIC-LENGTH *LEONARD STARR INTERVIEW*

 SIM

 TITLES

COMICRAFT's (JOE KUBERT) FONT

LETTERING

For international rights, contact livingthelinepublishing@gmail.com

**LTL**
www.LIVINGTHELINE.com

Sean Robinson, President & Publisher • Sean Robinson, Editor-in-Chief • Sean Robinson, EVP/Sr. Art Director • Sean Robinson, Chief Financial Officer • Sean Robinson, Chief Accounting Officer • Sean Robinson, SVP of Sales and Marketing • Sean Robinson, Associate Publisher • Sean Robinson, VP of New Product Development • Sean Robinson, VP of Digital Services • Sean Robinson, Editorial Director, Graphic Novels and Collections • Sean Robinson, Sr. Director, Licensing & Business Development

Sean Robinson, LTL Founder

Facebook: facebook.com/livingtheline • Twitter: @ltlpublishing • YouTube: youtube.com/ltlpublishing
Tumblr: tumblr.ltlpublishing.com • Instagram: instagram.com/ltlpublishing

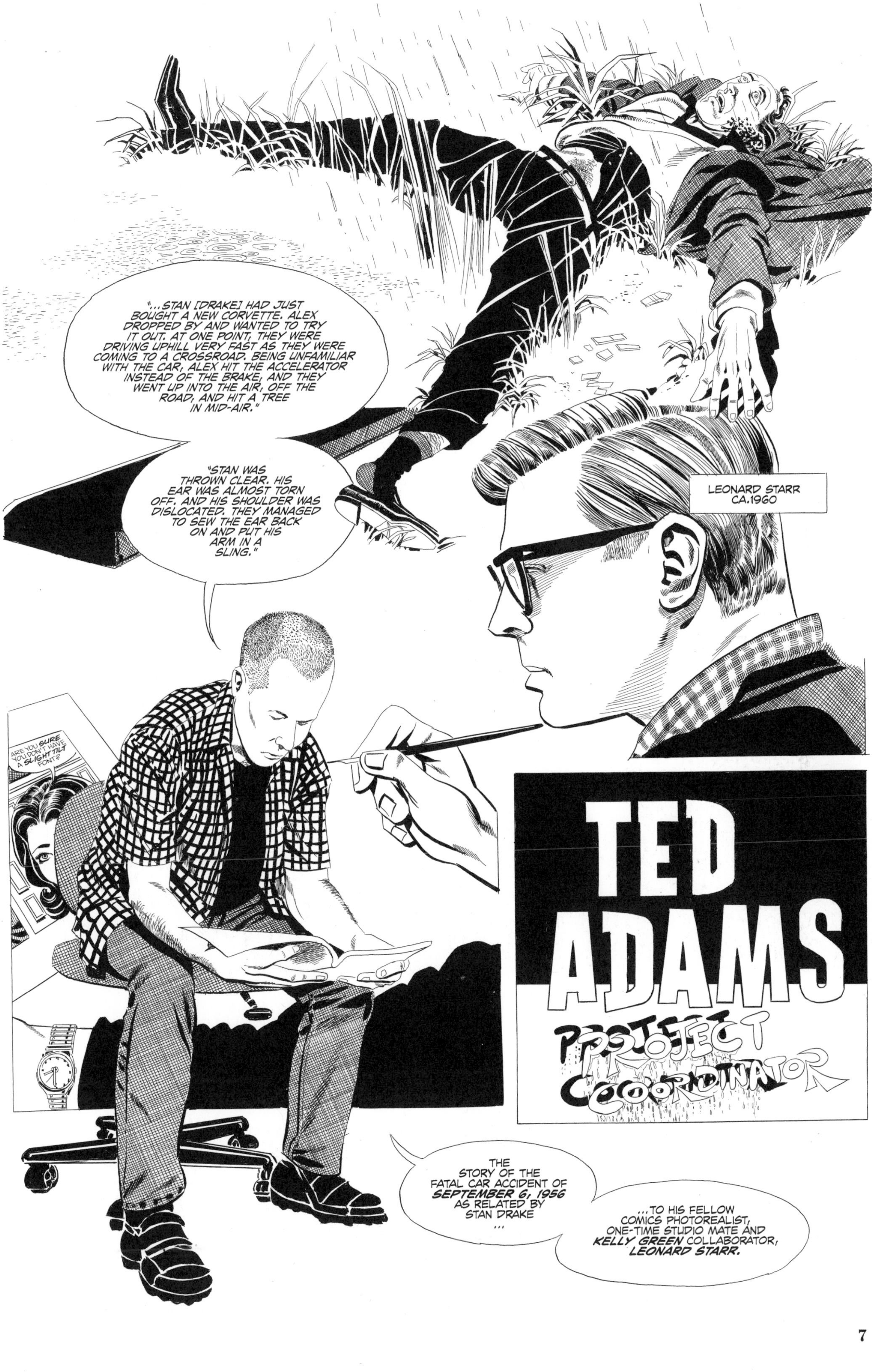
"...STAN [DRAKE] HAD JUST BOUGHT A NEW CORVETTE. ALEX DROPPED BY AND WANTED TO TRY IT OUT. AT ONE POINT, THEY WERE DRIVING UPHILL VERY FAST AS THEY WERE COMING TO A CROSSROAD. BEING UNFAMILIAR WITH THE CAR, ALEX HIT THE ACCELERATOR INSTEAD OF THE BRAKE, AND THEY WENT UP INTO THE AIR, OFF THE ROAD, AND HIT A TREE IN MID-AIR."
"STAN WAS THROWN CLEAR. HIS EAR WAS ALMOST TORN OFF. AND HIS SHOULDER WAS DISLOCATED. THEY MANAGED TO SEW THE EAR BACK ON AND PUT HIS ARM IN A SLING."
LEONARD STARR CA.1960
ARE YOU SURE YOU DON'T HAVE A SLIGHT TILT FONT?
TED ADAMS
PROJECT COORDINATOR
THE STORY OF THE FATAL CAR ACCIDENT OF SEPTEMBER 6, 1956 AS RELATED BY STAN DRAKE ...
...TO HIS FELLOW COMICS PHOTOREALIST, ONE-TIME STUDIO MATE AND KELLY GREEN COLLABORATOR, LEONARD STARR.

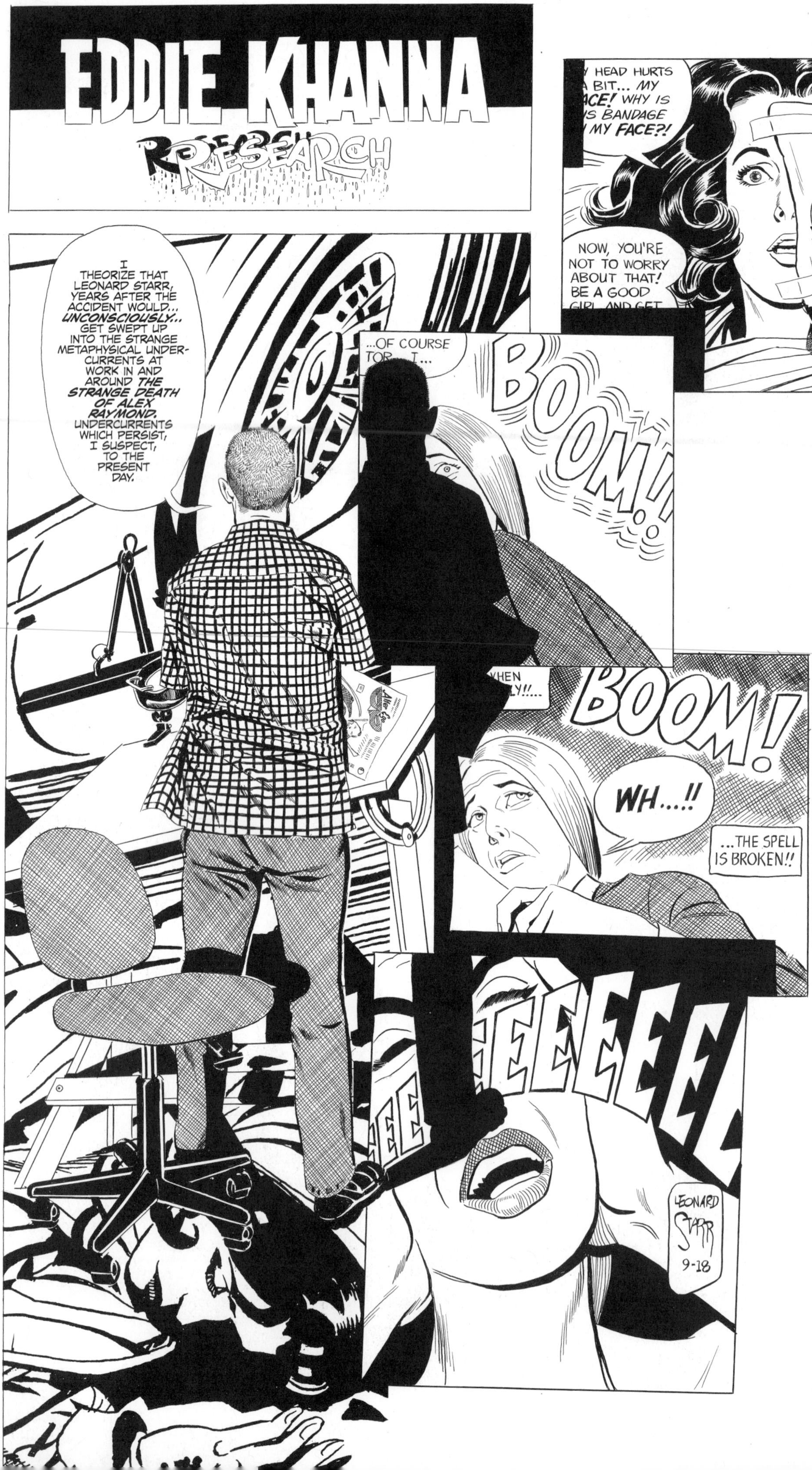
EDDIE KHANNA
RESEARCH
I THEORIZE THAT LEONARD STARR, YEARS AFTER THE ACCIDENT WOULD... UNCONSCIOUSLY... GET SWEPT UP INTO THE STRANGE METAPHYSICAL UNDER-CURRENTS AT WORK IN AND AROUND THE STRANGE DEATH OF ALEX RAYMOND. UNDERCURRENTS WHICH PERSIST, I SUSPECT, TO THE PRESENT DAY.
Y HEAD HURTS A BIT... MY ACE! WHY IS IS BANDAGE N MY FACE?!
NOW, YOU'RE NOT TO WORRY ABOUT THAT! BE A GOOD
...OF COURSE
BOOM!!
WHEN
BOOM!
WH...!!
...THE SPELL IS BROKEN!!
EEEEEEEEEL
LEONARD STARR 9-18

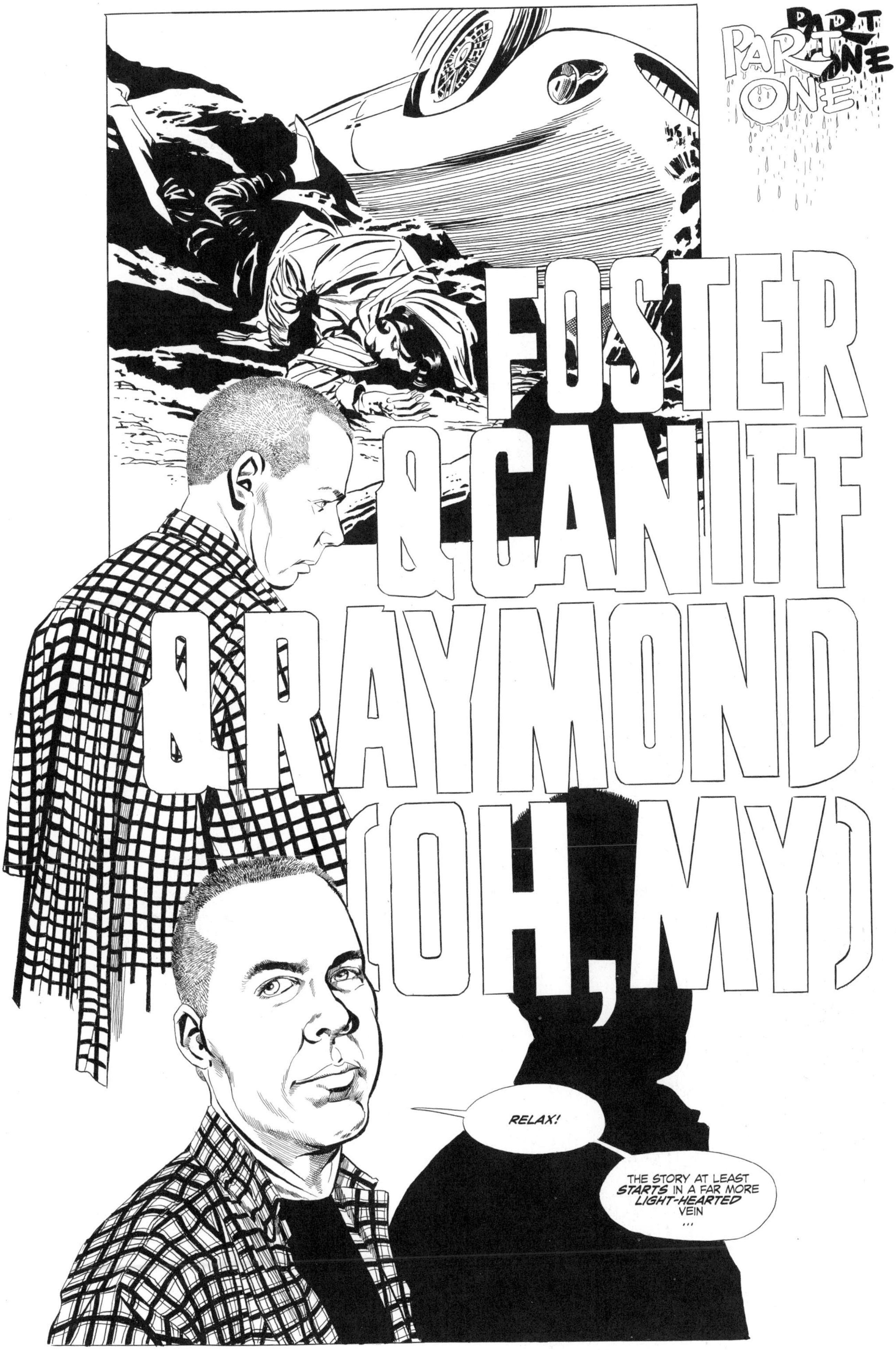
PART ONE
FOSTER & CANIFF & RAYMOND (OH, MY)
RELAX!
THE STORY AT LEAST STARTS IN A FAR MORE LIGHT-HEARTED VEIN ...

MAYBE...

AARDVARK-VANAHEIM presents

# glamourpuss

**1**
MAR

"TOP SECRET ORIGIN of glamourpuss!!"

YOU @*#!ING PUT ME ON THE COVER?!

FIRST APPEARANCE of SKANKO glamourpuss' EVIL TWIN!

SO, GLAMOURPUSS... HOW DOES IT FEEL TO STAR IN YOUR OWN COMIC BOOK?

FIRST APPEARANCE of DR. NORM

GOOD.

VERY GOOD.

FINE!

NEAR MINT, IN FACT!

SORRY ABOUT THAT, COMIC GEEK PEOPLE...

THEY DON'T LET GLAMOURPUSS WRITE HER OWN MATERIAL

...TOO... LIGHT-HEARTED.

TWITCH.

STILL TRYING TO FIGURE OUT HOW IT ALL WENT SO...*TERRIBLY WRONG*... ...SO...*QUICKLY*.

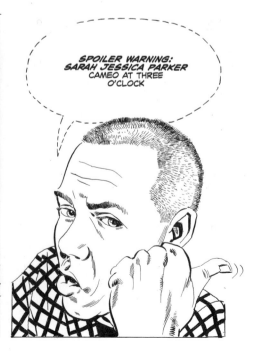

SPOILER WARNING: SARAH JESSICA PARKER CAMEO AT THREE O'CLOCK

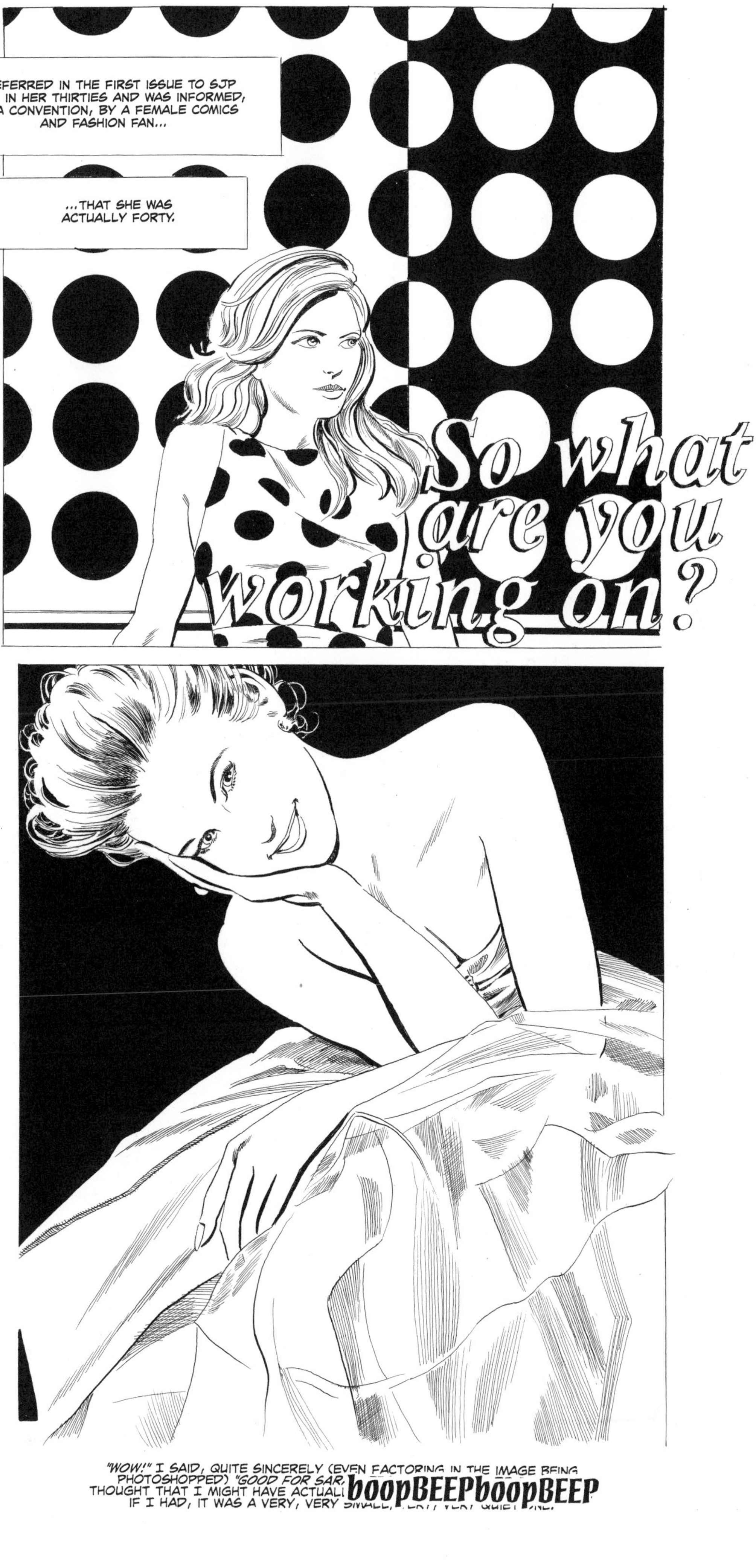

I REFERRED IN THE FIRST ISSUE TO SJP BEING IN HER THIRTIES AND WAS INFORMED, AT A CONVENTION, BY A FEMALE COMICS AND FASHION FAN...
...THAT SHE WAS ACTUALLY FORTY.
So what are you working on?
"WOW!" I SAID, QUITE SINCERELY (EVEN FACTORING IN THE IMAGE BEING
PHOTOSHOPPED) "GOOD FOR SAR,
THOUGHT THAT I MIGHT HAVE ACTUAL
IF I HAD, IT WAS A VERY, VERY
boopBEEPboopBEEP

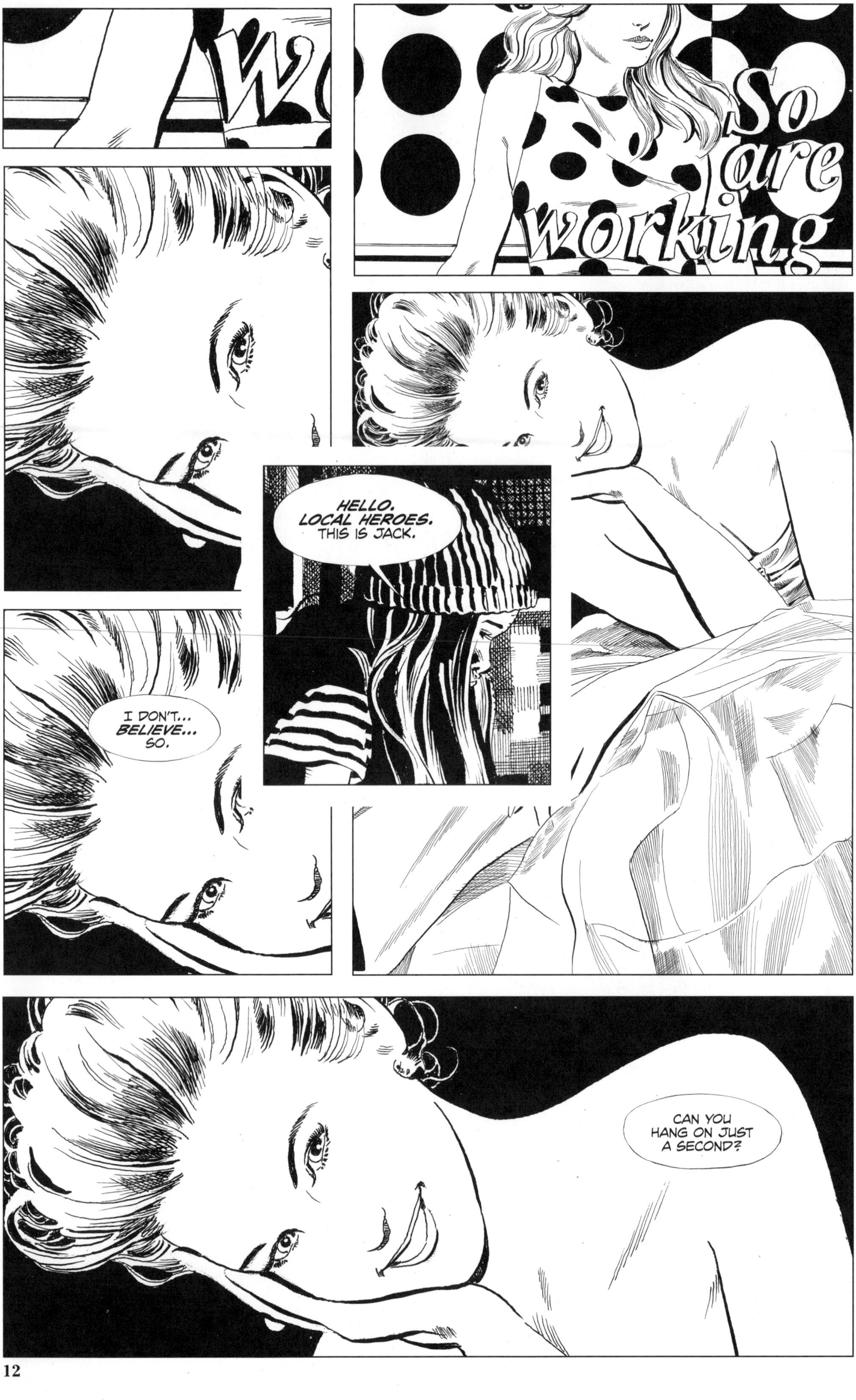
Wo
So
are
working
HELLO.
LOCAL HEROES.
THIS IS JACK.
I DON'T...
BELIEVE...
SO.
CAN YOU
HANG ON JUST
A SECOND?

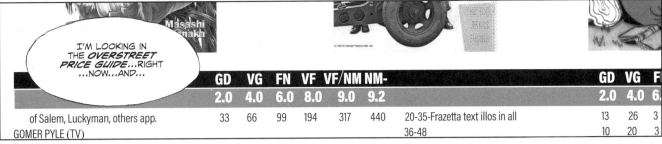

| | GD 2.0 | VG 4.0 | FN 6.0 | VF 8.0 | VF/NM 9.0 | NM- 9.2 | | GD 2.0 | VG 4.0 | F 6. |
|---|---|---|---|---|---|---|---|---|---|---|
| of Salem, Luckyman, others app. | 33 | 66 | 99 | 194 | 317 | 440 | 20-35-Frazetta text illos in all | 13 | 26 | 3 |
| GOMER PYLE (TV) | | | | | | | 36-48 | 10 | 20 | 3 |

**GOMER PYLE (TV)**
**Gold Key:** July, 1966 - No. 3, Oct, 1967

| | | | | | | |
|---|---|---|---|---|---|---|
| 1-Photo front/back-c | 7 | 14 | 21 | 46 | 86 | 125 |
| 2,3 | 5 | 10 | 15 | 34 | 60 | 85 |

**GON**
**DC Comics (Paradox Press):** July, 1996 - No. 4, Oct, 1996; No. 5, 1997 ($5.95, B&W, digest-size, limited series)
1-5: Misadventures of baby dinosaur; 1-Gon. 2-Gon Again. 3-Gon:Here Today,

36-48
**GOOFY SU**
**GOON, THE**
**Avatar Pre**
1-Eric Pow
2
3
.... Rough St
Rough St

nn-Tanaka-c/a/scripts                                              1
**GON WILD**
**DC Comics (Paradox Press):** 1997  ($9.95, B&W, digest-
nn-Tanaka-c/a/scripts in all. (Rep. Gon #3,4)                      1
**GOODBYE MR. CHIPS** (See Movie Comics)
**GOOD GIRL ART QUARTERLY**

"WOW! I SAID, QUITE SINCERELY (EVEN FACTORING IN THE IMAGE BEING PHOTOSHOPPED) "GOOD FOR SARAH JESSICA PARKER!" BRIEFLY, I THOUGHT THAT I MIGHT HAVE ACTUALLY REACHED A WHOLE NEW AUDIENCE. IF I HAD IT WAS A VERY, VERY SMALL, VERY, VERY QUIET ONE.

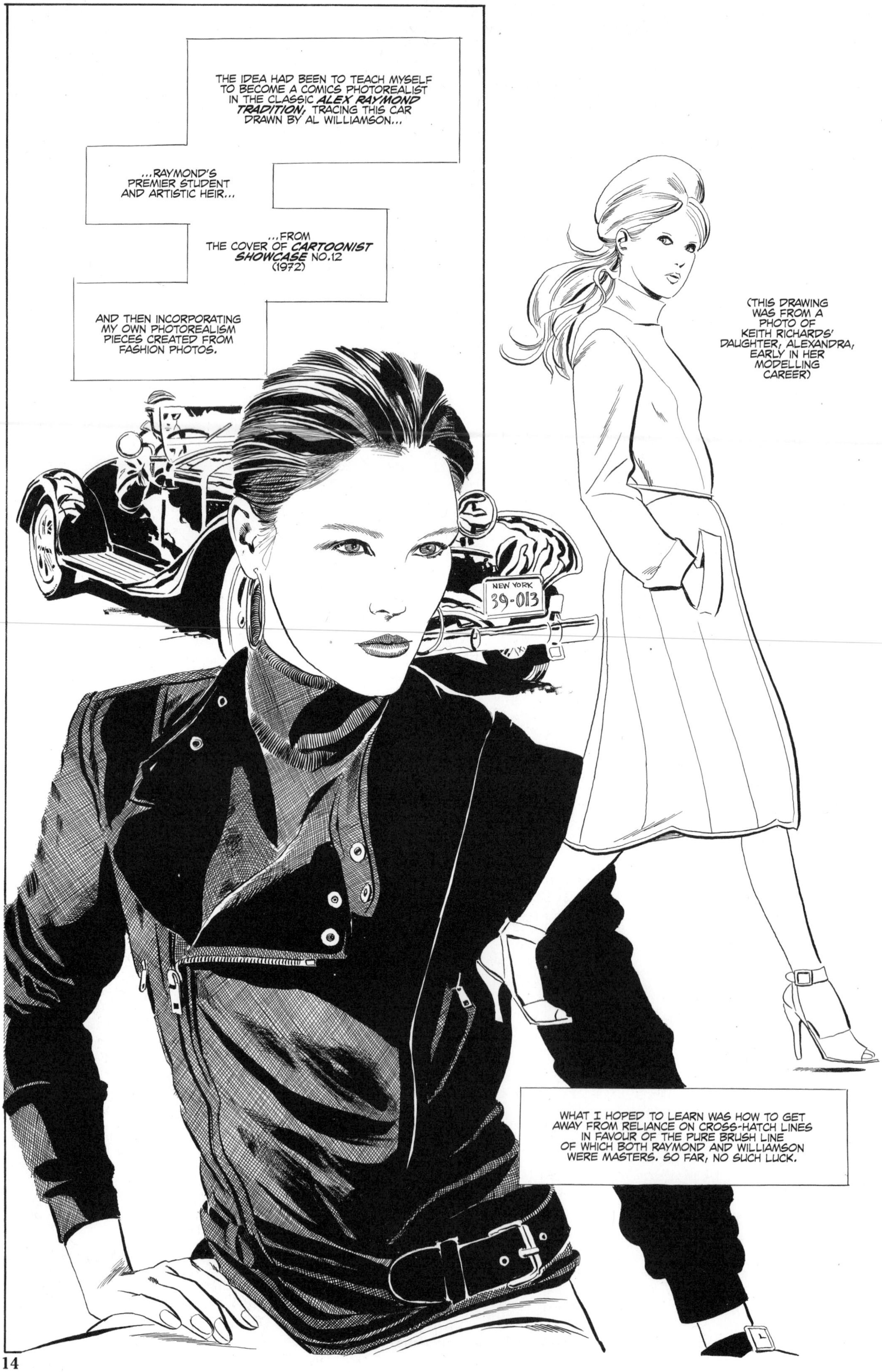
THE IDEA HAD BEEN TO TEACH MYSELF TO BECOME A COMICS PHOTOREALIST IN THE CLASSIC ALEX RAYMOND TRADITION, TRACING THIS CAR DRAWN BY AL WILLIAMSON...
...RAYMOND'S PREMIER STUDENT AND ARTISTIC HEIR...
...FROM THE COVER OF CARTOONIST SHOWCASE NO.12 (1972)
AND THEN INCORPORATING MY OWN PHOTOREALISM PIECES CREATED FROM FASHION PHOTOS.
(THIS DRAWING WAS FROM A PHOTO OF KEITH RICHARDS' DAUGHTER, ALEXANDRA, EARLY IN HER MODELLING CAREER)
NEW YORK
39-013
WHAT I HOPED TO LEARN WAS HOW TO GET AWAY FROM RELIANCE ON CROSS-HATCH LINES IN FAVOUR OF THE PURE BRUSH LINE OF WHICH BOTH RAYMOND AND WILLIAMSON WERE MASTERS. SO FAR, NO SUCH LUCK.

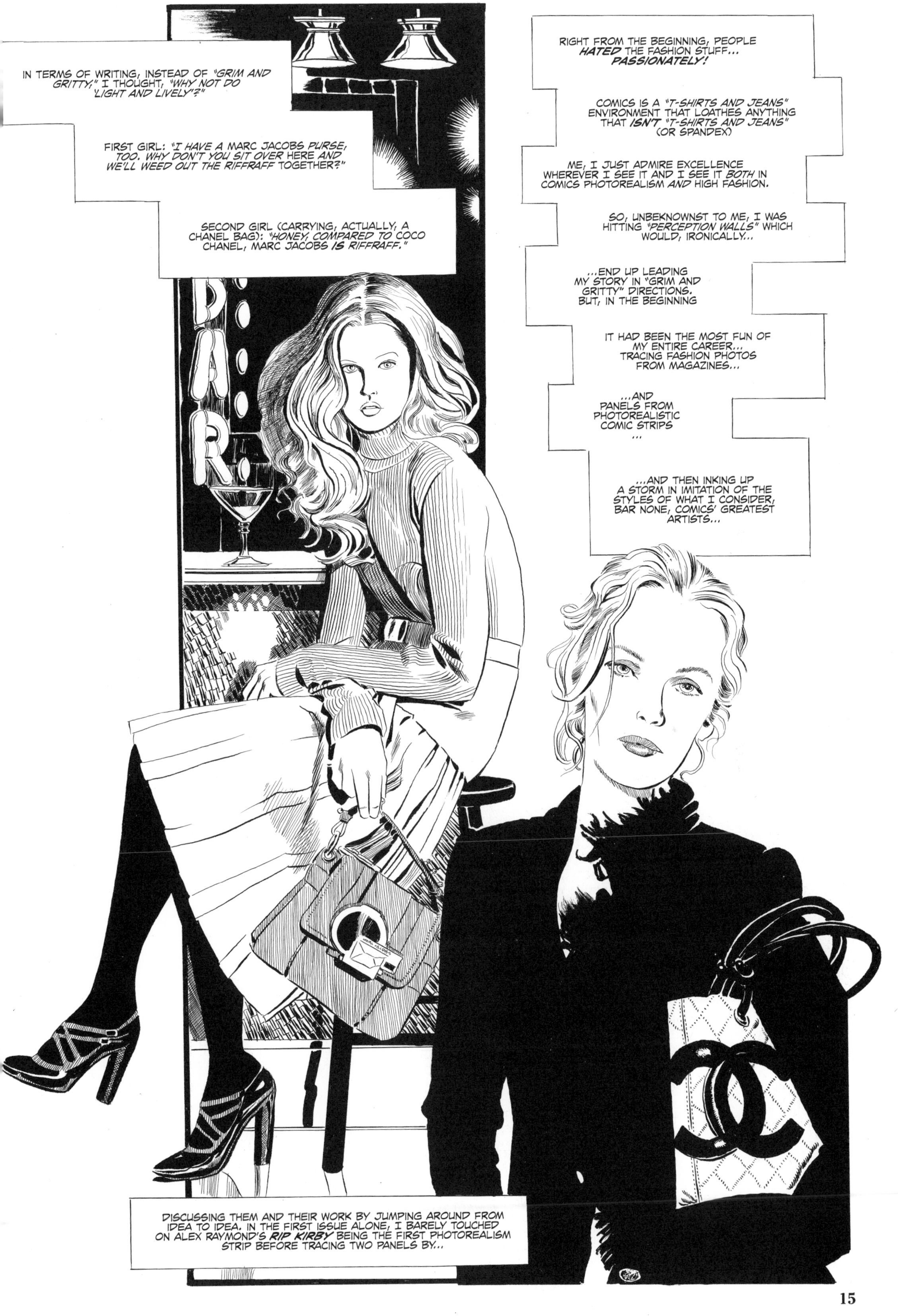
IN TERMS OF WRITING, INSTEAD OF "GRIM AND GRITTY," I THOUGHT, "WHY NOT DO 'LIGHT AND LIVELY'?"
FIRST GIRL: "I HAVE A MARC JACOBS PURSE, TOO. WHY DON'T YOU SIT OVER HERE AND WE'LL WEED OUT THE RIFFRAFF TOGETHER?"
SECOND GIRL (CARRYING, ACTUALLY, A CHANEL BAG): "HONEY, COMPARED TO COCO CHANEL, MARC JACOBS IS RIFFRAFF."
RIGHT FROM THE BEGINNING, PEOPLE HATED THE FASHION STUFF... PASSIONATELY!
COMICS IS A "T-SHIRTS AND JEANS" ENVIRONMENT THAT LOATHES ANYTHING THAT ISN'T "T-SHIRTS AND JEANS" (OR SPANDEX)
ME, I JUST ADMIRE EXCELLENCE WHEREVER I SEE IT AND I SEE IT BOTH IN COMICS PHOTOREALISM AND HIGH FASHION.
SO, UNBEKNOWNST TO ME, I WAS HITTING "PERCEPTION WALLS" WHICH WOULD, IRONICALLY...
...END UP LEADING MY STORY IN "GRIM AND GRITTY" DIRECTIONS. BUT, IN THE BEGINNING
IT HAD BEEN THE MOST FUN OF MY ENTIRE CAREER... TRACING FASHION PHOTOS FROM MAGAZINES...
...AND PANELS FROM PHOTOREALISTIC COMIC STRIPS ...
...AND THEN INKING UP A STORM IN IMITATION OF THE STYLES OF WHAT I CONSIDER, BAR NONE, COMICS' GREATEST ARTISTS...
BAR
DISCUSSING THEM AND THEIR WORK BY JUMPING AROUND FROM IDEA TO IDEA. IN THE FIRST ISSUE ALONE, I BARELY TOUCHED ON ALEX RAYMOND'S RIP KIRBY BEING THE FIRST PHOTOREALISM STRIP BEFORE TRACING TWO PANELS BY...

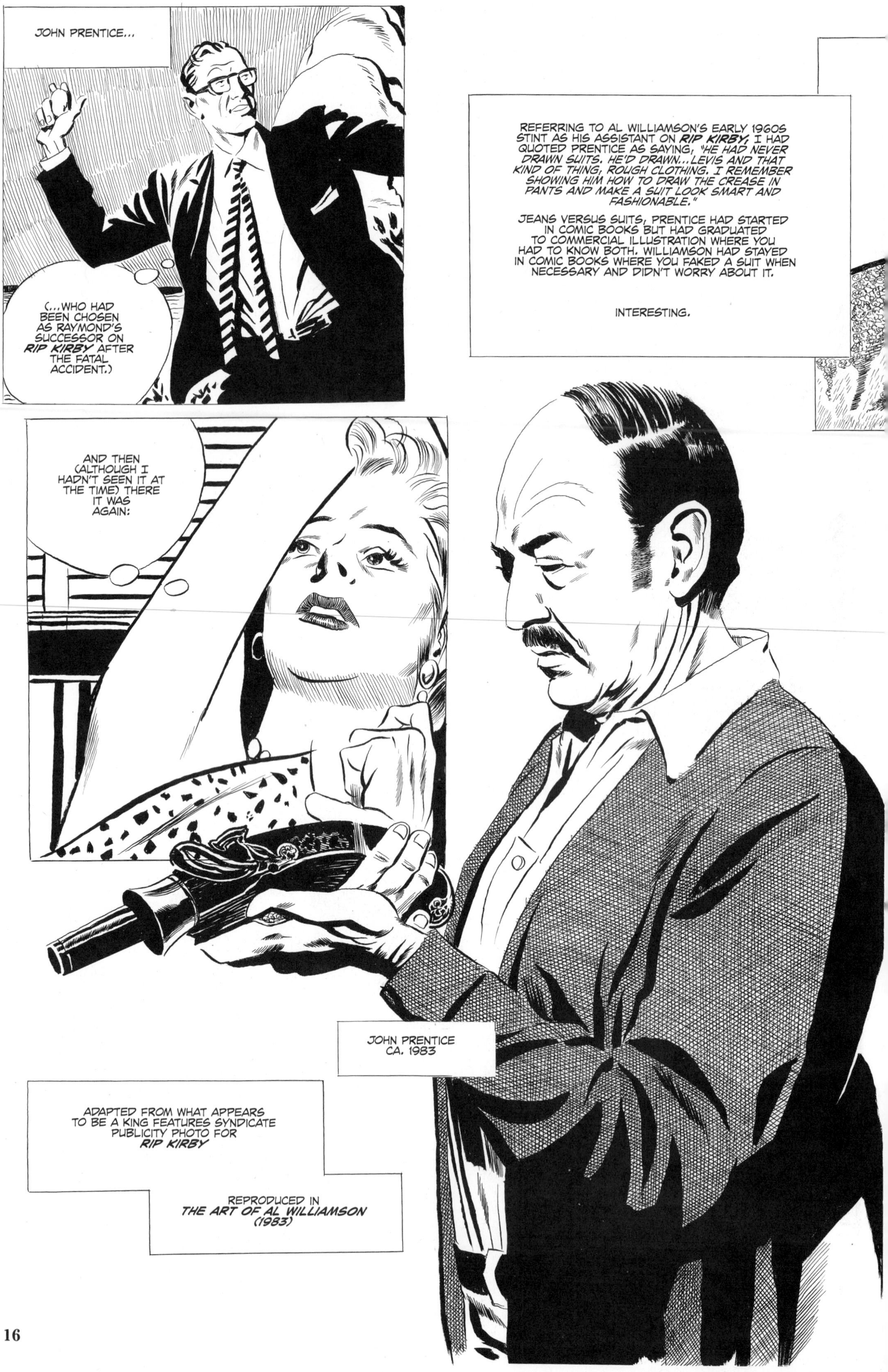
JOHN PRENTICE...
(...WHO HAD BEEN CHOSEN AS RAYMOND'S SUCCESSOR ON RIP KIRBY AFTER THE FATAL ACCIDENT.)
REFERRING TO AL WILLIAMSON'S EARLY 1960S STINT AS HIS ASSISTANT ON RIP KIRBY, I HAD QUOTED PRENTICE AS SAYING, "HE HAD NEVER DRAWN SUITS. HE'D DRAWN...LEVIS AND THAT KIND OF THING, ROUGH CLOTHING. I REMEMBER SHOWING HIM HOW TO DRAW THE CREASE IN PANTS AND MAKE A SUIT LOOK SMART AND FASHIONABLE."
JEANS VERSUS SUITS, PRENTICE HAD STARTED IN COMIC BOOKS BUT HAD GRADUATED TO COMMERCIAL ILLUSTRATION WHERE YOU HAD TO KNOW BOTH. WILLIAMSON HAD STAYED IN COMIC BOOKS WHERE YOU FAKED A SUIT WHEN NECESSARY AND DIDN'T WORRY ABOUT IT.
INTERESTING.
AND THEN (ALTHOUGH I HADN'T SEEN IT AT THE TIME) THERE IT WAS AGAIN:
JOHN PRENTICE CA. 1983
ADAPTED FROM WHAT APPEARS TO BE A KING FEATURES SYNDICATE PUBLICITY PHOTO FOR RIP KIRBY
REPRODUCED IN THE ART OF AL WILLIAMSON (1983)

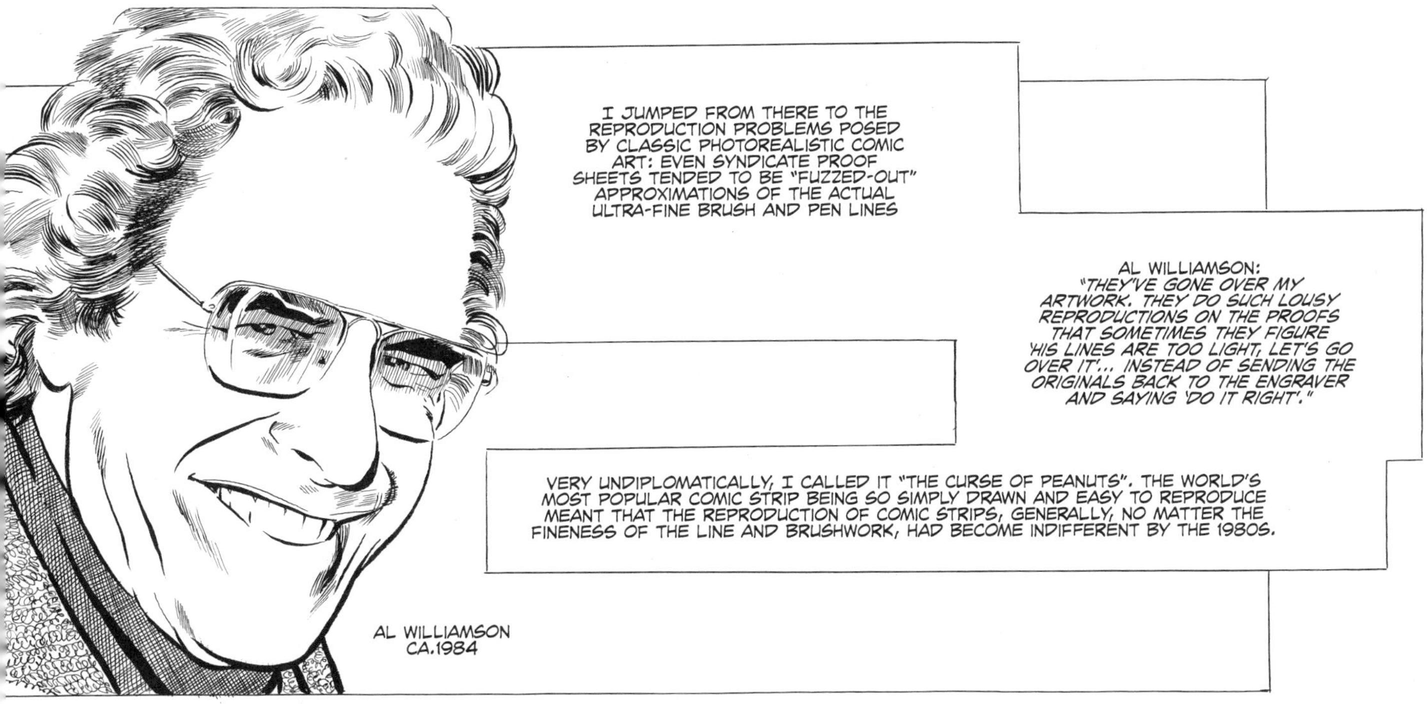
I JUMPED FROM THERE TO THE REPRODUCTION PROBLEMS POSED BY CLASSIC PHOTOREALISTIC COMIC ART: EVEN SYNDICATE PROOF SHEETS TENDED TO BE "FUZZED-OUT" APPROXIMATIONS OF THE ACTUAL ULTRA-FINE BRUSH AND PEN LINES
AL WILLIAMSON:
*"THEY'VE GONE OVER MY ARTWORK. THEY DO SUCH LOUSY REPRODUCTIONS ON THE PROOFS THAT SOMETIMES THEY FIGURE 'HIS LINES ARE TOO LIGHT, LET'S GO OVER IT'... INSTEAD OF SENDING THE ORIGINALS BACK TO THE ENGRAVER AND SAYING 'DO IT RIGHT'."*
VERY UNDIPLOMATICALLY, I CALLED IT "THE CURSE OF PEANUTS". THE WORLD'S MOST POPULAR COMIC STRIP BEING SO SIMPLY DRAWN AND EASY TO REPRODUCE MEANT THAT THE REPRODUCTION OF COMIC STRIPS, GENERALLY, NO MATTER THE FINENESS OF THE LINE AND BRUSHWORK, HAD BECOME INDIFFERENT BY THE 1980S.
AL WILLIAMSON CA.1984

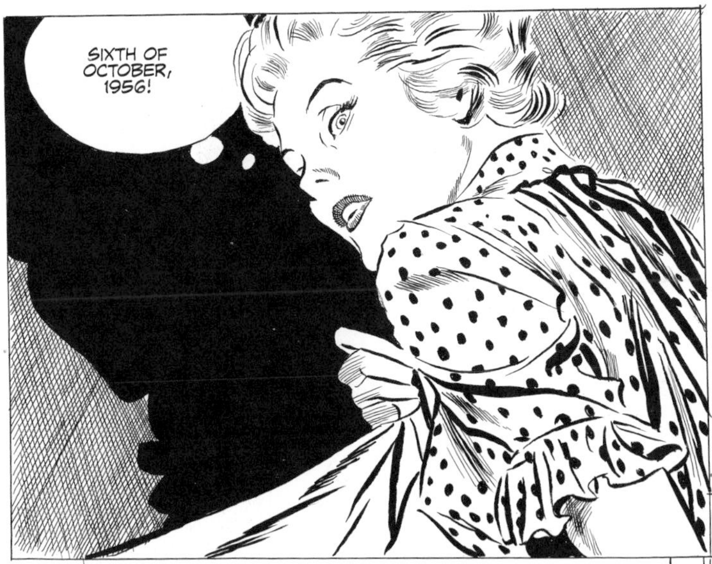
SIXTH OF OCTOBER, 1956!

I THEN JUMPED BACK TO JOHN PRENTICE...

...WHAT A ***REMARKABLE*** -- AND, BY THEN, COMPLETELY FORGOTTEN -- ACHIEVEMENT IT HAD BEEN FOR HIM TO TAKE OVER FROM ALEX RAYMOND. TO MASTER, IN LESS THAN TWO WEEKS, ONE OF THE MOST COMPLICATED COMIC-ART STYLES EVER CREATED AND TO FINISH THE LAST EIGHTEEN STRIPS IN A SEQUENCE WHICH HAD BEEN RUNNING SINCE JULY.

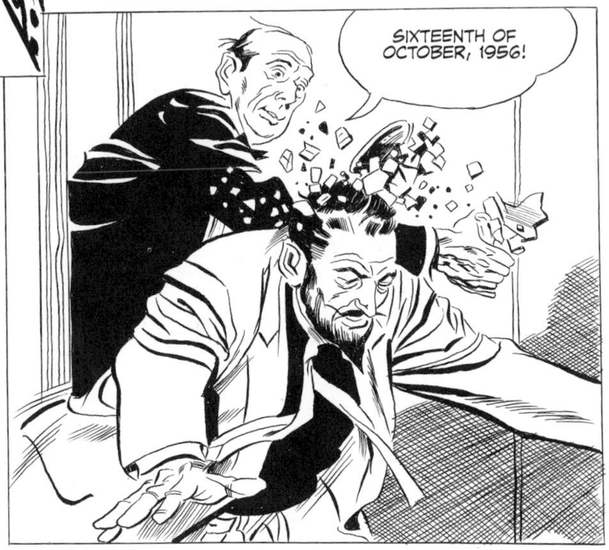
SIXTEENTH OF OCTOBER, 1956!

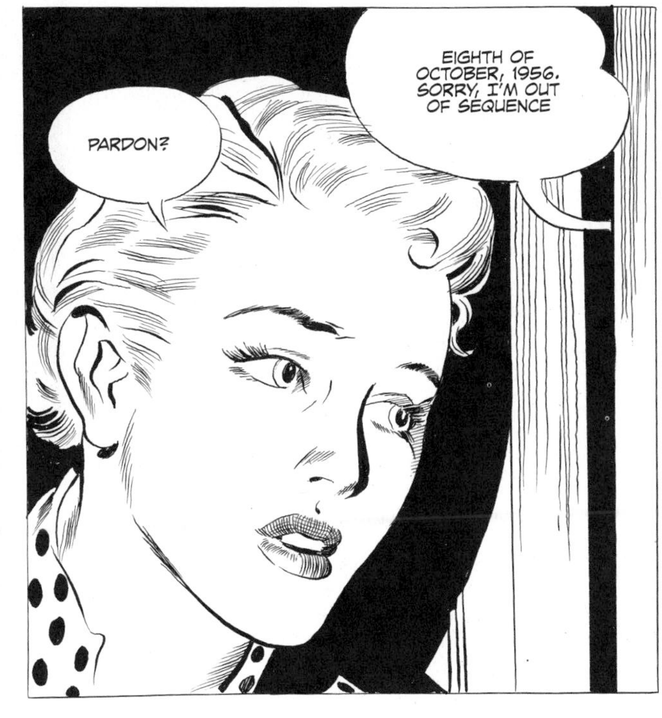
PARDON?
EIGHTH OF OCTOBER, 1956. SORRY, I'M OUT OF SEQUENCE

UNFORTUNATELY, MY "JEANS AND T-SHIRTS" AUDIENCE -- ALREADY GRIEVOUSLY REPELLED BY MY USE OF HIGH-FASHION IMAGES -- WAS SITTING THERE, FUMING:

*"WAIT A MINUTE, DAVE. WHAT EXACTLY DO YOU MEAN BY 'THE...**CURSE**...OF **PEANUTS**'?*

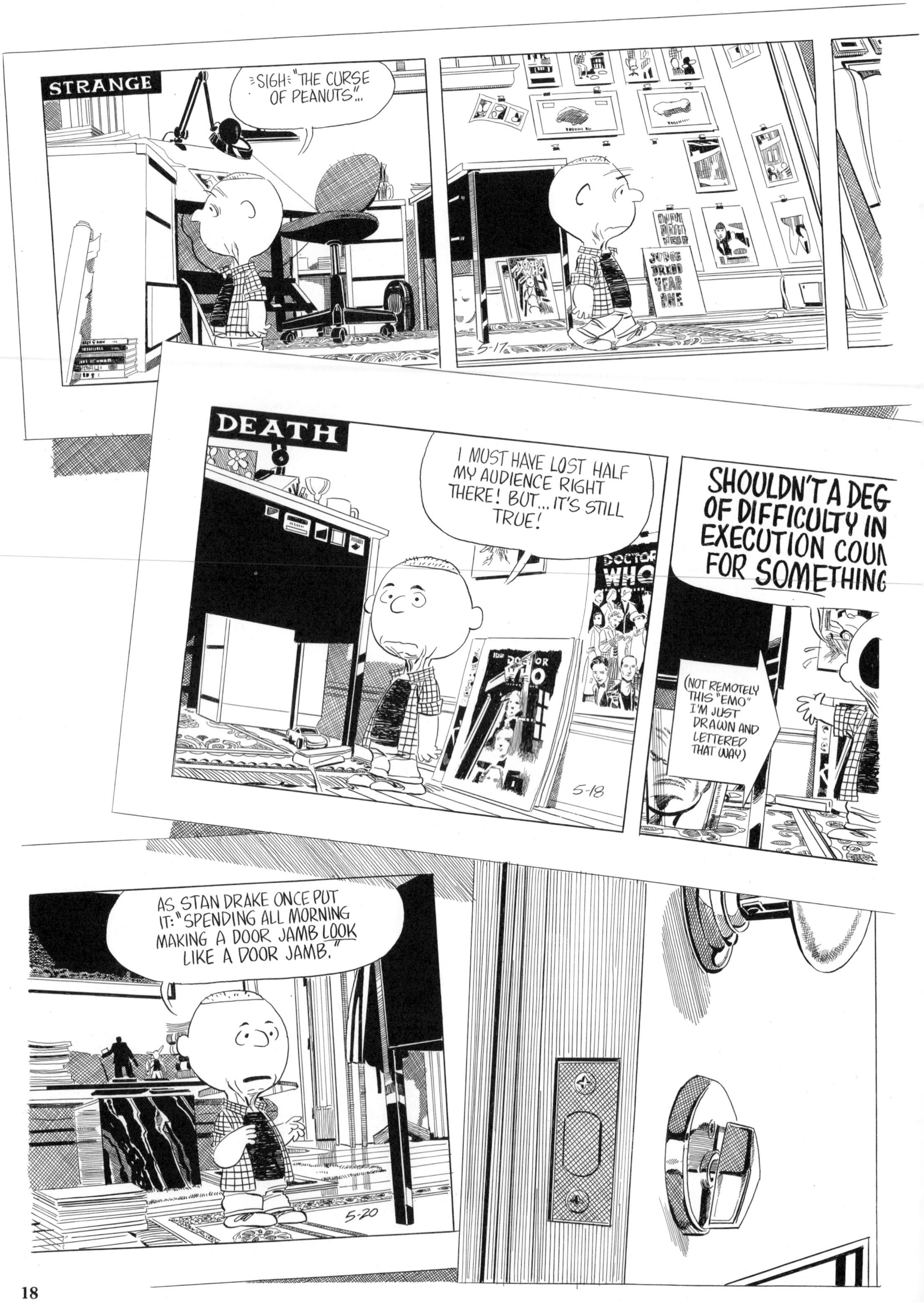
STRANGE
SIGH "THE CURSE OF PEANUTS"...
JUDGE DREDD YEAR ONE
5-17
DEATH
I MUST HAVE LOST HALF MY AUDIENCE RIGHT THERE! BUT... IT'S STILL TRUE!
DOCTOR WHO
5-18
SHOULDN'T A DEG
OF DIFFICULTY IN
EXECUTION COUN
FOR SOMETHING
(NOT REMOTELY THIS "EMO" I'M JUST DRAWN AND LETTERED THAT WAY)
AS STAN DRAKE ONCE PUT IT: "SPENDING ALL MORNING MAKING A DOOR JAMB LOOK LIKE A DOOR JAMB."
5-20

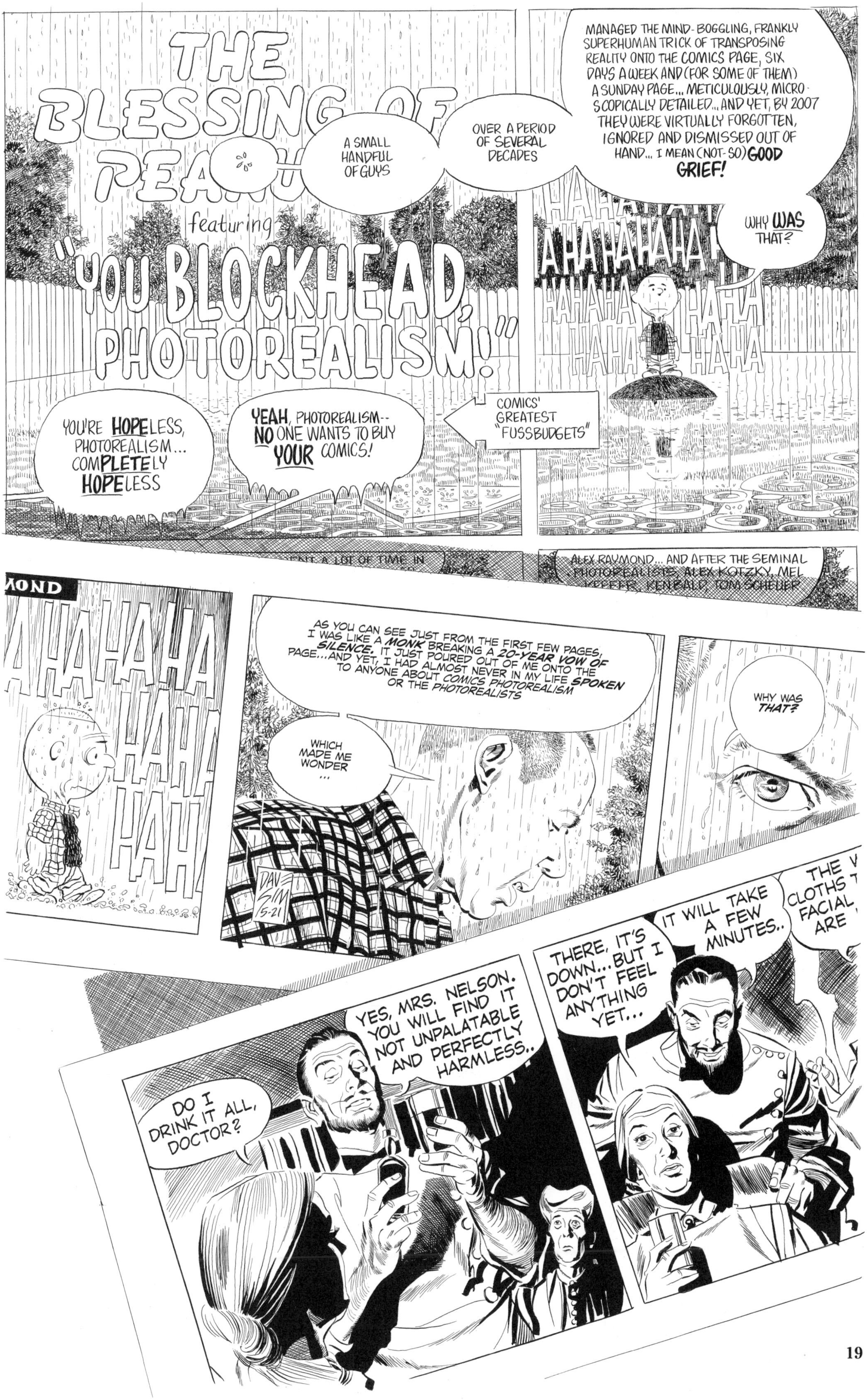
THE BLESSING OF PEA
featuring
"YOU BLOCKHEAD, PHOTOREALISM!"
A SMALL HANDFUL OF GUYS
OVER A PERIOD OF SEVERAL DECADES
MANAGED THE MIND-BOGGLING, FRANKLY SUPERHUMAN TRICK OF TRANSPOSING REALITY ONTO THE COMICS PAGE, SIX DAYS A WEEK AND (FOR SOME OF THEM) A SUNDAY PAGE... METICULOUSLY, MICROSCOPICALLY DETAILED... AND YET, BY 2007 THEY WERE VIRTUALLY FORGOTTEN, IGNORED AND DISMISSED OUT OF HAND... I MEAN (NOT-SO) GOOD GRIEF!
WHY WAS THAT?
HAHAHAHAHA
YOU'RE HOPELESS, PHOTOREALISM... COMPLETELY HOPELESS
YEAH, PHOTOREALISM-- NO ONE WANTS TO BUY YOUR COMICS!
COMICS' GREATEST "FUSSBUDGETS"
A LOT OF TIME IN
ALEX RAYMOND... AND AFTER THE SEMINAL PHOTOREALISTS, ALEX KOTZKY, MEL
KEN BALD, TOM SCHEUER
HAHAHA
AS YOU CAN SEE JUST FROM THE FIRST FEW PAGES, I WAS LIKE A MONK BREAKING A 20-YEAR VOW OF SILENCE. IT JUST POURED OUT OF ME ONTO THE PAGE... AND YET, I HAD ALMOST NEVER IN MY LIFE SPOKEN TO ANYONE ABOUT COMICS PHOTOREALISM OR THE PHOTOREALISTS
WHICH MADE ME WONDER ...
WHY WAS THAT?
DAVE SIM 5-21
DO I DRINK IT ALL, DOCTOR?
YES, MRS. NELSON. YOU WILL FIND IT NOT UNPALATABLE AND PERFECTLY HARMLESS..
THERE, IT'S DOWN... BUT I DON'T FEEL ANYTHING YET...
IT WILL TAKE A FEW MINUTES..

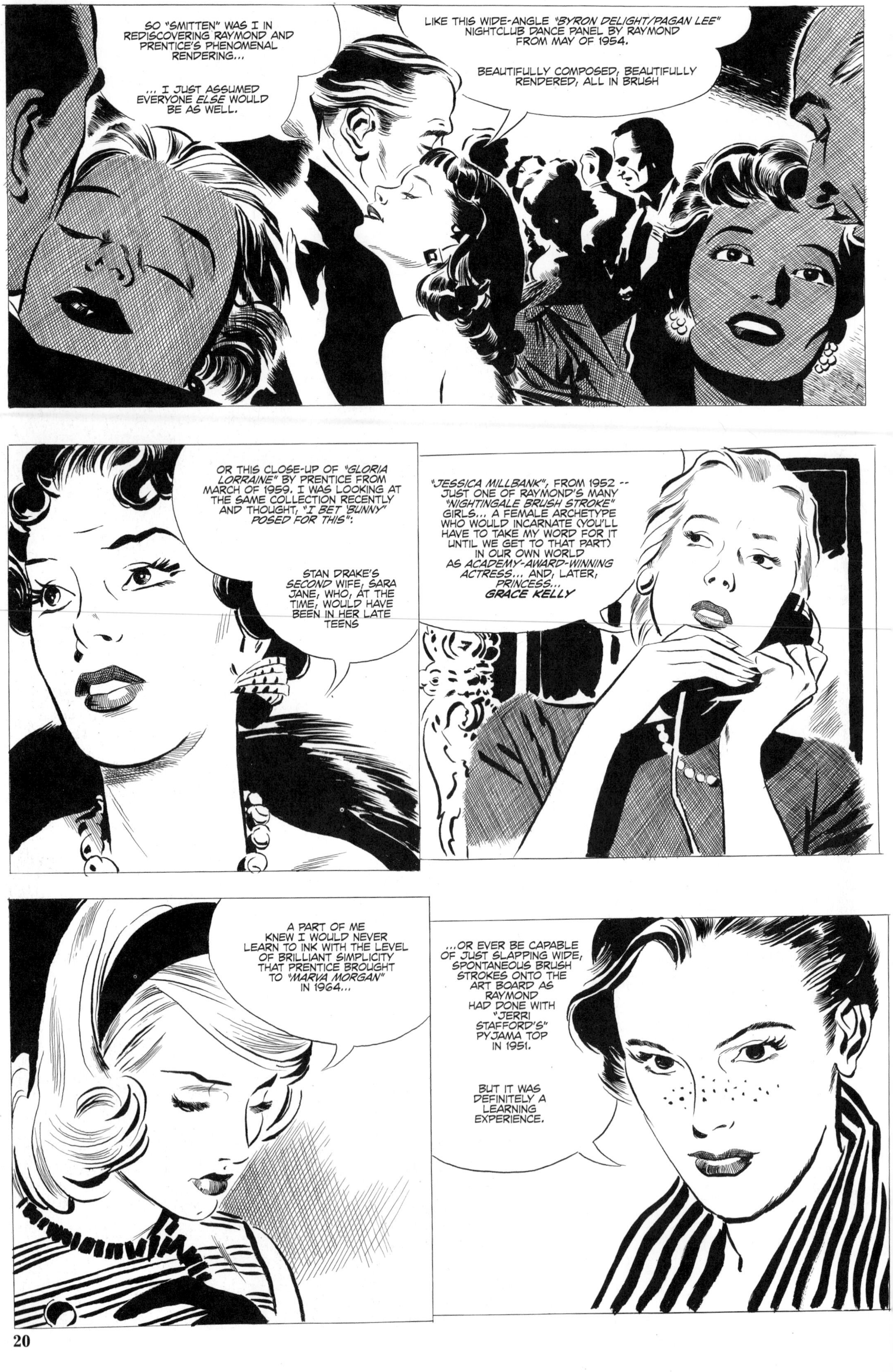
SO "SMITTEN" WAS I IN REDISCOVERING RAYMOND AND PRENTICE'S PHENOMENAL RENDERING...
... I JUST ASSUMED EVERYONE ELSE WOULD BE AS WELL.
LIKE THIS WIDE-ANGLE "BYRON DELIGHT/PAGAN LEE" NIGHTCLUB DANCE PANEL BY RAYMOND FROM MAY OF 1954.
BEAUTIFULLY COMPOSED, BEAUTIFULLY RENDERED, ALL IN BRUSH
OR THIS CLOSE-UP OF "GLORIA LORRAINE" BY PRENTICE FROM MARCH OF 1959. I WAS LOOKING AT THE SAME COLLECTION RECENTLY AND THOUGHT, "I BET 'BUNNY' POSED FOR THIS":
STAN DRAKE'S SECOND WIFE, SARA JANE, WHO, AT THE TIME, WOULD HAVE BEEN IN HER LATE TEENS
"JESSICA MILLBANK", FROM 1952 -- JUST ONE OF RAYMOND'S MANY "NIGHTINGALE BRUSH STROKE" GIRLS... A FEMALE ARCHETYPE WHO WOULD INCARNATE (YOU'LL HAVE TO TAKE MY WORD FOR IT UNTIL WE GET TO THAT PART) IN OUR OWN WORLD AS ACADEMY-AWARD-WINNING ACTRESS... AND, LATER, PRINCESS... GRACE KELLY
A PART OF ME KNEW I WOULD NEVER LEARN TO INK WITH THE LEVEL OF BRILLIANT SIMPLICITY THAT PRENTICE BROUGHT TO "MARVA MORGAN" IN 1964...
...OR EVER BE CAPABLE OF JUST SLAPPING WIDE, SPONTANEOUS BRUSH STROKES ONTO THE ART BOARD AS RAYMOND HAD DONE WITH "JERRI STAFFORD'S" PYJAMA TOP IN 1951.
BUT IT WAS DEFINITELY A LEARNING EXPERIENCE.

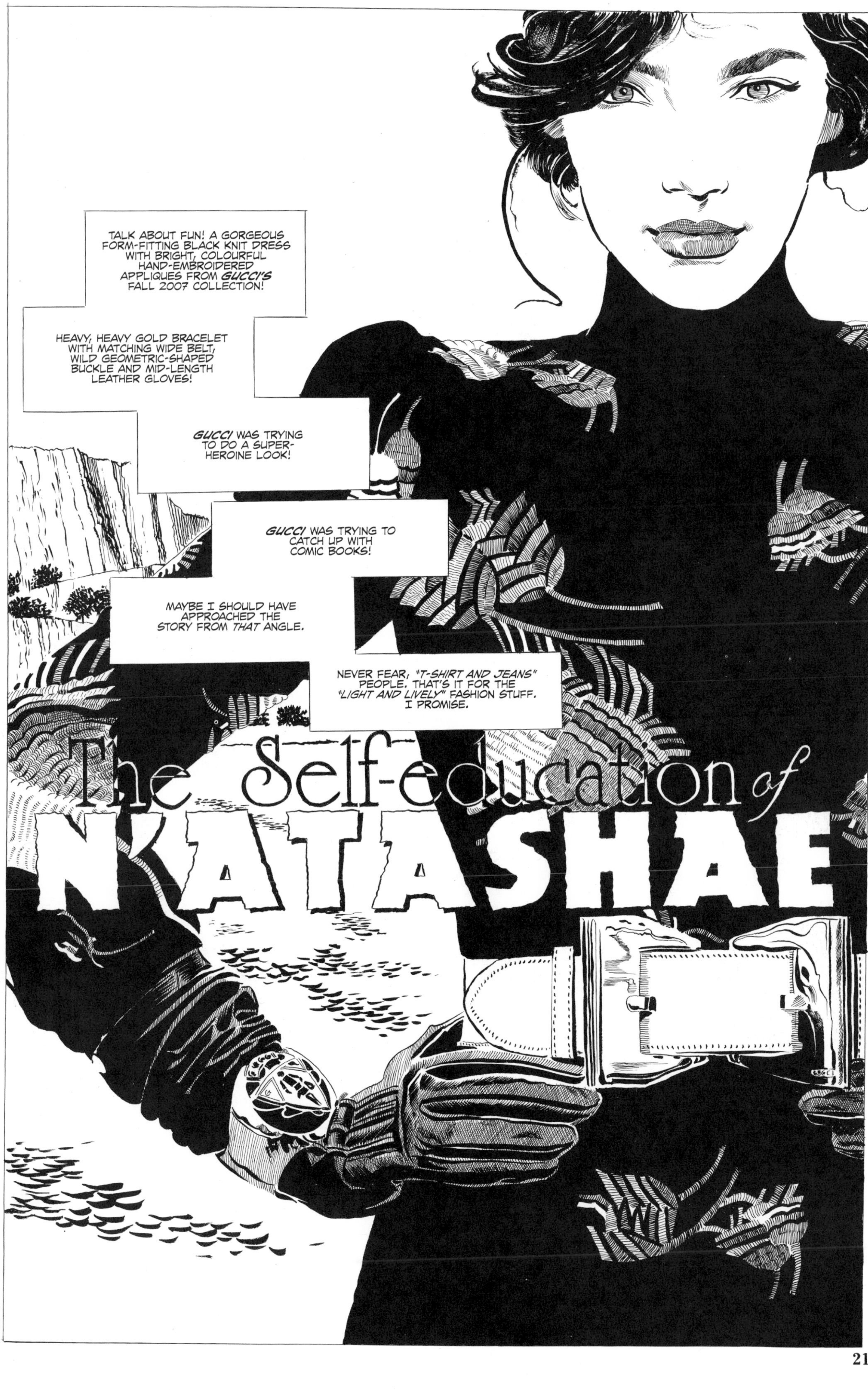

TALK ABOUT FUN! A GORGEOUS FORM-FITTING BLACK KNIT DRESS WITH BRIGHT, COLOURFUL HAND-EMBROIDERED APPLIQUES FROM GUCCI'S FALL 2007 COLLECTION!
HEAVY, HEAVY GOLD BRACELET WITH MATCHING WIDE BELT, WILD GEOMETRIC-SHAPED BUCKLE AND MID-LENGTH LEATHER GLOVES!
GUCCI WAS TRYING TO DO A SUPER-HEROINE LOOK!
GUCCI WAS TRYING TO CATCH UP WITH COMIC BOOKS!
MAYBE I SHOULD HAVE APPROACHED THE STORY FROM THAT ANGLE.
NEVER FEAR, "T-SHIRT AND JEANS" PEOPLE. THAT'S IT FOR THE "LIGHT AND LIVELY" FASHION STUFF. I PROMISE.
The Self-education of
N'ATASHAE

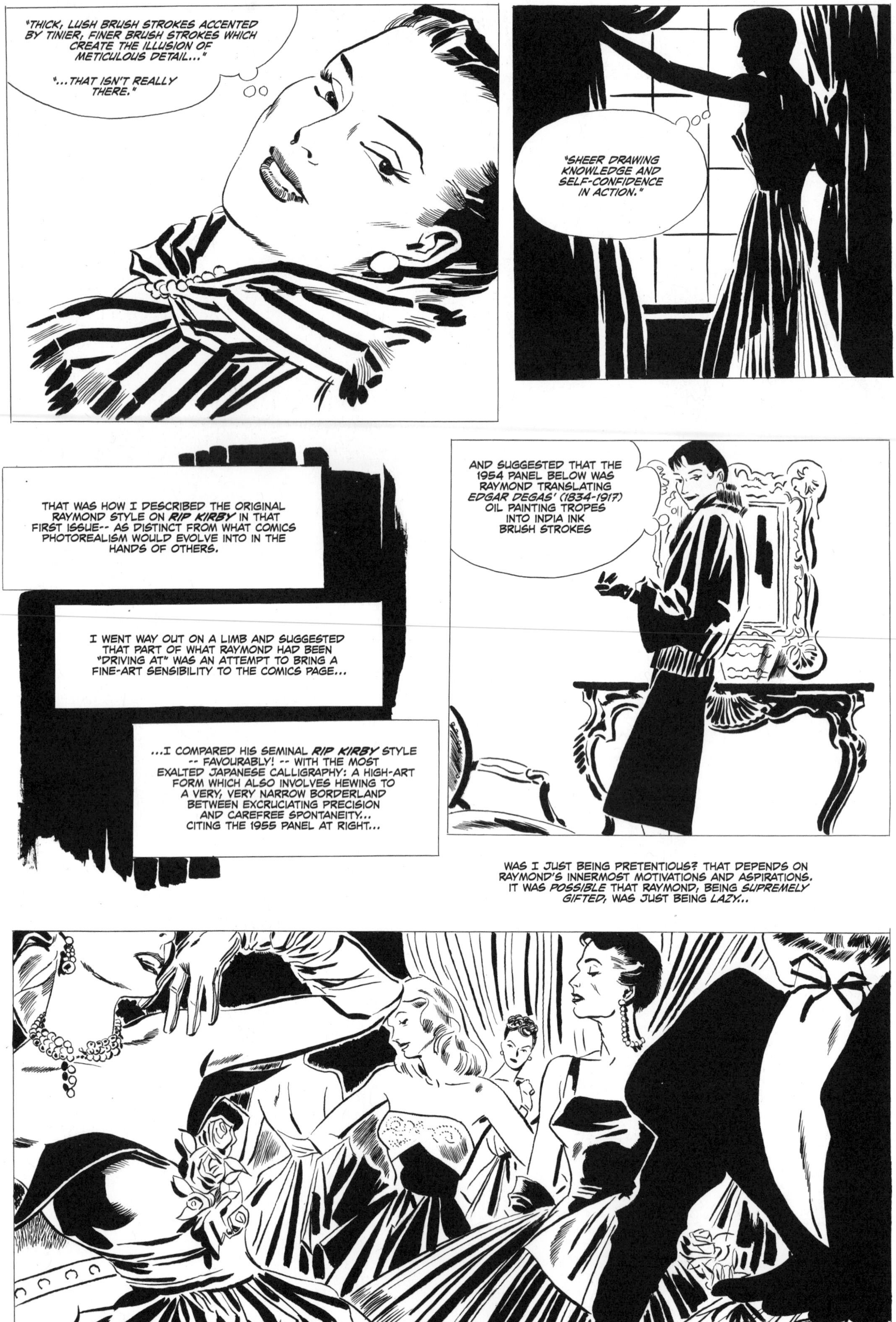
"THICK, LUSH BRUSH STROKES ACCENTED BY TINIER, FINER BRUSH STROKES WHICH CREATE THE ILLUSION OF METICULOUS DETAIL..."
"...THAT ISN'T REALLY THERE."
"SHEER DRAWING KNOWLEDGE AND SELF-CONFIDENCE IN ACTION."
THAT WAS HOW I DESCRIBED THE ORIGINAL RAYMOND STYLE ON *RIP KIRBY* IN THAT FIRST ISSUE-- AS DISTINCT FROM WHAT COMICS PHOTOREALISM WOULD EVOLVE INTO IN THE HANDS OF OTHERS.
I WENT WAY OUT ON A LIMB AND SUGGESTED THAT PART OF WHAT RAYMOND HAD BEEN "DRIVING AT" WAS AN ATTEMPT TO BRING A FINE-ART SENSIBILITY TO THE COMICS PAGE...
...I COMPARED HIS SEMINAL *RIP KIRBY* STYLE -- FAVOURABLY! -- WITH THE MOST EXALTED JAPANESE CALLIGRAPHY: A HIGH-ART FORM WHICH ALSO INVOLVES HEWING TO A VERY, VERY NARROW BORDERLAND BETWEEN EXCRUCIATING PRECISION AND CAREFREE SPONTANEITY... CITING THE 1955 PANEL AT RIGHT...
AND SUGGESTED THAT THE 1954 PANEL BELOW WAS RAYMOND TRANSLATING *EDGAR DEGAS' (1834-1917)* OIL PAINTING TROPES INTO INDIA INK BRUSH STROKES
WAS I JUST BEING PRETENTIOUS? THAT DEPENDS ON RAYMOND'S INNERMOST MOTIVATIONS AND ASPIRATIONS. IT WAS *POSSIBLE* THAT RAYMOND, BEING *SUPREMELY GIFTED*, WAS JUST BEING *LAZY*...

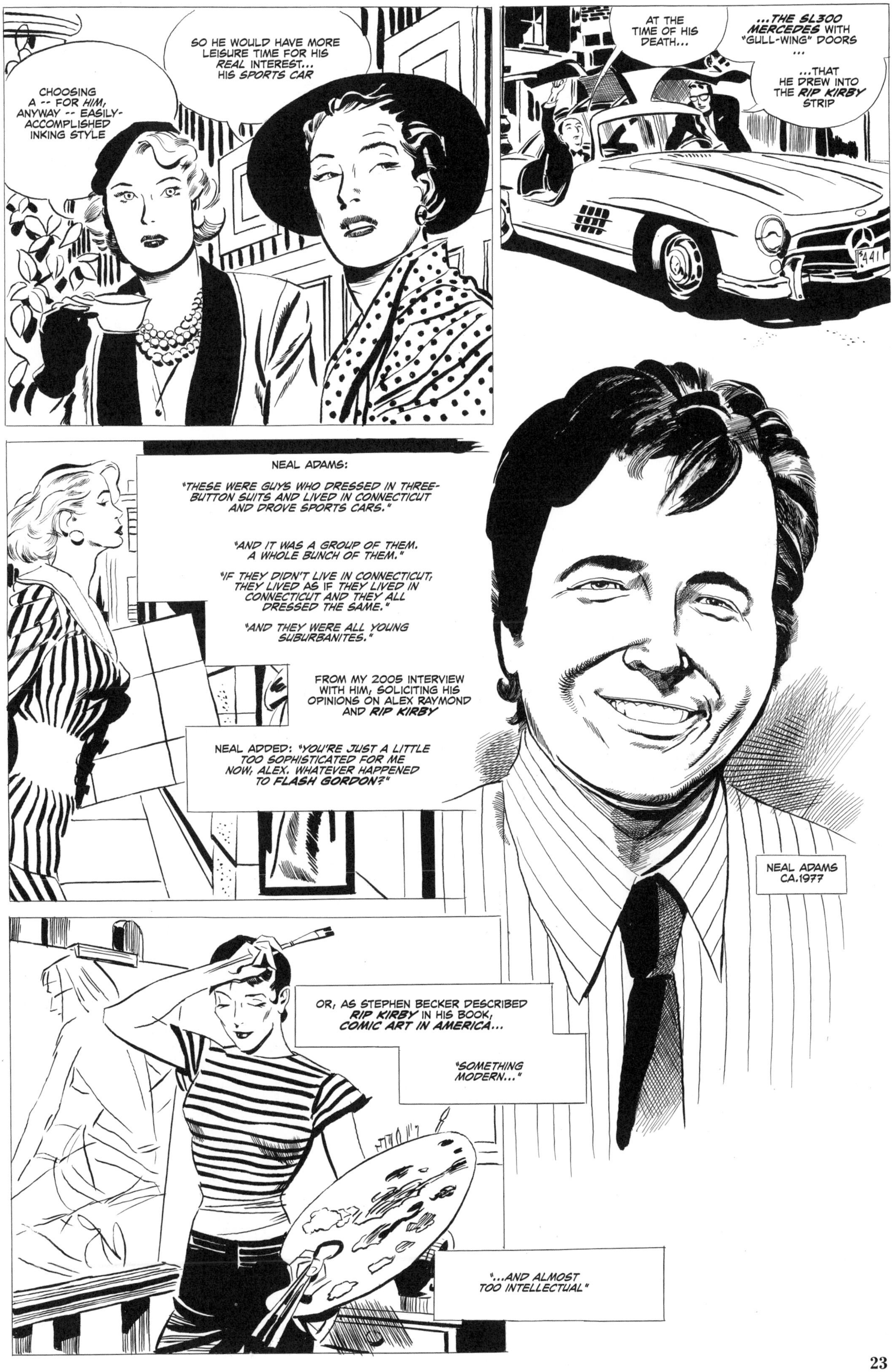

SO HE WOULD HAVE MORE LEISURE TIME FOR HIS REAL INTEREST... HIS SPORTS CAR
CHOOSING A -- FOR HIM, ANYWAY -- EASILY-ACCOMPLISHED INKING STYLE
AT THE TIME OF HIS DEATH...
...THE SL300 MERCEDES WITH "GULL-WING" DOORS ...
...THAT HE DREW INTO THE RIP KIRBY STRIP
NEAL ADAMS:
"THESE WERE GUYS WHO DRESSED IN THREE-BUTTON SUITS AND LIVED IN CONNECTICUT AND DROVE SPORTS CARS."
"AND IT WAS A GROUP OF THEM. A WHOLE BUNCH OF THEM."
"IF THEY DIDN'T LIVE IN CONNECTICUT, THEY LIVED AS IF THEY LIVED IN CONNECTICUT AND THEY ALL DRESSED THE SAME."
"AND THEY WERE ALL YOUNG SUBURBANITES."
FROM MY 2005 INTERVIEW WITH HIM, SOLICITING HIS OPINIONS ON ALEX RAYMOND AND RIP KIRBY
NEAL ADDED: "YOU'RE JUST A LITTLE TOO SOPHISTICATED FOR ME NOW, ALEX. WHATEVER HAPPENED TO FLASH GORDON?"
NEAL ADAMS CA.1977
OR, AS STEPHEN BECKER DESCRIBED RIP KIRBY IN HIS BOOK, COMIC ART IN AMERICA...
"SOMETHING MODERN..."
"...AND ALMOST TOO INTELLECTUAL"

IS THERE ANY GREAT DIFFERENCE BETWEEN THE *SPONTANEOUS HIGH-ART BRUSH STROKE* OF A *MASTER JAPANESE CALLIGRAPHER* ...

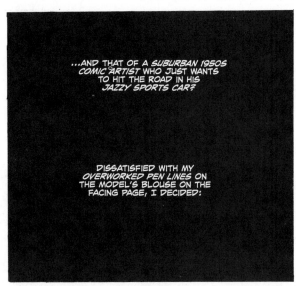

...AND THAT OF A *SUBURBAN 1950S COMIC ARTIST* WHO JUST WANTS TO HIT THE ROAD IN HIS *JAZZY SPORTS CAR?*

DISSATISFIED WITH MY *OVERWORKED PEN LINES* ON THE MODEL'S BLOUSE ON THE FACING PAGE, I DECIDED:

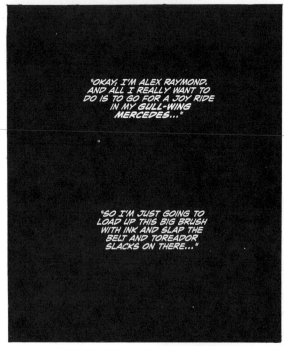

"OKAY, I'M ALEX RAYMOND, AND ALL I REALLY WANT TO DO IS TO GO FOR A JOY RIDE IN MY *GULL-WING MERCEDES*..."

"SO I'M JUST GOING TO LOAD UP THIS BIG BRUSH WITH INK AND SLAP THE BELT AND TOREADOR SLACKS ON THERE..."

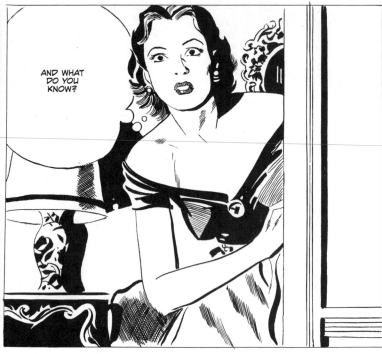

AND WHAT DO YOU KNOW?

IT TURNED OUT TO BE ONE OF THE *BEST THINGS* I'VE EVER DONE.

SIX YEARS LATER...

...IT STILL IS.

24

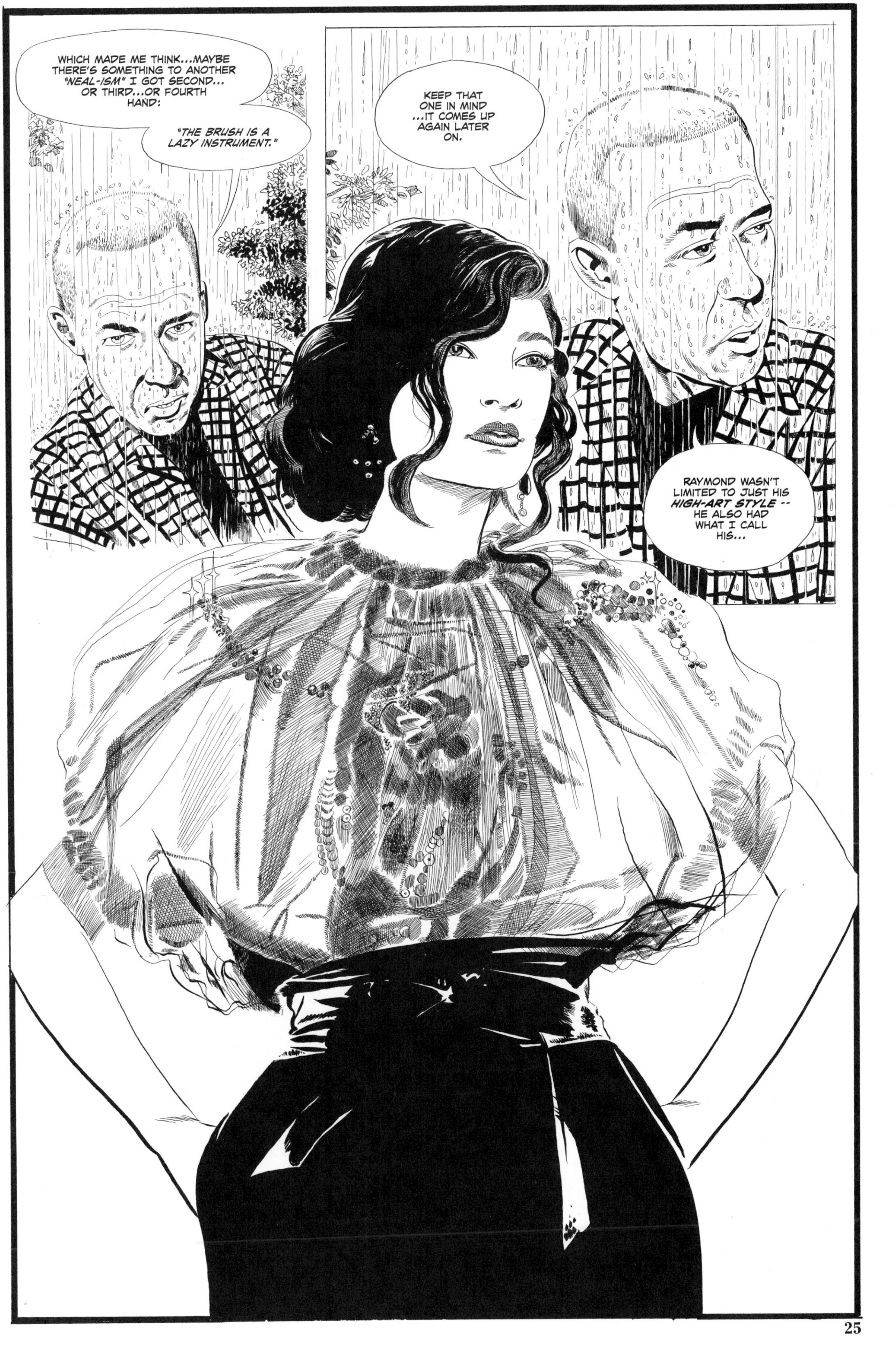
WHICH MADE ME THINK...MAYBE THERE'S SOMETHING TO ANOTHER "NEAL-ISM" I GOT SECOND... OR THIRD...OR FOURTH HAND:
"THE BRUSH IS A LAZY INSTRUMENT."
KEEP THAT ONE IN MIND ...IT COMES UP AGAIN LATER ON.
RAYMOND WASN'T LIMITED TO JUST HIS HIGH-ART STYLE -- HE ALSO HAD WHAT I CALL HIS...

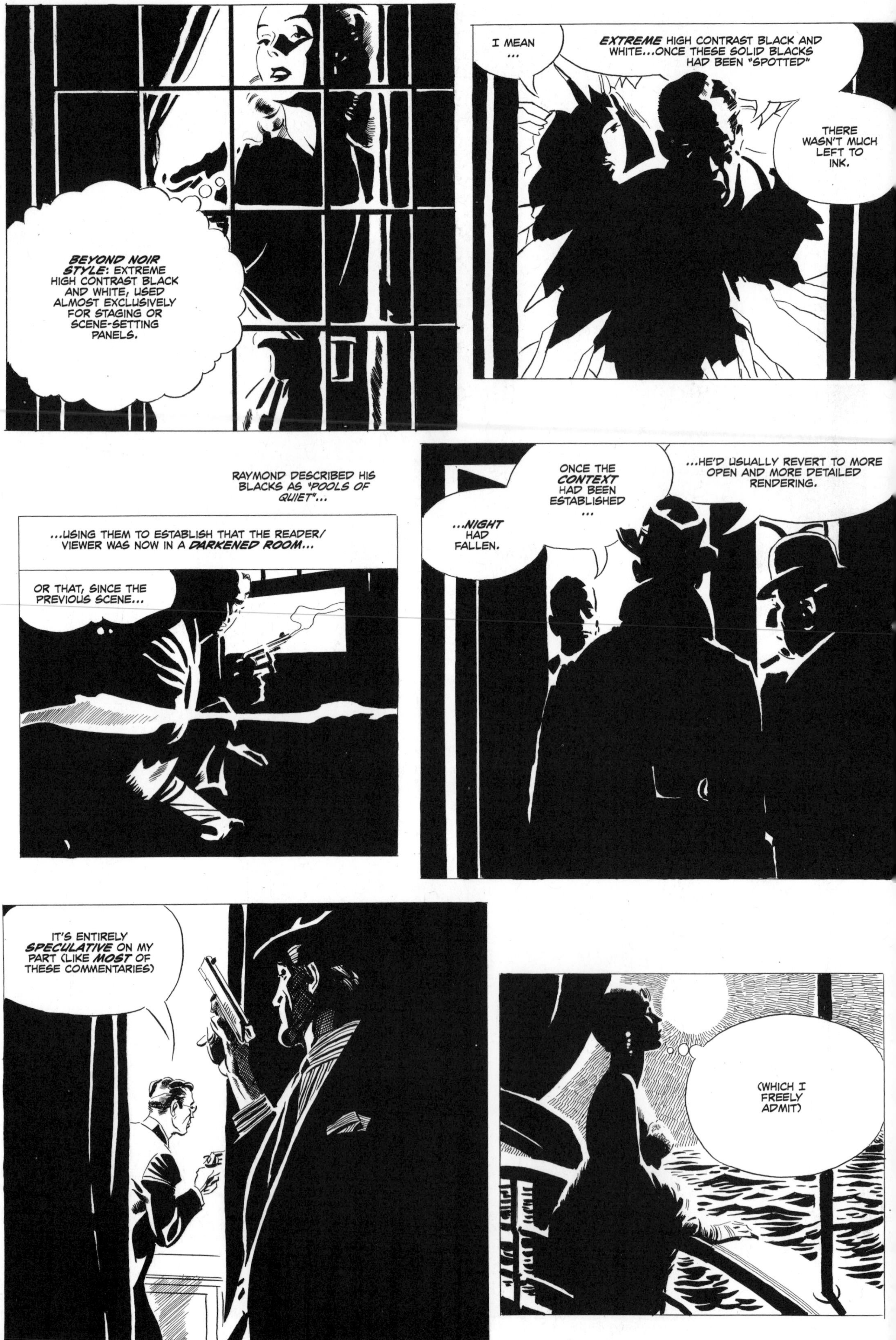
BEYOND NOIR STYLE: EXTREME HIGH CONTRAST BLACK AND WHITE, USED ALMOST EXCLUSIVELY FOR STAGING OR SCENE-SETTING PANELS.
I MEAN ...
EXTREME HIGH CONTRAST BLACK AND WHITE...ONCE THESE SOLID BLACKS HAD BEEN "SPOTTED"
THERE WASN'T MUCH LEFT TO INK.
RAYMOND DESCRIBED HIS BLACKS AS "POOLS OF QUIET"...
...USING THEM TO ESTABLISH THAT THE READER/ VIEWER WAS NOW IN A DARKENED ROOM...
OR THAT, SINCE THE PREVIOUS SCENE...
...NIGHT HAD FALLEN.
ONCE THE CONTEXT HAD BEEN ESTABLISHED ...
...HE'D USUALLY REVERT TO MORE OPEN AND MORE DETAILED RENDERING.
IT'S ENTIRELY SPECULATIVE ON MY PART (LIKE MOST OF THESE COMMENTARIES)
(WHICH I FREELY ADMIT)

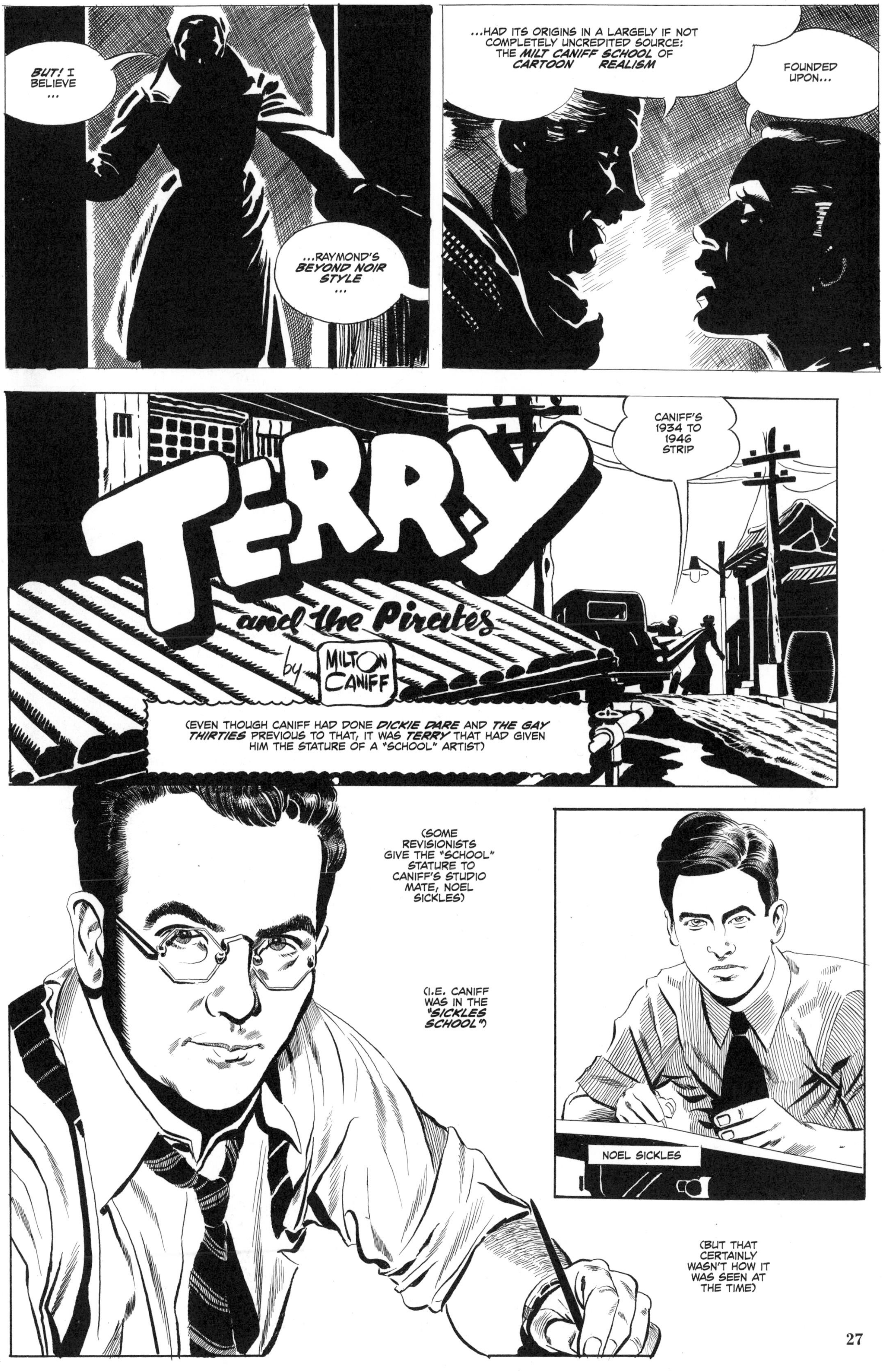
BUT! I BELIEVE ...
...RAYMOND'S BEYOND NOIR STYLE ...
...HAD ITS ORIGINS IN A LARGELY IF NOT COMPLETELY UNCREDITED SOURCE: THE MILT CANIFF SCHOOL OF CARTOON REALISM
FOUNDED UPON...
TERRY and the Pirates by MILTON CANIFF
CANIFF'S 1934 TO 1946 STRIP
(EVEN THOUGH CANIFF HAD DONE DICKIE DARE AND THE GAY THIRTIES PREVIOUS TO THAT, IT WAS TERRY THAT HAD GIVEN HIM THE STATURE OF A "SCHOOL" ARTIST)
(SOME REVISIONISTS GIVE THE "SCHOOL" STATURE TO CANIFF'S STUDIO MATE, NOEL SICKLES)
(I.E. CANIFF WAS IN THE "SICKLES SCHOOL")
NOEL SICKLES
(BUT THAT CERTAINLY WASN'T HOW IT WAS SEEN AT THE TIME)

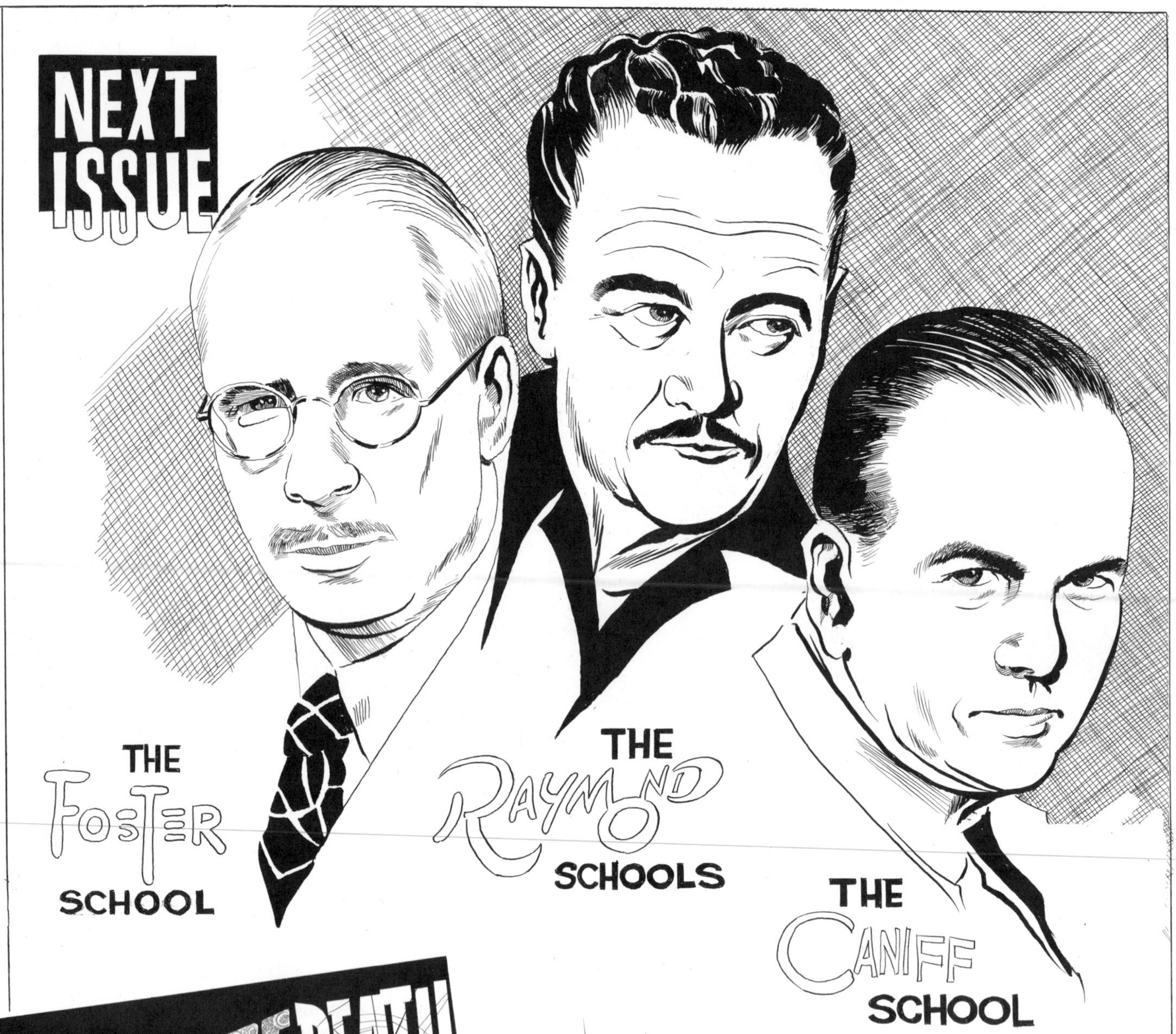
NEXT ISSUE
THE FOSTER SCHOOL
THE RAYMOND SCHOOLS
THE CANIFF SCHOOL

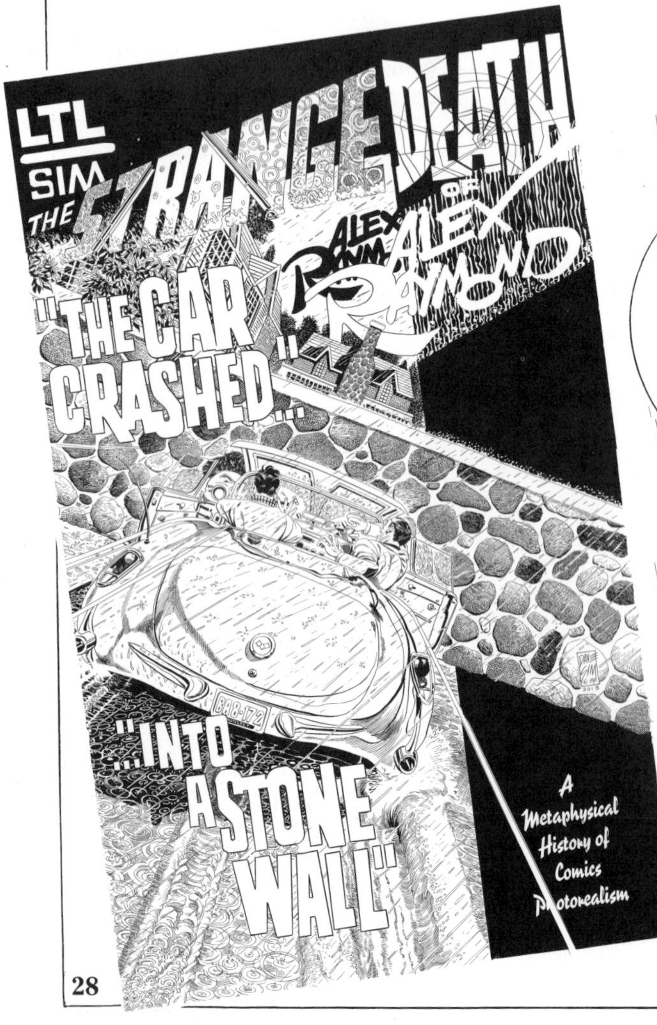
LTL
SIM
THE STRANGE DEATH OF ALEX RAYMOND
"THE CAR CRASHED"...
..."INTO A STONE WALL"
A Metaphysical History of Comics Photorealism

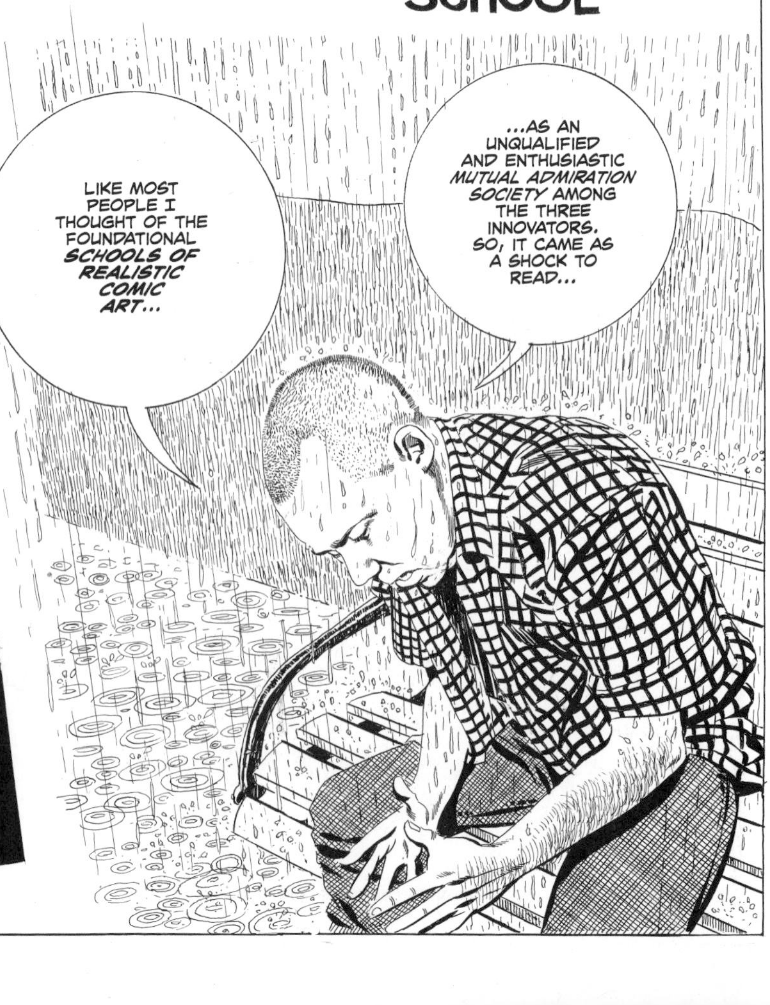
LIKE MOST PEOPLE I THOUGHT OF THE FOUNDATIONAL SCHOOLS OF REALISTIC COMIC ART...
...AS AN UNQUALIFIED AND ENTHUSIASTIC MUTUAL ADMIRATION SOCIETY AMONG THE THREE INNOVATORS. SO, IT CAME AS A SHOCK TO READ...

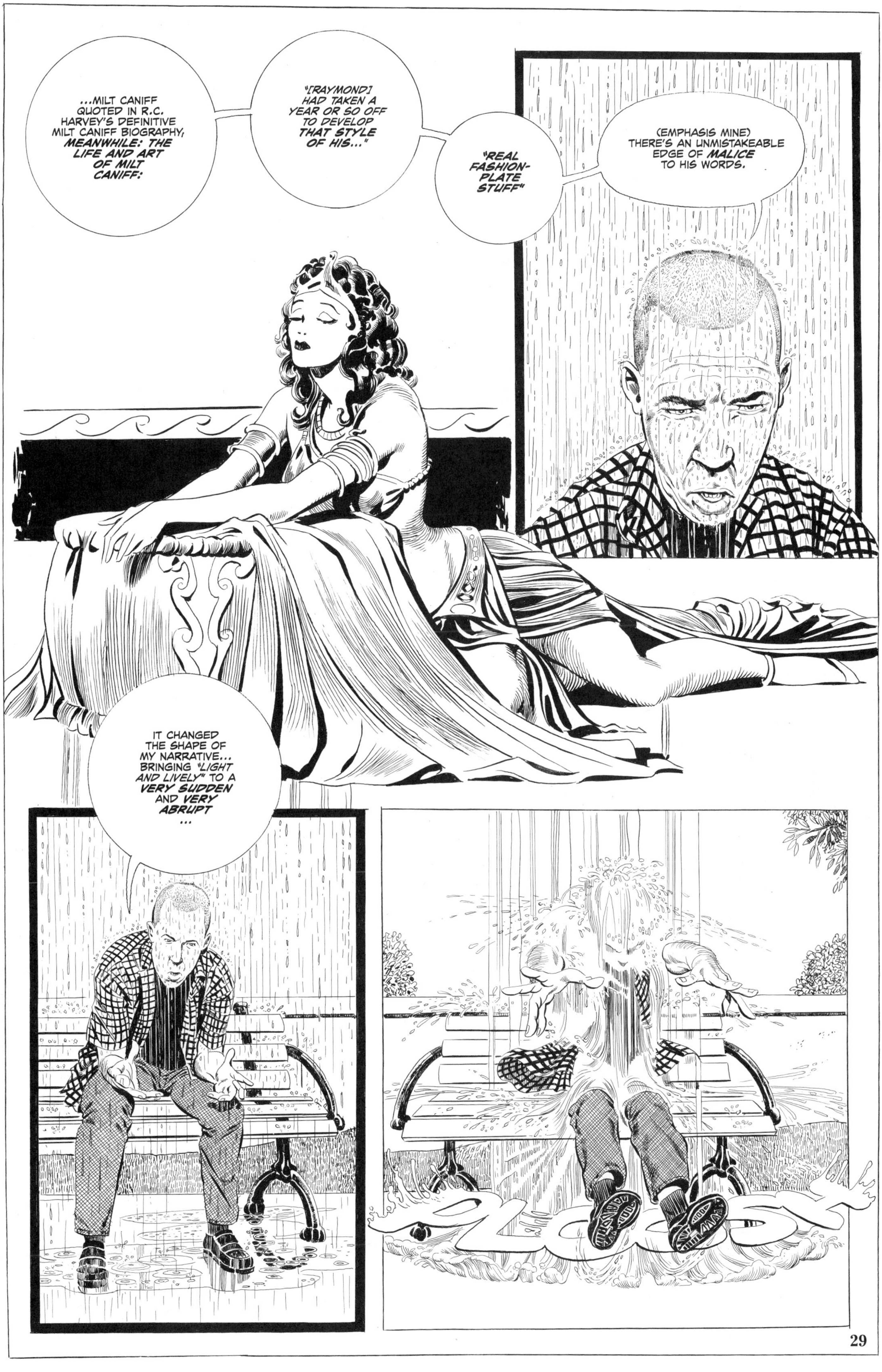
...MILT CANIFF QUOTED IN R.C. HARVEY'S DEFINITIVE MILT CANIFF BIOGRAPHY, MEANWHILE: THE LIFE AND ART OF MILT CANIFF:
"[RAYMOND] HAD TAKEN A YEAR OR SO OFF TO DEVELOP THAT STYLE OF HIS..."
"REAL FASHION-PLATE STUFF"
(EMPHASIS MINE) THERE'S AN UNMISTAKEABLE EDGE OF MALICE TO HIS WORDS.
IT CHANGED THE SHAPE OF MY NARRATIVE... BRINGING "LIGHT AND LIVELY" TO A VERY SUDDEN AND VERY ABRUPT ...

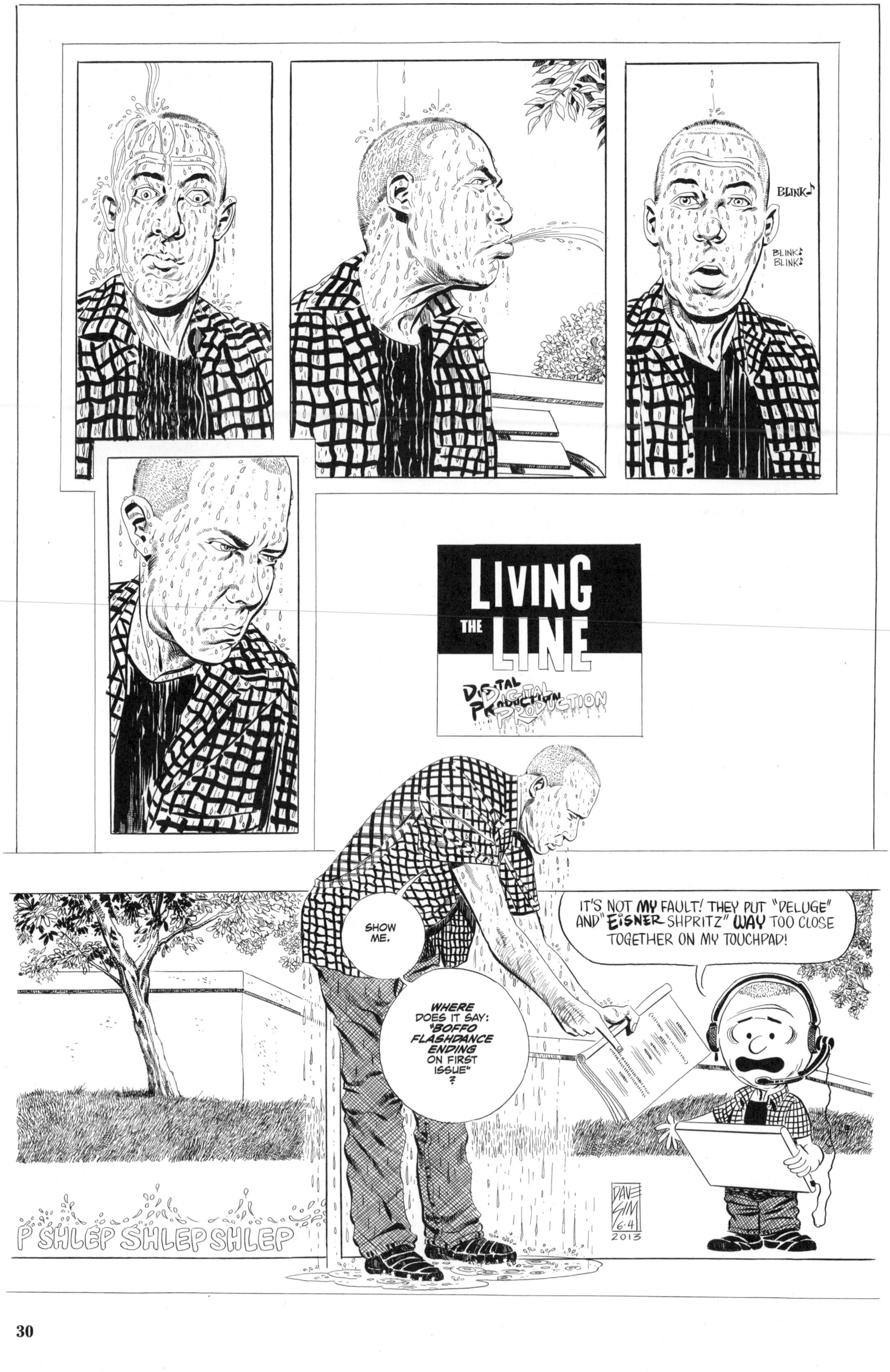
BLINK
BLINK
BLINK
LIVING THE LINE
DIGITAL PRODUCTION
SHOW ME.
WHERE DOES IT SAY: "BOFFO FLASHDANCE ENDING ON FIRST ISSUE"?
IT'S NOT MY FAULT! THEY PUT "DELUGE" AND "EISNER SHPRITZ" WAY TOO CLOSE TOGETHER ON MY TOUCHPAD!
P SHLEP SHLEP SHLEP
DAVE SIM 6-4 2013

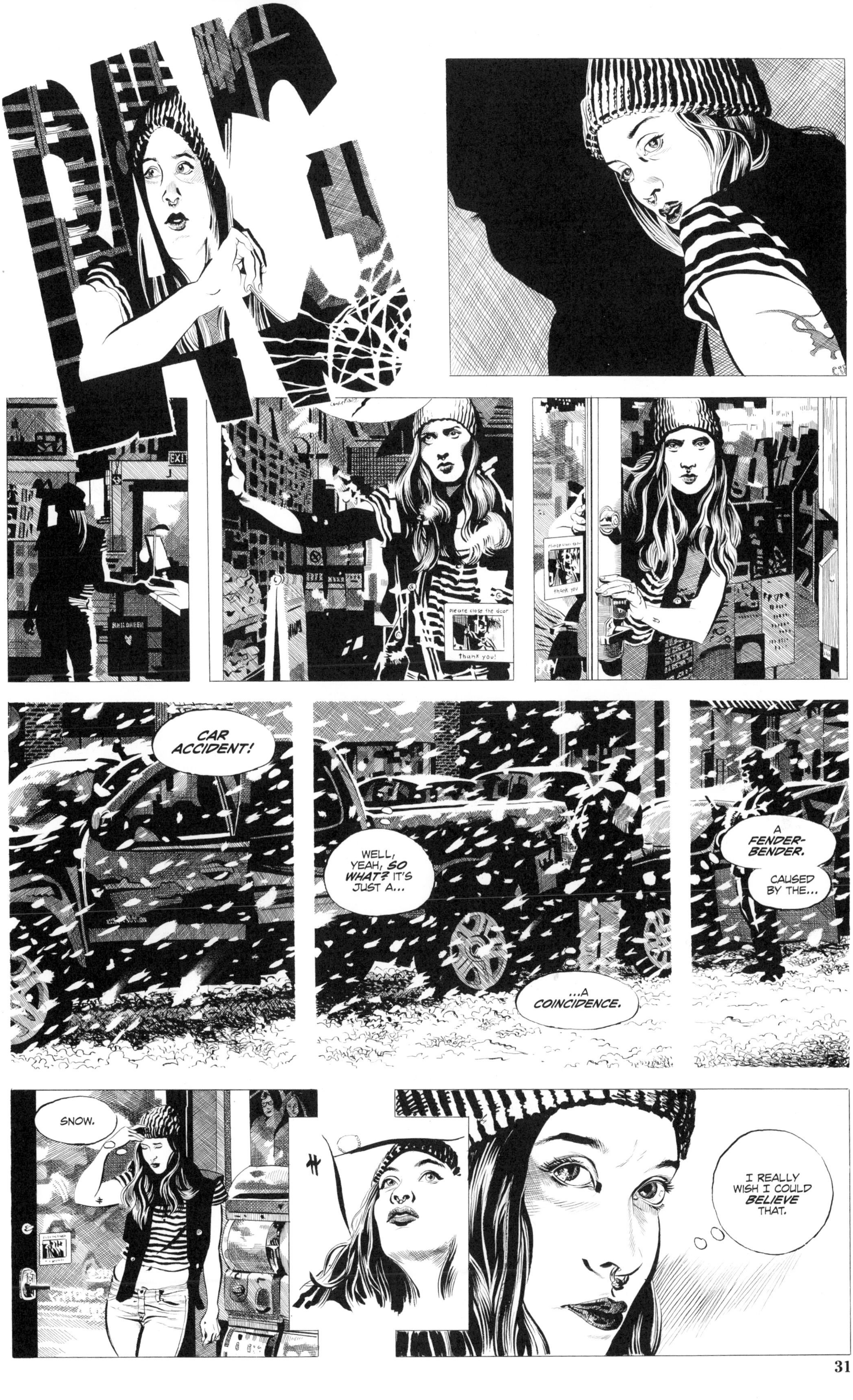
EXIT
please close the door
thank you!
CAR ACCIDENT!
WELL, YEAH, SO WHAT? IT'S JUST A...
...A COINCIDENCE.
A FENDER-BENDER.
CAUSED BY THE...
SNOW.
I REALLY WISH I COULD BELIEVE THAT.

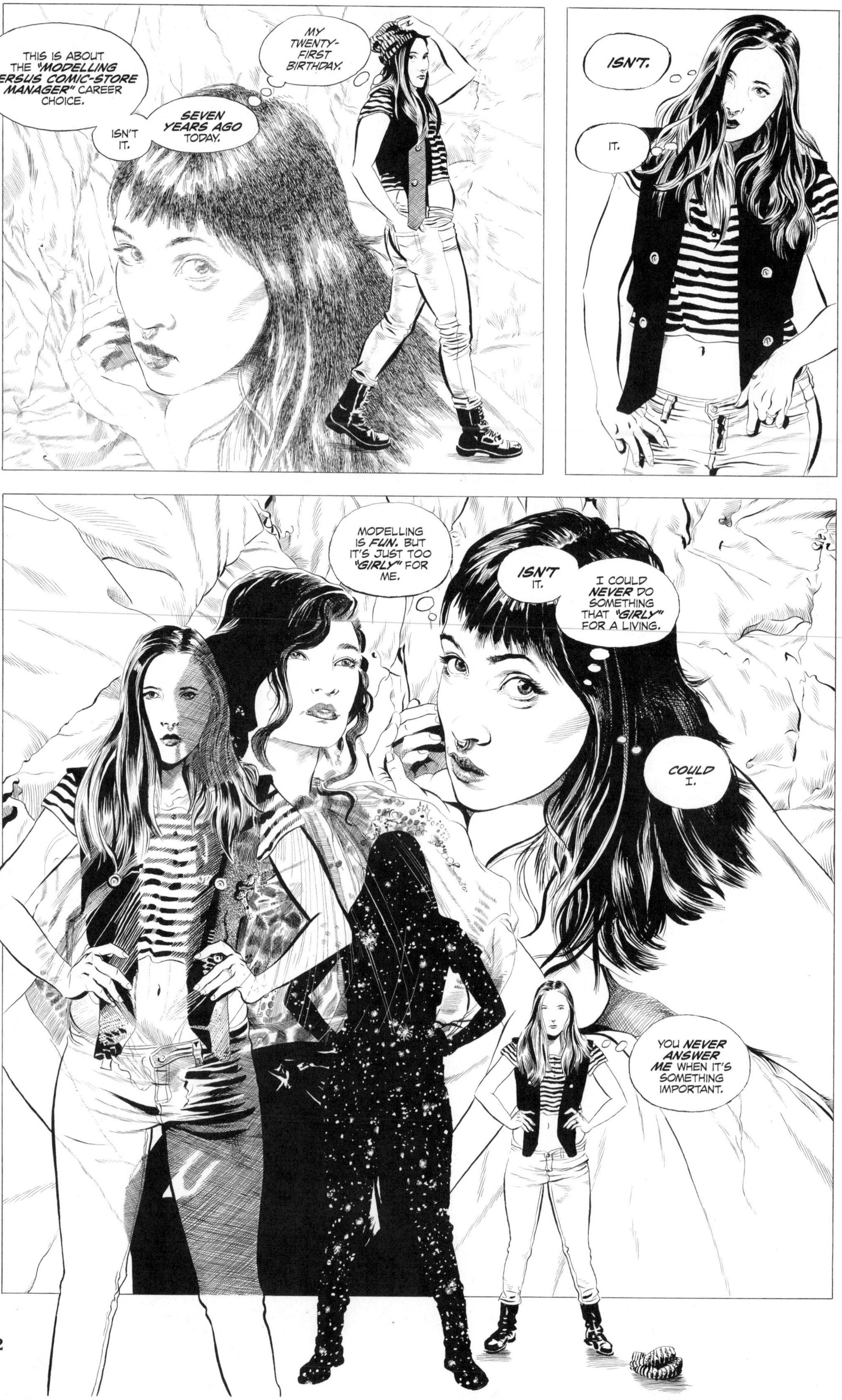
THIS IS ABOUT THE "MODELLING VERSUS COMIC-STORE MANAGER" CAREER CHOICE.
ISN'T IT.
MY TWENTY-FIRST BIRTHDAY.
SEVEN YEARS AGO TODAY.
ISN'T.
IT.
MODELLING IS FUN. BUT IT'S JUST TOO "GIRLY" FOR ME.
ISN'T IT.
I COULD NEVER DO SOMETHING THAT "GIRLY" FOR A LIVING.
COULD I.
YOU NEVER ANSWER ME WHEN IT'S SOMETHING IMPORTANT.

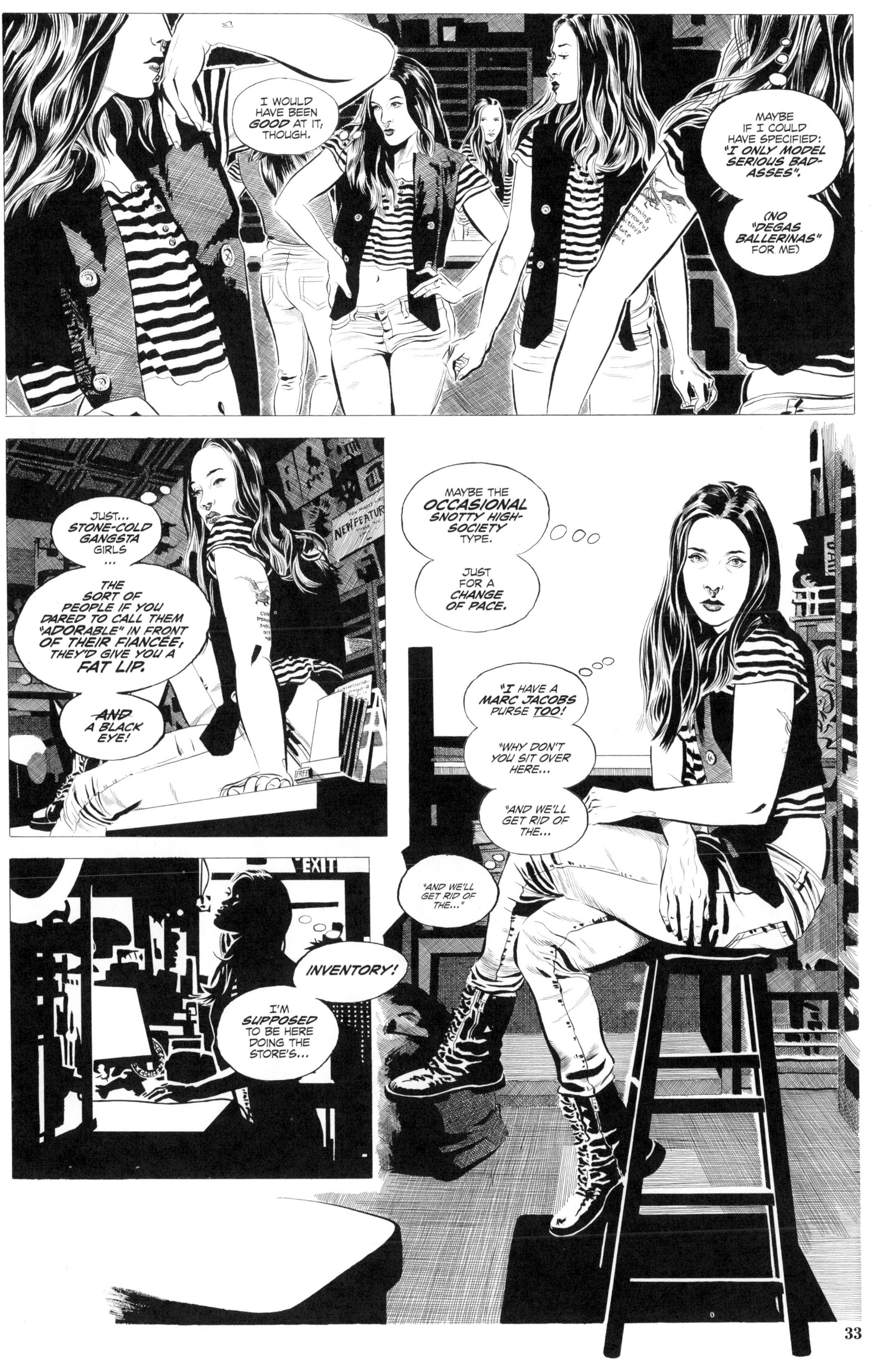
I WOULD HAVE BEEN GOOD AT IT, THOUGH.
MAYBE IF I COULD HAVE SPECIFIED: "I ONLY MODEL SERIOUS BAD-ASSES".
(NO "DEGAS BALLERINAS" FOR ME)
JUST... STONE-COLD GANGSTA GIRLS ...
THE SORT OF PEOPLE IF YOU DARED TO CALL THEM "ADORABLE" IN FRONT OF THEIR FIANCÉE, THEY'D GIVE YOU A FAT LIP.
AND A BLACK EYE!
MAYBE THE OCCASIONAL SNOTTY HIGH-SOCIETY TYPE.
JUST FOR A CHANGE OF PACE.
"I HAVE A MARC JACOBS PURSE TOO!
"WHY DON'T YOU SIT OVER HERE...
"AND WE'LL GET RID OF THE...
EXIT
"AND WE'LL GET RID OF THE..."
INVENTORY!
I'M SUPPOSED TO BE HERE DOING THE STORE'S...

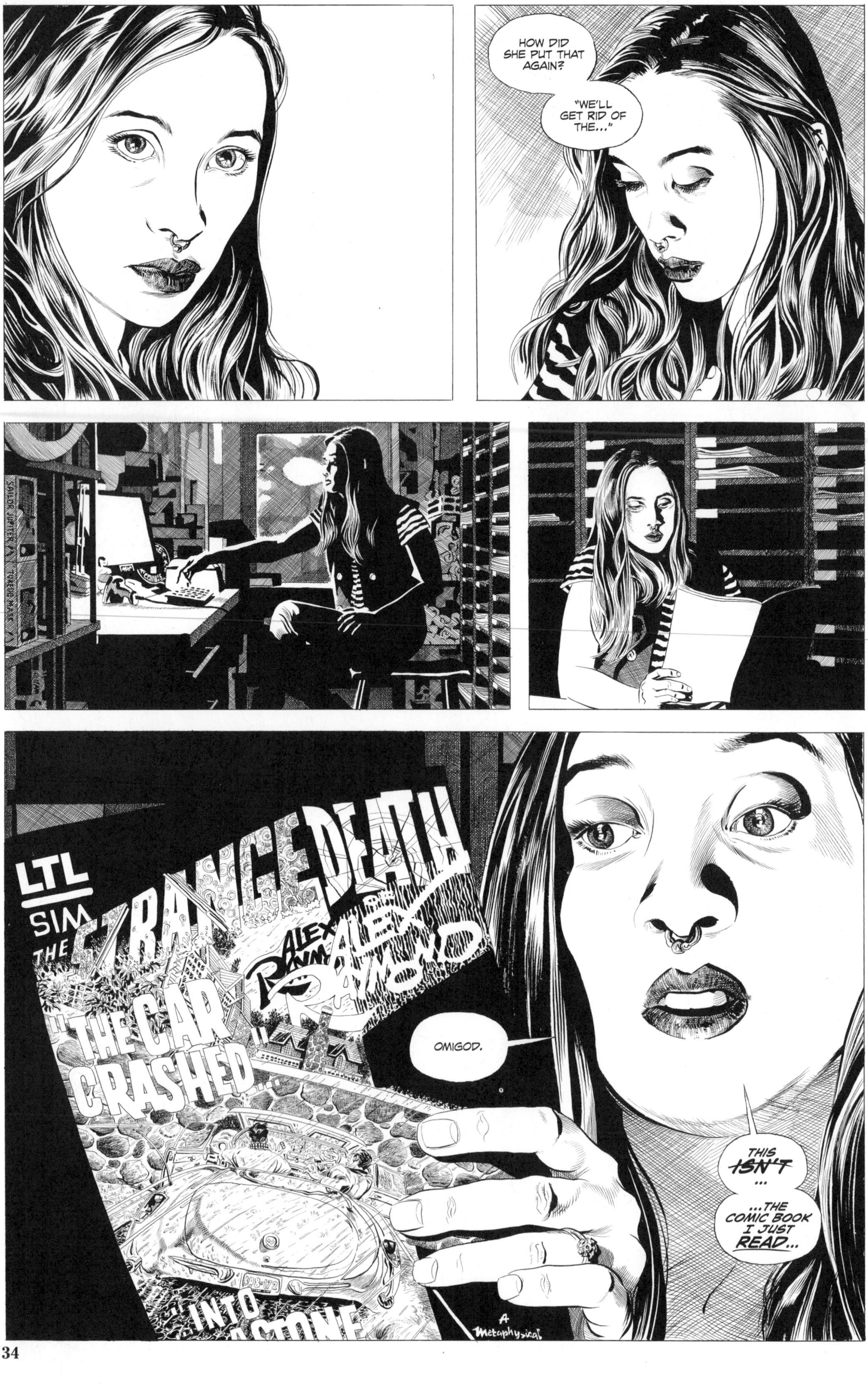
HOW DID SHE PUT THAT AGAIN?
"WE'LL GET RID OF THE..."
LTL
SIM
THE STRANGE DEATH
ALEX RAYMOND
"THE CAR CRASHED"
INTO
A Metaphysical
OMIGOD.
THIS ISN'T ...
...THE COMIC BOOK I JUST READ...

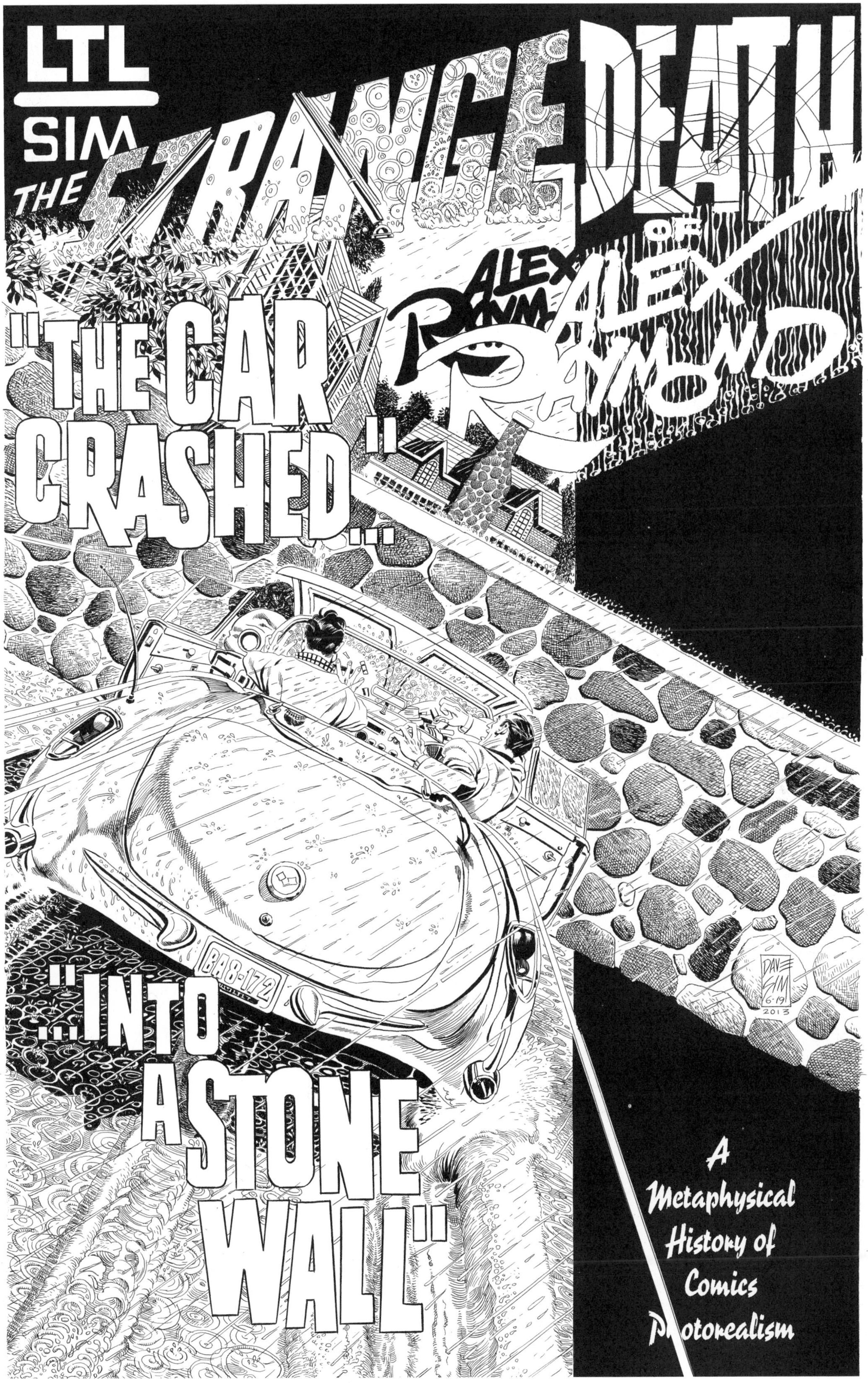
LTL
SIM
THE STRANGE DEATH OF ALEX RAYMOND
"THE CAR CRASHED..."
"...INTO A STONE WALL"
BA8-172
DAVE SIM 6-19 2013
A Metaphysical History of Comics Photorealism

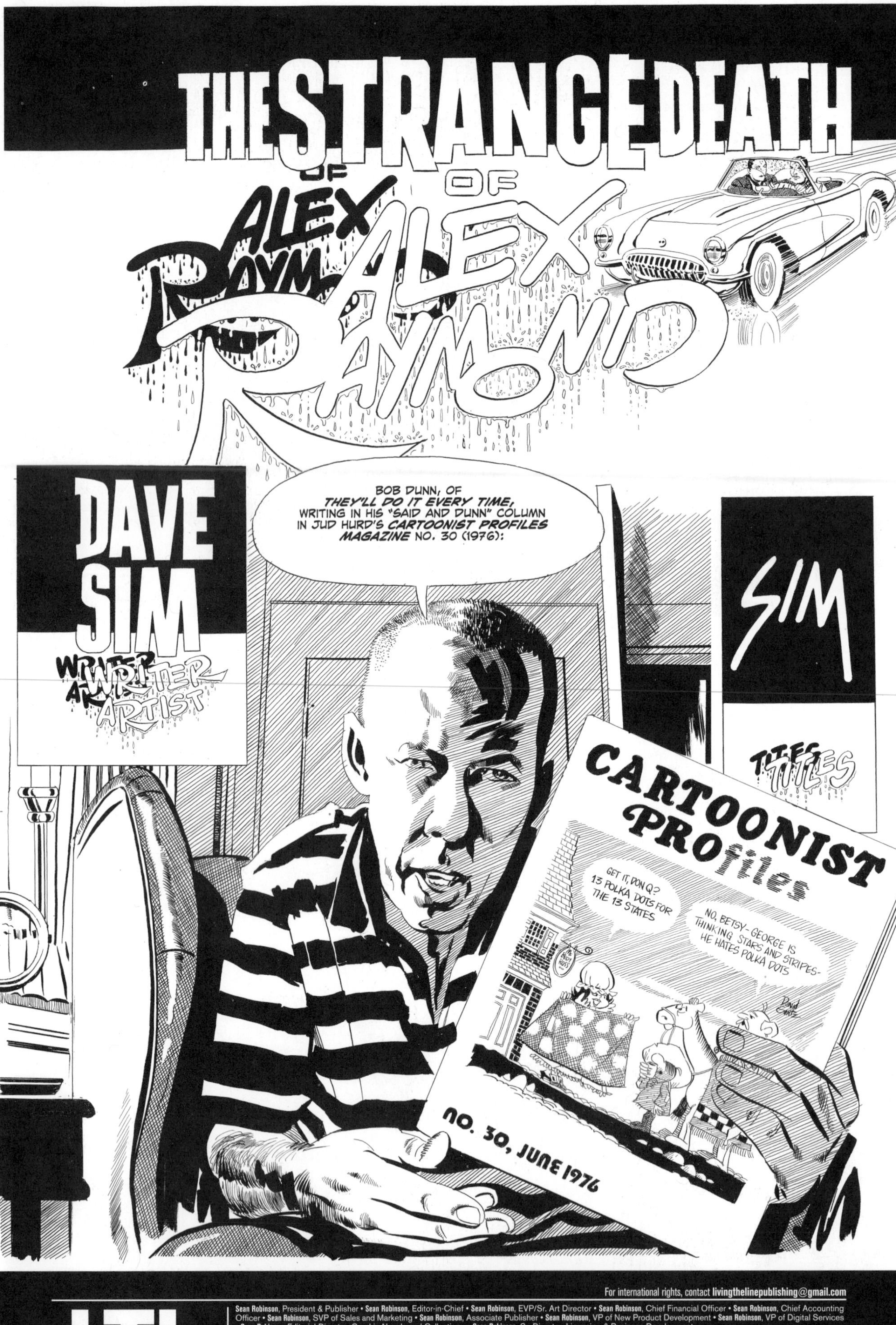
THE STRANGE DEATH OF ALEX RAYMOND
DAVE SIM
WRITER ARTIST
BOB DUNN, OF *THEY'LL DO IT EVERY TIME,* WRITING IN HIS "SAID AND DUNN" COLUMN IN JUD HURD'S *CARTOONIST PROFILES MAGAZINE* NO. 30 (1976):
SIM
TITLES
CARTOONIST PROfiles
GET IT, DON Q? 13 POLKA DOTS FOR THE 13 STATES
NO, BETSY- GEORGE IS THINKING STARS AND STRIPES- HE HATES POLKA DOTS
NO. 30, JUNE 1976

For international rights, contact livingthelinepublishing@gmail.com

LTL
www.LIVINGTHELINE.com

**Sean Robinson**, President & Publisher • **Sean Robinson**, Editor-in-Chief • **Sean Robinson**, EVP/Sr. Art Director • **Sean Robinson**, Chief Financial Officer • **Sean Robinson**, Chief Accounting Officer • **Sean Robinson**, SVP of Sales and Marketing • **Sean Robinson**, Associate Publisher • **Sean Robinson**, VP of New Product Development • **Sean Robinson**, VP of Digital Services • **Sean Robinson**, Editorial Director, Graphic Novels and Collections • **Sean Robinson**, Sr. Director, Licensing & Business Development

**Sean Robinson**, LTL Founder

Facebook: **facebook.com/livingtheline** • Twitter: **@ltlpublishing** • YouTube: **youtube.com/ltlpublishing**
Tumblr: **tumblr.ltlpublishing.com** • Instagram: **instagram.com/ltlpublishing**

THE STRANGE DEATH OF ALEX RAYMOND. JULY 2021. FIRST PRINTING.

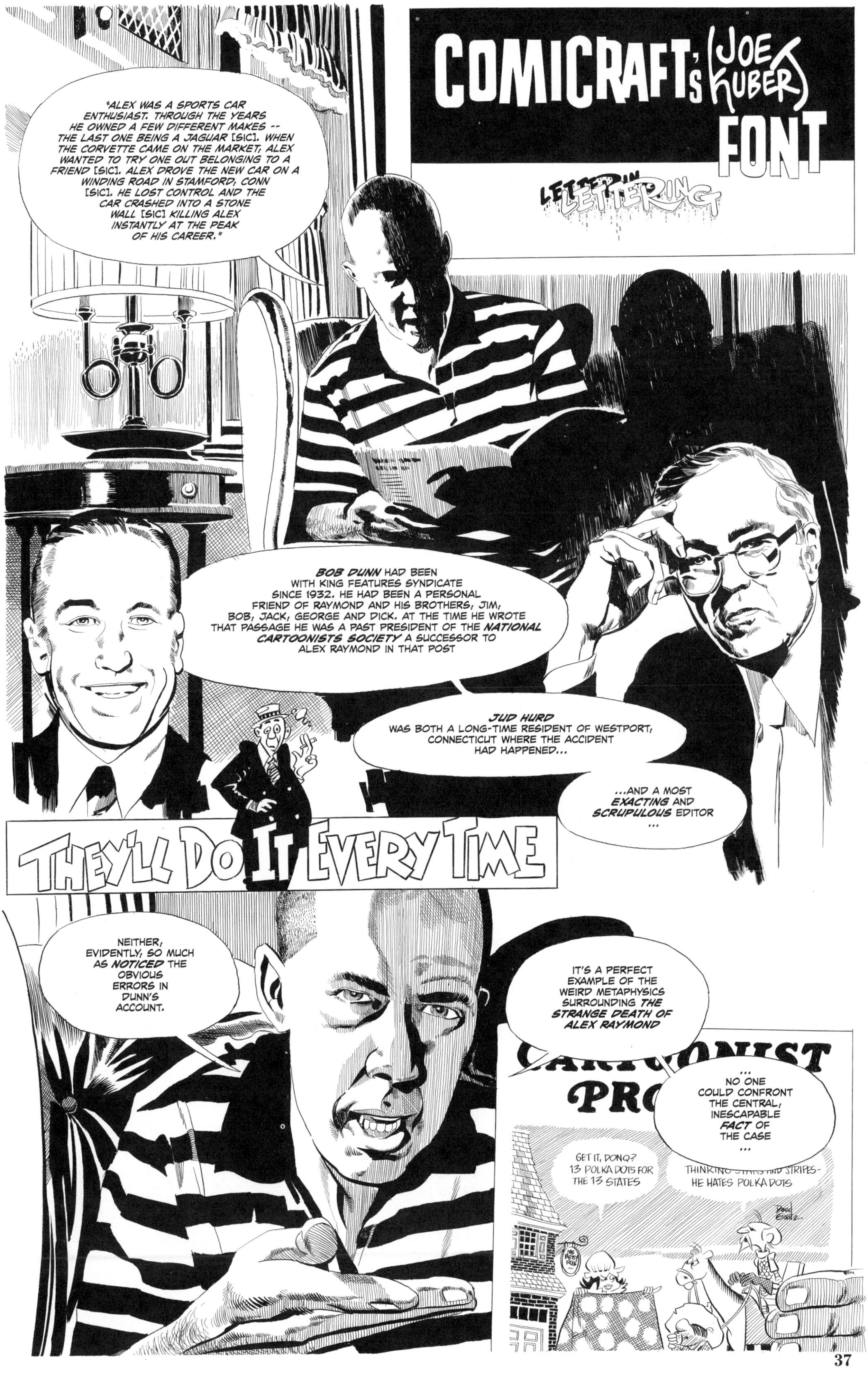
COMICRAFT'S JOE KUBERT FONT
"ALEX WAS A SPORTS CAR ENTHUSIAST. THROUGH THE YEARS HE OWNED A FEW DIFFERENT MAKES -- THE LAST ONE BEING A JAGUAR [SIC]. WHEN THE CORVETTE CAME ON THE MARKET, ALEX WANTED TO TRY ONE OUT BELONGING TO A FRIEND [SIC]. ALEX DROVE THE NEW CAR ON A WINDING ROAD IN STAMFORD, CONN [SIC]. HE LOST CONTROL AND THE CAR CRASHED INTO A STONE WALL [SIC] KILLING ALEX INSTANTLY AT THE PEAK OF HIS CAREER."
BOB DUNN HAD BEEN WITH KING FEATURES SYNDICATE SINCE 1932. HE HAD BEEN A PERSONAL FRIEND OF RAYMOND AND HIS BROTHERS, JIM, BOB, JACK, GEORGE AND DICK. AT THE TIME HE WROTE THAT PASSAGE HE WAS A PAST PRESIDENT OF THE NATIONAL CARTOONISTS SOCIETY A SUCCESSOR TO ALEX RAYMOND IN THAT POST
JUD HURD WAS BOTH A LONG-TIME RESIDENT OF WESTPORT, CONNECTICUT WHERE THE ACCIDENT HAD HAPPENED...
...AND A MOST EXACTING AND SCRUPULOUS EDITOR ...
THEY'LL DO IT EVERY TIME
NEITHER, EVIDENTLY, SO MUCH AS NOTICED THE OBVIOUS ERRORS IN DUNN'S ACCOUNT.
IT'S A PERFECT EXAMPLE OF THE WEIRD METAPHYSICS SURROUNDING THE STRANGE DEATH OF ALEX RAYMOND
PRO
... NO ONE COULD CONFRONT THE CENTRAL, INESCAPABLE FACT OF THE CASE ...
GET IT, DONQ? 13 POLKA DOTS FOR THE 13 STATES
THINKING STARS AND STRIPES- HE HATES POLKA DOTS

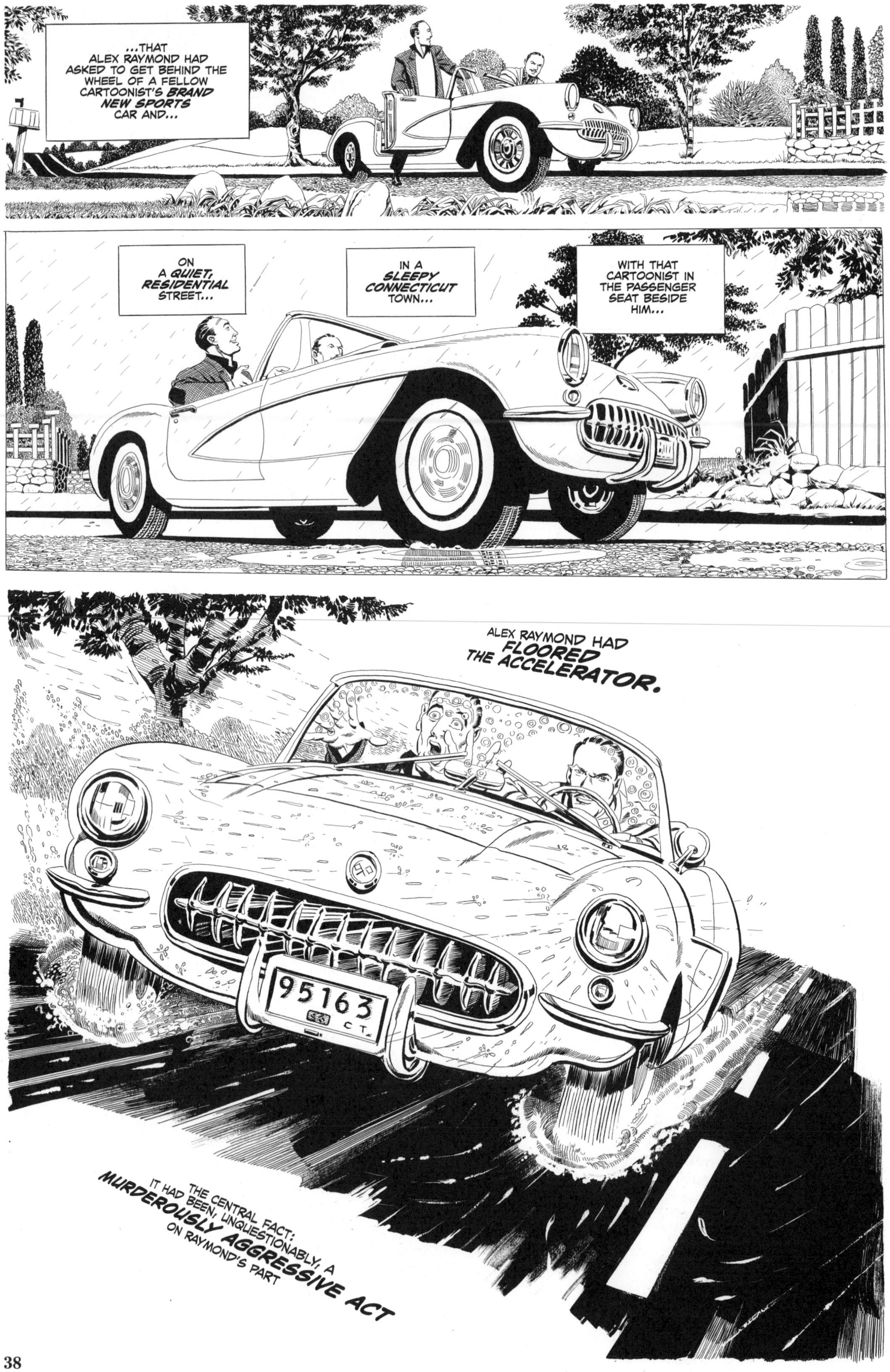
...THAT ALEX RAYMOND HAD ASKED TO GET BEHIND THE WHEEL OF A FELLOW CARTOONIST'S BRAND NEW SPORTS CAR AND...
ON A QUIET, RESIDENTIAL STREET...
IN A SLEEPY CONNECTICUT TOWN...
WITH THAT CARTOONIST IN THE PASSENGER SEAT BESIDE HIM...
ALEX RAYMOND HAD FLOORED THE ACCELERATOR.
95163
C.T.
THE CENTRAL FACT: IT HAD BEEN, UNQUESTIONABLY, A MURDEROUSLY AGGRESSIVE ACT ON RAYMOND'S PART

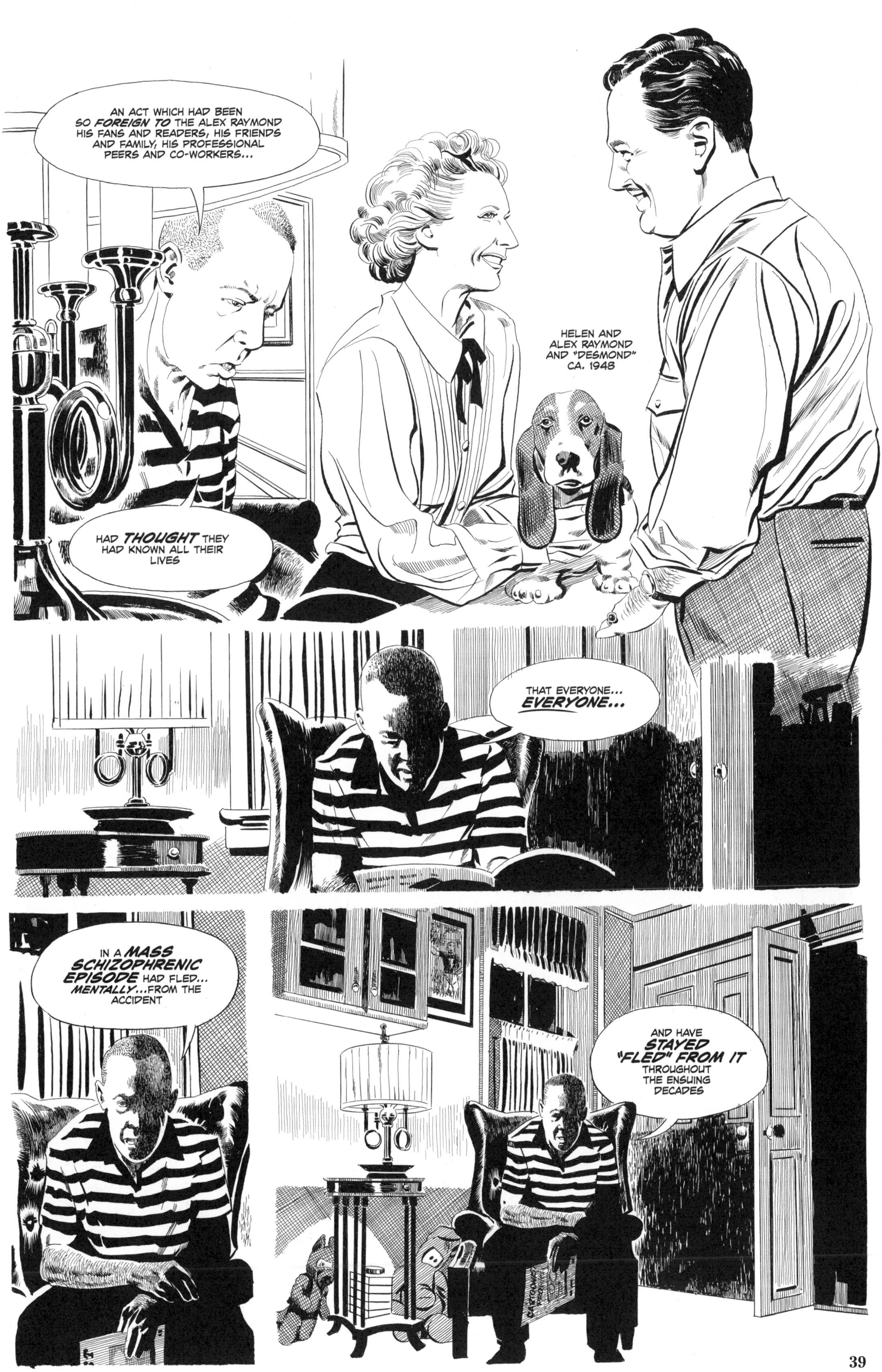

AN ACT WHICH HAD BEEN SO FOREIGN TO THE ALEX RAYMOND HIS FANS AND READERS, HIS FRIENDS AND FAMILY, HIS PROFESSIONAL PEERS AND CO-WORKERS...
HELEN AND ALEX RAYMOND AND "DESMOND" CA. 1948
HAD THOUGHT THEY HAD KNOWN ALL THEIR LIVES
THAT EVERYONE... EVERYONE...
IN A MASS SCHIZOPHRENIC EPISODE HAD FLED... MENTALLY...FROM THE ACCIDENT
AND HAVE STAYED "FLED" FROM IT THROUGHOUT THE ENSUING DECADES

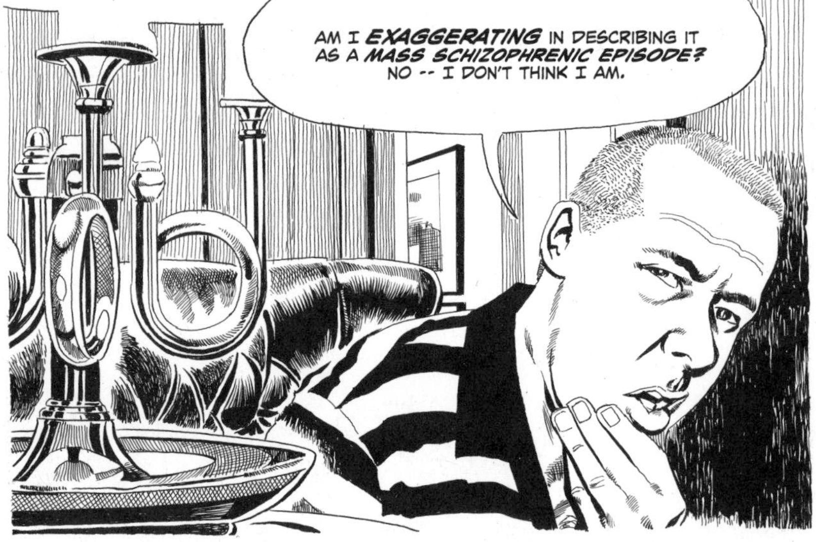
AM I *EXAGGERATING* IN DESCRIBING IT AS A *MASS SCHIZOPHRENIC EPISODE?* NO -- I DON'T THINK I AM.

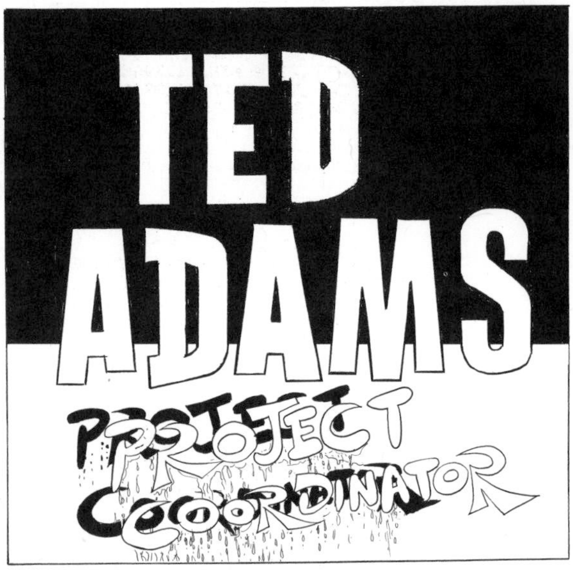
TED ADAMS
PROJECT COORDINATOR

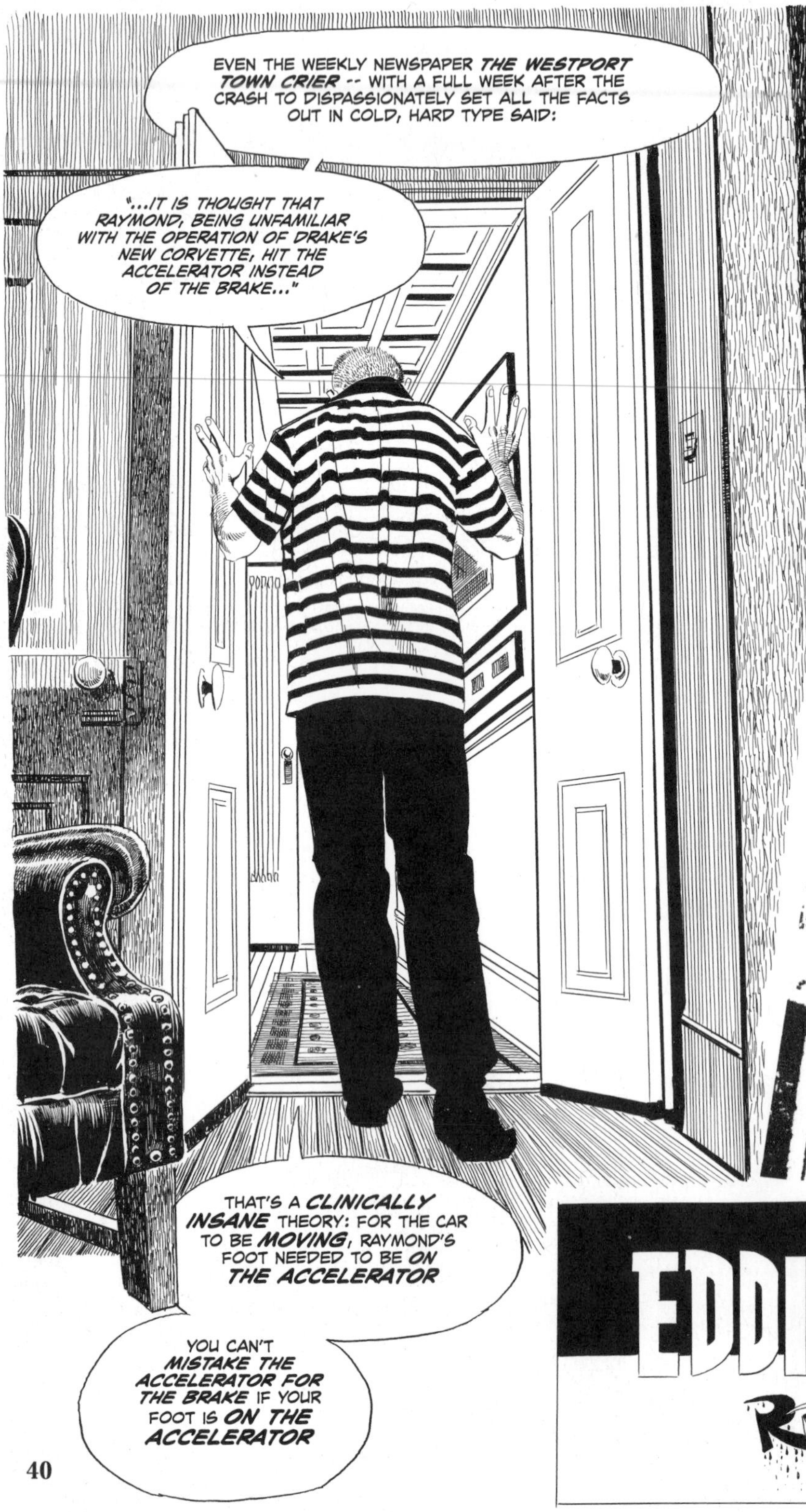
EVEN THE WEEKLY NEWSPAPER *THE WESTPORT TOWN CRIER* -- WITH A FULL WEEK AFTER THE CRASH TO DISPASSIONATELY SET ALL THE FACTS OUT IN COLD, HARD TYPE SAID:
*"...IT IS THOUGHT THAT RAYMOND, BEING UNFAMILIAR WITH THE OPERATION OF DRAKE'S NEW CORVETTE, HIT THE ACCELERATOR INSTEAD OF THE BRAKE..."*
THAT'S A *CLINICALLY INSANE* THEORY: FOR THE CAR TO BE *MOVING*, RAYMOND'S FOOT NEEDED TO BE *ON THE ACCELERATOR*
YOU CAN'T *MISTAKE THE ACCELERATOR FOR THE BRAKE* IF YOUR FOOT IS *ON THE ACCELERATOR*

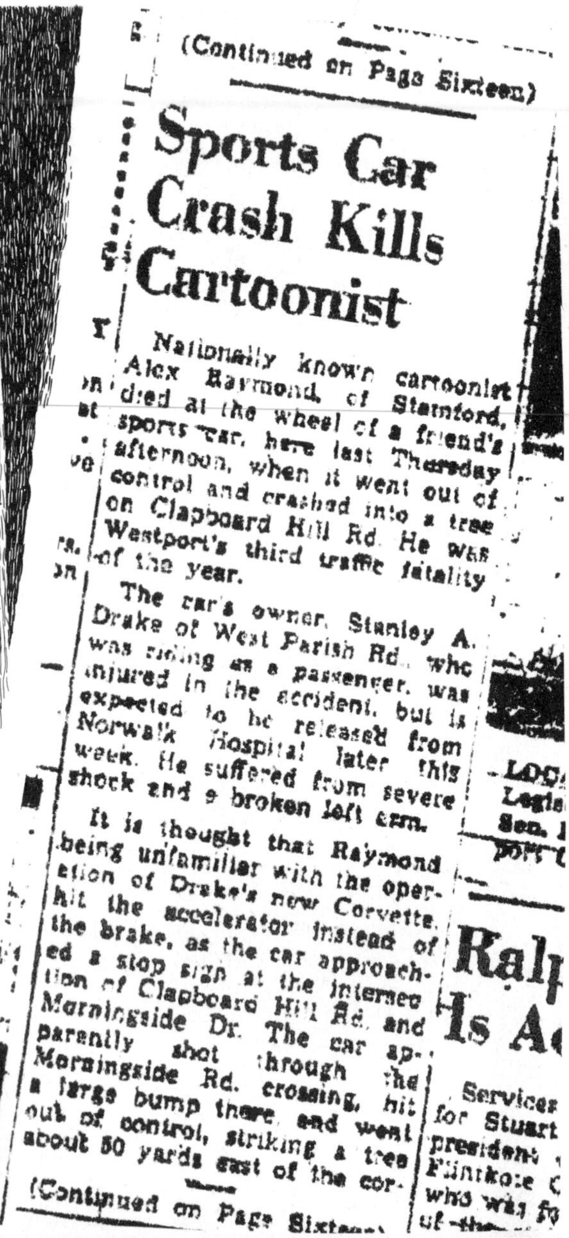
(Continued on Page Sixteen)

**Sports Car Crash Kills Cartoonist**

Nationally known cartoonist Alex Raymond, of Stamford, died at the wheel of a friend's sports car, here last Thursday afternoon, when it went out of control and crashed into a tree on Clapboard Hill Rd. He was Westport's third traffic fatality of the year.

The car's owner, Stanley A. Drake of West Parish Rd., who was riding as a passenger, was injured in the accident, but is expected to be released from Norwalk Hospital later this week. He suffered from severe shock and a broken left arm.

It is thought that Raymond being unfamiliar with the operation of Drake's new Corvette, hit the accelerator instead of the brake, as the car approached a stop sign at the intersection of Clapboard Hill Rd. and Morningside Dr. The car apparently shot through the Morningside Rd. crossing, hit a large bump there, and went out of control, striking a tree about 50 yards east of the corner.

(Continued on Page Sixteen)

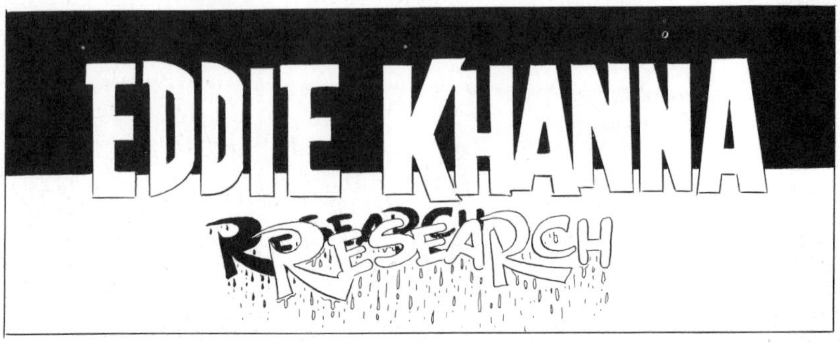
EDDIE KHANNA
RESEARCH

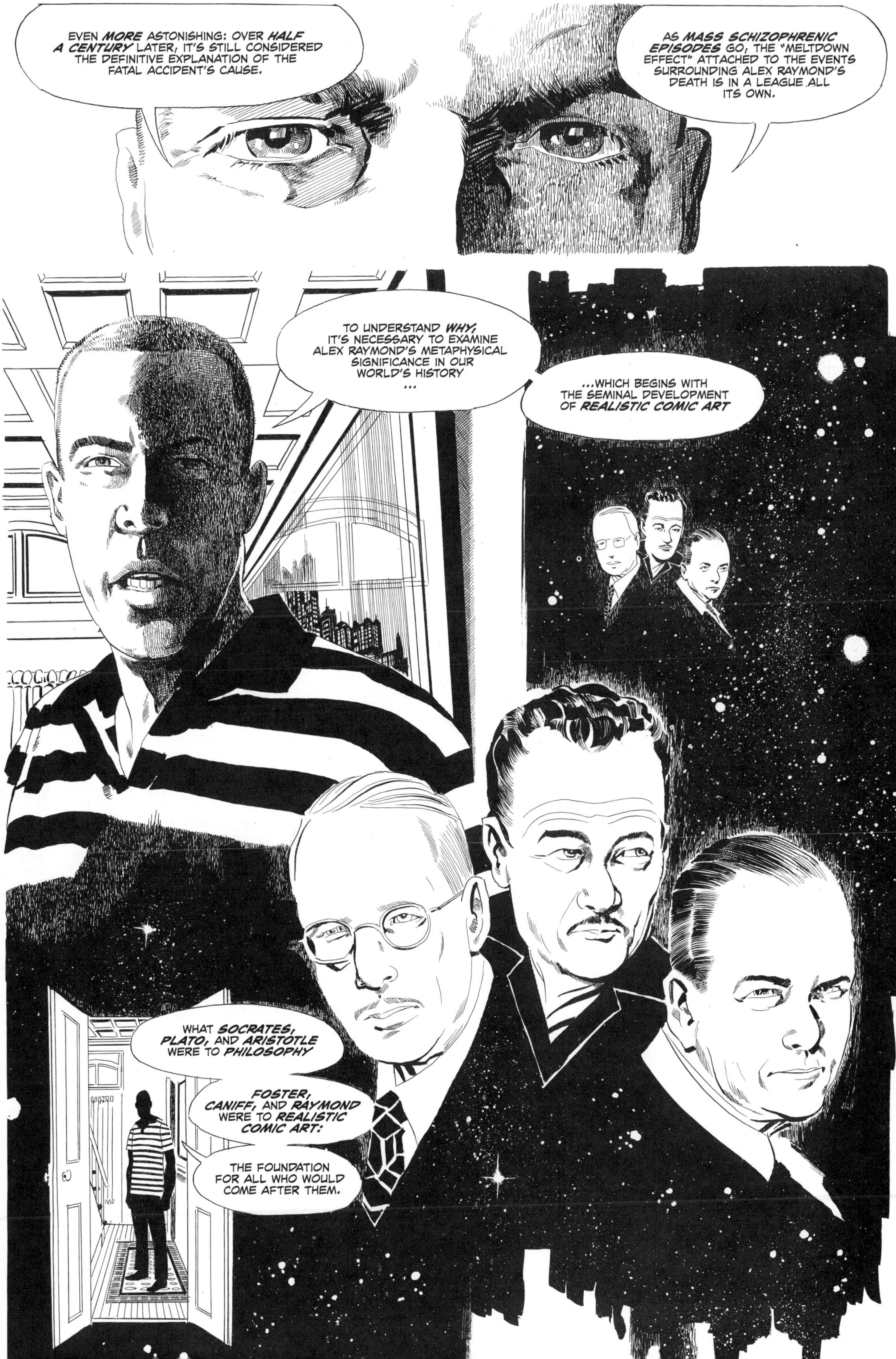
EVEN MORE ASTONISHING: OVER HALF A CENTURY LATER, IT'S STILL CONSIDERED THE DEFINITIVE EXPLANATION OF THE FATAL ACCIDENT'S CAUSE.
AS MASS SCHIZOPHRENIC EPISODES GO, THE "MELTDOWN EFFECT" ATTACHED TO THE EVENTS SURROUNDING ALEX RAYMOND'S DEATH IS IN A LEAGUE ALL ITS OWN.
TO UNDERSTAND WHY, IT'S NECESSARY TO EXAMINE ALEX RAYMOND'S METAPHYSICAL SIGNIFICANCE IN OUR WORLD'S HISTORY ...
...WHICH BEGINS WITH THE SEMINAL DEVELOPMENT OF REALISTIC COMIC ART
WHAT SOCRATES, PLATO, AND ARISTOTLE WERE TO PHILOSOPHY
FOSTER, CANIFF, AND RAYMOND WERE TO REALISTIC COMIC ART:
THE FOUNDATION FOR ALL WHO WOULD COME AFTER THEM.

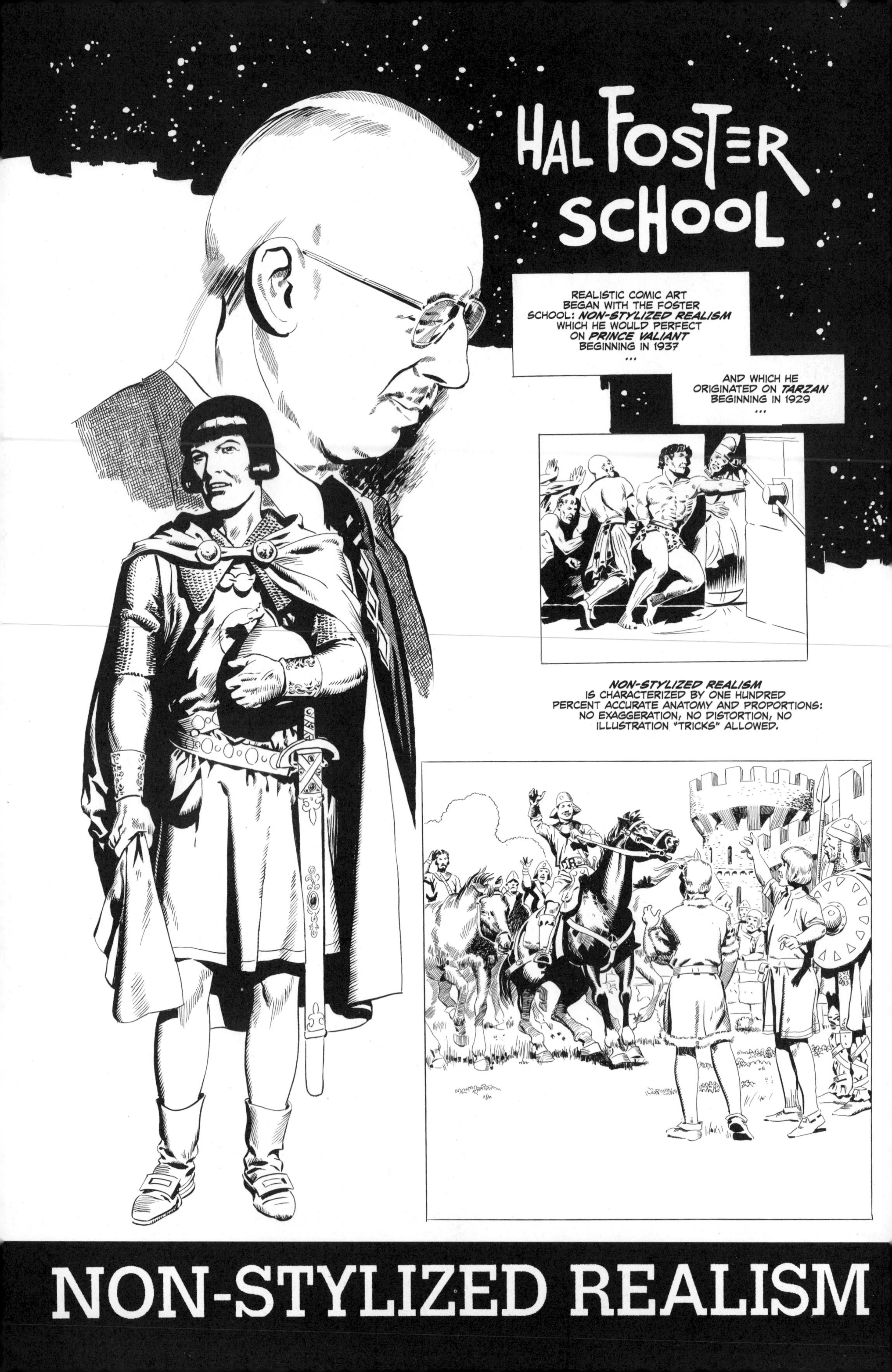
HAL FOSTER SCHOOL
REALISTIC COMIC ART BEGAN WITH THE FOSTER SCHOOL: NON-STYLIZED REALISM WHICH HE WOULD PERFECT ON PRINCE VALIANT BEGINNING IN 1937 ...
AND WHICH HE ORIGINATED ON TARZAN BEGINNING IN 1929 ...
NON-STYLIZED REALISM IS CHARACTERIZED BY ONE HUNDRED PERCENT ACCURATE ANATOMY AND PROPORTIONS: NO EXAGGERATION, NO DISTORTION, NO ILLUSTRATION "TRICKS" ALLOWED.
NON-STYLIZED REALISM

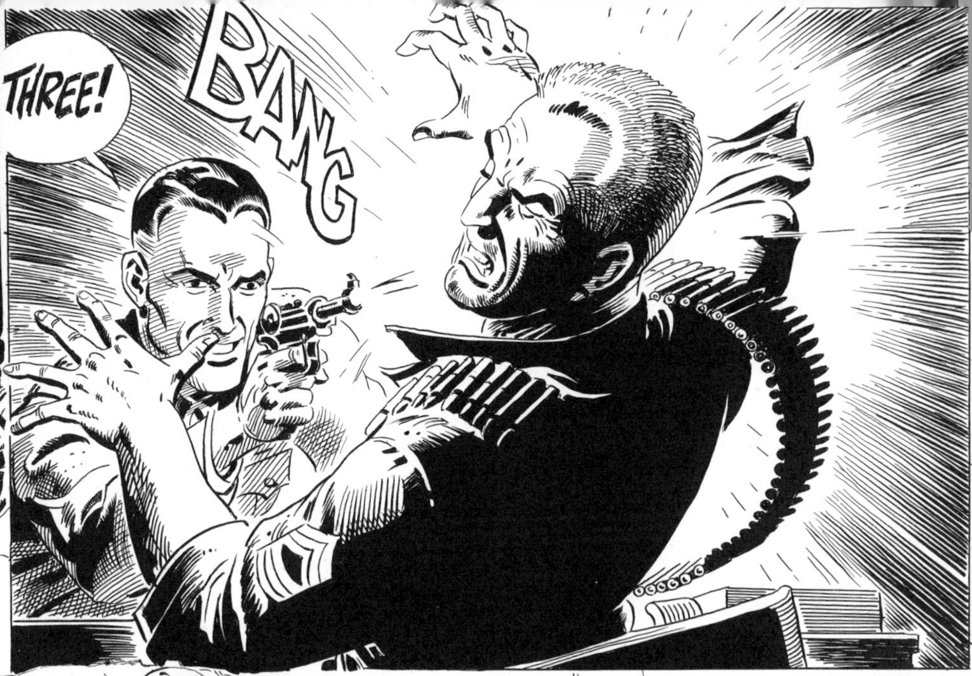
THREE!
BANG

RUSS HEATH

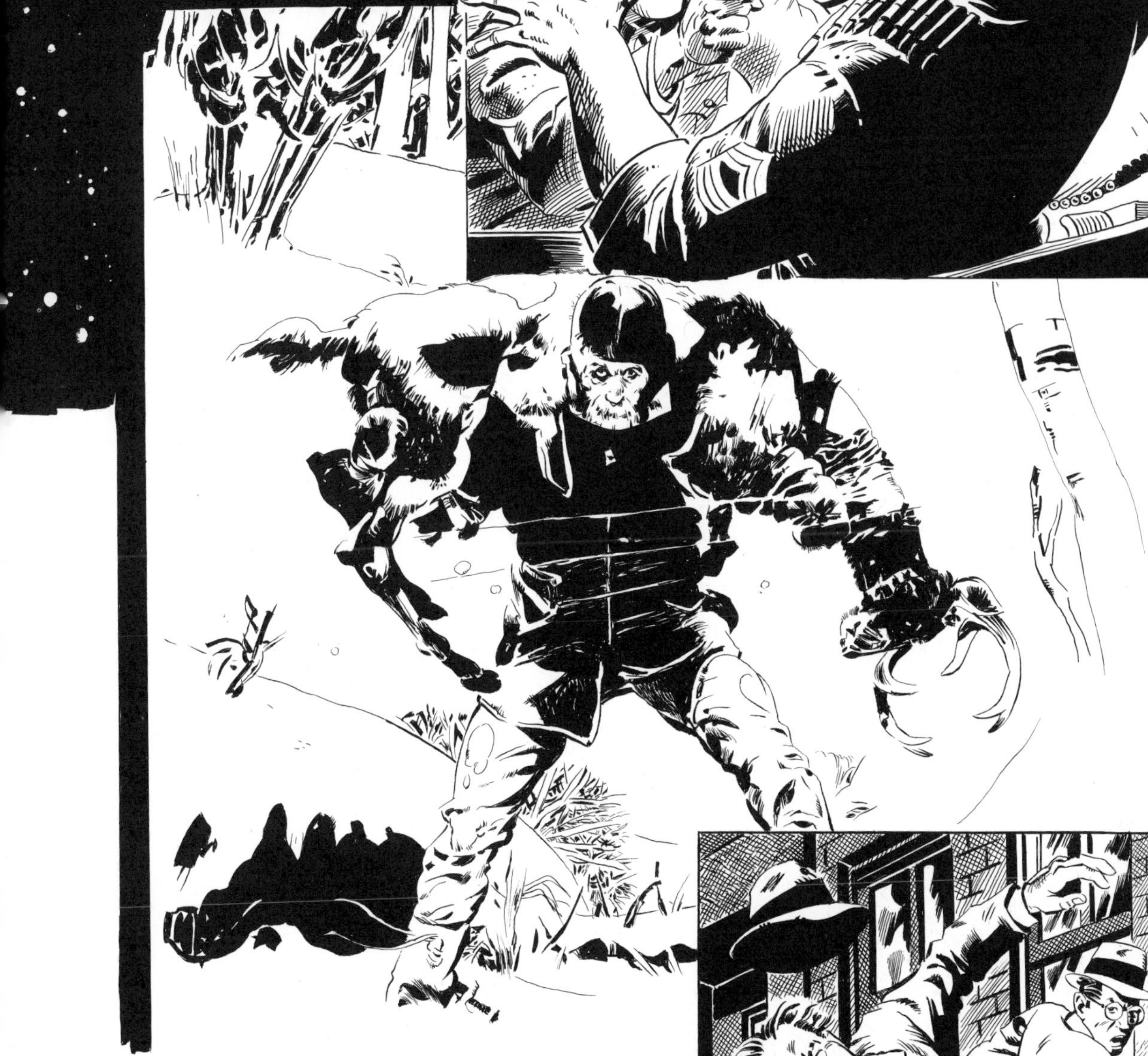

JEFF JONES

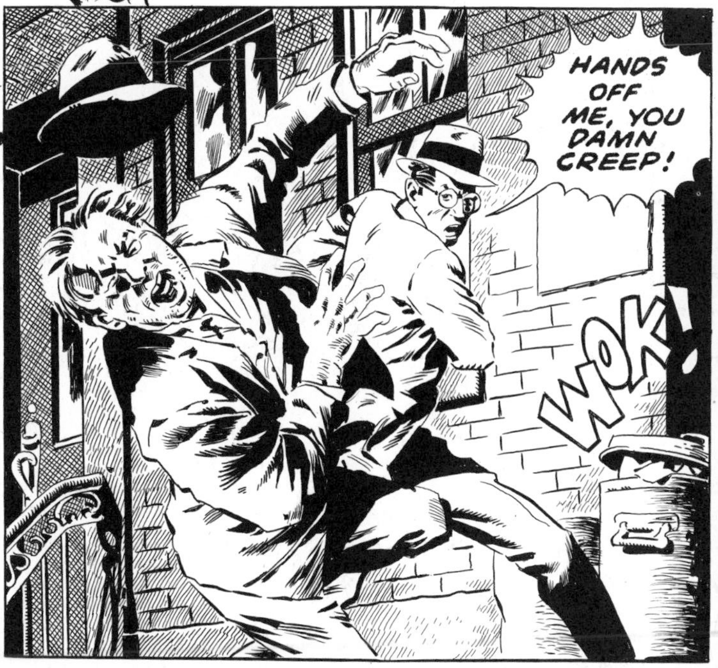
HANDS OFF ME, YOU DAMN CREEP!
WOK!

JOHN SEVERIN

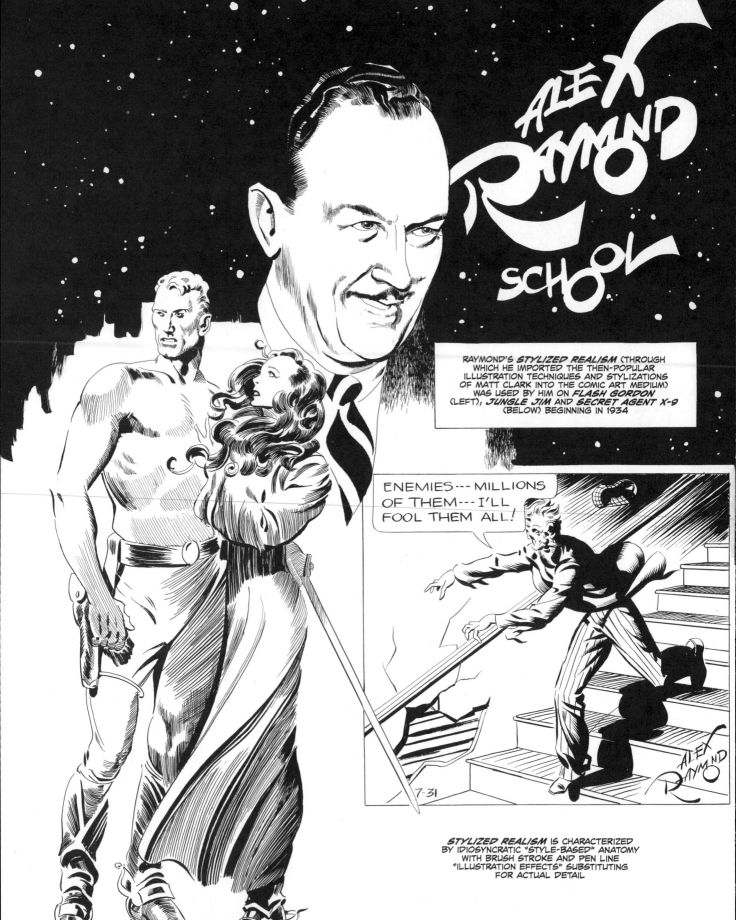

# ALEX RAYMOND SCHOOL

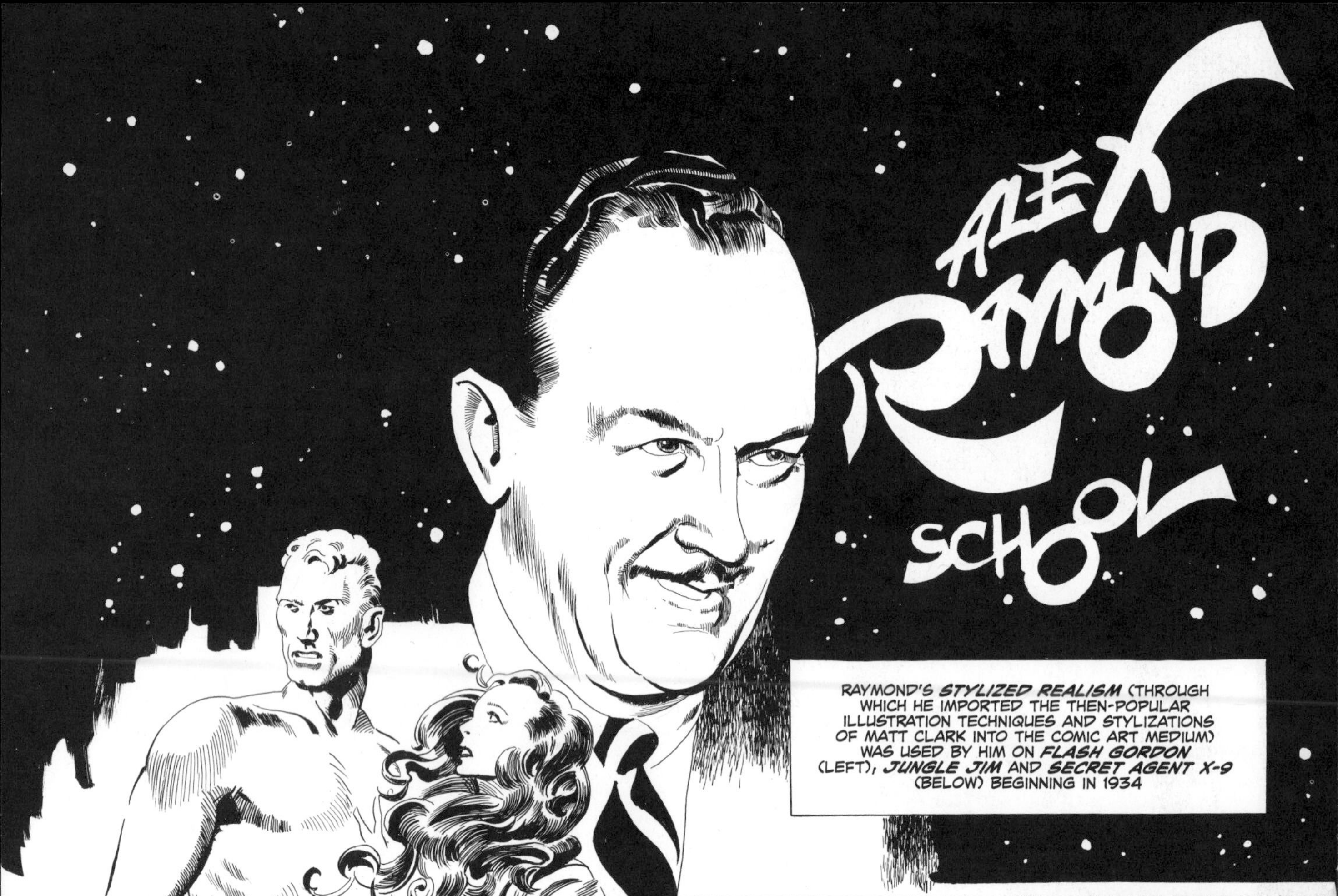
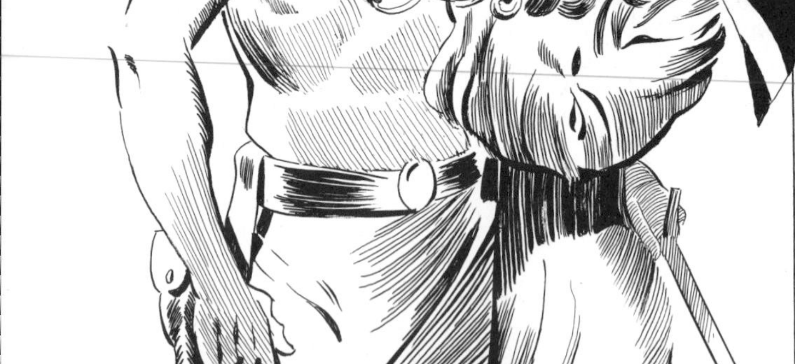

RAYMOND'S ***STYLIZED REALISM*** (THROUGH WHICH HE IMPORTED THE THEN-POPULAR ILLUSTRATION TECHNIQUES AND STYLIZATIONS OF MATT CLARK INTO THE COMIC ART MEDIUM) WAS USED BY HIM ON ***FLASH GORDON*** (LEFT); ***JUNGLE JIM*** AND ***SECRET AGENT X-9*** (BELOW) BEGINNING IN 1934

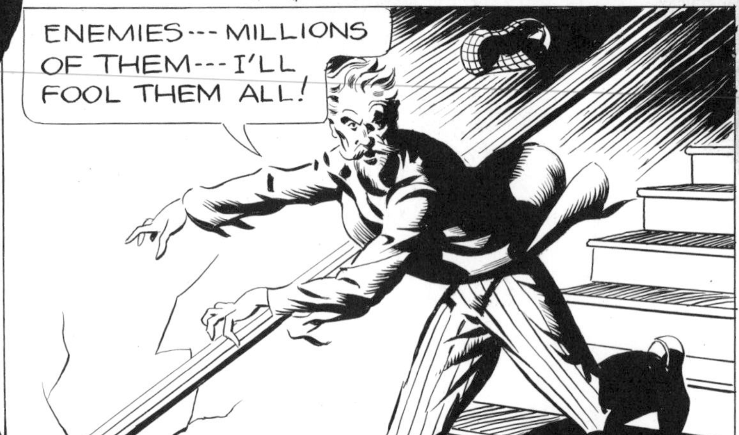
ENEMIES--- MILLIONS OF THEM--- I'LL FOOL THEM ALL!
ALEX RAYMOND
7-31

***STYLIZED REALISM*** IS CHARACTERIZED BY IDIOSYNCRATIC "STYLE-BASED" ANATOMY WITH BRUSH STROKE AND PEN LINE "ILLUSTRATION EFFECTS" SUBSTITUTING FOR ACTUAL DETAIL

IT WAS ONLY WHEN ***KING FEATURES SYNDICATE*** REFUSED TO ALLOW RAYMOND TO RETURN TO HIS CREATION, ***FLASH GORDON***, UPON HIS RETURN FROM MILITARY SERVICE IN WORLD WAR II THAT RAYMOND CREATED HIS SECOND SCHOOL, ***PHOTOREALISM***, ON ***RIP KIRBY***

# STYLIZED REALISM

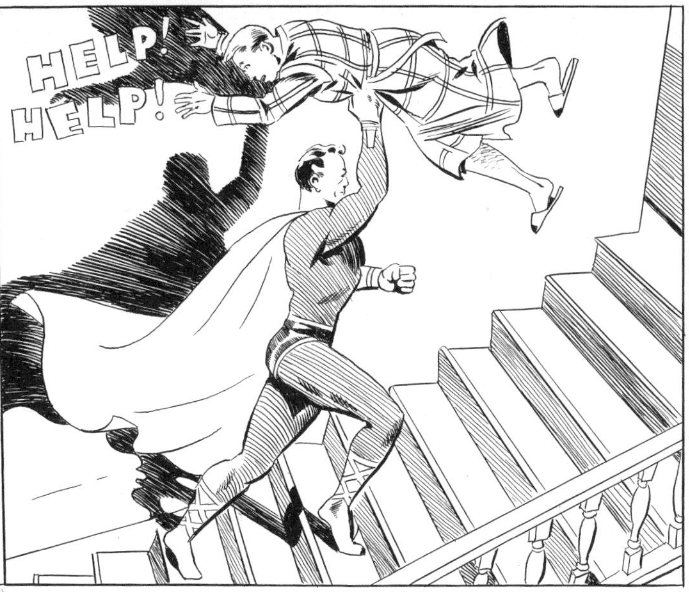
HELP!
HELP!

JOE SHUSTER

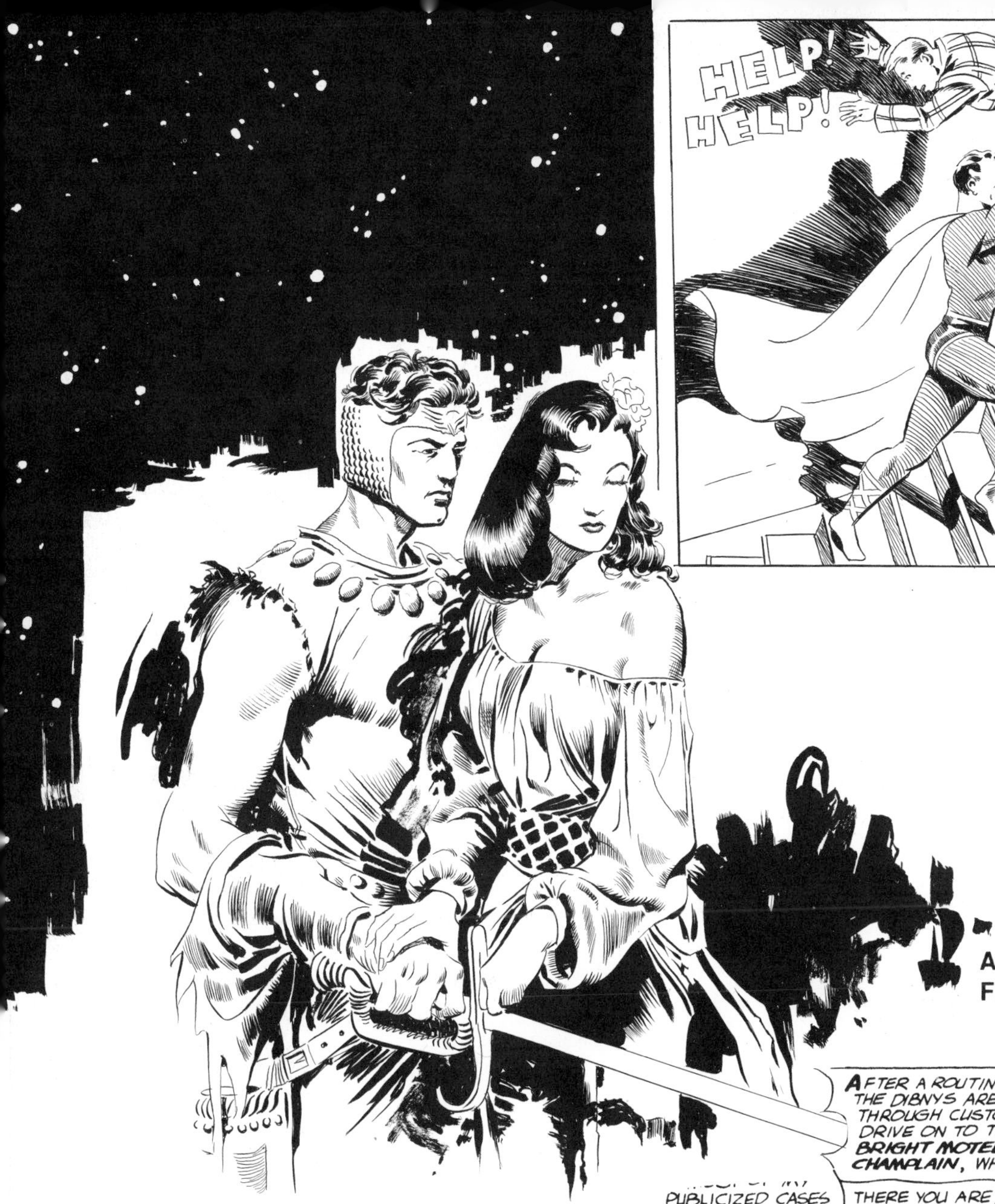

AL WILLIAMSON &
FRANK FRAZETTA

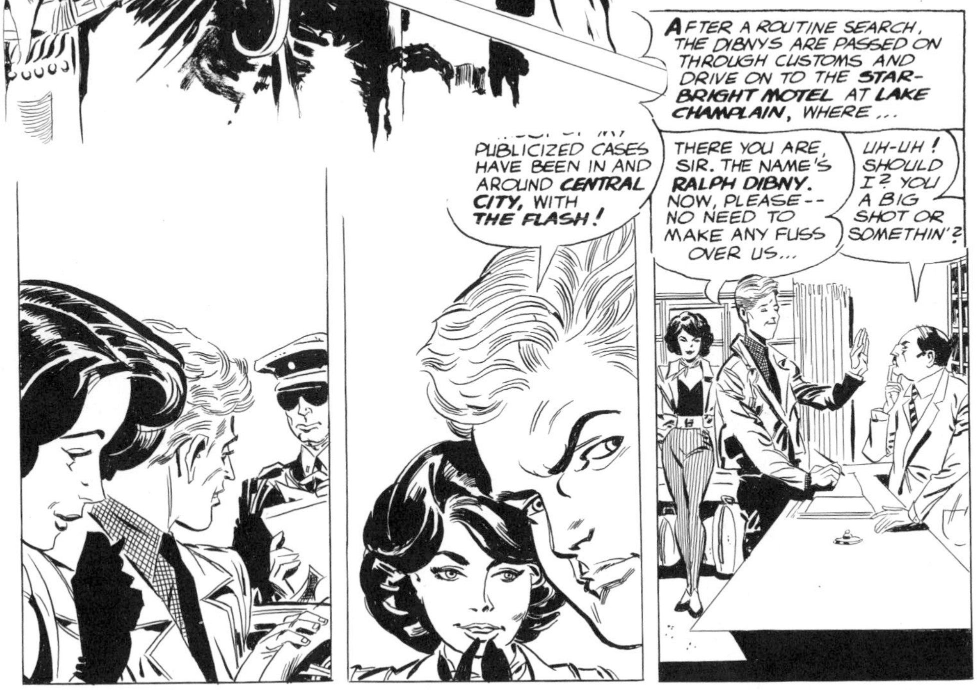
AFTER A ROUTINE SEARCH, THE DIBNYS ARE PASSED ON THROUGH CUSTOMS AND DRIVE ON TO THE STAR-BRIGHT MOTEL AT LAKE CHAMPLAIN, WHERE ...
PUBLICIZED CASES HAVE BEEN IN AND AROUND CENTRAL CITY, WITH THE FLASH!
THERE YOU ARE, SIR. THE NAME'S RALPH DIBNY. NOW, PLEASE-- NO NEED TO MAKE ANY FUSS OVER US...
UH-UH! SHOULD I? YOU A BIG SHOT OR SOMETHIN'?

CARMINE INFANTINO

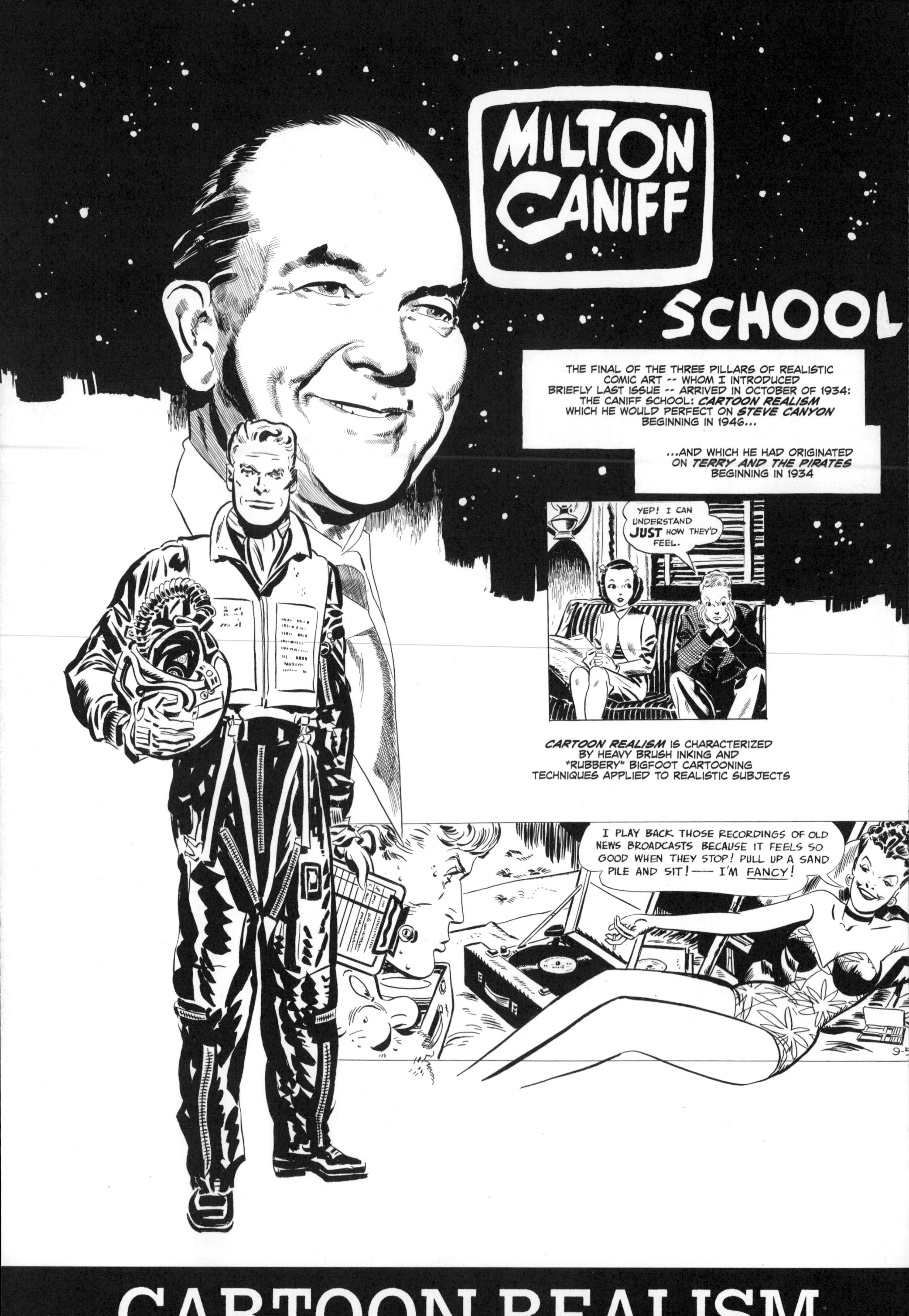
MILTON CANIFF
SCHOOL
THE FINAL OF THE THREE PILLARS OF REALISTIC COMIC ART -- WHOM I INTRODUCED BRIEFLY LAST ISSUE -- ARRIVED IN OCTOBER OF 1934: THE CANIFF SCHOOL: *CARTOON REALISM* WHICH HE WOULD PERFECT ON *STEVE CANYON* BEGINNING IN 1946...
...AND WHICH HE HAD ORIGINATED ON *TERRY AND THE PIRATES* BEGINNING IN 1934
YEP! I CAN UNDERSTAND **JUST** HOW THEY'D FEEL.
*CARTOON REALISM* IS CHARACTERIZED BY HEAVY BRUSH INKING AND "RUBBERY" BIGFOOT CARTOONING TECHNIQUES APPLIED TO REALISTIC SUBJECTS
I PLAY BACK THOSE RECORDINGS OF OLD NEWS BROADCASTS BECAUSE IT FEELS SO GOOD WHEN THEY STOP! PULL UP A SAND PILE AND SIT! —— I'M FANCY!

# CARTOON REALISM

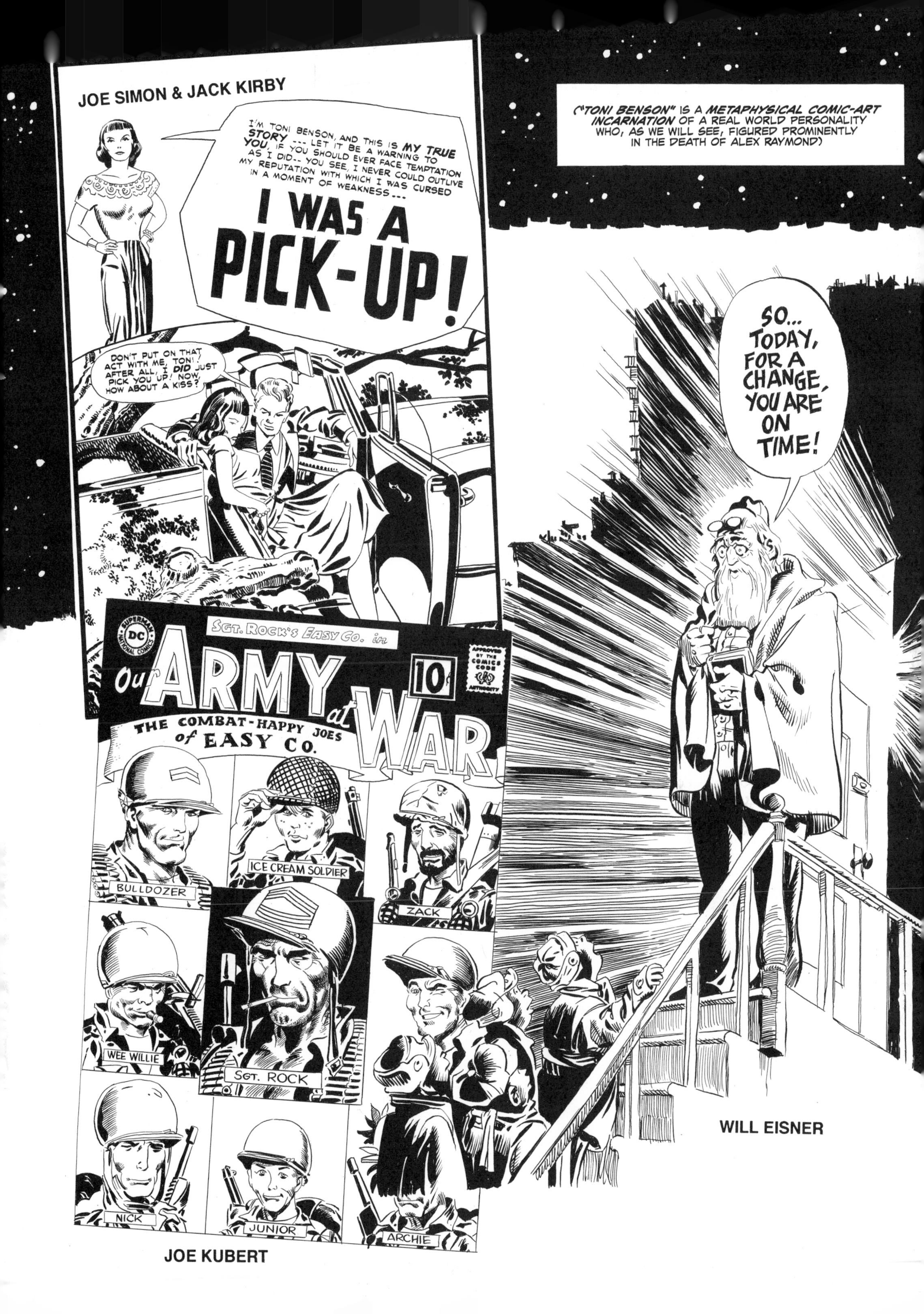
I'M TONI BENSON, AND THIS IS MY TRUE STORY --- LET IT BE A WARNING TO YOU, IF YOU SHOULD EVER FACE TEMPTATION AS I DID-- YOU SEE, I NEVER COULD OUTLIVE MY REPUTATION WITH WHICH I WAS CURSED IN A MOMENT OF WEAKNESS---
I WAS A PICK-UP!
DON'T PUT ON THAT ACT WITH ME, TONI! AFTER ALL, I DID JUST PICK YOU UP! NOW, HOW ABOUT A KISS?
SGT. ROCK'S EASY CO. in
Our ARMY at WAR
10¢
THE COMBAT-HAPPY JOES of EASY CO.
BULLDOZER
ICE CREAM SOLDIER
ZACK
WEE WILLIE
SGT. ROCK
NICK
JUNIOR
ARCHIE
("TONI BENSON" IS A METAPHYSICAL COMIC-ART INCARNATION OF A REAL WORLD PERSONALITY WHO, AS WE WILL SEE, FIGURED PROMINENTLY IN THE DEATH OF ALEX RAYMOND)
SO... TODAY, FOR A CHANGE, YOU ARE ON TIME!

JOE SIMON & JACK KIRBY

JOE KUBERT

WILL EISNER

AT THE RISK OF GETTING OFF-TOPIC:

THERE ARE INTERESTING MUTATIONS, PARTICULARLY AT THE MID-POINT BETWEEN ANY TWO SCHOOLS.

ROY CRANE'S ***BUZ SAWYER***, IN THE EARLY 1960S, OCCUPIED A POSITION HALFWAY BETWEEN NON-STYLIZED REALISM AND CARTOON REALISM...***(FOSTER/CANIFF)***

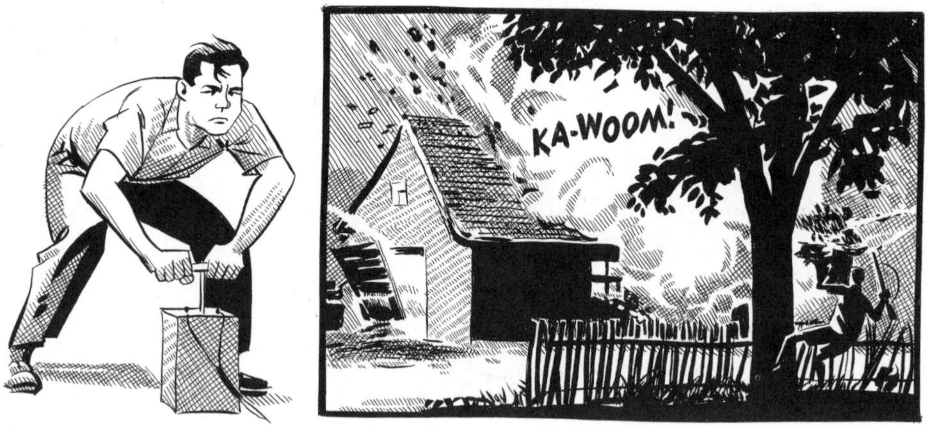
KA-WOOM!

WHILE HAROLD GRAY'S ***LITTLE ORPHAN ANNIE***, IN THE LATE 1930S, WAS ON THE SAME AXIS BUT COMING FROM THE OPPOSITE DIRECTION: CARTOON REALISM SKEWING TOWARDS NON-STYLIZED REALISM ***(CANIFF/FOSTER)***

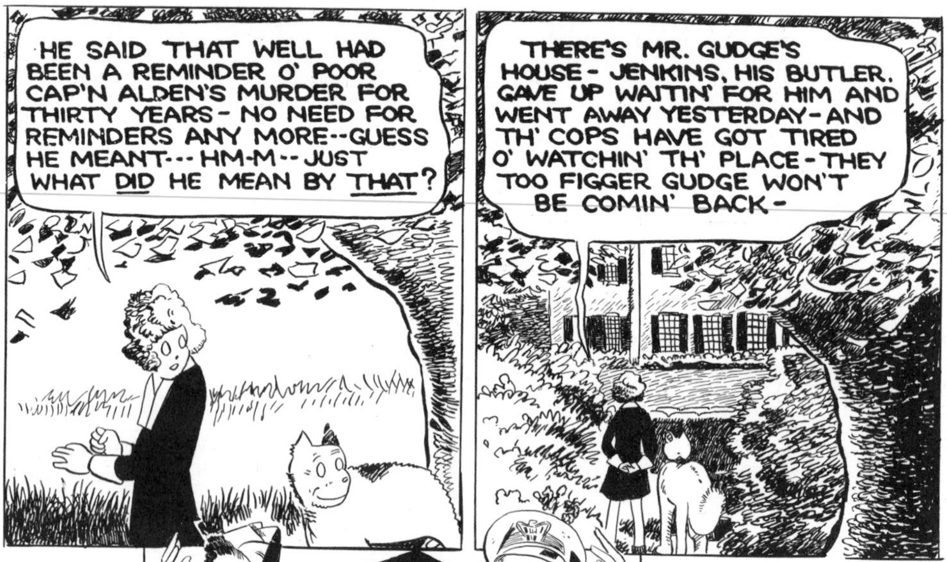
HE SAID THAT WELL HAD BEEN A REMINDER O' POOR CAP'N ALDEN'S MURDER FOR THIRTY YEARS- NO NEED FOR REMINDERS ANY MORE--GUESS HE MEANT--- HM-M--JUST WHAT DID HE MEAN BY THAT?
THERE'S MR. GUDGE'S HOUSE- JENKINS, HIS BUTLER, GAVE UP WAITIN' FOR HIM AND WENT AWAY YESTERDAY- AND TH' COPS HAVE GOT TIRED O' WATCHIN' TH' PLACE- THEY TOO FIGGER GUDGE WON'T BE COMIN' BACK-

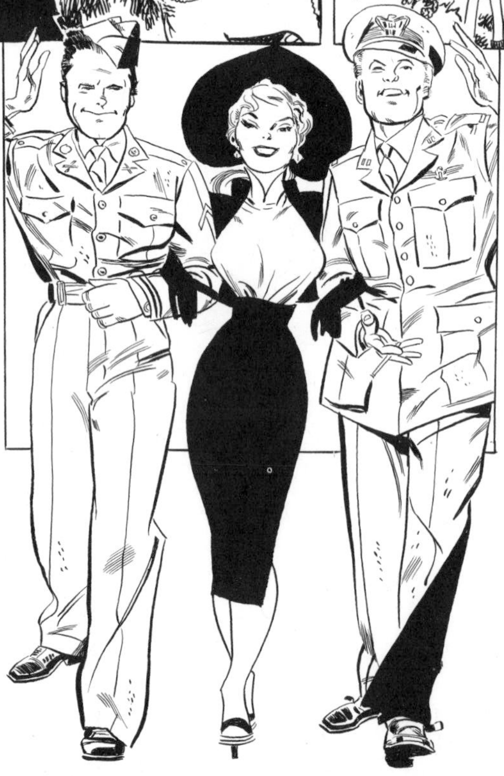

ALEX TOTH BEGAN AS A ***STYLIZED*** REALIST BUT SPENT MOST OF HIS CAREER AS A CARTOON REALIST ***(RAYMOND*** INTO ***CANIFF)***

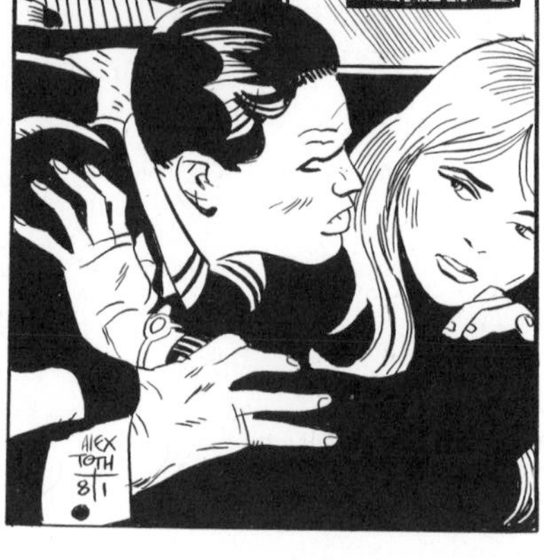
ALEX TOTH 8/1

(IT'S ALSO POSSIBLE TO DESCRIBE THE GENERAL HISTORY OF COMIC-BOOK ART IN THESE TERMS AS I ATTEMPTED TO DO IN ***GLAMOURPUSS*** NO. 2):

COMIC BOOKS IN THE 1960S AND 1970S WERE DOMINATED BY *JACK KIRBY* AND *NEAL ADAMS*: *CANIFF SCHOOL* VERSUS *RAYMOND SCHOOLS*. ADAMS, THROUGH HIS STUDIO, *CONTINUITY ASSOCIATES*, ACTUALLY CAME THE CLOSEST TO DEVELOPING HIS OWN SCHOOL BY APPRENTICING ARTISTS CAPABLE OF WORKING IN HIS STYLE

*MODIFIED CANIFF SCHOOL: CARTOON REALISM*

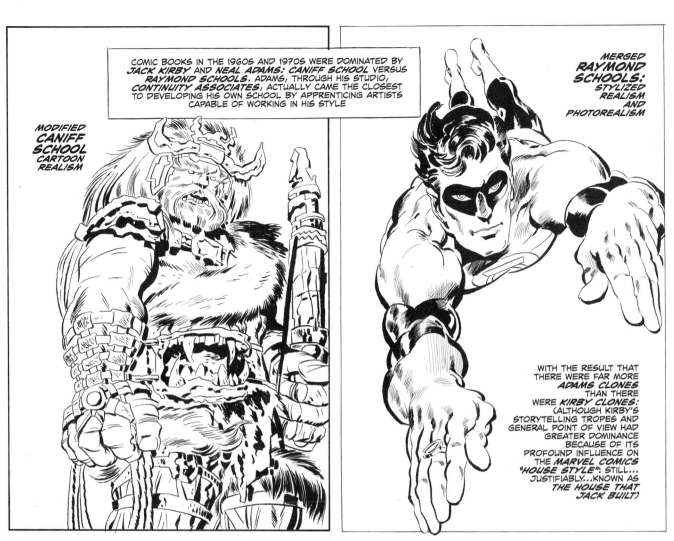

*MERGED RAYMOND SCHOOLS: STYLIZED REALISM AND PHOTOREALISM*

WITH THE RESULT THAT THERE WERE FAR MORE *ADAMS CLONES* THAN THERE WERE *KIRBY CLONES*: (ALTHOUGH KIRBY'S STORYTELLING TROPES AND GENERAL POINT OF VIEW HAD GREATER DOMINANCE BECAUSE OF ITS PROFOUND INFLUENCE ON THE *MARVEL COMICS* "HOUSE STYLE". STILL... JUSTIFIABLY...KNOWN AS *THE HOUSE THAT JACK BUILT*)

THE *KIRBY/ADAMS* DOMINANCE WOULD BE SUPPLANTED IN TWO DIRECTIONS IN THE 1990S:

*MODIFIED FOSTER SCHOOL: NON-STYLIZED REALISM*

THE CREATOR-FOUNDERS OF *IMAGE COMICS* WOULD TAKE THE SURFACE VENEER OF *ART ADAMS'* *FOSTER SCHOOL* STYLE

AND MODIFY IT INTO A MERGED *RAYMOND/ CANIFF* STYLE

*(STYLIZED CARTOON REALISM)* WHILE *BRUCE TIMM* WOULD ABANDON REALISM COMPLETELY BY IMPORTING *ANIMATED CARTOON SIMPLIFICATIONS* INTO COMIC-BOOK ART: *CARTOON ART*

BUT, GETTING BACK TO THE *ORIGINAL BIG THREE*:

49

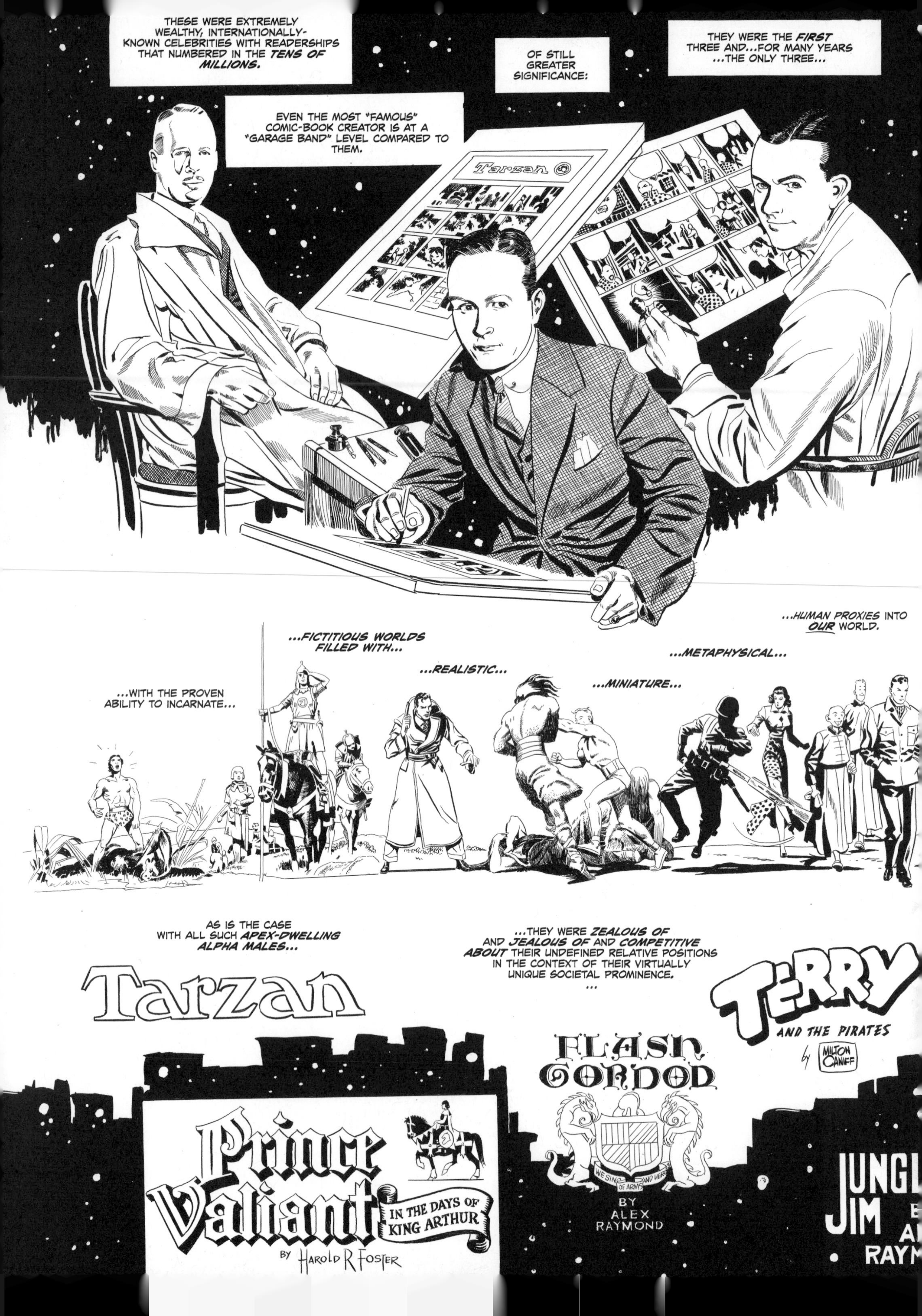
THESE WERE EXTREMELY WEALTHY, INTERNATIONALLY-KNOWN CELEBRITIES WITH READERSHIPS THAT NUMBERED IN THE TENS OF MILLIONS.
EVEN THE MOST "FAMOUS" COMIC-BOOK CREATOR IS AT A "GARAGE BAND" LEVEL COMPARED TO THEM.
OF STILL GREATER SIGNIFICANCE:
THEY WERE THE FIRST THREE AND...FOR MANY YEARS ...THE ONLY THREE...
Tarzan
...WITH THE PROVEN ABILITY TO INCARNATE...
...FICTITIOUS WORLDS FILLED WITH...
...REALISTIC...
...MINIATURE...
...METAPHYSICAL...
...HUMAN PROXIES INTO OUR WORLD.
AS IS THE CASE WITH ALL SUCH APEX-DWELLING ALPHA MALES...
...THEY WERE ZEALOUS OF AND JEALOUS OF AND COMPETITIVE ABOUT THEIR UNDEFINED RELATIVE POSITIONS IN THE CONTEXT OF THEIR VIRTUALLY UNIQUE SOCIETAL PROMINENCE. ...
TARZAN
TERRY AND THE PIRATES by MILTON CANIFF
Prince Valiant IN THE DAYS OF KING ARTHUR BY HAROLD R FOSTER
FLASH GORDON BY ALEX RAYMOND
JUNGLE JIM BY ALEX RAYMOND

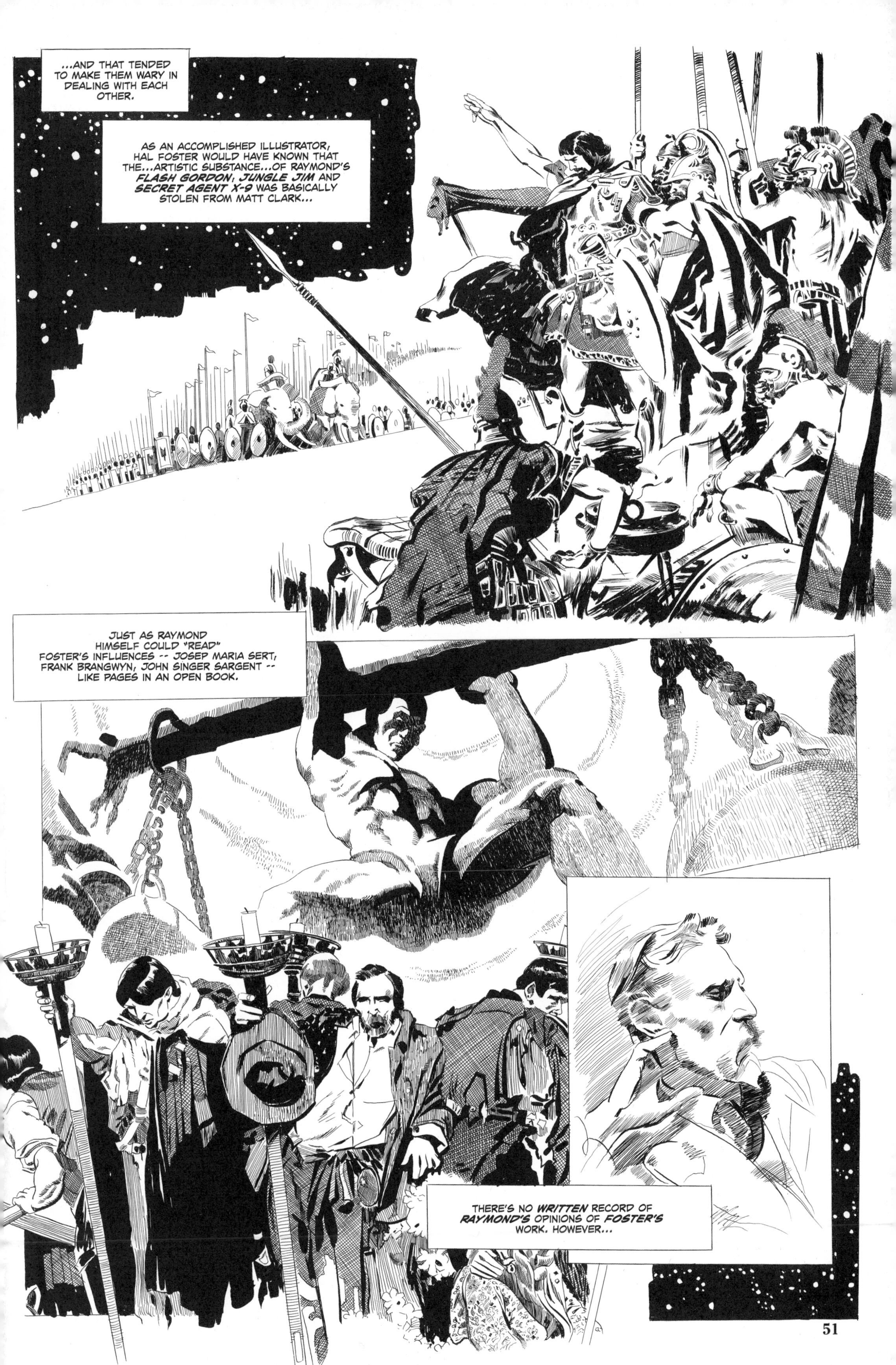

...AND THAT TENDED TO MAKE THEM WARY IN DEALING WITH EACH OTHER.
AS AN ACCOMPLISHED ILLUSTRATOR, HAL FOSTER WOULD HAVE KNOWN THAT THE...ARTISTIC SUBSTANCE...OF RAYMOND'S FLASH GORDON, JUNGLE JIM AND SECRET AGENT X-9 WAS BASICALLY STOLEN FROM MATT CLARK...
JUST AS RAYMOND HIMSELF COULD "READ" FOSTER'S INFLUENCES -- JOSEP MARIA SERT, FRANK BRANGWYN, JOHN SINGER SARGENT -- LIKE PAGES IN AN OPEN BOOK.
THERE'S NO WRITTEN RECORD OF RAYMOND'S OPINIONS OF FOSTER'S WORK. HOWEVER...

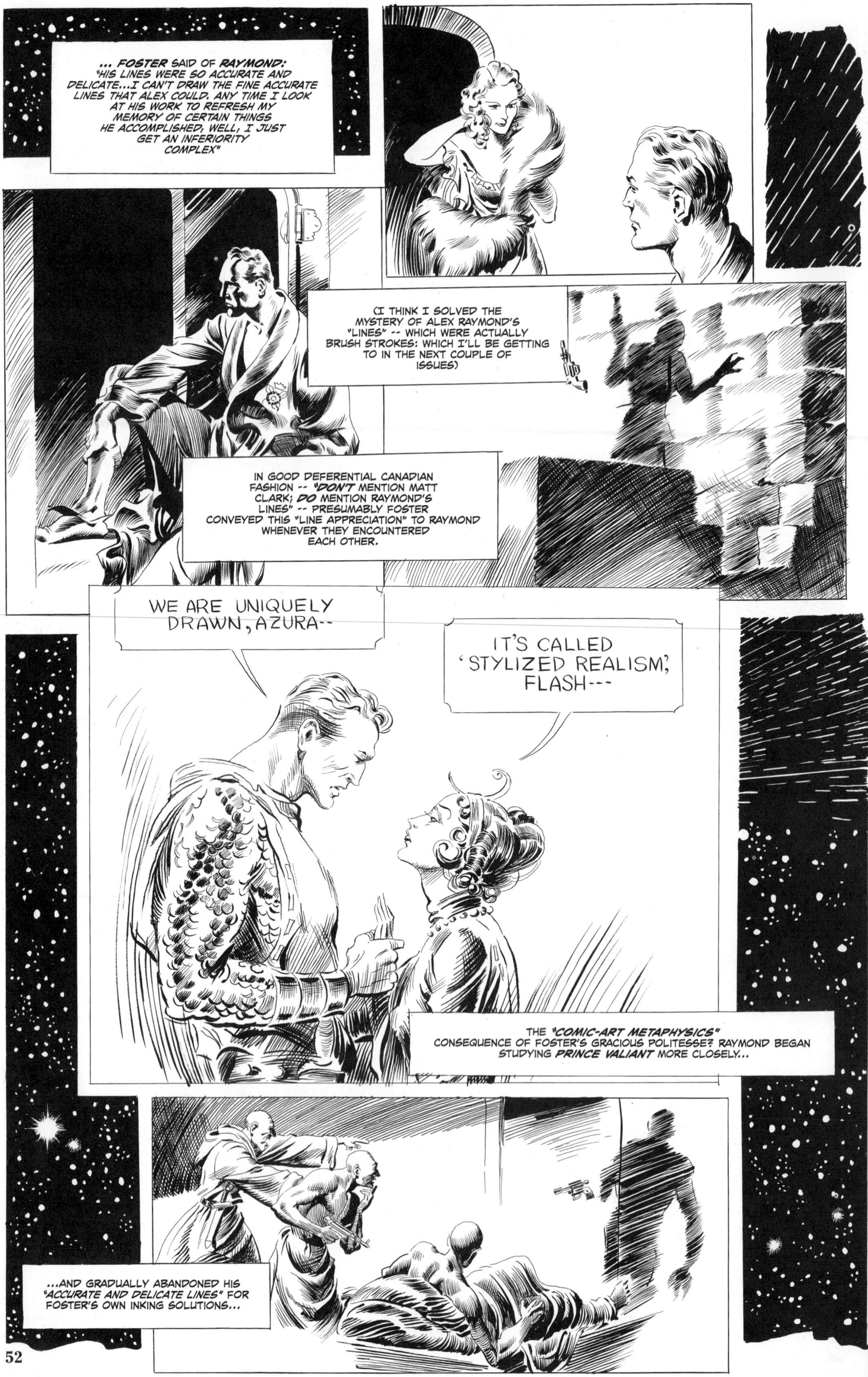
... FOSTER SAID OF RAYMOND: "HIS LINES WERE SO ACCURATE AND DELICATE...I CAN'T DRAW THE FINE ACCURATE LINES THAT ALEX COULD. ANY TIME I LOOK AT HIS WORK TO REFRESH MY MEMORY OF CERTAIN THINGS HE ACCOMPLISHED, WELL, I JUST GET AN INFERIORITY COMPLEX"
(I THINK I SOLVED THE MYSTERY OF ALEX RAYMOND'S "LINES" -- WHICH WERE ACTUALLY BRUSH STROKES: WHICH I'LL BE GETTING TO IN THE NEXT COUPLE OF ISSUES)
IN GOOD DEFERENTIAL CANADIAN FASHION -- "DON'T MENTION MATT CLARK; DO MENTION RAYMOND'S LINES" -- PRESUMABLY FOSTER CONVEYED THIS "LINE APPRECIATION" TO RAYMOND WHENEVER THEY ENCOUNTERED EACH OTHER.
WE ARE UNIQUELY DRAWN, AZURA--
IT'S CALLED 'STYLIZED REALISM', FLASH---
THE "COMIC-ART METAPHYSICS" CONSEQUENCE OF FOSTER'S GRACIOUS POLITESSE? RAYMOND BEGAN STUDYING PRINCE VALIANT MORE CLOSELY...
...AND GRADUALLY ABANDONED HIS "ACCURATE AND DELICATE LINES" FOR FOSTER'S OWN INKING SOLUTIONS...

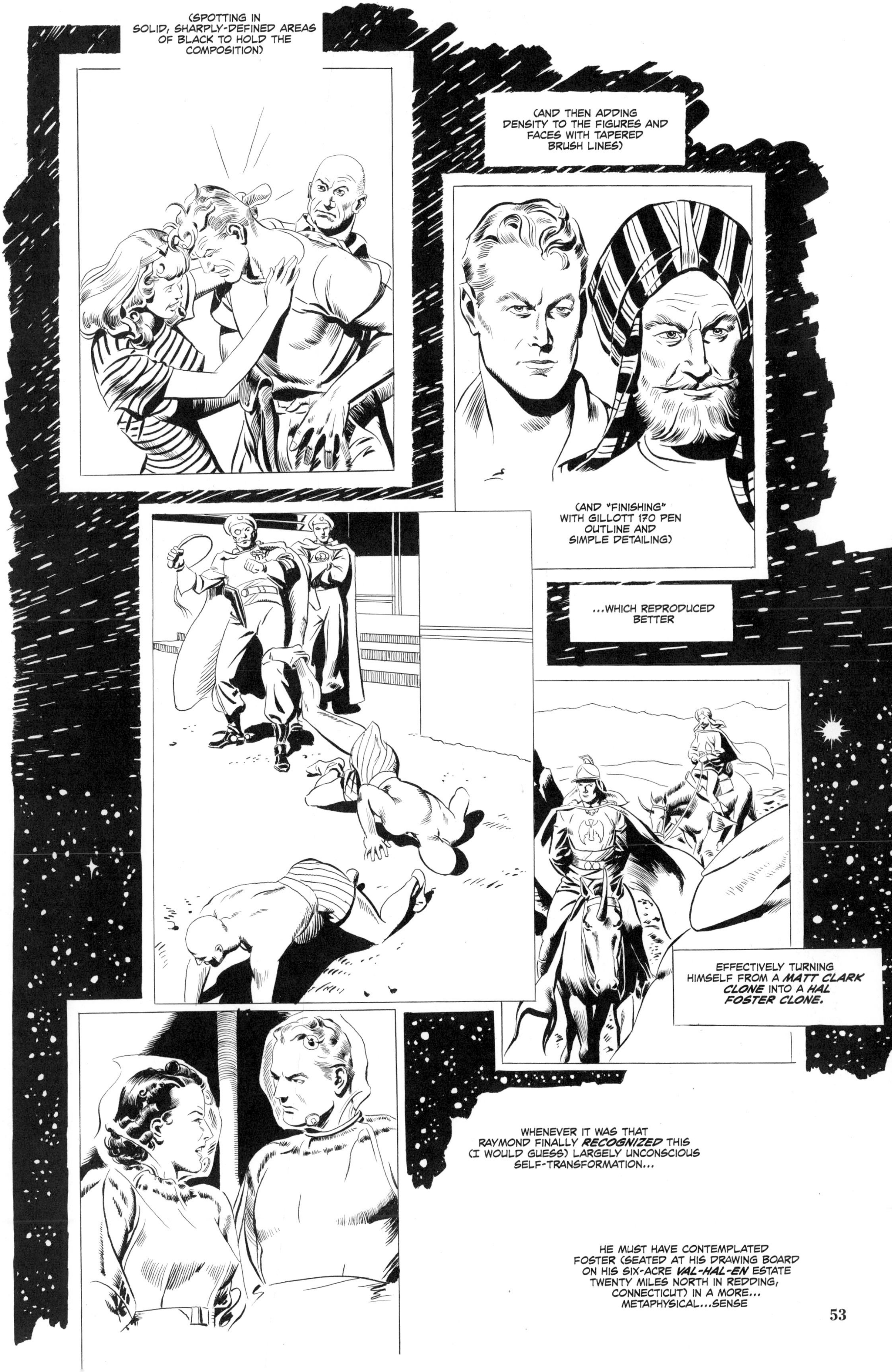
(SPOTTING IN SOLID, SHARPLY-DEFINED AREAS OF BLACK TO HOLD THE COMPOSITION)
(AND THEN ADDING DENSITY TO THE FIGURES AND FACES WITH TAPERED BRUSH LINES)
(AND "FINISHING" WITH GILLOTT 170 PEN OUTLINE AND SIMPLE DETAILING)
...WHICH REPRODUCED BETTER
EFFECTIVELY TURNING HIMSELF FROM A ***MATT CLARK CLONE*** INTO A ***HAL FOSTER CLONE.***
WHENEVER IT WAS THAT RAYMOND FINALLY ***RECOGNIZED*** THIS (I WOULD GUESS) LARGELY UNCONSCIOUS SELF-TRANSFORMATION...
HE MUST HAVE CONTEMPLATED FOSTER (SEATED AT HIS DRAWING BOARD ON HIS SIX-ACRE ***VAL-HAL-EN*** ESTATE TWENTY MILES NORTH IN REDDING, CONNECTICUT) IN A MORE... METAPHYSICAL...SENSE

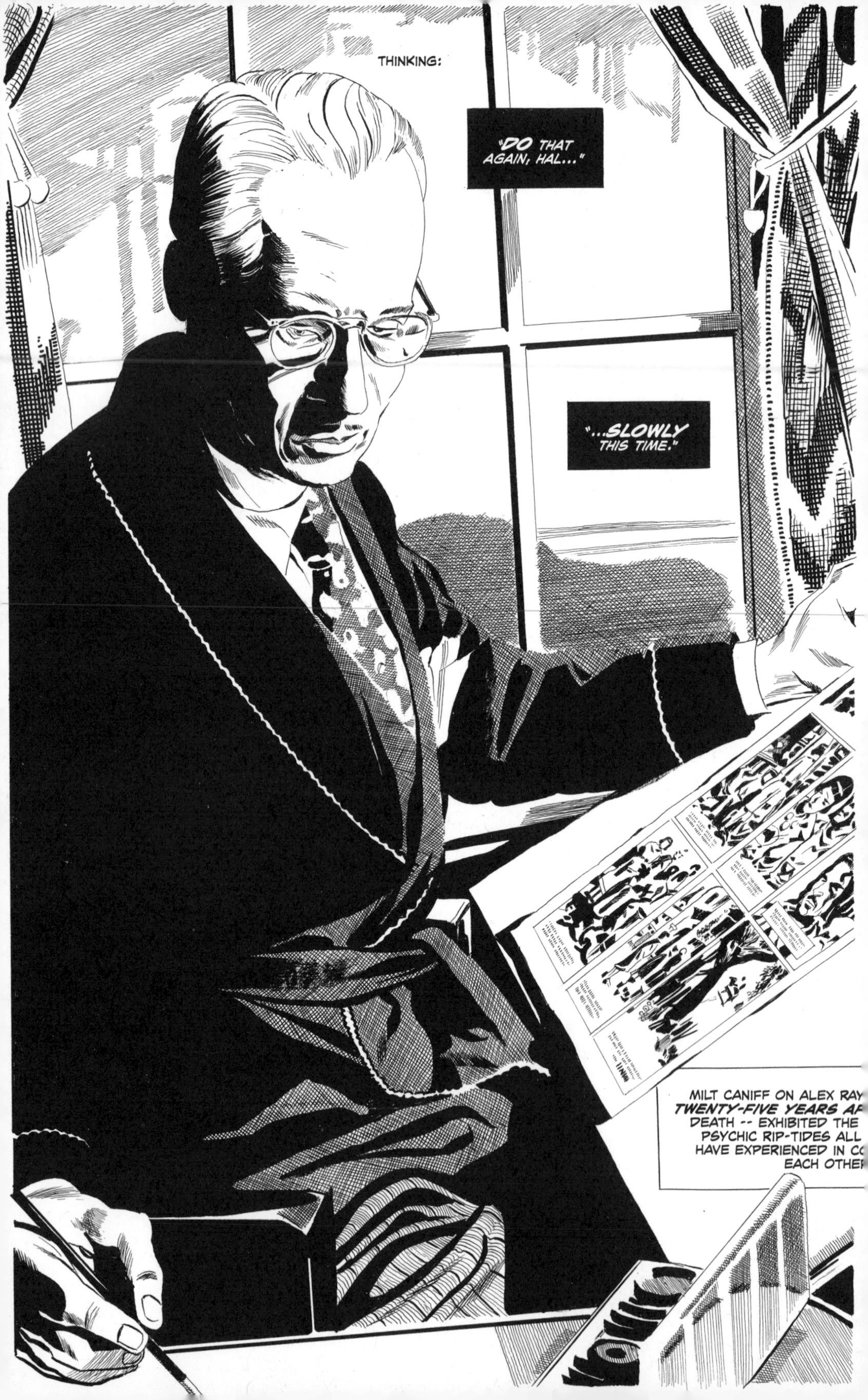
THINKING:
"DO THAT AGAIN, HAL..."
"...SLOWLY THIS TIME."
MILT CANIFF ON ALEX RAY
TWENTY-FIVE YEARS AF
DEATH -- EXHIBITED THE
PSYCHIC RIP-TIDES ALL
HAVE EXPERIENCED IN CO
EACH OTHER

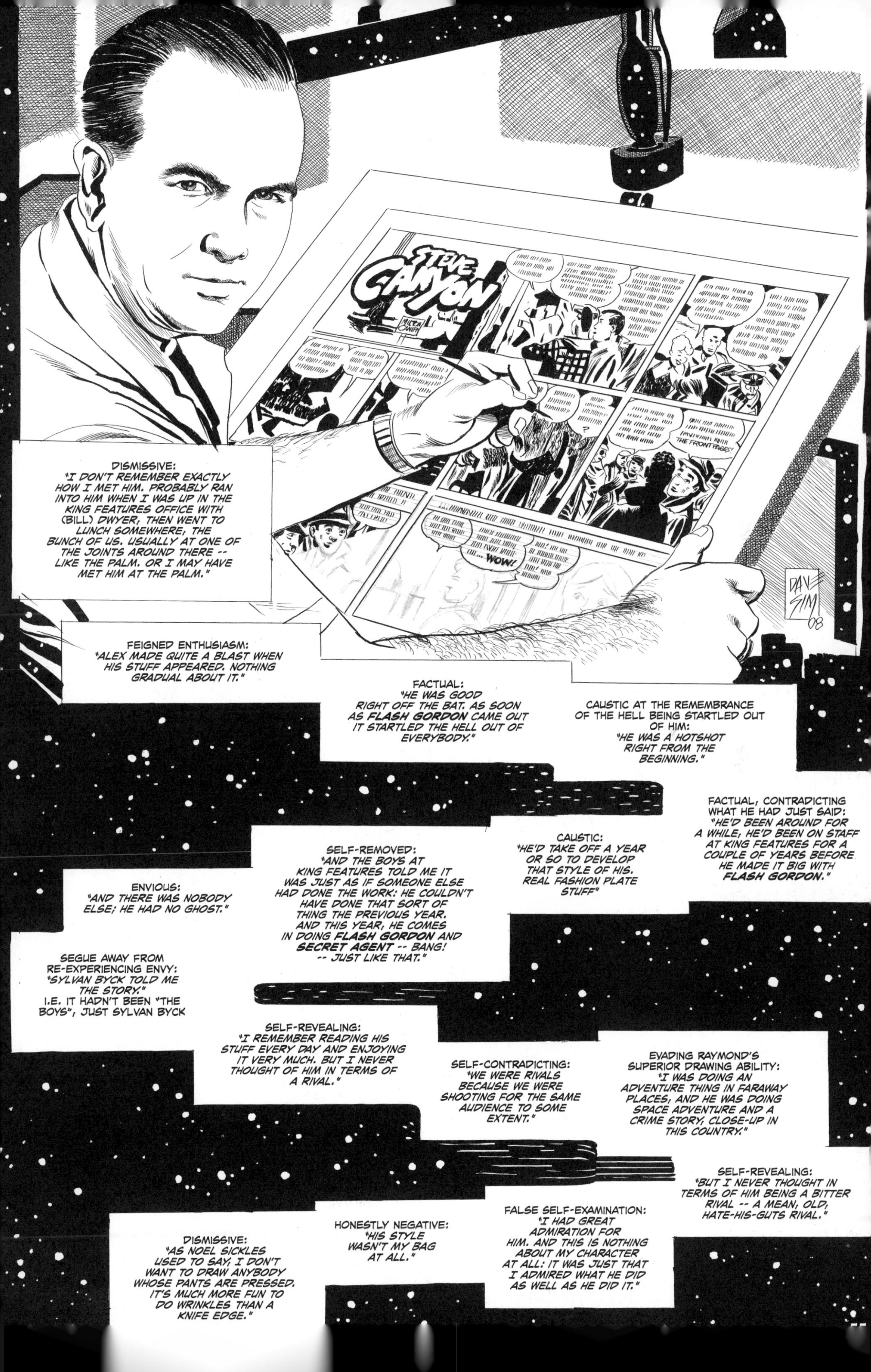
STEVE CANYON
...WOW!
THE FRONT PAGES!
DAVE SIM 08
DISMISSIVE: "I DON'T REMEMBER EXACTLY HOW I MET HIM. PROBABLY RAN INTO HIM WHEN I WAS UP IN THE KING FEATURES OFFICE WITH (BILL) DWYER, THEN WENT TO LUNCH SOMEWHERE, THE BUNCH OF US. USUALLY AT ONE OF THE JOINTS AROUND THERE -- LIKE THE PALM. OR I MAY HAVE MET HIM AT THE PALM."
FEIGNED ENTHUSIASM: "ALEX MADE QUITE A BLAST WHEN HIS STUFF APPEARED. NOTHING GRADUAL ABOUT IT."
FACTUAL: "HE WAS GOOD RIGHT OFF THE BAT. AS SOON AS FLASH GORDON CAME OUT IT STARTLED THE HELL OUT OF EVERYBODY."
CAUSTIC AT THE REMEMBRANCE OF THE HELL BEING STARTLED OUT OF HIM: "HE WAS A HOTSHOT RIGHT FROM THE BEGINNING."
FACTUAL, CONTRADICTING WHAT HE HAD JUST SAID: "HE'D BEEN AROUND FOR A WHILE, HE'D BEEN ON STAFF AT KING FEATURES FOR A COUPLE OF YEARS BEFORE HE MADE IT BIG WITH FLASH GORDON."
CAUSTIC: "HE'D TAKE OFF A YEAR OR SO TO DEVELOP THAT STYLE OF HIS. REAL FASHION PLATE STUFF"
SELF-REMOVED: "AND THE BOYS AT KING FEATURES TOLD ME IT WAS JUST AS IF SOMEONE ELSE HAD DONE THE WORK: HE COULDN'T HAVE DONE THAT SORT OF THING THE PREVIOUS YEAR. AND THIS YEAR, HE COMES IN DOING FLASH GORDON AND SECRET AGENT -- BANG! -- JUST LIKE THAT."
ENVIOUS: "AND THERE WAS NOBODY ELSE; HE HAD NO GHOST."
SEGUE AWAY FROM RE-EXPERIENCING ENVY: "SYLVAN BYCK TOLD ME THE STORY." I.E. IT HADN'T BEEN "THE BOYS", JUST SYLVAN BYCK
SELF-REVEALING: "I REMEMBER READING HIS STUFF EVERY DAY AND ENJOYING IT VERY MUCH. BUT I NEVER THOUGHT OF HIM IN TERMS OF A RIVAL."
SELF-CONTRADICTING: "WE WERE RIVALS BECAUSE WE WERE SHOOTING FOR THE SAME AUDIENCE TO SOME EXTENT."
EVADING RAYMOND'S SUPERIOR DRAWING ABILITY: "I WAS DOING AN ADVENTURE THING IN FARAWAY PLACES, AND HE WAS DOING SPACE ADVENTURE AND A CRIME STORY, CLOSE-UP IN THIS COUNTRY."
SELF-REVEALING: "BUT I NEVER THOUGHT IN TERMS OF HIM BEING A BITTER RIVAL -- A MEAN, OLD, HATE-HIS-GUTS RIVAL."
FALSE SELF-EXAMINATION: "I HAD GREAT ADMIRATION FOR HIM. AND THIS IS NOTHING ABOUT MY CHARACTER AT ALL: IT WAS JUST THAT I ADMIRED WHAT HE DID AS WELL AS HE DID IT."
HONESTLY NEGATIVE: "HIS STYLE WASN'T MY BAG AT ALL."
DISMISSIVE: "AS NOEL SICKLES USED TO SAY, I DON'T WANT TO DRAW ANYBODY WHOSE PANTS ARE PRESSED. IT'S MUCH MORE FUN TO DO WRINKLES THAN A KNIFE EDGE."

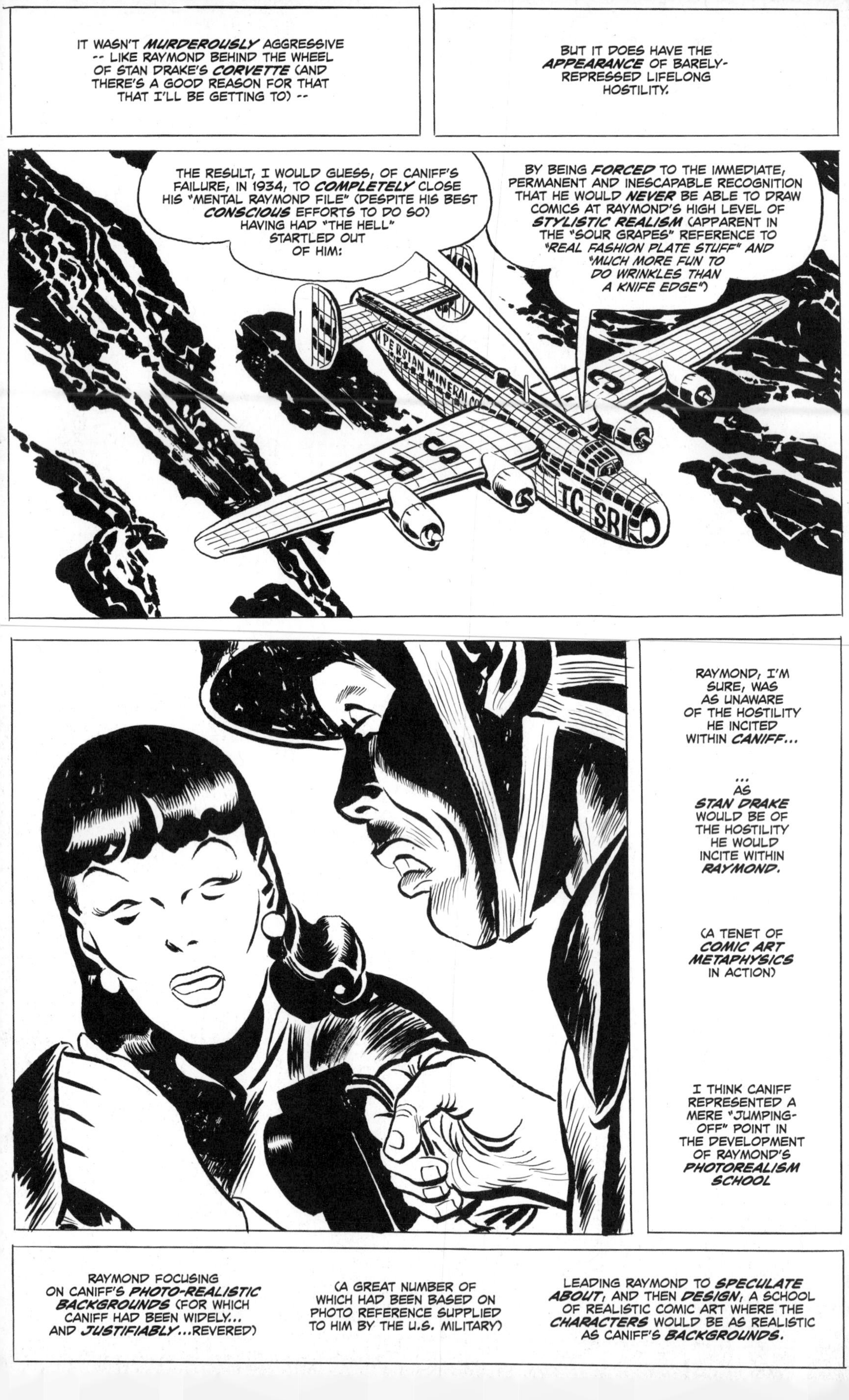
IT WASN'T MURDEROUSLY AGGRESSIVE -- LIKE RAYMOND BEHIND THE WHEEL OF STAN DRAKE'S CORVETTE (AND THERE'S A GOOD REASON FOR THAT THAT I'LL BE GETTING TO) --
BUT IT DOES HAVE THE APPEARANCE OF BARELY-REPRESSED LIFELONG HOSTILITY.
THE RESULT, I WOULD GUESS, OF CANIFF'S FAILURE, IN 1934, TO COMPLETELY CLOSE HIS "MENTAL RAYMOND FILE" (DESPITE HIS BEST CONSCIOUS EFFORTS TO DO SO) HAVING HAD "THE HELL" STARTLED OUT OF HIM:
BY BEING FORCED TO THE IMMEDIATE, PERMANENT AND INESCAPABLE RECOGNITION THAT HE WOULD NEVER BE ABLE TO DRAW COMICS AT RAYMOND'S HIGH LEVEL OF STYLISTIC REALISM (APPARENT IN THE "SOUR GRAPES" REFERENCE TO "REAL FASHION PLATE STUFF" AND "MUCH MORE FUN TO DO WRINKLES THAN A KNIFE EDGE")
PERSIAN MINERAL CO.
TC SRI
RAYMOND, I'M SURE, WAS AS UNAWARE OF THE HOSTILITY HE INCITED WITHIN CANIFF...
... AS STAN DRAKE WOULD BE OF THE HOSTILITY HE WOULD INCITE WITHIN RAYMOND.
(A TENET OF COMIC ART METAPHYSICS IN ACTION)
I THINK CANIFF REPRESENTED A MERE "JUMPING-OFF" POINT IN THE DEVELOPMENT OF RAYMOND'S PHOTOREALISM SCHOOL
RAYMOND FOCUSING ON CANIFF'S PHOTO-REALISTIC BACKGROUNDS (FOR WHICH CANIFF HAD BEEN WIDELY... AND JUSTIFIABLY...REVERED)
(A GREAT NUMBER OF WHICH HAD BEEN BASED ON PHOTO REFERENCE SUPPLIED TO HIM BY THE U.S. MILITARY)
LEADING RAYMOND TO SPECULATE ABOUT, AND THEN DESIGN, A SCHOOL OF REALISTIC COMIC ART WHERE THE CHARACTERS WOULD BE AS REALISTIC AS CANIFF'S BACKGROUNDS.

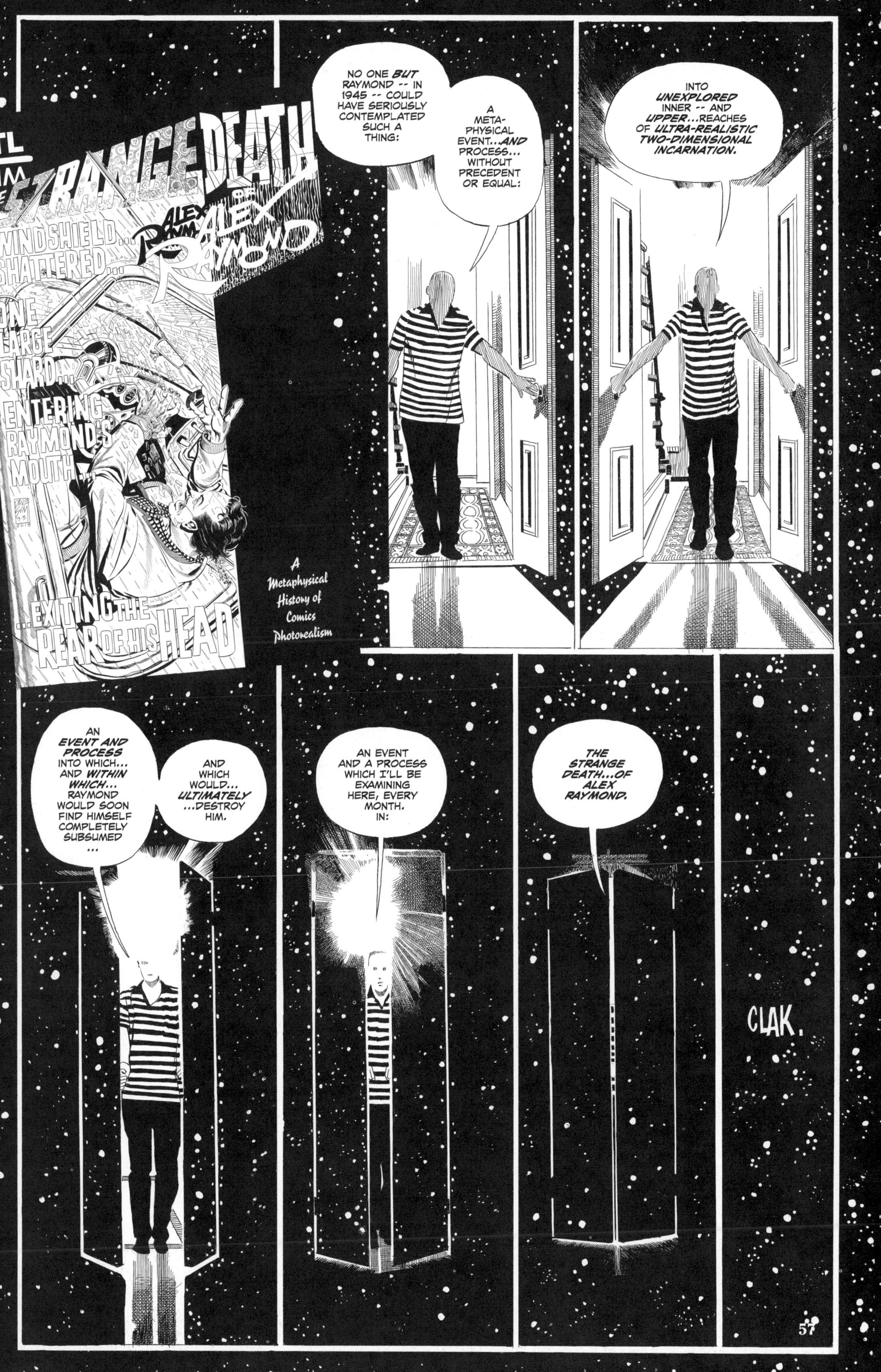
LTL
SIM
THE STRANGE DEATH OF ALEX RAYMOND
WINDSHIELD... SHATTERED...
ONE LARGE SHARD... ENTERING RAYMOND'S MOUTH...
...EXITING THE REAR OF HIS HEAD
A Metaphysical History of Comics Photorealism
NO ONE *BUT* RAYMOND -- IN 1945 -- COULD HAVE SERIOUSLY CONTEMPLATED SUCH A THING:
A META-PHYSICAL EVENT...*AND* PROCESS... WITHOUT PRECEDENT OR EQUAL:
INTO *UNEXPLORED* INNER -- AND *UPPER*...REACHES OF *ULTRA-REALISTIC TWO-DIMENSIONAL INCARNATION.*
AN *EVENT AND PROCESS* INTO WHICH... AND *WITHIN WHICH*... RAYMOND WOULD SOON FIND HIMSELF COMPLETELY SUBSUMED ...
AND WHICH WOULD... *ULTIMATELY* ...DESTROY HIM.
AN EVENT AND A PROCESS WHICH I'LL BE EXAMINING HERE, EVERY MONTH. IN:
*THE STRANGE DEATH...OF ALEX RAYMOND.*
CLAK.

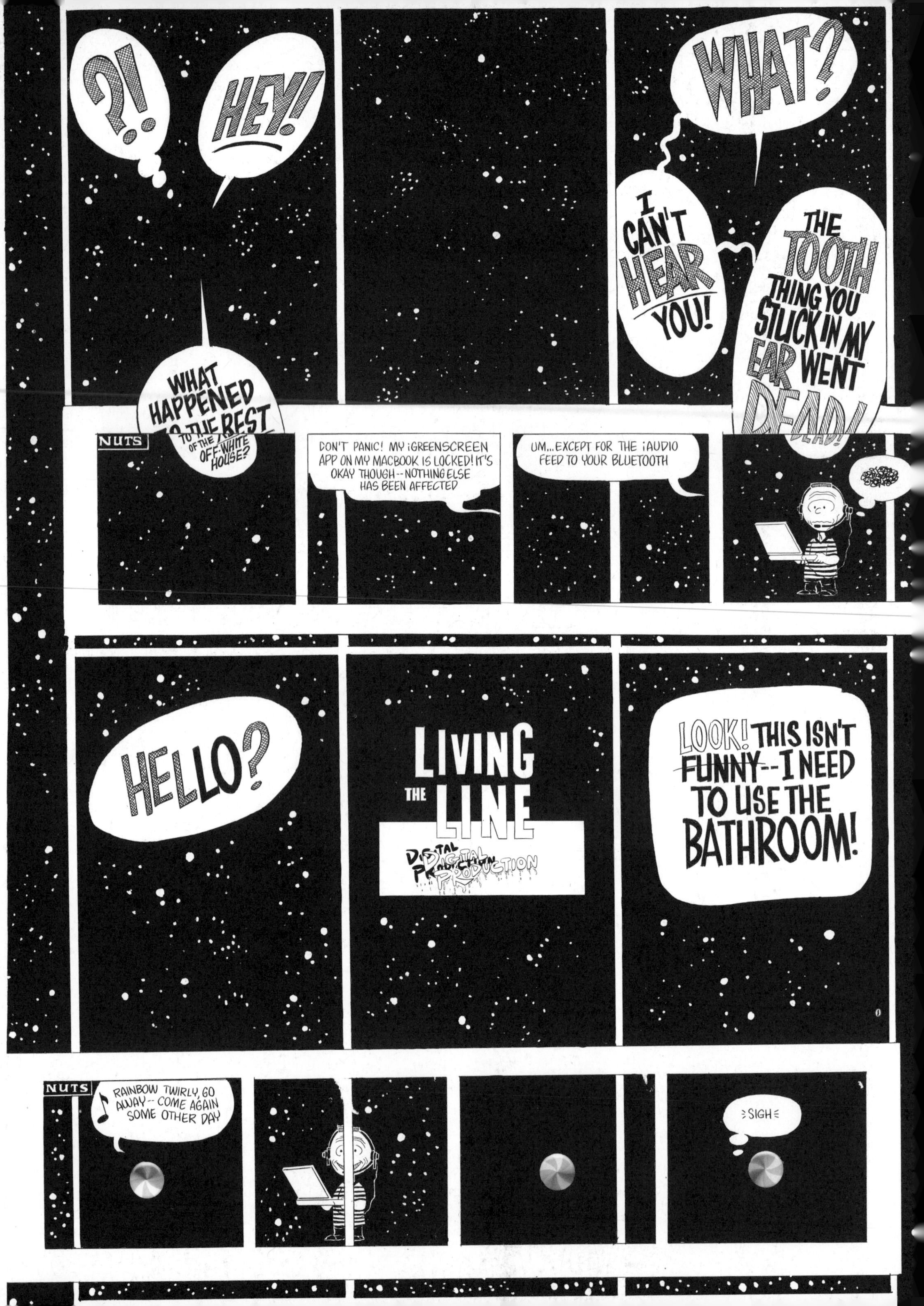
?!
HEY!
WHAT?
I CAN'T HEAR YOU!
THE TOOTH THING YOU STUCK IN MY EAR WENT DEAD!
WHAT HAPPENED TO THE REST OF THE OFF-WHITE HOUSE?
NUTS
DON'T PANIC! MY iGREENSCREEN APP ON MY MACBOOK IS LOCKED! IT'S OKAY THOUGH--NOTHING ELSE HAS BEEN AFFECTED
UM... EXCEPT FOR THE iAUDIO FEED TO YOUR BLUETOOTH
HELLO?
LIVING THE LINE
DIGITAL PRODUCTION
LOOK! THIS ISN'T FUNNY--I NEED TO USE THE BATHROOM!
NUTS
RAINBOW TWIRLY, GO AWAY--COME AGAIN SOME OTHER DAY
SIGH

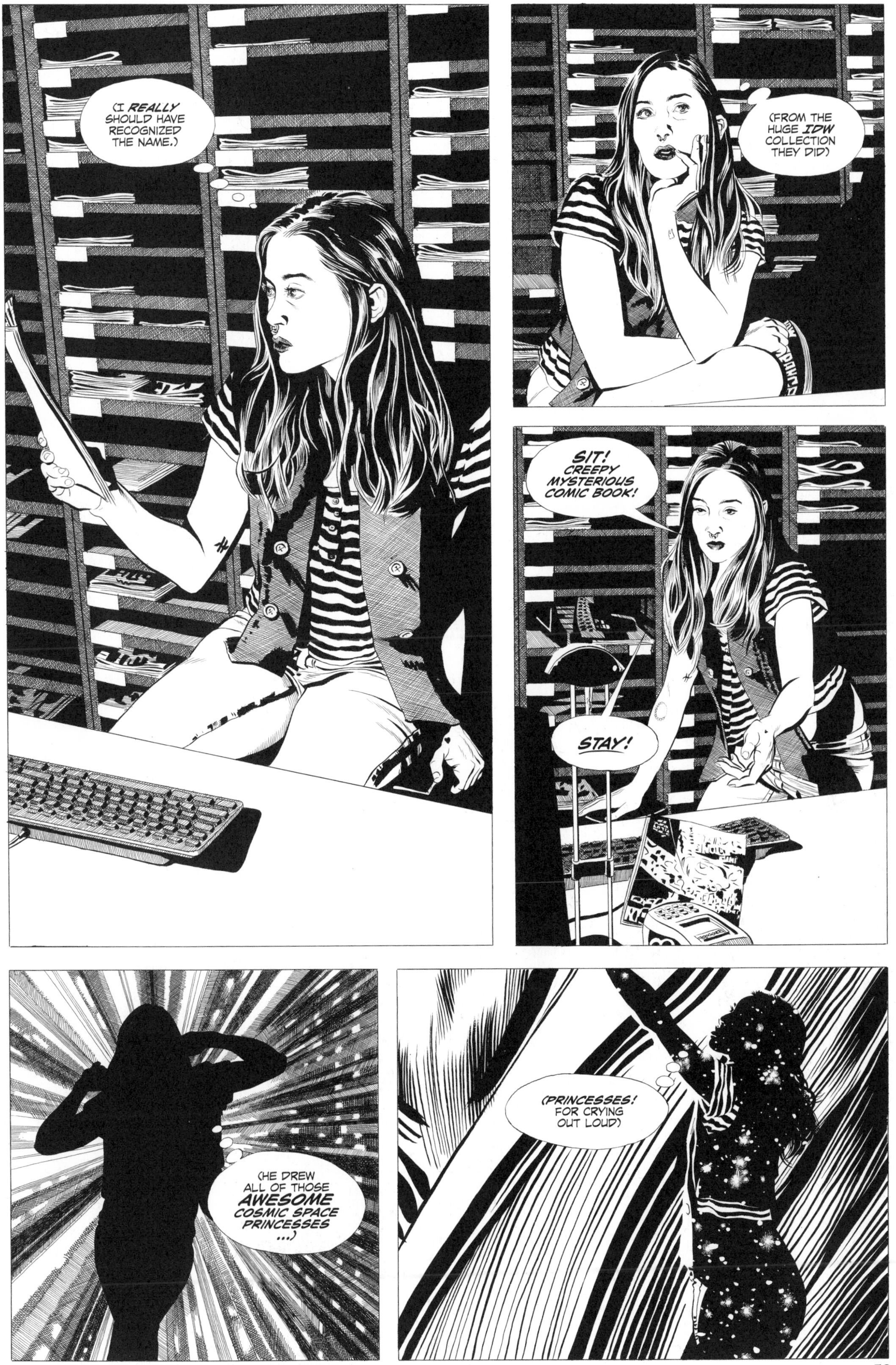
(I REALLY SHOULD HAVE RECOGNIZED THE NAME.)
(FROM THE HUGE IDW COLLECTION THEY DID)
SIT! CREEPY MYSTERIOUS COMIC BOOK!
STAY!
(HE DREW ALL OF THOSE AWESOME COSMIC SPACE PRINCESSES ...)
(PRINCESSES! FOR CRYING OUT LOUD)

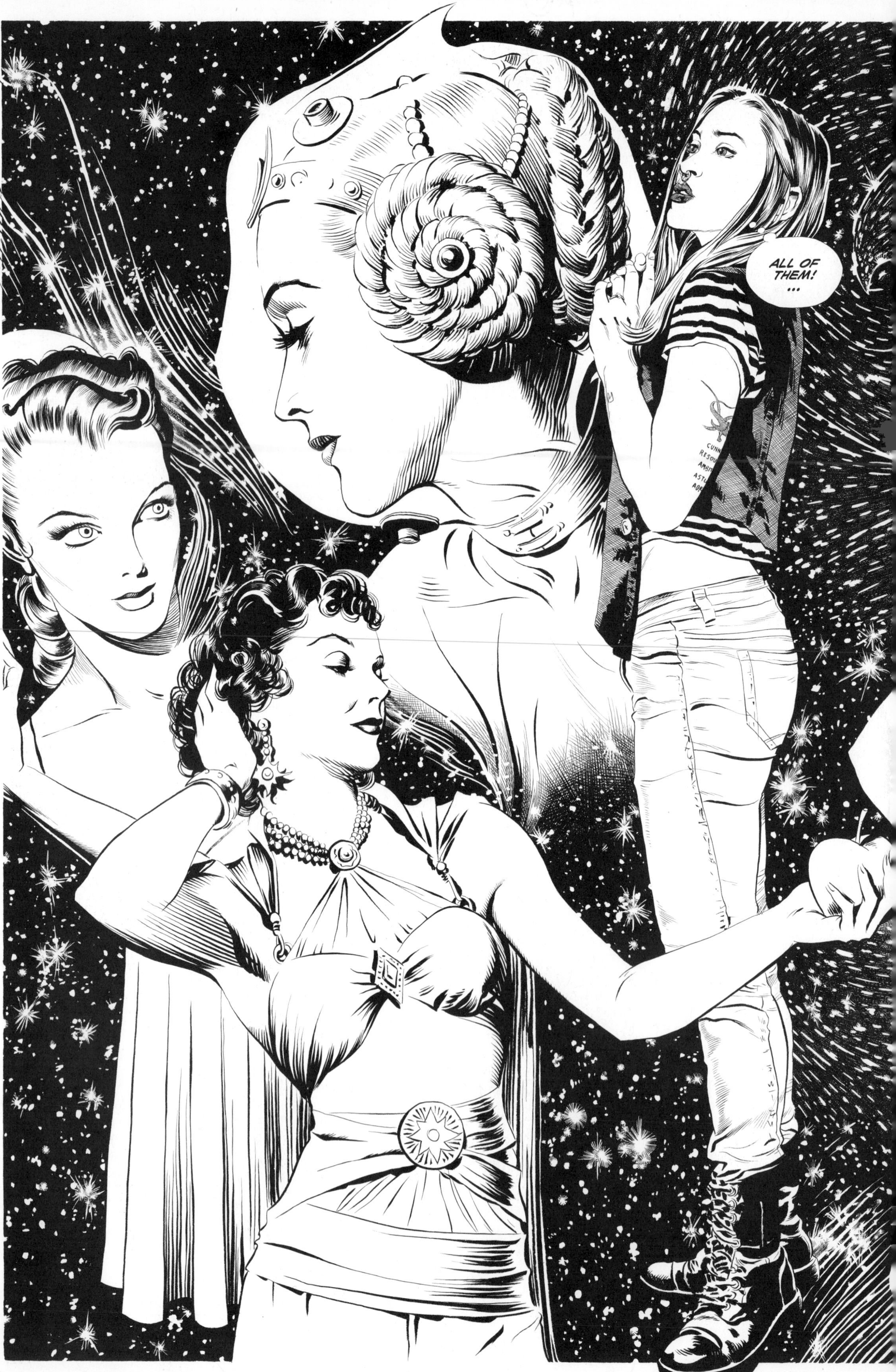
ALL OF THEM! ...

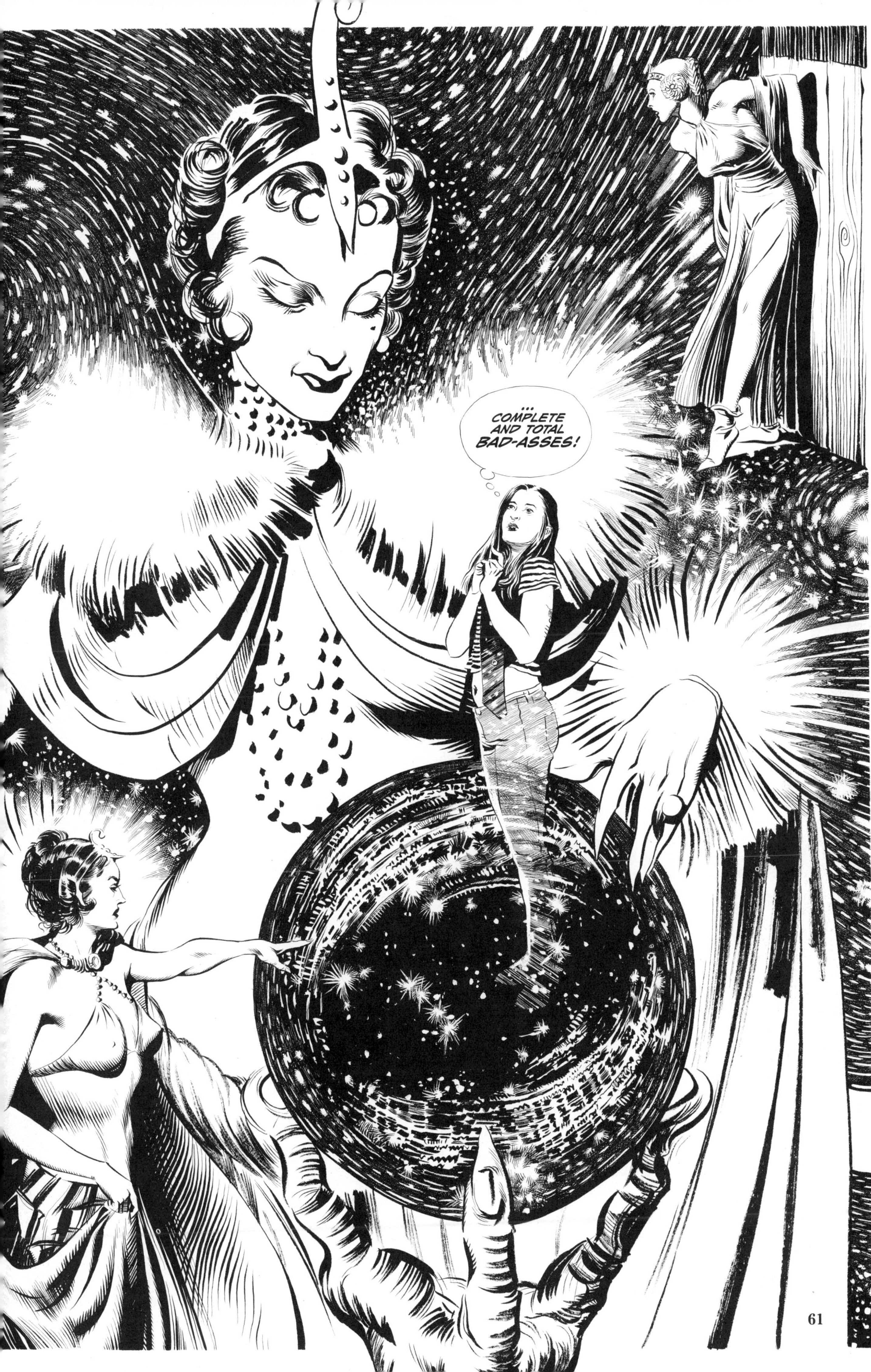
...COMPLETE AND TOTAL BAD-ASSES!

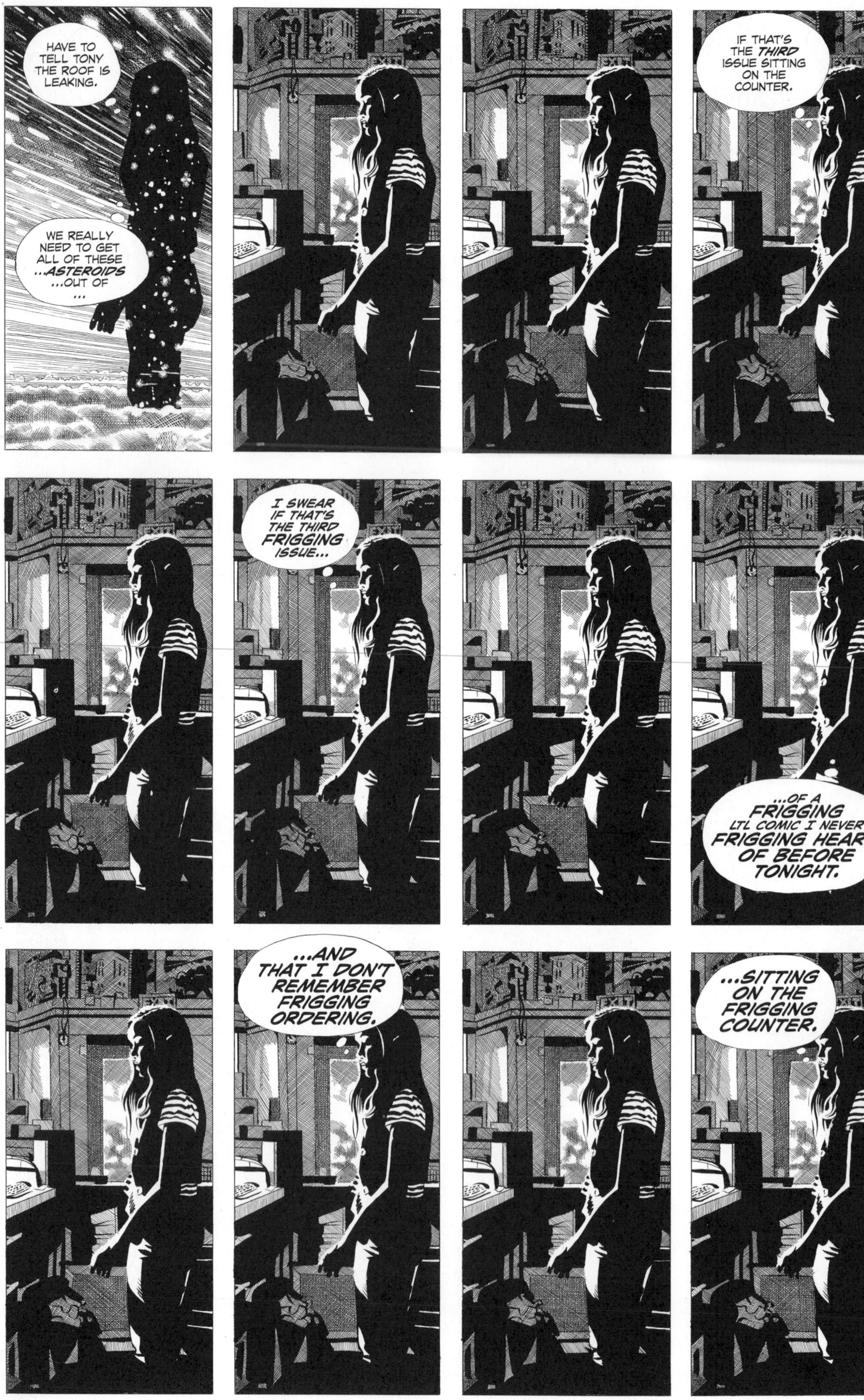
HAVE TO TELL TONY THE ROOF IS LEAKING.
WE REALLY NEED TO GET ALL OF THESE ...ASTEROIDS ...OUT OF ...
IF THAT'S THE THIRD ISSUE SITTING ON THE COUNTER.
I SWEAR IF THAT'S THE THIRD FRIGGING ISSUE...
...OF A FRIGGING LTL COMIC I NEVER FRIGGING HEARD OF BEFORE TONIGHT.
...AND THAT I DON'T REMEMBER FRIGGING ORDERING.
...SITTING ON THE FRIGGING COUNTER.

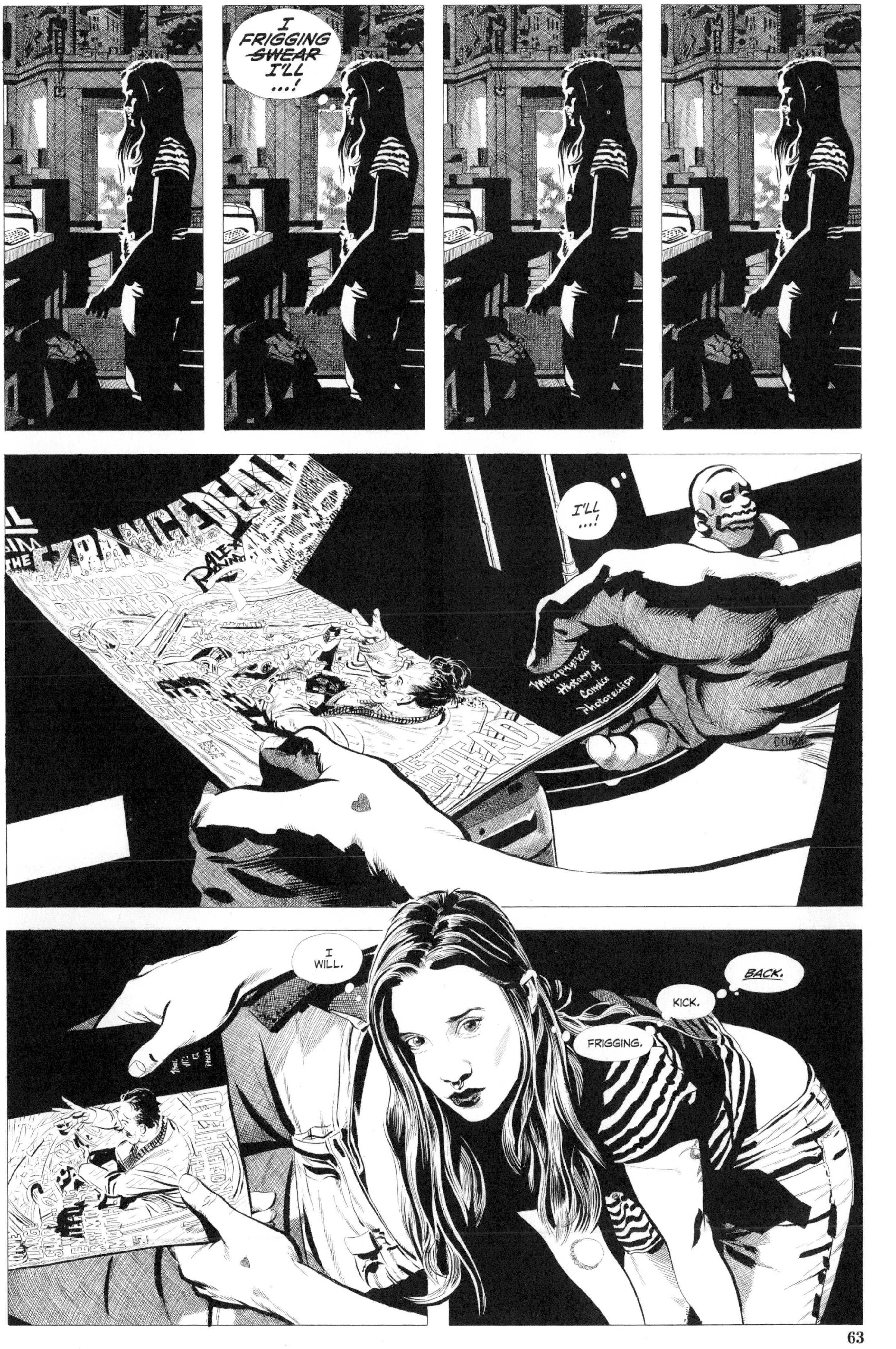
I FRIGGING SWEAR I'LL ...!
I'LL ...!
Metaphysical History of Comics Photorealism
I WILL.
FRIGGING.
KICK.
BACK.

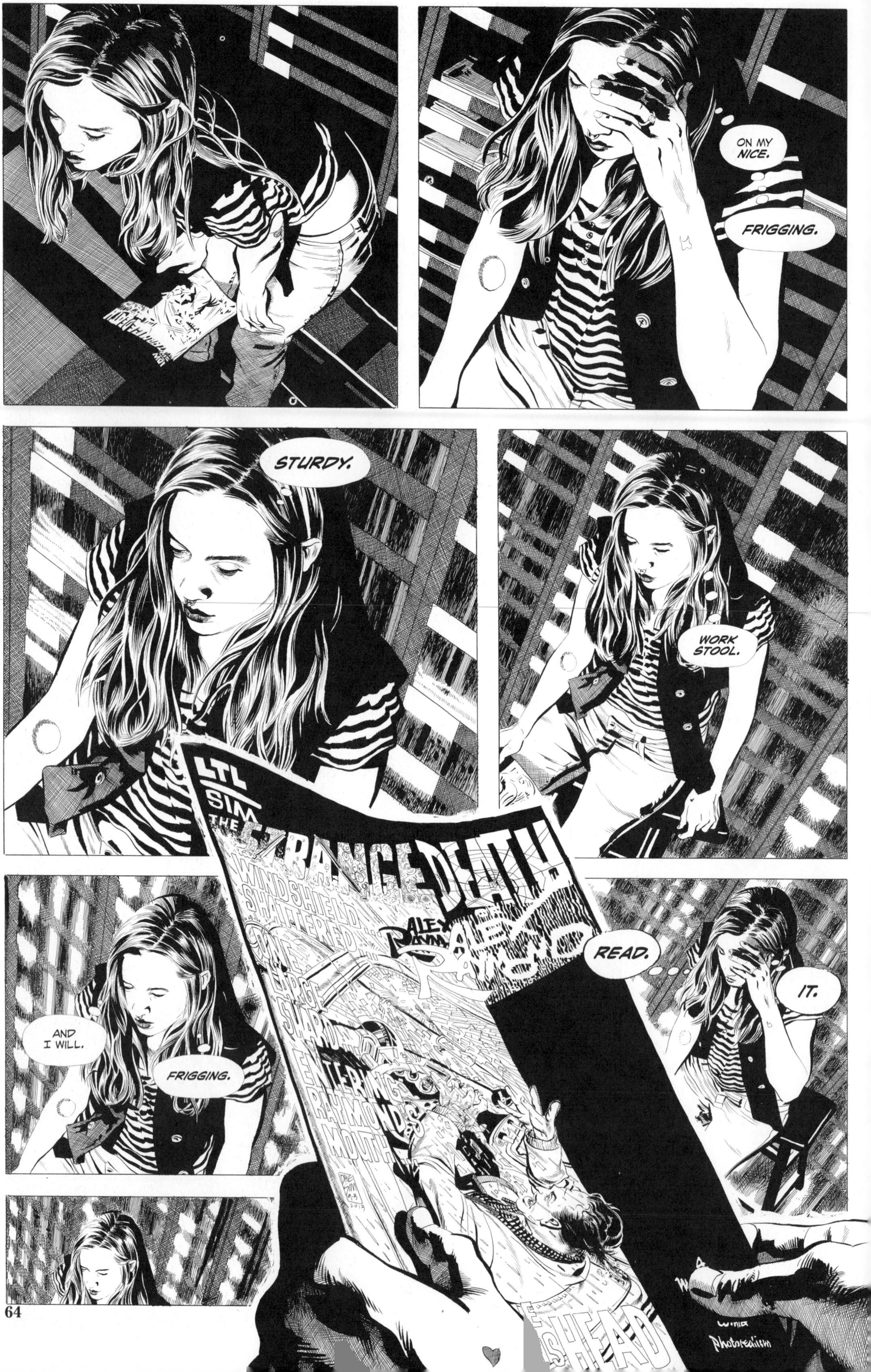
ON MY NICE.
FRIGGING.
STURDY.
WORK STOOL.
AND I WILL.
FRIGGING.
READ.
IT.
LTL
SIM
DEATH
WINDSHIELD SHATTERED
ENTERING RAYMOND'S MOUTH

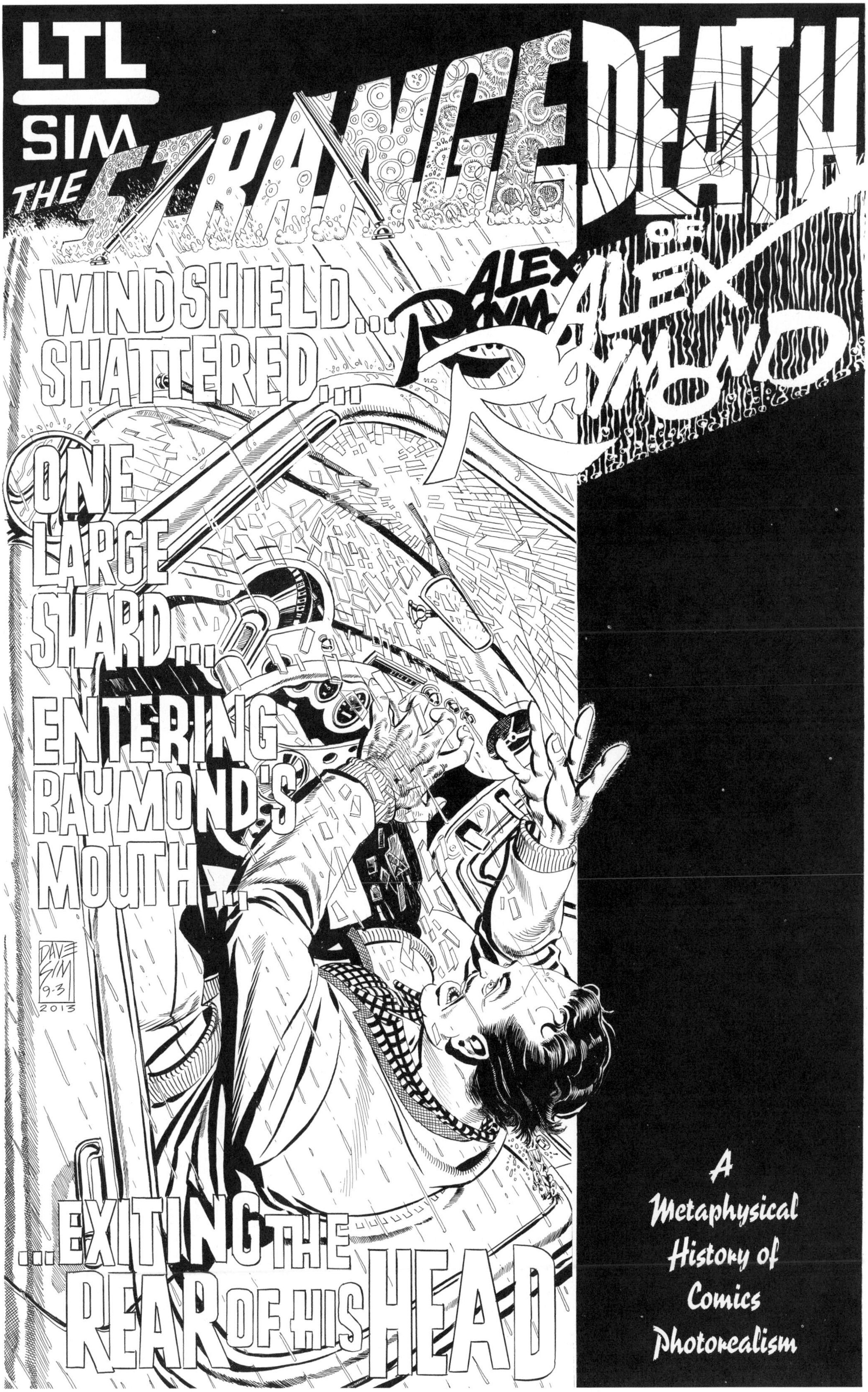
LTL
SIM
THE STRANGE DEATH OF ALEX RAYMOND
WINDSHIELD... SHATTERED...
ONE LARGE SHARD...
ENTERING RAYMOND'S MOUTH...
...EXITING THE REAR OF HIS HEAD
DAVE SIM 9-3 2013
A Metaphysical History of Comics Photorealism

# THE STRANGE DEATH OF ALEX RAYMOND

DAVE SIM · FIRST CANADIAN TOUR 1983

DAVE SIM WRITER ARTIST

DENI and DAVE SIM AMERICAN 1984

"ALEX RAYMOND'S LAST RIDE" BY ARLEN SCHUMER

...

AS IT APPEARED IN TOM HEINTJES' *HOGAN'S ALLEY* NO. 3, BACK IN 1996

## Alex Raymond's Last Ride

Stan Drake bottles about remembering the fatal car wreck that took Alex Raymond's life — was it accident or suicide?

*By Arlen Schumer*

Portrait of Alex Raymond, 1952

# LTL

www.LIVINGTHELINE.com

Sean Robinson, President & Publisher • Sean Robinson, Editor-in-Chief • Sean Robinson, EVP/Sr. Art Director • Sean Robinson, Chief Financial Officer • Sean Robinson, SVP of Sales and Marketing • Sean Robinson, Associate Publisher • Sean Robinson, VP of New Product Development • Sean Robinson, Sr. Director, Licensing & Business Development • Sean Robinson, Editorial Director, Graphic Novels and Collections • Sean Robinson, Sr. Director, Licensing & Business Development

Sean Robinson, LTL Founder

Facebook: facebook.com/livingtheline • Twitter: @ltlpublishing • YouTube: youtube.com/ltlpublishing
Tumblr: tumblr.ltlpublishing.com • Instagram: instagram.com/ltlpublishing

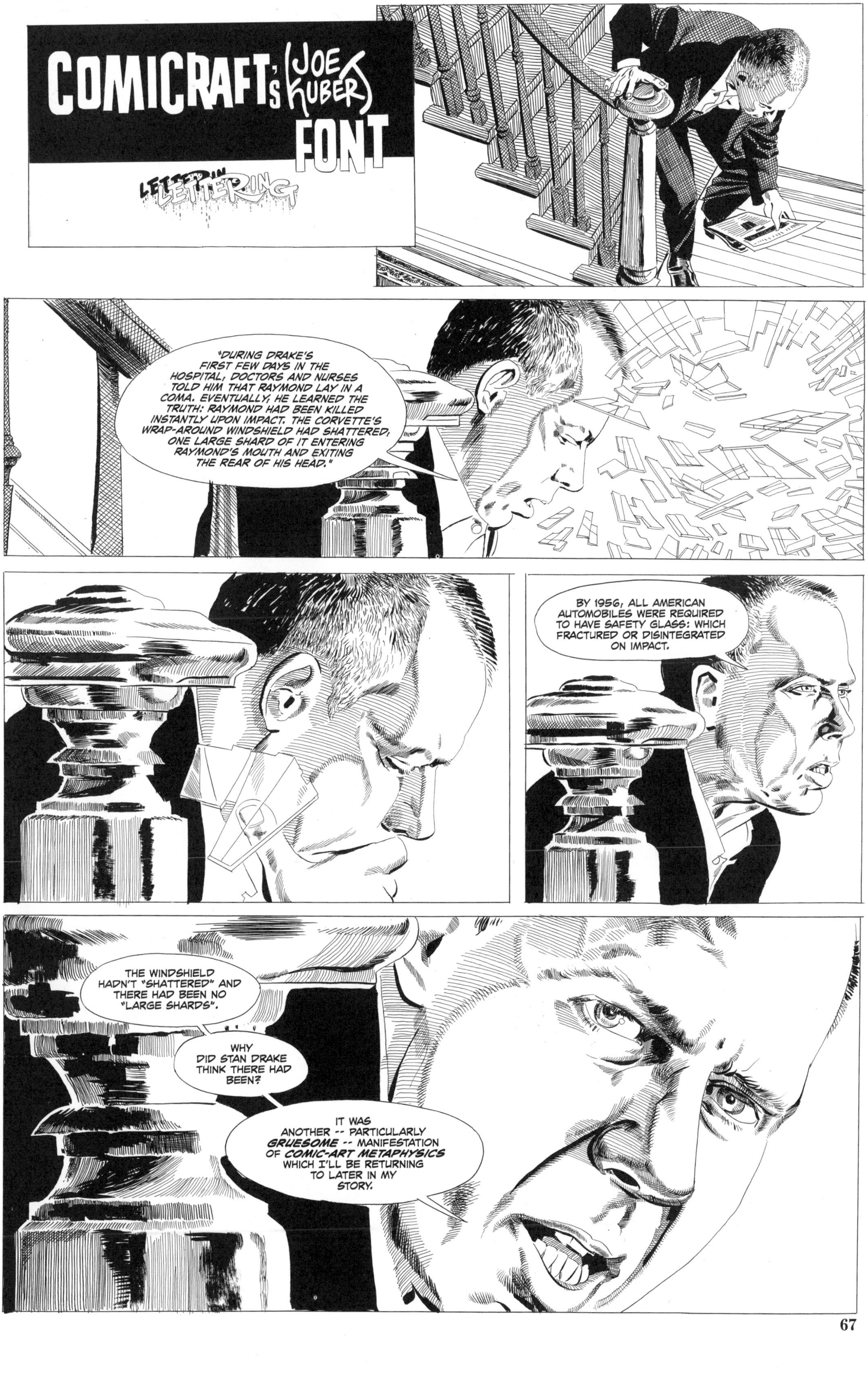

COMICRAFT'S JOE KUBERT FONT
LETTERING
"DURING DRAKE'S FIRST FEW DAYS IN THE HOSPITAL, DOCTORS AND NURSES TOLD HIM THAT RAYMOND LAY IN A COMA. EVENTUALLY, HE LEARNED THE TRUTH: RAYMOND HAD BEEN KILLED INSTANTLY UPON IMPACT. THE CORVETTE'S WRAP-AROUND WINDSHIELD HAD SHATTERED, ONE LARGE SHARD OF IT ENTERING RAYMOND'S MOUTH AND EXITING THE REAR OF HIS HEAD."
BY 1956, ALL AMERICAN AUTOMOBILES WERE REQUIRED TO HAVE SAFETY GLASS: WHICH FRACTURED OR DISINTEGRATED ON IMPACT.
THE WINDSHIELD HADN'T "SHATTERED" AND THERE HAD BEEN NO "LARGE SHARDS".
WHY DID STAN DRAKE THINK THERE HAD BEEN?
IT WAS ANOTHER -- PARTICULARLY GRUESOME -- MANIFESTATION OF COMIC-ART METAPHYSICS WHICH I'LL BE RETURNING TO LATER IN MY STORY.

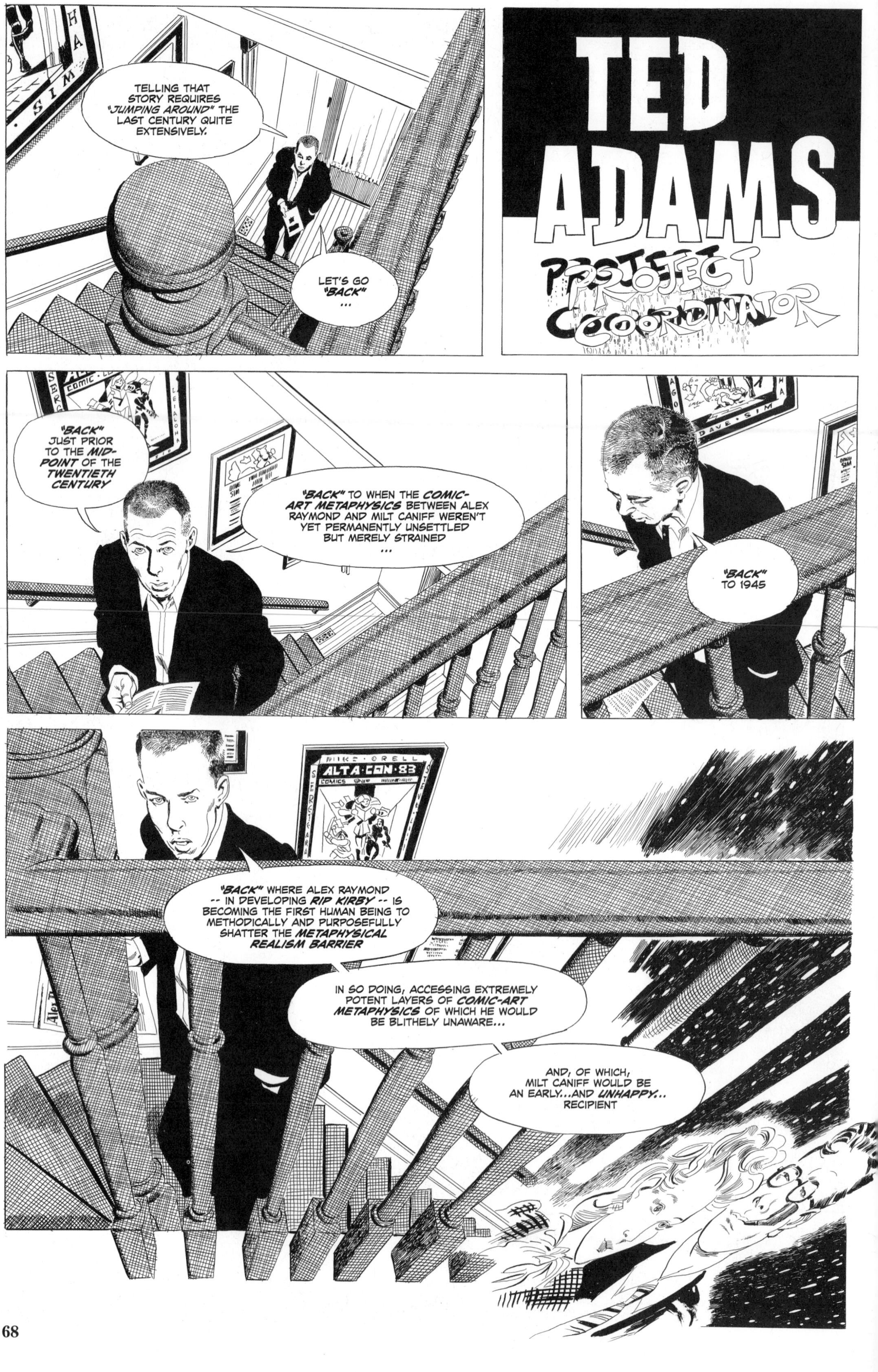
TELLING THAT STORY REQUIRES "JUMPING AROUND" THE LAST CENTURY QUITE EXTENSIVELY.
LET'S GO "BACK" ...
TED ADAMS
PROJECT COORDINATOR
"BACK" JUST PRIOR TO THE MID-POINT OF THE TWENTIETH CENTURY
"BACK" TO WHEN THE COMIC-ART METAPHYSICS BETWEEN ALEX RAYMOND AND MILT CANIFF WEREN'T YET PERMANENTLY UNSETTLED BUT MERELY STRAINED ...
"BACK" TO 1945
ALTA·CON·83
"BACK" WHERE ALEX RAYMOND -- IN DEVELOPING RIP KIRBY -- IS BECOMING THE FIRST HUMAN BEING TO METHODICALLY AND PURPOSEFULLY SHATTER THE METAPHYSICAL REALISM BARRIER
IN SO DOING, ACCESSING EXTREMELY POTENT LAYERS OF COMIC-ART METAPHYSICS OF WHICH HE WOULD BE BLITHELY UNAWARE...
AND, OF WHICH, MILT CANIFF WOULD BE AN EARLY...AND UNHAPPY... RECIPIENT

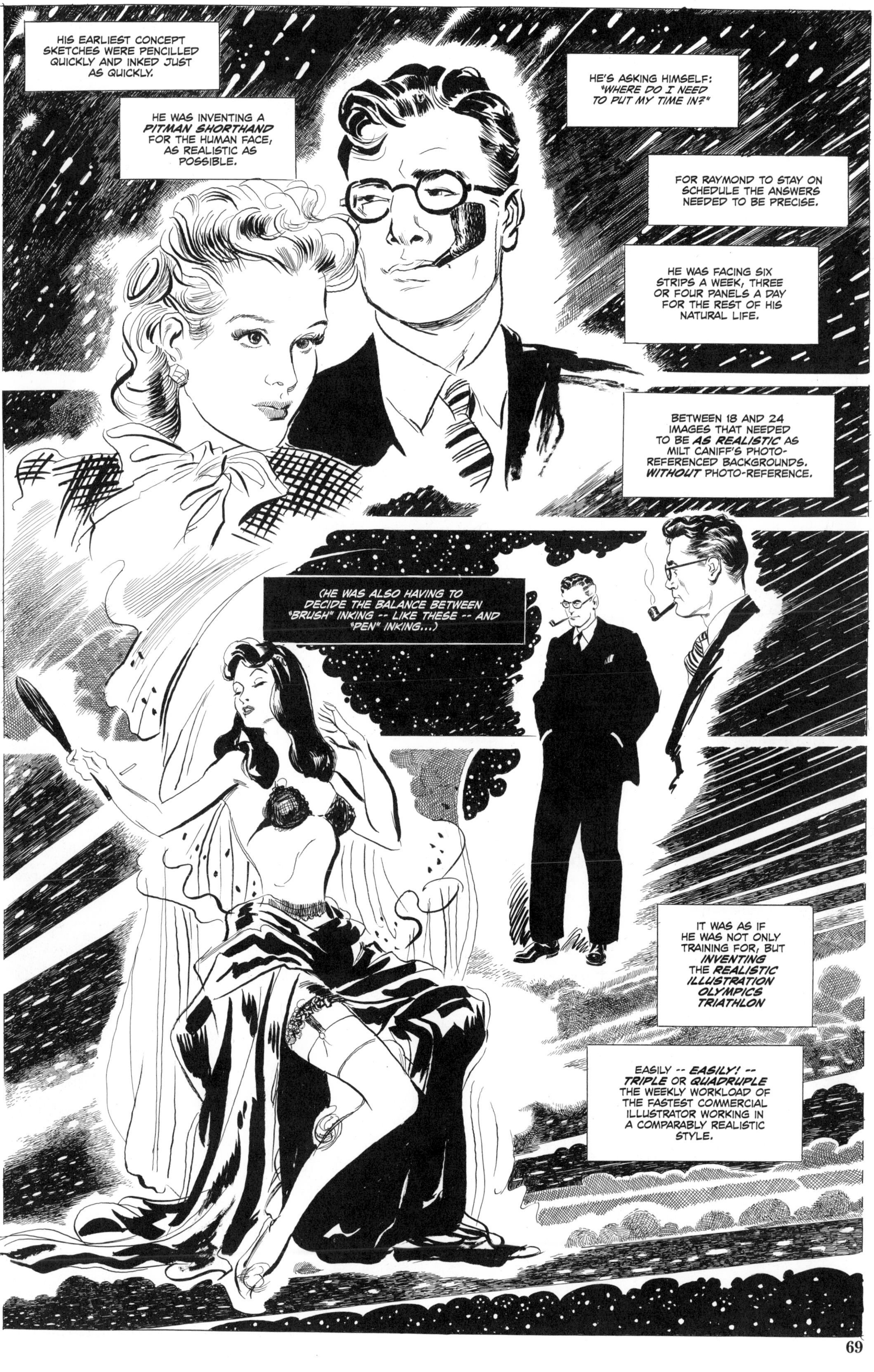

HIS EARLIEST CONCEPT SKETCHES WERE PENCILLED QUICKLY AND INKED JUST AS QUICKLY.
HE WAS INVENTING A PITMAN SHORTHAND FOR THE HUMAN FACE, AS REALISTIC AS POSSIBLE.
HE'S ASKING HIMSELF: "WHERE DO I NEED TO PUT MY TIME IN?"
FOR RAYMOND TO STAY ON SCHEDULE THE ANSWERS NEEDED TO BE PRECISE.
HE WAS FACING SIX STRIPS A WEEK, THREE OR FOUR PANELS A DAY FOR THE REST OF HIS NATURAL LIFE.
BETWEEN 18 AND 24 IMAGES THAT NEEDED TO BE AS REALISTIC AS MILT CANIFF'S PHOTO-REFERENCED BACKGROUNDS. WITHOUT PHOTO-REFERENCE.
(HE WAS ALSO HAVING TO DECIDE THE BALANCE BETWEEN "BRUSH" INKING -- LIKE THESE -- AND "PEN" INKING...)
IT WAS AS IF HE WAS NOT ONLY TRAINING FOR, BUT INVENTING THE REALISTIC ILLUSTRATION OLYMPICS TRIATHLON
EASILY -- EASILY! -- TRIPLE OR QUADRUPLE THE WEEKLY WORKLOAD OF THE FASTEST COMMERCIAL ILLUSTRATOR WORKING IN A COMPARABLY REALISTIC STYLE.

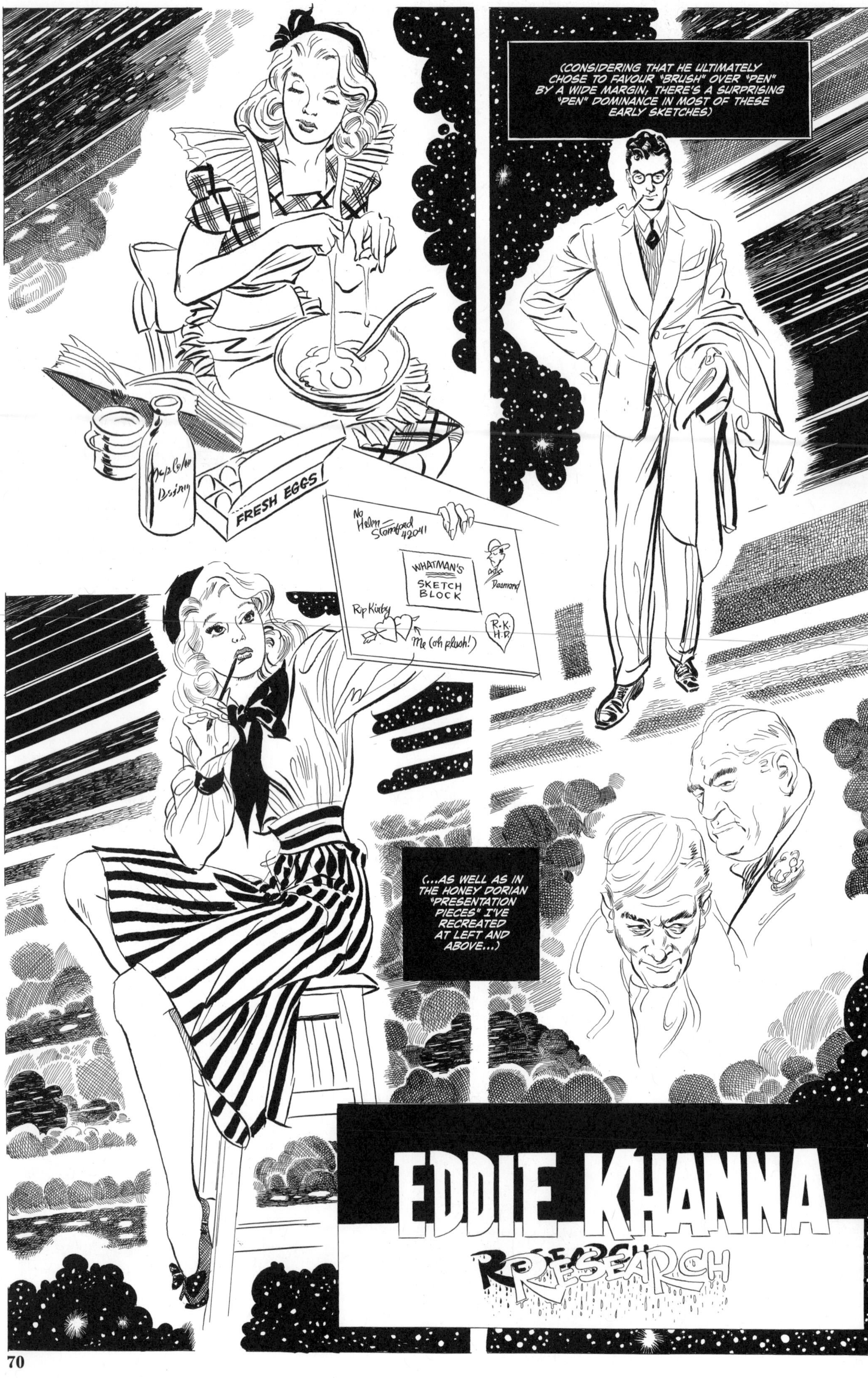
(CONSIDERING THAT HE ULTIMATELY CHOSE TO FAVOUR "BRUSH" OVER "PEN" BY A WIDE MARGIN, THERE'S A SURPRISING "PEN" DOMINANCE IN MOST OF THESE EARLY SKETCHES)
FRESH EGGS
No Helen — Stamford 42041
WHATMAN'S SKETCH BLOCK
Desmond
Rip Kirby
Me (oh plush!)
R.K. H.D.
(...AS WELL AS IN THE HONEY DORIAN "PRESENTATION PIECES" I'VE RECREATED AT LEFT AND ABOVE...)
EDDIE KHANNA
RESEARCH

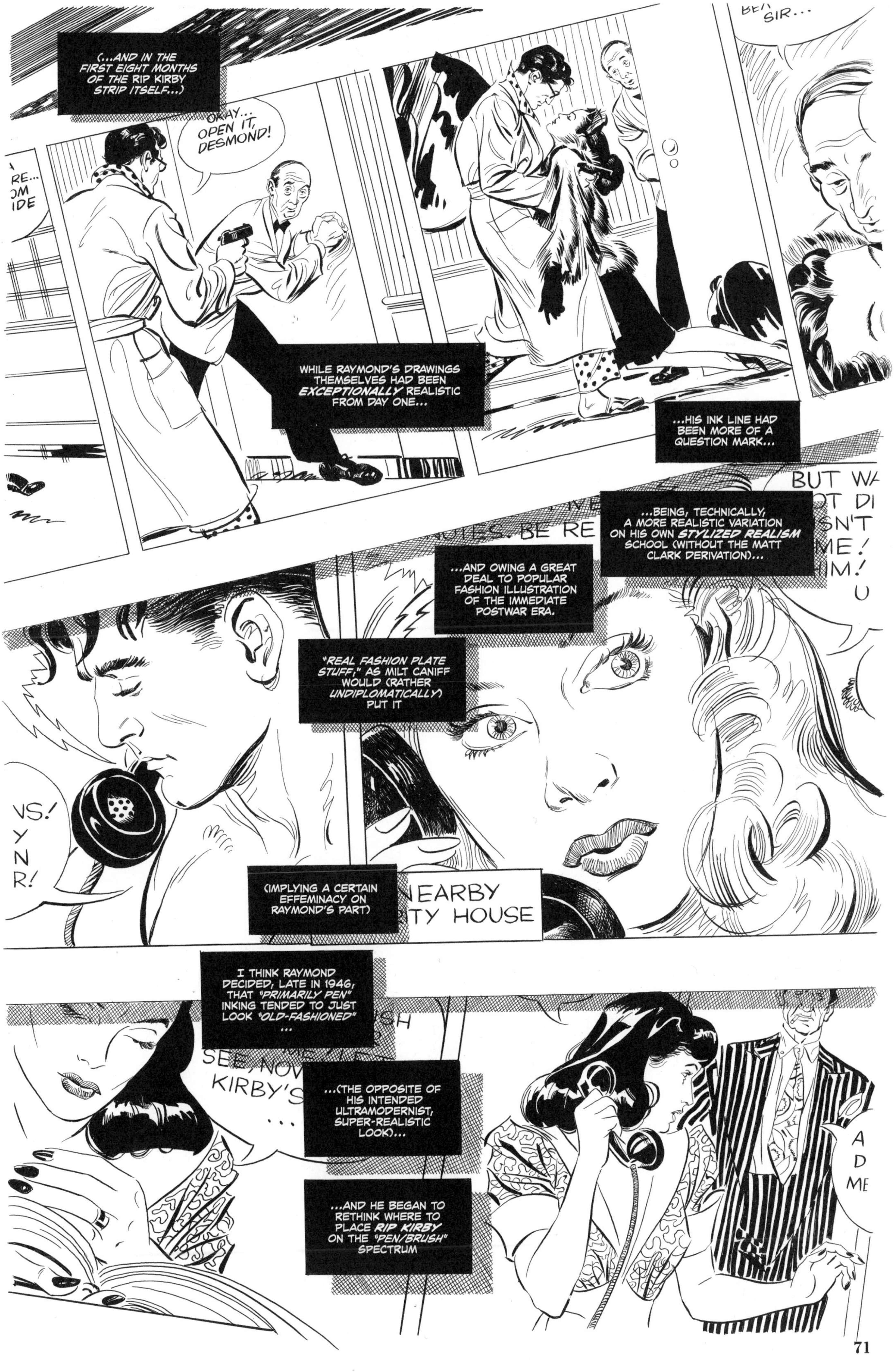
(...AND IN THE FIRST EIGHT MONTHS OF THE RIP KIRBY STRIP ITSELF...)
OKAY... OPEN IT, DESMOND!
WHILE RAYMOND'S DRAWINGS THEMSELVES HAD BEEN *EXCEPTIONALLY* REALISTIC FROM DAY ONE...
...HIS INK LINE HAD BEEN MORE OF A QUESTION MARK...
...BEING, TECHNICALLY, A MORE REALISTIC VARIATION ON HIS OWN *STYLIZED REALISM* SCHOOL (WITHOUT THE MATT CLARK DERIVATION)...
...AND OWING A GREAT DEAL TO POPULAR FASHION ILLUSTRATION OF THE IMMEDIATE POSTWAR ERA.
*"REAL FASHION PLATE STUFF,"* AS MILT CANIFF WOULD (RATHER *UNDIPLOMATICALLY*) PUT IT
(IMPLYING A CERTAIN EFFEMINACY ON RAYMOND'S PART)
I THINK RAYMOND DECIDED, LATE IN 1946, THAT *"PRIMARILY PEN"* INKING TENDED TO JUST LOOK *"OLD-FASHIONED"* ...
...(THE OPPOSITE OF HIS INTENDED ULTRAMODERNIST, SUPER-REALISTIC LOOK)...
...AND HE BEGAN TO RETHINK WHERE TO PLACE *RIP KIRBY* ON THE *"PEN/BRUSH"* SPECTRUM

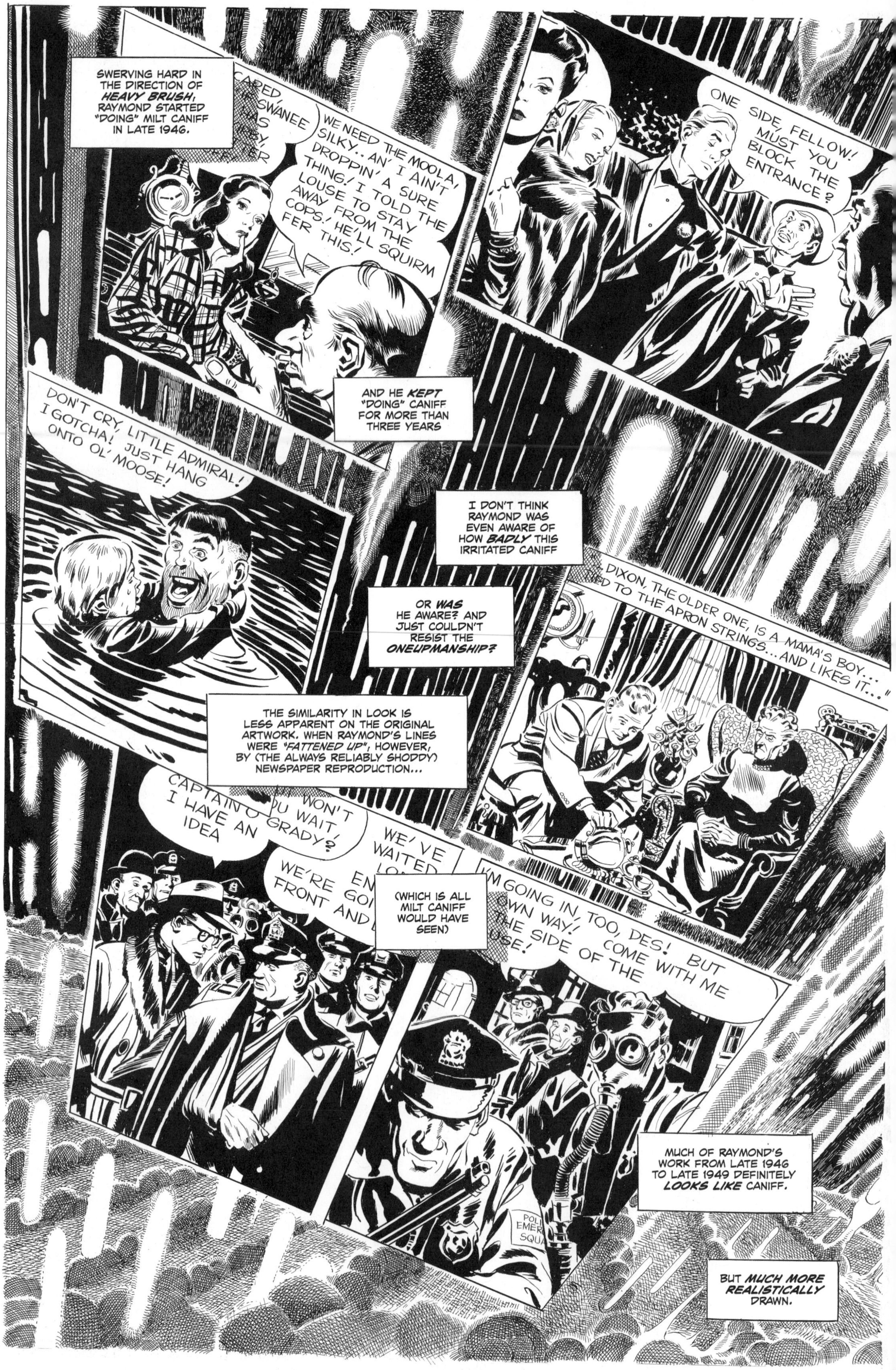
SWERVING HARD IN THE DIRECTION OF ***HEAVY BRUSH***, RAYMOND STARTED "DOING" MILT CANIFF IN LATE 1946.
WE NEED THE MOOLA, SILKY.. AN' I AIN'T DROPPIN' A SURE THING! I TOLD THE LOUSE TO STAY AWAY FROM THE COPS! HE'LL SQUIRM FER THIS!
ONE SIDE, FELLOW! MUST YOU BLOCK THE ENTRANCE?
AND HE ***KEPT*** "DOING" CANIFF FOR MORE THAN THREE YEARS
DON'T CRY, LITTLE ADMIRAL! I GOTCHA! JUST HANG ONTO OL' MOOSE!
I DON'T THINK RAYMOND WAS EVEN AWARE OF HOW ***BADLY*** THIS IRRITATED CANIFF
OR ***WAS*** HE AWARE? AND JUST COULDN'T RESIST THE ***ONEUPMANSHIP?***
DIXON, THE OLDER ONE, IS A MAMA'S BOY... TIED TO THE APRON STRINGS... AND LIKES IT..."
THE SIMILARITY IN LOOK IS LESS APPARENT ON THE ORIGINAL ARTWORK. WHEN RAYMOND'S LINES WERE *"FATTENED UP"*, HOWEVER, BY (THE ALWAYS RELIABLY SHODDY) NEWSPAPER REPRODUCTION...
CAPTAIN O'GRADY?
I HAVE AN IDEA
WON'T YOU WAIT,
WE'VE WAITED
WE'RE GOI FRONT AND
(WHICH IS ALL MILT CANIFF WOULD HAVE SEEN)
I'M GOING IN, TOO, DES! BUT OWN WAY! COME WITH ME THE SIDE OF THE USE!
MUCH OF RAYMOND'S WORK FROM LATE 1946 TO LATE 1949 DEFINITELY ***LOOKS LIKE*** CANIFF.
BUT ***MUCH MORE REALISTICALLY*** DRAWN.

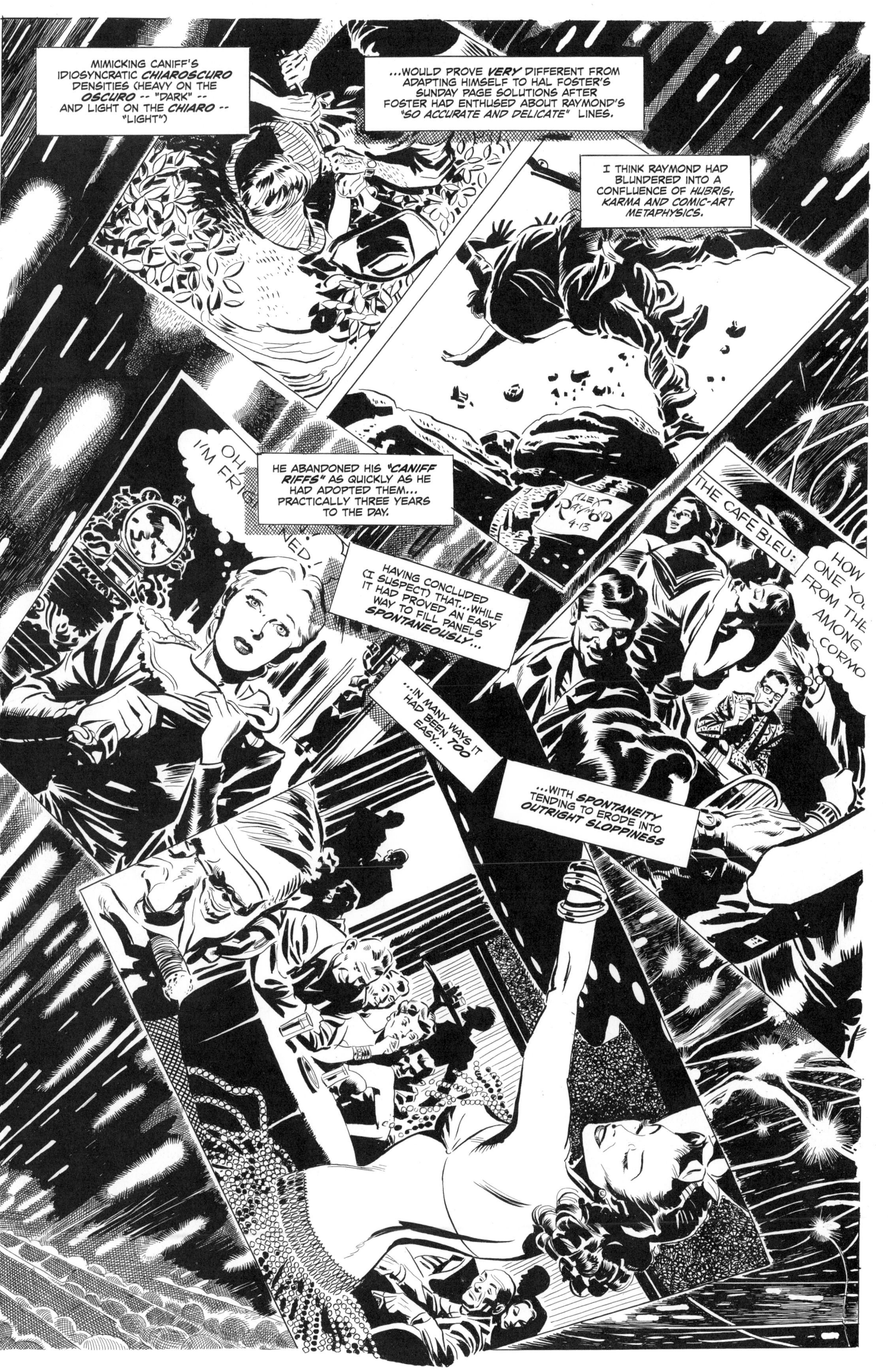
MIMICKING CANIFF'S IDIOSYNCRATIC CHIAROSCURO DENSITIES (HEAVY ON THE OSCURO -- "DARK" -- AND LIGHT ON THE CHIARO -- "LIGHT")
...WOULD PROVE VERY DIFFERENT FROM ADAPTING HIMSELF TO HAL FOSTER'S SUNDAY PAGE SOLUTIONS AFTER FOSTER HAD ENTHUSED ABOUT RAYMOND'S "SO ACCURATE AND DELICATE" LINES.
I THINK RAYMOND HAD BLUNDERED INTO A CONFLUENCE OF HUBRIS, KARMA AND COMIC-ART METAPHYSICS.
HE ABANDONED HIS "CANIFF RIFFS" AS QUICKLY AS HE HAD ADOPTED THEM... PRACTICALLY THREE YEARS TO THE DAY.
ALEX RAYMOND 4-13
HAVING CONCLUDED (I SUSPECT) THAT...WHILE IT HAD PROVED AN EASY WAY TO FILL PANELS SPONTANEOUSLY...
...IN MANY WAYS IT HAD BEEN TOO EASY...
THE CAFE BLEU:
...WITH SPONTANEITY TENDING TO ERODE INTO OUTRIGHT SLOPPINESS

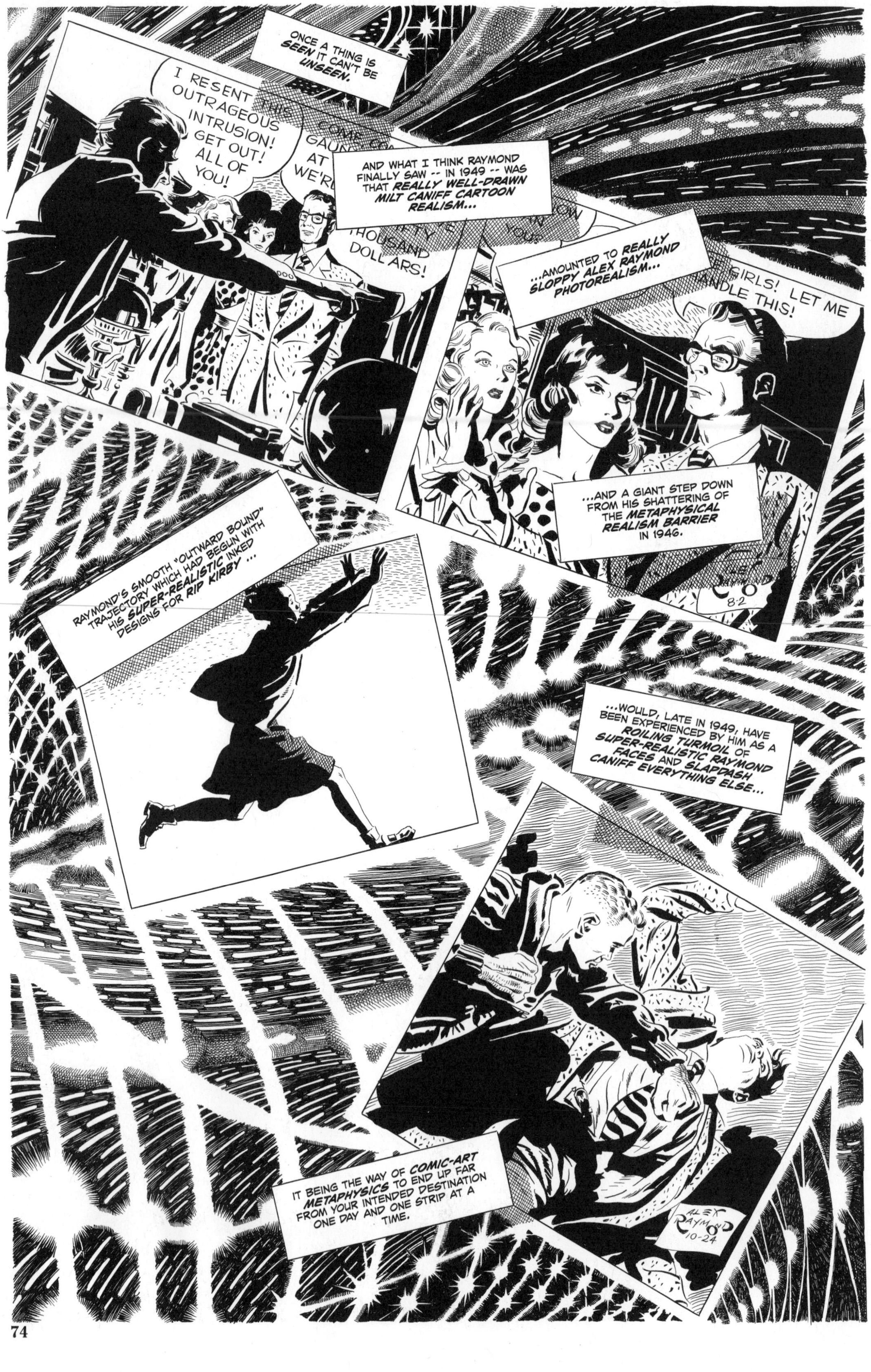
ONCE A THING IS SEEN IT CAN'T BE UNSEEN.
I RESENT THIS OUTRAGEOUS INTRUSION! GET OUT! ALL OF YOU!
AND WHAT I THINK RAYMOND FINALLY SAW -- IN 1949 -- WAS THAT REALLY WELL-DRAWN MILT CANIFF CARTOON REALISM...
THOUSAND DOLLARS!
...AMOUNTED TO REALLY SLOPPY ALEX RAYMOND PHOTOREALISM...
GIRLS! LET ME
THIS!
...AND A GIANT STEP DOWN FROM HIS SHATTERING OF THE METAPHYSICAL REALISM BARRIER IN 1946.
RAYMOND'S SMOOTH "OUTWARD BOUND" TRAJECTORY WHICH HAD BEGUN WITH HIS SUPER-REALISTIC INKED DESIGNS FOR RIP KIRBY ...
...WOULD, LATE IN 1949, HAVE BEEN EXPERIENCED BY HIM AS A ROILING TURMOIL OF SUPER-REALISTIC RAYMOND FACES AND SLAPDASH CANIFF EVERYTHING ELSE...
IT BEING THE WAY OF COMIC-ART METAPHYSICS TO END UP FAR FROM YOUR INTENDED DESTINATION ONE DAY AND ONE STRIP AT A TIME.
ALEX RAYMOND 10-24

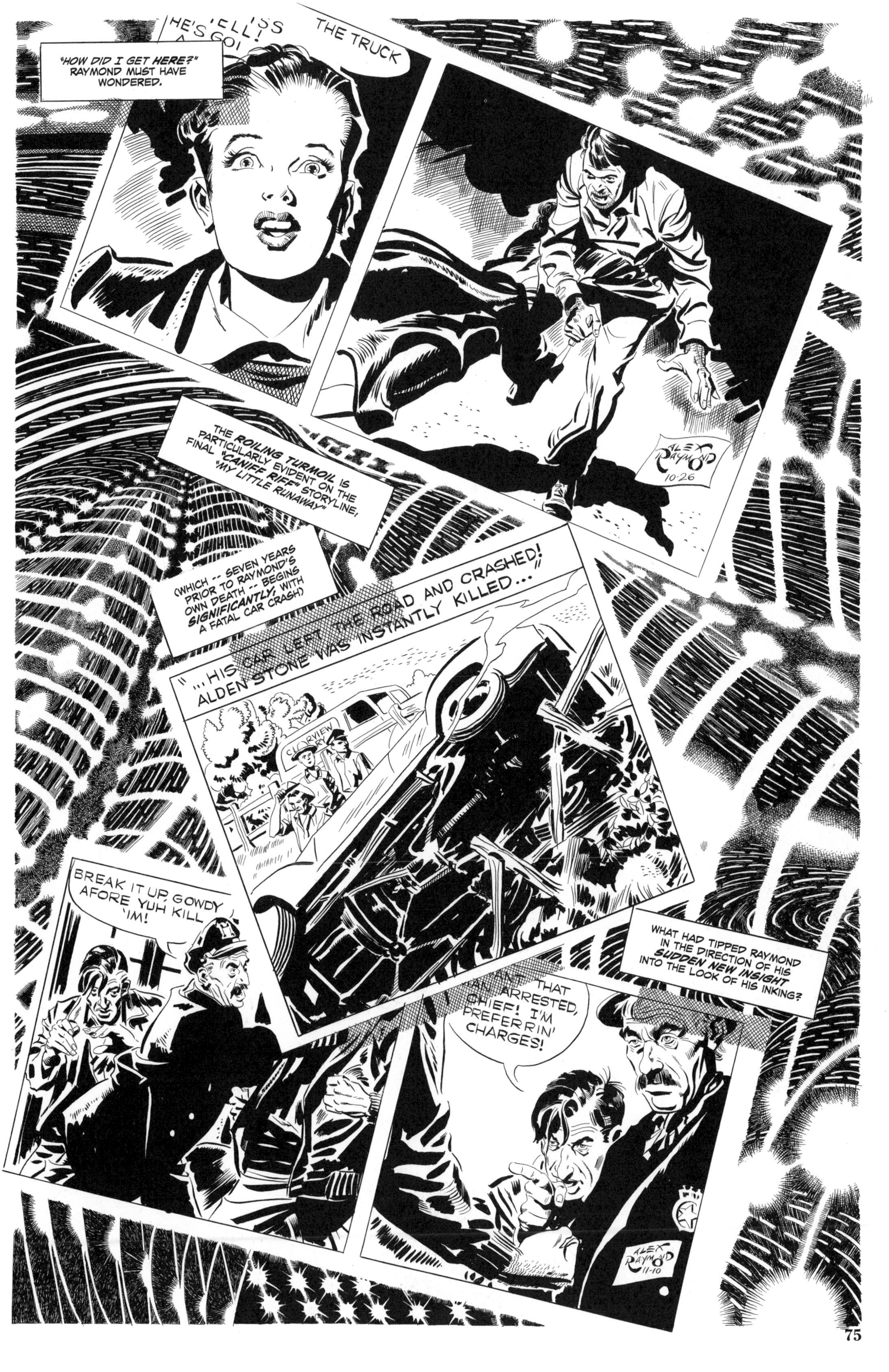
"HOW DID I GET HERE?" RAYMOND MUST HAVE WONDERED.
THE TRUCK
ALEX RAYMOND 10-26
THE ROILING TURMOIL IS PARTICULARLY EVIDENT ON THE FINAL "CANIFF RIFF" STORYLINE, "MY LITTLE RUNAWAY"
(WHICH -- SEVEN YEARS PRIOR TO RAYMOND'S OWN DEATH -- BEGINS SIGNIFICANTLY, WITH A FATAL CAR CRASH)
"...HIS CAR LEFT THE ROAD AND CRASHED! ALDEN STONE WAS INSTANTLY KILLED..."
BREAK IT UP, GOWDY AFORE YUH KILL 'IM!
WHAT HAD TIPPED RAYMOND IN THE DIRECTION OF HIS SUDDEN NEW INSIGHT INTO THE LOOK OF HIS INKING?
THAT ARRESTED, CHIEF! I'M PREFERRIN' CHARGES!
ALEX RAYMOND 11-10

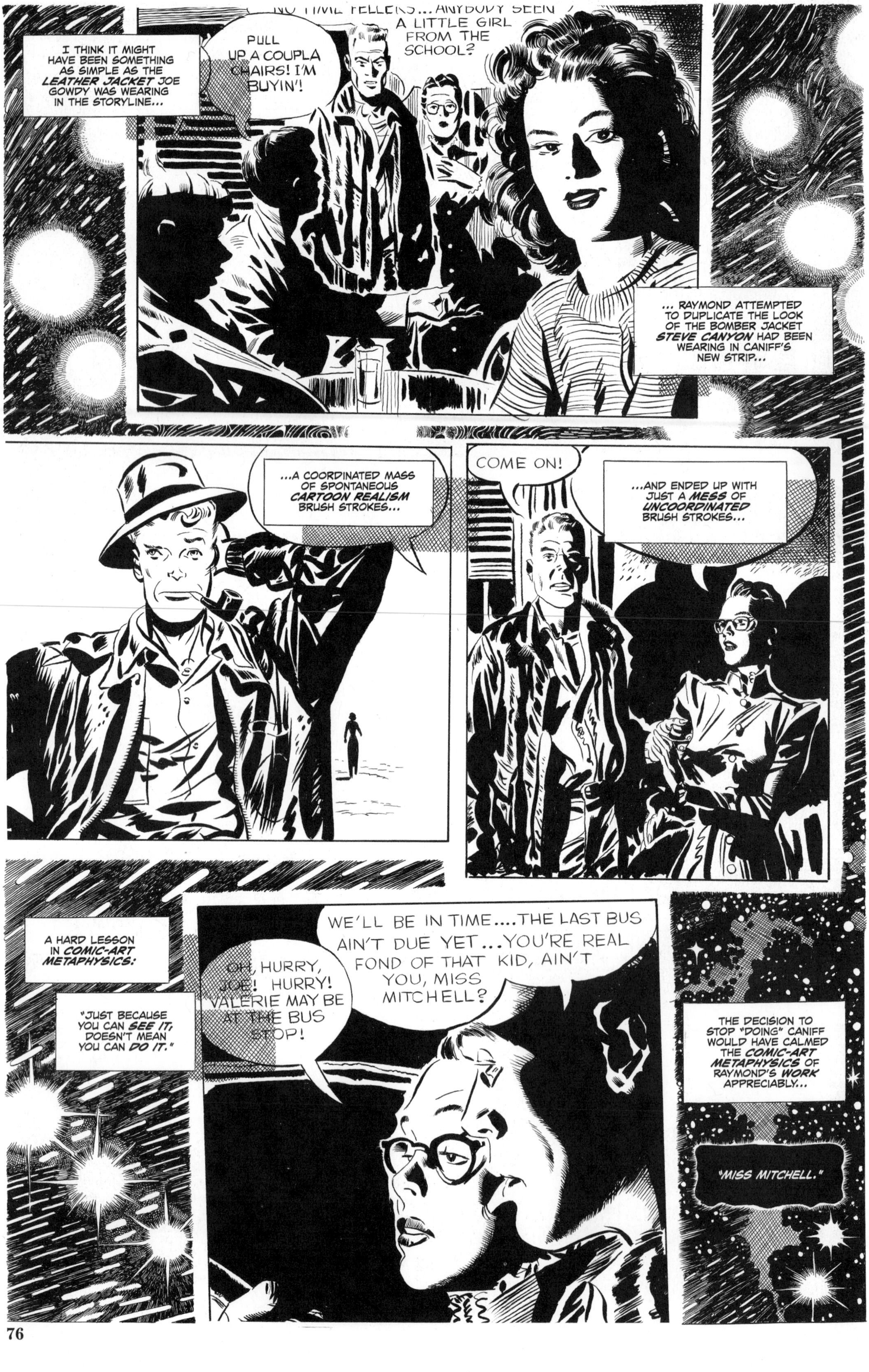

I THINK IT MIGHT HAVE BEEN SOMETHING AS SIMPLE AS THE LEATHER JACKET JOE GOWDY WAS WEARING IN THE STORYLINE...
PULL UP A COUPLA CHAIRS! I'M BUYIN'!
NO TIME FELLERS... ANYBODY SEEN A LITTLE GIRL FROM THE SCHOOL?
... RAYMOND ATTEMPTED TO DUPLICATE THE LOOK OF THE BOMBER JACKET STEVE CANYON HAD BEEN WEARING IN CANIFF'S NEW STRIP...
...A COORDINATED MASS OF SPONTANEOUS CARTOON REALISM BRUSH STROKES...
COME ON!
...AND ENDED UP WITH JUST A MESS OF UNCOORDINATED BRUSH STROKES...
A HARD LESSON IN COMIC-ART METAPHYSICS:
"JUST BECAUSE YOU CAN SEE IT, DOESN'T MEAN YOU CAN DO IT."
OH, HURRY, JOE! HURRY! VALERIE MAY BE AT THE BUS STOP!
WE'LL BE IN TIME.... THE LAST BUS AIN'T DUE YET... YOU'RE REAL FOND OF THAT KID, AIN'T YOU, MISS MITCHELL?
THE DECISION TO STOP "DOING" CANIFF WOULD HAVE CALMED THE COMIC-ART METAPHYSICS OF RAYMOND'S WORK APPRECIABLY...
"MISS MITCHELL."

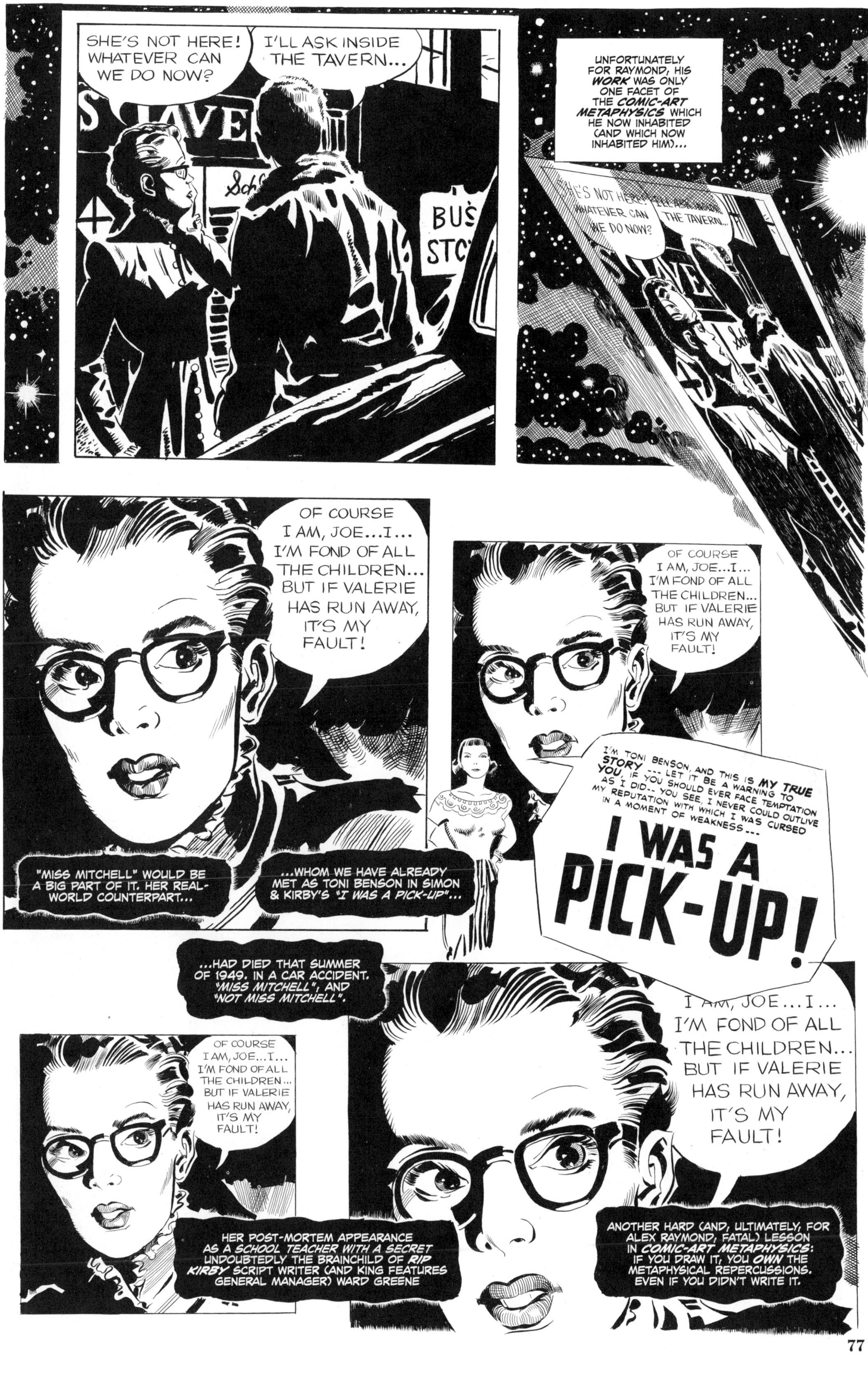
SHE'S NOT HERE! WHATEVER CAN WE DO NOW?
I'LL ASK INSIDE THE TAVERN...
BUS STO
UNFORTUNATELY FOR RAYMOND, HIS WORK WAS ONLY ONE FACET OF THE COMIC-ART METAPHYSICS WHICH HE NOW INHABITED (AND WHICH NOW INHABITED HIM)...
SHE'S NOT HERE! WHATEVER CAN WE DO NOW?
I'LL ASK INSIDE THE TAVERN...
OF COURSE I AM, JOE...I... I'M FOND OF ALL THE CHILDREN... BUT IF VALERIE HAS RUN AWAY, IT'S MY FAULT!
"MISS MITCHELL" WOULD BE A BIG PART OF IT. HER REAL-WORLD COUNTERPART...
OF COURSE I AM, JOE...I... I'M FOND OF ALL THE CHILDREN... BUT IF VALERIE HAS RUN AWAY, IT'S MY FAULT!
...WHOM WE HAVE ALREADY MET AS TONI BENSON IN SIMON & KIRBY'S "I WAS A PICK-UP"...
I'M TONI BENSON, AND THIS IS MY TRUE STORY --- LET IT BE A WARNING TO YOU, IF YOU SHOULD EVER FACE TEMPTATION AS I DID-- YOU SEE, I NEVER COULD OUTLIVE MY REPUTATION WITH WHICH I WAS CURSED IN A MOMENT OF WEAKNESS...
I WAS A PICK-UP!
...HAD DIED THAT SUMMER OF 1949. IN A CAR ACCIDENT. "MISS MITCHELL", AND "NOT MISS MITCHELL".
OF COURSE I AM, JOE...I... I'M FOND OF ALL THE CHILDREN... BUT IF VALERIE HAS RUN AWAY, IT'S MY FAULT!
HER POST-MORTEM APPEARANCE AS A SCHOOL TEACHER WITH A SECRET UNDOUBTEDLY THE BRAINCHILD OF RIP KIRBY SCRIPT WRITER (AND KING FEATURES GENERAL MANAGER) WARD GREENE
I AM, JOE...I... I'M FOND OF ALL THE CHILDREN... BUT IF VALERIE HAS RUN AWAY, IT'S MY FAULT!
ANOTHER HARD (AND, ULTIMATELY, FOR ALEX RAYMOND, FATAL) LESSON IN COMIC-ART METAPHYSICS: IF YOU DRAW IT, YOU OWN THE METAPHYSICAL REPERCUSSIONS. EVEN IF YOU DIDN'T WRITE IT.

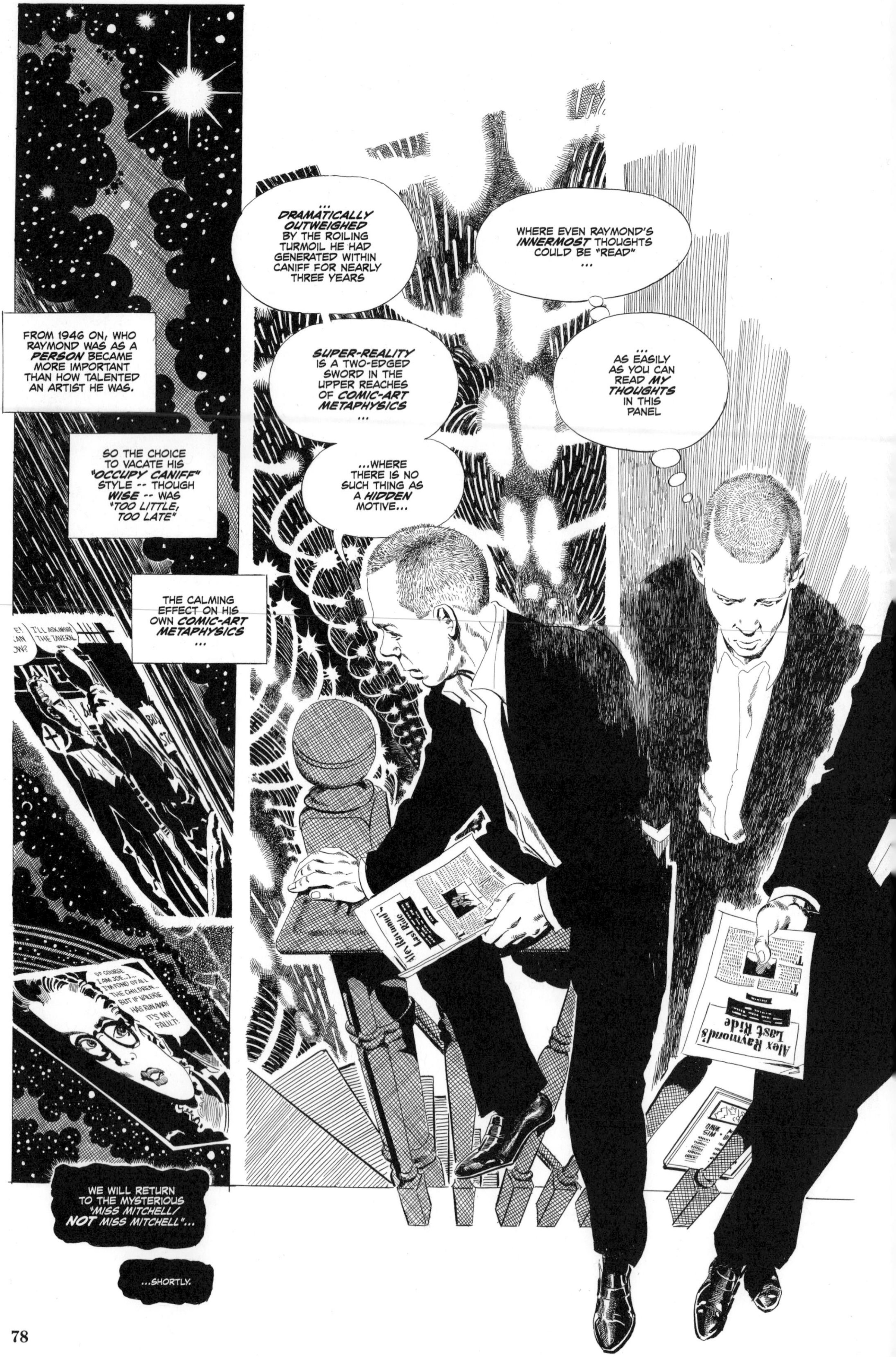
FROM 1946 ON, WHO RAYMOND WAS AS A PERSON BECAME MORE IMPORTANT THAN HOW TALENTED AN ARTIST HE WAS.
SO THE CHOICE TO VACATE HIS "OCCUPY CANIFF" STYLE -- THOUGH WISE -- WAS "TOO LITTLE, TOO LATE"
THE CALMING EFFECT ON HIS OWN COMIC-ART METAPHYSICS ...
I'LL ASK INSIDE THE TAVERN.
OF COURSE I AM JOE... I... I'M FOND OF ALL THE CHILDREN... BUT IF VALERIE HAS RUN AWAY IT'S MY FAULT!
... DRAMATICALLY OUTWEIGHED BY THE ROILING TURMOIL HE HAD GENERATED WITHIN CANIFF FOR NEARLY THREE YEARS
SUPER-REALITY IS A TWO-EDGED SWORD IN THE UPPER REACHES OF COMIC-ART METAPHYSICS ...
...WHERE THERE IS NO SUCH THING AS A HIDDEN MOTIVE...
WHERE EVEN RAYMOND'S INNERMOST THOUGHTS COULD BE "READ" ...
... AS EASILY AS YOU CAN READ MY THOUGHTS IN THIS PANEL
Alex Raymond's Last Ride
Alex Raymond's Last Ride
WE WILL RETURN TO THE MYSTERIOUS "MISS MITCHELL/ NOT MISS MITCHELL"...
...SHORTLY.

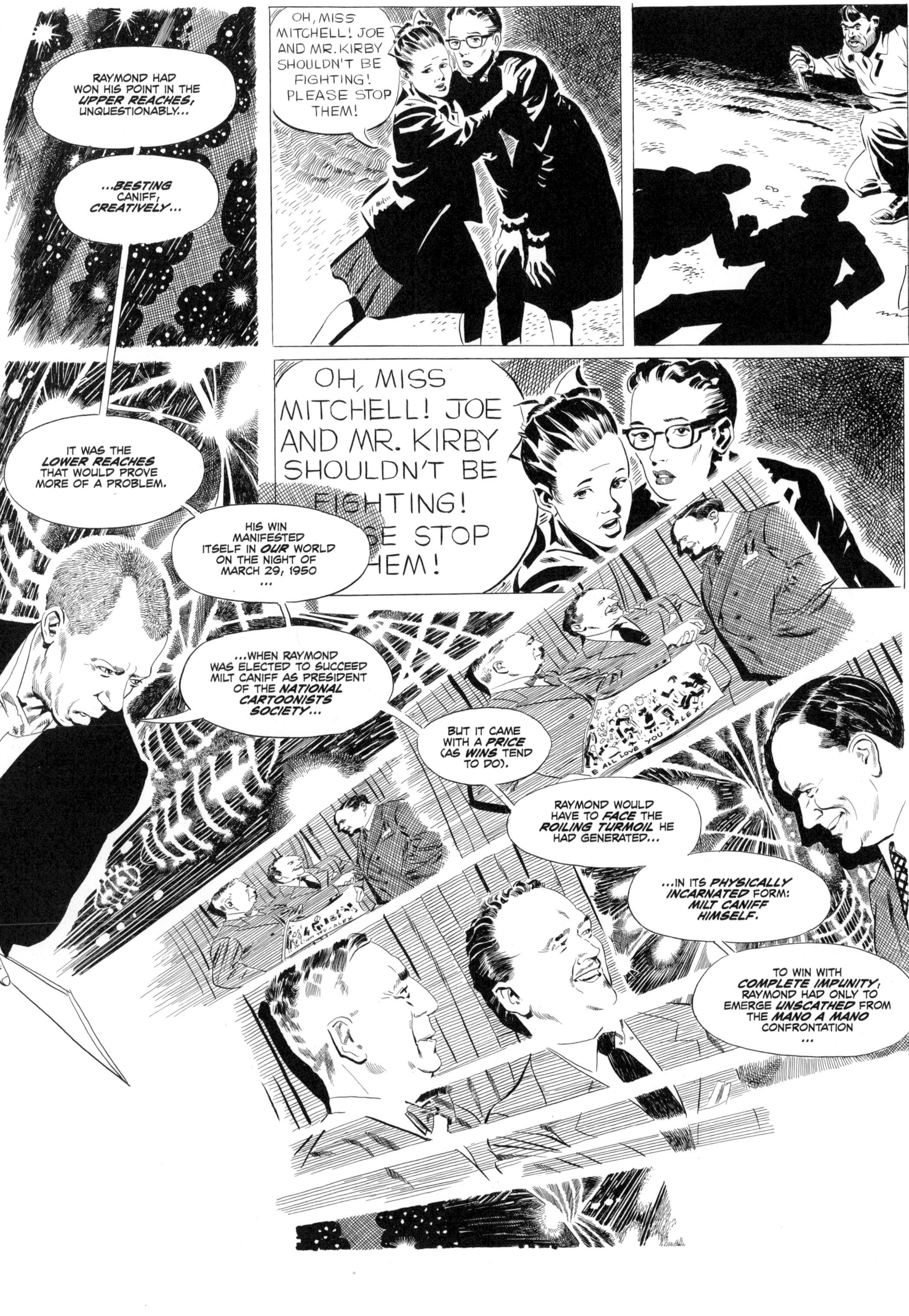
RAYMOND HAD WON HIS POINT IN THE UPPER REACHES, UNQUESTIONABLY...
OH, MISS MITCHELL! JOE AND MR. KIRBY SHOULDN'T BE FIGHTING! PLEASE STOP THEM!
...BESTING CANIFF, CREATIVELY...
OH, MISS MITCHELL! JOE AND MR. KIRBY SHOULDN'T BE FIGHTING!
IT WAS THE LOWER REACHES THAT WOULD PROVE MORE OF A PROBLEM.
HIS WIN MANIFESTED ITSELF IN OUR WORLD ON THE NIGHT OF MARCH 29, 1950 ...
...WHEN RAYMOND WAS ELECTED TO SUCCEED MILT CANIFF AS PRESIDENT OF THE NATIONAL CARTOONISTS SOCIETY...
BUT IT CAME WITH A PRICE (AS WINS TEND TO DO).
RAYMOND WOULD HAVE TO FACE THE ROILING TURMOIL HE HAD GENERATED...
...IN ITS PHYSICALLY INCARNATED FORM: MILT CANIFF HIMSELF.
TO WIN WITH COMPLETE IMPUNITY, RAYMOND HAD ONLY TO EMERGE UNSCATHED FROM THE MANO A MANO CONFRONTATION ...

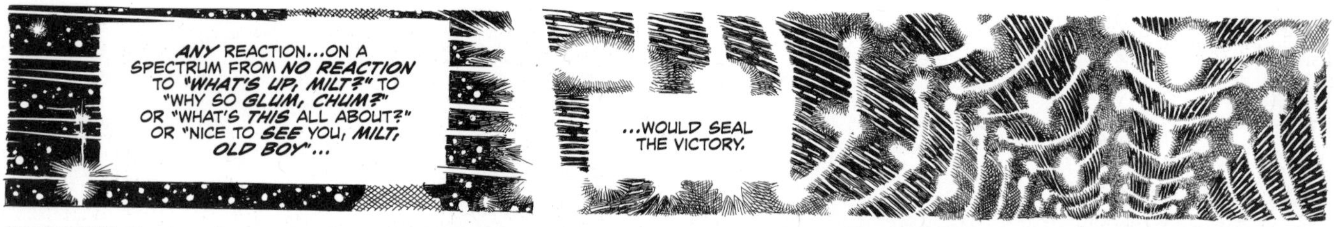
ANY REACTION...ON A SPECTRUM FROM NO REACTION TO "WHAT'S UP, MILT?" TO "WHY SO GLUM, CHUM?" OR "WHAT'S THIS ALL ABOUT?" OR "NICE TO SEE YOU, MILT, OLD BOY"...
...WOULD SEAL THE VICTORY.

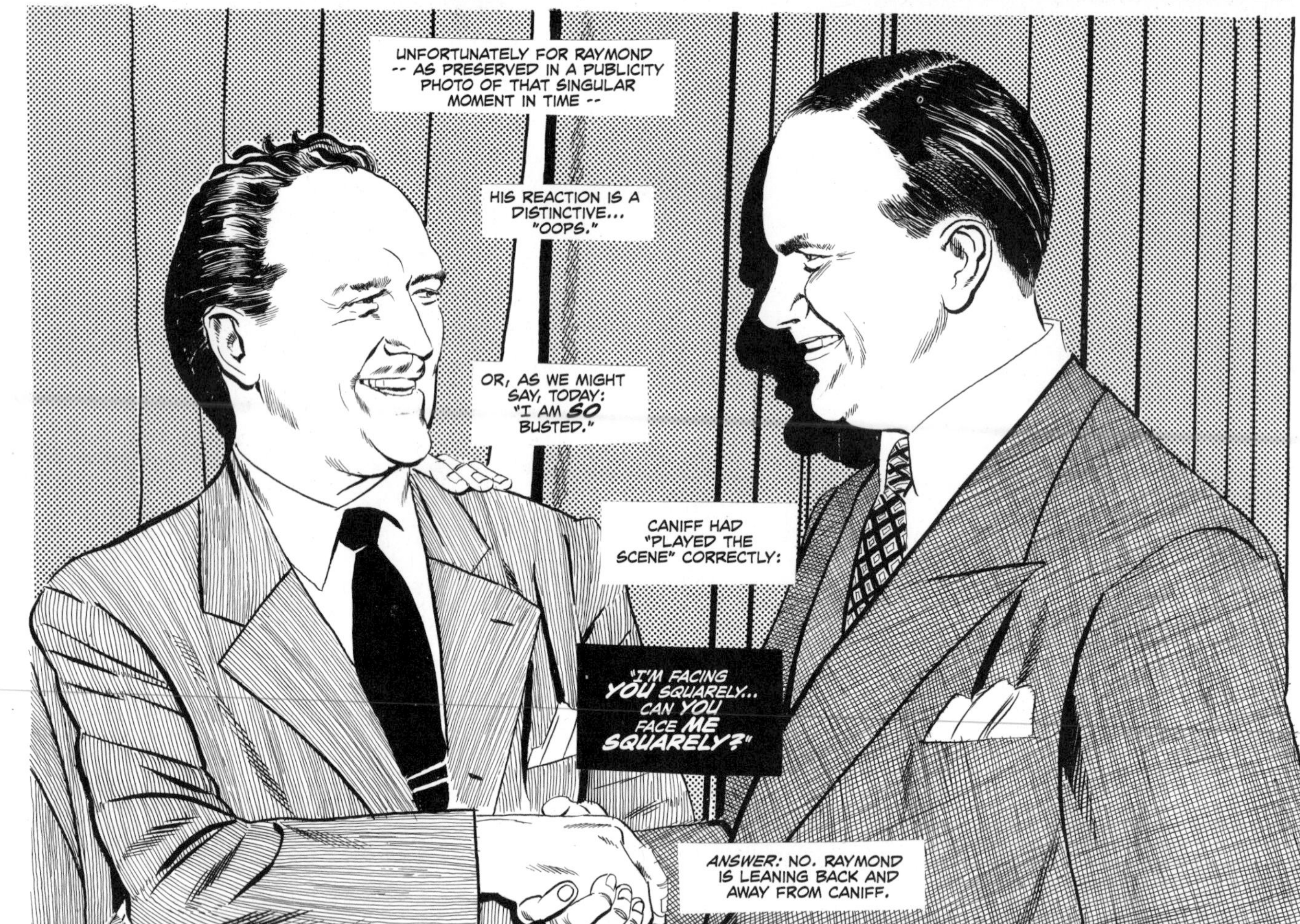
UNFORTUNATELY FOR RAYMOND -- AS PRESERVED IN A PUBLICITY PHOTO OF THAT SINGULAR MOMENT IN TIME --
HIS REACTION IS A DISTINCTIVE... "OOPS."
OR, AS WE MIGHT SAY, TODAY: "I AM SO BUSTED."
CANIFF HAD "PLAYED THE SCENE" CORRECTLY:
"I'M FACING YOU SQUARELY... CAN YOU FACE ME SQUARELY?"
ANSWER: NO. RAYMOND IS LEANING BACK AND AWAY FROM CANIFF.
"I'M LOOKING YOU SQUARE IN THE EYE...CAN YOU LOOK ME SQUARE IN THE EYE?"
ALL LOVE YOU - ALEX!

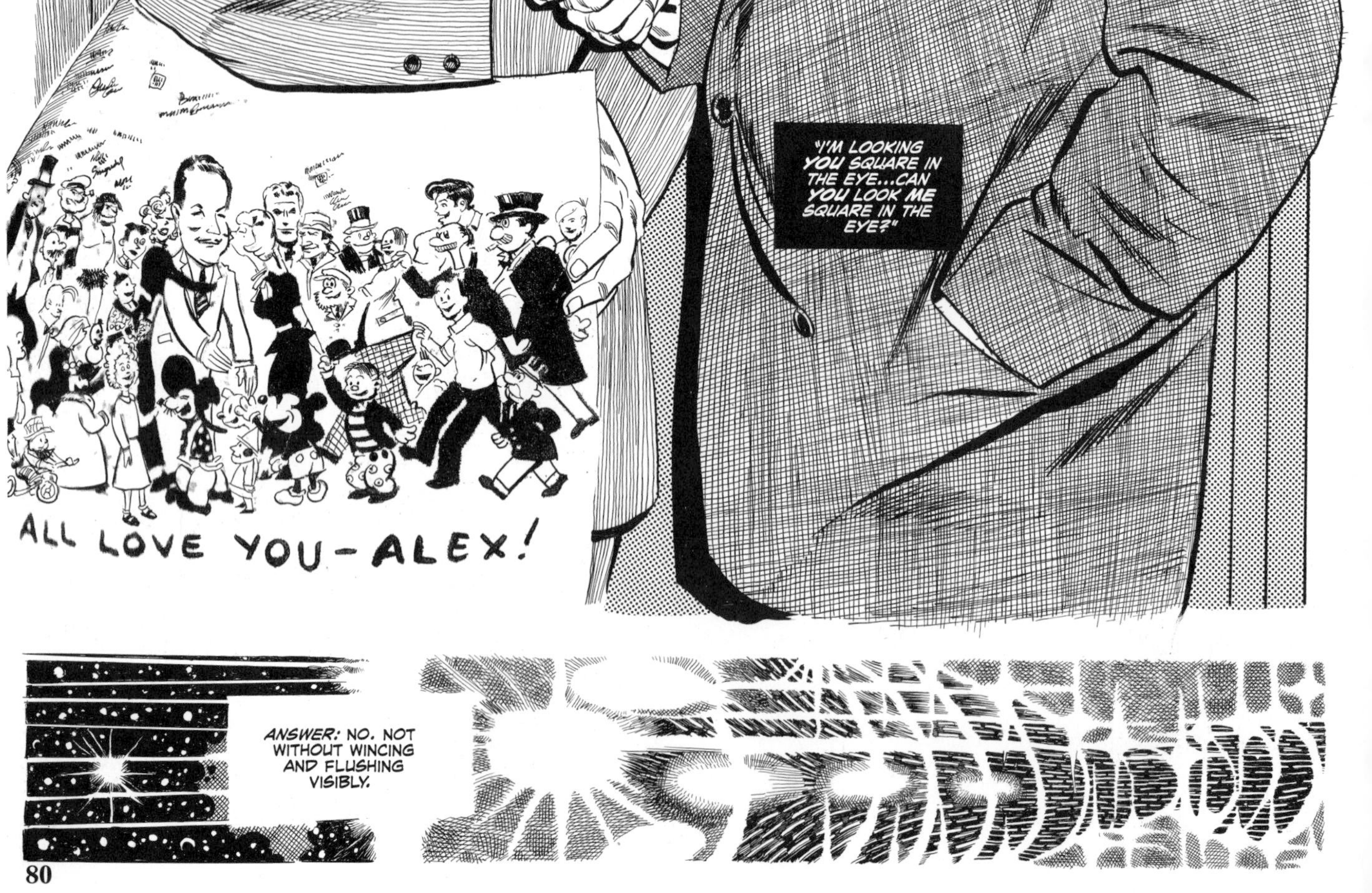
ANSWER: NO. NOT WITHOUT WINCING AND FLUSHING VISIBLY.

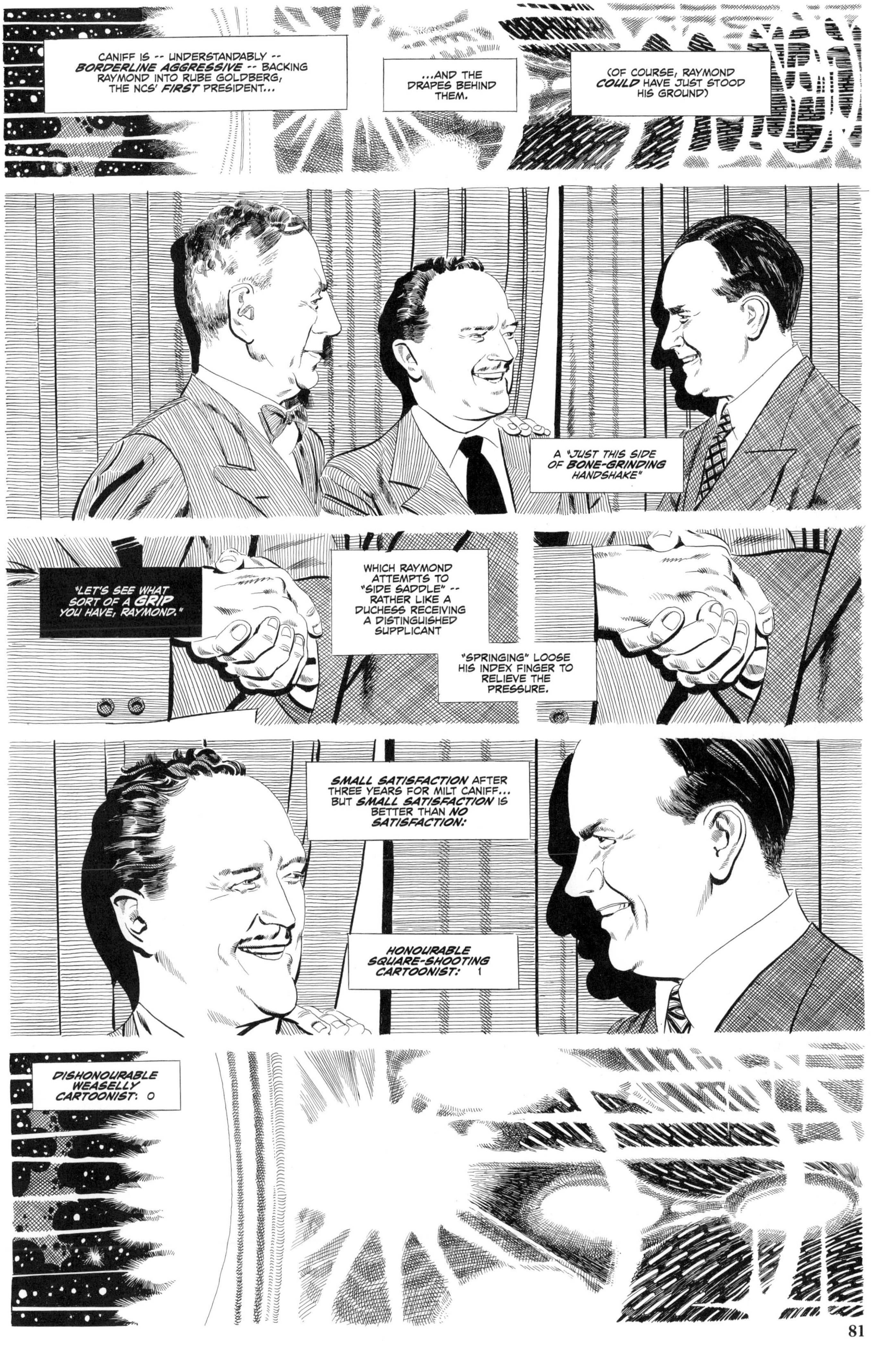
CANIFF IS -- UNDERSTANDABLY -- BORDERLINE AGGRESSIVE -- BACKING RAYMOND INTO RUBE GOLDBERG, THE NCS' FIRST PRESIDENT...
...AND THE DRAPES BEHIND THEM.
(OF COURSE, RAYMOND COULD HAVE JUST STOOD HIS GROUND)
A "JUST THIS SIDE OF BONE-GRINDING HANDSHAKE"
"LET'S SEE WHAT SORT OF A GRIP YOU HAVE, RAYMOND."
WHICH RAYMOND ATTEMPTS TO "SIDE SADDLE" -- RATHER LIKE A DUCHESS RECEIVING A DISTINGUISHED SUPPLICANT
"SPRINGING" LOOSE HIS INDEX FINGER TO RELIEVE THE PRESSURE.
SMALL SATISFACTION AFTER THREE YEARS FOR MILT CANIFF... BUT SMALL SATISFACTION IS BETTER THAN NO SATISFACTION:
HONOURABLE SQUARE-SHOOTING CARTOONIST: 1
DISHONOURABLE WEASELLY CARTOONIST: 0

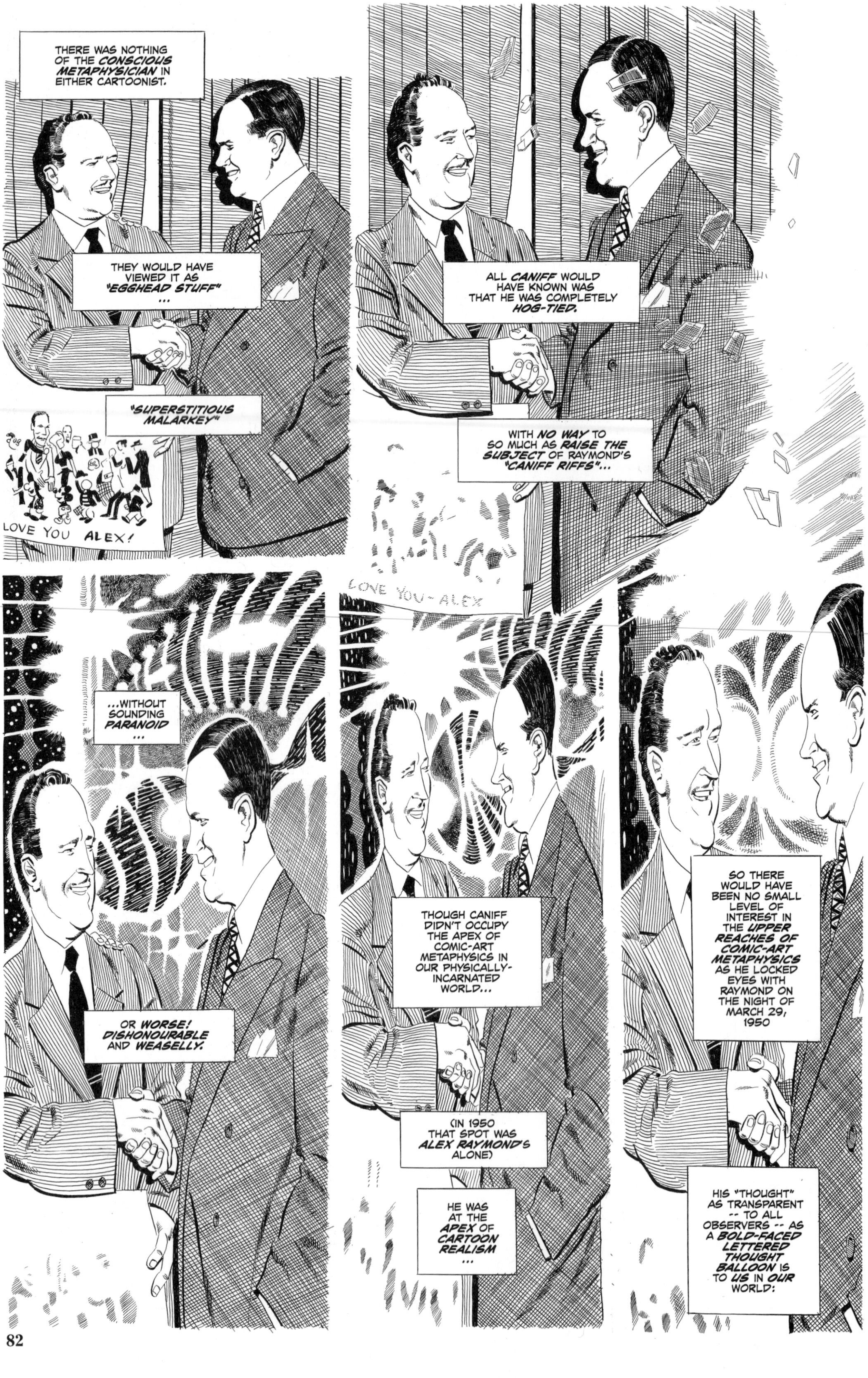
THERE WAS NOTHING OF THE CONSCIOUS METAPHYSICIAN IN EITHER CARTOONIST.
THEY WOULD HAVE VIEWED IT AS "EGGHEAD STUFF" ...
"SUPERSTITIOUS MALARKEY"
LOVE YOU ALEX!
ALL CANIFF WOULD HAVE KNOWN WAS THAT HE WAS COMPLETELY HOG-TIED.
WITH NO WAY TO SO MUCH AS RAISE THE SUBJECT OF RAYMOND'S "CANIFF RIFFS"...
LOVE YOU - ALEX
...WITHOUT SOUNDING PARANOID ...
OR WORSE! DISHONOURABLE AND WEASELLY.
THOUGH CANIFF DIDN'T OCCUPY THE APEX OF COMIC-ART METAPHYSICS IN OUR PHYSICALLY-INCARNATED WORLD...
(IN 1950 THAT SPOT WAS ALEX RAYMOND'S ALONE)
HE WAS AT THE APEX OF CARTOON REALISM ...
SO THERE WOULD HAVE BEEN NO SMALL LEVEL OF INTEREST IN THE UPPER REACHES OF COMIC-ART METAPHYSICS AS HE LOCKED EYES WITH RAYMOND ON THE NIGHT OF MARCH 29, 1950
HIS "THOUGHT" AS TRANSPARENT -- TO ALL OBSERVERS -- AS A BOLD-FACED LETTERED THOUGHT BALLOON IS TO US IN OUR WORLD:

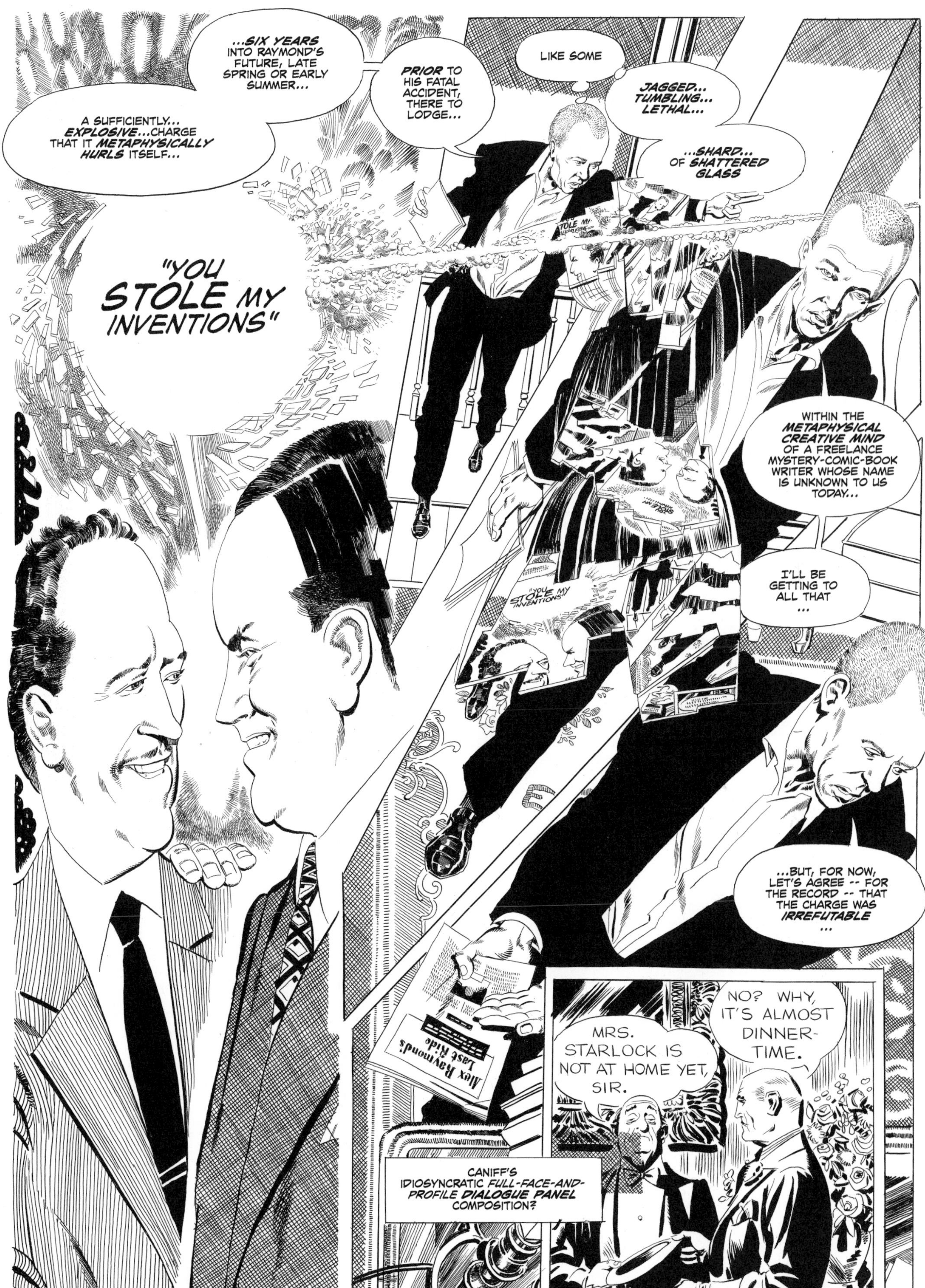

A SUFFICIENTLY... EXPLOSIVE...CHARGE THAT IT METAPHYSICALLY HURLS ITSELF...
...SIX YEARS INTO RAYMOND'S FUTURE, LATE SPRING OR EARLY SUMMER...
PRIOR TO HIS FATAL ACCIDENT, THERE TO LODGE...
LIKE SOME
JAGGED... TUMBLING... LETHAL...
...SHARD... OF SHATTERED GLASS
"YOU STOLE MY INVENTIONS"
WITHIN THE METAPHYSICAL CREATIVE MIND OF A FREELANCE MYSTERY-COMIC-BOOK WRITER WHOSE NAME IS UNKNOWN TO US TODAY...
I'LL BE GETTING TO ALL THAT ...
...BUT, FOR NOW, LET'S AGREE -- FOR THE RECORD -- THAT THE CHARGE WAS IRREFUTABLE ...
Alex Raymond's Last Ride
NO? WHY, IT'S ALMOST DINNER-TIME.
MRS. STARLOCK IS NOT AT HOME YET, SIR.
CANIFF'S IDIOSYNCRATIC FULL-FACE-AND-PROFILE DIALOGUE PANEL COMPOSITION?
CHECK.

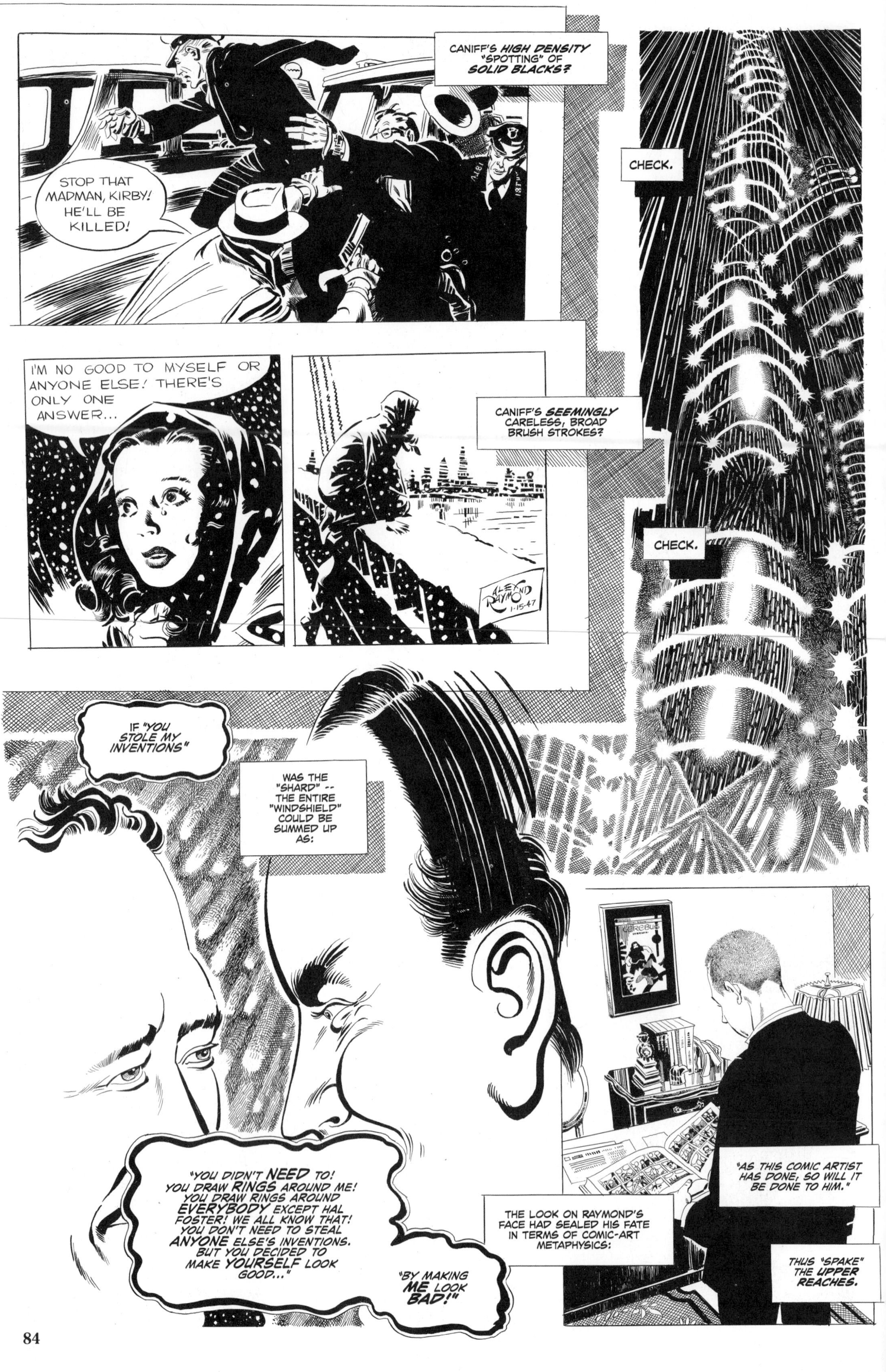
CANIFF'S HIGH DENSITY "SPOTTING" OF SOLID BLACKS?
STOP THAT MADMAN, KIRBY! HE'LL BE KILLED!
CHECK.
I'M NO GOOD TO MYSELF OR ANYONE ELSE! THERE'S ONLY ONE ANSWER...
CANIFF'S SEEMINGLY CARELESS, BROAD BRUSH STROKES?
ALEX RAYMOND 1-15-47
CHECK.
IF "YOU STOLE MY INVENTIONS"
WAS THE "SHARD" -- THE ENTIRE "WINDSHIELD" COULD BE SUMMED UP AS:
"YOU DIDN'T NEED TO! YOU DRAW RINGS AROUND ME! YOU DRAW RINGS AROUND EVERYBODY EXCEPT HAL FOSTER! WE ALL KNOW THAT! YOU DON'T NEED TO STEAL ANYONE ELSE'S INVENTIONS. BUT YOU DECIDED TO MAKE YOURSELF LOOK GOOD..."
"BY MAKING ME LOOK BAD!"
"AS THIS COMIC ARTIST HAS DONE, SO WILL IT BE DONE TO HIM."
THE LOOK ON RAYMOND'S FACE HAD SEALED HIS FATE IN TERMS OF COMIC-ART METAPHYSICS:
THUS "SPAKE" THE UPPER REACHES.

WHY *HAD* RAYMOND DONE IT?

*Here they are!*

Two of t... ...lor-ful char... ...ew daily a... ...ture by MILTON CANIFF

STEVE CANYON

This is in reply to the thousands of MILTON CANIFF fans who have asked "What will it be?" and "When will it start?"

The starting date is Monday, January 13th, 1947 for the Daily, and January 19th for the Sunday feature.

WOUNDED VANITY, I SUSPECT. WORD HAD LEAKED OUT IN 1945 THAT CANIFF WOULD BE DOING A NEW STRIP IN 1947 ...

...LEADING TO A GROUNDSWELL OF PUBLICITY THAT QUICKLY DWARFED THE PUBLIC RESPONSE TO THE 1946 LAUNCH OF *RIP KIRBY*.

RAYMOND COULD HAVE -- *SHOULD* HAVE -- JUST LEFT IT ALONE...CONTENT THAT RIP KIRBY HAD BEEN THE FASTEST LAUNCH OF ANY *KING FEATURES* STRIP ...

EVERYTHING HE DID IN AN ATTEMPT TO *DIMINISH* CANIFF...

...TO EMPHASIZE HIS OWN CLEARLY SUPERIOR ARTISTIC "CHOPS"...

...SERVED MERELY TO FURTHER *ELEVATE* CANIFF...

RIP KIRBY

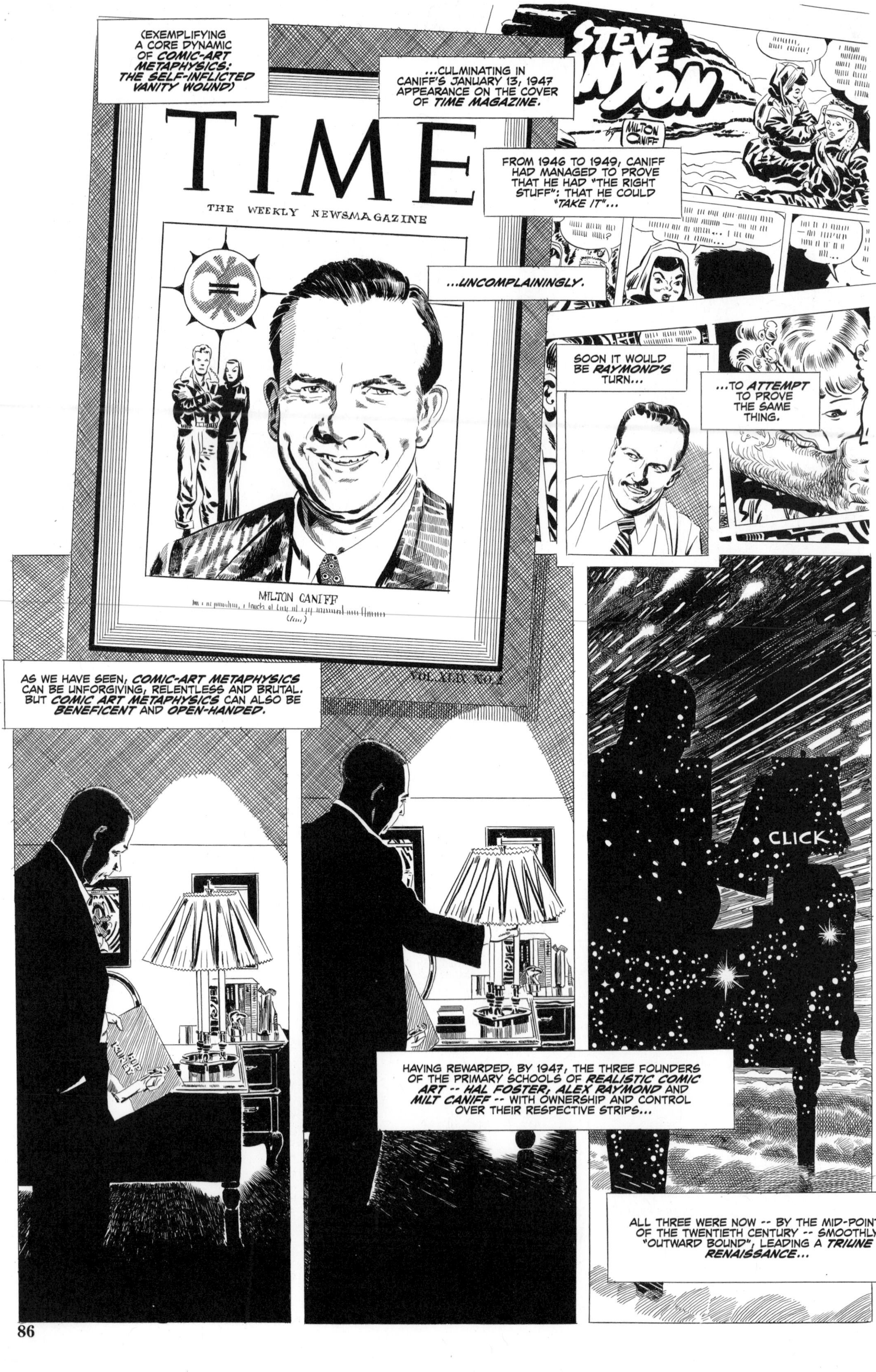
(EXEMPLIFYING A CORE DYNAMIC OF COMIC-ART METAPHYSICS: THE SELF-INFLICTED VANITY WOUND)
...CULMINATING IN CANIFF'S JANUARY 13, 1947 APPEARANCE ON THE COVER OF TIME MAGAZINE.
TIME
THE WEEKLY NEWSMAGAZINE
MILTON CANIFF
FROM 1946 TO 1949, CANIFF HAD MANAGED TO PROVE THAT HE HAD "THE RIGHT STUFF": THAT HE COULD "TAKE IT"...
...UNCOMPLAININGLY.
SOON IT WOULD BE RAYMOND'S TURN...
...TO ATTEMPT TO PROVE THE SAME THING.
AS WE HAVE SEEN, COMIC-ART METAPHYSICS CAN BE UNFORGIVING, RELENTLESS AND BRUTAL. BUT COMIC ART METAPHYSICS CAN ALSO BE BENEFICENT AND OPEN-HANDED.
CLICK
HAVING REWARDED, BY 1947, THE THREE FOUNDERS OF THE PRIMARY SCHOOLS OF REALISTIC COMIC ART -- HAL FOSTER, ALEX RAYMOND AND MILT CANIFF -- WITH OWNERSHIP AND CONTROL OVER THEIR RESPECTIVE STRIPS...
ALL THREE WERE NOW -- BY THE MID-POINT OF THE TWENTIETH CENTURY -- SMOOTHLY "OUTWARD BOUND", LEADING A TRIUNE RENAISSANCE...

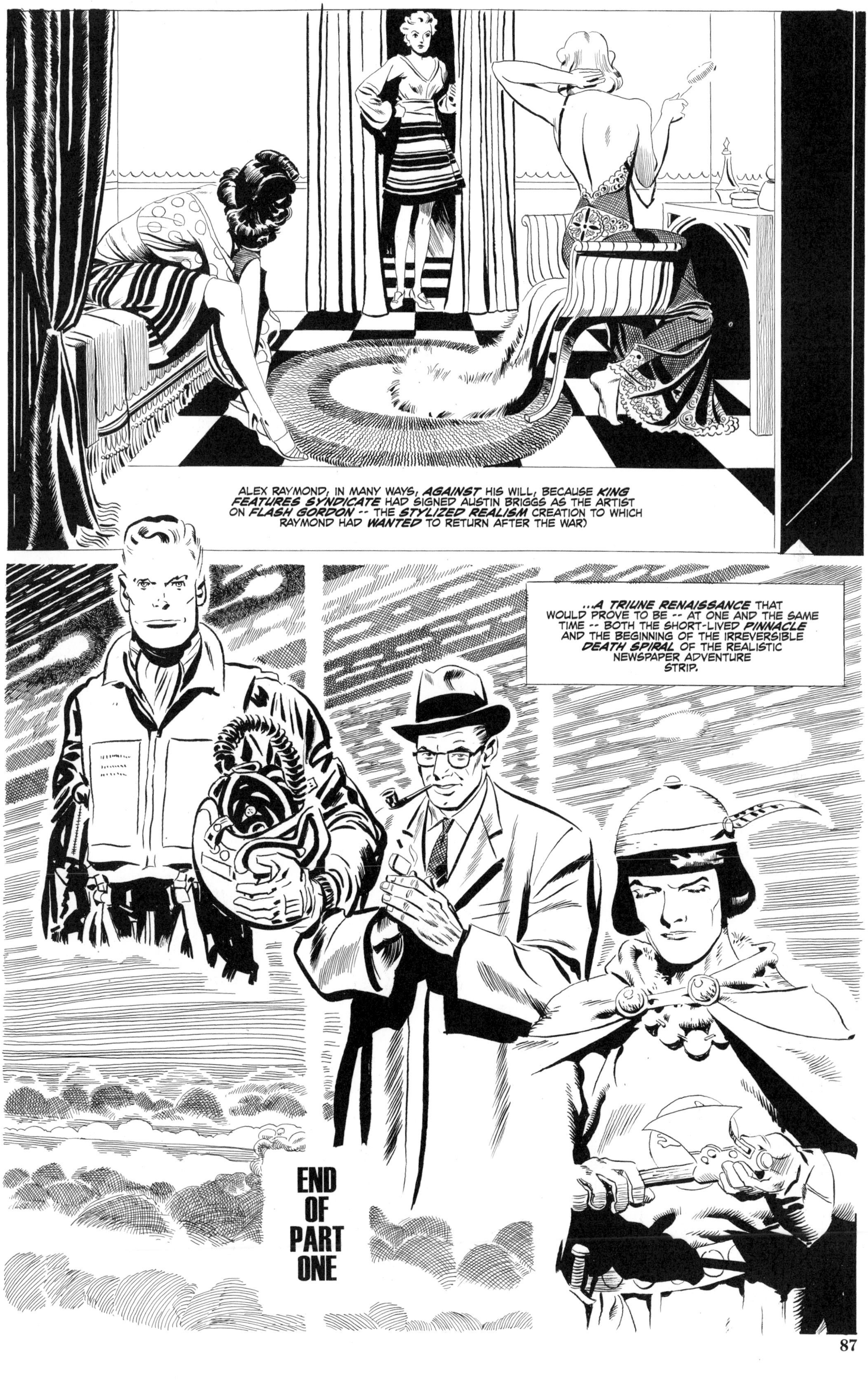
ALEX RAYMOND, IN MANY WAYS, AGAINST HIS WILL, BECAUSE KING FEATURES SYNDICATE HAD SIGNED AUSTIN BRIGGS AS THE ARTIST ON FLASH GORDON -- THE STYLIZED REALISM CREATION TO WHICH RAYMOND HAD WANTED TO RETURN AFTER THE WAR)
...A TRIUNE RENAISSANCE THAT WOULD PROVE TO BE -- AT ONE AND THE SAME TIME -- BOTH THE SHORT-LIVED PINNACLE AND THE BEGINNING OF THE IRREVERSIBLE DEATH SPIRAL OF THE REALISTIC NEWSPAPER ADVENTURE STRIP.
END OF PART ONE

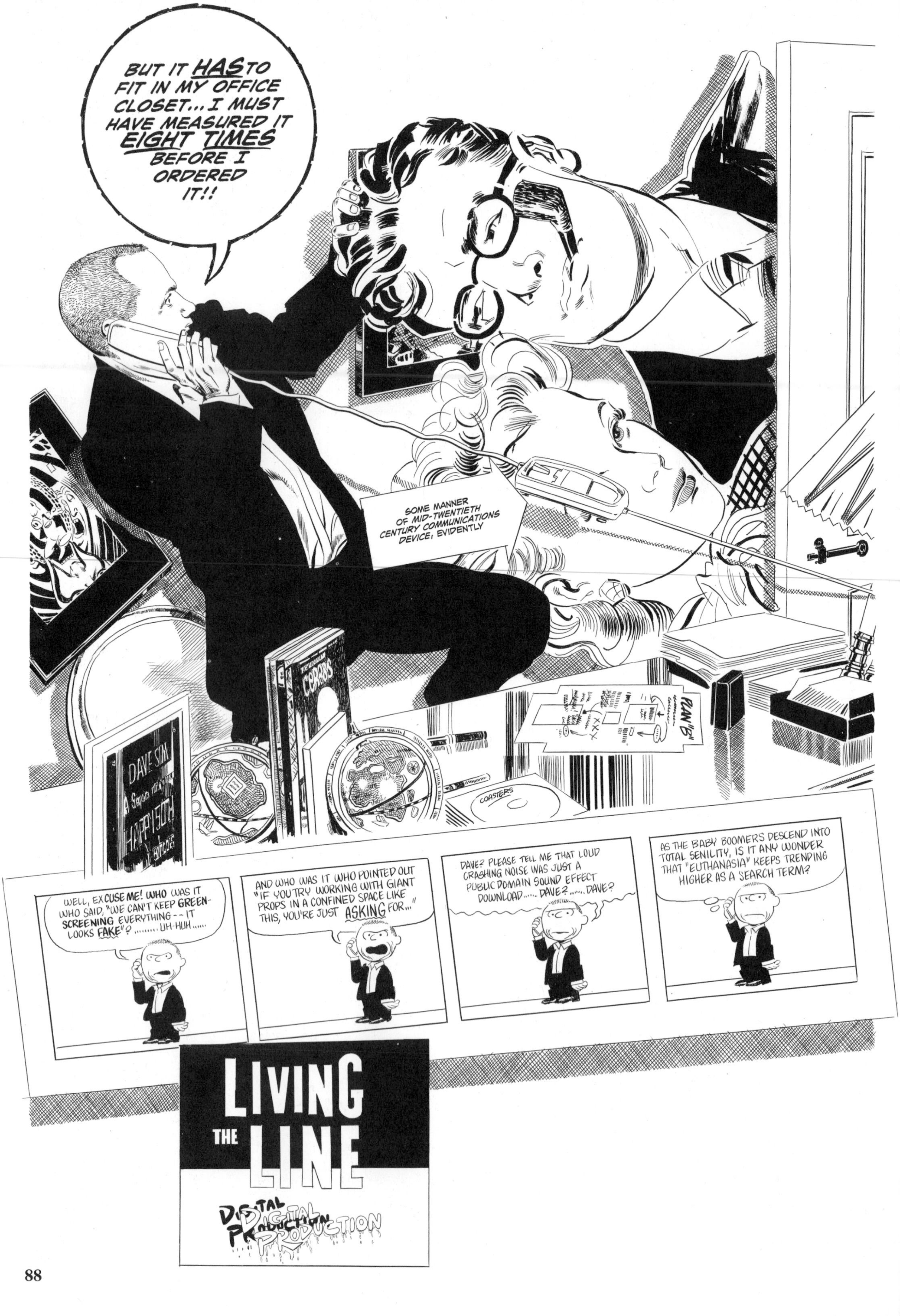
BUT IT HAS TO FIT IN MY OFFICE CLOSET... I MUST HAVE MEASURED IT EIGHT TIMES BEFORE I ORDERED IT!!
SOME MANNER OF MID-TWENTIETH CENTURY COMMUNICATIONS DEVICE, EVIDENTLY
CEREBUS
PLAN "B"
DAVE SIM
HAPPY 50TH
COASTERS
WELL, EXCUSE ME! WHO WAS IT WHO SAID, "WE CAN'T KEEP GREEN-SCREENING EVERYTHING -- IT LOOKS FAKE"? ......... UH-HUH ......
AND WHO WAS IT WHO POINTED OUT "IF YOU TRY WORKING WITH GIANT PROPS IN A CONFINED SPACE LIKE THIS, YOU'RE JUST ASKING FOR..."
DAVE? PLEASE TELL ME THAT LOUD CRASHING NOISE WAS JUST A PUBLIC DOMAIN SOUND EFFECT DOWNLOAD...... DAVE? ...... DAVE?
AS THE BABY BOOMERS DESCEND INTO TOTAL SENILITY, IS IT ANY WONDER THAT "EUTHANASIA" KEEPS TRENDING HIGHER AS A SEARCH TERM?
LIVING THE LINE
DIGITAL PRODUCTION

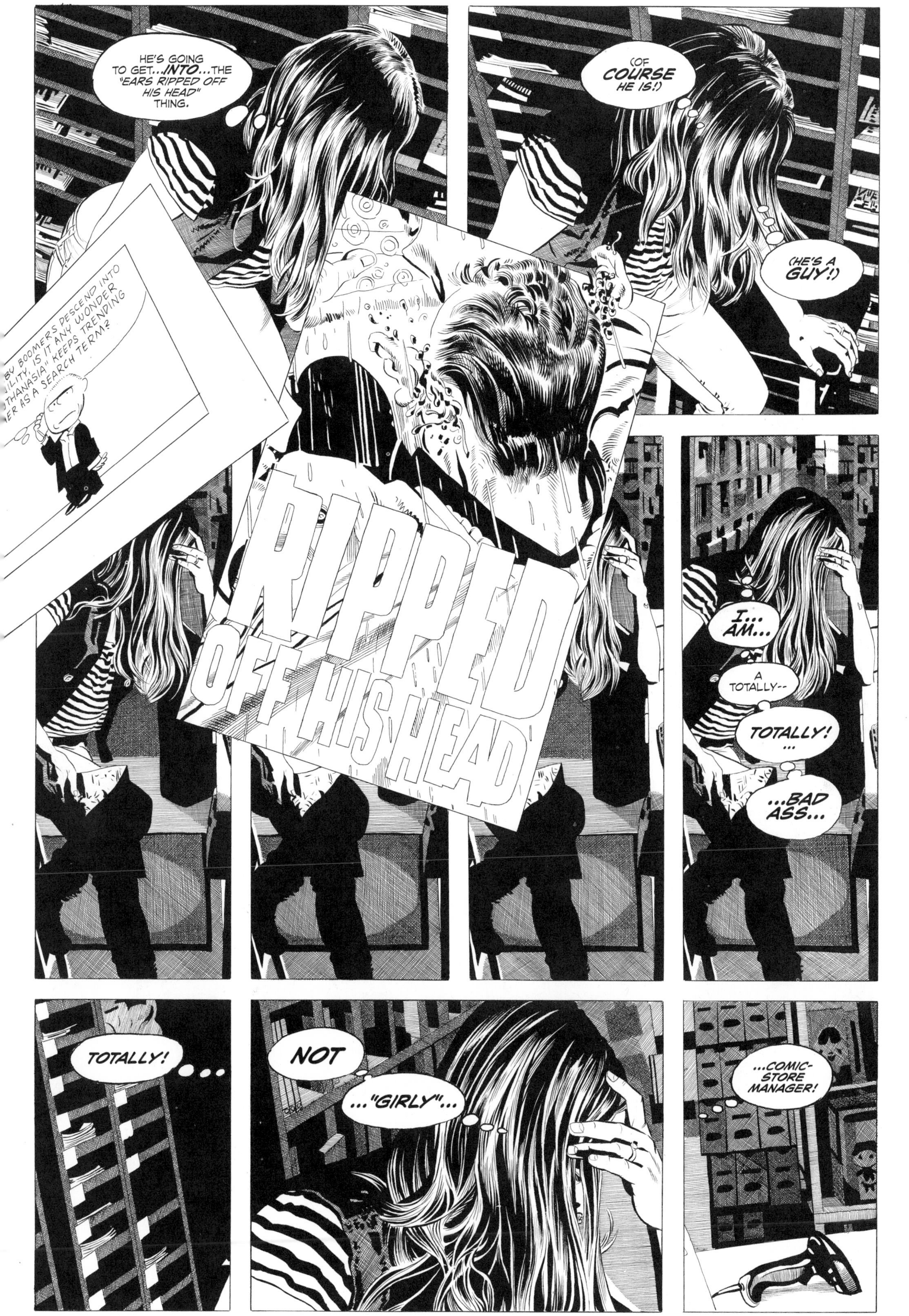

HE'S GOING TO GET...INTO...THE "EARS RIPPED OFF HIS HEAD" THING.
(OF COURSE HE IS!)
(HE'S A GUY!)
BY BOOMERS DESCEND INTO
ILITY, IS IT ANY WONDER
THANASIA" KEEPS TRENDING
ER AS A SEARCH TERM?
RIPPED OFF HIS HEAD
I... AM...
A TOTALLY--
TOTALLY! ...
...BAD ASS...
TOTALLY!...
NOT
..."GIRLY"...
...COMIC-STORE MANAGER!

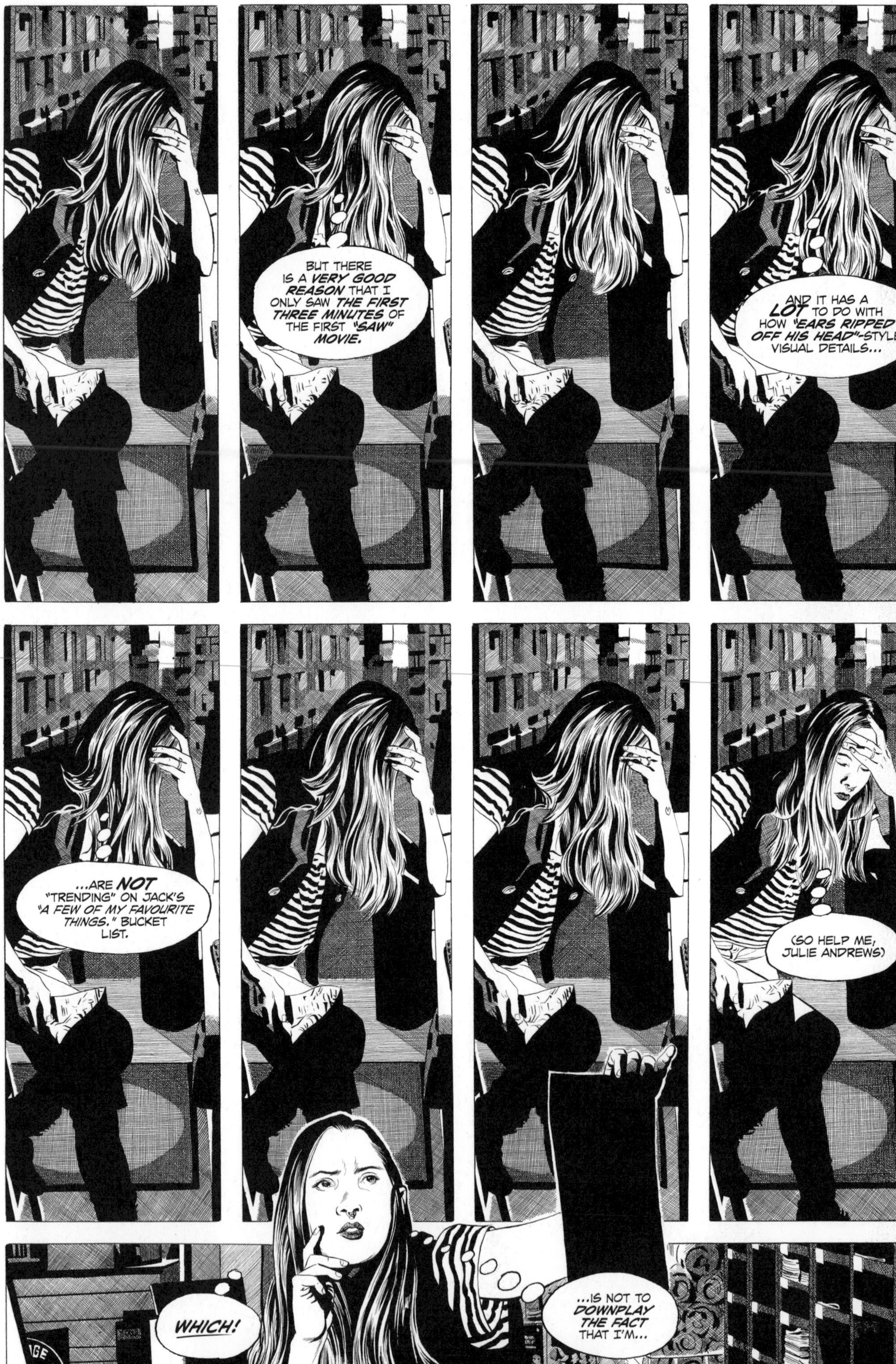
BUT THERE IS A VERY GOOD REASON THAT I ONLY SAW THE FIRST THREE MINUTES OF THE FIRST "SAW" MOVIE.
AND IT HAS A LOT TO DO WITH HOW "EARS RIPPED OFF HIS HEAD"-STYLE VISUAL DETAILS...
...ARE NOT "TRENDING" ON JACK'S "A FEW OF MY FAVOURITE THINGS." BUCKET LIST.
(SO HELP ME, JULIE ANDREWS)
WHICH!
...IS NOT TO DOWNPLAY THE FACT THAT I'M...
COMICS

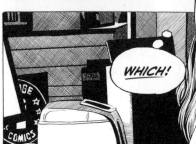

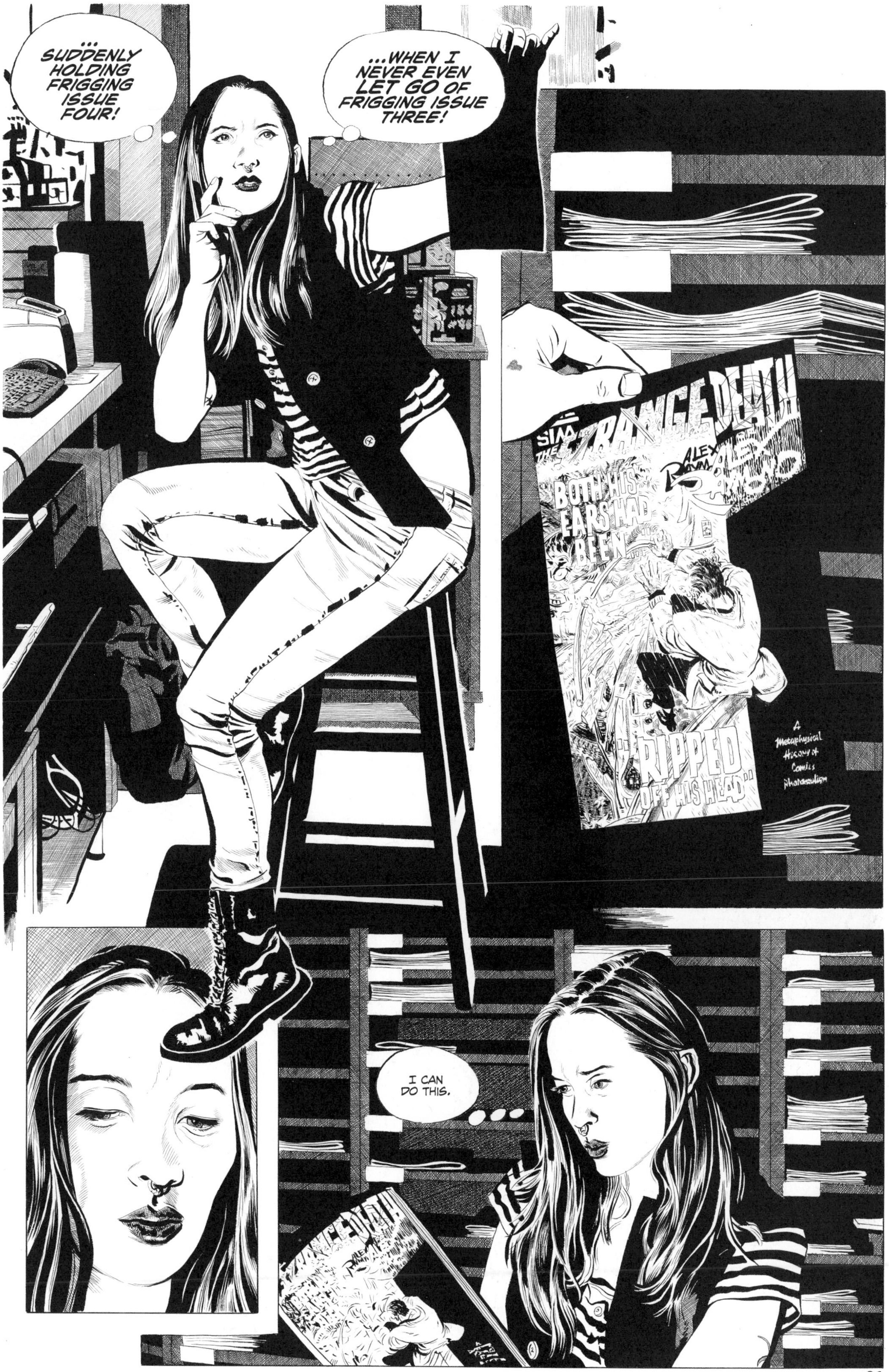
...SUDDENLY HOLDING FRIGGING ISSUE FOUR!
...WHEN I NEVER EVEN LET GO OF FRIGGING ISSUE THREE!
"BOTH HIS EARS HAD BEEN..."
"...RIPPED OFF HIS HEAD"
A Metaphysical History of Comics Photorealism
I CAN DO THIS.

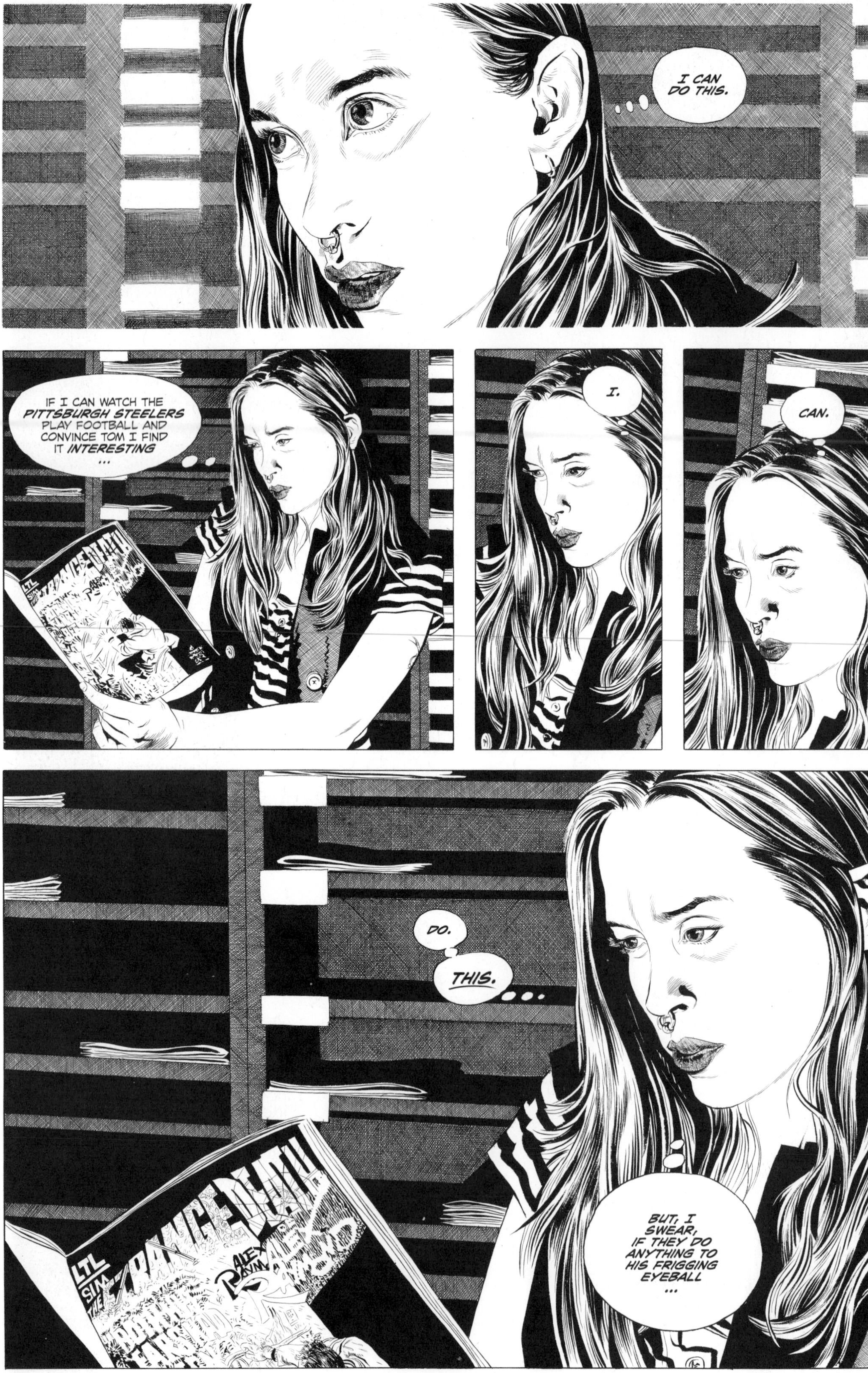
I CAN DO THIS.
IF I CAN WATCH THE PITTSBURGH STEELERS PLAY FOOTBALL AND CONVINCE TOM I FIND IT INTERESTING ...
I.
CAN.
DO.
THIS.
BUT, I SWEAR, IF THEY DO ANYTHING TO HIS FRIGGING EYEBALL ...

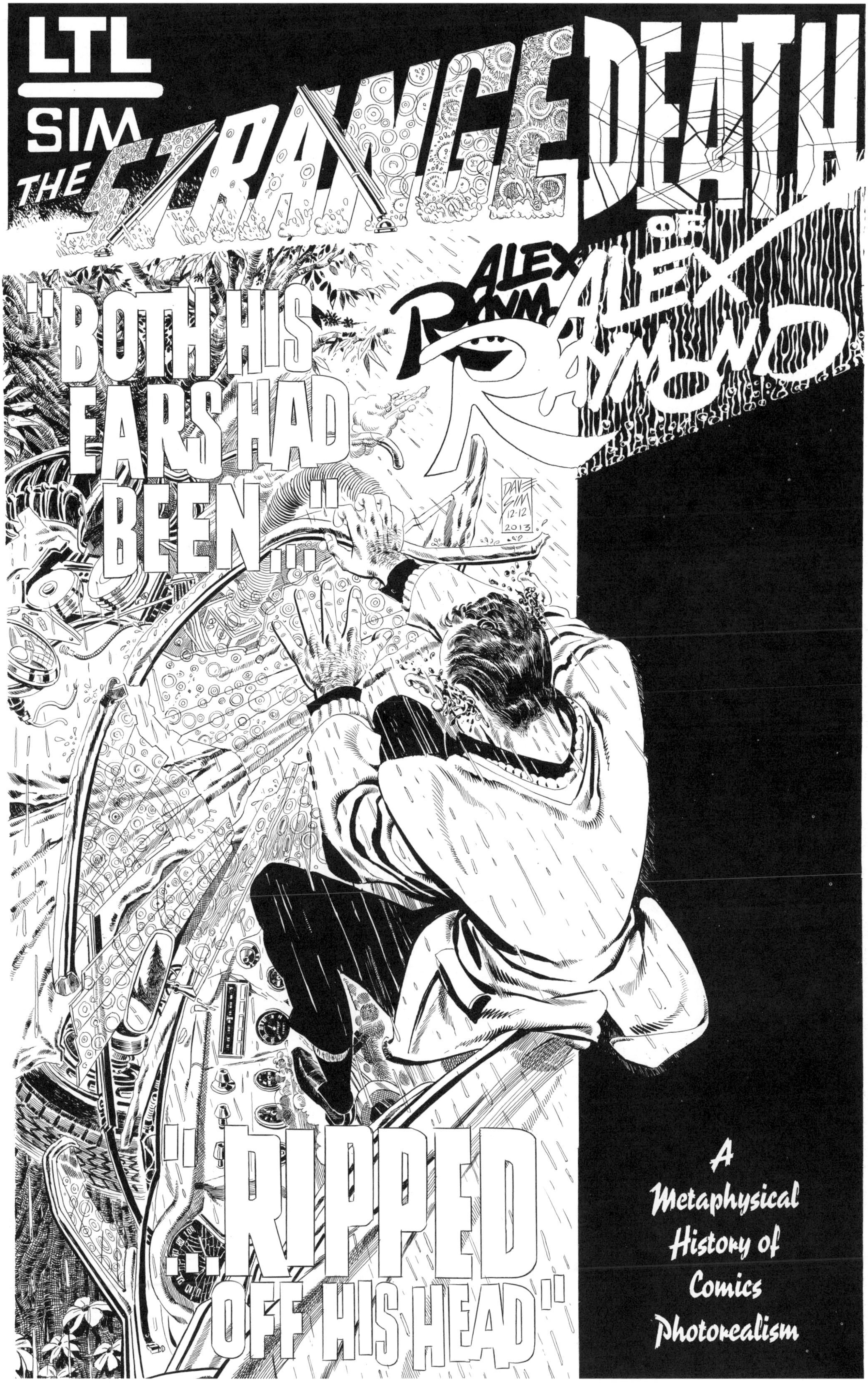
LTL
SIM
THE STRANGE DEATH OF ALEX RAYMOND
"BOTH HIS EARS HAD BEEN..."
"...RIPPED OFF HIS HEAD"
A Metaphysical History of Comics Photorealism

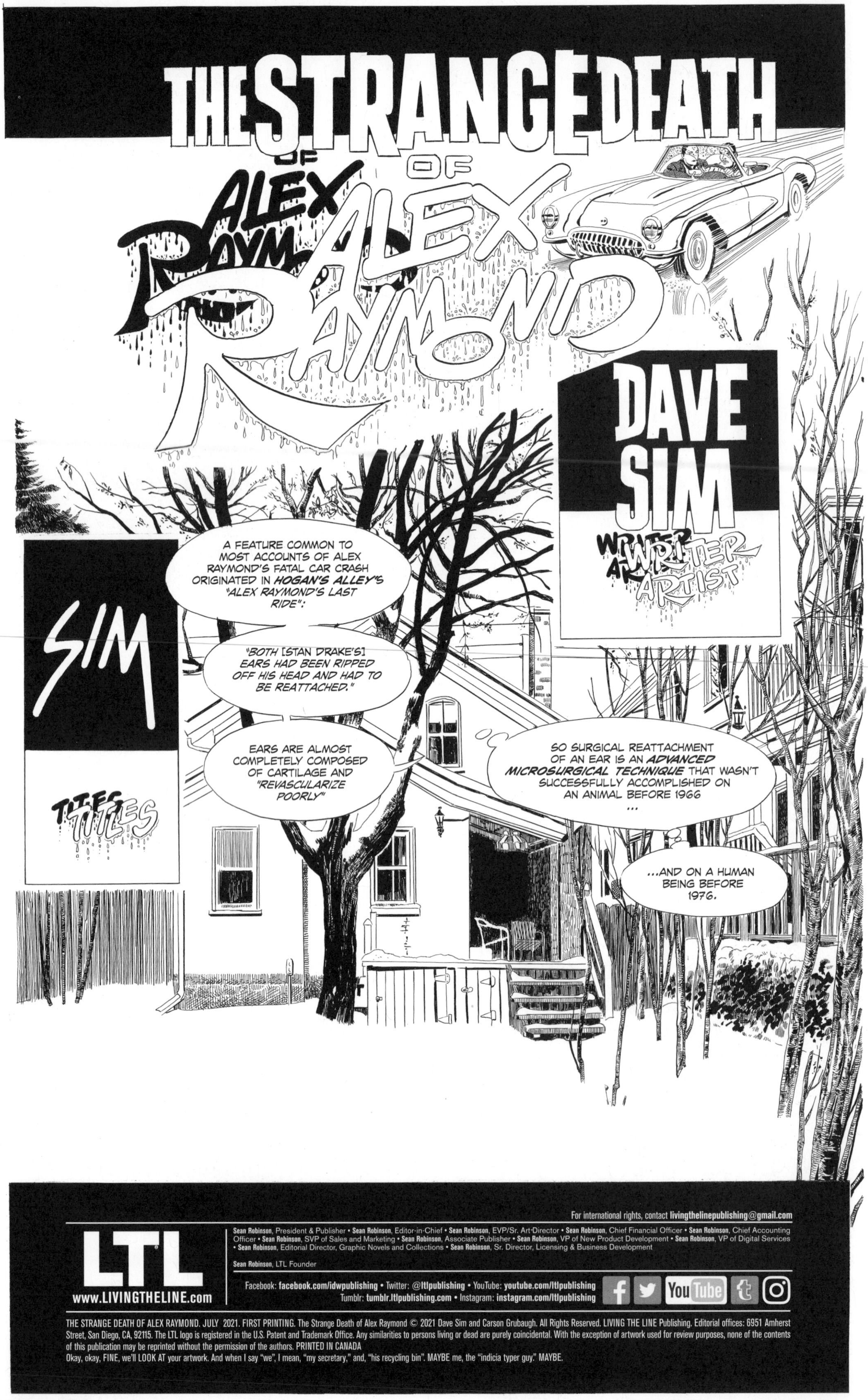
THE STRANGE DEATH OF ALEX RAYMOND
DAVE SIM
WRITER ARTIST
SIM
TITLES
A FEATURE COMMON TO MOST ACCOUNTS OF ALEX RAYMOND'S FATAL CAR CRASH ORIGINATED IN *HOGAN'S ALLEY*'S *"ALEX RAYMOND'S LAST RIDE"*:
*"BOTH [STAN DRAKE'S] EARS HAD BEEN RIPPED OFF HIS HEAD AND HAD TO BE REATTACHED."*
EARS ARE ALMOST COMPLETELY COMPOSED OF CARTILAGE AND *"REVASCULARIZE POORLY"*
SO SURGICAL REATTACHMENT OF AN EAR IS AN ***ADVANCED MICROSURGICAL TECHNIQUE*** THAT WASN'T SUCCESSFULLY ACCOMPLISHED ON AN ANIMAL BEFORE 1966 ...
...AND ON A HUMAN BEING BEFORE 1976.

For international rights, contact **livingthelinepublishing@gmail.com**

LTL
www.LIVINGTHELINE.com

**Sean Robinson**, President & Publisher • **Sean Robinson**, Editor-in-Chief • **Sean Robinson**, EVP/Sr. Art Director • **Sean Robinson**, Chief Financial Officer • **Sean Robinson**, Chief Accounting Officer • **Sean Robinson**, SVP of Sales and Marketing • **Sean Robinson**, Associate Publisher • **Sean Robinson**, VP of New Product Development • **Sean Robinson**, VP of Digital Services • **Sean Robinson**, Editorial Director, Graphic Novels and Collections • **Sean Robinson**, Sr. Director, Licensing & Business Development

**Sean Robinson**, LTL Founder

Facebook: **facebook.com/idwpublishing** • Twitter: **@ltlpublishing** • YouTube: **youtube.com/ltlpublishing**
Tumblr: **tumblr.ltlpublishing.com** • Instagram: **instagram.com/ltlpublishing**

THE STRANGE DEATH OF ALEX RAYMOND. JULY 2021. FIRST PRINTING.  LIVING THE LINE Publishing. Editorial offices: 6951 Amherst Street, San Diego, CA, 92115.  PRINTED IN CANADA
Okay, okay, FINE, we'll LOOK AT your artwork. And when I say "we", I mean, "my secretary," and, "his recycling bin". MAYBE me, the "indicia typer guy." MAYBE.

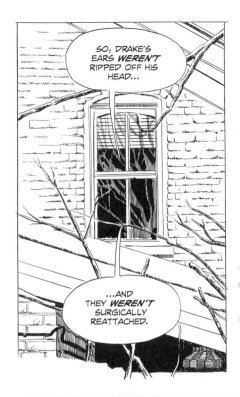

SO, DRAKE'S EARS *WEREN'T* RIPPED OFF HIS HEAD...

...AND THEY *WEREN'T* SURGICALLY REATTACHED.

WHY, FORTY YEARS AFTER THE ACCIDENT, DID HE BELIEVE THAT THEY *HAD BEEN?*

MYSTERIES WITHIN *MYSTERIES* WITHIN *MYSTERIES* ...

THE INTERWOVEN ESSENCES OF *COMIC-ART* METAPHYSICS.

THE *CREATOR* SHAPES THE *COMIC ART* ...

...AND THE *COMIC ART,* IN ITS TURN, SHAPES THE *CREATOR.*

**COMICRAFT'S (JOE KUBERT) FONT**

LETTER IN LETTERING

PART TWO

WHICH BRINGS US TO ONE OF THOSE MYSTERIES WHICH ALEX RAYMOND *DEFINED* AND WHICH *DEFINED* ALEX RAYMOND

"NIGHTINGALE BRUSH STROKES"

HIS *EXTRAORDINARY* BRUSH STROKES.

"SO ACCURATE AND DELICATE" THAT THEY GAVE HAL FOSTER "AN INFERIORITY COMPLEX."

HAL FOSTER WASN'T *ALONE* IN THAT.

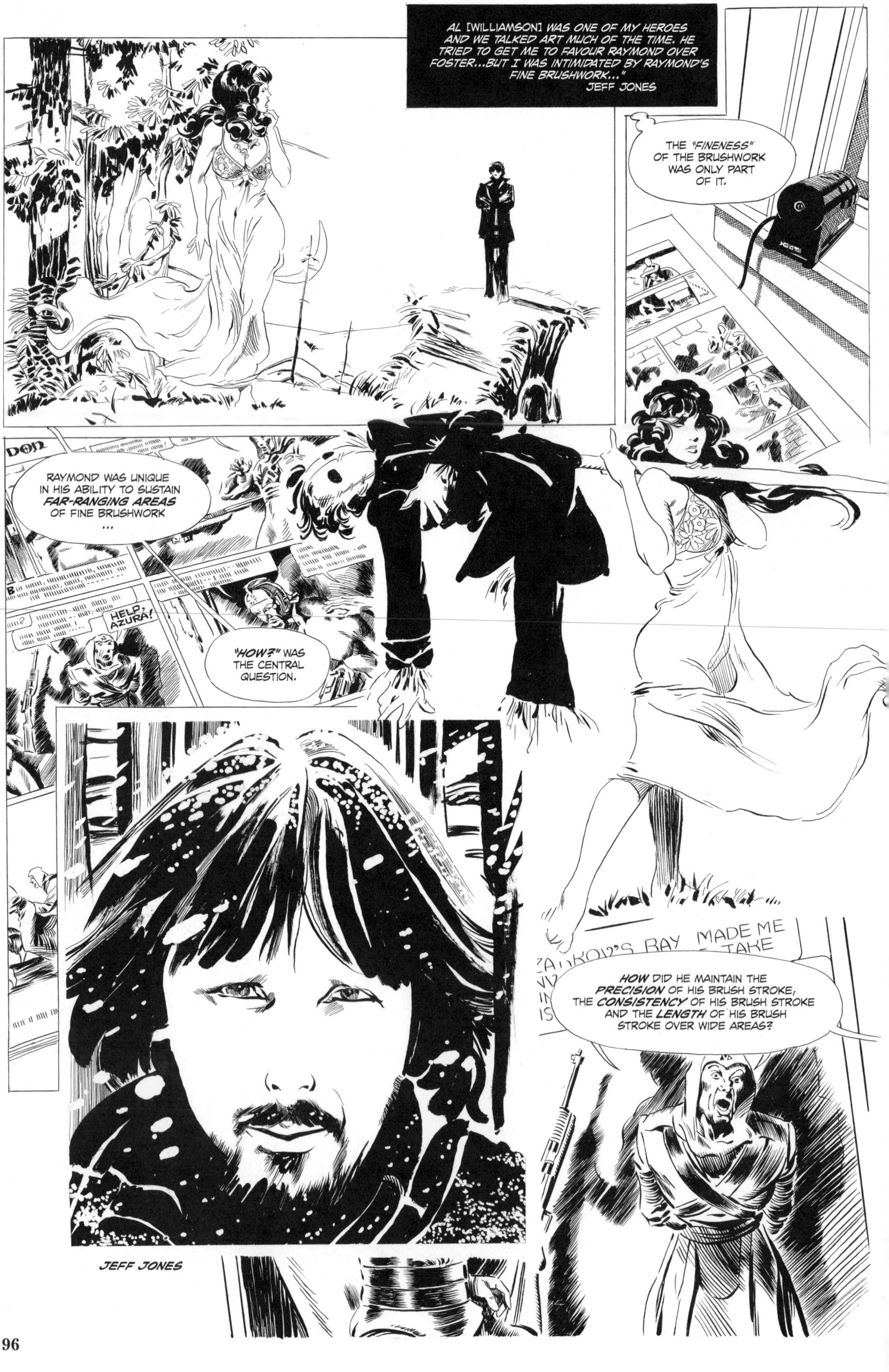
AL [WILLIAMSON] WAS ONE OF MY HEROES AND WE TALKED ART MUCH OF THE TIME. HE TRIED TO GET ME TO FAVOUR RAYMOND OVER FOSTER...BUT I WAS INTIMIDATED BY RAYMOND'S FINE BRUSHWORK..." JEFF JONES
THE "FINENESS" OF THE BRUSHWORK WAS ONLY PART OF IT.
RAYMOND WAS UNIQUE IN HIS ABILITY TO SUSTAIN FAR-RANGING AREAS OF FINE BRUSHWORK ...
HELP, AZURA!
"HOW?" WAS THE CENTRAL QUESTION.
HOW DID HE MAINTAIN THE PRECISION OF HIS BRUSH STROKE, THE CONSISTENCY OF HIS BRUSH STROKE AND THE LENGTH OF HIS BRUSH STROKE OVER WIDE AREAS?
JEFF JONES

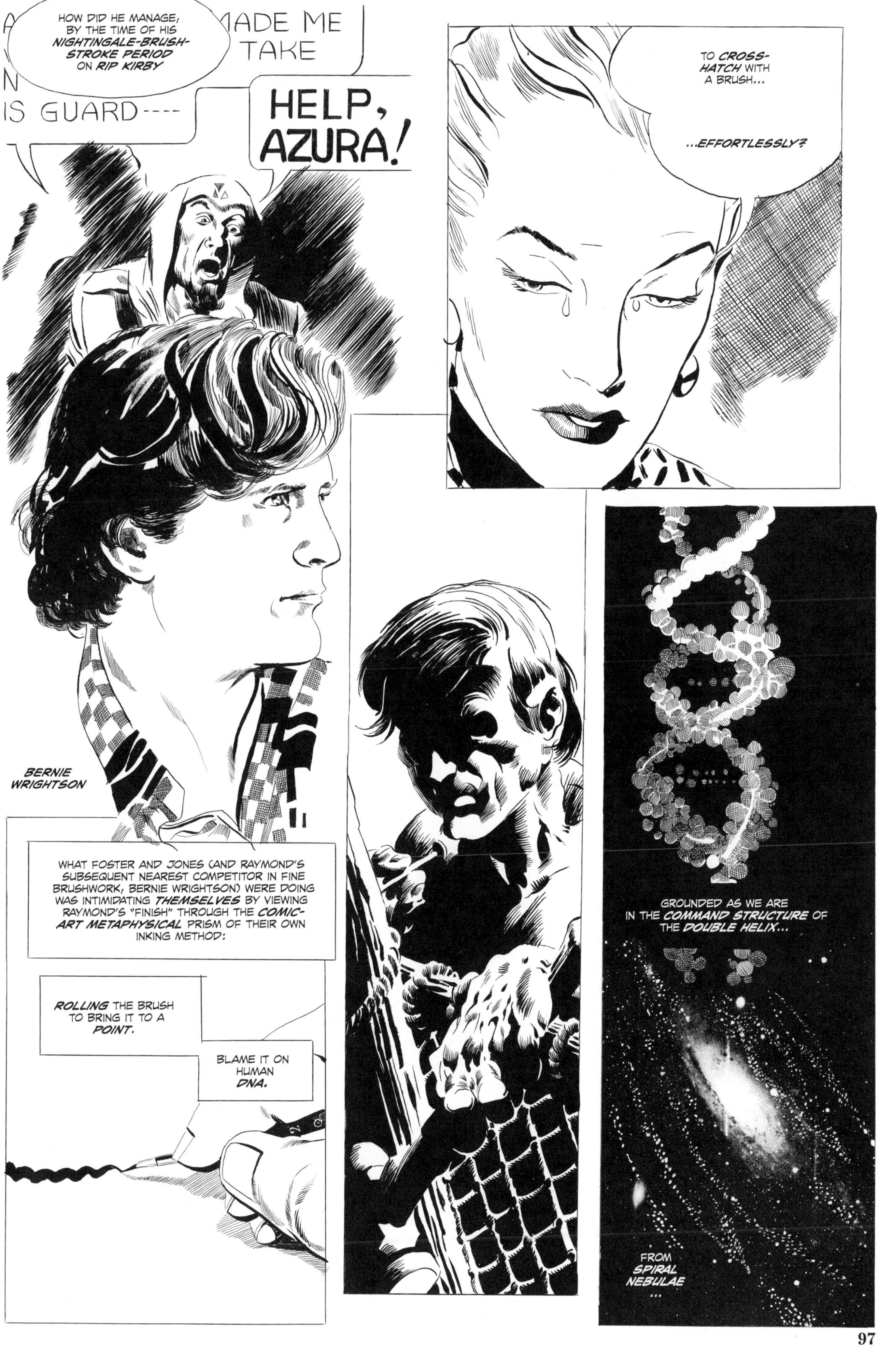

HOW DID HE MANAGE, BY THE TIME OF HIS NIGHTINGALE-BRUSH-STROKE PERIOD ON RIP KIRBY
MADE ME
TAKE
IS GUARD----
HELP, AZURA!
TO CROSS-HATCH WITH A BRUSH...
...EFFORTLESSLY?
BERNIE WRIGHTSON
WHAT FOSTER AND JONES (AND RAYMOND'S SUBSEQUENT NEAREST COMPETITOR IN FINE BRUSHWORK, BERNIE WRIGHTSON) WERE DOING WAS INTIMIDATING THEMSELVES BY VIEWING RAYMOND'S "FINISH" THROUGH THE COMIC-ART METAPHYSICAL PRISM OF THEIR OWN INKING METHOD:
ROLLING THE BRUSH TO BRING IT TO A POINT.
BLAME IT ON HUMAN DNA.
GROUNDED AS WE ARE IN THE COMMAND STRUCTURE OF THE DOUBLE HELIX...
FROM SPIRAL NEBULAE ...

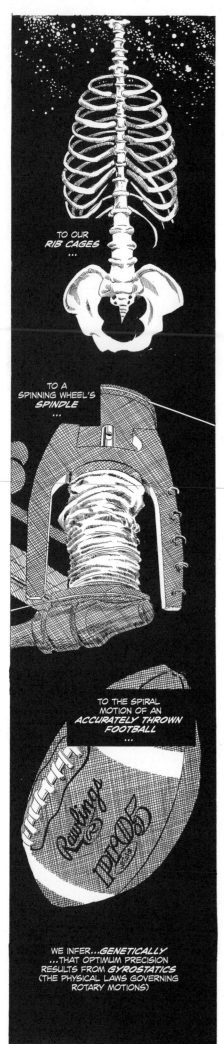

TO OUR *RIB CAGES* ...

TO A SPINNING WHEEL'S *SPINDLE* ...

TO THE SPIRAL MOTION OF AN *ACCURATELY THROWN* FOOTBALL ...

WE INFER...*GENETICALLY* ...THAT OPTIMUM PRECISION RESULTS FROM *GYROSTATICS* (THE PHYSICAL LAWS GOVERNING ROTARY MOTIONS)

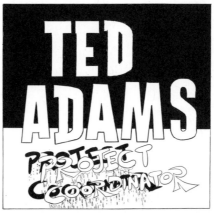

# TED ADAMS
### PROJECT COOORDINATOR

WHICH IS *TRUE*...

...UP TO A *POINT* (NYUCK NYUCK NYUCK)

IF YOU DIP A *SERIES SEVEN NUMBER TWO BRUSH* INTO INDIA INK...

...AND *ROLL* THE TIP ON A TEST SHEET, YOU *CAN* BRING IT TO A *SHARP POINT.*

HOWEVER, AS SOON AS YOU START *INKING* WITH IT YOU HAVE LESS INK ON THE BRUSH *"HOLDING"* THE POINT...

AND THE BRISTLES QUICKLY BEGIN TO *UNROLL.*

SO YOU HAVE TO *RINSE* THE INK OFF, *DRY* THE BRUSH, *DIP* IT AGAIN AND *ROLL* IT AGAIN.

*THAT'S* WHAT INTIMIDATED *EVERYONE* ABOUT RAYMOND'S INKING: HE MUST HAVE SPENT MOST OF HIS LIFE ON BASIC BRUSH MAINTENANCE!

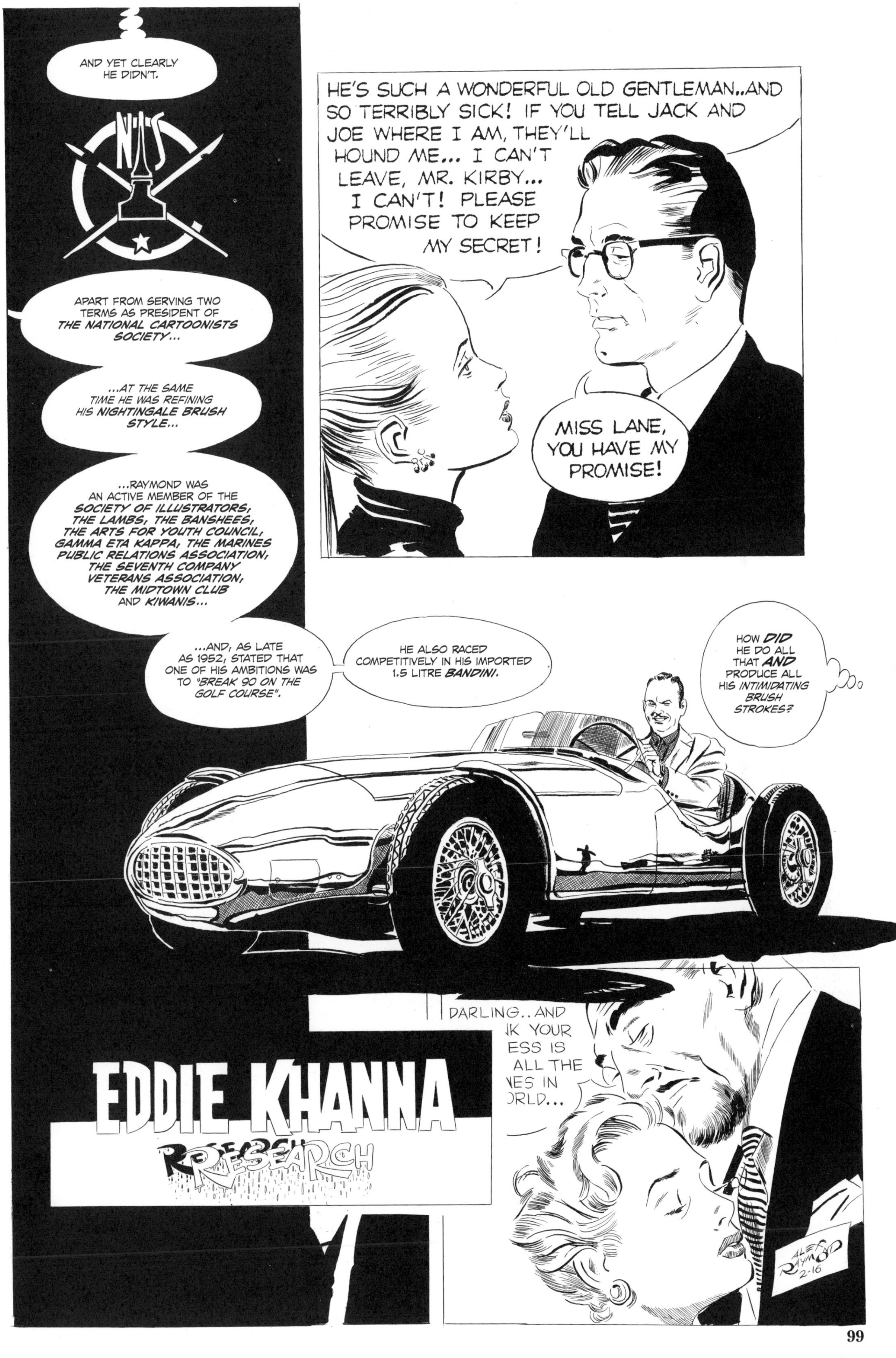
AND YET CLEARLY HE DIDN'T.
HE'S SUCH A WONDERFUL OLD GENTLEMAN..AND SO TERRIBLY SICK! IF YOU TELL JACK AND JOE WHERE I AM, THEY'LL HOUND ME... I CAN'T LEAVE, MR. KIRBY... I CAN'T! PLEASE PROMISE TO KEEP MY SECRET!
MISS LANE, YOU HAVE MY PROMISE!
APART FROM SERVING TWO TERMS AS PRESIDENT OF *THE NATIONAL CARTOONISTS SOCIETY*...
...AT THE SAME TIME HE WAS REFINING HIS *NIGHTINGALE BRUSH STYLE*...
...RAYMOND WAS AN ACTIVE MEMBER OF THE *SOCIETY OF ILLUSTRATORS, THE LAMBS, THE BANSHEES, THE ARTS FOR YOUTH COUNCIL, GAMMA ETA KAPPA, THE MARINES PUBLIC RELATIONS ASSOCIATION, THE SEVENTH COMPANY VETERANS ASSOCIATION, THE MIDTOWN CLUB* AND *KIWANIS*...
...AND, AS LATE AS 1952, STATED THAT ONE OF HIS AMBITIONS WAS TO *"BREAK 90 ON THE GOLF COURSE"*.
HE ALSO RACED COMPETITIVELY IN HIS IMPORTED 1.5 LITRE *BANDINI*.
HOW *DID* HE DO ALL THAT *AND* PRODUCE ALL HIS *INTIMIDATING BRUSH STROKES?*
DARLING..AND
NK YOUR
ESS IS
ALL THE
NES IN
ORLD...
EDDIE KHANNA
RESEARCH
ALEX RAYMOND 2-16

I'M *PRETTY SURE* THIS IS HOW:

RAYMOND WOULD DIP HIS *NUMBER TWO BRUSH* ROUGHLY A QUARTER OF AN INCH INTO THE INDIA INK, THEN...

...RESTING THE *ENTIRE* QUARTER INCH ON HIS TEST SHEET...

...*LIGHTLY*...

...HE WOULD SLIDE IT SIDEWAYS TO THE RIGHT, ATTEMPTING TO RENDER A *PERFECT RECTANGLE.*

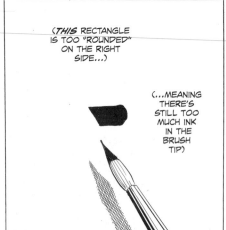

(*THIS* RECTANGLE IS TOO "ROUNDED" ON THE RIGHT SIDE...)

(...MEANING THERE'S STILL TOO MUCH INK IN THE BRUSH TIP)

*SUCCESSFULLY* RENDERING A PERFECT RECTANGLE TOLD HIM THAT HE NOW HAD A *PERFECTLY SHARP* BRUSH POINT *AND*...

...A FULL "RESERVOIR" OF INK READY TO FEED IT *AND*...

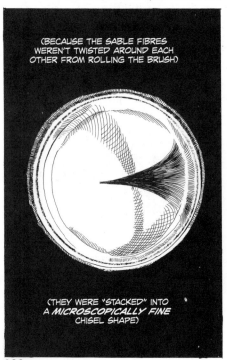

(BECAUSE THE SABLE FIBRES WEREN'T TWISTED AROUND EACH OTHER FROM ROLLING THE BRUSH)

(THEY WERE "STACKED" INTO A *MICROSCOPICALLY FINE* CHISEL SHAPE)

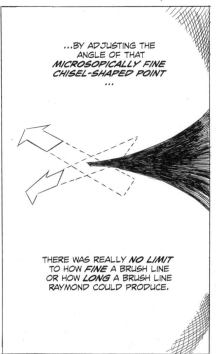

...BY ADJUSTING THE ANGLE OF THAT *MICROSCOPICALLY FINE CHISEL-SHAPED POINT* ...

THERE WAS REALLY *NO LIMIT* TO HOW *FINE* A BRUSH LINE OR HOW *LONG* A BRUSH LINE RAYMOND COULD PRODUCE.

*VOILA!*

*NIGHTINGALE BRUSH STROKES UNLIMITED!*

AN ADVANTAGE TO RAYMOND'S TECHNIQUE IS THAT THE *MICROSCOPICALLY FINE CHISEL-SHAPED POINT...*

...COMPRESSES ITSELF ALONG ITS *VERTICAL AXIS* AS YOU INK.

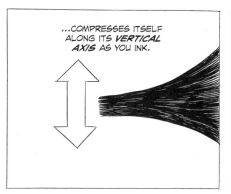

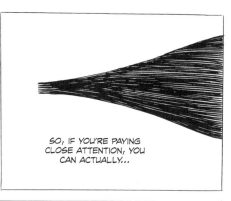

SO, IF YOU'RE PAYING CLOSE ATTENTION, YOU CAN ACTUALLY...

(ONCE YOU'VE ACHIEVED YOUR *IDEAL NIGHTINGALE-BRUSH-STROKE DENSITY*)

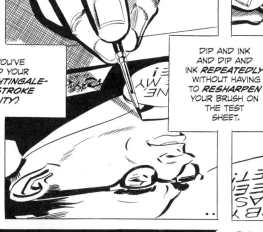

DIP AND INK AND DIP AND INK *REPEATEDLY* WITHOUT HAVING TO *RESHARPEN* YOUR BRUSH ON THE TEST SHEET.

I ONLY FIGURED OUT RAYMOND'S TECHNIQUE BECAUSE HE STARTED ACTUALLY SHARPENING HIS BRUSH, ON OCCASION, INSIDE THE STRIP ITSELF.

I FIRST SAW IT ON GRAVES' ASCOT IN PANEL ONE OF THE 23 JUNE 53 STRIP ON A FULL-SIZED PRINT-OUT OF RAYMOND'S ORIGINAL ART DOWNLOADED FROM *HERITAGE AUCTIONS'* WEBSITE (*HA.COM*)

RIP KIRBY'S GOING TO DRIVE FOR YOU IN THE INTERNATIONAL? JET, MY DEAR, HE HASN'T A CHANCE...I BEG OF YOU...GIVE UP THIS DANGEROUS AND EXPENSIVE PASTIME...

GRAVES, YOU'RE OVERSTEPPING...

(...AND THIS *STRIPE*, SQUARE ON *BOTH* ENDS, TOLD ME WHAT I WAS LOOKING AT)

(THESE *TWO STRIPES*, ROUNDED ON THEIR RIGHT ENDS...)

AFTER THAT, I SAW THE *DASHES AND RECTANGLES* JUST ABOUT EVERYWHERE

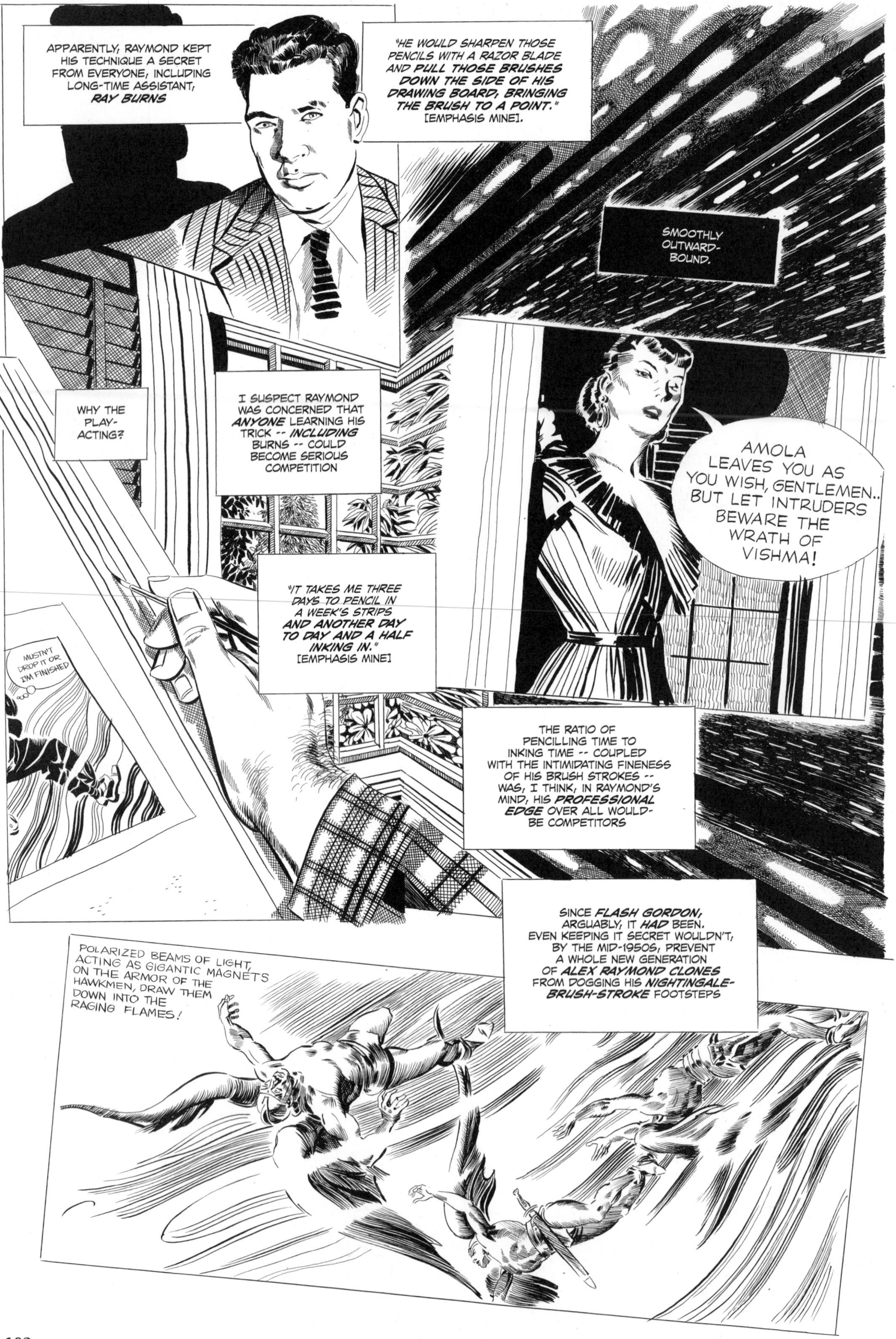

APPARENTLY, RAYMOND KEPT HIS TECHNIQUE A SECRET FROM EVERYONE, INCLUDING LONG-TIME ASSISTANT, RAY BURNS
"HE WOULD SHARPEN THOSE PENCILS WITH A RAZOR BLADE AND PULL THOSE BRUSHES DOWN THE SIDE OF HIS DRAWING BOARD, BRINGING THE BRUSH TO A POINT." [EMPHASIS MINE].
SMOOTHLY OUTWARD-BOUND.
WHY THE PLAY-ACTING?
I SUSPECT RAYMOND WAS CONCERNED THAT ANYONE LEARNING HIS TRICK -- INCLUDING BURNS -- COULD BECOME SERIOUS COMPETITION
AMOLA LEAVES YOU AS YOU WISH, GENTLEMEN.. BUT LET INTRUDERS BEWARE THE WRATH OF VISHMA!
"IT TAKES ME THREE DAYS TO PENCIL IN A WEEK'S STRIPS AND ANOTHER DAY TO DAY AND A HALF INKING IN." [EMPHASIS MINE]
MUSTN'T DROP IT OR I'M FINISHED
THE RATIO OF PENCILLING TIME TO INKING TIME -- COUPLED WITH THE INTIMIDATING FINENESS OF HIS BRUSH STROKES -- WAS, I THINK, IN RAYMOND'S MIND, HIS PROFESSIONAL EDGE OVER ALL WOULD-BE COMPETITORS
SINCE FLASH GORDON, ARGUABLY, IT HAD BEEN. EVEN KEEPING IT SECRET WOULDN'T, BY THE MID-1950S, PREVENT A WHOLE NEW GENERATION OF ALEX RAYMOND CLONES FROM DOGGING HIS NIGHTINGALE-BRUSH-STROKE FOOTSTEPS
POLARIZED BEAMS OF LIGHT, ACTING AS GIGANTIC MAGNETS ON THE ARMOR OF THE HAWKMEN, DRAW THEM DOWN INTO THE RAGING FLAMES!

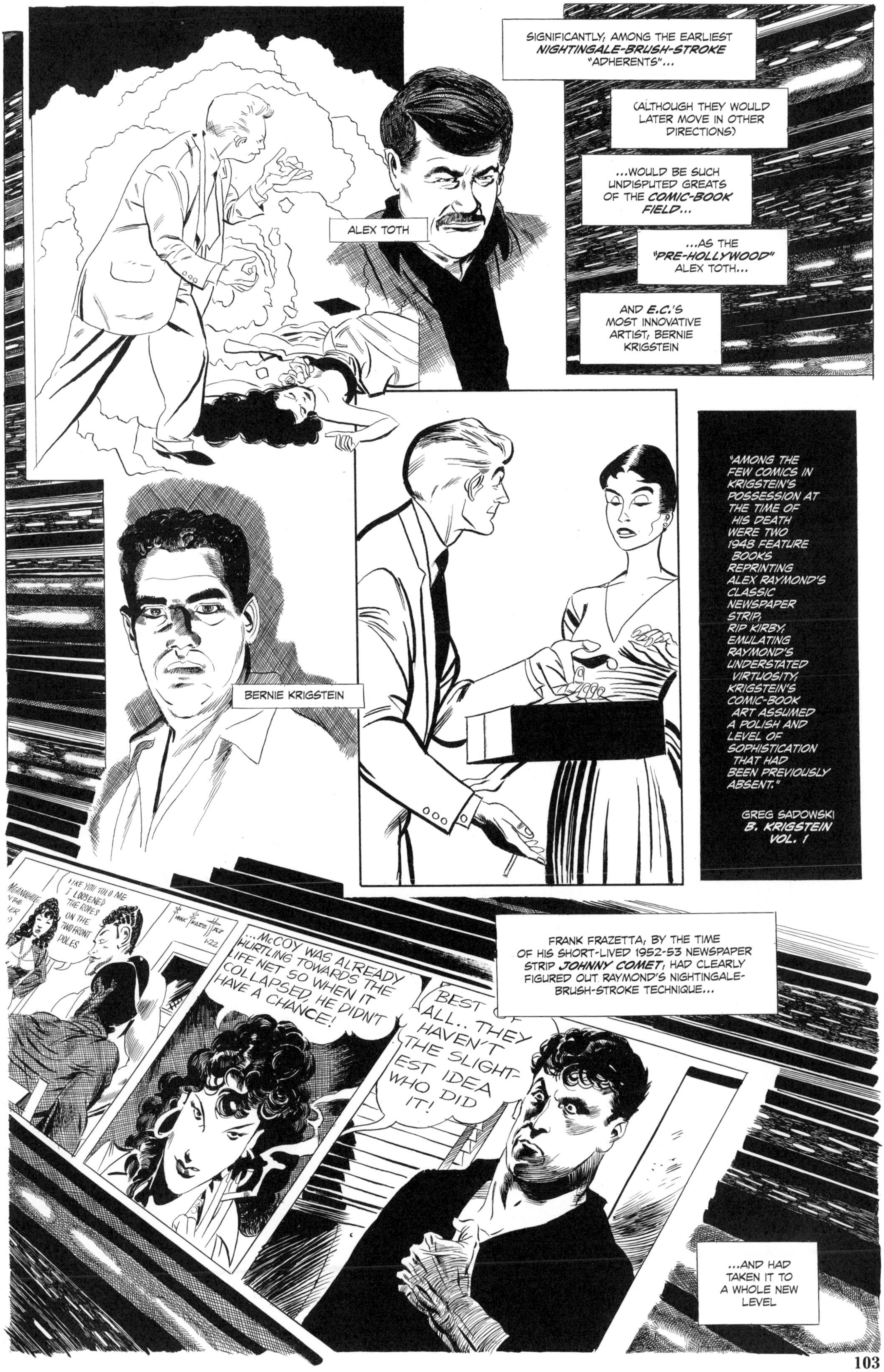
SIGNIFICANTLY, AMONG THE EARLIEST NIGHTINGALE-BRUSH-STROKE "ADHERENTS"...
(ALTHOUGH THEY WOULD LATER MOVE IN OTHER DIRECTIONS)
...WOULD BE SUCH UNDISPUTED GREATS OF THE COMIC-BOOK FIELD...
...AS THE "PRE-HOLLYWOOD" ALEX TOTH...
AND E.C.'S MOST INNOVATIVE ARTIST, BERNIE KRIGSTEIN
ALEX TOTH
BERNIE KRIGSTEIN
"AMONG THE FEW COMICS IN KRIGSTEIN'S POSSESSION AT THE TIME OF HIS DEATH WERE TWO 1948 FEATURE BOOKS REPRINTING ALEX RAYMOND'S CLASSIC NEWSPAPER STRIP, RIP KIRBY; EMULATING RAYMOND'S UNDERSTATED VIRTUOSITY, KRIGSTEIN'S COMIC-BOOK ART ASSUMED A POLISH AND LEVEL OF SOPHISTICATION THAT HAD BEEN PREVIOUSLY ABSENT."
GREG SADOWSKI
B. KRIGSTEIN VOL. 1
I LOOSENED THE ROPES ON THE TWO FRONT POLES
1-22
...McCOY WAS ALREADY HURTLING TOWARDS THE LIFE NET SO WHEN IT COLLAPSED, HE DIDN'T HAVE A CHANCE!
ALL.. THEY HAVEN'T THE SLIGHT-EST IDEA WHO DID IT!
FRANK FRAZETTA, BY THE TIME OF HIS SHORT-LIVED 1952-53 NEWSPAPER STRIP JOHNNY COMET, HAD CLEARLY FIGURED OUT RAYMOND'S NIGHTINGALE-BRUSH-STROKE TECHNIQUE...
...AND HAD TAKEN IT TO A WHOLE NEW LEVEL

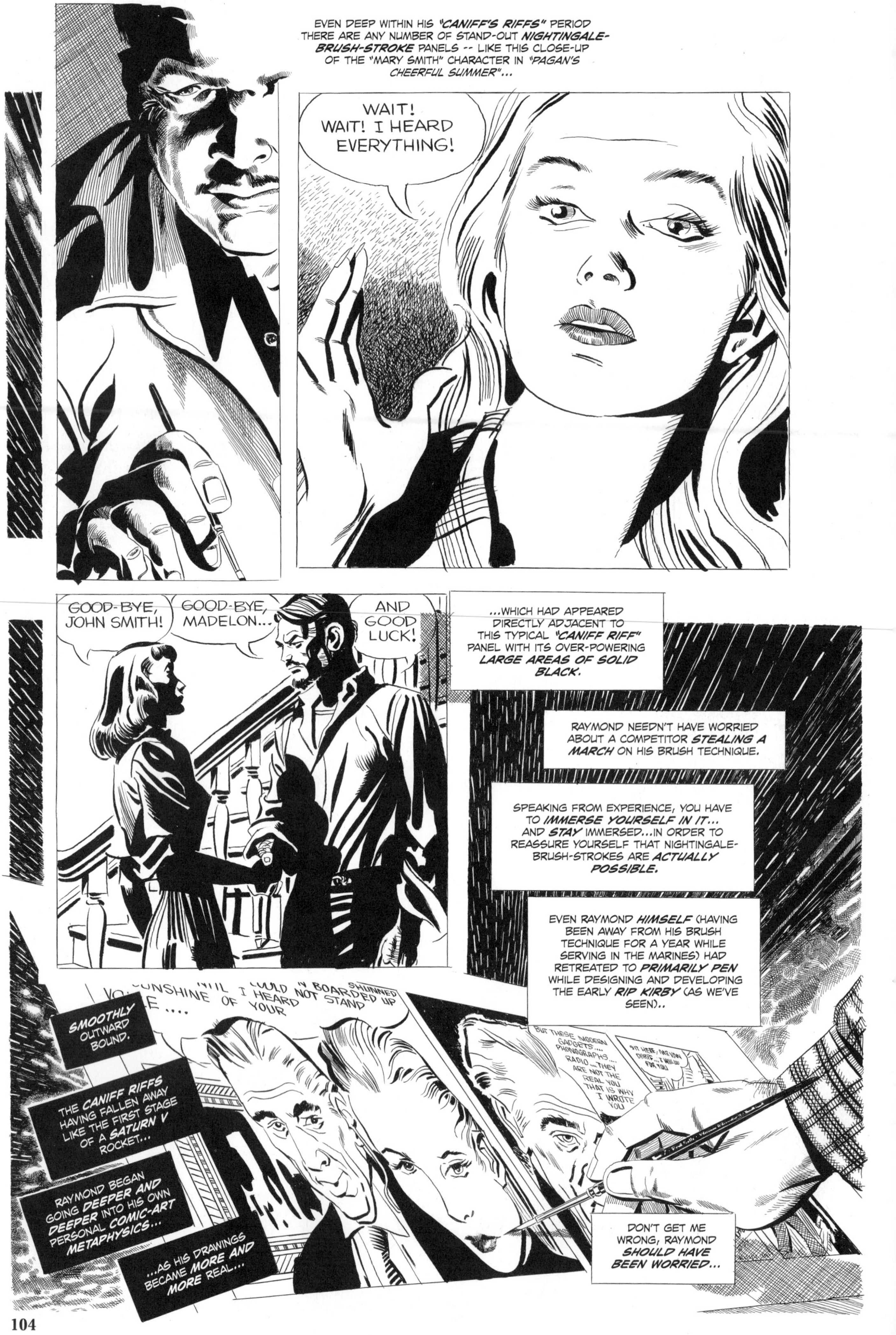
EVEN DEEP WITHIN HIS "CANIFF'S RIFFS" PERIOD THERE ARE ANY NUMBER OF STAND-OUT NIGHTINGALE-BRUSH-STROKE PANELS -- LIKE THIS CLOSE-UP OF THE "MARY SMITH" CHARACTER IN "PAGAN'S CHEERFUL SUMMER"...
WAIT! WAIT! I HEARD EVERYTHING!
GOOD-BYE, JOHN SMITH!
GOOD-BYE, MADELON...
AND GOOD LUCK!
...WHICH HAD APPEARED DIRECTLY ADJACENT TO THIS TYPICAL "CANIFF RIFF" PANEL WITH ITS OVER-POWERING LARGE AREAS OF SOLID BLACK.
RAYMOND NEEDN'T HAVE WORRIED ABOUT A COMPETITOR STEALING A MARCH ON HIS BRUSH TECHNIQUE.
SPEAKING FROM EXPERIENCE, YOU HAVE TO IMMERSE YOURSELF IN IT... AND STAY IMMERSED...IN ORDER TO REASSURE YOURSELF THAT NIGHTINGALE-BRUSH-STROKES ARE ACTUALLY POSSIBLE.
EVEN RAYMOND HIMSELF (HAVING BEEN AWAY FROM HIS BRUSH TECHNIQUE FOR A YEAR WHILE SERVING IN THE MARINES) HAD RETREATED TO PRIMARILY PEN WHILE DESIGNING AND DEVELOPING THE EARLY RIP KIRBY (AS WE'VE SEEN)..
SMOOTHLY OUTWARD BOUND.
BUT THESE MODERN GADGETS PHONOGRAPHS... RADIO... THEY ARE NOT THE REAL YOU THAT IS WHY I WROTE YOU
THE CANIFF RIFFS HAVING FALLEN AWAY LIKE THE FIRST STAGE OF A SATURN V ROCKET...
RAYMOND BEGAN GOING DEEPER AND DEEPER INTO HIS OWN PERSONAL COMIC-ART METAPHYSICS...
...AS HIS DRAWINGS BECAME MORE AND MORE REAL...
DON'T GET ME WRONG, RAYMOND SHOULD HAVE BEEN WORRIED...

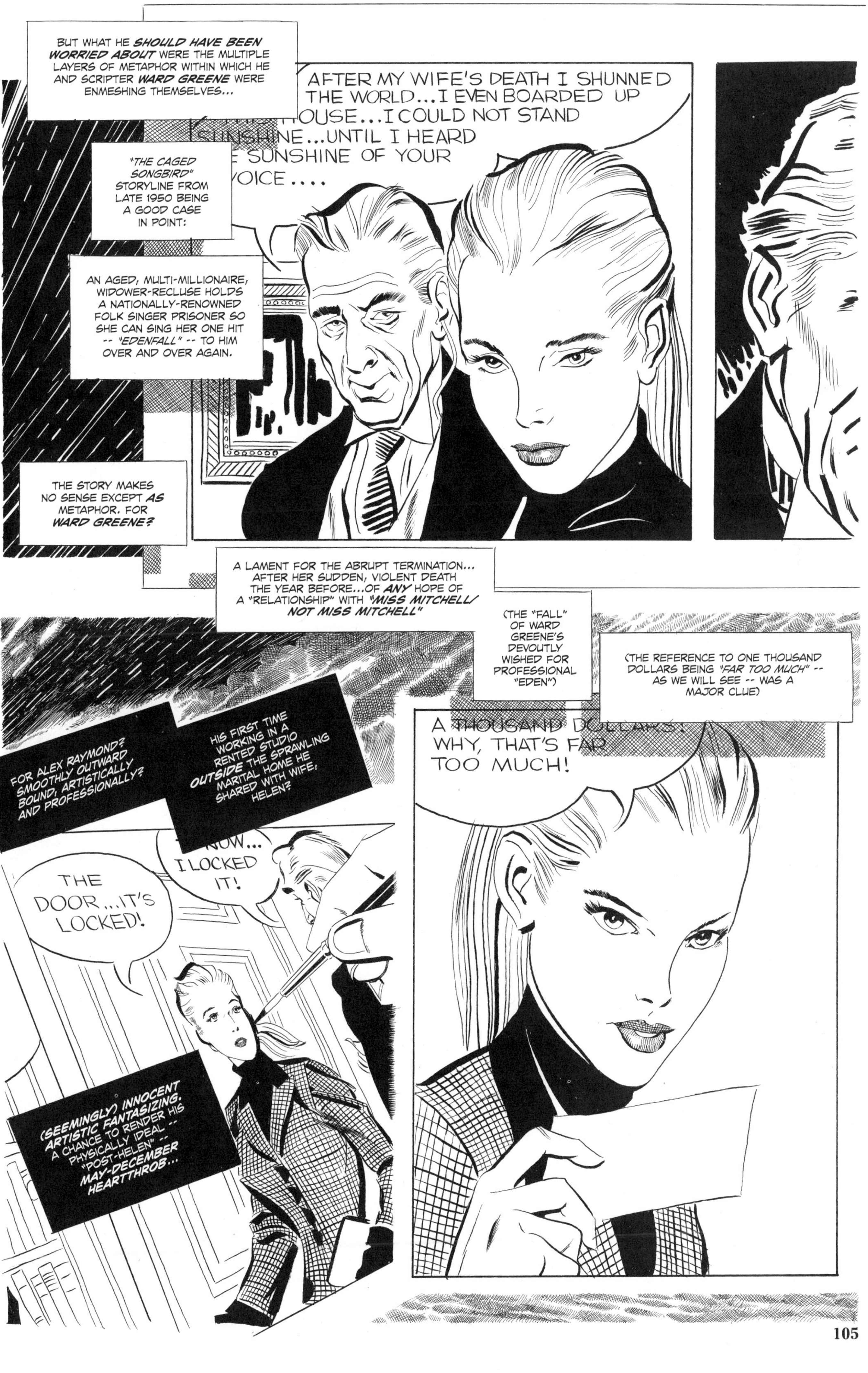
BUT WHAT HE SHOULD HAVE BEEN WORRIED ABOUT WERE THE MULTIPLE LAYERS OF METAPHOR WITHIN WHICH HE AND SCRIPTER WARD GREENE WERE ENMESHING THEMSELVES...
AFTER MY WIFE'S DEATH I SHUNNED THE WORLD...I EVEN BOARDED UP HOUSE...I COULD NOT STAND SUNSHINE...UNTIL I HEARD SUNSHINE OF YOUR VOICE....
"THE CAGED SONGBIRD" STORYLINE FROM LATE 1950 BEING A GOOD CASE IN POINT:
AN AGED, MULTI-MILLIONAIRE, WIDOWER-RECLUSE HOLDS A NATIONALLY-RENOWNED FOLK SINGER PRISONER SO SHE CAN SING HER ONE HIT -- "EDENFALL" -- TO HIM OVER AND OVER AGAIN.
THE STORY MAKES NO SENSE EXCEPT AS METAPHOR. FOR WARD GREENE?
A LAMENT FOR THE ABRUPT TERMINATION... AFTER HER SUDDEN, VIOLENT DEATH THE YEAR BEFORE...OF ANY HOPE OF A "RELATIONSHIP" WITH "MISS MITCHELL/ NOT MISS MITCHELL"
(THE "FALL" OF WARD GREENE'S DEVOUTLY WISHED FOR PROFESSIONAL "EDEN")
(THE REFERENCE TO ONE THOUSAND DOLLARS BEING "FAR TOO MUCH" -- AS WE WILL SEE -- WAS A MAJOR CLUE)
FOR ALEX RAYMOND? SMOOTHLY OUTWARD BOUND, ARTISTICALLY AND PROFESSIONALLY?
HIS FIRST TIME WORKING IN A RENTED STUDIO OUTSIDE THE SPRAWLING MARITAL HOME HE SHARED WITH WIFE, HELEN?
THE DOOR...IT'S LOCKED!
NOW... I LOCKED IT!
A THOUSAND DOLLARS! WHY, THAT'S FAR TOO MUCH!
(SEEMINGLY) INNOCENT ARTISTIC FANTASIZING. A CHANCE TO RENDER HIS PHYSICALLY IDEAL -- "POST-HELEN" -- MAY-DECEMBER HEARTTHROB...

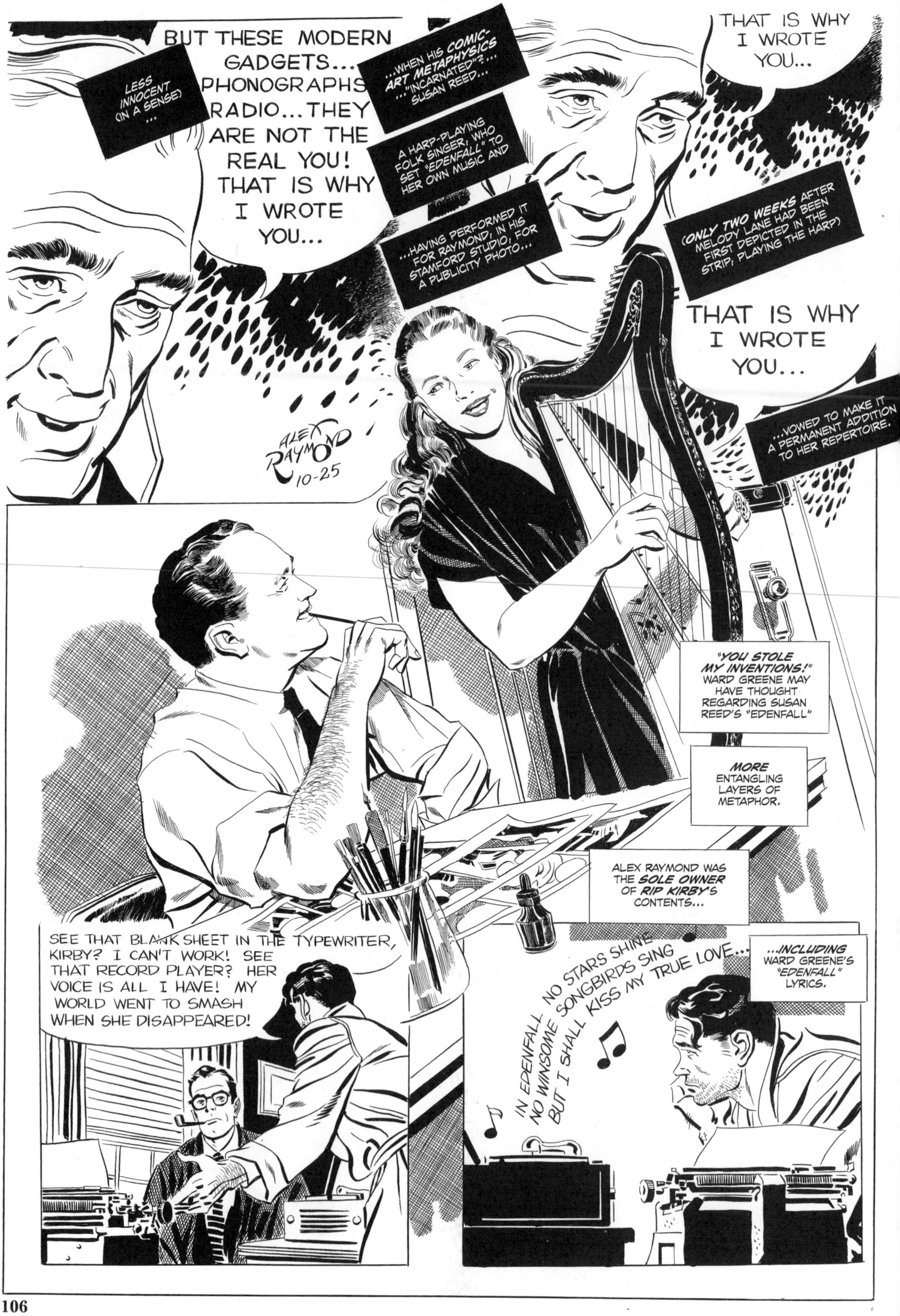
LESS INNOCENT (IN A SENSE) ...
BUT THESE MODERN GADGETS... PHONOGRAPHS RADIO... THEY ARE NOT THE REAL YOU! THAT IS WHY I WROTE YOU...
...WHEN HIS COMIC-ART METAPHYSICS ..."INCARNATED"?... SUSAN REED...
A HARP-PLAYING FOLK SINGER, WHO SET "EDENFALL" TO HER OWN MUSIC AND
...HAVING PERFORMED IT FOR RAYMOND, IN HIS STAMFORD STUDIO, FOR A PUBLICITY PHOTO...
THAT IS WHY I WROTE YOU...
(ONLY TWO WEEKS AFTER MELODY LANE HAD BEEN FIRST DEPICTED IN THE STRIP, PLAYING THE HARP)
THAT IS WHY I WROTE YOU...
...VOWED TO MAKE IT A PERMANENT ADDITION TO HER REPERTOIRE.
ALEX RAYMOND 10-25
"YOU STOLE MY INVENTIONS!" WARD GREENE MAY HAVE THOUGHT REGARDING SUSAN REED'S "EDENFALL"
MORE ENTANGLING LAYERS OF METAPHOR.
ALEX RAYMOND WAS THE SOLE OWNER OF RIP KIRBY'S CONTENTS...
SEE THAT BLANK SHEET IN THE TYPEWRITER, KIRBY? I CAN'T WORK! SEE THAT RECORD PLAYER? HER VOICE IS ALL I HAVE! MY WORLD WENT TO SMASH WHEN SHE DISAPPEARED!
IN EDENFALL NO STARS SHINE NO WINSOME SONGBIRDS SING BUT I SHALL KISS MY TRUE LOVE...
...INCLUDING WARD GREENE'S "EDENFALL" LYRICS.

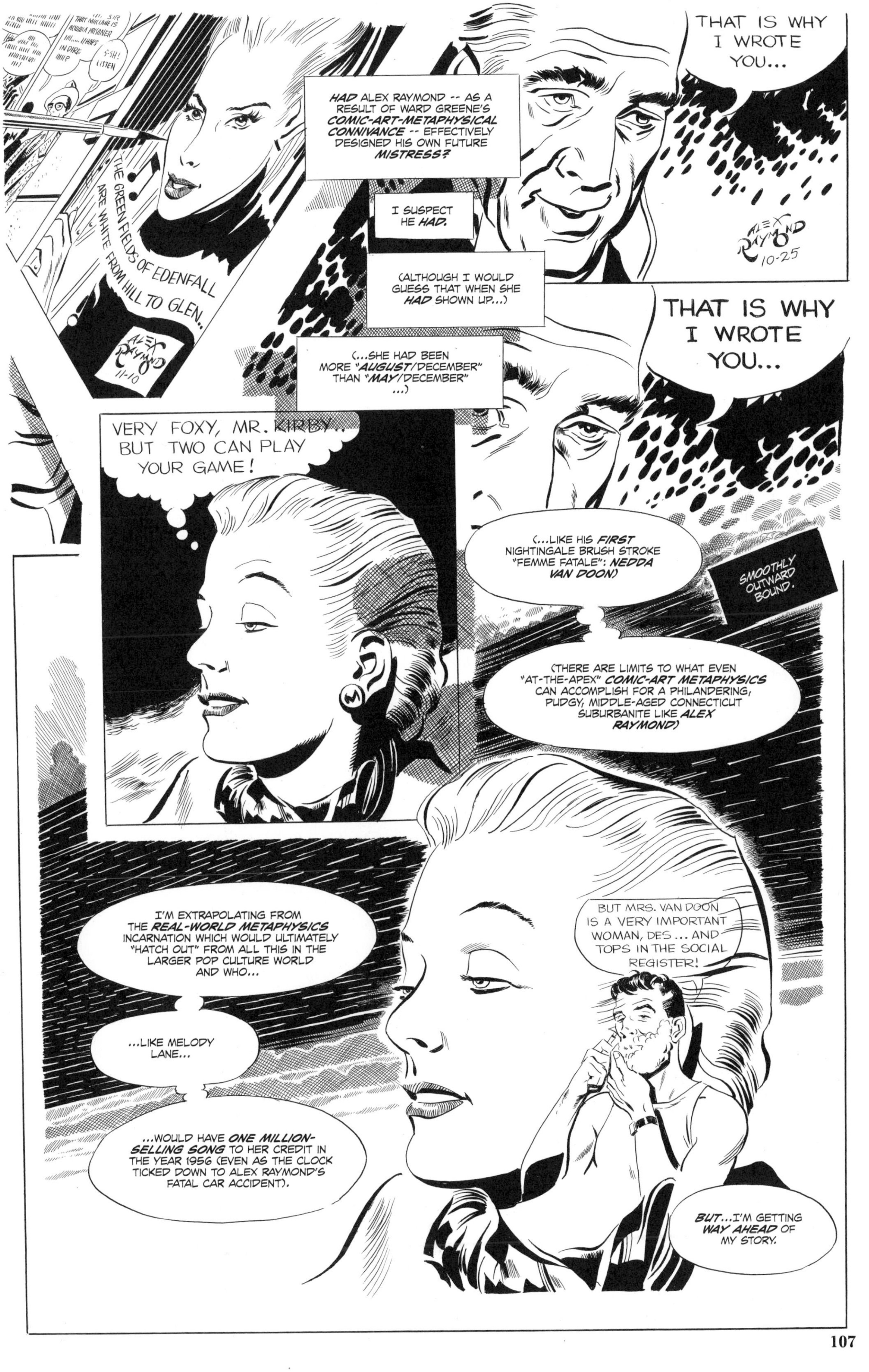
S-SH! LISTEN
THE GREEN FIELDS OF EDENFALL ARE WHITE FROM HILL TO GLEN...
ALEX RAYMOND 11-10
HAD ALEX RAYMOND -- AS A RESULT OF WARD GREENE'S COMIC-ART-METAPHYSICAL CONNIVANCE -- EFFECTIVELY DESIGNED HIS OWN FUTURE MISTRESS?
I SUSPECT HE HAD.
THAT IS WHY I WROTE YOU...
ALEX RAYMOND 10-25
(ALTHOUGH I WOULD GUESS THAT WHEN SHE HAD SHOWN UP...)
(...SHE HAD BEEN MORE "AUGUST/DECEMBER" THAN "MAY/DECEMBER" ...)
THAT IS WHY I WROTE YOU...
VERY FOXY, MR. KIRBY... BUT TWO CAN PLAY YOUR GAME!
(...LIKE HIS FIRST NIGHTINGALE BRUSH STROKE "FEMME FATALE": NEDDA VAN DOON)
SMOOTHLY OUTWARD BOUND.
(THERE ARE LIMITS TO WHAT EVEN "AT-THE-APEX" COMIC-ART METAPHYSICS CAN ACCOMPLISH FOR A PHILANDERING, PUDGY, MIDDLE-AGED CONNECTICUT SUBURBANITE LIKE ALEX RAYMOND)
I'M EXTRAPOLATING FROM THE REAL-WORLD METAPHYSICS INCARNATION WHICH WOULD ULTIMATELY "HATCH OUT" FROM ALL THIS IN THE LARGER POP CULTURE WORLD AND WHO...
...LIKE MELODY LANE...
...WOULD HAVE ONE MILLION-SELLING SONG TO HER CREDIT IN THE YEAR 1956 (EVEN AS THE CLOCK TICKED DOWN TO ALEX RAYMOND'S FATAL CAR ACCIDENT).
BUT MRS. VAN DOON IS A VERY IMPORTANT WOMAN, DES... AND TOPS IN THE SOCIAL REGISTER!
BUT...I'M GETTING WAY AHEAD OF MY STORY.

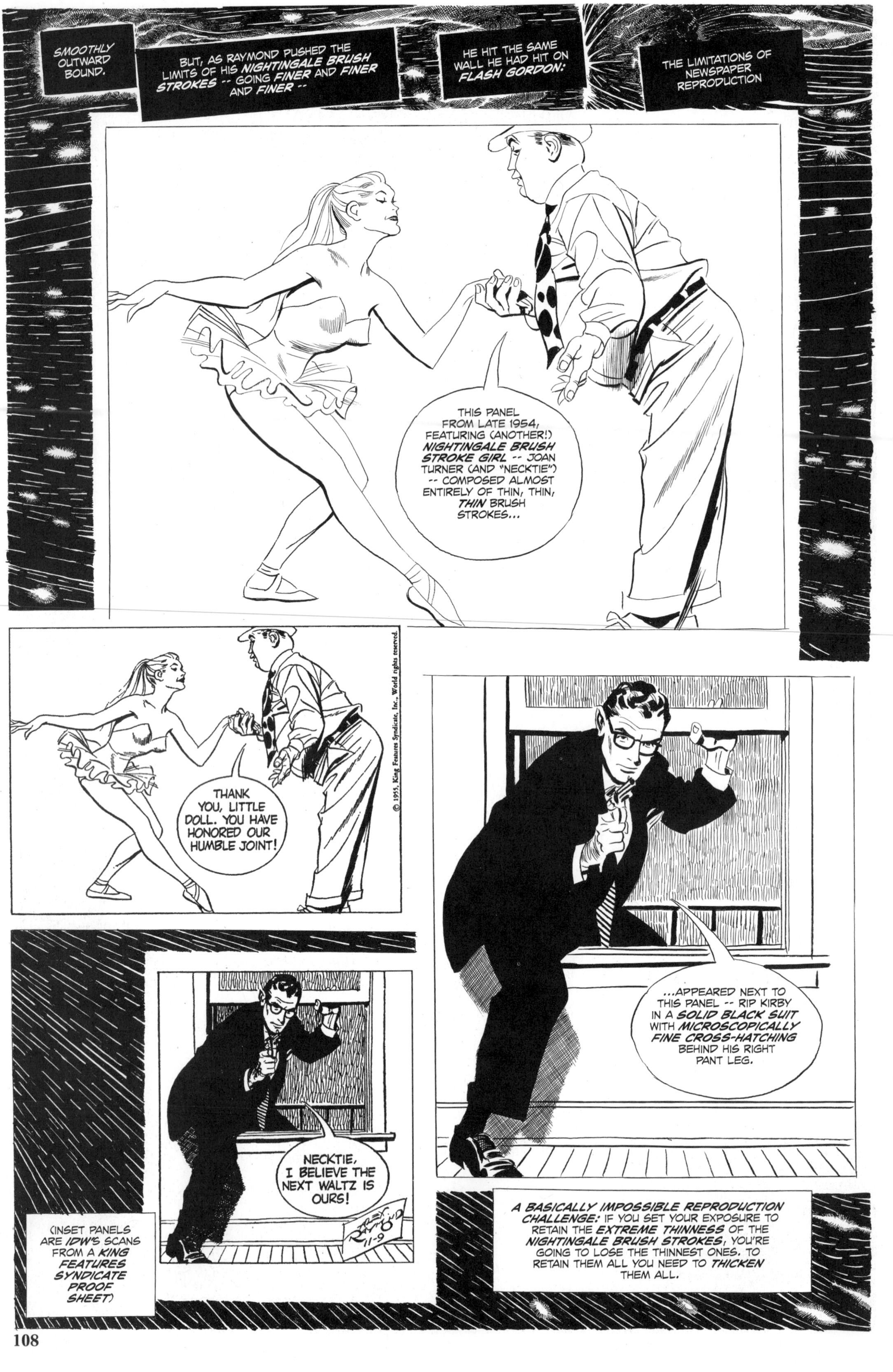
SMOOTHLY OUTWARD BOUND.
BUT, AS RAYMOND PUSHED THE LIMITS OF HIS NIGHTINGALE BRUSH STROKES -- GOING FINER AND FINER AND FINER --
HE HIT THE SAME WALL HE HAD HIT ON FLASH GORDON:
THE LIMITATIONS OF NEWSPAPER REPRODUCTION
THIS PANEL FROM LATE 1954, FEATURING (ANOTHER!) NIGHTINGALE BRUSH STROKE GIRL -- JOAN TURNER (AND "NECKTIE") -- COMPOSED ALMOST ENTIRELY OF THIN, THIN, THIN BRUSH STROKES...
THANK YOU, LITTLE DOLL. YOU HAVE HONORED OUR HUMBLE JOINT!
© 1955, King Features Syndicate, Inc., World rights reserved.
...APPEARED NEXT TO THIS PANEL -- RIP KIRBY IN A SOLID BLACK SUIT WITH MICROSCOPICALLY FINE CROSS-HATCHING BEHIND HIS RIGHT PANT LEG.
NECKTIE, I BELIEVE THE NEXT WALTZ IS OURS!
(INSET PANELS ARE IDW'S SCANS FROM A KING FEATURES SYNDICATE PROOF SHEET)
A BASICALLY IMPOSSIBLE REPRODUCTION CHALLENGE: IF YOU SET YOUR EXPOSURE TO RETAIN THE EXTREME THINNESS OF THE NIGHTINGALE BRUSH STROKES, YOU'RE GOING TO LOSE THE THINNEST ONES. TO RETAIN THEM ALL YOU NEED TO THICKEN THEM ALL.

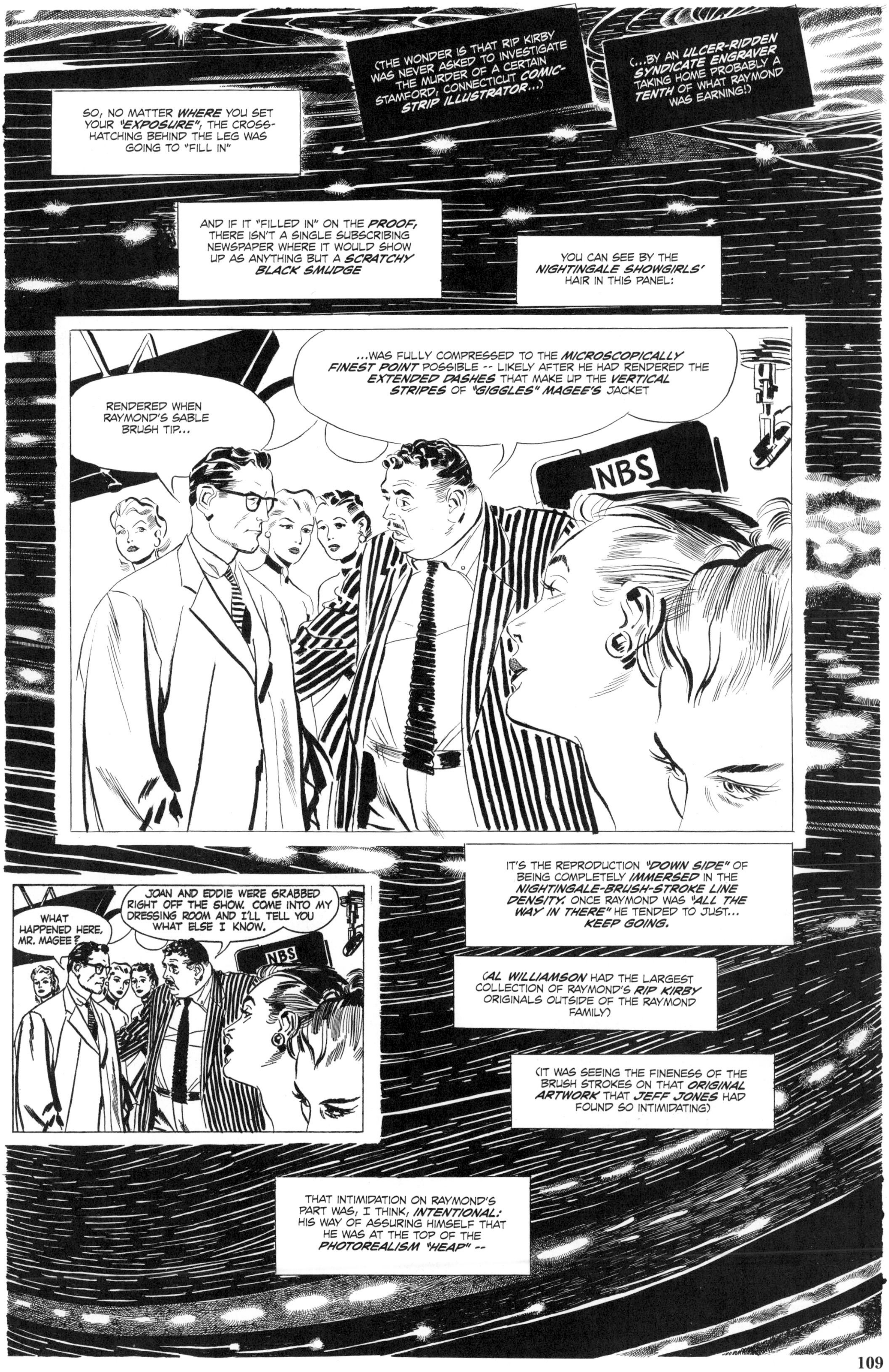
SO, NO MATTER WHERE YOU SET YOUR "EXPOSURE", THE CROSS-HATCHING BEHIND THE LEG WAS GOING TO "FILL IN"
(THE WONDER IS THAT RIP KIRBY WAS NEVER ASKED TO INVESTIGATE THE MURDER OF A CERTAIN STAMFORD, CONNECTICUT COMIC-STRIP ILLUSTRATOR...)
(...BY AN ULCER-RIDDEN SYNDICATE ENGRAVER TAKING HOME PROBABLY A TENTH OF WHAT RAYMOND WAS EARNING!)
AND IF IT "FILLED IN" ON THE PROOF, THERE ISN'T A SINGLE SUBSCRIBING NEWSPAPER WHERE IT WOULD SHOW UP AS ANYTHING BUT A SCRATCHY BLACK SMUDGE
YOU CAN SEE BY THE NIGHTINGALE SHOWGIRLS' HAIR IN THIS PANEL:
RENDERED WHEN RAYMOND'S SABLE BRUSH TIP...
...WAS FULLY COMPRESSED TO THE MICROSCOPICALLY FINEST POINT POSSIBLE -- LIKELY AFTER HE HAD RENDERED THE EXTENDED DASHES THAT MAKE UP THE VERTICAL STRIPES OF "GIGGLES" MAGEE'S JACKET
NBS
WHAT HAPPENED HERE, MR. MAGEE?
JOAN AND EDDIE WERE GRABBED RIGHT OFF THE SHOW. COME INTO MY DRESSING ROOM AND I'LL TELL YOU WHAT ELSE I KNOW.
NBS
IT'S THE REPRODUCTION "DOWN SIDE" OF BEING COMPLETELY IMMERSED IN THE NIGHTINGALE-BRUSH-STROKE LINE DENSITY. ONCE RAYMOND WAS "ALL THE WAY IN THERE" HE TENDED TO JUST... KEEP GOING.
(AL WILLIAMSON HAD THE LARGEST COLLECTION OF RAYMOND'S RIP KIRBY ORIGINALS OUTSIDE OF THE RAYMOND FAMILY)
(IT WAS SEEING THE FINENESS OF THE BRUSH STROKES ON THAT ORIGINAL ARTWORK THAT JEFF JONES HAD FOUND SO INTIMIDATING)
THAT INTIMIDATION ON RAYMOND'S PART WAS, I THINK, INTENTIONAL: HIS WAY OF ASSURING HIMSELF THAT HE WAS AT THE TOP OF THE PHOTOREALISM "HEAP" --

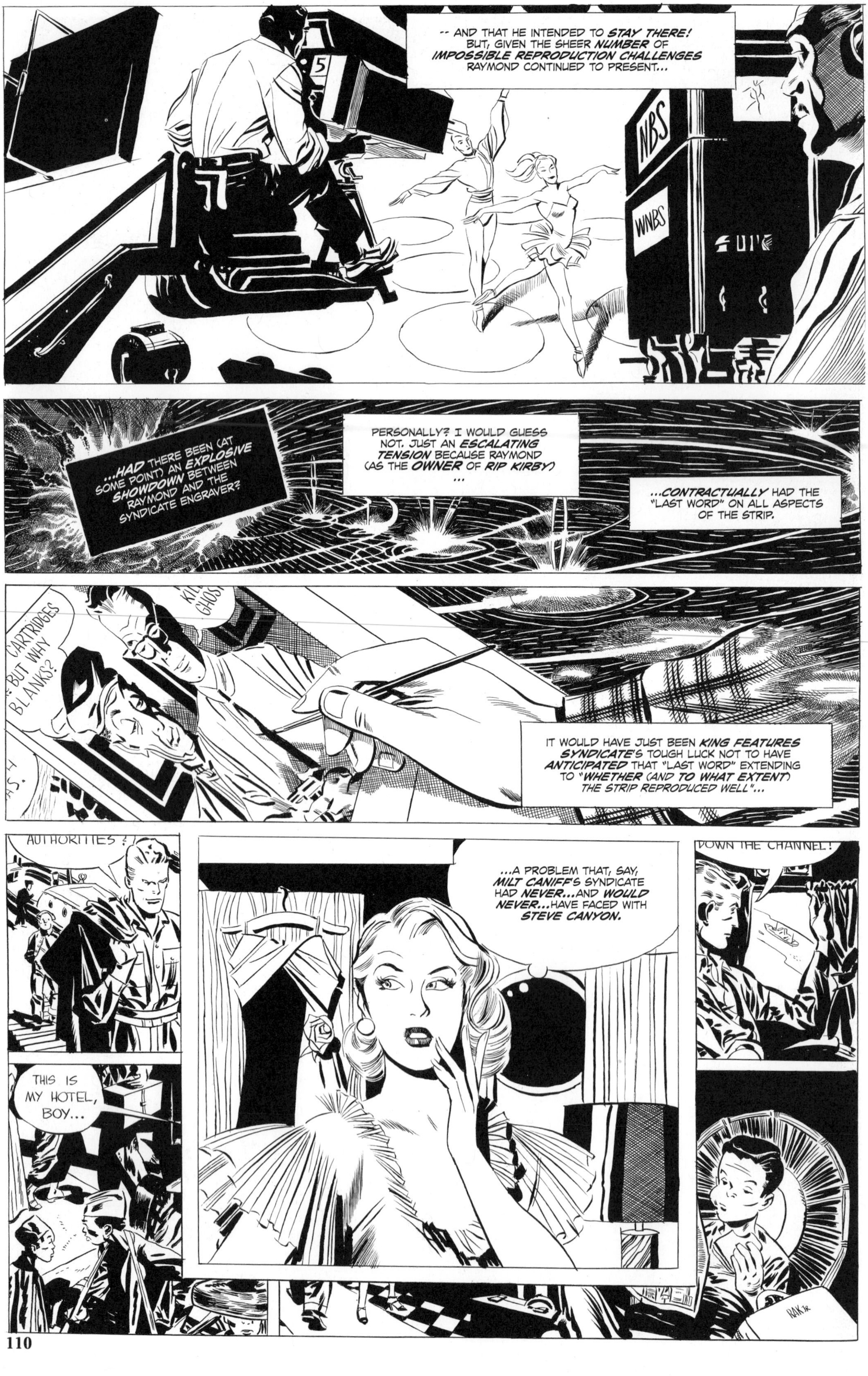

-- AND THAT HE INTENDED TO STAY THERE! BUT, GIVEN THE SHEER NUMBER OF IMPOSSIBLE REPRODUCTION CHALLENGES RAYMOND CONTINUED TO PRESENT...
5
NBS
WNBS
...HAD THERE BEEN (AT SOME POINT) AN EXPLOSIVE SHOWDOWN BETWEEN RAYMOND AND THE SYNDICATE ENGRAVER?
PERSONALLY? I WOULD GUESS NOT. JUST AN ESCALATING TENSION BECAUSE RAYMOND (AS THE OWNER OF RIP KIRBY) ...
...CONTRACTUALLY HAD THE "LAST WORD" ON ALL ASPECTS OF THE STRIP.
CARTRIDGES ...BUT WHY BLANKS?
IT WOULD HAVE JUST BEEN KING FEATURES SYNDICATE'S TOUGH LUCK NOT TO HAVE ANTICIPATED THAT "LAST WORD" EXTENDING TO "WHETHER (AND TO WHAT EXTENT) THE STRIP REPRODUCED WELL"...
AUTHORITIES?
...A PROBLEM THAT, SAY, MILT CANIFF'S SYNDICATE HAD NEVER...AND WOULD NEVER...HAVE FACED WITH STEVE CANYON.
DOWN THE CHANNEL!
THIS IS MY HOTEL, BOY...

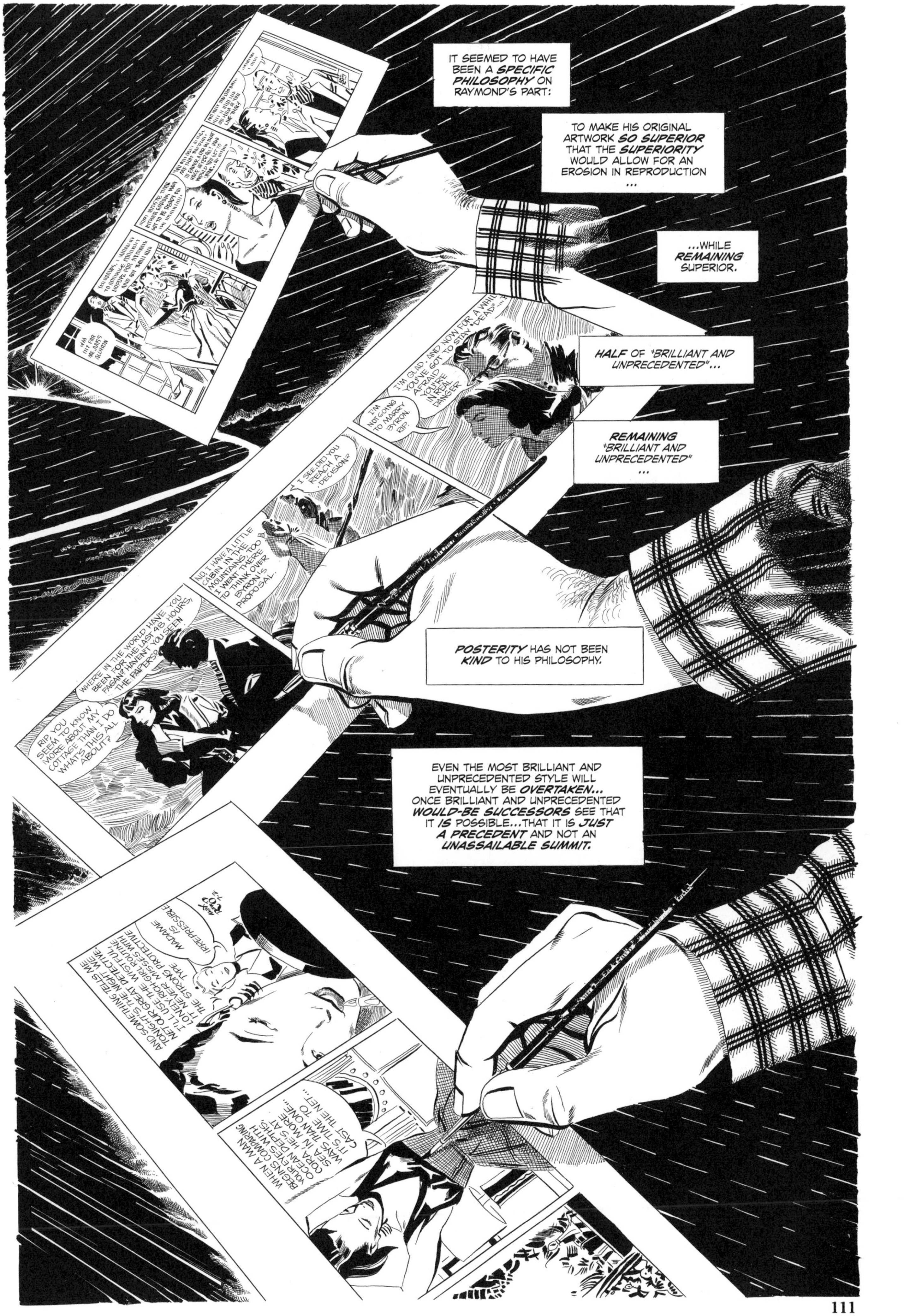
IT SEEMED TO HAVE BEEN A ***SPECIFIC PHILOSOPHY*** ON RAYMOND'S PART:
TO MAKE HIS ORIGINAL ARTWORK ***SO SUPERIOR*** THAT THE ***SUPERIORITY*** WOULD ALLOW FOR AN EROSION IN REPRODUCTION ...
...WHILE ***REMAINING*** SUPERIOR.
***HALF*** OF *"BRILLIANT AND UNPRECEDENTED"*...
***REMAINING*** *"BRILLIANT AND UNPRECEDENTED"* ...
I'M GLAD - AND NOW FOR A WHILE YOU'VE GOT TO STAY "DEAD"... AFRAID YOU'RE IN REAL DANGER
I'M NOT GOING TO MARRY BYRON, RIP.
I SEE. DID YOU REACH A DECISION?
I HAVE A LITTLE CABIN IN THE MOUNTAINS. I WENT THERE TO THINK OVER BYRON'S PROPOSAL.
WHERE IN THE WORLD HAVE YOU BEEN FOR THE LAST 48 HOURS, FAGAN? HAVEN'T YOU SEEN THE PAPERS?
RIP, YOU SEEM TO KNOW MORE ABOUT MY COTTAGE THAN I DO. WHAT'S THIS ALL ABOUT?
***POSTERITY*** HAS NOT BEEN ***KIND*** TO HIS PHILOSOPHY.
EVEN THE MOST BRILLIANT AND UNPRECEDENTED STYLE WILL EVENTUALLY BE ***OVERTAKEN...*** ONCE BRILLIANT AND UNPRECEDENTED ***WOULD-BE SUCCESSORS*** SEE THAT IT ***IS*** POSSIBLE...THAT IT IS ***JUST A PRECEDENT*** AND NOT AN ***UNASSAILABLE SUMMIT.***

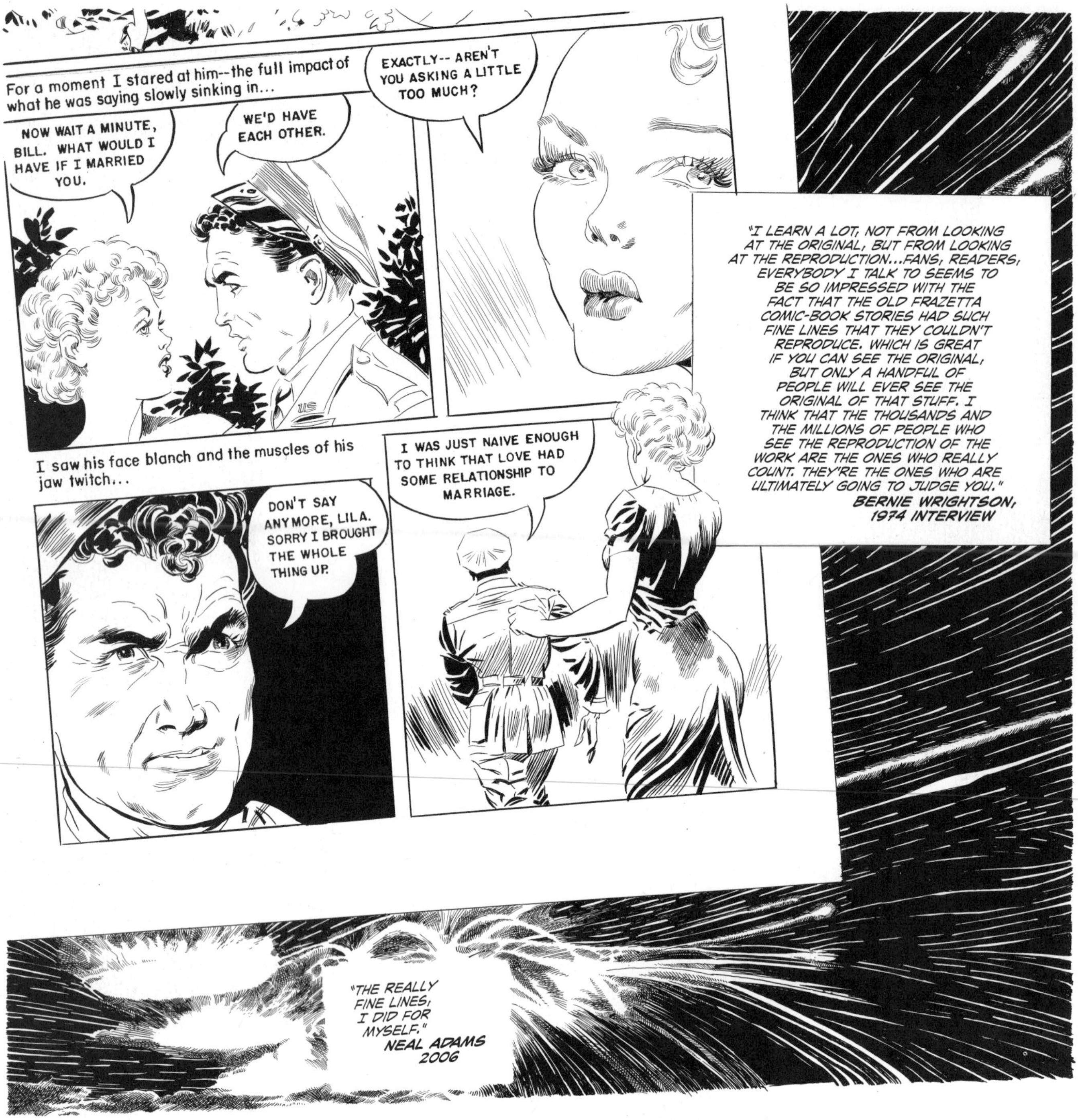
For a moment I stared at him--the full impact of what he was saying slowly sinking in...
NOW WAIT A MINUTE, BILL. WHAT WOULD I HAVE IF I MARRIED YOU.
WE'D HAVE EACH OTHER.
EXACTLY-- AREN'T YOU ASKING A LITTLE TOO MUCH?
I saw his face blanch and the muscles of his jaw twitch...
DON'T SAY ANYMORE, LILA. SORRY I BROUGHT THE WHOLE THING UP.
I WAS JUST NAIVE ENOUGH TO THINK THAT LOVE HAD SOME RELATIONSHIP TO MARRIAGE.

*"I LEARN A LOT, NOT FROM LOOKING AT THE ORIGINAL, BUT FROM LOOKING AT THE REPRODUCTION...FANS, READERS, EVERYBODY I TALK TO SEEMS TO BE SO IMPRESSED WITH THE FACT THAT THE OLD FRAZETTA COMIC-BOOK STORIES HAD SUCH FINE LINES THAT THEY COULDN'T REPRODUCE. WHICH IS GREAT IF YOU CAN SEE THE ORIGINAL, BUT ONLY A HANDFUL OF PEOPLE WILL EVER SEE THE ORIGINAL OF THAT STUFF. I THINK THAT THE THOUSANDS AND THE MILLIONS OF PEOPLE WHO SEE THE REPRODUCTION OF THE WORK ARE THE ONES WHO REALLY COUNT. THEY'RE THE ONES WHO ARE ULTIMATELY GOING TO JUDGE YOU."*
***BERNIE WRIGHTSON, 1974 INTERVIEW***

*"THE REALLY FINE LINES, I DID FOR MYSELF."*
***NEAL ADAMS 2006***

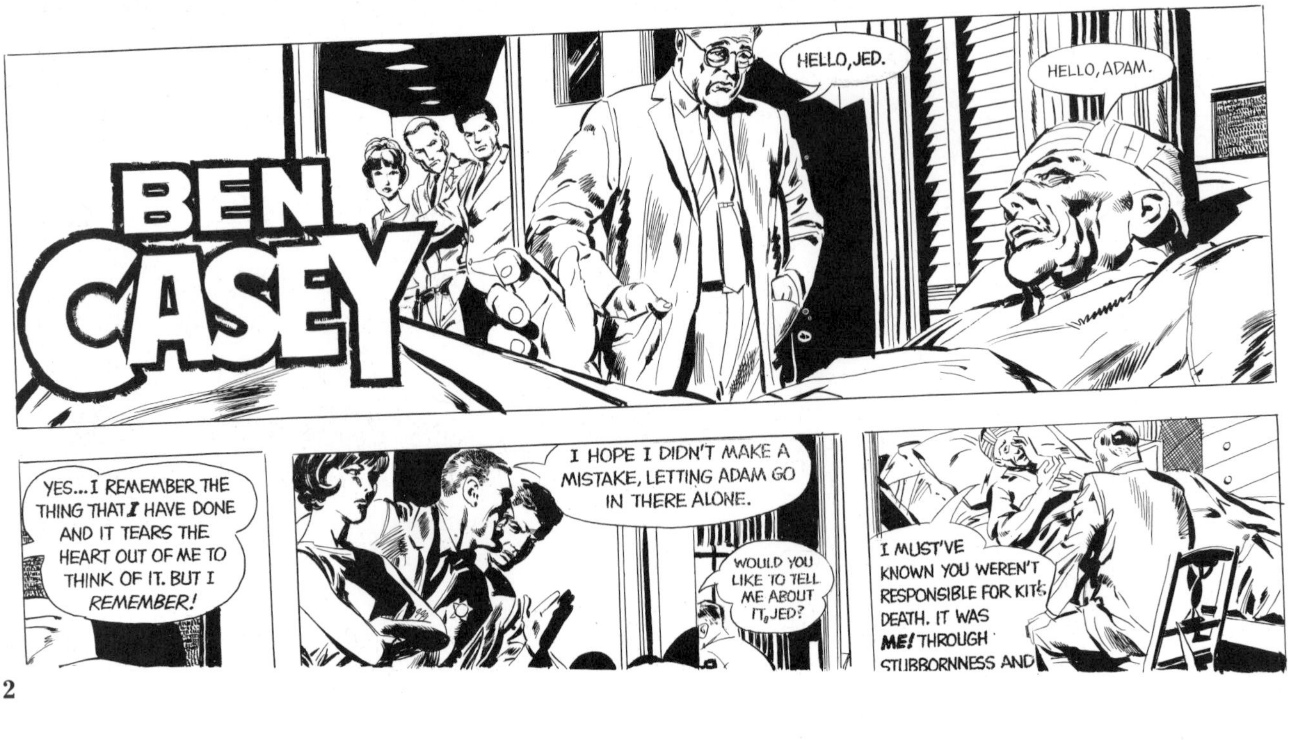
BEN CASEY
HELLO, JED.
HELLO, ADAM.
YES...I REMEMBER THE THING THAT I HAVE DONE AND IT TEARS THE HEART OUT OF ME TO THINK OF IT. BUT I REMEMBER!
I HOPE I DIDN'T MAKE A MISTAKE, LETTING ADAM GO IN THERE ALONE.
WOULD YOU LIKE TO TELL ME ABOUT IT, JED?
I MUST'VE KNOWN YOU WEREN'T RESPONSIBLE FOR KIT'S DEATH. IT WAS ME! THROUGH STUBBORNNESS AND

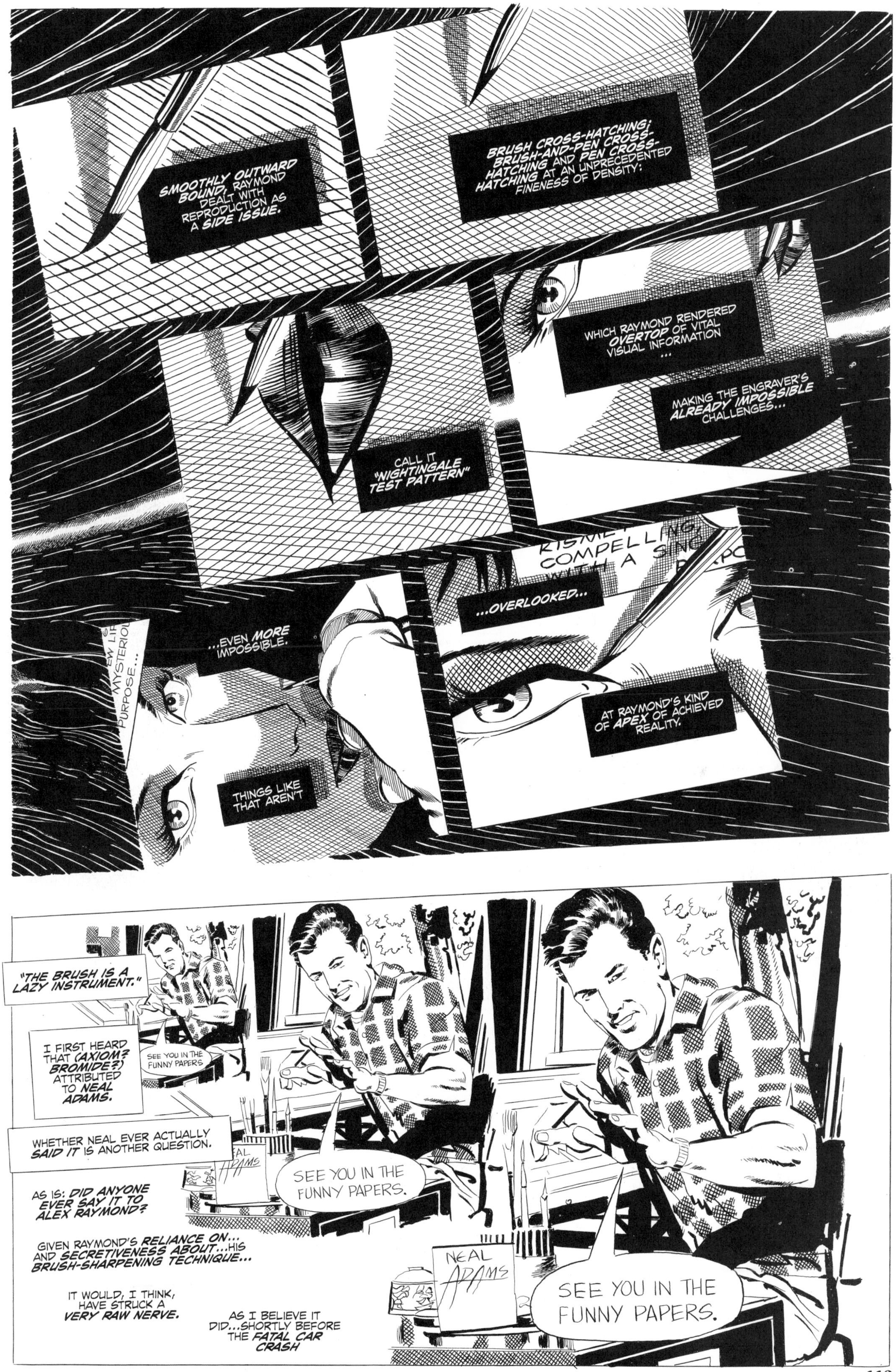

SMOOTHLY OUTWARD BOUND, RAYMOND DEALT WITH REPRODUCTION AS A SIDE ISSUE.
BRUSH CROSS-HATCHING; BRUSH-AND-PEN CROSS-HATCHING AND PEN CROSS-HATCHING AT AN UNPRECEDENTED FINENESS OF DENSITY;
CALL IT "NIGHTINGALE TEST PATTERN"
WHICH RAYMOND RENDERED OVERTOP OF VITAL VISUAL INFORMATION ...
MAKING THE ENGRAVER'S ALREADY IMPOSSIBLE CHALLENGES...
...EVEN MORE IMPOSSIBLE.
THINGS LIKE THAT AREN'T
...OVERLOOKED...
AT RAYMOND'S KIND OF APEX OF ACHIEVED REALITY.
"THE BRUSH IS A LAZY INSTRUMENT."
I FIRST HEARD THAT (AXIOM? BROMIDE?) ATTRIBUTED TO NEAL ADAMS.
SEE YOU IN THE FUNNY PAPERS
WHETHER NEAL EVER ACTUALLY SAID IT IS ANOTHER QUESTION.
NEAL ADAMS
SEE YOU IN THE FUNNY PAPERS.
AS IS: DID ANYONE EVER SAY IT TO ALEX RAYMOND?
GIVEN RAYMOND'S RELIANCE ON... AND SECRETIVENESS ABOUT...HIS BRUSH-SHARPENING TECHNIQUE...
IT WOULD, I THINK, HAVE STRUCK A VERY RAW NERVE.
AS I BELIEVE IT DID...SHORTLY BEFORE THE FATAL CAR CRASH
NEAL ADAMS
SEE YOU IN THE FUNNY PAPERS.

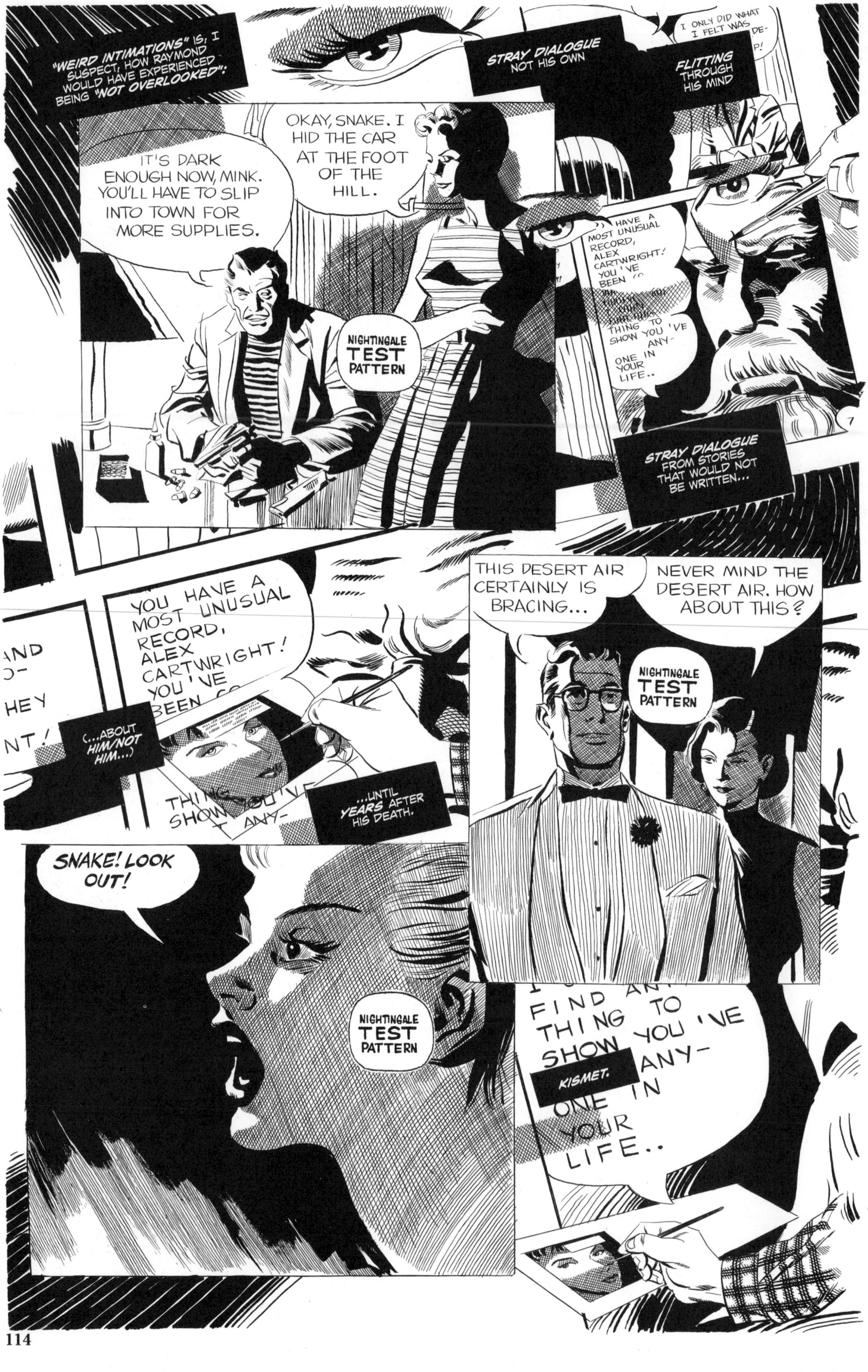
"WEIRD INTIMATIONS" IS, I SUSPECT, HOW RAYMOND WOULD HAVE EXPERIENCED BEING "NOT OVERLOOKED".
STRAY DIALOGUE NOT HIS OWN
I ONLY DID WHAT I FELT WAS
FLITTING THROUGH HIS MIND
IT'S DARK ENOUGH NOW, MINK. YOU'LL HAVE TO SLIP INTO TOWN FOR MORE SUPPLIES.
OKAY, SNAKE. I HID THE CAR AT THE FOOT OF THE HILL.
NIGHTINGALE TEST PATTERN
HAVE A MOST UNUSUAL RECORD, ALEX CARTWRIGHT! YOU'VE BEEN
THING TO SHOW YOU'VE ANY- ONE IN YOUR LIFE..
STRAY DIALOGUE FROM STORIES THAT WOULD NOT BE WRITTEN...
YOU HAVE A MOST UNUSUAL RECORD, ALEX CARTWRIGHT! YOU'VE
(...ABOUT HIM/NOT HIM...)
...UNTIL YEARS AFTER HIS DEATH.
THIS DESERT AIR CERTAINLY IS BRACING...
NEVER MIND THE DESERT AIR. HOW ABOUT THIS?
NIGHTINGALE TEST PATTERN
SNAKE! LOOK OUT!
NIGHTINGALE TEST PATTERN
FIND
THING TO SHOW YOU'VE ANY- ONE IN YOUR LIFE..
KISMET.

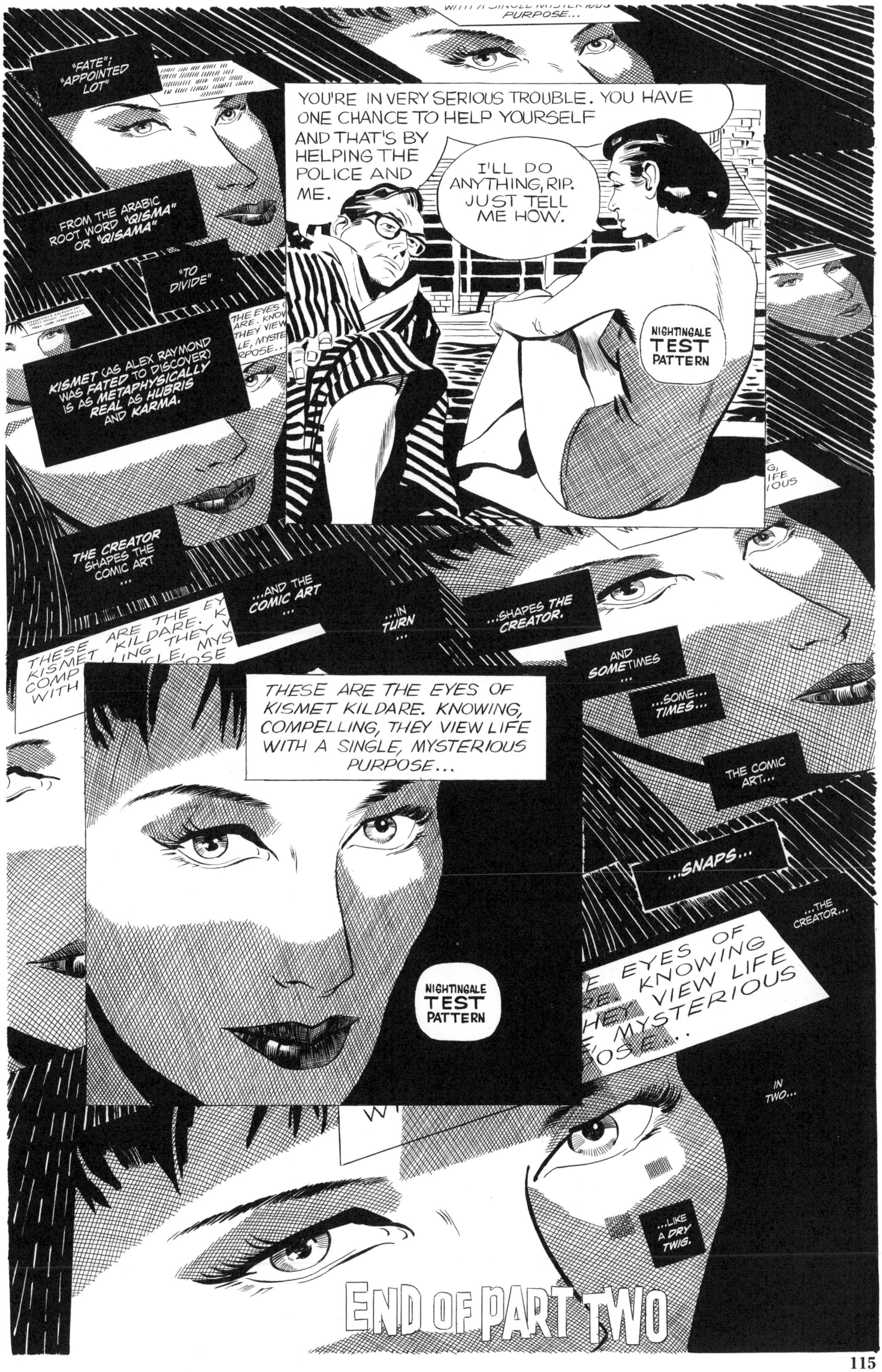
WITH A SINGLE MYSTERIOUS PURPOSE...
"FATE": "APPOINTED LOT"
YOU'RE IN VERY SERIOUS TROUBLE. YOU HAVE ONE CHANCE TO HELP YOURSELF AND THAT'S BY HELPING THE POLICE AND ME.
I'LL DO ANYTHING, RIP. JUST TELL ME HOW.
FROM THE ARABIC ROOT WORD "QISMA" OR "QISAMA"
"TO DIVIDE"
KISMET (AS ALEX RAYMOND WAS FATED TO DISCOVER) IS AS METAPHYSICALLY REAL AS HUBRIS AND KARMA.
NIGHTINGALE TEST PATTERN
THE CREATOR SHAPES THE COMIC ART ...
...AND THE COMIC ART ...
...IN TURN ...
...SHAPES THE CREATOR.
AND SOMETIMES ...
...SOME... TIMES...
THESE ARE THE EYES OF KISMET KILDARE. KNOWING, COMPELLING, THEY VIEW LIFE WITH A SINGLE, MYSTERIOUS PURPOSE...
THE COMIC ART...
...SNAPS...
...THE CREATOR...
NIGHTINGALE TEST PATTERN
IN TWO...
...LIKE A DRY TWIG.
END OF PART TWO

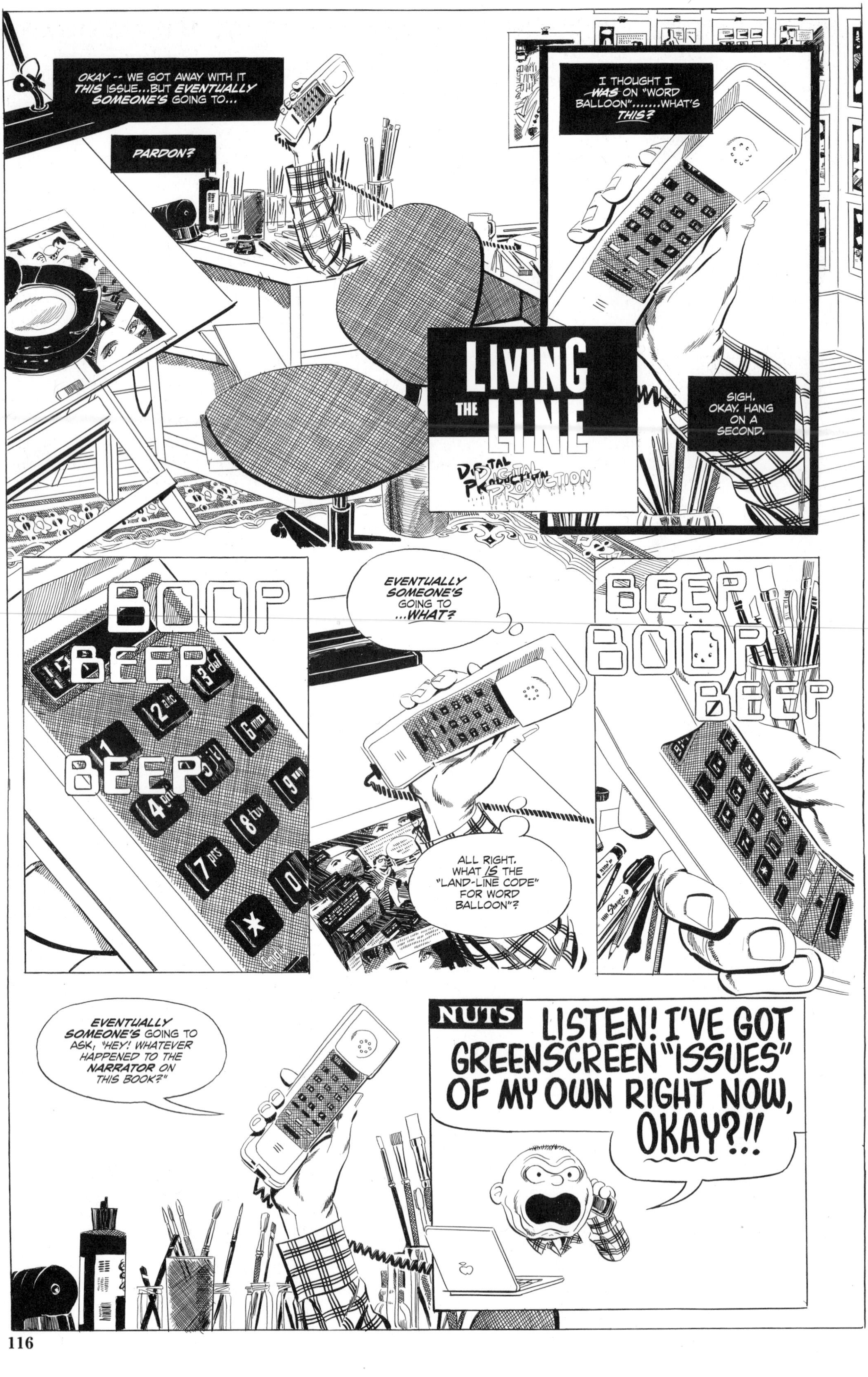
OKAY -- WE GOT AWAY WITH IT THIS ISSUE...BUT EVENTUALLY SOMEONE'S GOING TO...
PARDON?
I THOUGHT I WAS ON "WORD BALLOON"......WHAT'S THIS?
LIVING THE LINE
DIGITAL PRODUCTION
SIGH. OKAY. HANG ON A SECOND.
BOOP
BEEP
BEEP
EVENTUALLY SOMEONE'S GOING TO ...WHAT?
ALL RIGHT. WHAT IS THE "LAND-LINE CODE" FOR WORD BALLOON"?
BEEP
BOOP
BEEP
EVENTUALLY SOMEONE'S GOING TO ASK, "HEY! WHATEVER HAPPENED TO THE NARRATOR ON THIS BOOK?"
NUTS
LISTEN! I'VE GOT GREENSCREEN "ISSUES" OF MY OWN RIGHT NOW, OKAY?!!

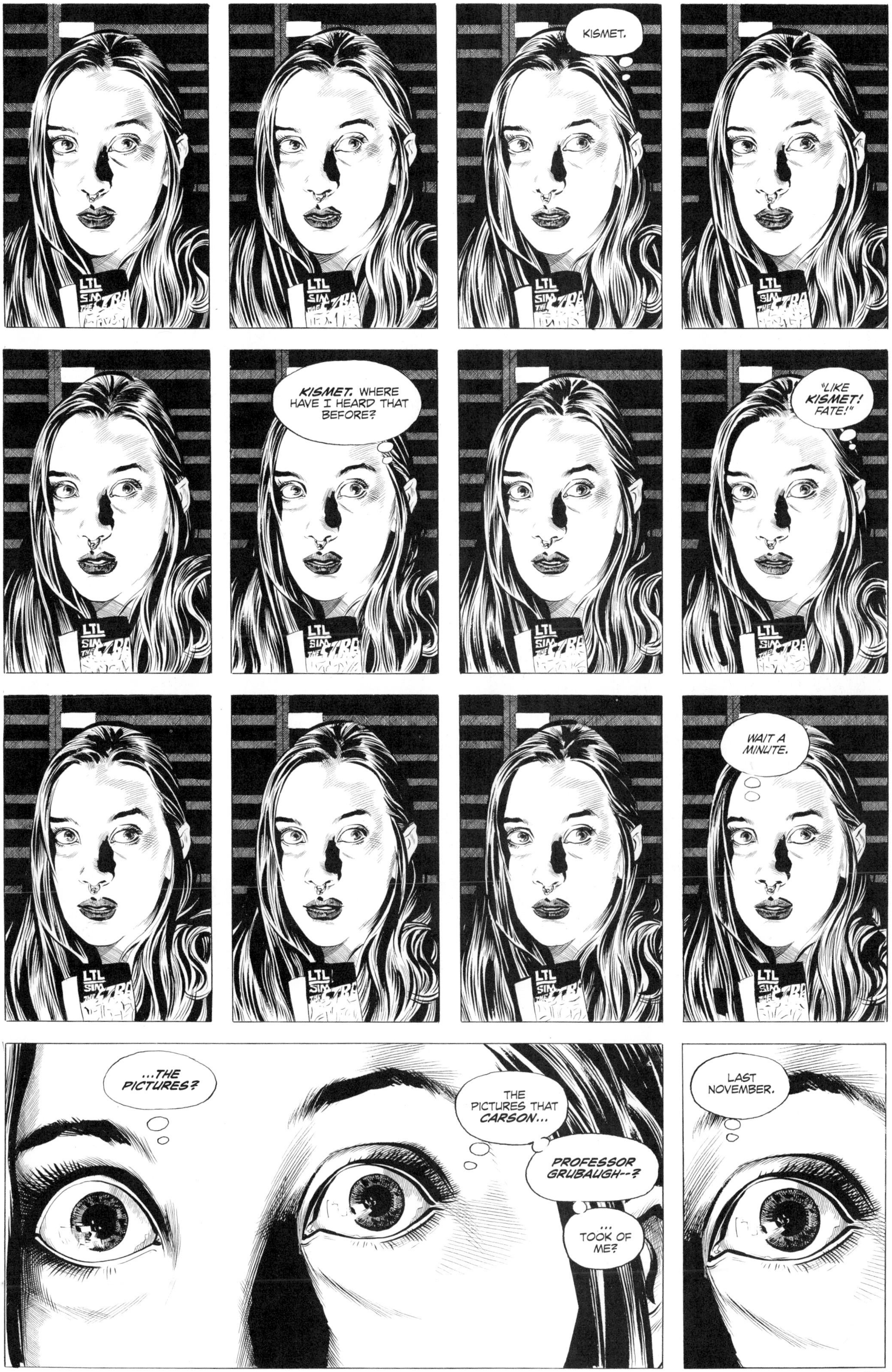
KISMET.
KISMET. WHERE HAVE I HEARD THAT BEFORE?
"LIKE KISMET! FATE!"
WAIT A MINUTE.
...THE PICTURES?
THE PICTURES THAT CARSON...
PROFESSOR GRUBAUGH--?
... TOOK OF ME?
LAST NOVEMBER.

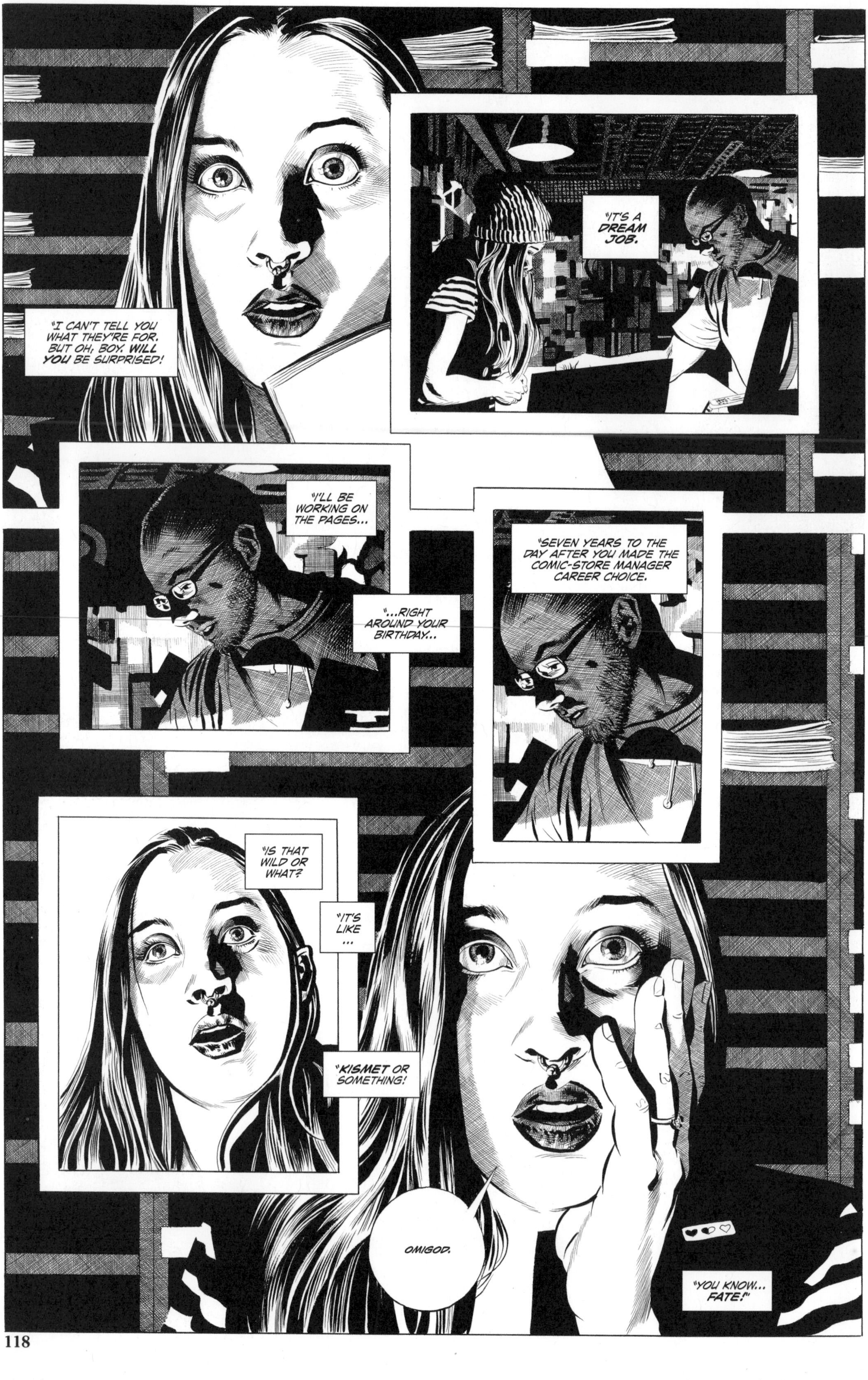
"I CAN'T TELL YOU WHAT THEY'RE FOR. BUT OH, BOY. WILL YOU BE SURPRISED!
"IT'S A DREAM JOB.
"I'LL BE WORKING ON THE PAGES...
"...RIGHT AROUND YOUR BIRTHDAY...
"SEVEN YEARS TO THE DAY AFTER YOU MADE THE COMIC-STORE MANAGER CAREER CHOICE.
"IS THAT WILD OR WHAT?
"IT'S LIKE ...
"KISMET OR SOMETHING!
OMIGOD.
"YOU KNOW... FATE!"

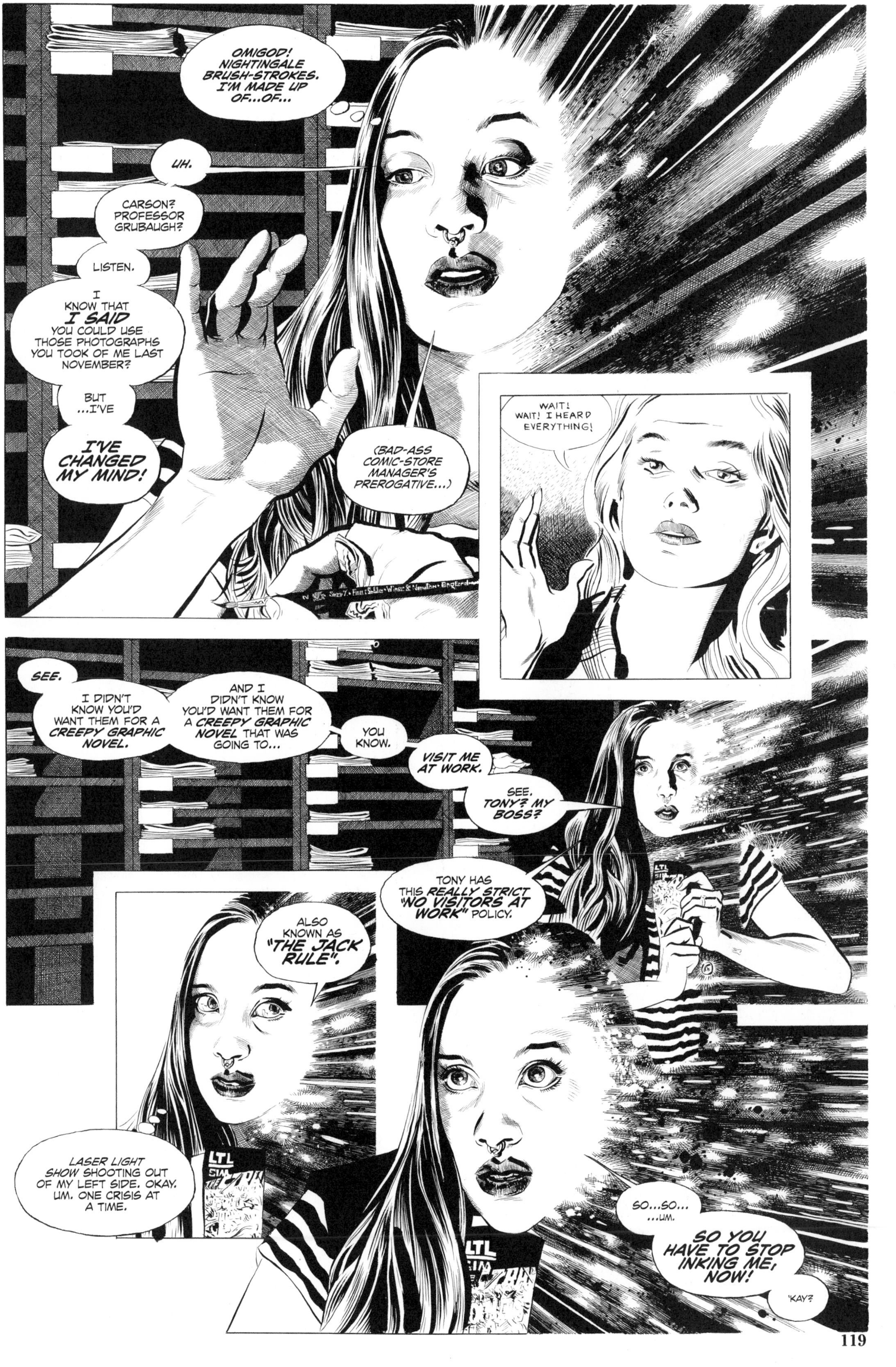

OMIGOD! NIGHTINGALE BRUSH-STROKES. I'M MADE UP OF...OF...
UH.
CARSON? PROFESSOR GRUBAUGH?
LISTEN.
I KNOW THAT I SAID YOU COULD USE THOSE PHOTOGRAPHS YOU TOOK OF ME LAST NOVEMBER?
BUT ...I'VE
I'VE CHANGED MY MIND!
(BAD-ASS COMIC-STORE MANAGER'S PREROGATIVE...)
WAIT! WAIT! I HEARD EVERYTHING!
SEE.
I DIDN'T KNOW YOU'D WANT THEM FOR A CREEPY GRAPHIC NOVEL.
AND I DIDN'T KNOW YOU'D WANT THEM FOR A CREEPY GRAPHIC NOVEL THAT WAS GOING TO...
YOU KNOW.
VISIT ME AT WORK.
SEE. TONY? MY BOSS?
TONY HAS THIS REALLY STRICT "NO VISITORS AT WORK" POLICY.
ALSO KNOWN AS "THE JACK RULE".
LASER LIGHT SHOW SHOOTING OUT OF MY LEFT SIDE. OKAY. UM. ONE CRISIS AT A TIME.
SO...SO... ...UM.
SO YOU HAVE TO STOP INKING ME, NOW!
'KAY?

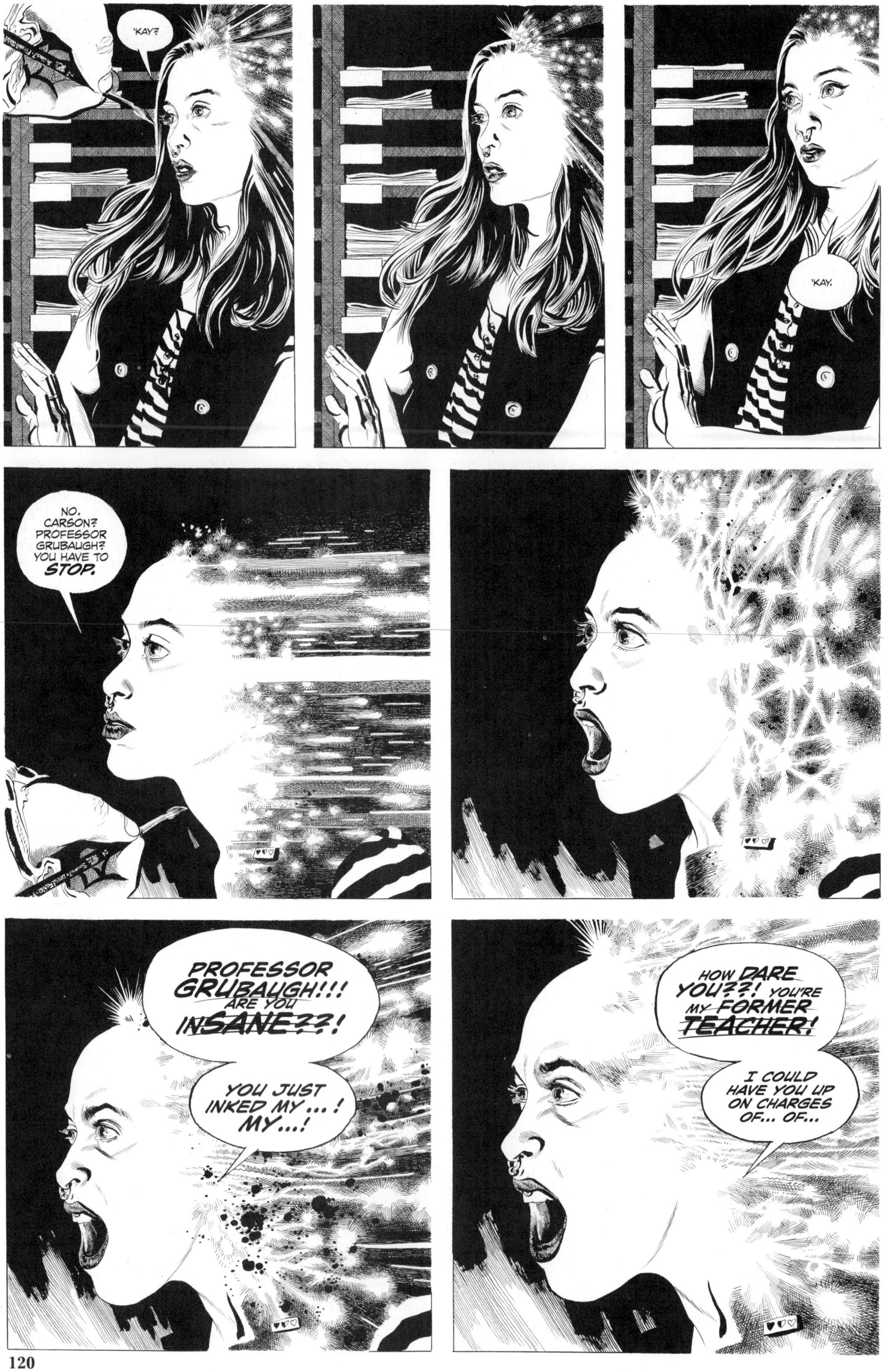
'KAY?
'KAY.
NO. CARSON? PROFESSOR GRUBAUGH? YOU HAVE TO STOP.
PROFESSOR GRUBAUGH!!! ARE YOU INSANE??!
YOU JUST INKED MY ... ! MY...!
HOW DARE YOU??! YOU'RE MY FORMER TEACHER!
I COULD HAVE YOU UP ON CHARGES OF... OF...

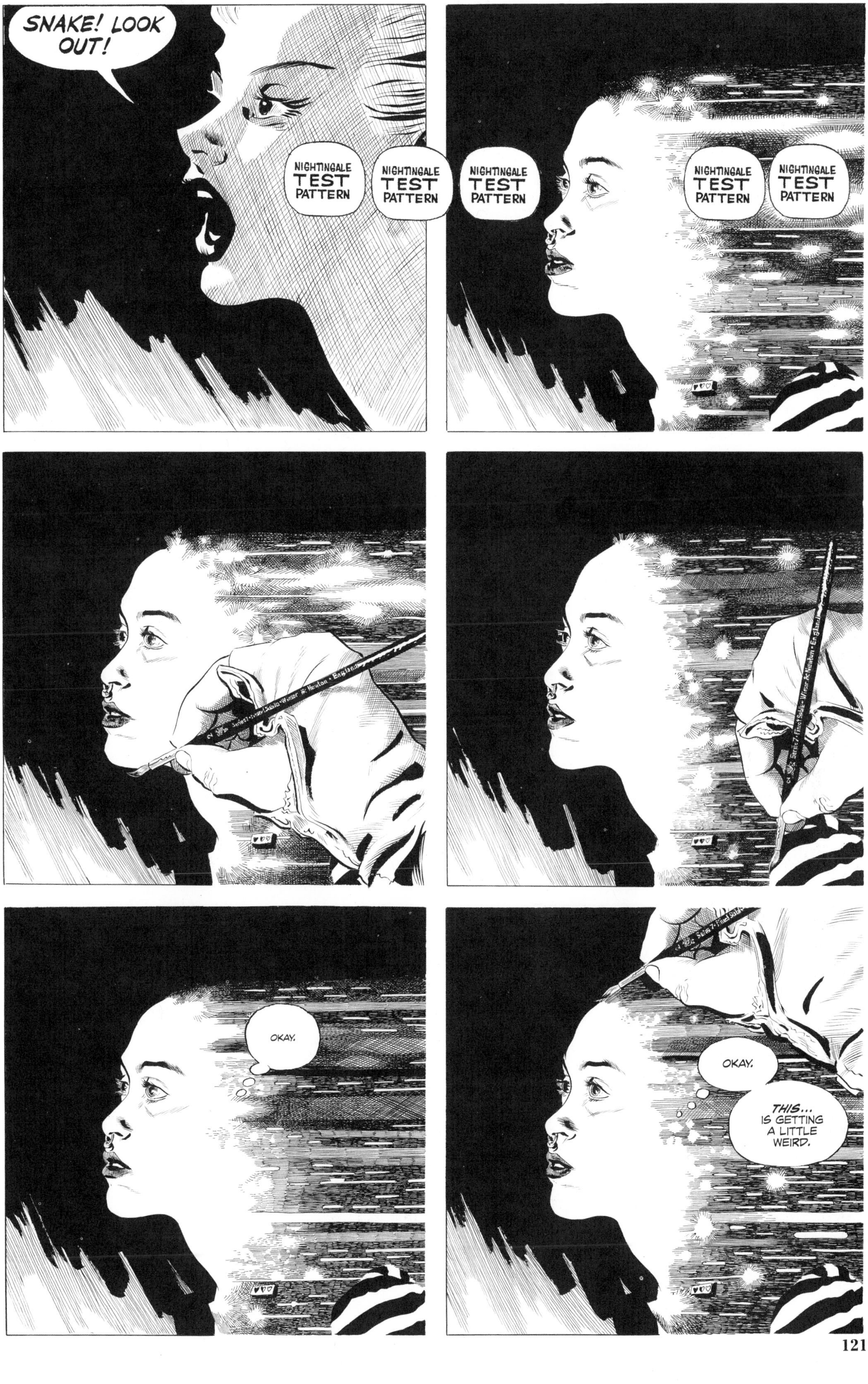

SNAKE! LOOK OUT!
NIGHTINGALE TEST PATTERN
NIGHTINGALE TEST PATTERN
NIGHTINGALE TEST PATTERN
NIGHTINGALE TEST PATTERN
NIGHTINGALE TEST PATTERN
OKAY.
OKAY.
THIS... IS GETTING A LITTLE WEIRD.

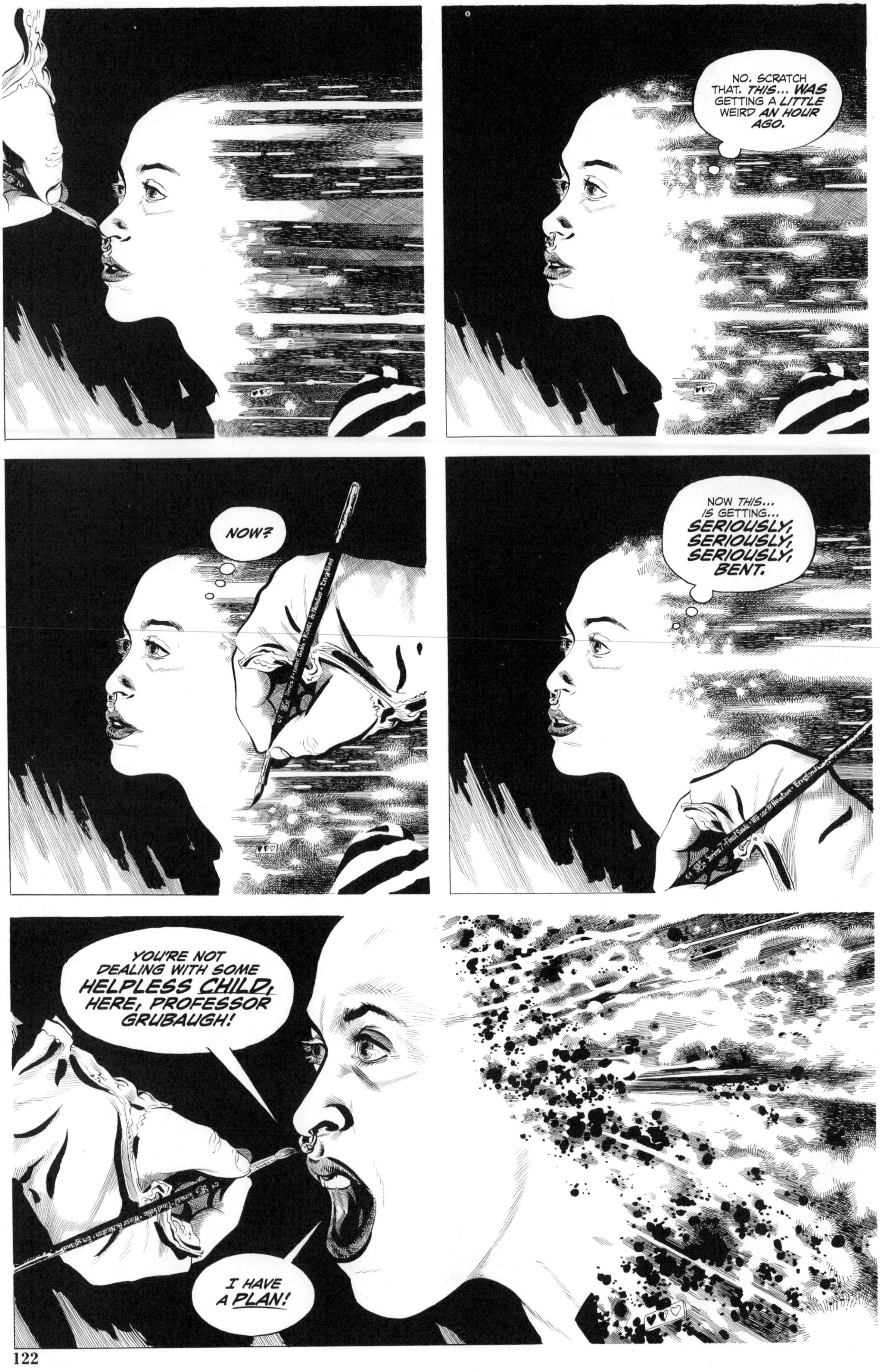
NO. SCRATCH THAT. THIS... WAS GETTING A LITTLE WEIRD AN HOUR AGO.
NOW?
NOW THIS... IS GETTING... SERIOUSLY, SERIOUSLY, SERIOUSLY, BENT.
YOU'RE NOT DEALING WITH SOME HELPLESS CHILD, HERE, PROFESSOR GRUBAUGH!
I HAVE A PLAN!

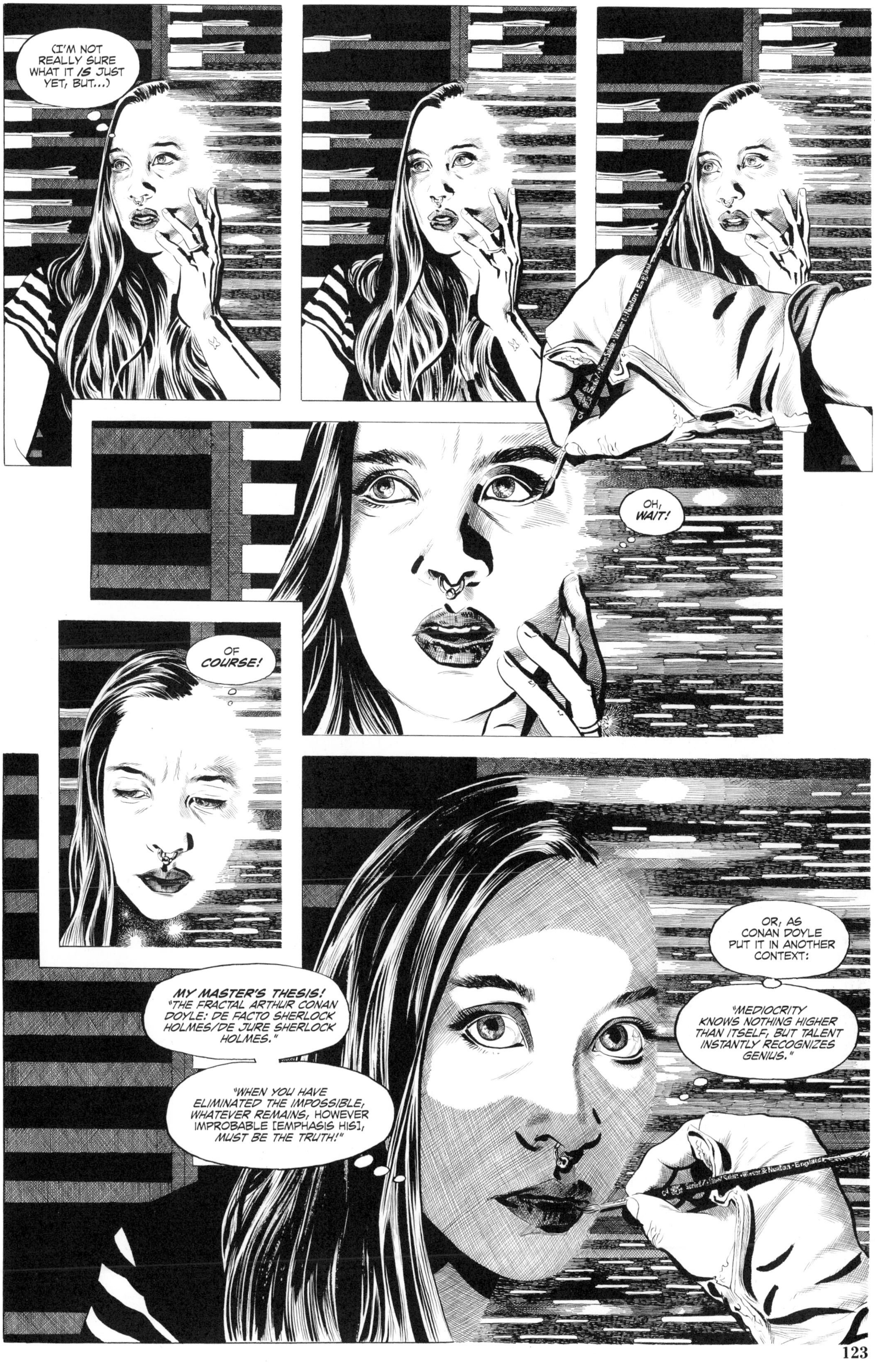

(I'M NOT REALLY SURE WHAT IT *IS* JUST YET, BUT...)
OH, *WAIT!*
OF *COURSE!*
OR, AS CONAN DOYLE PUT IT IN ANOTHER CONTEXT:
"MEDIOCRITY KNOWS NOTHING HIGHER THAN ITSELF, BUT TALENT INSTANTLY RECOGNIZES GENIUS."
**MY MASTER'S THESIS!** "THE FRACTAL ARTHUR CONAN DOYLE: DE FACTO SHERLOCK HOLMES/DE JURE SHERLOCK HOLMES."
"WHEN YOU HAVE ELIMINATED THE IMPOSSIBLE, WHATEVER REMAINS, HOWEVER IMPROBABLE [EMPHASIS HIS], MUST BE THE TRUTH!"

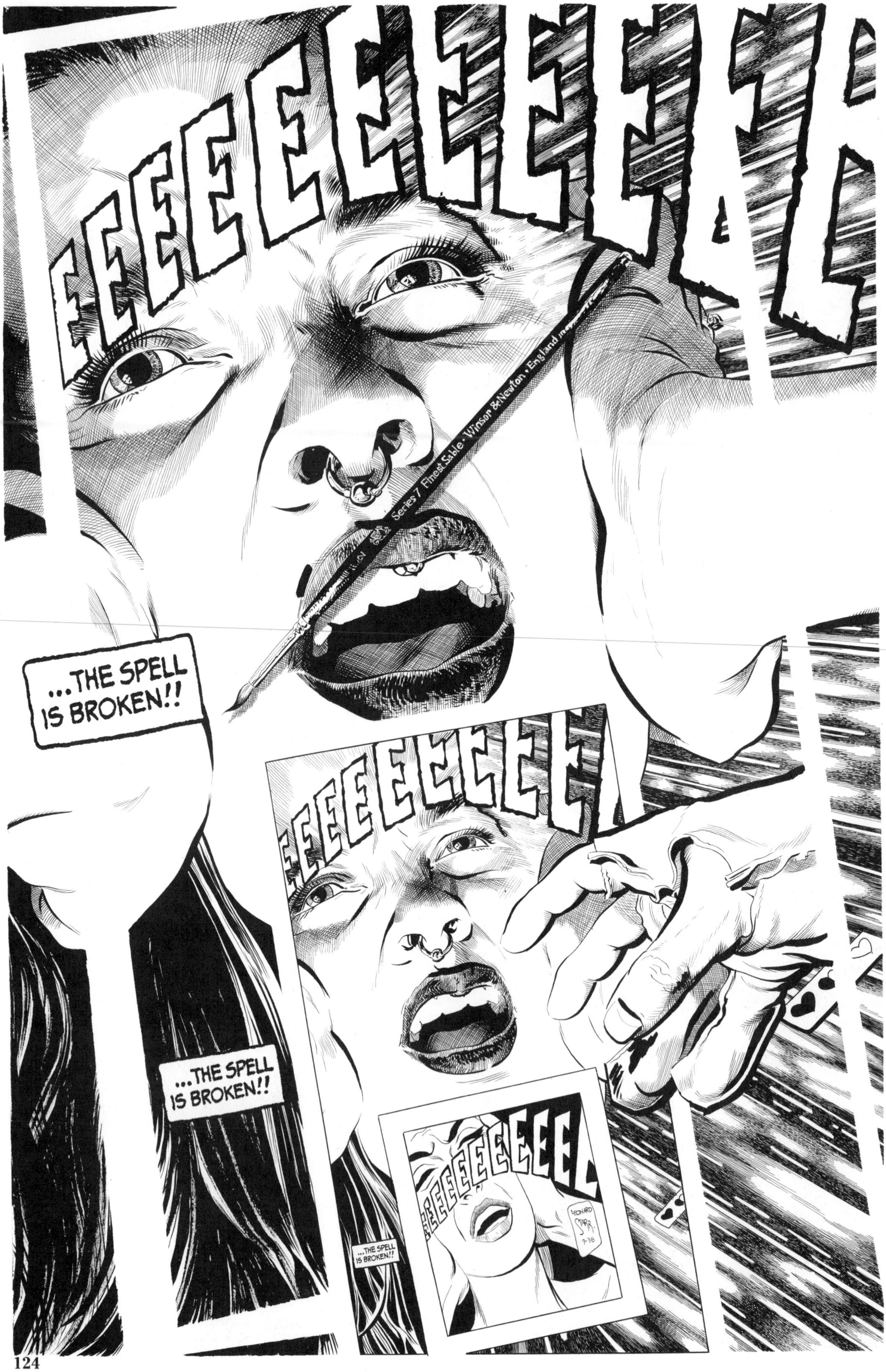
Series 7 Finest Sable · Winsor & Newton · England
...THE SPELL IS BROKEN!!
...THE SPELL IS BROKEN!!
...THE SPELL IS BROKEN!!

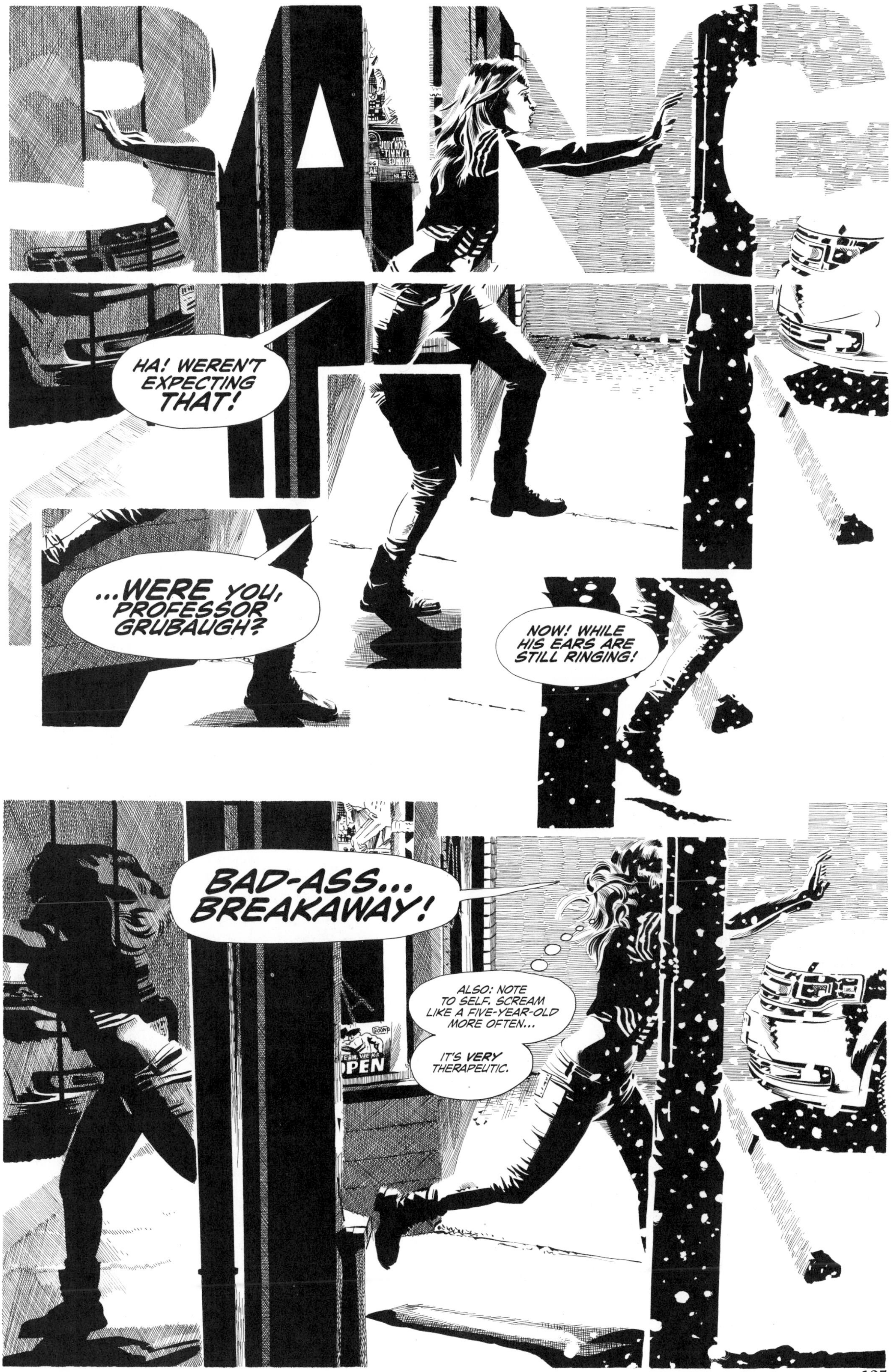
BANG
HA! WEREN'T EXPECTING THAT!
...WERE YOU, PROFESSOR GRUBAUGH?
NOW! WHILE HIS EARS ARE STILL RINGING!
BAD-ASS... BREAKAWAY!
ALSO: NOTE TO SELF. SCREAM LIKE A FIVE-YEAR-OLD MORE OFTEN...
IT'S VERY THERAPEUTIC.
OPEN

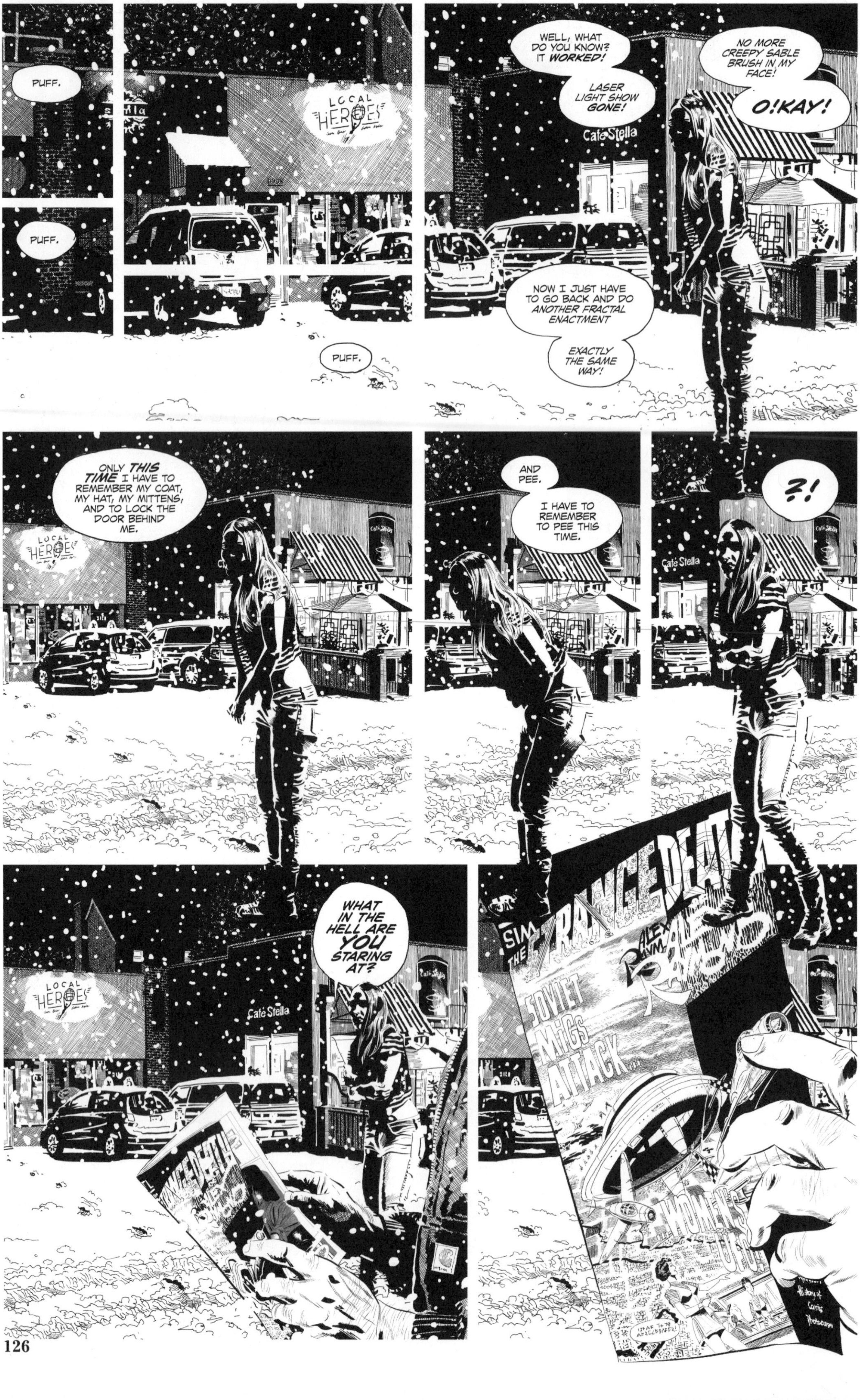
PUFF.
PUFF.
PUFF.
LOCAL HEROES
Café Stella
WELL, WHAT DO YOU KNOW? IT WORKED!
LASER LIGHT SHOW GONE!
NO MORE CREEPY SABLE BRUSH IN MY FACE!
O!KAY!
NOW I JUST HAVE TO GO BACK AND DO ANOTHER FRACTAL ENACTMENT
EXACTLY THE SAME WAY!
ONLY THIS TIME I HAVE TO REMEMBER MY COAT, MY HAT, MY MITTENS, AND TO LOCK THE DOOR BEHIND ME.
AND PEE.
I HAVE TO REMEMBER TO PEE THIS TIME.
?!
WHAT IN THE HELL ARE YOU STARING AT?
SOVIET MIGS ATTACK

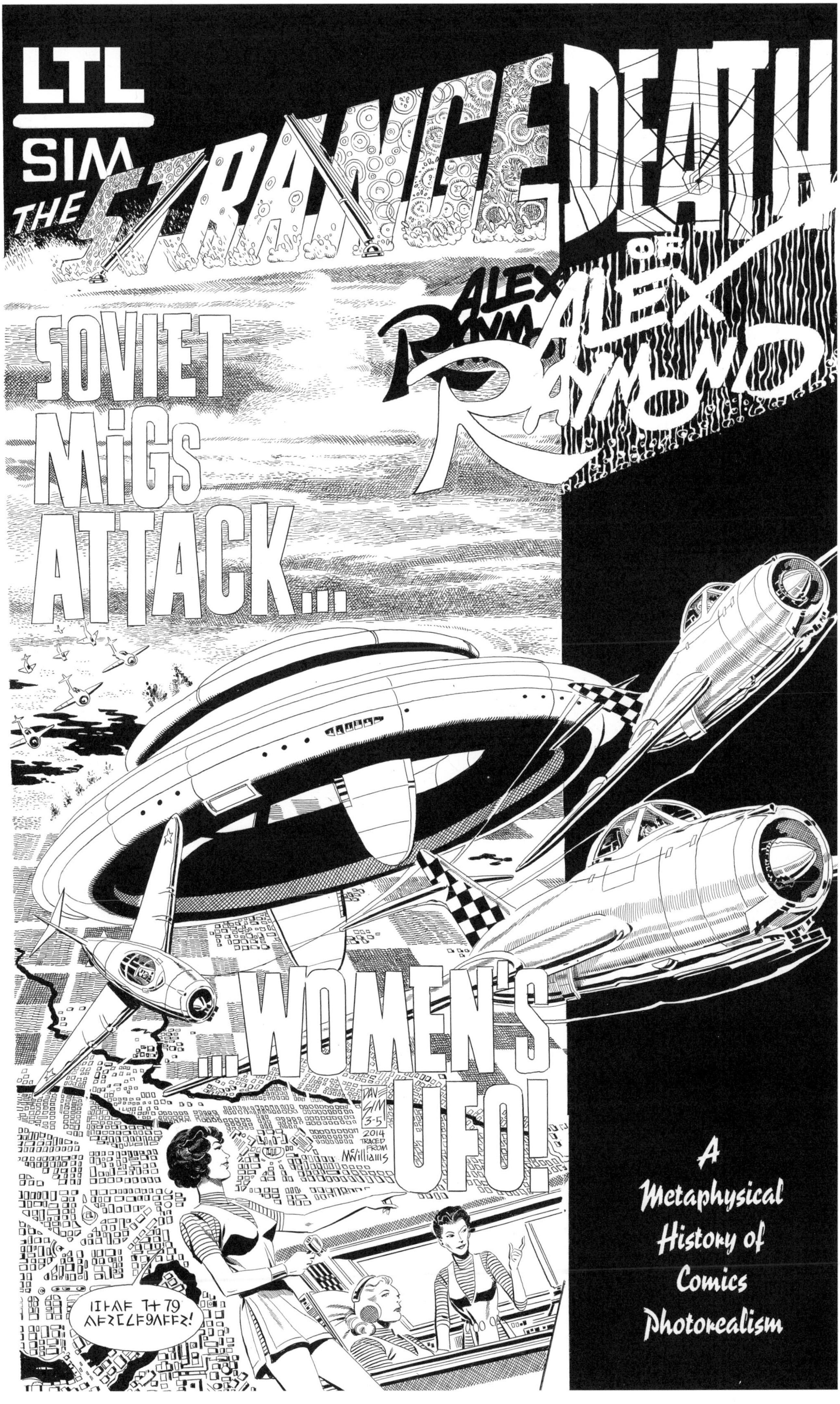
LTL
SIM
THE STRANGE DEATH
OF
ALEX RAYMOND
ALEX RAYMOND
SOVIET MiGS ATTACK...
...WOMEN'S UFO!
DAVE SIM 3-5 2014 TRACED FROM McWilliams
A Metaphysical History of Comics Photorealism

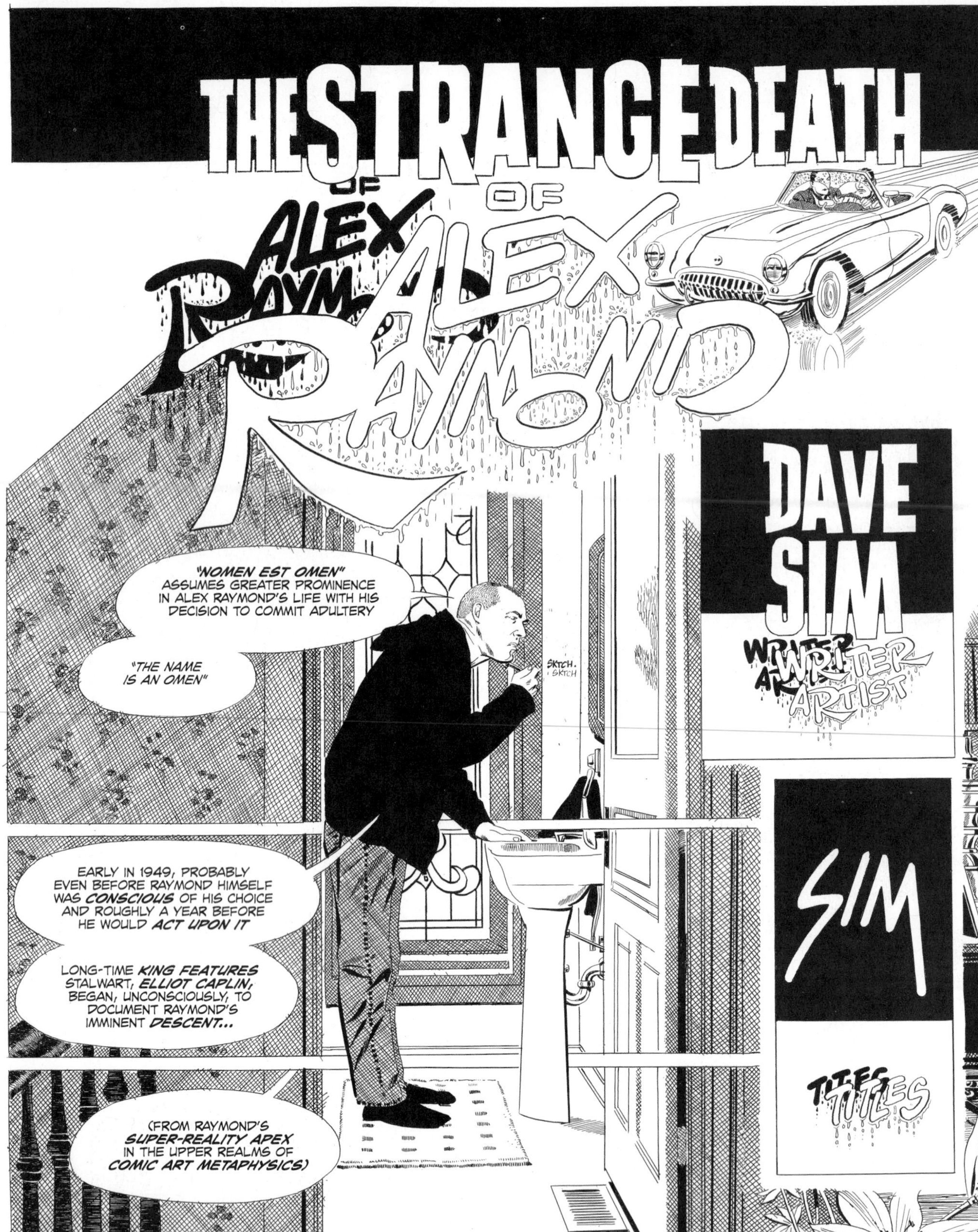
THE STRANGE DEATH OF ALEX RAYMOND
DAVE SIM
WRITER ARTIST
"NOMEN EST OMEN" ASSUMES GREATER PROMINENCE IN ALEX RAYMOND'S LIFE WITH HIS DECISION TO COMMIT ADULTERY
"THE NAME IS AN OMEN"
SKTCH. SKTCH
EARLY IN 1949, PROBABLY EVEN BEFORE RAYMOND HIMSELF WAS CONSCIOUS OF HIS CHOICE AND ROUGHLY A YEAR BEFORE HE WOULD ACT UPON IT
LONG-TIME KING FEATURES STALWART, ELLIOT CAPLIN, BEGAN, UNCONSCIOUSLY, TO DOCUMENT RAYMOND'S IMMINENT DESCENT...
(FROM RAYMOND'S SUPER-REALITY APEX IN THE UPPER REALMS OF COMIC ART METAPHYSICS)
SIM
TITLES

For international rights, contact **livingthelinepublishing@gmail.com**

LTL

www.LIVINGTHELINE.com

**Sean Robinson**, President & Publisher • **Sean Robinson**, Editor-in-Chief • **Sean Robinson**, EVP/Sr. Art Director • **Sean Robinson**, Chief Financial Officer • **Sean Robinson**, Chief Accounting Officer • **Sean Robinson**, SVP of Sales and Marketing • **Sean Robinson**, Associate Publisher • **Sean Robinson**, VP of New Product Development • **Sean Robinson**, VP of Digital Services • **Sean Robinson**, Editorial Director, Graphic Novels and Collections • **Sean Robinson**, Sr. Director, Licensing & Business Development

**Sean Robinson**, LTL Founder

Facebook: **facebook.com/livingtheline**• Twitter: **@ltlpublishing** • YouTube: **youtube.com/ltlpublishing**
Tumblr: **tumblr.ltlpublishing.com** • Instagram: **instagram.com/ltlpublishing**

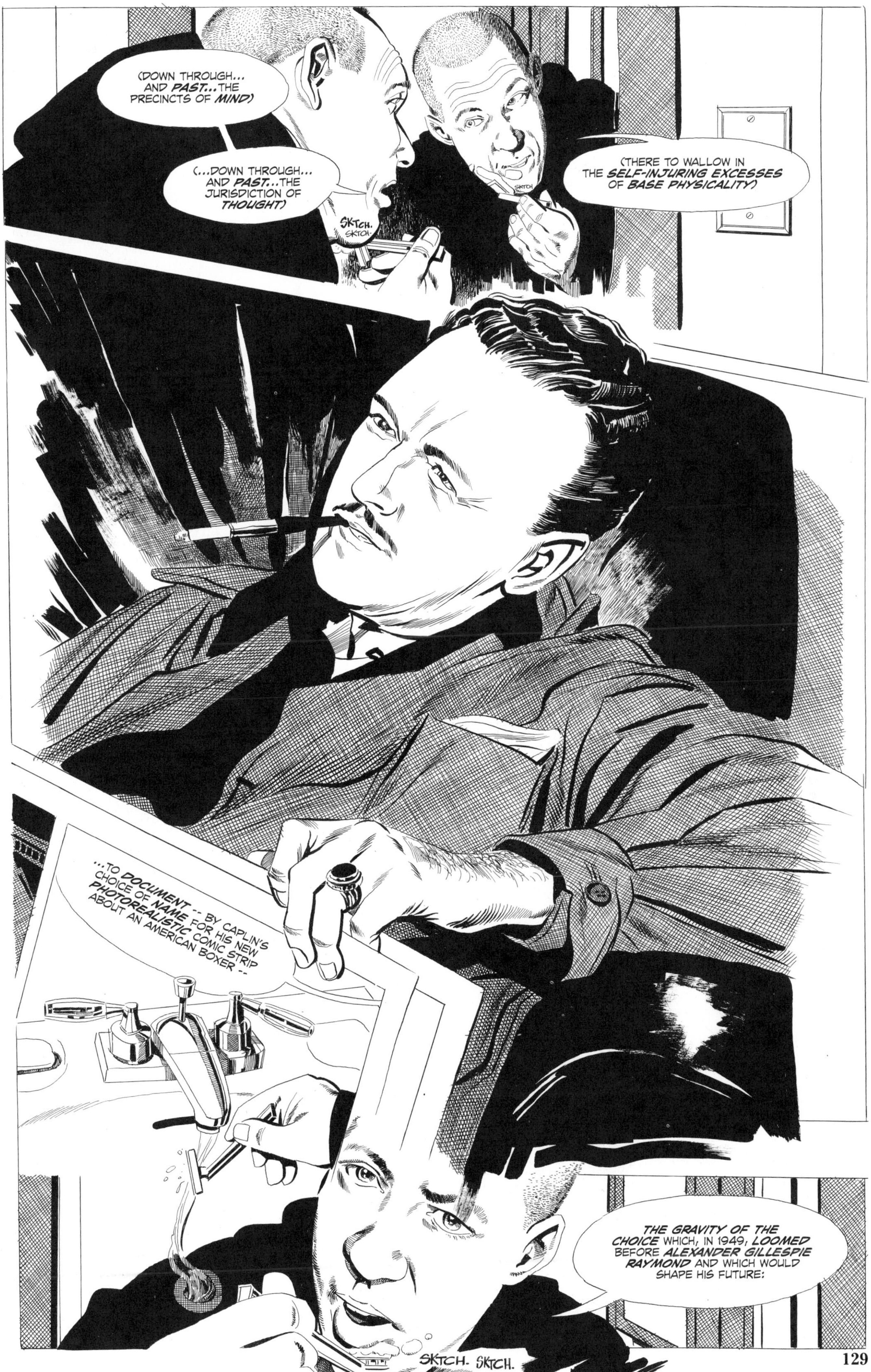
(DOWN THROUGH... AND PAST...THE PRECINCTS OF MIND)
(...DOWN THROUGH... AND PAST...THE JURISDICTION OF THOUGHT)
SKTCH. SKTCH.
SKTCH
(THERE TO WALLOW IN THE SELF-INJURING EXCESSES OF BASE PHYSICALITY)
...TO DOCUMENT -- BY CAPLIN'S CHOICE OF NAME FOR HIS NEW PHOTOREALISTIC COMIC STRIP ABOUT AN AMERICAN BOXER --
THE GRAVITY OF THE CHOICE WHICH, IN 1949, LOOMED BEFORE ALEXANDER GILLESPIE RAYMOND AND WHICH WOULD SHAPE HIS FUTURE:
SKTCH. SKTCH.

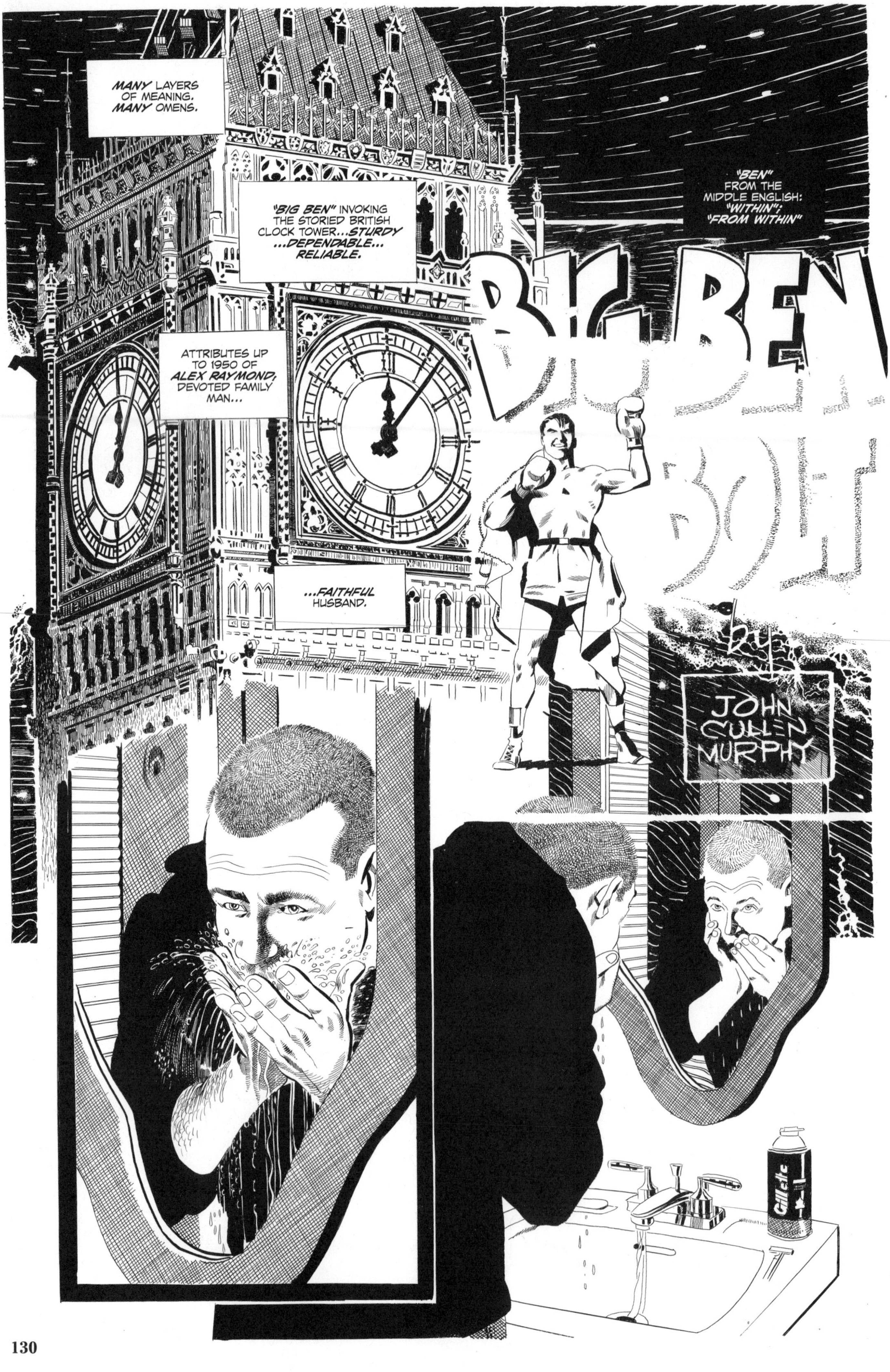

MANY LAYERS OF MEANING. MANY OMENS.
"BIG BEN" INVOKING THE STORIED BRITISH CLOCK TOWER...STURDY ...DEPENDABLE... RELIABLE.
ATTRIBUTES UP TO 1950 OF ALEX RAYMOND, DEVOTED FAMILY MAN...
...FAITHFUL HUSBAND.
"BEN" FROM THE MIDDLE ENGLISH: "WITHIN": "FROM WITHIN"
BIG BEN BOLT
by
JOHN CULLEN MURPHY

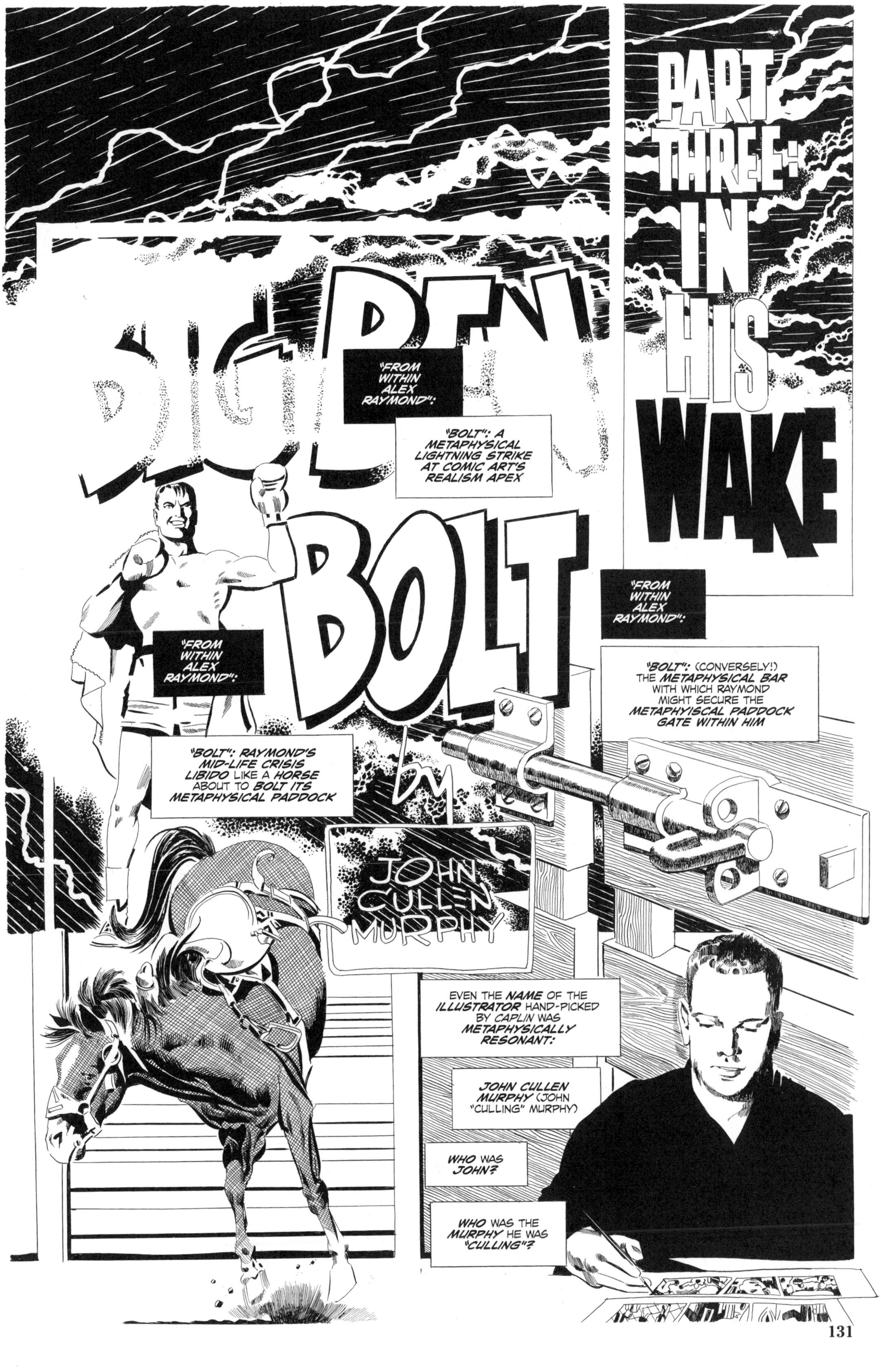
PART THREE: IN HIS WAKE
"FROM WITHIN ALEX RAYMOND":
"BOLT": A METAPHYSICAL LIGHTNING STRIKE AT COMIC ART'S REALISM APEX
BOLT
"FROM WITHIN ALEX RAYMOND":
"BOLT": RAYMOND'S MID-LIFE CRISIS LIBIDO LIKE A HORSE ABOUT TO BOLT ITS METAPHYSICAL PADDOCK
by
JOHN CULLEN MURPHY
"FROM WITHIN ALEX RAYMOND":
"BOLT": (CONVERSELY!) THE METAPHYSICAL BAR WITH WHICH RAYMOND MIGHT SECURE THE METAPHYISCAL PADDOCK GATE WITHIN HIM
EVEN THE NAME OF THE ILLUSTRATOR HAND-PICKED BY CAPLIN WAS METAPHYSICALLY RESONANT:
JOHN CULLEN MURPHY (JOHN "CULLING" MURPHY)
WHO WAS JOHN?
WHO WAS THE MURPHY HE WAS "CULLING"?

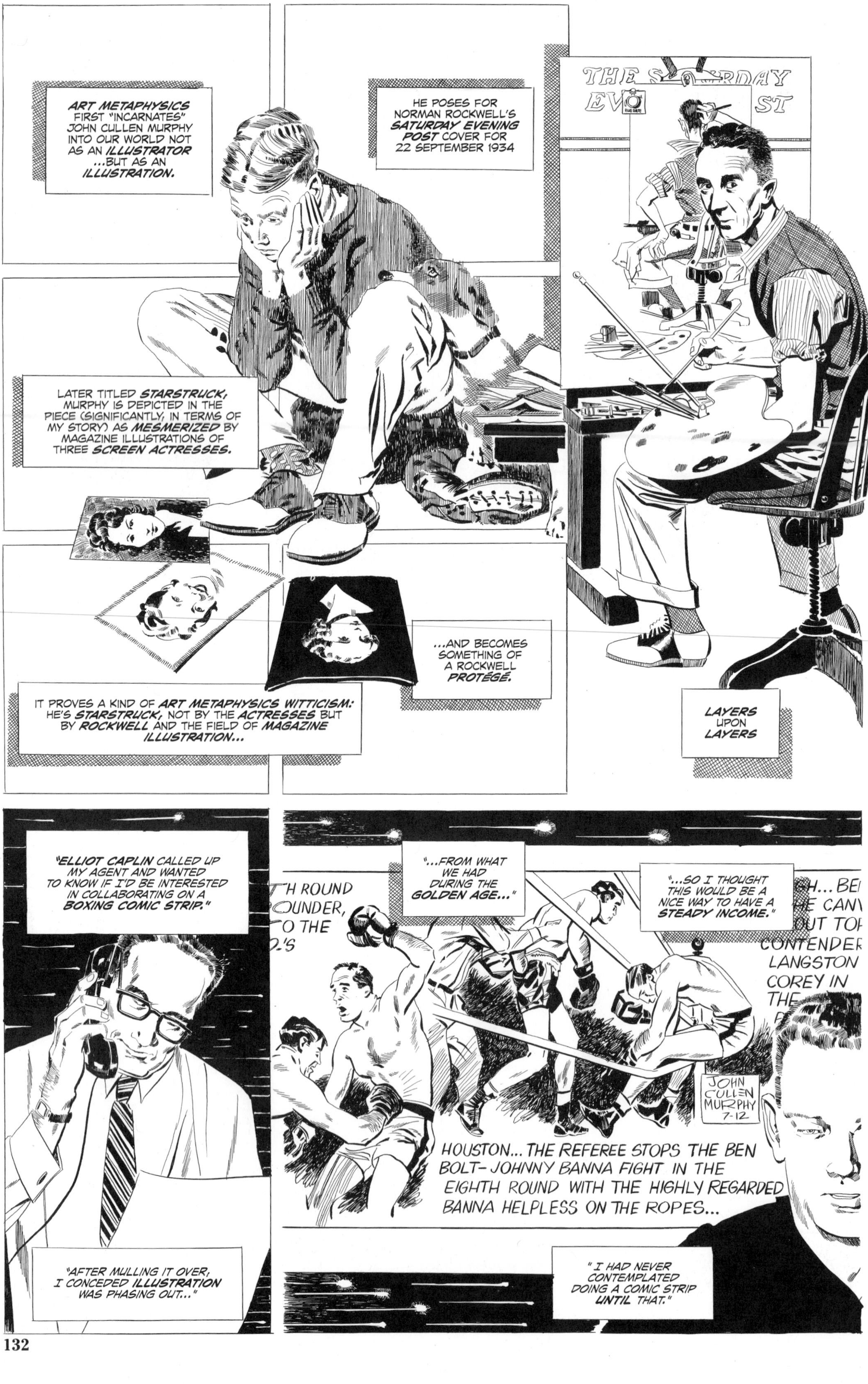
ART METAPHYSICS FIRST "INCARNATES" JOHN CULLEN MURPHY INTO OUR WORLD NOT AS AN ILLUSTRATOR ...BUT AS AN ILLUSTRATION.
HE POSES FOR NORMAN ROCKWELL'S SATURDAY EVENING POST COVER FOR 22 SEPTEMBER 1934
LATER TITLED STARSTRUCK, MURPHY IS DEPICTED IN THE PIECE (SIGNIFICANTLY, IN TERMS OF MY STORY) AS MESMERIZED BY MAGAZINE ILLUSTRATIONS OF THREE SCREEN ACTRESSES.
IT PROVES A KIND OF ART METAPHYSICS WITTICISM: HE'S STARSTRUCK, NOT BY THE ACTRESSES BUT BY ROCKWELL AND THE FIELD OF MAGAZINE ILLUSTRATION...
...AND BECOMES SOMETHING OF A ROCKWELL PROTÉGÉ.
LAYERS UPON LAYERS
"ELLIOT CAPLIN CALLED UP MY AGENT AND WANTED TO KNOW IF I'D BE INTERESTED IN COLLABORATING ON A BOXING COMIC STRIP."
"...FROM WHAT WE HAD DURING THE GOLDEN AGE..."
"...SO I THOUGHT THIS WOULD BE A NICE WAY TO HAVE A STEADY INCOME."
JOHN CULLEN MURPHY 7-12
HOUSTON... THE REFEREE STOPS THE BEN BOLT- JOHNNY BANNA FIGHT IN THE EIGHTH ROUND WITH THE HIGHLY REGARDED BANNA HELPLESS ON THE ROPES...
"AFTER MULLING IT OVER, I CONCEDED ILLUSTRATION WAS PHASING OUT..."
"I HAD NEVER CONTEMPLATED DOING A COMIC STRIP UNTIL THAT."

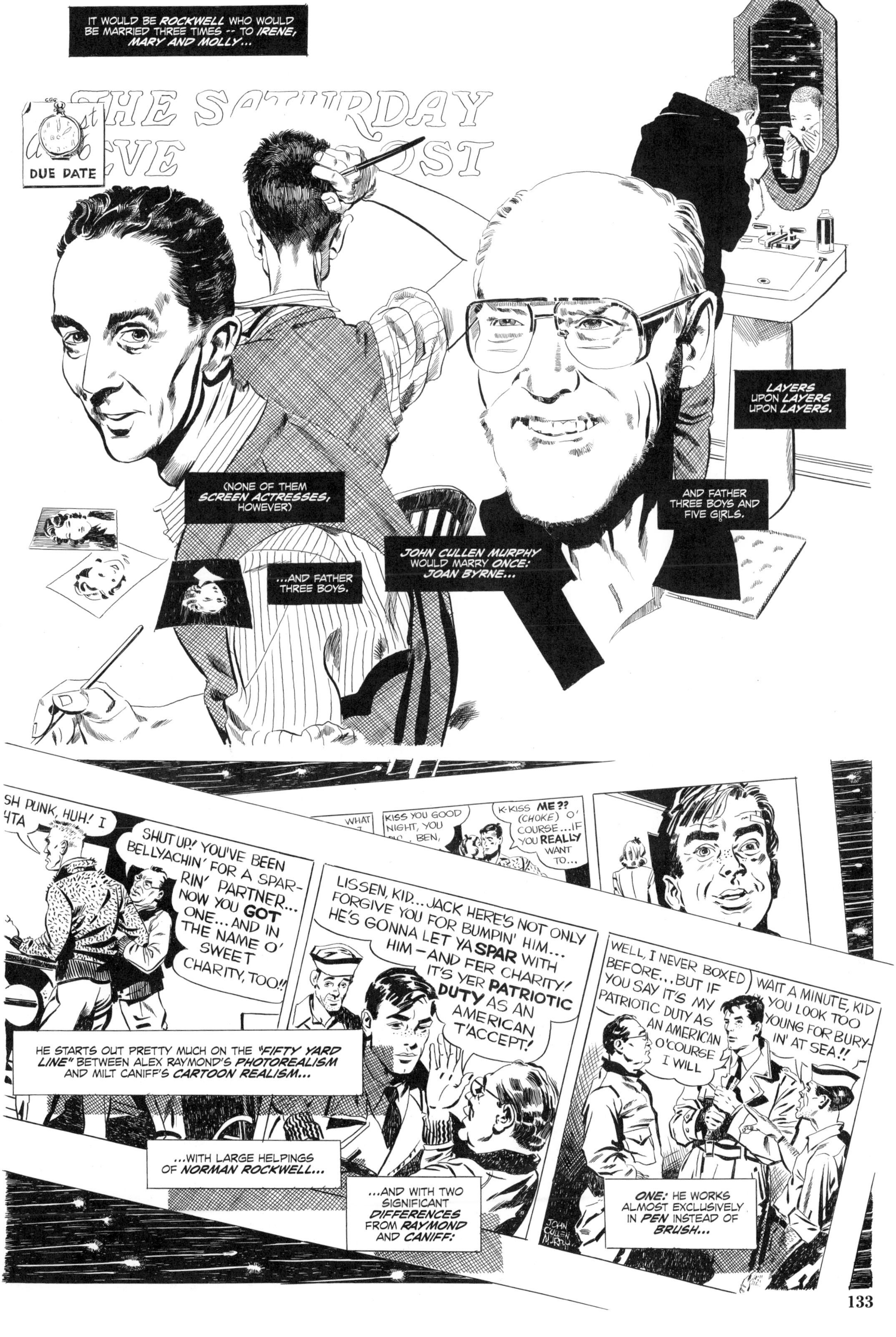

IT WOULD BE ROCKWELL WHO WOULD BE MARRIED THREE TIMES -- TO IRENE, MARY AND MOLLY...
THE SATURDAY EVE POST
DUE DATE
LAYERS UPON LAYERS UPON LAYERS.
(NONE OF THEM SCREEN ACTRESSES, HOWEVER)
AND FATHER THREE BOYS AND FIVE GIRLS.
...AND FATHER THREE BOYS.
JOHN CULLEN MURPHY WOULD MARRY ONCE: JOAN BYRNE...
SH PUNK, HUH! I
SHUT UP! YOU'VE BEEN BELLYACHIN' FOR A SPAR-RIN' PARTNER... NOW YOU GOT ONE... AND IN THE NAME O' SWEET CHARITY, TOO!!
KISS YOU GOOD NIGHT, YOU BEN,
K-KISS ME?? (CHOKE) O' COURSE...IF YOU REALLY WANT TO...
LISSEN, KID... JACK HERE'S NOT ONLY FORGIVE YOU FOR BUMPIN' HIM... HE'S GONNA LET YA SPAR WITH HIM – AND FER CHARITY! IT'S YER PATRIOTIC DUTY AS AN AMERICAN T'ACCEPT!
WELL, I NEVER BOXED BEFORE...BUT IF YOU SAY IT'S MY PATRIOTIC DUTY AS AN AMERICAN O'COURSE I WILL
WAIT A MINUTE, KID YOU LOOK TOO YOUNG FOR BURY-IN' AT SEA!!
HE STARTS OUT PRETTY MUCH ON THE "FIFTY YARD LINE" BETWEEN ALEX RAYMOND'S PHOTOREALISM AND MILT CANIFF'S CARTOON REALISM...
...WITH LARGE HELPINGS OF NORMAN ROCKWELL...
...AND WITH TWO SIGNIFICANT DIFFERENCES FROM RAYMOND AND CANIFF:
ONE: HE WORKS ALMOST EXCLUSIVELY IN PEN INSTEAD OF BRUSH...
JOHN CULLEN MURPHY

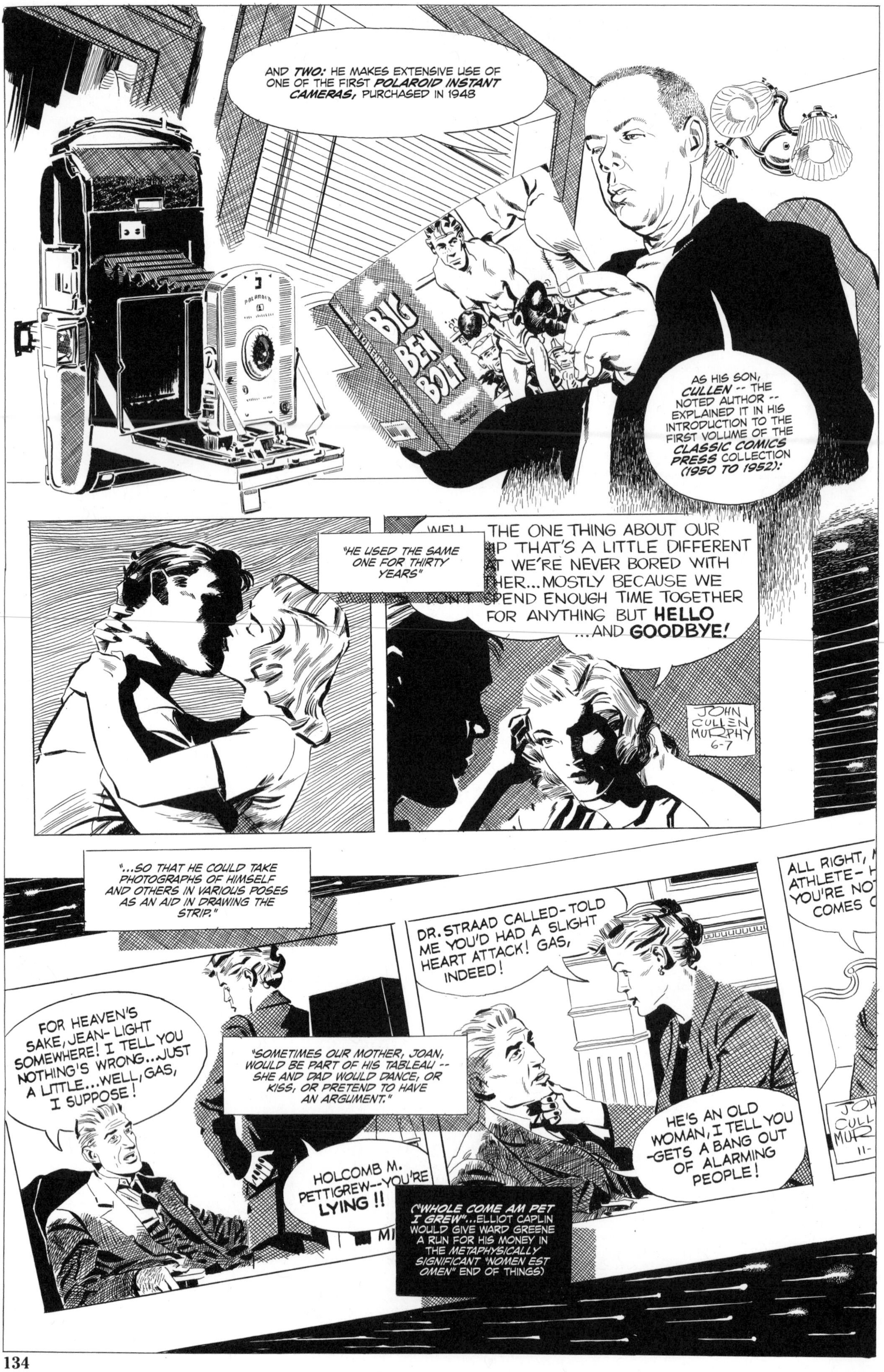
AND TWO: HE MAKES EXTENSIVE USE OF ONE OF THE FIRST POLAROID INSTANT CAMERAS, PURCHASED IN 1948
BIG BEN BOLT
AS HIS SON, CULLEN -- THE NOTED AUTHOR -- EXPLAINED IT IN HIS INTRODUCTION TO THE FIRST VOLUME OF THE CLASSIC COMICS PRESS COLLECTION (1950 TO 1952):
"HE USED THE SAME ONE FOR THIRTY YEARS"
THE ONE THING ABOUT OUR
THAT'S A LITTLE DIFFERENT
WE'RE NEVER BORED WITH
...MOSTLY BECAUSE WE
SPEND ENOUGH TIME TOGETHER FOR ANYTHING BUT HELLO ...AND GOODBYE!
JOHN CULLEN MURPHY 6-7
"...SO THAT HE COULD TAKE PHOTOGRAPHS OF HIMSELF AND OTHERS IN VARIOUS POSES AS AN AID IN DRAWING THE STRIP."
FOR HEAVEN'S SAKE, JEAN- LIGHT SOMEWHERE! I TELL YOU NOTHING'S WRONG...JUST A LITTLE...WELL, GAS, I SUPPOSE!
"SOMETIMES OUR MOTHER, JOAN, WOULD BE PART OF HIS TABLEAU -- SHE AND DAD WOULD DANCE, OR KISS, OR PRETEND TO HAVE AN ARGUMENT."
HOLCOMB M. PETTIGREW--YOU'RE LYING !!
("WHOLE COME AM PET I GREW"...ELLIOT CAPLIN WOULD GIVE WARD GREENE A RUN FOR HIS MONEY IN THE METAPHYSICALLY SIGNIFICANT "NOMEN EST OMEN" END OF THINGS)
DR. STRAAD CALLED- TOLD ME YOU'D HAD A SLIGHT HEART ATTACK! GAS, INDEED!
HE'S AN OLD WOMAN, I TELL YOU -GETS A BANG OUT OF ALARMING PEOPLE!
ALL RIGHT,

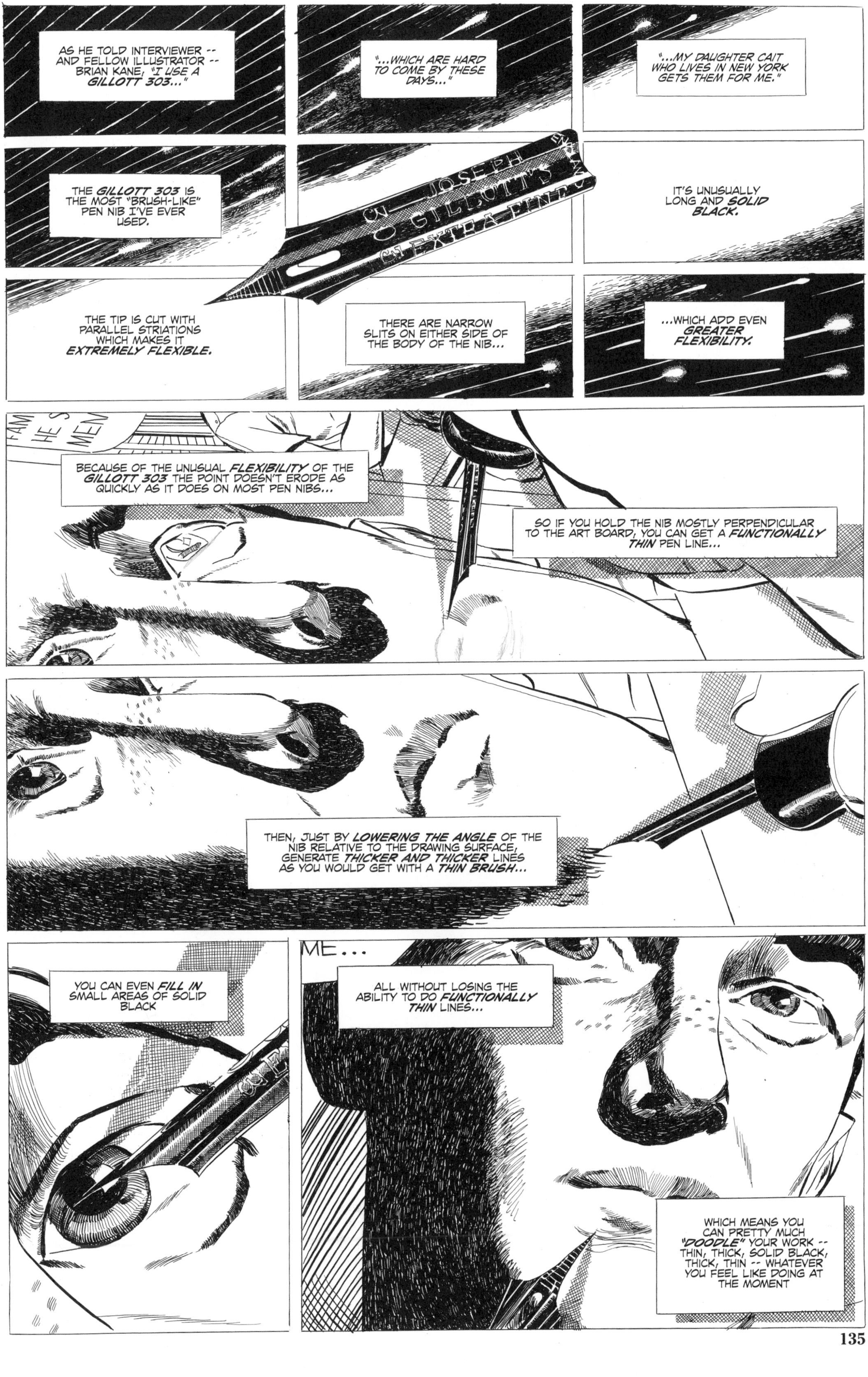
AS HE TOLD INTERVIEWER -- AND FELLOW ILLUSTRATOR -- BRIAN KANE, "I USE A GILLOTT 303..."
"...WHICH ARE HARD TO COME BY THESE DAYS..."
"...MY DAUGHTER CAIT WHO LIVES IN NEW YORK GETS THEM FOR ME."
THE GILLOTT 303 IS THE MOST "BRUSH-LIKE" PEN NIB I'VE EVER USED.
IT'S UNUSUALLY LONG AND SOLID BLACK.
THE TIP IS CUT WITH PARALLEL STRIATIONS WHICH MAKES IT EXTREMELY FLEXIBLE.
THERE ARE NARROW SLITS ON EITHER SIDE OF THE BODY OF THE NIB...
...WHICH ADD EVEN GREATER FLEXIBILITY.
BECAUSE OF THE UNUSUAL FLEXIBILITY OF THE GILLOTT 303 THE POINT DOESN'T ERODE AS QUICKLY AS IT DOES ON MOST PEN NIBS...
SO IF YOU HOLD THE NIB MOSTLY PERPENDICULAR TO THE ART BOARD, YOU CAN GET A FUNCTIONALLY THIN PEN LINE...
THEN, JUST BY LOWERING THE ANGLE OF THE NIB RELATIVE TO THE DRAWING SURFACE, GENERATE THICKER AND THICKER LINES AS YOU WOULD GET WITH A THIN BRUSH...
YOU CAN EVEN FILL IN SMALL AREAS OF SOLID BLACK
ALL WITHOUT LOSING THE ABILITY TO DO FUNCTIONALLY THIN LINES...
WHICH MEANS YOU CAN PRETTY MUCH "DOODLE" YOUR WORK -- THIN, THICK, SOLID BLACK, THICK, THIN -- WHATEVER YOU FEEL LIKE DOING AT THE MOMENT

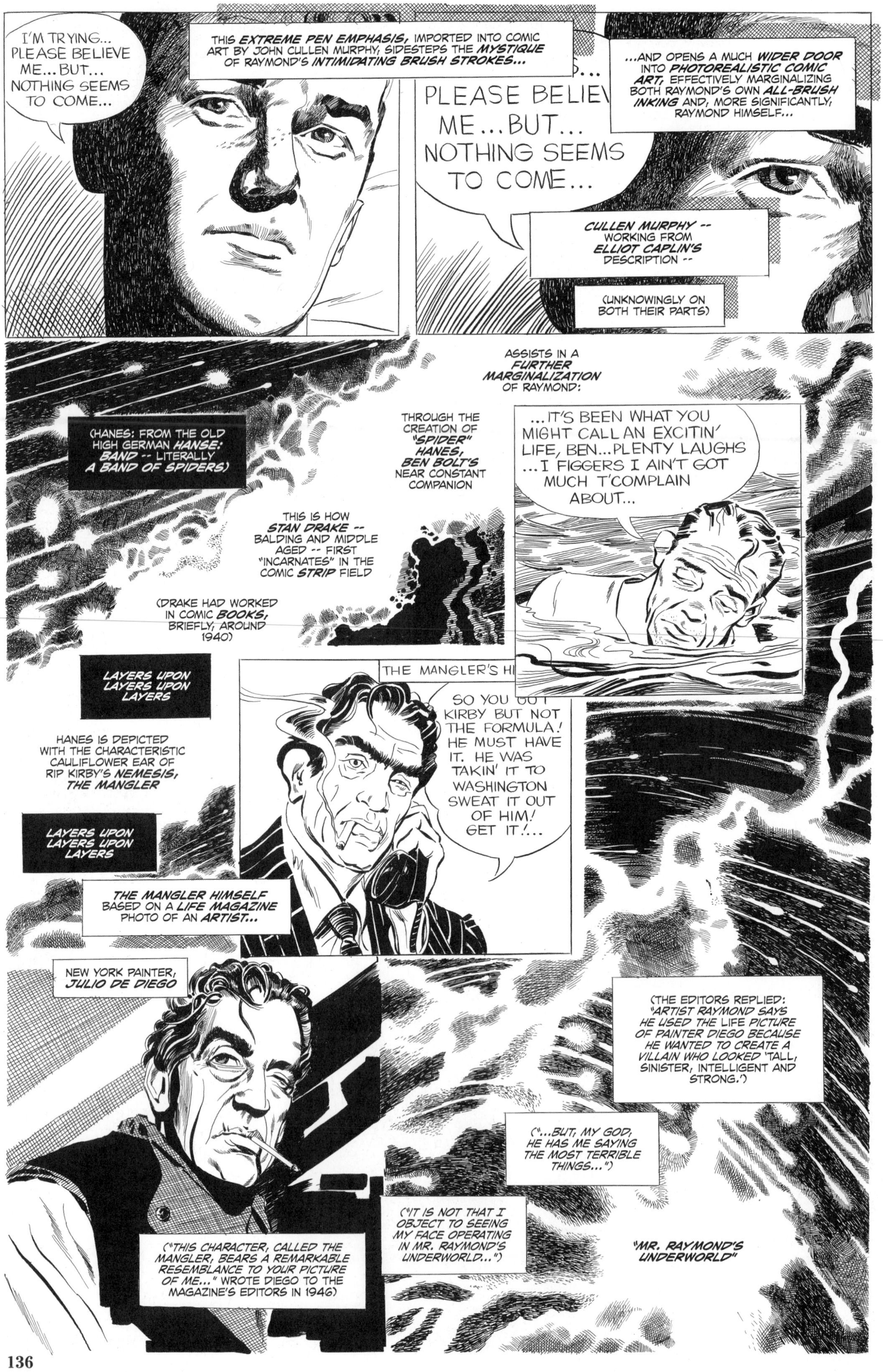

I'M TRYING... PLEASE BELIEVE ME...BUT... NOTHING SEEMS TO COME...
THIS EXTREME PEN EMPHASIS, IMPORTED INTO COMIC ART BY JOHN CULLEN MURPHY, SIDESTEPS THE MYSTIQUE OF RAYMOND'S INTIMIDATING BRUSH STROKES...
PLEASE BELIEV ME...BUT... NOTHING SEEMS TO COME...
...AND OPENS A MUCH WIDER DOOR INTO PHOTOREALISTIC COMIC ART, EFFECTIVELY MARGINALIZING BOTH RAYMOND'S OWN ALL-BRUSH INKING AND, MORE SIGNIFICANTLY, RAYMOND HIMSELF...
CULLEN MURPHY -- WORKING FROM ELLIOT CAPLIN'S DESCRIPTION --
(UNKNOWINGLY ON BOTH THEIR PARTS)
ASSISTS IN A FURTHER MARGINALIZATION OF RAYMOND:
(HANES: FROM THE OLD HIGH GERMAN HANSE: BAND -- LITERALLY A BAND OF SPIDERS)
THROUGH THE CREATION OF "SPIDER" HANES, BEN BOLT'S NEAR CONSTANT COMPANION
...IT'S BEEN WHAT YOU MIGHT CALL AN EXCITIN' LIFE, BEN...PLENTY LAUGHS ...I FIGGERS I AIN'T GOT MUCH T'COMPLAIN ABOUT...
THIS IS HOW STAN DRAKE -- BALDING AND MIDDLE AGED -- FIRST "INCARNATES" IN THE COMIC STRIP FIELD
(DRAKE HAD WORKED IN COMIC BOOKS, BRIEFLY, AROUND 1940)
LAYERS UPON LAYERS UPON LAYERS
THE MANGLER'S HI
SO YOU GOT KIRBY BUT NOT THE FORMULA! HE MUST HAVE IT. HE WAS TAKIN' IT TO WASHINGTON SWEAT IT OUT OF HIM! GET IT!...
HANES IS DEPICTED WITH THE CHARACTERISTIC CAULIFLOWER EAR OF RIP KIRBY'S NEMESIS, THE MANGLER
LAYERS UPON LAYERS UPON LAYERS
THE MANGLER HIMSELF BASED ON A LIFE MAGAZINE PHOTO OF AN ARTIST...
NEW YORK PAINTER, JULIO DE DIEGO
(THE EDITORS REPLIED: "ARTIST RAYMOND SAYS HE USED THE LIFE PICTURE OF PAINTER DIEGO BECAUSE HE WANTED TO CREATE A VILLAIN WHO LOOKED 'TALL, SINISTER, INTELLIGENT AND STRONG.'")
("...BUT, MY GOD, HE HAS ME SAYING THE MOST TERRIBLE THINGS...")
("IT IS NOT THAT I OBJECT TO SEEING MY FACE OPERATING IN MR. RAYMOND'S UNDERWORLD...")
"MR. RAYMOND'S UNDERWORLD"
("THIS CHARACTER, CALLED THE MANGLER, BEARS A REMARKABLE RESEMBLANCE TO YOUR PICTURE OF ME..." WROTE DIEGO TO THE MAGAZINE'S EDITORS IN 1946)

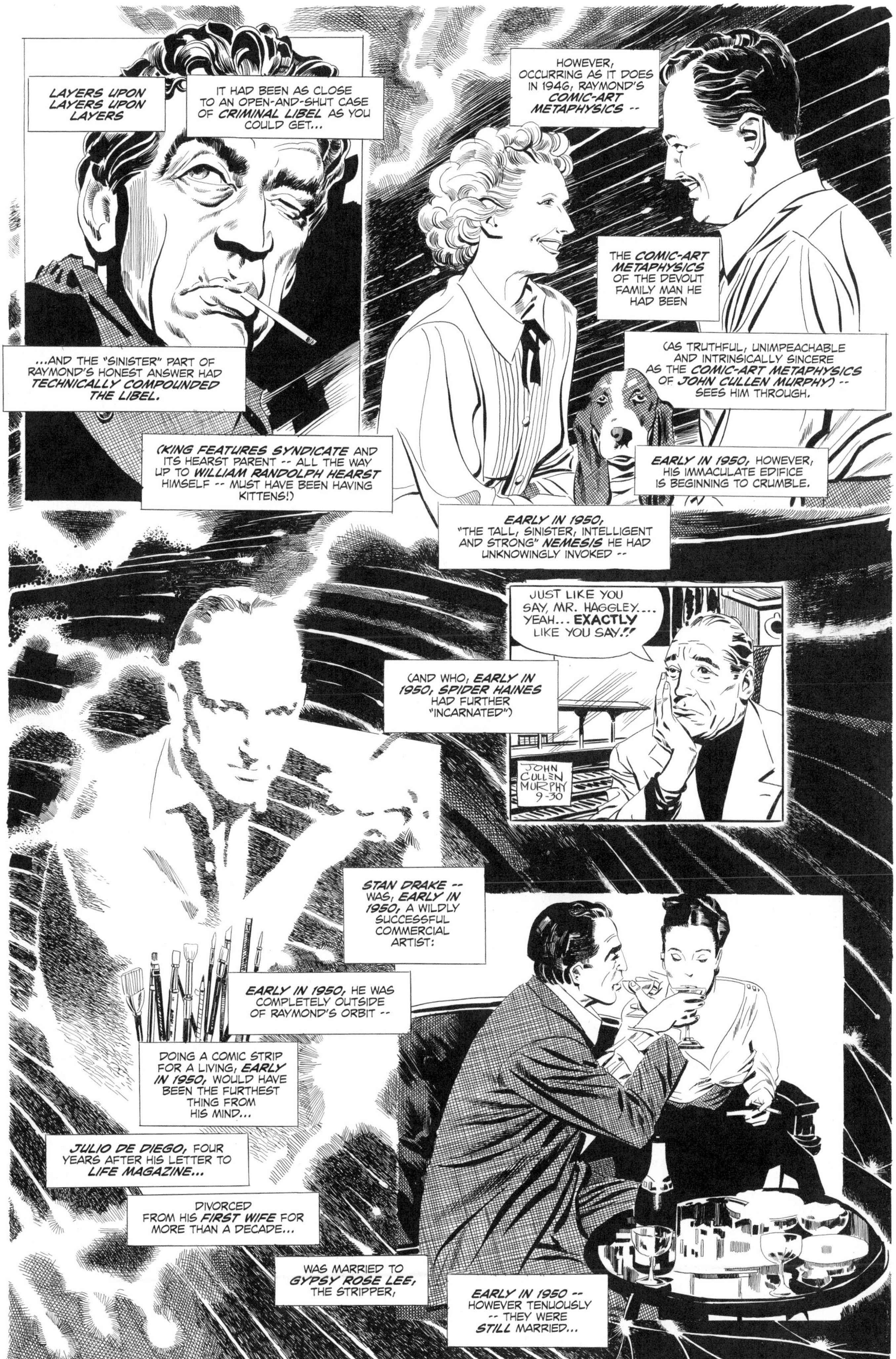
LAYERS UPON LAYERS UPON LAYERS
IT HAD BEEN AS CLOSE TO AN OPEN-AND-SHUT CASE OF CRIMINAL LIBEL AS YOU COULD GET...
...AND THE "SINISTER" PART OF RAYMOND'S HONEST ANSWER HAD TECHNICALLY COMPOUNDED THE LIBEL.
(KING FEATURES SYNDICATE AND ITS HEARST PARENT -- ALL THE WAY UP TO WILLIAM RANDOLPH HEARST HIMSELF -- MUST HAVE BEEN HAVING KITTENS!)
HOWEVER, OCCURRING AS IT DOES IN 1946, RAYMOND'S COMIC-ART METAPHYSICS --
THE COMIC-ART METAPHYSICS OF THE DEVOUT FAMILY MAN HE HAD BEEN
(AS TRUTHFUL, UNIMPEACHABLE AND INTRINSICALLY SINCERE AS THE COMIC-ART METAPHYSICS OF JOHN CULLEN MURPHY) -- SEES HIM THROUGH.
EARLY IN 1950, HOWEVER, HIS IMMACULATE EDIFICE IS BEGINNING TO CRUMBLE.
EARLY IN 1950, "THE TALL, SINISTER, INTELLIGENT AND STRONG" NEMESIS HE HAD UNKNOWINGLY INVOKED --
JUST LIKE YOU SAY, MR. HAGGLEY.... YEAH... EXACTLY LIKE YOU SAY!!
(AND WHO, EARLY IN 1950, SPIDER HAINES HAD FURTHER "INCARNATED")
JOHN CULLEN MURPHY 9-30
STAN DRAKE -- WAS, EARLY IN 1950, A WILDLY SUCCESSFUL COMMERCIAL ARTIST:
EARLY IN 1950, HE WAS COMPLETELY OUTSIDE OF RAYMOND'S ORBIT --
DOING A COMIC STRIP FOR A LIVING, EARLY IN 1950, WOULD HAVE BEEN THE FURTHEST THING FROM HIS MIND...
JULIO DE DIEGO, FOUR YEARS AFTER HIS LETTER TO LIFE MAGAZINE...
DIVORCED FROM HIS FIRST WIFE FOR MORE THAN A DECADE...
WAS MARRIED TO GYPSY ROSE LEE, THE STRIPPER,
EARLY IN 1950 -- HOWEVER TENUOUSLY -- THEY WERE STILL MARRIED...

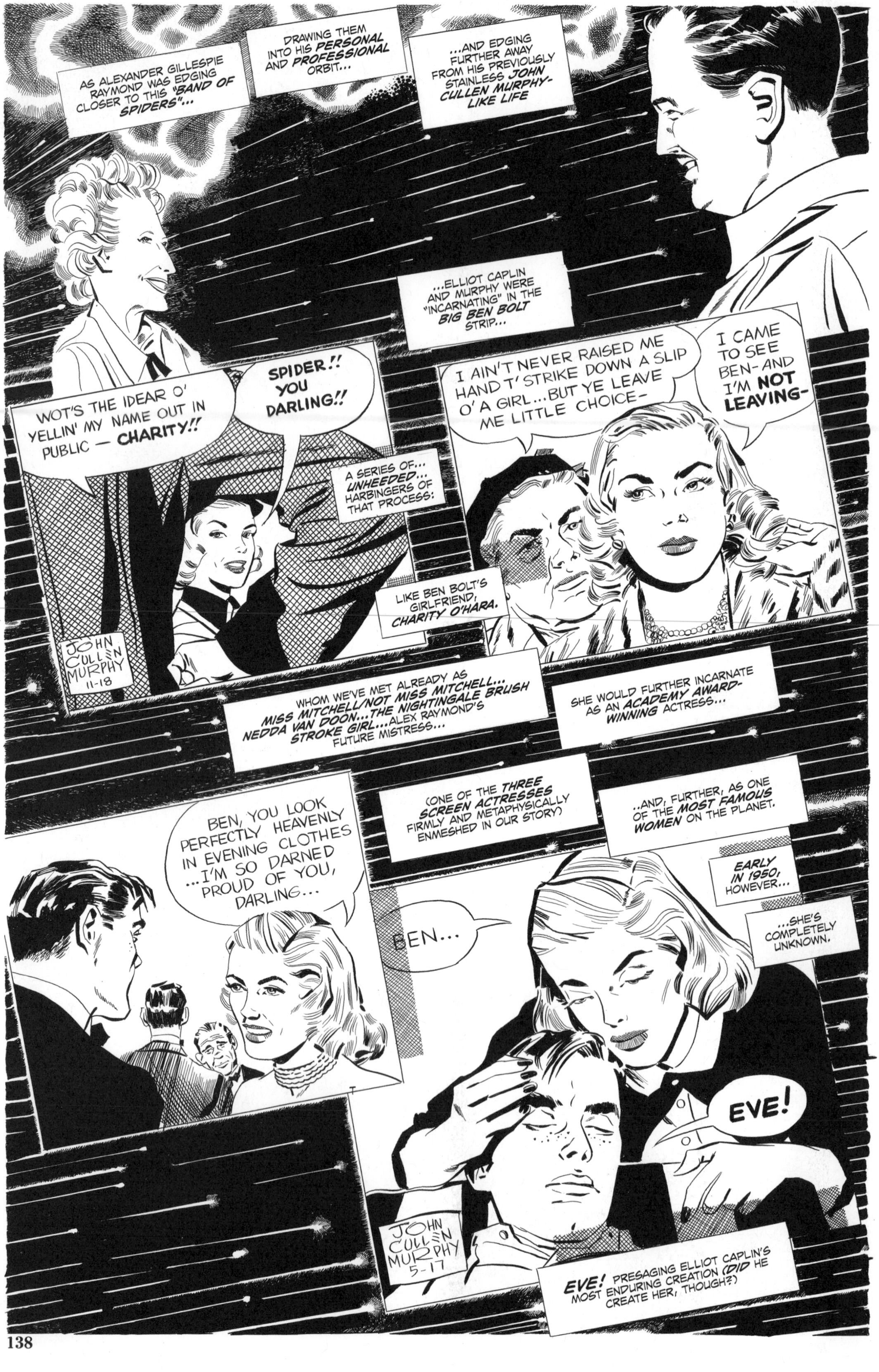

AS ALEXANDER GILLESPIE RAYMOND WAS EDGING CLOSER TO THIS "BAND OF SPIDERS"...
DRAWING THEM INTO HIS PERSONAL AND PROFESSIONAL ORBIT...
...AND EDGING FURTHER AWAY FROM HIS PREVIOUSLY STAINLESS JOHN CULLEN MURPHY-LIKE LIFE
...ELLIOT CAPLIN AND MURPHY WERE "INCARNATING" IN THE BIG BEN BOLT STRIP...
WOT'S THE IDEAR O' YELLIN' MY NAME OUT IN PUBLIC — CHARITY!!
SPIDER!! YOU DARLING!!
A SERIES OF... UNHEEDED... HARBINGERS OF THAT PROCESS:
LIKE BEN BOLT'S GIRLFRIEND, CHARITY O'HARA.
JOHN CULLEN MURPHY 11-18
I AIN'T NEVER RAISED ME HAND T' STRIKE DOWN A SLIP O' A GIRL...BUT YE LEAVE ME LITTLE CHOICE-
I CAME TO SEE BEN-AND I'M NOT LEAVING-
WHOM WE'VE MET ALREADY AS MISS MITCHELL/NOT MISS MITCHELL... NEDDA VAN DOON...THE NIGHTINGALE BRUSH STROKE GIRL...ALEX RAYMOND'S FUTURE MISTRESS...
SHE WOULD FURTHER INCARNATE AS AN ACADEMY AWARD-WINNING ACTRESS...
(ONE OF THE THREE SCREEN ACTRESSES FIRMLY AND METAPHYSICALLY ENMESHED IN OUR STORY)
..AND, FURTHER, AS ONE OF THE MOST FAMOUS WOMEN ON THE PLANET.
BEN, YOU LOOK PERFECTLY HEAVENLY IN EVENING CLOTHES ...I'M SO DARNED PROUD OF YOU, DARLING...
BEN...
EARLY IN 1950, HOWEVER...
...SHE'S COMPLETELY UNKNOWN.
EVE!
JOHN CULLEN MURPHY 5-17
EVE! PRESAGING ELLIOT CAPLIN'S MOST ENDURING CREATION (DID HE CREATE HER, THOUGH?)

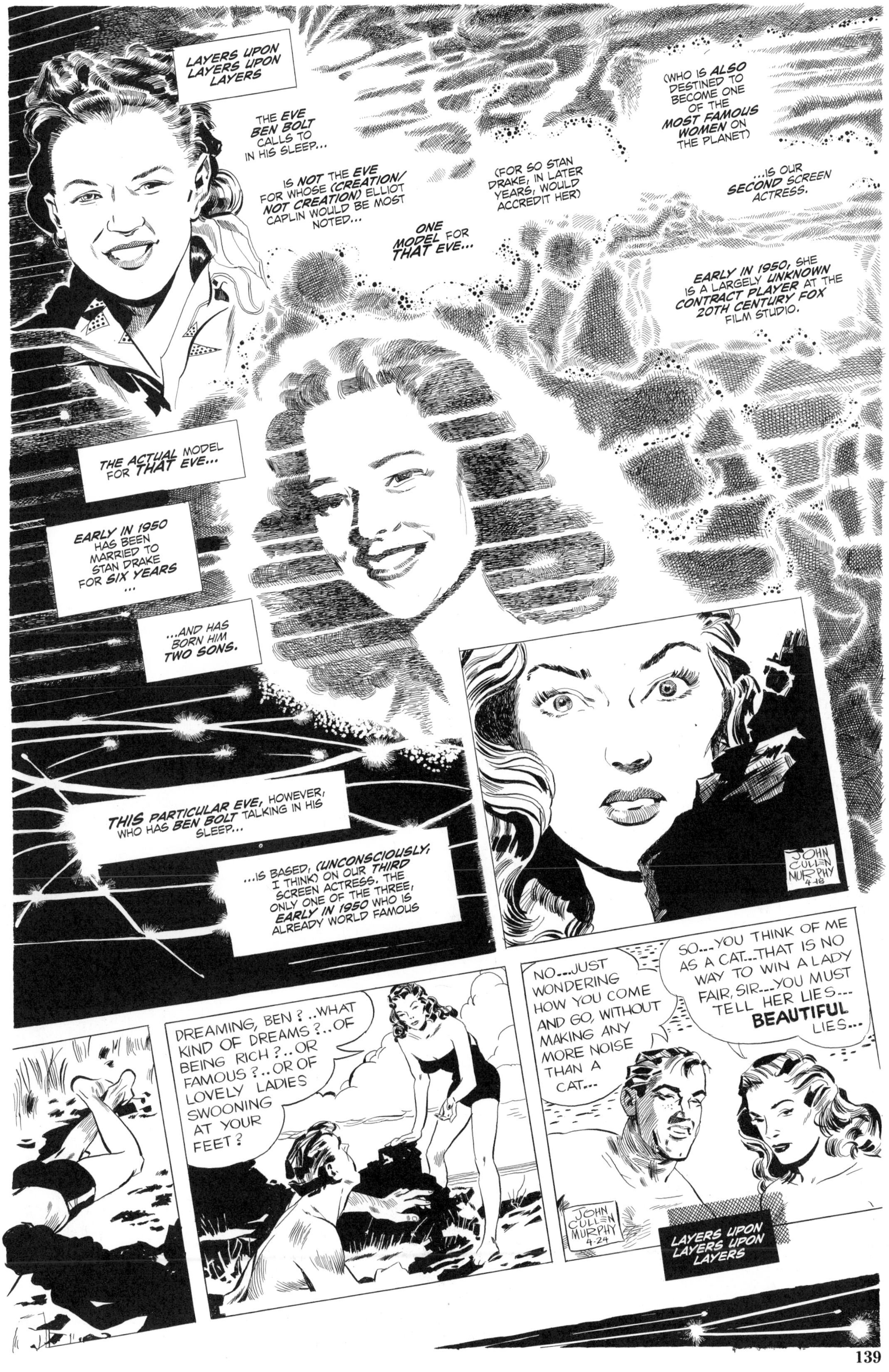

LAYERS UPON LAYERS UPON LAYERS
THE EVE BEN BOLT CALLS TO IN HIS SLEEP...
IS NOT THE EVE FOR WHOSE (CREATION/ NOT CREATION) ELLIOT CAPLIN WOULD BE MOST NOTED...
ONE MODEL FOR THAT EVE...
(FOR SO STAN DRAKE, IN LATER YEARS, WOULD ACCREDIT HER)
(WHO IS ALSO DESTINED TO BECOME ONE OF THE MOST FAMOUS WOMEN ON THE PLANET)
...IS OUR SECOND SCREEN ACTRESS.
EARLY IN 1950, SHE IS A LARGELY UNKNOWN CONTRACT PLAYER AT THE 20TH CENTURY FOX FILM STUDIO.
THE ACTUAL MODEL FOR THAT EVE...
EARLY IN 1950 HAS BEEN MARRIED TO STAN DRAKE FOR SIX YEARS ...
...AND HAS BORN HIM TWO SONS.
THIS PARTICULAR EVE, HOWEVER, WHO HAS BEN BOLT TALKING IN HIS SLEEP...
...IS BASED, (UNCONSCIOUSLY, I THINK) ON OUR THIRD SCREEN ACTRESS. THE ONLY ONE OF THE THREE, EARLY IN 1950 WHO IS ALREADY WORLD FAMOUS
JOHN CULLEN MURPHY 4-18
DREAMING, BEN? ..WHAT KIND OF DREAMS?..OF BEING RICH?..OR FAMOUS?..OR OF LOVELY LADIES SWOONING AT YOUR FEET?
NO...JUST WONDERING HOW YOU COME AND GO, WITHOUT MAKING ANY MORE NOISE THAN A CAT...
SO...YOU THINK OF ME AS A CAT...THAT IS NO WAY TO WIN A LADY FAIR, SIR...YOU MUST TELL HER LIES... BEAUTIFUL LIES...
JOHN CULLEN MURPHY 4-24
LAYERS UPON LAYERS UPON LAYERS

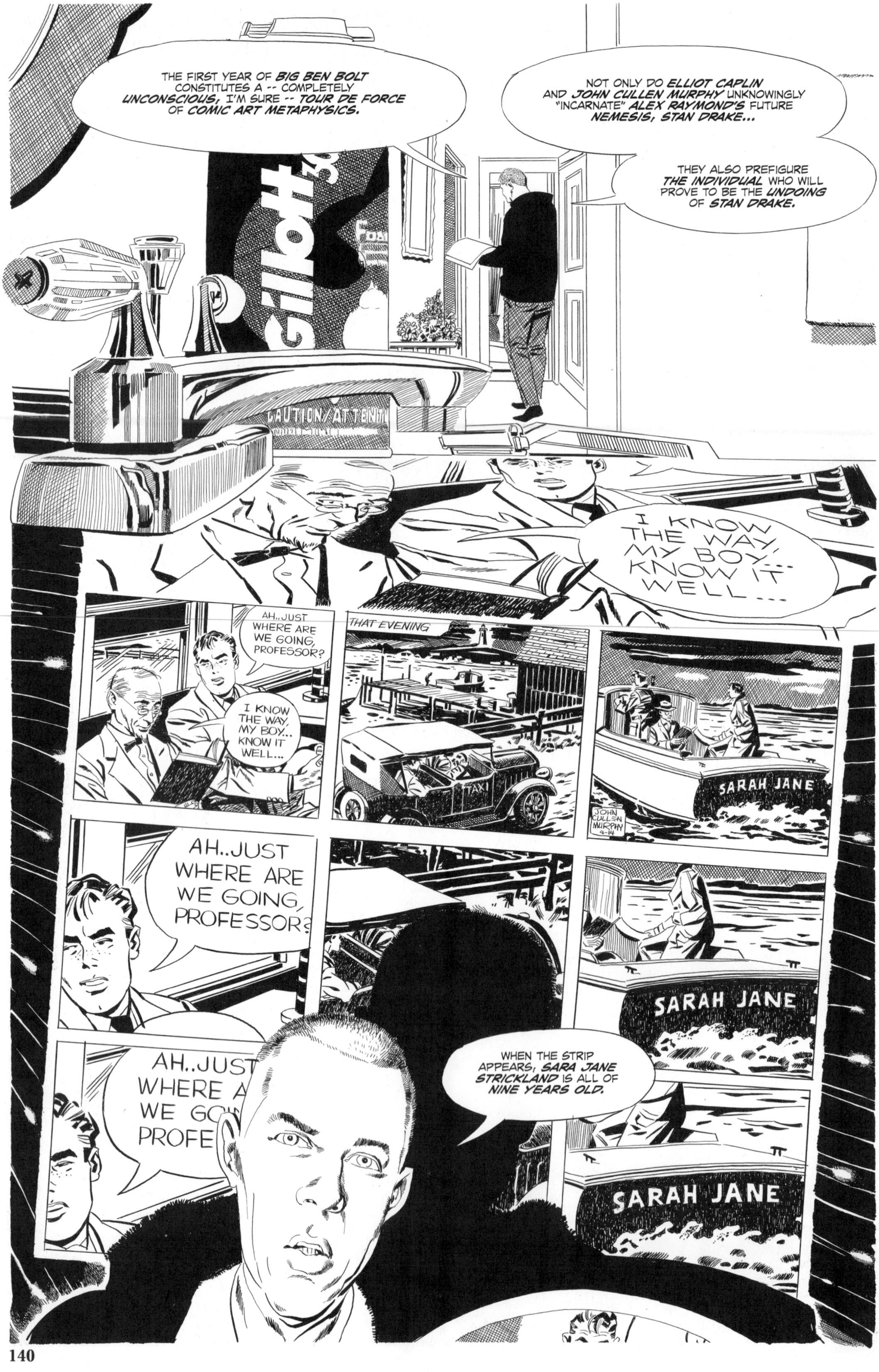
THE FIRST YEAR OF BIG BEN BOLT CONSTITUTES A -- COMPLETELY UNCONSCIOUS, I'M SURE -- TOUR DE FORCE OF COMIC ART METAPHYSICS.
NOT ONLY DO ELLIOT CAPLIN AND JOHN CULLEN MURPHY UNKNOWINGLY "INCARNATE" ALEX RAYMOND'S FUTURE NEMESIS, STAN DRAKE...
THEY ALSO PREFIGURE THE INDIVIDUAL WHO WILL PROVE TO BE THE UNDOING OF STAN DRAKE.
CAUTION/ATTENT
I KNOW THE WAY, MY BOY... KNOW IT WELL...
AH..JUST WHERE ARE WE GOING, PROFESSOR?
I KNOW THE WAY, MY BOY... KNOW IT WELL...
THAT EVENING
TAXI
SARAH JANE
JOHN CULLEN MURPHY 4-14
AH..JUST WHERE ARE WE GOING, PROFESSOR?
SARAH JANE
AH..JUST WHERE A WE GOIN PROFE
WHEN THE STRIP APPEARS, SARA JANE STRICKLAND IS ALL OF NINE YEARS OLD.
SARAH JANE

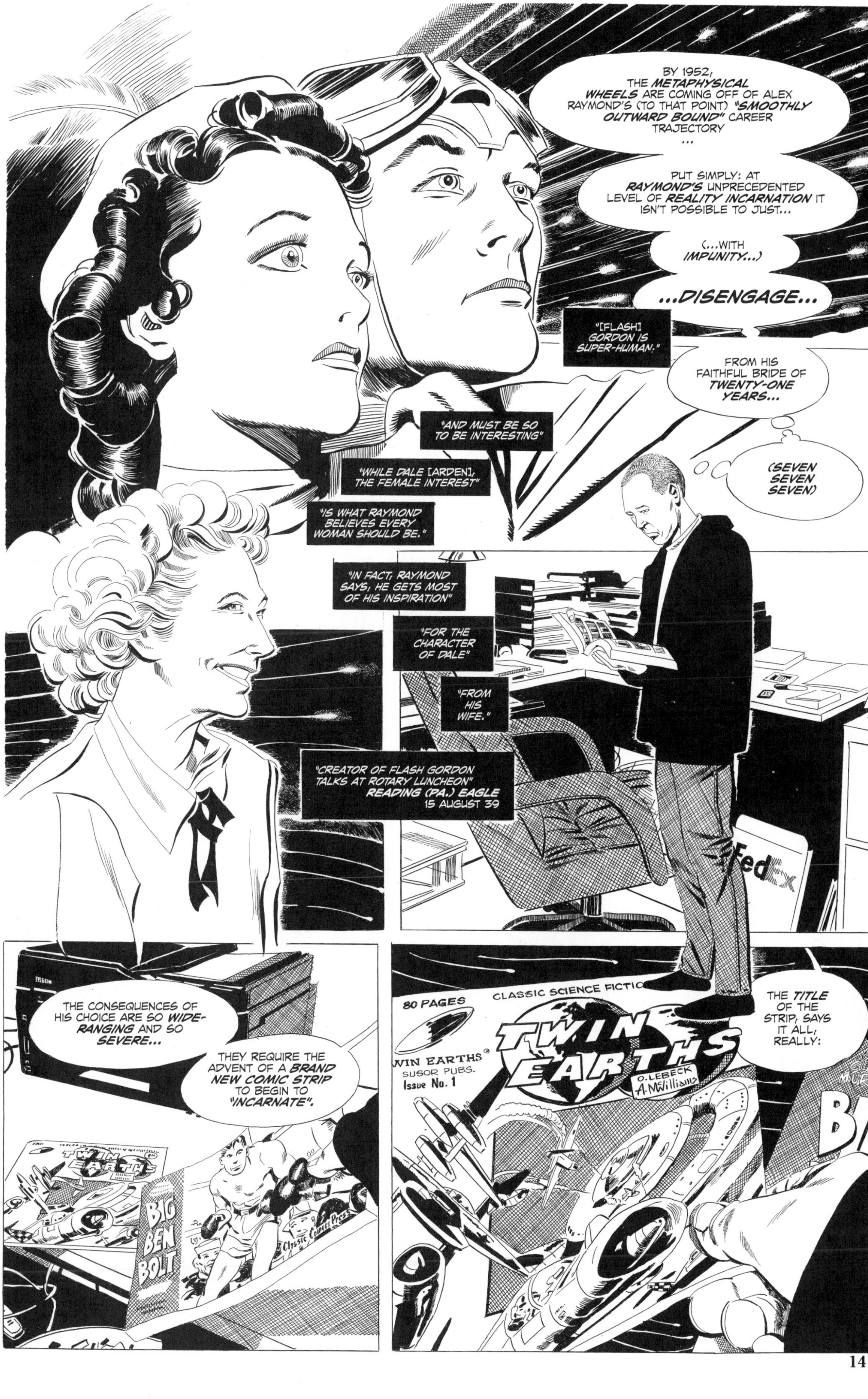

BY 1952, THE METAPHYSICAL WHEELS ARE COMING OFF OF ALEX RAYMOND'S (TO THAT POINT) "SMOOTHLY OUTWARD BOUND" CAREER TRAJECTORY ...
PUT SIMPLY: AT RAYMOND'S UNPRECEDENTED LEVEL OF REALITY INCARNATION IT ISN'T POSSIBLE TO JUST...
(...WITH IMPUNITY...)
...DISENGAGE...
"[FLASH] GORDON IS SUPER-HUMAN."
FROM HIS FAITHFUL BRIDE OF TWENTY-ONE YEARS...
"AND MUST BE SO TO BE INTERESTING"
(SEVEN SEVEN SEVEN)
"WHILE DALE [ARDEN], THE FEMALE INTEREST"
"IS WHAT RAYMOND BELIEVES EVERY WOMAN SHOULD BE."
"IN FACT, RAYMOND SAYS, HE GETS MOST OF HIS INSPIRATION"
"FOR THE CHARACTER OF DALE"
"FROM HIS WIFE."
"CREATOR OF FLASH GORDON TALKS AT ROTARY LUNCHEON" READING (PA.) EAGLE 15 AUGUST 39
FedEx
THE CONSEQUENCES OF HIS CHOICE ARE SO WIDE-RANGING AND SO SEVERE...
THEY REQUIRE THE ADVENT OF A BRAND NEW COMIC STRIP TO BEGIN TO "INCARNATE".
BIG BEN BOLT
Classic Comics Press
80 PAGES
CLASSIC SCIENCE FICTIO
TWIN EARTHS
WIN EARTHS
SUSOR PUBS.
Issue No. 1
O. LEBECK
A. McWilliams
THE TITLE OF THE STRIP, SAYS IT ALL, REALLY:

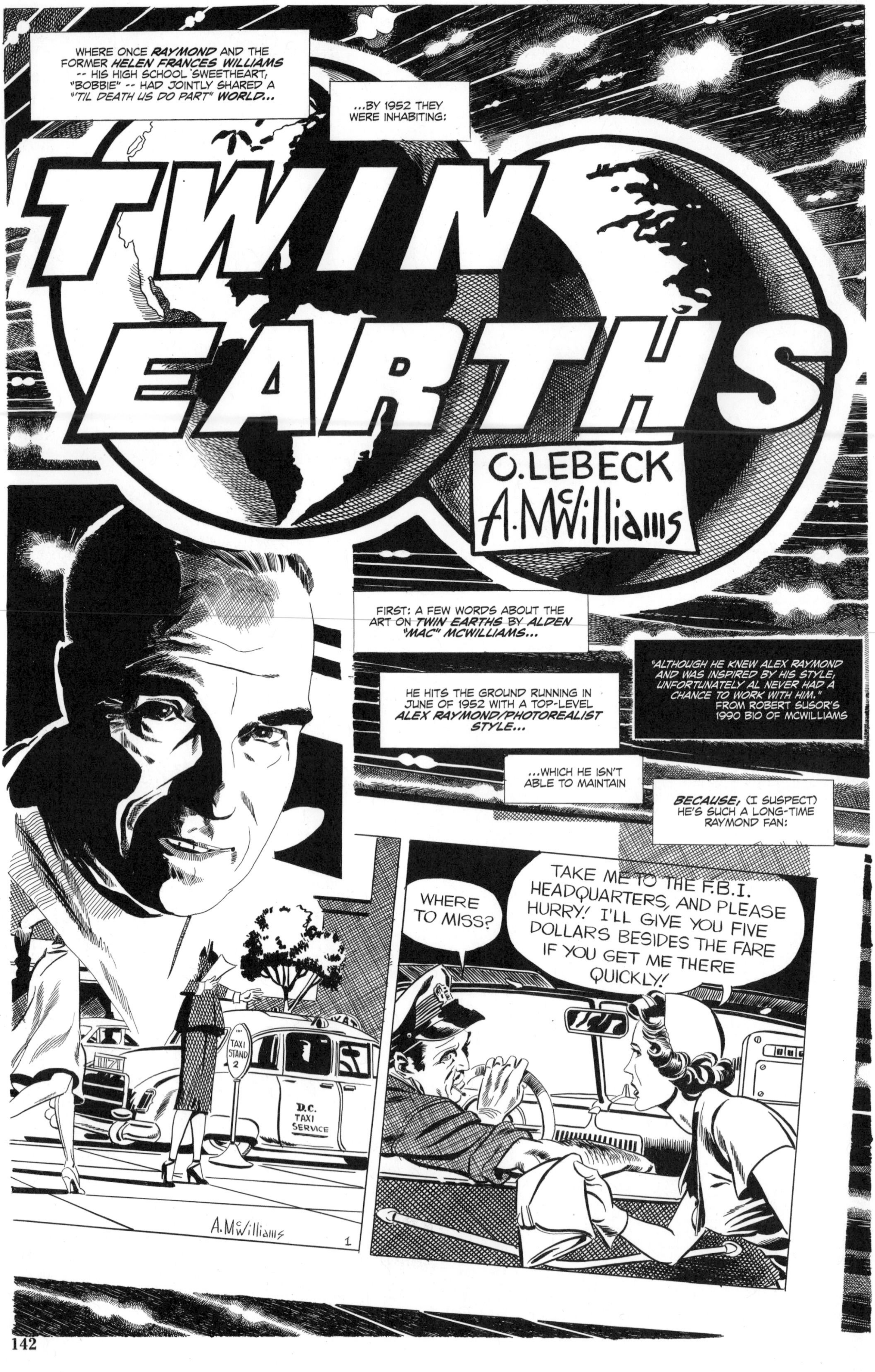

WHERE ONCE RAYMOND AND THE FORMER HELEN FRANCES WILLIAMS -- HIS HIGH SCHOOL SWEETHEART, "BOBBIE" -- HAD JOINTLY SHARED A "'TIL DEATH US DO PART" WORLD...
...BY 1952 THEY WERE INHABITING:
TWIN EARTHS
O. LEBECK
A. McWilliams
FIRST: A FEW WORDS ABOUT THE ART ON TWIN EARTHS BY ALDEN "MAC" MCWILLIAMS...
"ALTHOUGH HE KNEW ALEX RAYMOND AND WAS INSPIRED BY HIS STYLE, UNFORTUNATELY AL NEVER HAD A CHANCE TO WORK WITH HIM." FROM ROBERT SUSOR'S 1990 BIO OF MCWILLIAMS
HE HITS THE GROUND RUNNING IN JUNE OF 1952 WITH A TOP-LEVEL ALEX RAYMOND/PHOTOREALIST STYLE...
...WHICH HE ISN'T ABLE TO MAINTAIN
BECAUSE, (I SUSPECT) HE'S SUCH A LONG-TIME RAYMOND FAN:
TAXI STAND 2
D.C. TAXI SERVICE
WHERE TO MISS?
TAKE ME TO THE F.B.I. HEADQUARTERS, AND PLEASE HURRY! I'LL GIVE YOU FIVE DOLLARS BESIDES THE FARE IF YOU GET ME THERE QUICKLY!
A. McWilliams
1

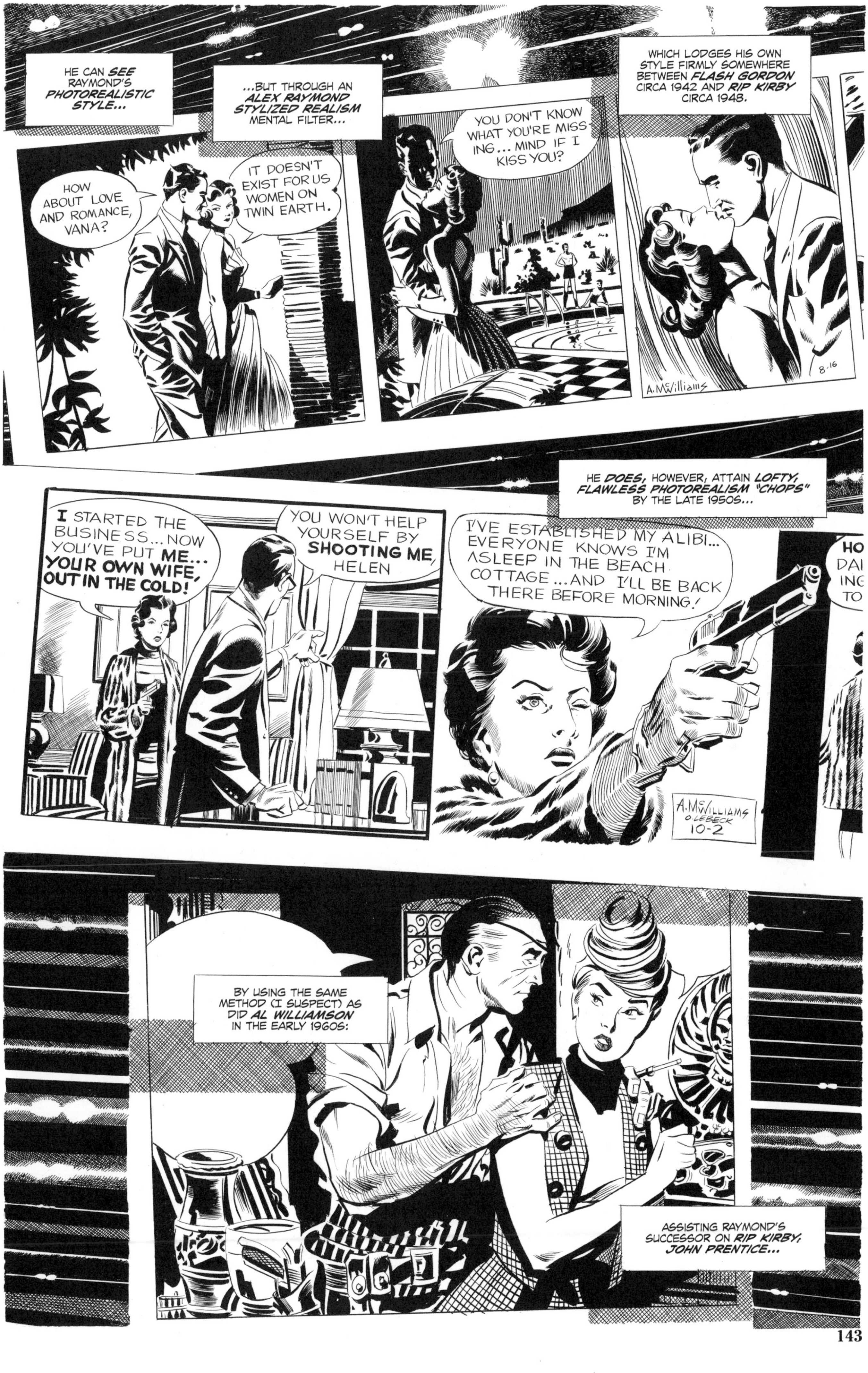

HE CAN ***SEE*** RAYMOND'S ***PHOTOREALISTIC STYLE...***
...BUT THROUGH AN ***ALEX RAYMOND STYLIZED REALISM*** MENTAL FILTER...
HOW ABOUT LOVE AND ROMANCE, VANA?
IT DOESN'T EXIST FOR US WOMEN ON TWIN EARTH.
YOU DON'T KNOW WHAT YOU'RE MISS-ING... MIND IF I KISS YOU?
WHICH LODGES HIS OWN STYLE FIRMLY SOMEWHERE BETWEEN ***FLASH GORDON*** CIRCA 1942 AND ***RIP KIRBY*** CIRCA 1948.
A. McWilliams
8-16
HE ***DOES,*** HOWEVER, ATTAIN ***LOFTY, FLAWLESS PHOTOREALISM "CHOPS"*** BY THE LATE 1950S...
**I** STARTED THE BUSINESS... NOW YOU'VE PUT **ME... YOUR OWN WIFE, OUT IN THE COLD!**
YOU WON'T HELP YOURSELF BY **SHOOTING ME,** HELEN
I'VE ESTABLISHED MY ALIBI... EVERYONE KNOWS I'M ASLEEP IN THE BEACH COTTAGE... AND I'LL BE BACK THERE BEFORE MORNING!
A. McWilliams
O. LEBECK
10-2
BY USING THE SAME METHOD (I SUSPECT) AS DID ***AL WILLIAMSON*** IN THE EARLY 1960S:
ASSISTING RAYMOND'S SUCCESSOR ON ***RIP KIRBY, JOHN PRENTICE...***

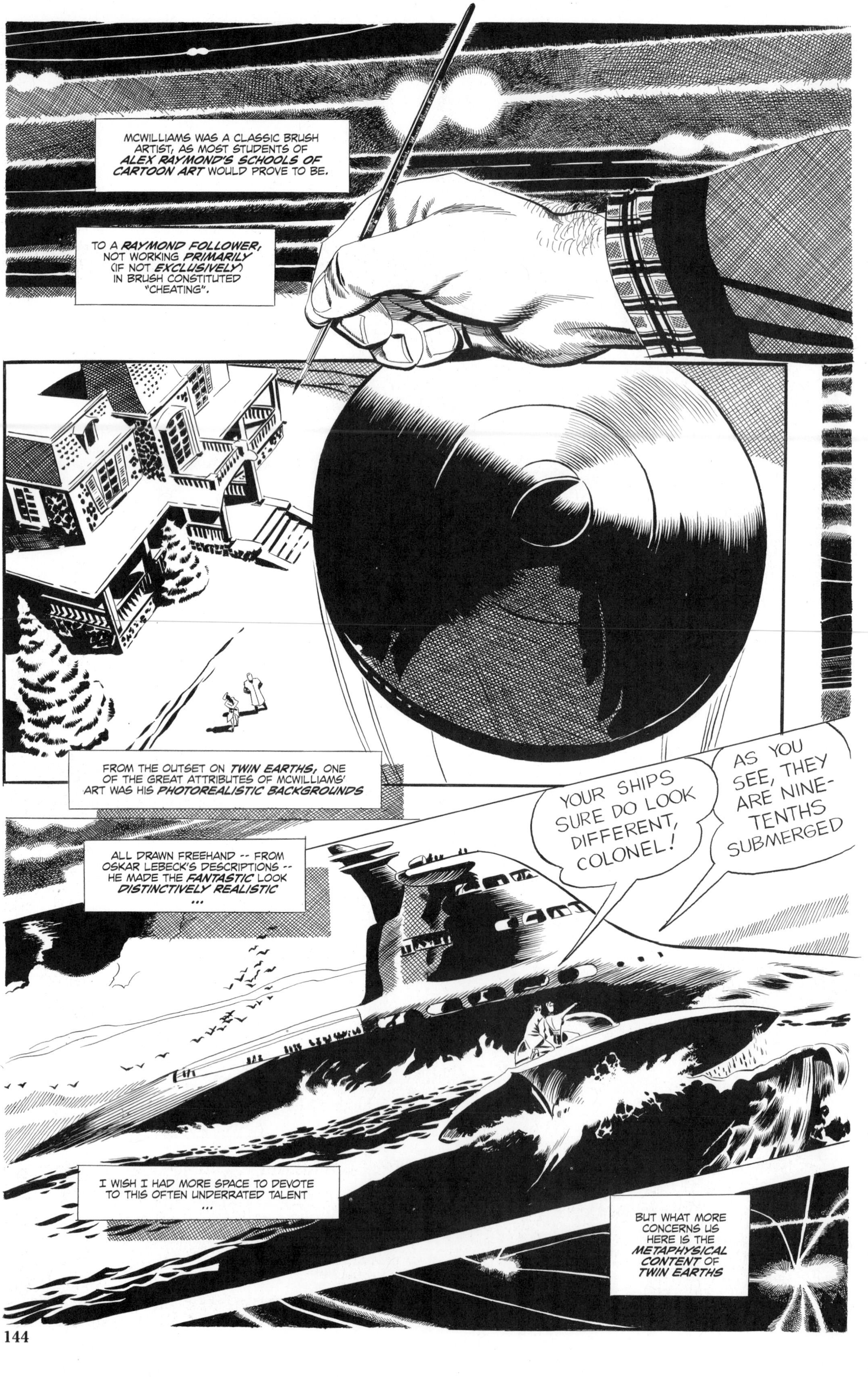

MCWILLIAMS WAS A CLASSIC BRUSH ARTIST, AS MOST STUDENTS OF ALEX RAYMOND'S SCHOOLS OF CARTOON ART WOULD PROVE TO BE.
TO A RAYMOND FOLLOWER, NOT WORKING PRIMARILY (IF NOT EXCLUSIVELY) IN BRUSH CONSTITUTED "CHEATING".
FROM THE OUTSET ON TWIN EARTHS, ONE OF THE GREAT ATTRIBUTES OF MCWILLIAMS' ART WAS HIS PHOTOREALISTIC BACKGROUNDS
ALL DRAWN FREEHAND -- FROM OSKAR LEBECK'S DESCRIPTIONS -- HE MADE THE FANTASTIC LOOK DISTINCTIVELY REALISTIC ...
YOUR SHIPS SURE DO LOOK DIFFERENT, COLONEL!
AS YOU SEE, THEY ARE NINE-TENTHS SUBMERGED
I WISH I HAD MORE SPACE TO DEVOTE TO THIS OFTEN UNDERRATED TALENT ...
BUT WHAT MORE CONCERNS US HERE IS THE METAPHYSICAL CONTENT OF TWIN EARTHS

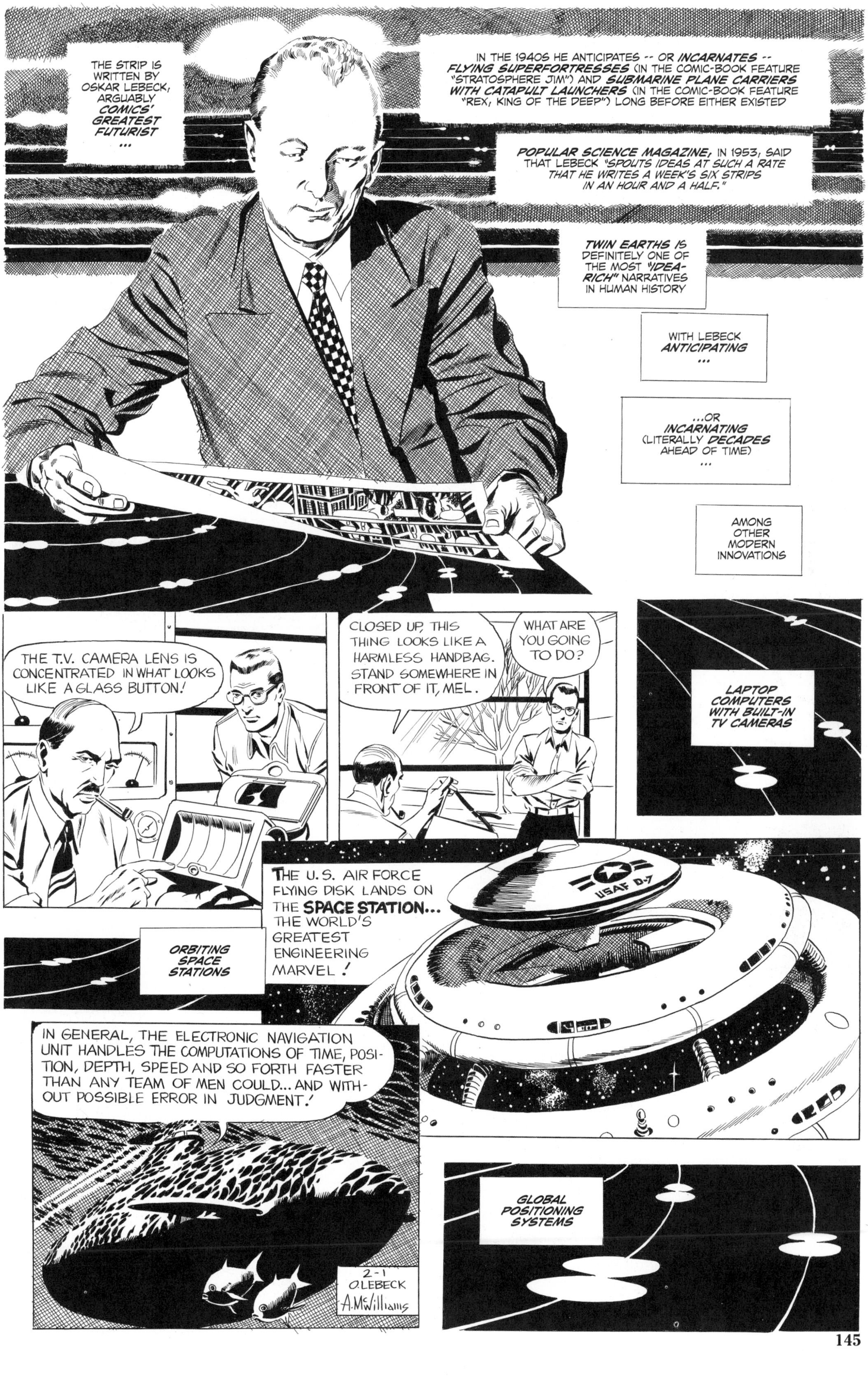
THE STRIP IS WRITTEN BY OSKAR LEBECK, ARGUABLY COMICS' GREATEST FUTURIST ...
IN THE 1940S HE ANTICIPATES -- OR INCARNATES -- FLYING SUPERFORTRESSES (IN THE COMIC-BOOK FEATURE "STRATOSPHERE JIM") AND SUBMARINE PLANE CARRIERS WITH CATAPULT LAUNCHERS (IN THE COMIC-BOOK FEATURE "REX, KING OF THE DEEP") LONG BEFORE EITHER EXISTED
POPULAR SCIENCE MAGAZINE, IN 1953, SAID THAT LEBECK "SPOUTS IDEAS AT SUCH A RATE THAT HE WRITES A WEEK'S SIX STRIPS IN AN HOUR AND A HALF."
TWIN EARTHS IS DEFINITELY ONE OF THE MOST "IDEA-RICH" NARRATIVES IN HUMAN HISTORY
WITH LEBECK ANTICIPATING ...
...OR INCARNATING (LITERALLY DECADES AHEAD OF TIME) ...
AMONG OTHER MODERN INNOVATIONS
THE T.V. CAMERA LENS IS CONCENTRATED IN WHAT LOOKS LIKE A GLASS BUTTON!
CLOSED UP, THIS THING LOOKS LIKE A HARMLESS HANDBAG. STAND SOMEWHERE IN FRONT OF IT, MEL.
WHAT ARE YOU GOING TO DO?
LAPTOP COMPUTERS WITH BUILT-IN TV CAMERAS
THE U. S. AIR FORCE FLYING DISK LANDS ON THE SPACE STATION... THE WORLD'S GREATEST ENGINEERING MARVEL!
USAF D-7
ORBITING SPACE STATIONS
IN GENERAL, THE ELECTRONIC NAVIGATION UNIT HANDLES THE COMPUTATIONS OF TIME, POSITION, DEPTH, SPEED AND SO FORTH FASTER THAN ANY TEAM OF MEN COULD... AND WITHOUT POSSIBLE ERROR IN JUDGMENT!
2-1
O.LEBECK
A.McWilliams
GLOBAL POSITIONING SYSTEMS

THE NEWLY ARRIVED PASSENGERS ARE WHISKED FROM SHIP TO TERMINAL VIA MOVING RAMPS

O. LEBECK
A. McWilliams
4-10

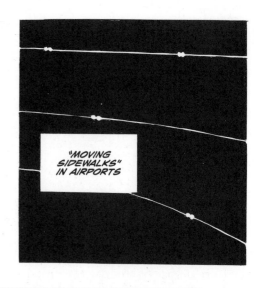

"MOVING SIDEWALKS" IN AIRPORTS

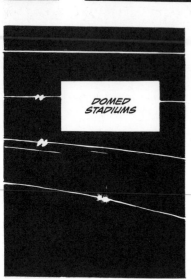

DOMED STADIUMS

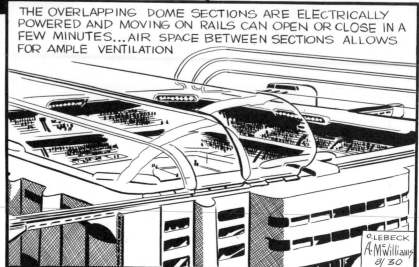

THE OVERLAPPING DOME SECTIONS ARE ELECTRICALLY POWERED AND MOVING ON RAILS CAN OPEN OR CLOSE IN A FEW MINUTES...AIR SPACE BETWEEN SECTIONS ALLOWS FOR AMPLE VENTILATION

O. LEBECK
A. McWilliams
8/30

THE INTERNET

ALL RIGHT, GARRY...YOU KNOW HOW TO OPERATE TELE-BRAIN'S KEYBOARD CONTROLS... GO TO IT!

THE STRANGE STORY of 'BIRDY' MURPHY

("BIRDIE" MURPHY IS THE "MURPHY" THAT *JOHN CULLEN MURPHY* WAS "CULLING")

(LAYERS UPON LAYERS UPON LAYERS)

(METAPHORICALLY, AS WE WILL SEE, HE WAS -- AT ONE AND THE SAME TIME -- BOTH *ALEX RAYMOND*) ...

(STORIES WITHIN STORIES WITHIN STORIES)

(...AND *ALSO* ONE OF THE MOST FAMOUS *POP* CULTURE FIGURES OF THE TWENTIETH CENTURY)

(TWIN EARTHS AND TWIN EARTHS AND TWIN EARTHS)

(WHO WOULD *BURST UPON THE NATIONAL SCENE* THREE DAYS AFTER RAYMOND'S FATAL CAR ACCIDENT)

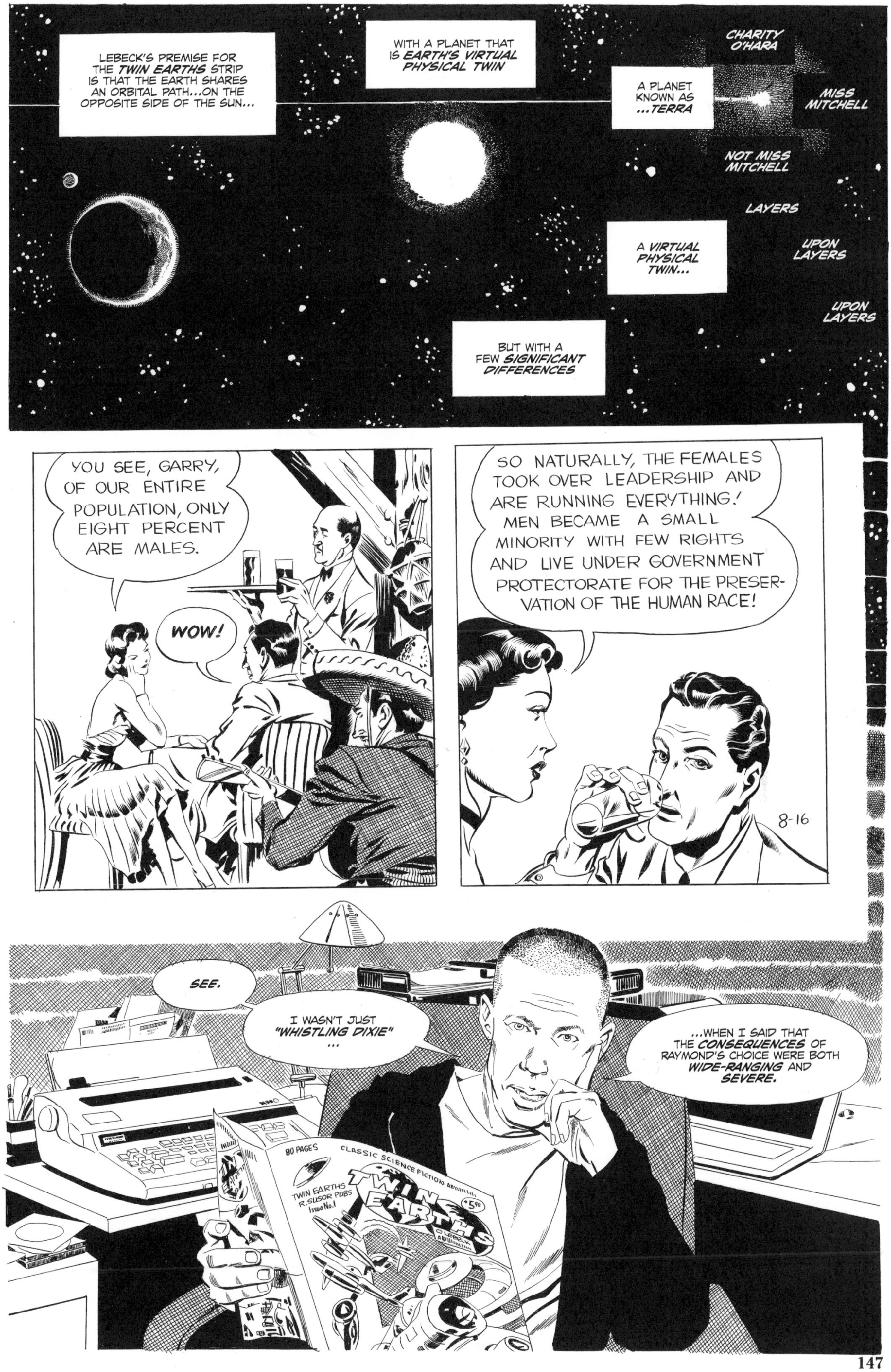
LEBECK'S PREMISE FOR THE TWIN EARTHS STRIP IS THAT THE EARTH SHARES AN ORBITAL PATH...ON THE OPPOSITE SIDE OF THE SUN...
WITH A PLANET THAT IS EARTH'S VIRTUAL PHYSICAL TWIN
A PLANET KNOWN AS ...TERRA
CHARITY O'HARA
MISS MITCHELL
NOT MISS MITCHELL
LAYERS
A VIRTUAL PHYSICAL TWIN...
UPON LAYERS
UPON LAYERS
BUT WITH A FEW SIGNIFICANT DIFFERENCES
YOU SEE, GARRY, OF OUR ENTIRE POPULATION, ONLY EIGHT PERCENT ARE MALES.
WOW!
SO NATURALLY, THE FEMALES TOOK OVER LEADERSHIP AND ARE RUNNING EVERYTHING! MEN BECAME A SMALL MINORITY WITH FEW RIGHTS AND LIVE UNDER GOVERNMENT PROTECTORATE FOR THE PRESER-VATION OF THE HUMAN RACE!
8-16
SEE.
I WASN'T JUST "WHISTLING DIXIE" ...
...WHEN I SAID THAT THE CONSEQUENCES OF RAYMOND'S CHOICE WERE BOTH WIDE-RANGING AND SEVERE.
80 PAGES
CLASSIC SCIENCE FICTION
TWIN EARTHS
TWIN EARTHS
R. SUSOR PUBS
Issue No. 1

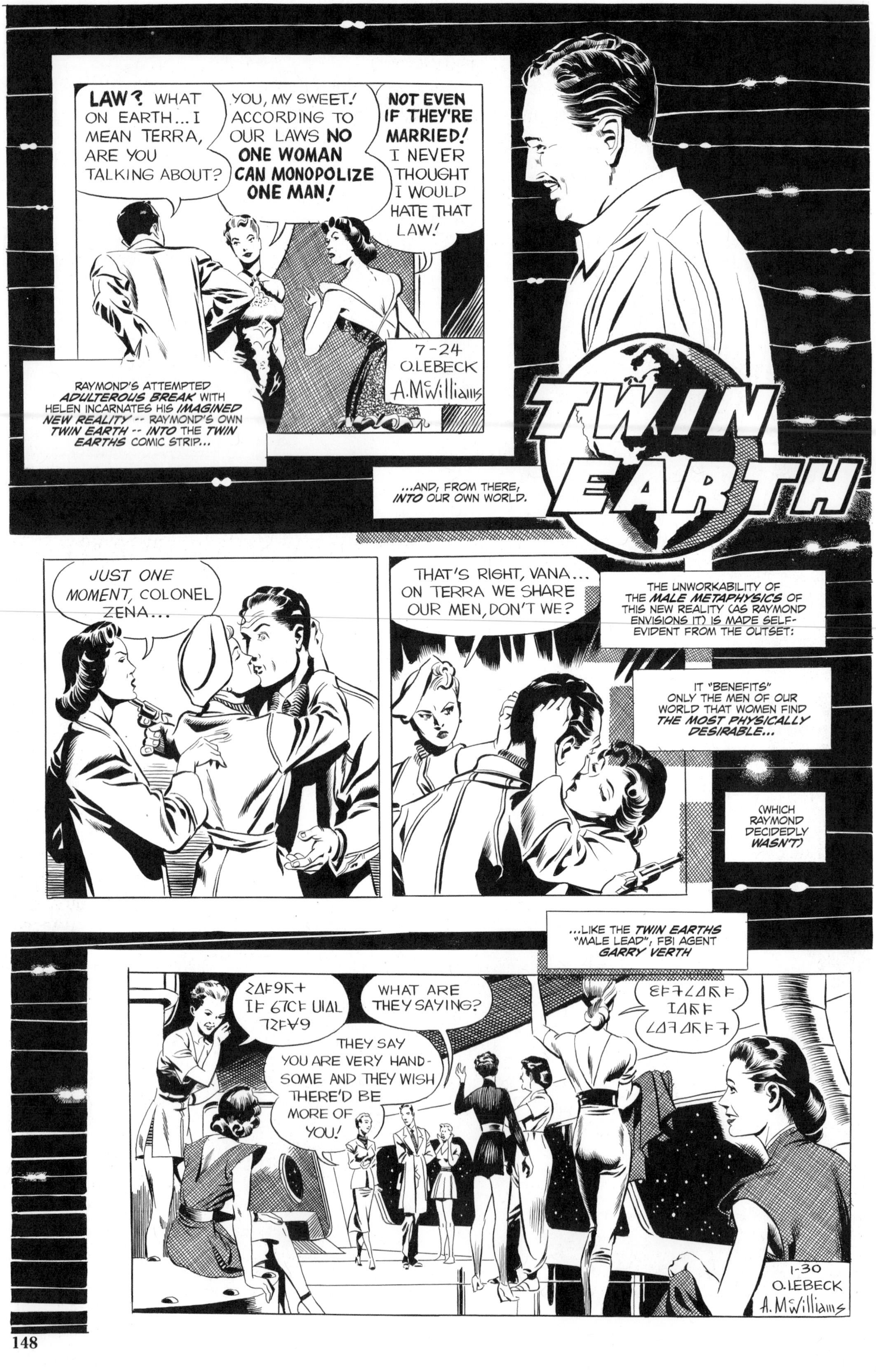
LAW? WHAT ON EARTH... I MEAN TERRA, ARE YOU TALKING ABOUT?
YOU, MY SWEET! ACCORDING TO OUR LAWS NO ONE WOMAN CAN MONOPOLIZE ONE MAN!
NOT EVEN IF THEY'RE MARRIED! I NEVER THOUGHT I WOULD HATE THAT LAW!
7-24 O.LEBECK A.McWilliams
RAYMOND'S ATTEMPTED ADULTEROUS BREAK WITH HELEN INCARNATES HIS IMAGINED NEW REALITY -- RAYMOND'S OWN TWIN EARTH -- INTO THE TWIN EARTHS COMIC STRIP...
TWIN EARTH
...AND, FROM THERE, INTO OUR OWN WORLD.
JUST ONE MOMENT, COLONEL ZENA...
THAT'S RIGHT, VANA... ON TERRA WE SHARE OUR MEN, DON'T WE?
THE UNWORKABILITY OF THE MALE METAPHYSICS OF THIS NEW REALITY (AS RAYMOND ENVISIONS IT) IS MADE SELF-EVIDENT FROM THE OUTSET:
IT "BENEFITS" ONLY THE MEN OF OUR WORLD THAT WOMEN FIND THE MOST PHYSICALLY DESIRABLE...
(WHICH RAYMOND DECIDEDLY WASN'T)
...LIKE THE TWIN EARTHS "MALE LEAD", FBI AGENT GARRY VERTH
WHAT ARE THEY SAYING?
THEY SAY YOU ARE VERY HANDSOME AND THEY WISH THERE'D BE MORE OF YOU!
1-30 O.LEBECK A.McWilliams

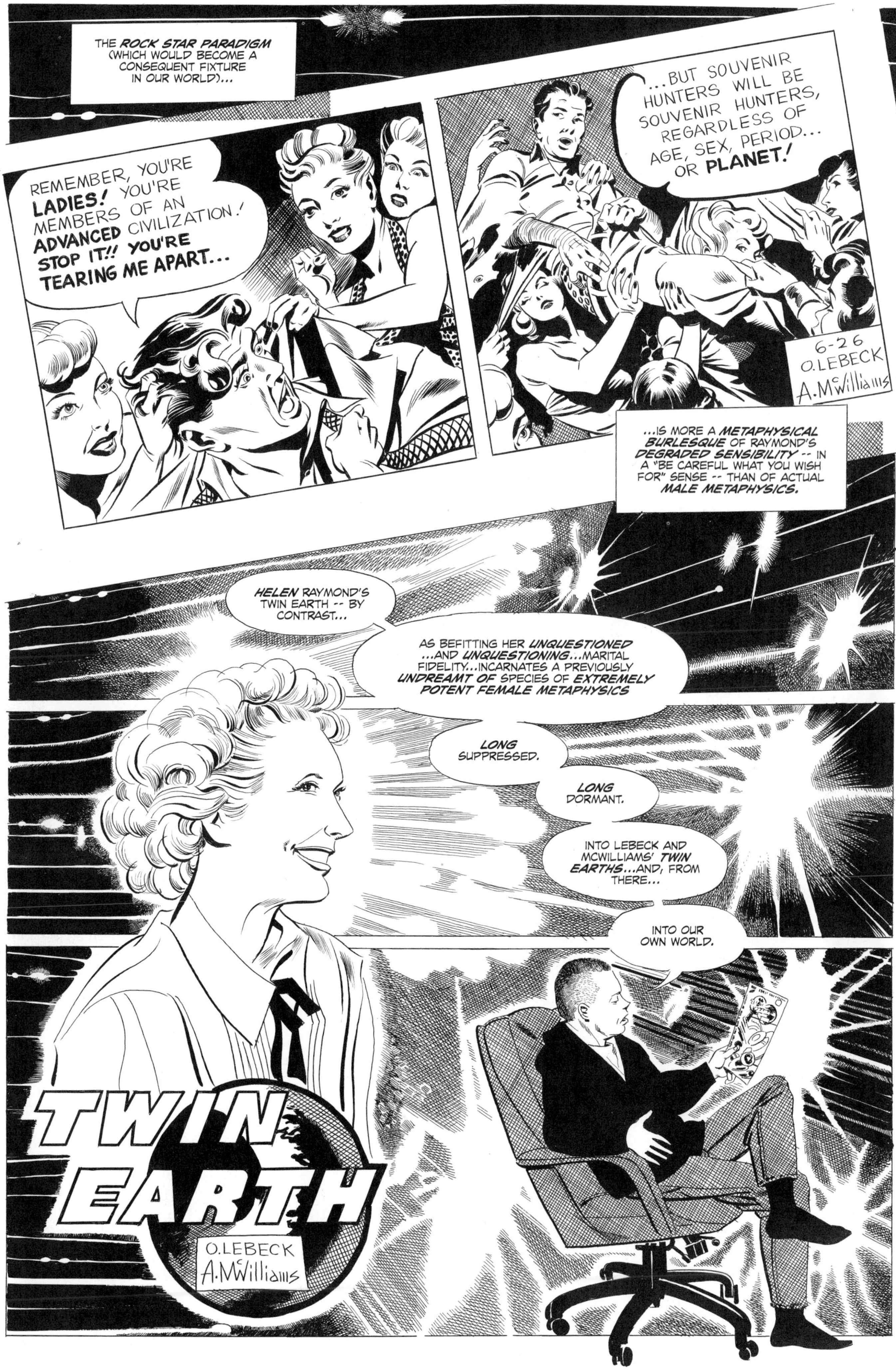

THE ROCK STAR PARADIGM (WHICH WOULD BECOME A CONSEQUENT FIXTURE IN OUR WORLD)...
REMEMBER, YOU'RE LADIES! YOU'RE MEMBERS OF AN ADVANCED CIVILIZATION! STOP IT!! YOU'RE TEARING ME APART...
...BUT SOUVENIR HUNTERS WILL BE SOUVENIR HUNTERS, REGARDLESS OF AGE, SEX, PERIOD... OR PLANET!
6-26
O.LEBECK
A. McWilliams
...IS MORE A METAPHYSICAL BURLESQUE OF RAYMOND'S DEGRADED SENSIBILITY -- IN A "BE CAREFUL WHAT YOU WISH FOR" SENSE -- THAN OF ACTUAL MALE METAPHYSICS.
HELEN RAYMOND'S TWIN EARTH -- BY CONTRAST...
AS BEFITTING HER UNQUESTIONED ...AND UNQUESTIONING...MARITAL FIDELITY...INCARNATES A PREVIOUSLY UNDREAMT OF SPECIES OF EXTREMELY POTENT FEMALE METAPHYSICS
LONG SUPPRESSED.
LONG DORMANT.
INTO LEBECK AND MCWILLIAMS' TWIN EARTHS...AND, FROM THERE...
INTO OUR OWN WORLD.
TWIN EARTH
O.LEBECK
A. McWilliams

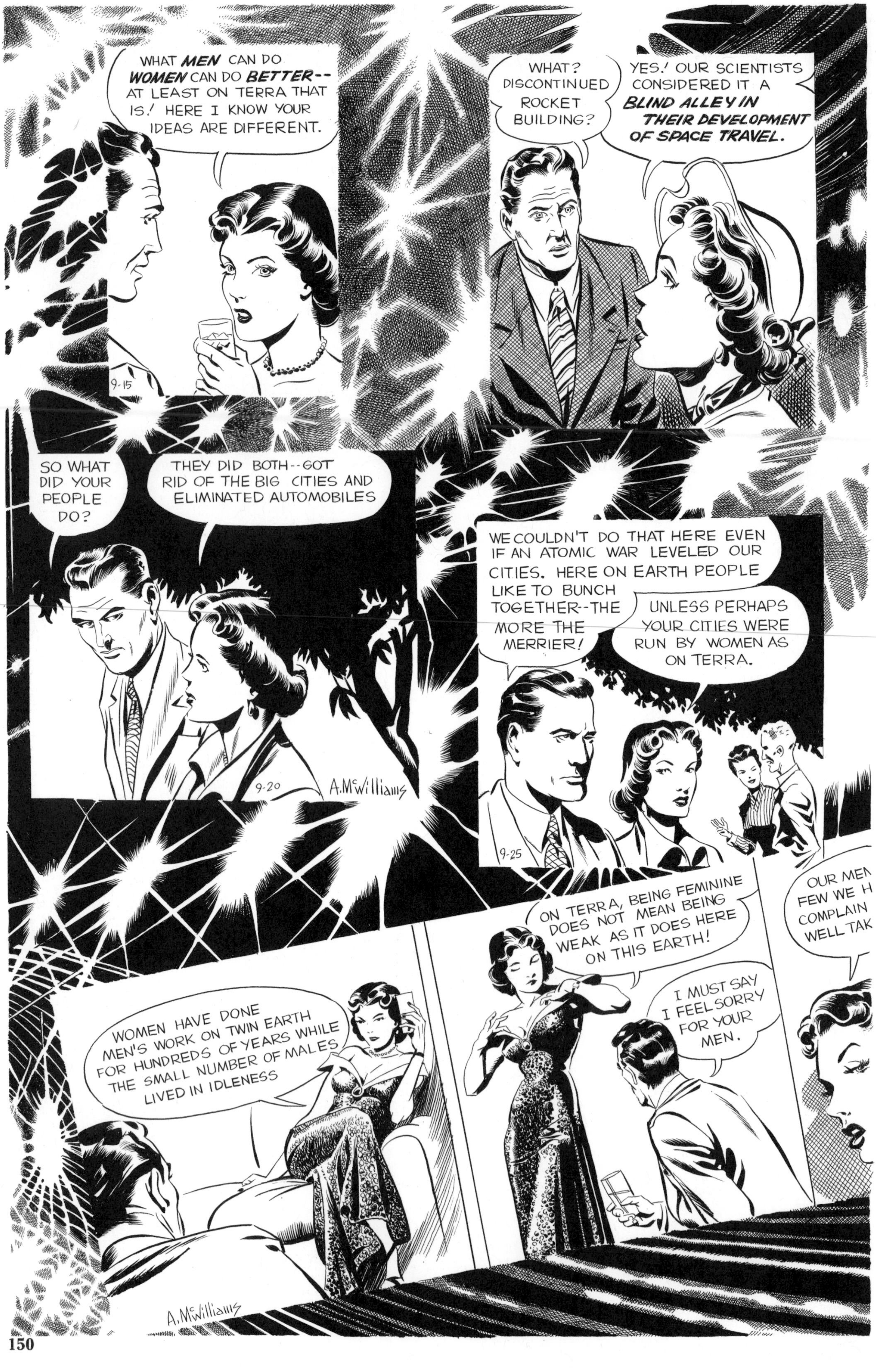
WHAT **MEN** CAN DO **WOMEN** CAN DO **BETTER**-- AT LEAST ON TERRA THAT IS! HERE I KNOW YOUR IDEAS ARE DIFFERENT.
WHAT? DISCONTINUED ROCKET BUILDING?
YES! OUR SCIENTISTS CONSIDERED IT A **BLIND ALLEY IN THEIR DEVELOPMENT OF SPACE TRAVEL.**
SO WHAT DID YOUR PEOPLE DO?
THEY DID BOTH--GOT RID OF THE BIG CITIES AND ELIMINATED AUTOMOBILES
WE COULDN'T DO THAT HERE EVEN IF AN ATOMIC WAR LEVELED OUR CITIES. HERE ON EARTH PEOPLE LIKE TO BUNCH TOGETHER--THE MORE THE MERRIER!
UNLESS PERHAPS YOUR CITIES WERE RUN BY WOMEN AS ON TERRA.
WOMEN HAVE DONE MEN'S WORK ON TWIN EARTH FOR HUNDREDS OF YEARS WHILE THE SMALL NUMBER OF MALES LIVED IN IDLENESS
ON TERRA, BEING FEMININE DOES NOT MEAN BEING WEAK AS IT DOES HERE ON THIS EARTH!
I MUST SAY I FEEL SORRY FOR YOUR MEN.
OUR MEN
FEW WE H
COMPLAIN
WELL TAK

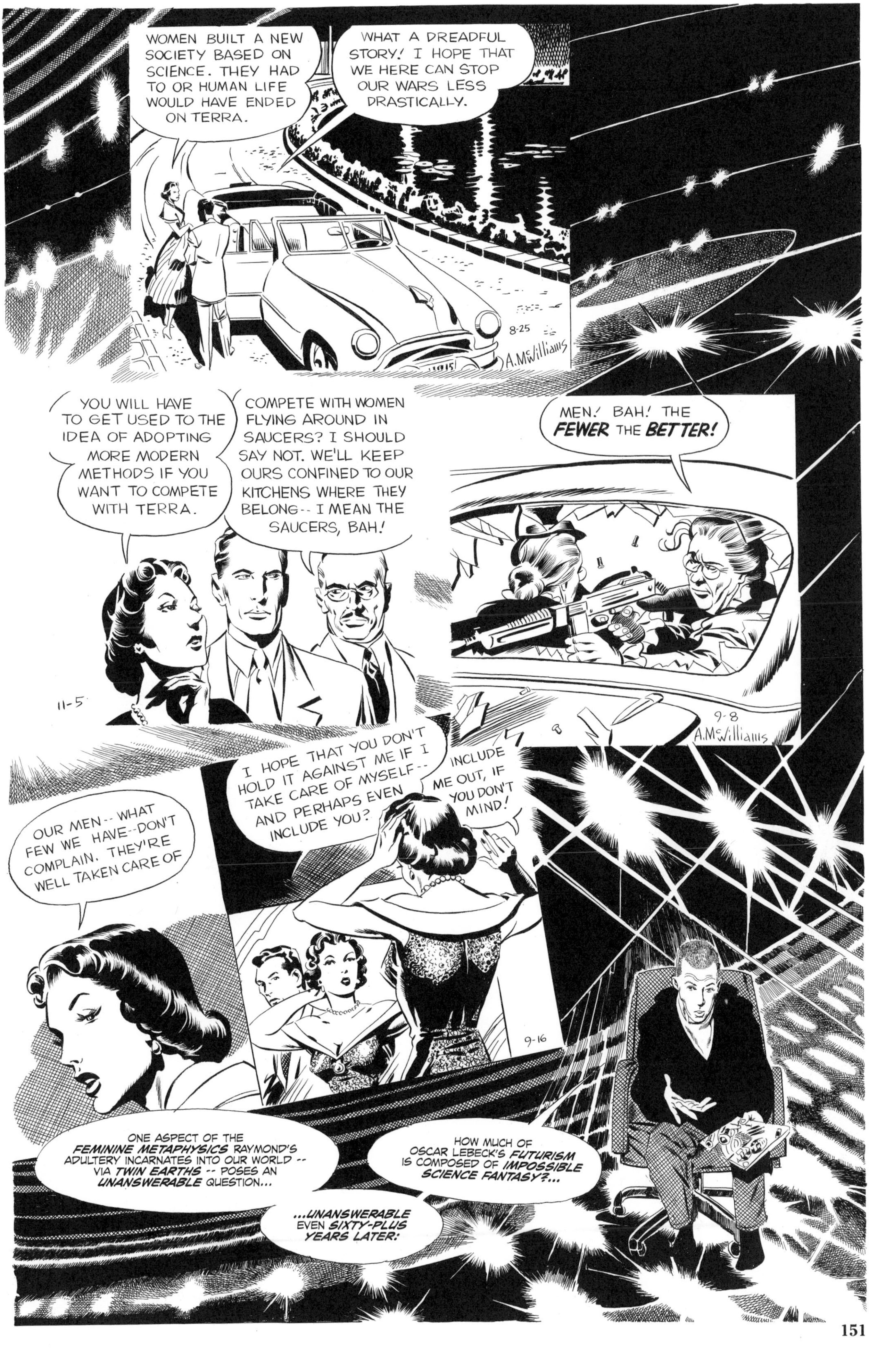
WOMEN BUILT A NEW SOCIETY BASED ON SCIENCE. THEY HAD TO OR HUMAN LIFE WOULD HAVE ENDED ON TERRA.
WHAT A DREADFUL STORY! I HOPE THAT WE HERE CAN STOP OUR WARS LESS DRASTICALLY.
8-25
A. McWilliams
YOU WILL HAVE TO GET USED TO THE IDEA OF ADOPTING MORE MODERN METHODS IF YOU WANT TO COMPETE WITH TERRA.
COMPETE WITH WOMEN FLYING AROUND IN SAUCERS? I SHOULD SAY NOT. WE'LL KEEP OURS CONFINED TO OUR KITCHENS WHERE THEY BELONG-- I MEAN THE SAUCERS, BAH!
11-5
MEN! BAH! THE FEWER THE BETTER!
9-8
A. McWilliams
OUR MEN-- WHAT FEW WE HAVE--DON'T COMPLAIN. THEY'RE WELL TAKEN CARE OF
I HOPE THAT YOU DON'T HOLD IT AGAINST ME IF I TAKE CARE OF MYSELF-- AND PERHAPS EVEN INCLUDE YOU?
INCLUDE ME OUT, IF YOU DON'T MIND!
9-16
ONE ASPECT OF THE FEMININE METAPHYSICS RAYMOND'S ADULTERY INCARNATES INTO OUR WORLD -- VIA TWIN EARTHS -- POSES AN UNANSWERABLE QUESTION...
...UNANSWERABLE EVEN SIXTY-PLUS YEARS LATER:
HOW MUCH OF OSCAR LEBECK'S FUTURISM IS COMPOSED OF IMPOSSIBLE SCIENCE FANTASY?...

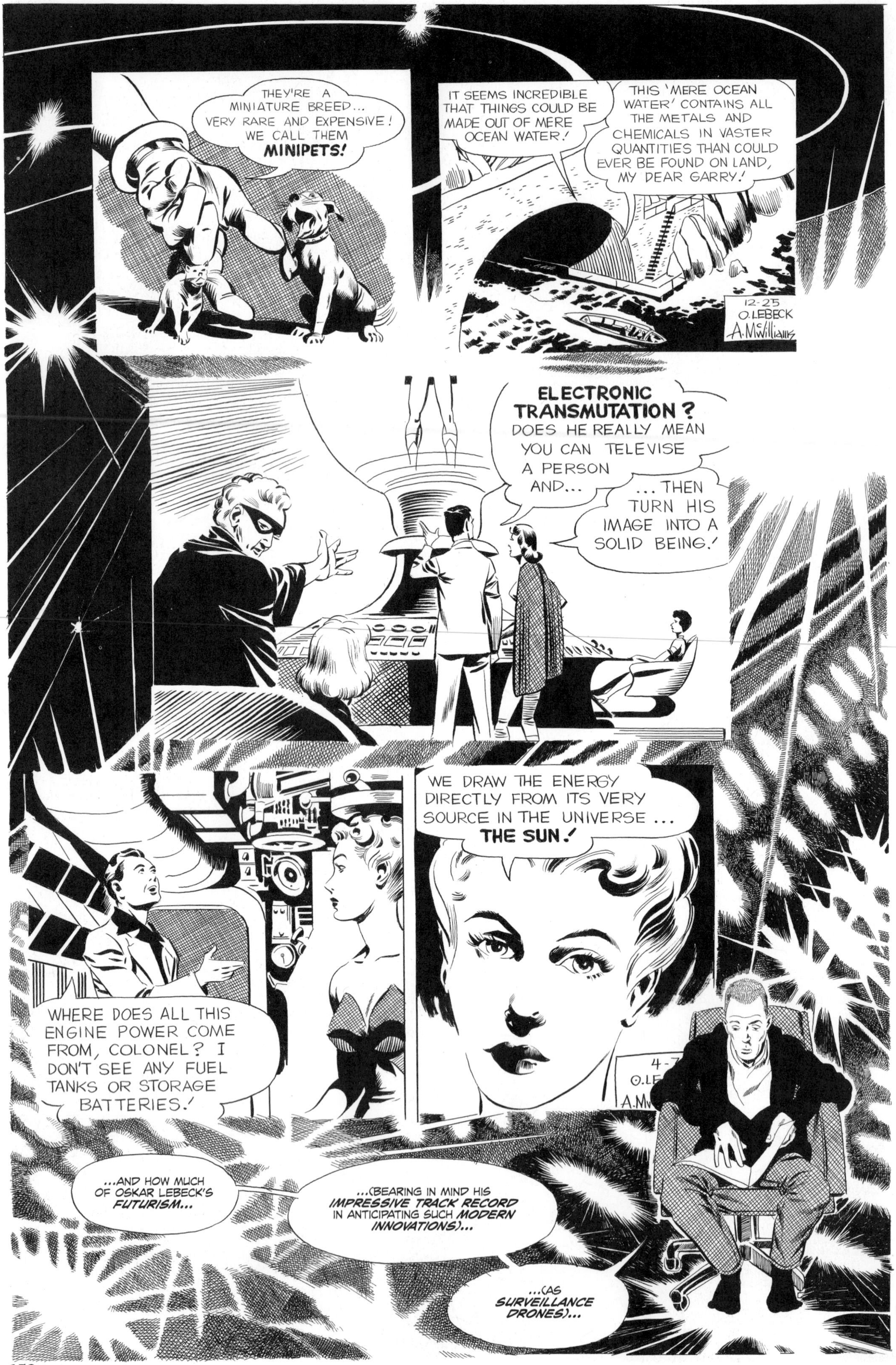
THEY'RE A MINIATURE BREED... VERY RARE AND EXPENSIVE! WE CALL THEM **MINIPETS!**
IT SEEMS INCREDIBLE THAT THINGS COULD BE MADE OUT OF MERE OCEAN WATER!
THIS 'MERE OCEAN WATER' CONTAINS ALL THE METALS AND CHEMICALS IN VASTER QUANTITIES THAN COULD EVER BE FOUND ON LAND, MY DEAR GARRY!
12-25 O. LEBECK A. McWilliams
**ELECTRONIC TRANSMUTATION?** DOES HE REALLY MEAN YOU CAN TELEVISE A PERSON AND...
...THEN TURN HIS IMAGE INTO A SOLID BEING!
WHERE DOES ALL THIS ENGINE POWER COME FROM, COLONEL? I DON'T SEE ANY FUEL TANKS OR STORAGE BATTERIES!
WE DRAW THE ENERGY DIRECTLY FROM ITS VERY SOURCE IN THE UNIVERSE ... **THE SUN!**
...AND HOW MUCH OF OSKAR LEBECK'S ***FUTURISM...***
...(BEARING IN MIND HIS ***IMPRESSIVE TRACK RECORD*** IN ANTICIPATING SUCH ***MODERN INNOVATIONS***)...
...(AS ***SURVEILLANCE DRONES***)...

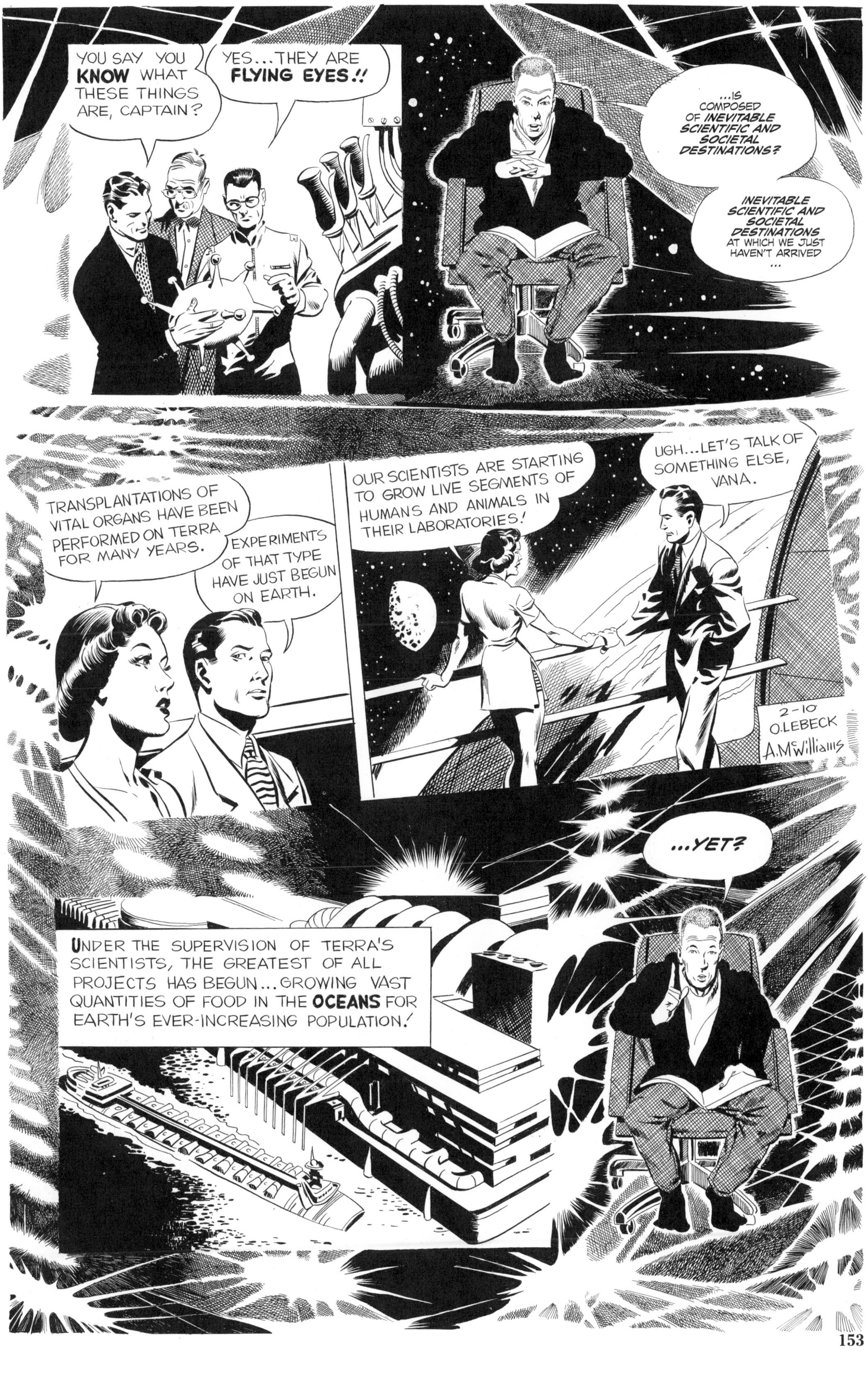
YOU SAY YOU KNOW WHAT THESE THINGS ARE, CAPTAIN?
YES... THEY ARE FLYING EYES.!!
...IS COMPOSED OF INEVITABLE SCIENTIFIC AND SOCIETAL DESTINATIONS?
INEVITABLE SCIENTIFIC AND SOCIETAL DESTINATIONS AT WHICH WE JUST HAVEN'T ARRIVED ...
TRANSPLANTATIONS OF VITAL ORGANS HAVE BEEN PERFORMED ON TERRA FOR MANY YEARS.
EXPERIMENTS OF THAT TYPE HAVE JUST BEGUN ON EARTH.
OUR SCIENTISTS ARE STARTING TO GROW LIVE SEGMENTS OF HUMANS AND ANIMALS IN THEIR LABORATORIES!
UGH...LET'S TALK OF SOMETHING ELSE, VANA.
2-10
O.LEBECK
A.McWilliams
...YET?
UNDER THE SUPERVISION OF TERRA'S SCIENTISTS, THE GREATEST OF ALL PROJECTS HAS BEGUN... GROWING VAST QUANTITIES OF FOOD IN THE OCEANS FOR EARTH'S EVER-INCREASING POPULATION!

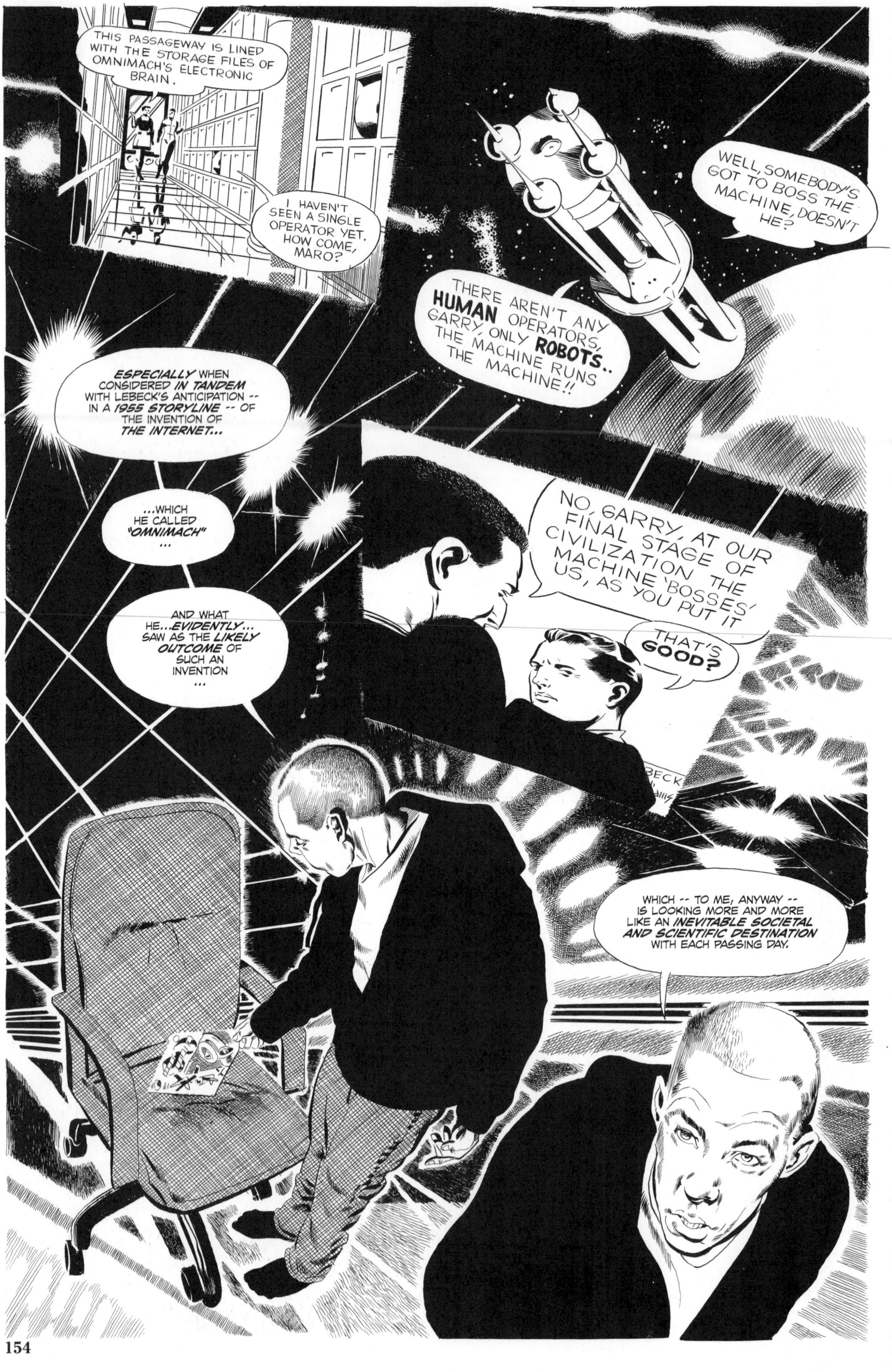
THIS PASSAGEWAY IS LINED WITH THE STORAGE FILES OF OMNIMACH'S ELECTRONIC BRAIN.
I HAVEN'T SEEN A SINGLE OPERATOR YET. HOW COME, MARO?
WELL, SOMEBODY'S GOT TO BOSS THE MACHINE, DOESN'T HE?
THERE AREN'T ANY HUMAN OPERATORS, GARRY, ONLY ROBOTS.. THE MACHINE RUNS THE MACHINE!!
ESPECIALLY WHEN CONSIDERED IN TANDEM WITH LEBECK'S ANTICIPATION -- IN A 1955 STORYLINE -- OF THE INVENTION OF THE INTERNET...
...WHICH HE CALLED "OMNIMACH" ...
AND WHAT HE...EVIDENTLY... SAW AS THE LIKELY OUTCOME OF SUCH AN INVENTION ...
NO, GARRY, AT OUR FINAL STAGE OF CIVILIZATION THE MACHINE 'BOSSES' US, AS YOU PUT IT
THAT'S GOOD?
WHICH -- TO ME, ANYWAY -- IS LOOKING MORE AND MORE LIKE AN INEVITABLE SOCIETAL AND SCIENTIFIC DESTINATION WITH EACH PASSING DAY.

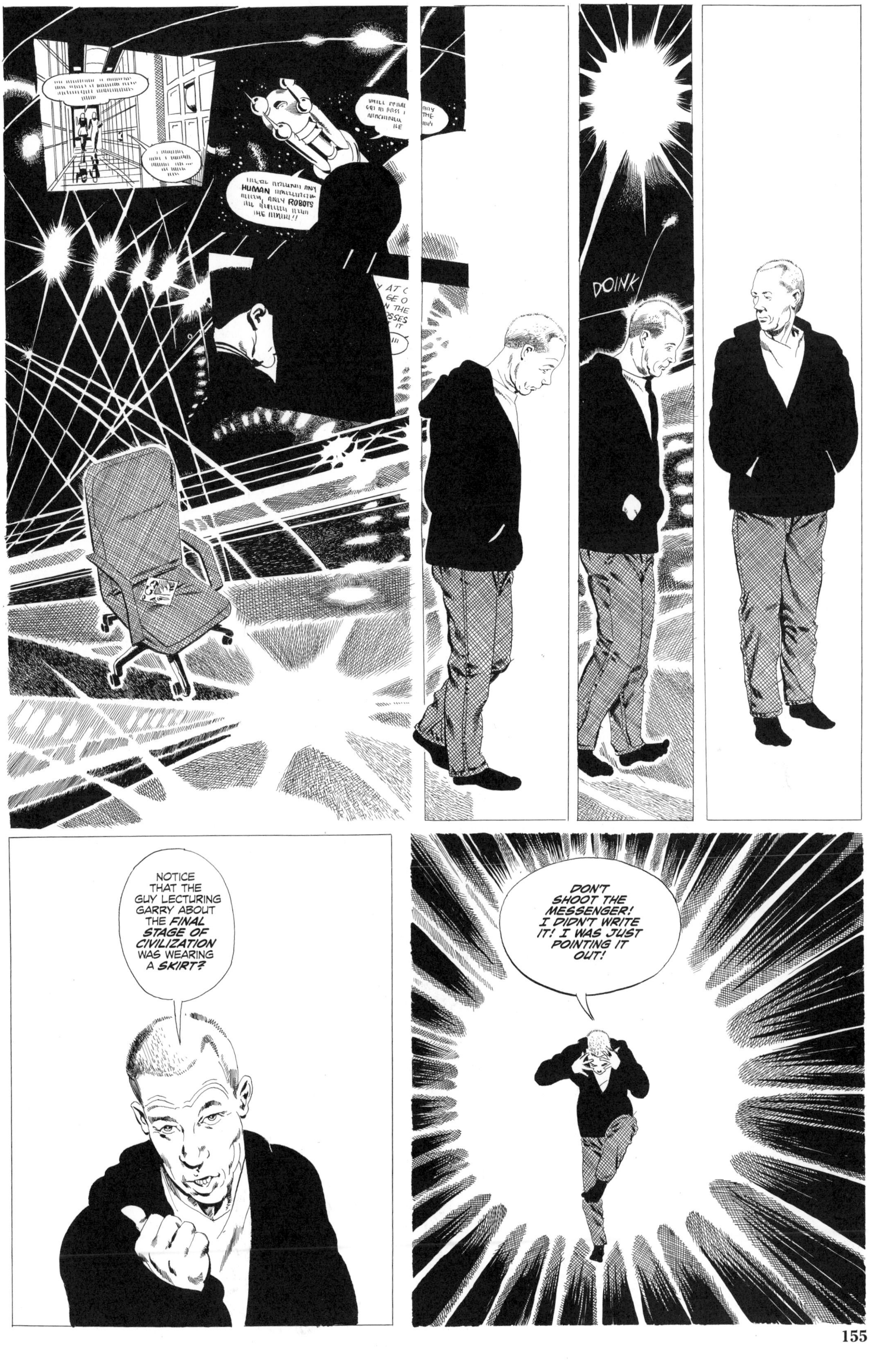
DOINK
NOTICE THAT THE GUY LECTURING GARRY ABOUT THE *FINAL STAGE OF CIVILIZATION* WAS WEARING A *SKIRT?*
*DON'T SHOOT THE MESSENGER! I DIDN'T WRITE IT! I WAS JUST POINTING IT OUT!*

SLOWLY THE THOUGHT-RECEIVING REEL BEGINS TO TURN...DRAWING THE ANSWERS FROM THE MEMORY CELLS WITHIN HIS BRAIN...

GARRY'S FACE REVEALS THE AGONY OF THE MENTAL STRAIN INDUCED BY THE MECHANICAL BRAIN-PROBING PROCESS!!

ACTUALLY, IF LEBECK IS RIGHT, *THOUGHT-RECORDING MACHINES* ARE ALSO IN OUR FUTURE, MACHINES THAT CAN DETERMINE...*FLAWLESSLY*...IF YOU'RE THINKING THE *WRONG WAY!*

WHAT'S HAPPENED? CRIPES! I FEEL AS IF I'VE BEEN THROUGH A *WRINGER!*

YOU HAVE... A *MENTAL WRINGER!*

FOR ALL OF YOU WHO BELIEVE I SHOULDN'T BE *ALLOWED TO THINK* THERE'S SOMETHING *WRONG* WITH A MAN WEARING A SKIRT

HERE ARE YOUR RECORDED SUBCONSCIOUS ANSWERS... THEY WILL DECIDE *YOUR FUTURE!*

I COULDN'T CARE LESS!

O... BU... YOU WILL...THE ... P...NISHMENT FOR A CRIM... AGAINST THE STATE IS A COMPLETE *BRAIN-WASH!!* NOT A PLEASANT PROCESS, AS I SHALL SHOW YOU!!

11-4 O. LEBECK
A M°Williams

WHAT A FIENDISH THING! YOU'VE DESTROYED HIS MIND!

GOO GOO...

CORRECTION, PLEASE... OUR *BRAIN-WASHER* ONLY CLEANED OUT THE MENTAL MESS...

*DEFINITELY* SOMETHING TO LOOK FORWARD TO.

IT REMOVED 97 YARDS OF MEMORY RECORDING TAPE FROM HIS BRAIN--SUCH DEPRAVITY AND POLITICAL GARBAGE. TUT, TUT

YOUR ATTITUDE TURNS MY STOMACH!

MY NARRATIVE REGARDING *THE STRANGE DEATH OF ALEX RAYMOND* IS, NECESSARILY, *INCOMPLETE.*

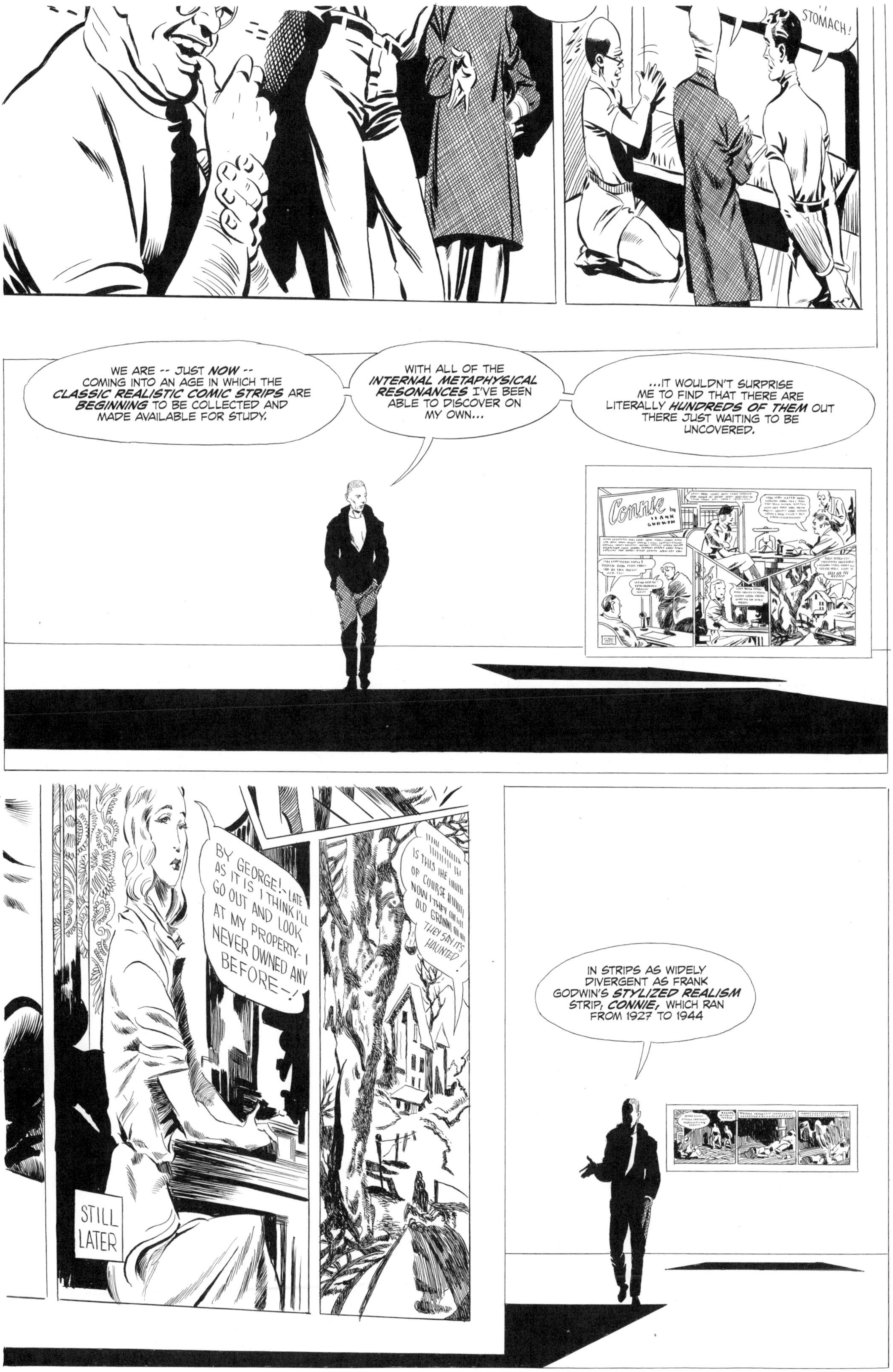
STOMACH!
WE ARE -- JUST NOW -- COMING INTO AN AGE IN WHICH THE CLASSIC REALISTIC COMIC STRIPS ARE BEGINNING TO BE COLLECTED AND MADE AVAILABLE FOR STUDY.
WITH ALL OF THE INTERNAL METAPHYSICAL RESONANCES I'VE BEEN ABLE TO DISCOVER ON MY OWN...
...IT WOULDN'T SURPRISE ME TO FIND THAT THERE ARE LITERALLY HUNDREDS OF THEM OUT THERE JUST WAITING TO BE UNCOVERED.
BY GEORGE! - LATE AS IT IS I THINK I'LL GO OUT AND LOOK AT MY PROPERTY - I NEVER OWNED ANY BEFORE -!
THEY SAY IT'S HAUNTED
STILL LATER
IN STRIPS AS WIDELY DIVERGENT AS FRANK GODWIN'S STYLIZED REALISM STRIP, CONNIE, WHICH RAN FROM 1927 TO 1944

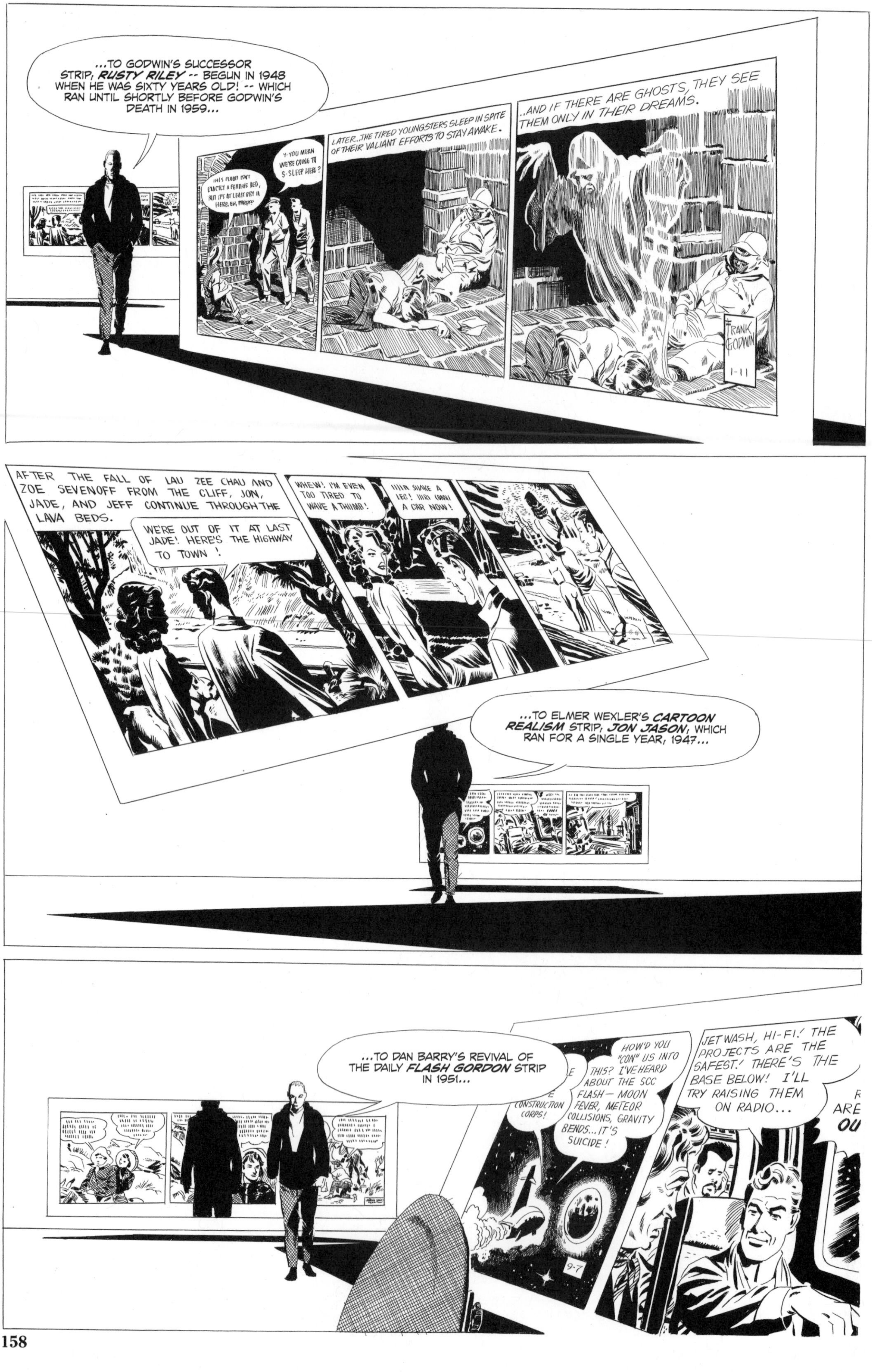
...TO GODWIN'S SUCCESSOR STRIP, RUSTY RILEY -- BEGUN IN 1948 WHEN HE WAS SIXTY YEARS OLD! -- WHICH RAN UNTIL SHORTLY BEFORE GODWIN'S DEATH IN 1959...
THIS FLOOR ISN'T EXACTLY A FEATHER BED, BUT IT'S AT LEAST DRY IN HERE, EH, PARDS?
Y-YOU MEAN WE'RE GOING TO S-SLEEP HERE?
LATER...THE TIRED YOUNGSTERS SLEEP IN SPITE OF THEIR VALIANT EFFORTS TO STAY AWAKE.
..AND IF THERE ARE GHOSTS, THEY SEE THEM ONLY IN THEIR DREAMS.
FRANK GODWIN
1-11
AFTER THE FALL OF LAU ZEE CHAU AND ZOE SEVENOFF FROM THE CLIFF, JON, JADE, AND JEFF CONTINUE THROUGH THE LAVA BEDS.
WE'RE OUT OF IT AT LAST JADE! HERE'S THE HIGHWAY TO TOWN!
WHEW! I'M EVEN TOO TIRED TO WAVE A THUMB!
...TO ELMER WEXLER'S CARTOON REALISM STRIP, JON JASON, WHICH RAN FOR A SINGLE YEAR, 1947...
...TO DAN BARRY'S REVIVAL OF THE DAILY FLASH GORDON STRIP IN 1951...
HOW'D YOU "CON" US INTO THIS? I'VE HEARD ABOUT THE SCC FLASH— MOON FEVER, METEOR COLLISIONS, GRAVITY BENDS...IT'S SUICIDE!
JET WASH, HI-FI! THE PROJECTS ARE THE SAFEST! THERE'S THE BASE BELOW! I'LL TRY RAISING THEM ON RADIO...
9-7

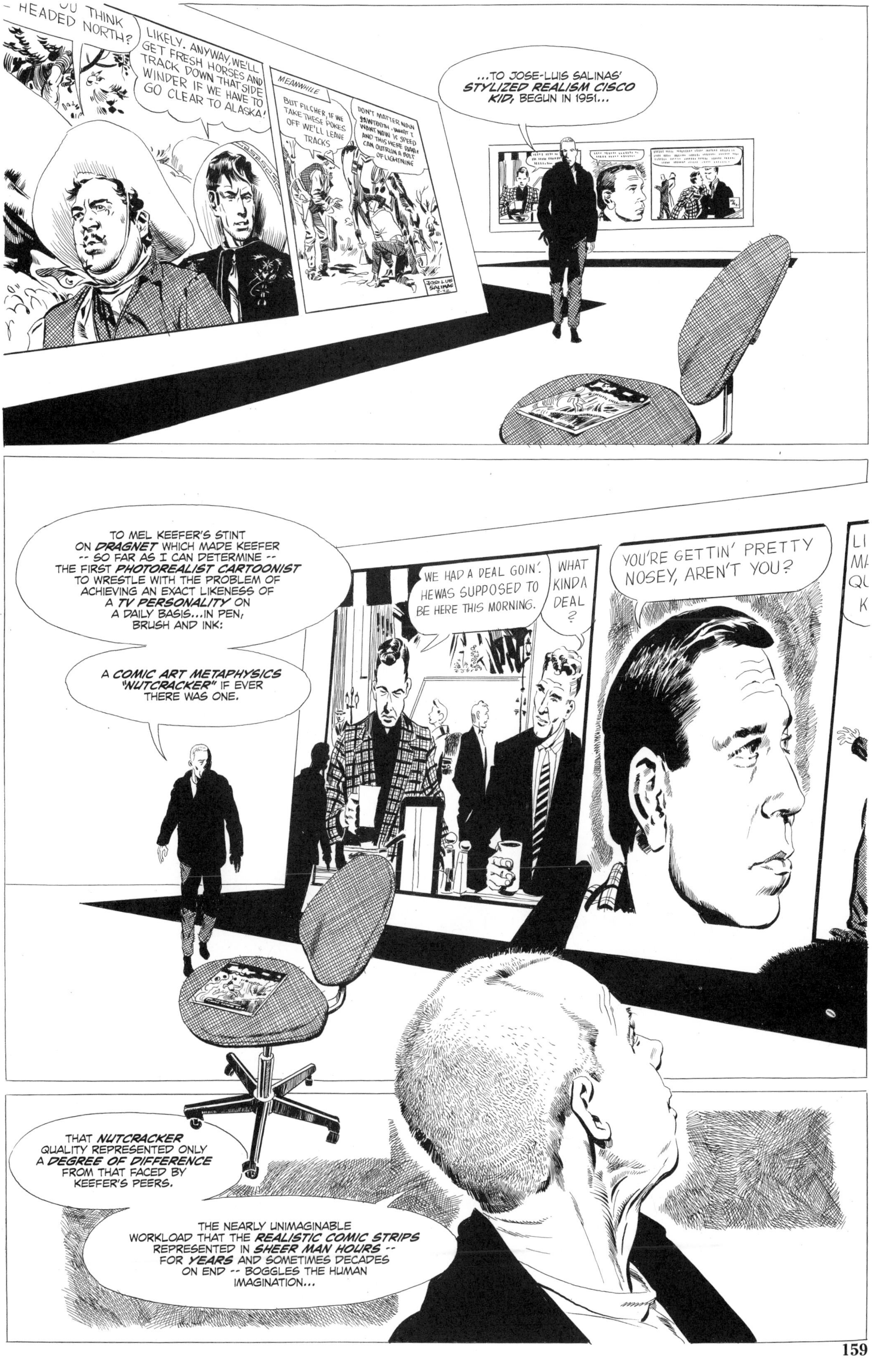
HEADED NORTH?
LIKELY. ANYWAY, WE'LL GET FRESH HORSES AND TRACK DOWN THAT SIDE WINDER IF WE HAVE TO GO CLEAR TO ALASKA!
MEANWHILE
BUT FILCHER, IF WE TAKE THESE POKES OFF WE'LL LEAVE TRACKS
DON'T MATTER NOW SAWTOOTH, WHAT I WANT NOW IS SPEED AND THIS HERE DIABLO CAN OUTRUN A BOLT OF LIGHTNING
...TO JOSE-LUIS SALINAS' STYLIZED REALISM CISCO KID, BEGUN IN 1951...
TO MEL KEEFER'S STINT ON DRAGNET WHICH MADE KEEFER -- SO FAR AS I CAN DETERMINE -- THE FIRST PHOTOREALIST CARTOONIST TO WRESTLE WITH THE PROBLEM OF ACHIEVING AN EXACT LIKENESS OF A TV PERSONALITY ON A DAILY BASIS...IN PEN, BRUSH AND INK:
A COMIC ART METAPHYSICS "NUTCRACKER" IF EVER THERE WAS ONE.
WE HAD A DEAL GOIN'. HE WAS SUPPOSED TO BE HERE THIS MORNING.
WHAT KINDA DEAL?
YOU'RE GETTIN' PRETTY NOSEY, AREN'T YOU?
THAT NUTCRACKER QUALITY REPRESENTED ONLY A DEGREE OF DIFFERENCE FROM THAT FACED BY KEEFER'S PEERS.
THE NEARLY UNIMAGINABLE WORKLOAD THAT THE REALISTIC COMIC STRIPS REPRESENTED IN SHEER MAN HOURS -- FOR YEARS AND SOMETIMES DECADES ON END -- BOGGLES THE HUMAN IMAGINATION...

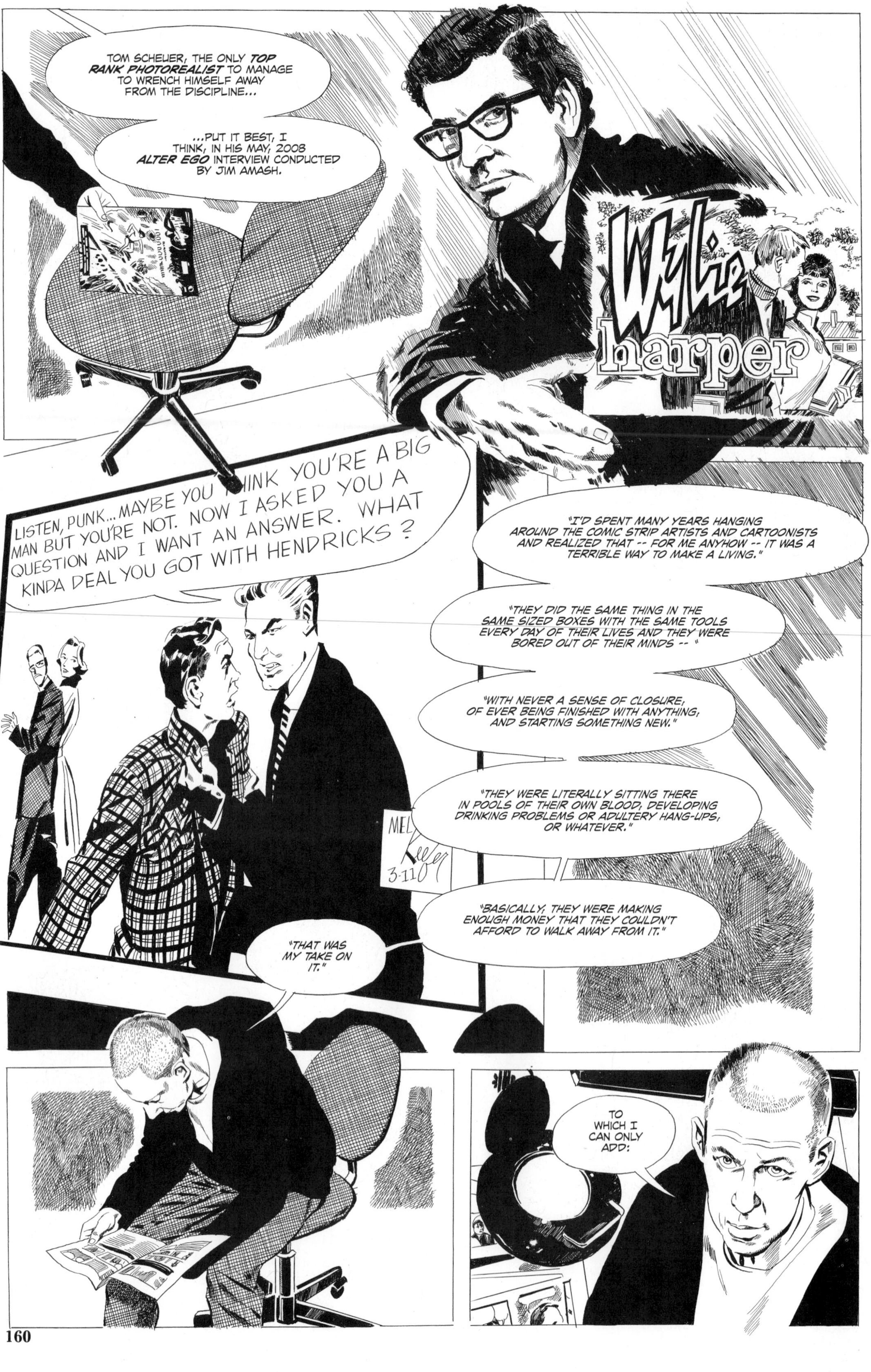
TOM SCHEUER, THE ONLY TOP RANK PHOTOREALIST TO MANAGE TO WRENCH HIMSELF AWAY FROM THE DISCIPLINE...
...PUT IT BEST, I THINK, IN HIS MAY, 2008 ALTER EGO INTERVIEW CONDUCTED BY JIM AMASH.
Wylie harper
LISTEN, PUNK... MAYBE YOU THINK YOU'RE A BIG MAN BUT YOU'RE NOT. NOW I ASKED YOU A QUESTION AND I WANT AN ANSWER. WHAT KINDA DEAL YOU GOT WITH HENDRICKS ?
"I'D SPENT MANY YEARS HANGING AROUND THE COMIC STRIP ARTISTS AND CARTOONISTS AND REALIZED THAT -- FOR ME ANYHOW -- IT WAS A TERRIBLE WAY TO MAKE A LIVING."
"THEY DID THE SAME THING IN THE SAME SIZED BOXES WITH THE SAME TOOLS EVERY DAY OF THEIR LIVES AND THEY WERE BORED OUT OF THEIR MINDS -- "
"WITH NEVER A SENSE OF CLOSURE, OF EVER BEING FINISHED WITH ANYTHING, AND STARTING SOMETHING NEW."
"THEY WERE LITERALLY SITTING THERE IN POOLS OF THEIR OWN BLOOD, DEVELOPING DRINKING PROBLEMS OR ADULTERY HANG-UPS, OR WHATEVER."
"BASICALLY, THEY WERE MAKING ENOUGH MONEY THAT THEY COULDN'T AFFORD TO WALK AWAY FROM IT."
"THAT WAS MY TAKE ON IT."
TO WHICH I CAN ONLY ADD:

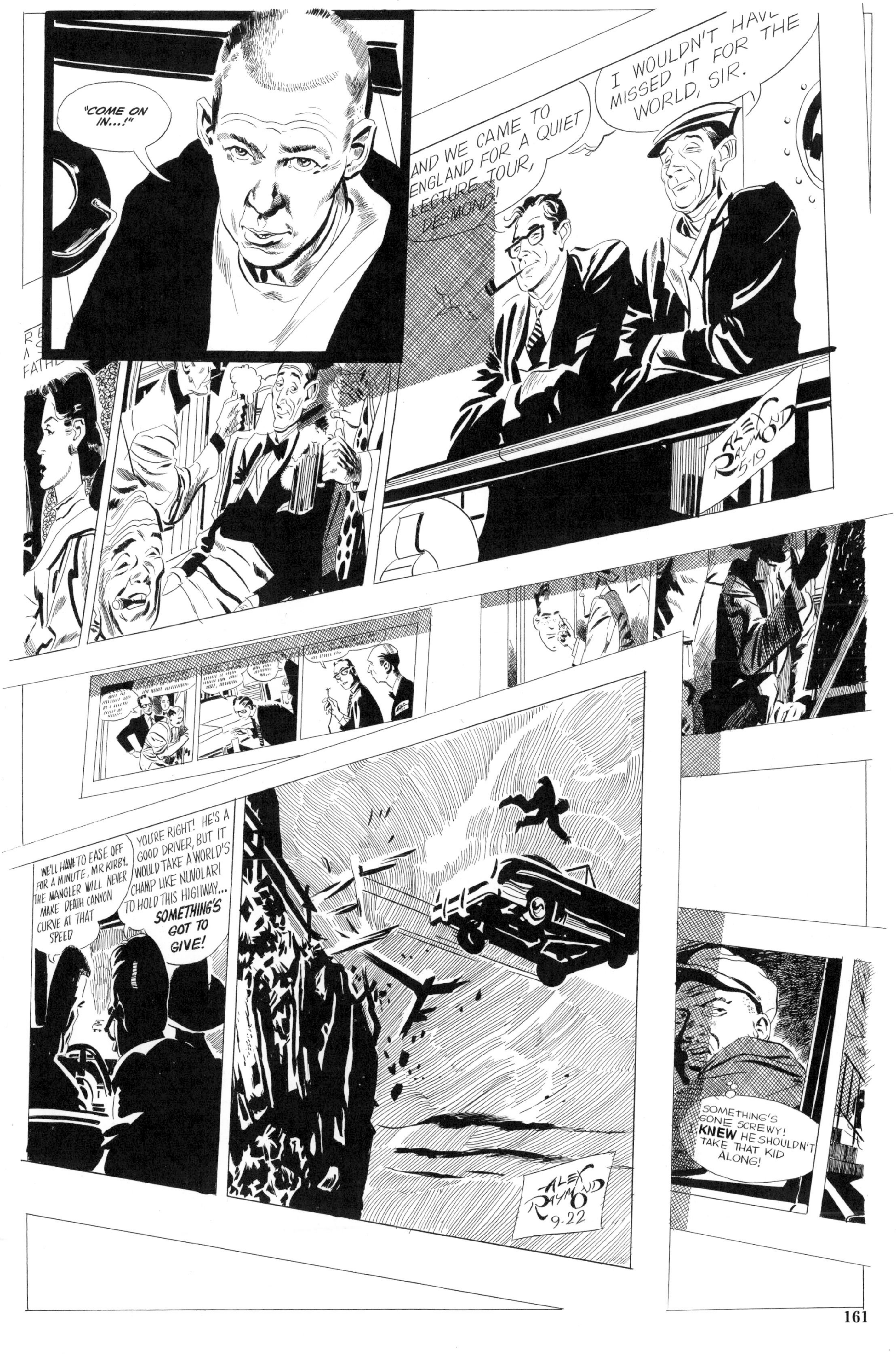
"COME ON IN...!"
AND WE CAME TO ENGLAND FOR A QUIET LECTURE TOUR, DESMOND!
I WOULDN'T HAVE MISSED IT FOR THE WORLD, SIR.
ALEX RAYMOND 5-19
WE'LL HAVE TO EASE OFF FOR A MINUTE, MR KIRBY.. THE MANGLER WILL NEVER MAKE DEATH CANYON CURVE AT THAT SPEED
YOU'RE RIGHT! HE'S A GOOD DRIVER, BUT IT WOULD TAKE A WORLD'S CHAMP LIKE NUVOLARI TO HOLD THIS HIGHWAY... SOMETHING'S GOT TO GIVE!
ALEX RAYMOND 9-22
SOMETHING'S GONE SCREWY! KNEW HE SHOULDN'T TAKE THAT KID ALONG!

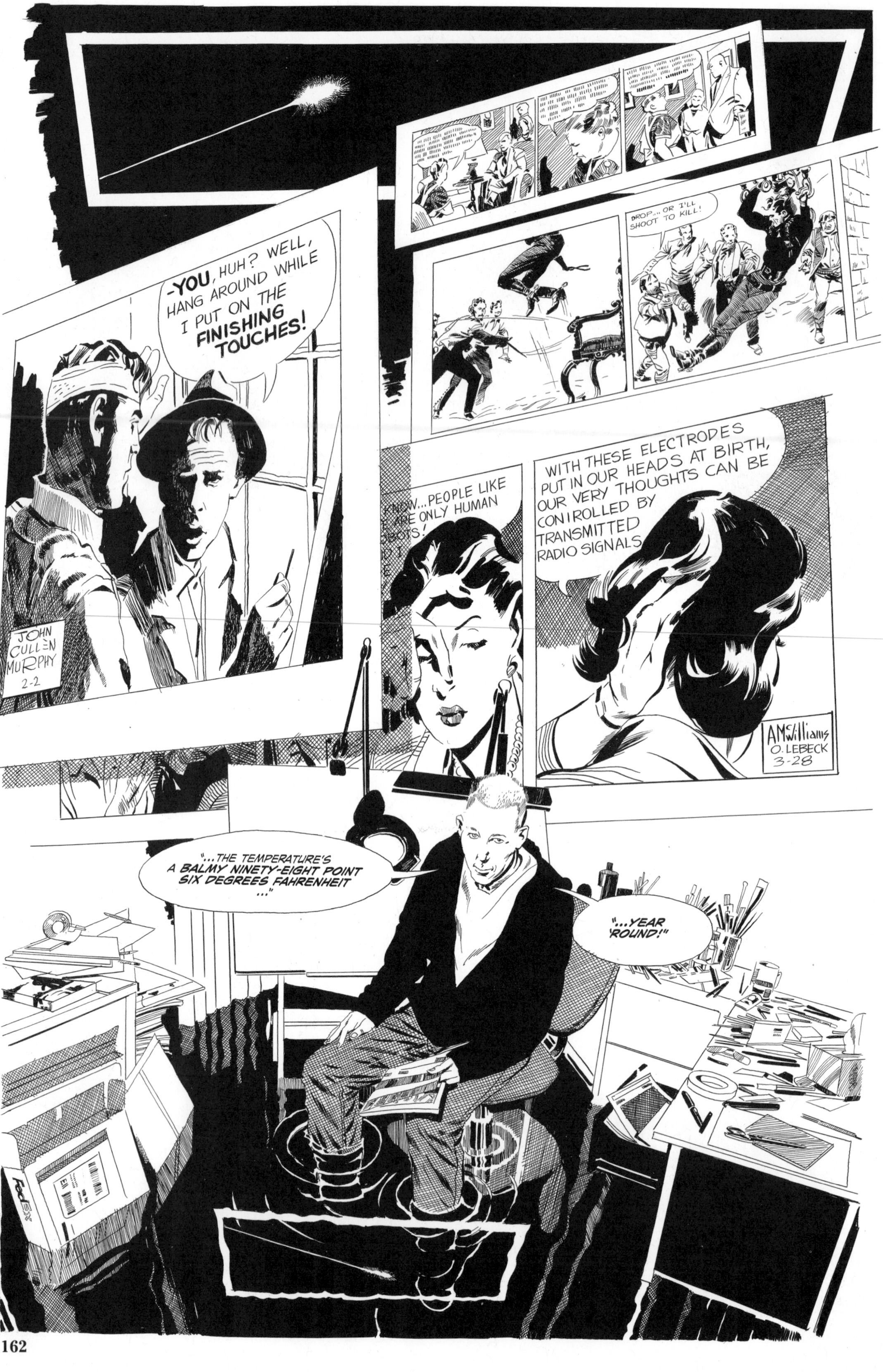
-YOU, HUH? WELL, HANG AROUND WHILE I PUT ON THE FINISHING TOUCHES!
JOHN CULLEN MURPHY 2-2
DROP... OR I'LL SHOOT TO KILL!
KNOW... PEOPLE LIKE
ARE ONLY HUMAN
WITH THESE ELECTRODES PUT IN OUR HEADS AT BIRTH, OUR VERY THOUGHTS CAN BE CONTROLLED BY TRANSMITTED RADIO SIGNALS
AMcWilliams O. LEBECK 3-28
"...THE TEMPERATURE'S A BALMY NINETY-EIGHT POINT SIX DEGREES FAHRENHEIT ..."
"...YEAR 'ROUND!"

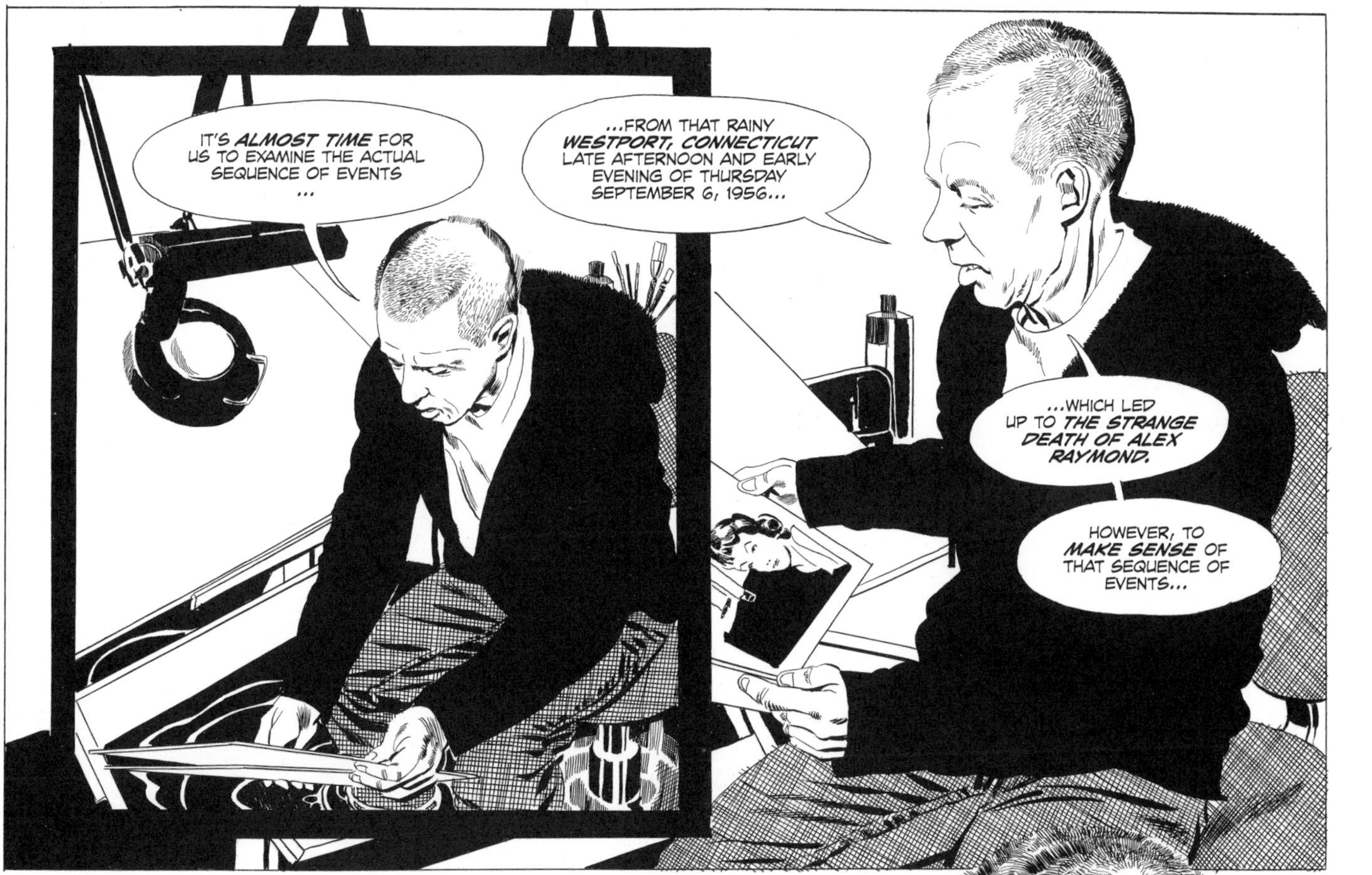
IT'S ALMOST TIME FOR US TO EXAMINE THE ACTUAL SEQUENCE OF EVENTS ...
...FROM THAT RAINY WESTPORT, CONNECTICUT LATE AFTERNOON AND EARLY EVENING OF THURSDAY SEPTEMBER 6, 1956...
...WHICH LED UP TO THE STRANGE DEATH OF ALEX RAYMOND.
HOWEVER, TO MAKE SENSE OF THAT SEQUENCE OF EVENTS...

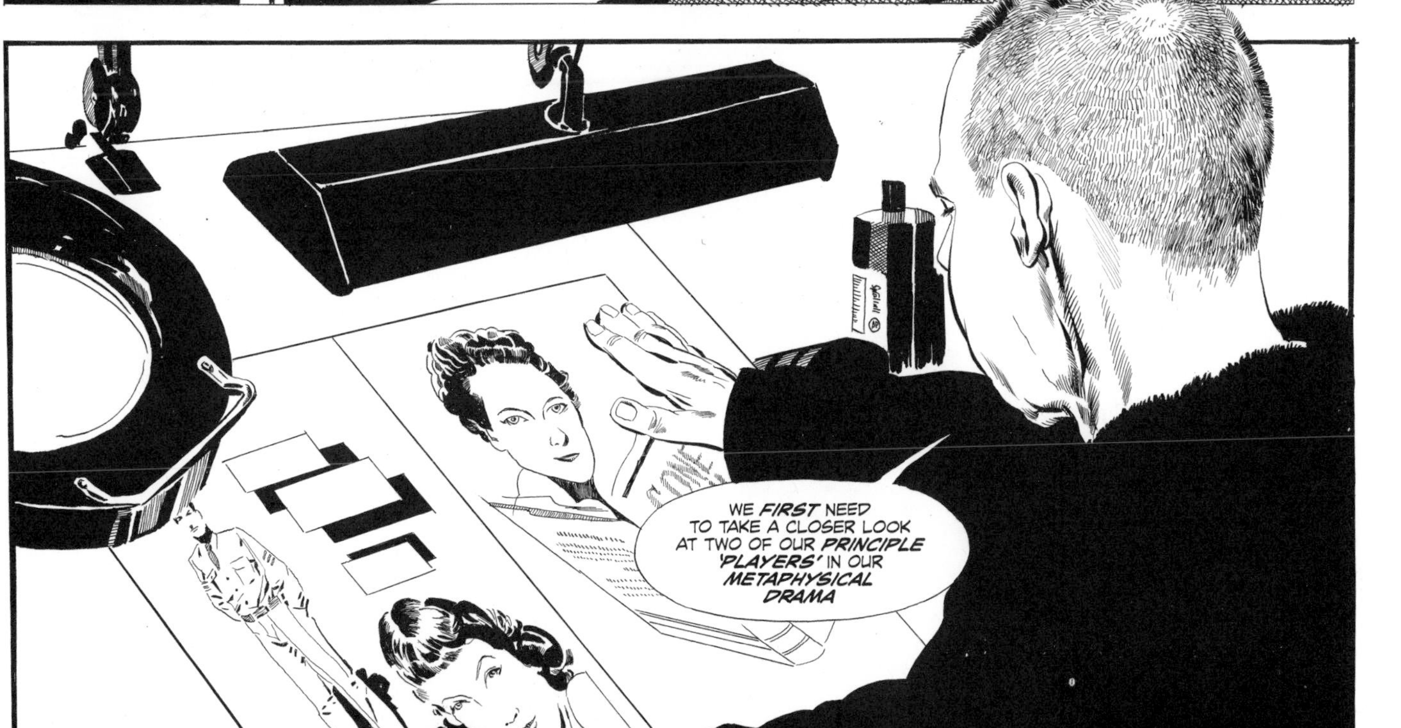
WE FIRST NEED TO TAKE A CLOSER LOOK AT TWO OF OUR PRINCIPLE 'PLAYERS' IN OUR METAPHYSICAL DRAMA

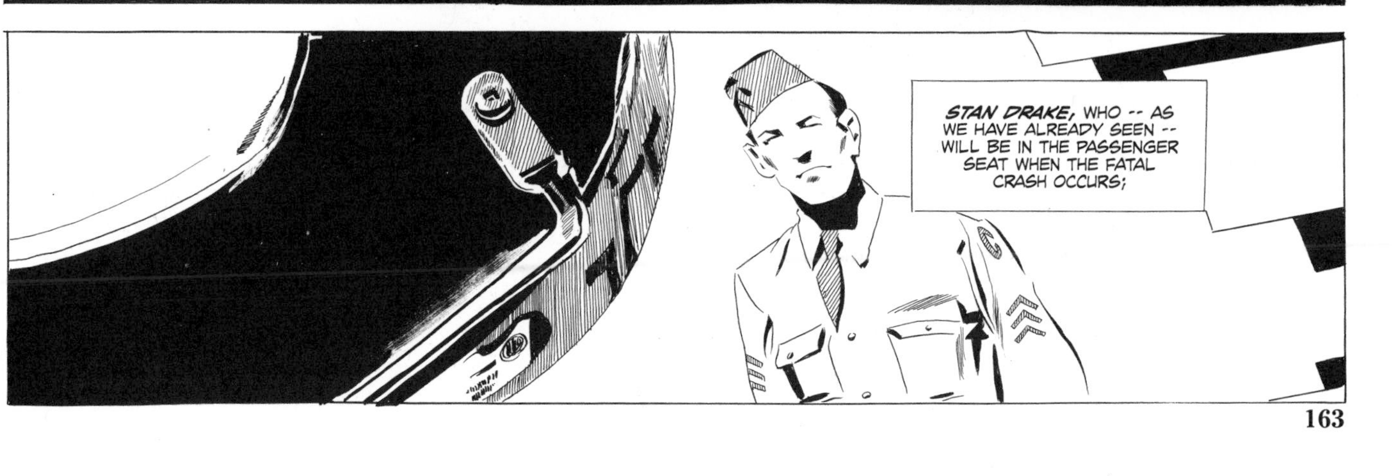
STAN DRAKE, WHO -- AS WE HAVE ALREADY SEEN -- WILL BE IN THE PASSENGER SEAT WHEN THE FATAL CRASH OCCURS;

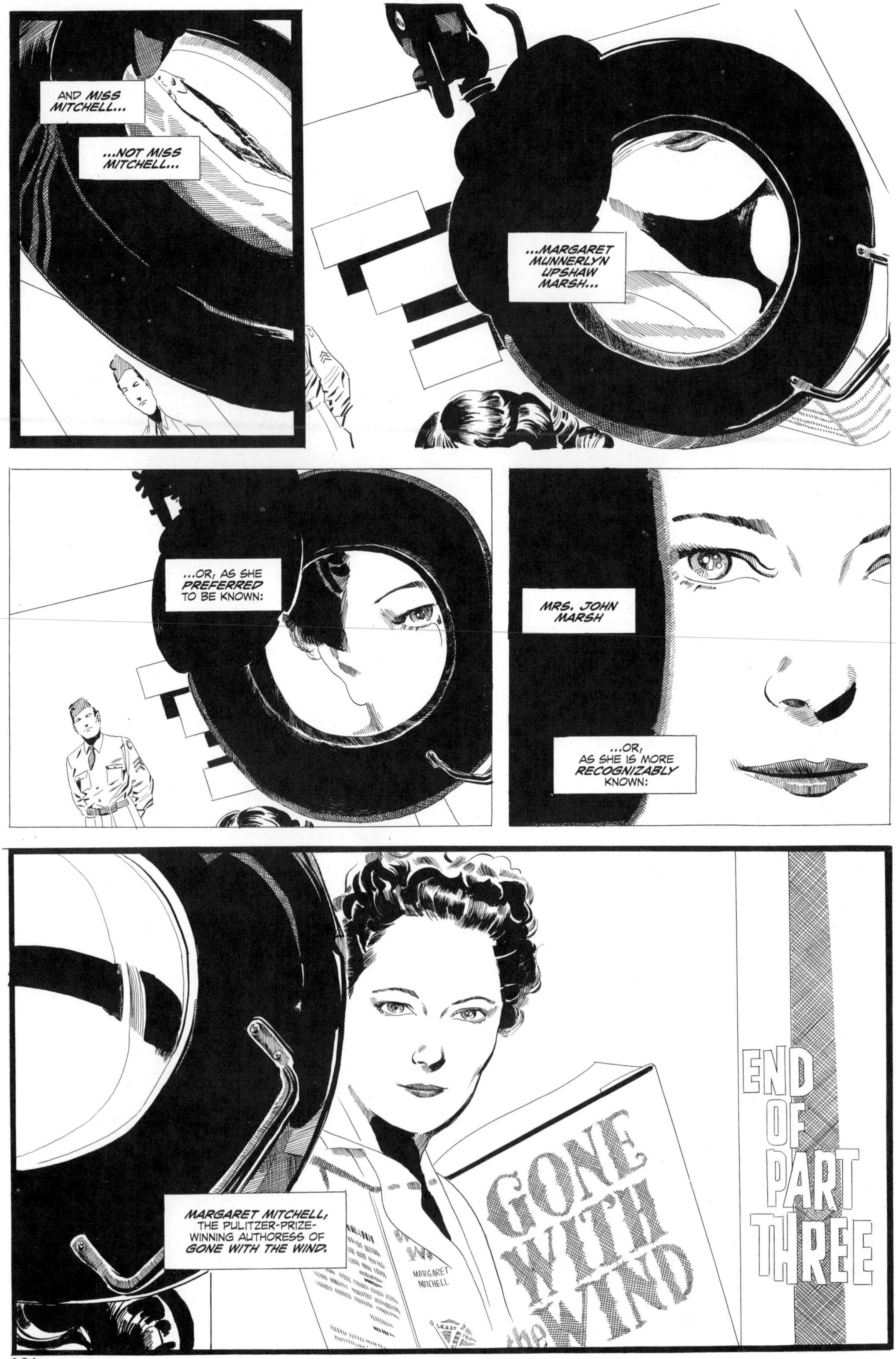
AND MISS MITCHELL...
...NOT MISS MITCHELL...
...MARGARET MUNNERLYN UPSHAW MARSH...
...OR, AS SHE PREFERRED TO BE KNOWN:
MRS. JOHN MARSH
...OR, AS SHE IS MORE RECOGNIZABLY KNOWN:
MARGARET MITCHELL, THE PULITZER-PRIZE-WINNING AUTHORESS OF GONE WITH THE WIND.
MARGARET MITCHELL
GONE WITH the WIND
END OF PART THREE

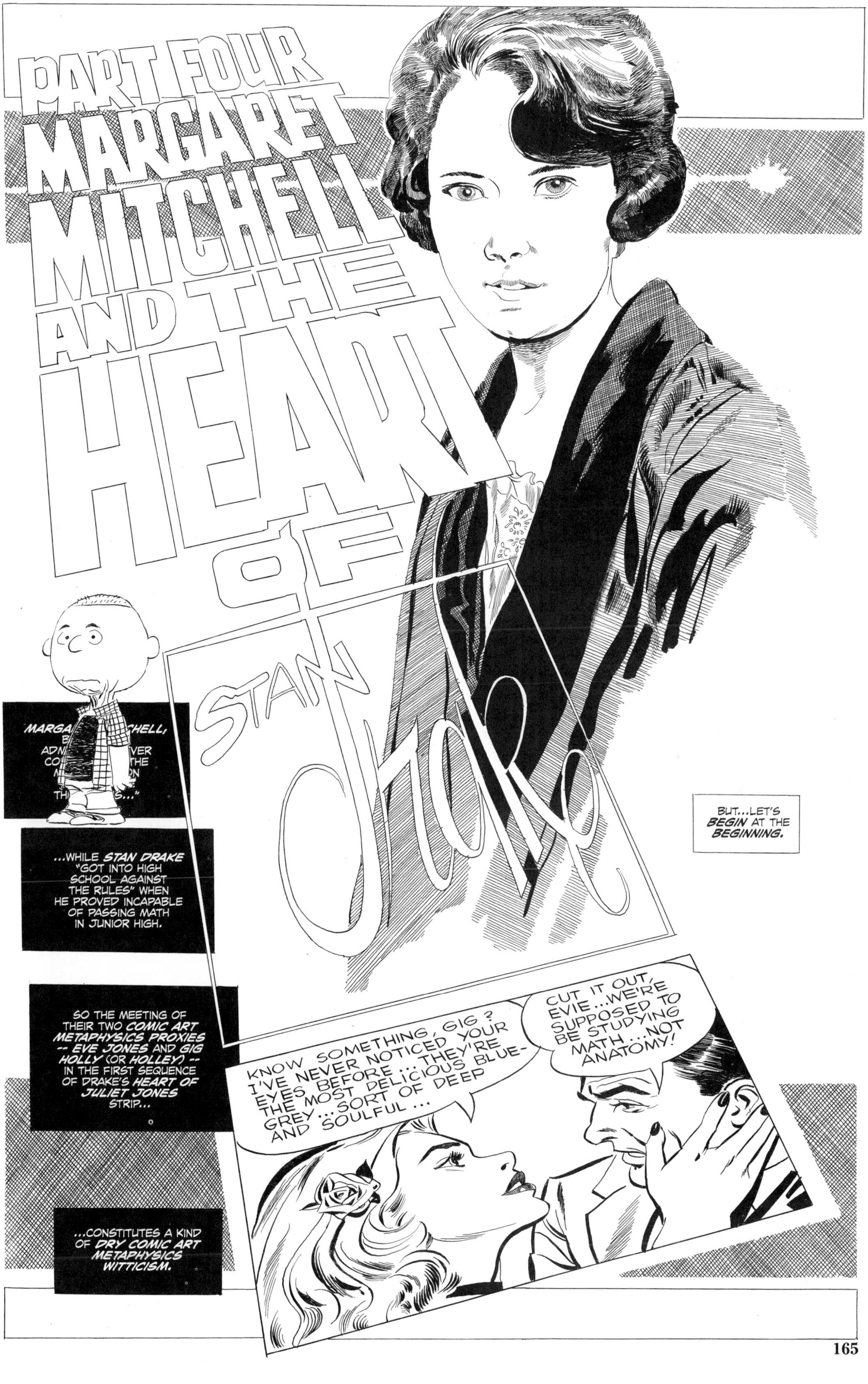

PART FOUR
MARGARET MITCHELL AND THE HEART OF
STAN DRAKE
...WHILE STAN DRAKE "GOT INTO HIGH SCHOOL AGAINST THE RULES" WHEN HE PROVED INCAPABLE OF PASSING MATH IN JUNIOR HIGH.
BUT...LET'S BEGIN AT THE BEGINNING.
SO THE MEETING OF THEIR TWO COMIC ART METAPHYSICS PROXIES -- EVE JONES AND GIG HOLLY (OR HOLLEY) -- IN THE FIRST SEQUENCE OF DRAKE'S HEART OF JULIET JONES STRIP...
KNOW SOMETHING, GIG? I'VE NEVER NOTICED YOUR EYES BEFORE... THEY'RE THE MOST DELICIOUS BLUE-GREY... SORT OF DEEP AND SOULFUL...
CUT IT OUT, EVIE... WE'RE SUPPOSED TO BE STUDYING MATH... NOT ANATOMY!
...CONSTITUTES A KIND OF DRY COMIC ART METAPHYSICS WITTICISM.

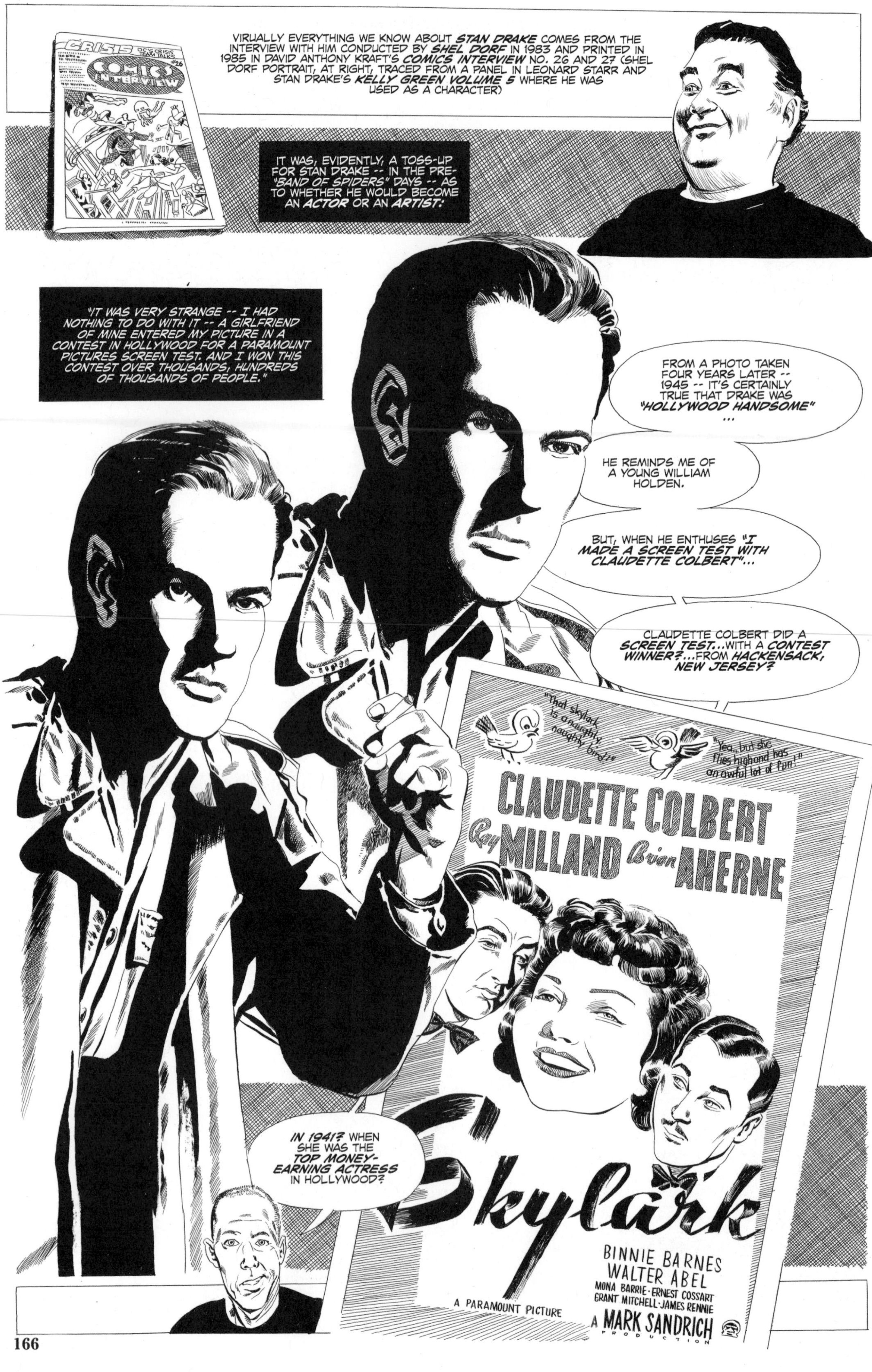
CRISIS
COMICS INTERVIEW
#26
VIRUALLY EVERYTHING WE KNOW ABOUT STAN DRAKE COMES FROM THE INTERVIEW WITH HIM CONDUCTED BY SHEL DORF IN 1983 AND PRINTED IN 1985 IN DAVID ANTHONY KRAFT'S COMICS INTERVIEW NO. 26 AND 27 (SHEL DORF PORTRAIT, AT RIGHT, TRACED FROM A PANEL IN LEONARD STARR AND STAN DRAKE'S KELLY GREEN VOLUME 5 WHERE HE WAS USED AS A CHARACTER)
IT WAS, EVIDENTLY, A TOSS-UP FOR STAN DRAKE -- IN THE PRE-"BAND OF SPIDERS" DAYS -- AS TO WHETHER HE WOULD BECOME AN ACTOR OR AN ARTIST:
"IT WAS VERY STRANGE -- I HAD NOTHING TO DO WITH IT -- A GIRLFRIEND OF MINE ENTERED MY PICTURE IN A CONTEST IN HOLLYWOOD FOR A PARAMOUNT PICTURES SCREEN TEST. AND I WON THIS CONTEST OVER THOUSANDS, HUNDREDS OF THOUSANDS OF PEOPLE."
FROM A PHOTO TAKEN FOUR YEARS LATER -- 1945 -- IT'S CERTAINLY TRUE THAT DRAKE WAS "HOLLYWOOD HANDSOME" ...
HE REMINDS ME OF A YOUNG WILLIAM HOLDEN.
BUT, WHEN HE ENTHUSES "I MADE A SCREEN TEST WITH CLAUDETTE COLBERT"...
CLAUDETTE COLBERT DID A SCREEN TEST...WITH A CONTEST WINNER?...FROM HACKENSACK, NEW JERSEY?
"That skylark is a naughty, naughty bird!"
"Yea.. but she flies highand has an awful lot of fun!"
CLAUDETTE COLBERT
Ray MILLAND Brian AHERNE
Skylark
BINNIE BARNES
WALTER ABEL
MONA BARRIE · ERNEST COSSART
GRANT MITCHELL · JAMES RENNIE
A PARAMOUNT PICTURE
A MARK SANDRICH PRODUCTION
IN 1941? WHEN SHE WAS THE TOP MONEY-EARNING ACTRESS IN HOLLYWOOD?

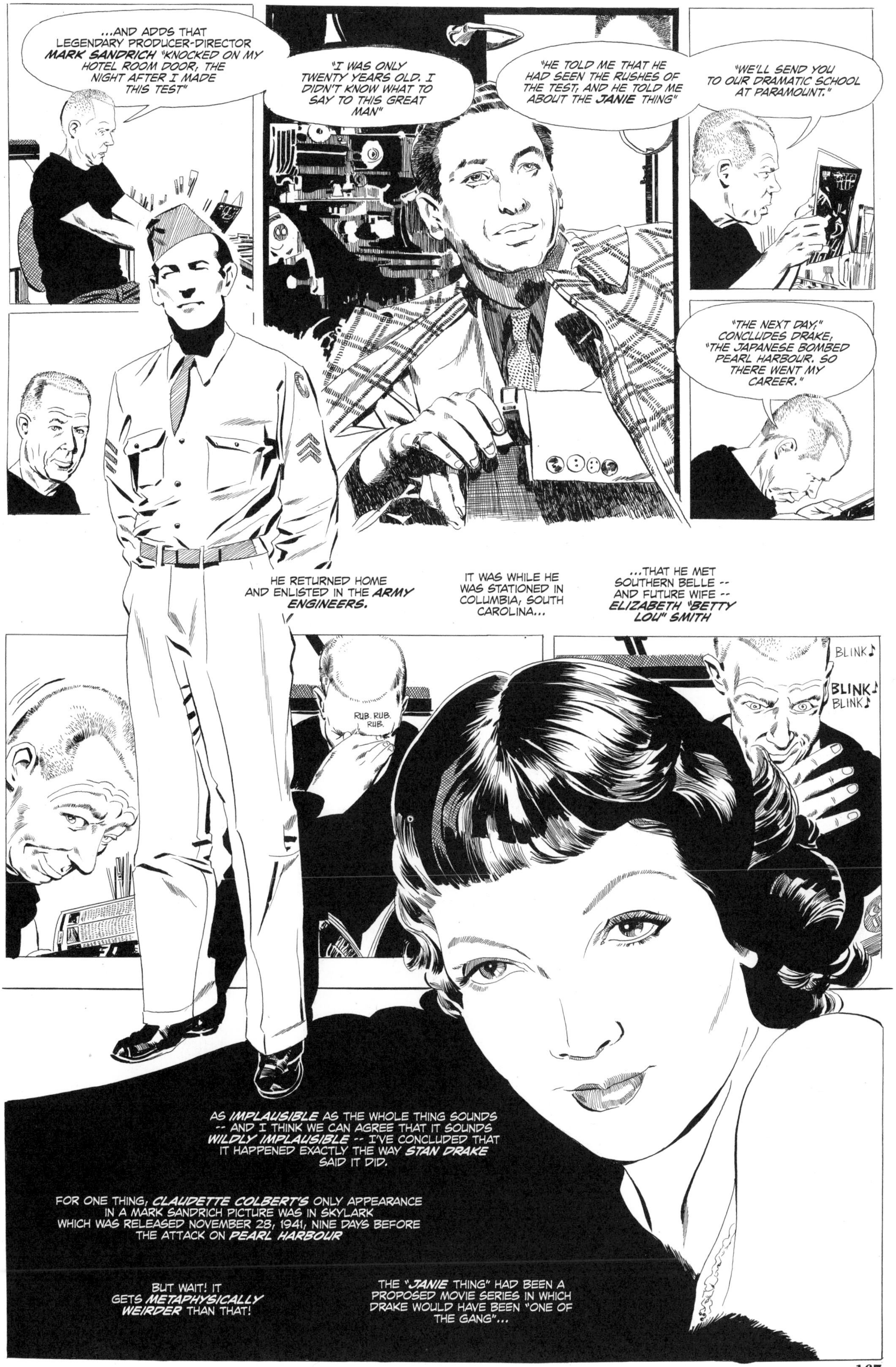
...AND ADDS THAT LEGENDARY PRODUCER-DIRECTOR MARK SANDRICH "KNOCKED ON MY HOTEL ROOM DOOR, THE NIGHT AFTER I MADE THIS TEST"
"I WAS ONLY TWENTY YEARS OLD. I DIDN'T KNOW WHAT TO SAY TO THIS GREAT MAN"
"HE TOLD ME THAT HE HAD SEEN THE RUSHES OF THE TEST, AND HE TOLD ME ABOUT THE JANIE THING"
"WE'LL SEND YOU TO OUR DRAMATIC SCHOOL AT PARAMOUNT."
"THE NEXT DAY," CONCLUDES DRAKE, "THE JAPANESE BOMBED PEARL HARBOUR. SO THERE WENT MY CAREER."
HE RETURNED HOME AND ENLISTED IN THE ARMY ENGINEERS.
IT WAS WHILE HE WAS STATIONED IN COLUMBIA, SOUTH CAROLINA...
...THAT HE MET SOUTHERN BELLE -- AND FUTURE WIFE -- ELIZABETH "BETTY LOU" SMITH
RUB. RUB. RUB.
BLINK♪
BLINK♪
BLINK♪
AS IMPLAUSIBLE AS THE WHOLE THING SOUNDS -- AND I THINK WE CAN AGREE THAT IT SOUNDS WILDLY IMPLAUSIBLE -- I'VE CONCLUDED THAT IT HAPPENED EXACTLY THE WAY STAN DRAKE SAID IT DID.
FOR ONE THING, CLAUDETTE COLBERT'S ONLY APPEARANCE IN A MARK SANDRICH PICTURE WAS IN SKYLARK WHICH WAS RELEASED NOVEMBER 28, 1941, NINE DAYS BEFORE THE ATTACK ON PEARL HARBOUR
BUT WAIT! IT GETS METAPHYSICALLY WEIRDER THAN THAT!
THE "JANIE THING" HAD BEEN A PROPOSED MOVIE SERIES IN WHICH DRAKE WOULD HAVE BEEN "ONE OF THE GANG"...

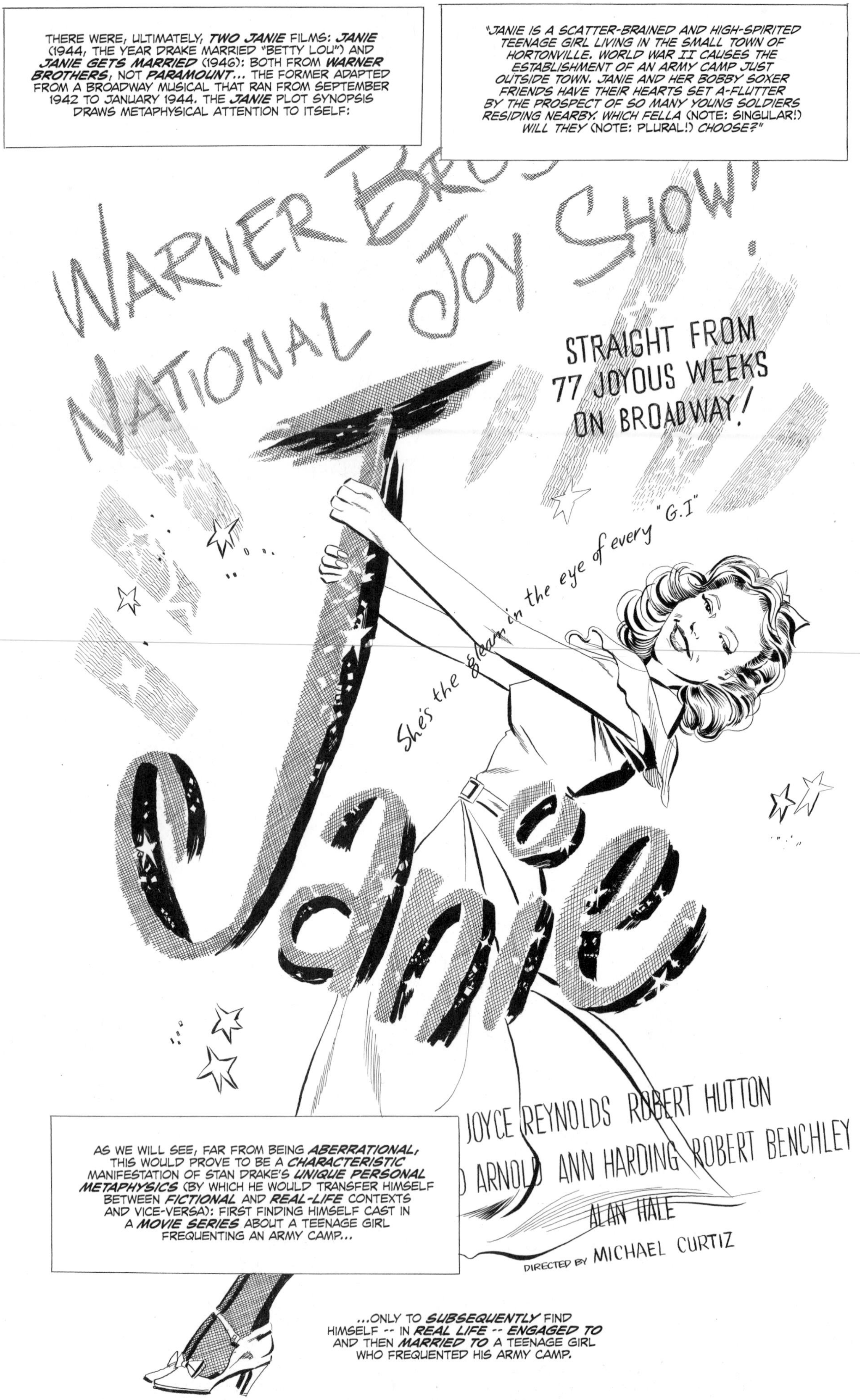

THERE WERE, ULTIMATELY, TWO JANIE FILMS: JANIE (1944, THE YEAR DRAKE MARRIED "BETTY LOU") AND JANIE GETS MARRIED (1946): BOTH FROM WARNER BROTHERS, NOT PARAMOUNT... THE FORMER ADAPTED FROM A BROADWAY MUSICAL THAT RAN FROM SEPTEMBER 1942 TO JANUARY 1944. THE JANIE PLOT SYNOPSIS DRAWS METAPHYSICAL ATTENTION TO ITSELF:
"JANIE IS A SCATTER-BRAINED AND HIGH-SPIRITED TEENAGE GIRL LIVING IN THE SMALL TOWN OF HORTONVILLE. WORLD WAR II CAUSES THE ESTABLISHMENT OF AN ARMY CAMP JUST OUTSIDE TOWN. JANIE AND HER BOBBY SOXER FRIENDS HAVE THEIR HEARTS SET A-FLUTTER BY THE PROSPECT OF SO MANY YOUNG SOLDIERS RESIDING NEARBY. WHICH FELLA (NOTE: SINGULAR!) WILL THEY (NOTE: PLURAL!) CHOOSE?"
WARNER BROS
NATIONAL JOY SHOW!
STRAIGHT FROM 77 JOYOUS WEEKS ON BROADWAY!
She's the gleam in the eye of every "G.I"
Janie
JOYCE REYNOLDS ROBERT HUTTON
ARNOLD ANN HARDING ROBERT BENCHLEY
ALAN HALE
DIRECTED BY MICHAEL CURTIZ
AS WE WILL SEE, FAR FROM BEING ABERRATIONAL, THIS WOULD PROVE TO BE A CHARACTERISTIC MANIFESTATION OF STAN DRAKE'S UNIQUE PERSONAL METAPHYSICS (BY WHICH HE WOULD TRANSFER HIMSELF BETWEEN FICTIONAL AND REAL-LIFE CONTEXTS AND VICE-VERSA): FIRST FINDING HIMSELF CAST IN A MOVIE SERIES ABOUT A TEENAGE GIRL FREQUENTING AN ARMY CAMP...
...ONLY TO SUBSEQUENTLY FIND HIMSELF -- IN REAL LIFE -- ENGAGED TO AND THEN MARRIED TO A TEENAGE GIRL WHO FREQUENTED HIS ARMY CAMP.

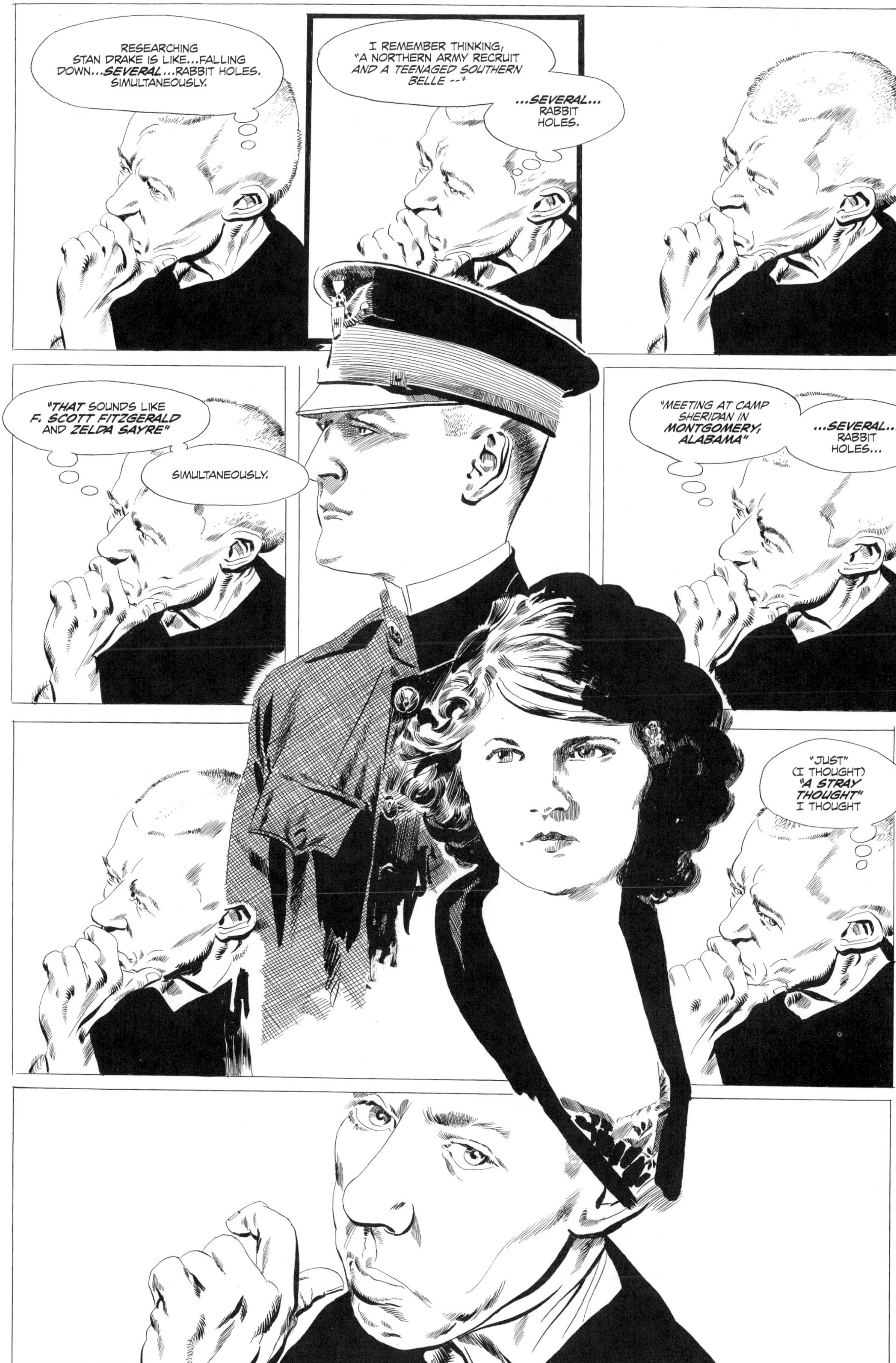

RESEARCHING STAN DRAKE IS LIKE...FALLING DOWN...SEVERAL...RABBIT HOLES. SIMULTANEOUSLY.
I REMEMBER THINKING, "A NORTHERN ARMY RECRUIT AND A TEENAGED SOUTHERN BELLE --"
...SEVERAL... RABBIT HOLES.
"THAT SOUNDS LIKE F. SCOTT FITZGERALD AND ZELDA SAYRE"
SIMULTANEOUSLY.
"MEETING AT CAMP SHERIDAN IN MONTGOMERY, ALABAMA"
...SEVERAL... RABBIT HOLES...
"JUST" (I THOUGHT) "A STRAY THOUGHT" I THOUGHT

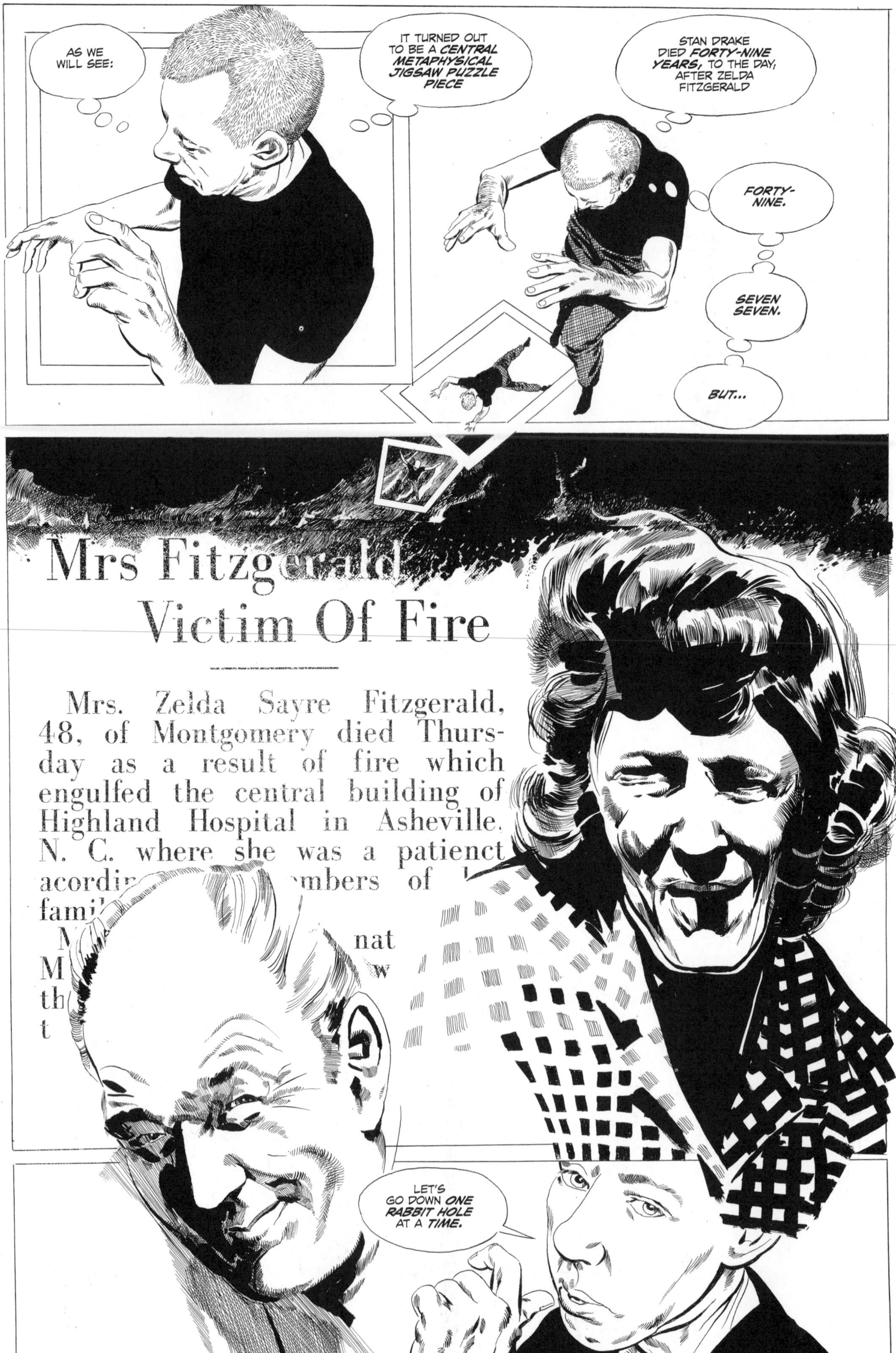

AS WE WILL SEE:
IT TURNED OUT TO BE A CENTRAL METAPHYSICAL JIGSAW PUZZLE PIECE
STAN DRAKE DIED FORTY-NINE YEARS, TO THE DAY, AFTER ZELDA FITZGERALD
FORTY-NINE.
SEVEN SEVEN.
BUT...
Mrs Fitzgerald Victim Of Fire
Mrs. Zelda Sayre Fitzgerald, 48, of Montgomery died Thursday as a result of fire which engulfed the central building of Highland Hospital in Asheville, N. C. where she was a patienct
LET'S GO DOWN ONE RABBIT HOLE AT A TIME.

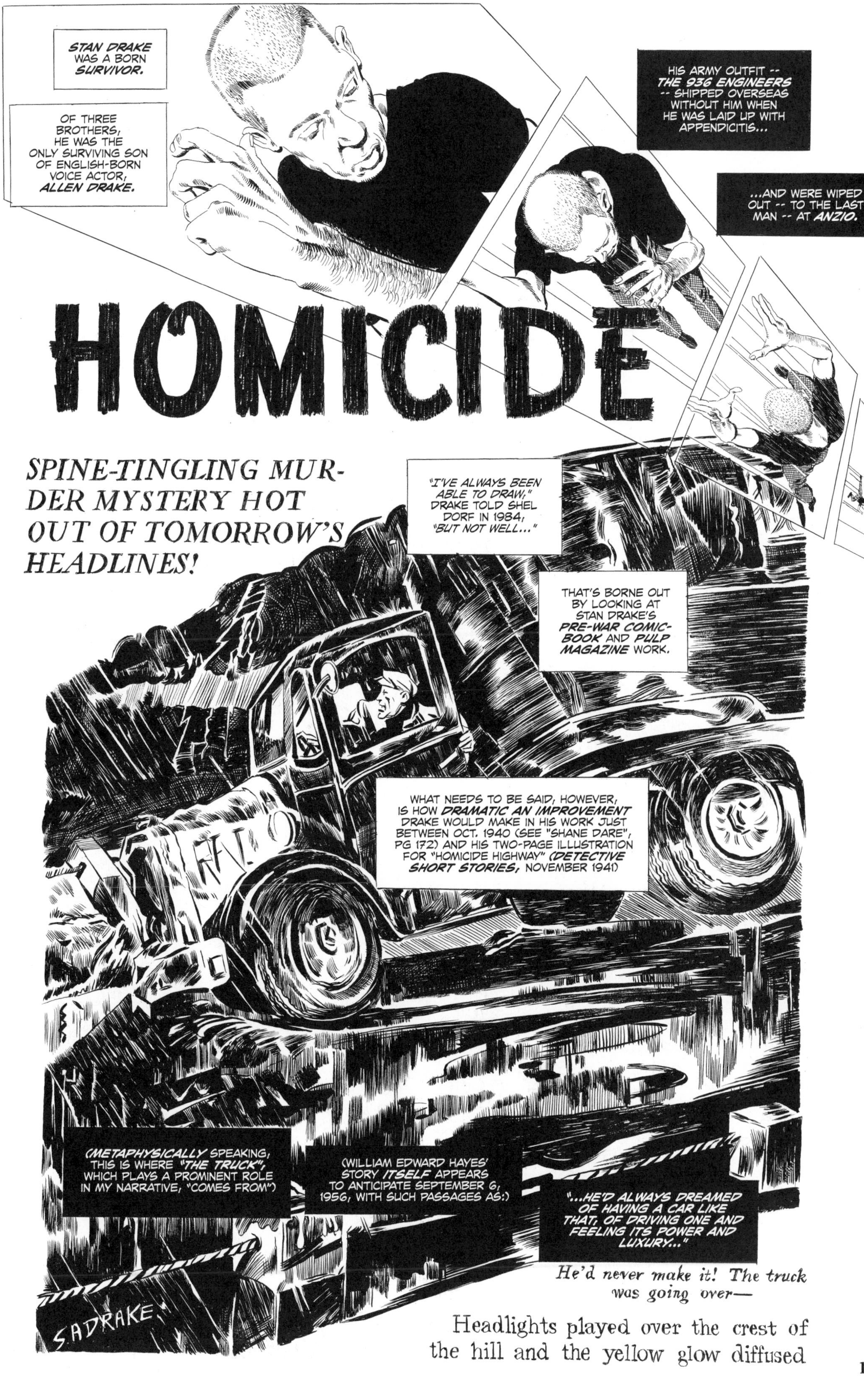
STAN DRAKE WAS A BORN SURVIVOR.
OF THREE BROTHERS, HE WAS THE ONLY SURVIVING SON OF ENGLISH-BORN VOICE ACTOR, ALLEN DRAKE.
HIS ARMY OUTFIT -- THE 936 ENGINEERS -- SHIPPED OVERSEAS WITHOUT HIM WHEN HE WAS LAID UP WITH APPENDICITIS...
...AND WERE WIPED OUT -- TO THE LAST MAN -- AT ANZIO.
HOMICIDE
SPINE-TINGLING MURDER MYSTERY HOT OUT OF TOMORROW'S HEADLINES!
"I'VE ALWAYS BEEN ABLE TO DRAW," DRAKE TOLD SHEL DORF IN 1984, "BUT NOT WELL..."
THAT'S BORNE OUT BY LOOKING AT STAN DRAKE'S PRE-WAR COMIC-BOOK AND PULP MAGAZINE WORK.
WHAT NEEDS TO BE SAID, HOWEVER, IS HOW DRAMATIC AN IMPROVEMENT DRAKE WOULD MAKE IN HIS WORK JUST BETWEEN OCT. 1940 (SEE "SHANE DARE", PG 172) AND HIS TWO-PAGE ILLUSTRATION FOR "HOMICIDE HIGHWAY" (DETECTIVE SHORT STORIES, NOVEMBER 1941)
(METAPHYSICALLY SPEAKING, THIS IS WHERE "THE TRUCK", WHICH PLAYS A PROMINENT ROLE IN MY NARRATIVE, "COMES FROM")
(WILLIAM EDWARD HAYES' STORY ITSELF APPEARS TO ANTICIPATE SEPTEMBER 6, 1956, WITH SUCH PASSAGES AS:)
"...HE'D ALWAYS DREAMED OF HAVING A CAR LIKE THAT, OF DRIVING ONE AND FEELING ITS POWER AND LUXURY..."
He'd never make it! The truck was going over—
S.A. DRAKE
Headlights played over the crest of the hill and the yellow glow diffused

"...HE PUSHED HIS FOOT TO THE FLOOR. RATHER HE PRESSED IT HARDER AGAINST THE FLOOR BECAUSE HE HAD ALREADY HAD HIS GAS ALL THE WAY DOWN..."

"...GOING INTO HIGH GEAR FOR THE DESCENT OF DEAD MAN'S DIVE. IT MUST BE SOMEONE WHO DIDN'T KNOW WHAT A DROP THAT WAS..."

"...BOUNCED, SPUN WHEELS IN THIN AIR, CAME DOWN ON THE WET PAVEMENT AND BOUNCED AGAIN..."

"...HIS FOREHEAD CLUNKED AGAINST THE WINDSHIELD, THE STEERING WHEEL KNOCKED THE WIND OUT OF HIM AND CONSCIOUSNESS DEPARTED..."

"...A MAN LAY CRUSHED TO A PULP BEHIND THE WHEEL. A FORMLESS THING WITH ONLY A HIDEOUS FACE..."

# HIGHWAY

(REMEMBER THE MYSTERIOUS *EVE* WHO APPEARS OUT OF NOWHERE TO *BIG BEN BOLT*?)

DREAMING, BEN?..WHAT KIND OF DREAMS?..OF BEING RICH?..OR FAMOUS?..OR OF LOVELY LADIES SWOONING AT YOUR FEET?

OH! SAVE ME... ...THEY-GOING TO DROWN ME... I-I......

NEVER MIND EXPLAINING NOW—WAIT 'TILL WE GET SAFE LY TO SHORE

REACHING LAND—SHANE CARRIES THE NOW UNCONCIOUS GIRL UP ON THE BEACH

(THIS IS, METAPHYSICALLY SPEAKING, WHERE *SHE* "CAME FROM": "SHANE DARE" BY STANLEY ALLEN DRAKE IN CENTAUR COMICS' *FANTOMAN* NO. 3 OCTOBER 1940)

WHERE-- OH! YOU SAV-HOW AM I GOING TO THANK YOU? BUT WAIT-I-

HEY—HOLD ON, NOT SO FAST. FROM WHAT I GATHER YOU'RE IN SOME SORT OF TROUBLE AND MAYBE I CAN HELP-BUT TAKE IT SLOW—SO I CAN UNDERSTAND.

ıout moving his
a sound. When
himself that he
e, why then he
ɡ or nobody had
ɡney. Not yet!
he shoulder and

Only Jimmy wasn't driving a truck any more. Mr. Banion had just told him that afternoon how sorry he was, sat down. He fumbled in his pockets for the limp sack of granulated tobacco, the soiled book of papers. He fashioned

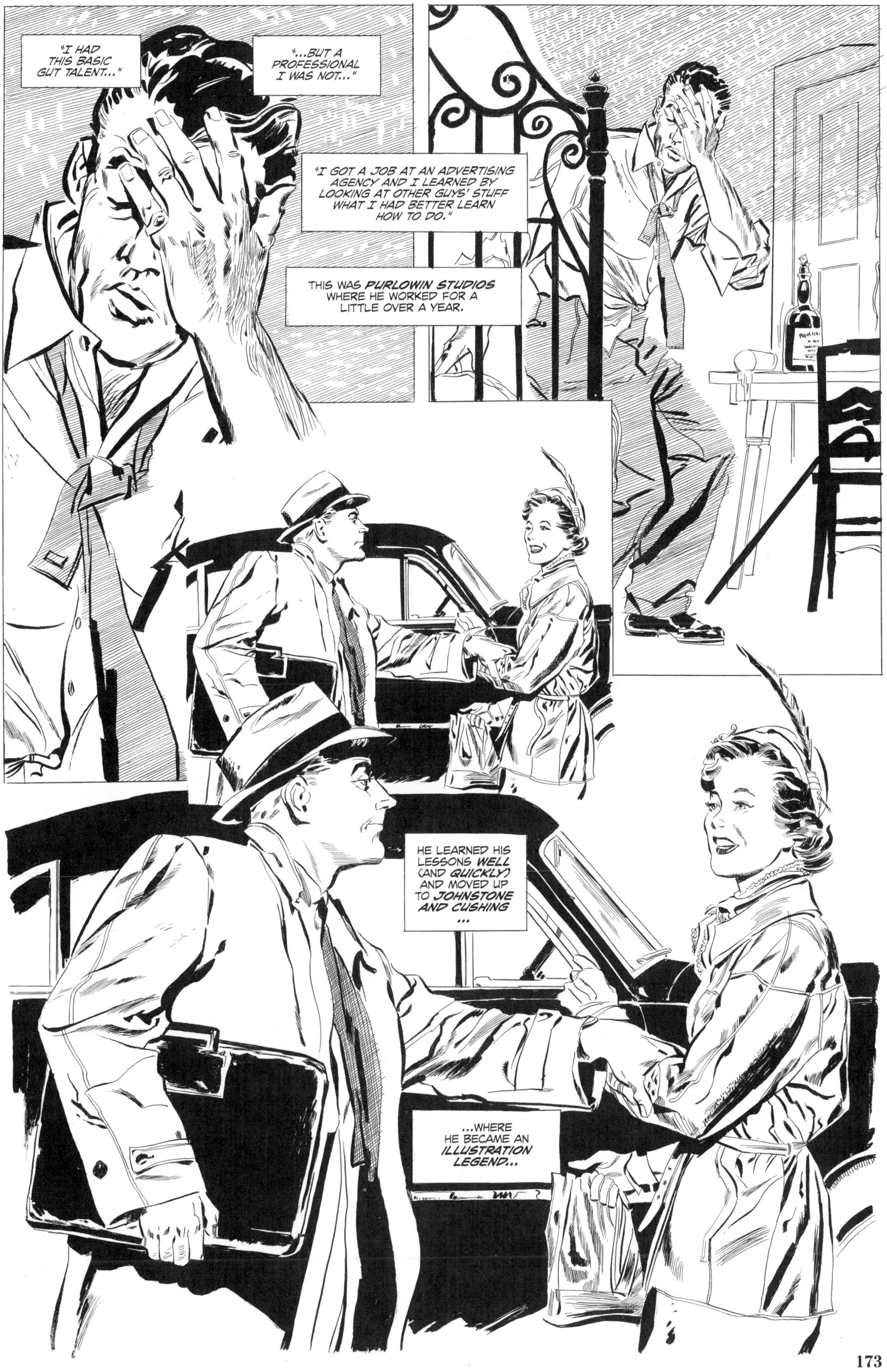
"I HAD THIS BASIC GUT TALENT..."
"...BUT A PROFESSIONAL I WAS NOT..."
"I GOT A JOB AT AN ADVERTISING AGENCY AND I LEARNED BY LOOKING AT OTHER GUYS' STUFF WHAT I HAD BETTER LEARN HOW TO DO."
THIS WAS PURLOWIN STUDIOS WHERE HE WORKED FOR A LITTLE OVER A YEAR.
HE LEARNED HIS LESSONS WELL (AND QUICKLY) AND MOVED UP TO JOHNSTONE AND CUSHING ...
...WHERE HE BECAME AN ILLUSTRATION LEGEND...

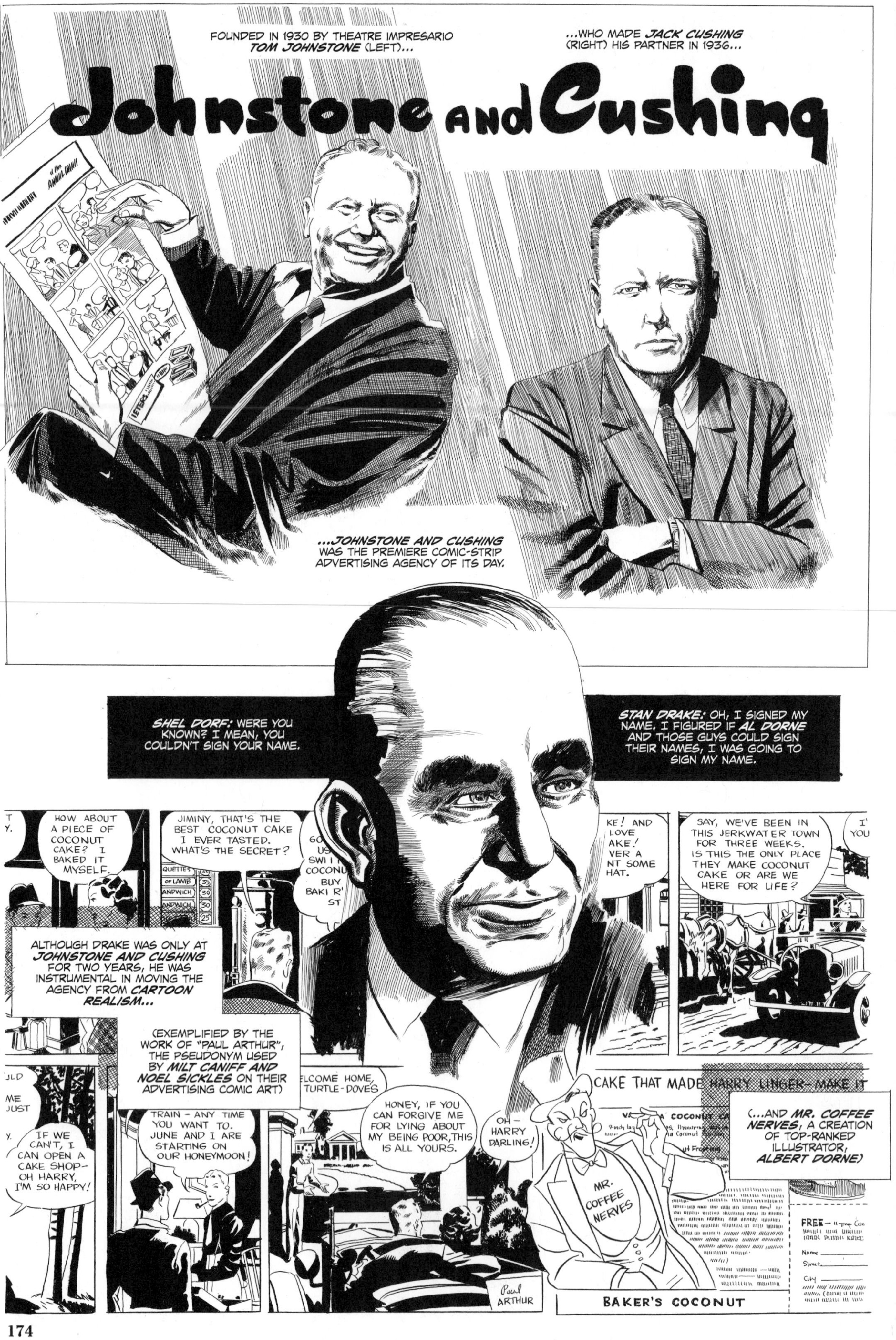

FOUNDED IN 1930 BY THEATRE IMPRESARIO TOM JOHNSTONE (LEFT)...
...WHO MADE JACK CUSHING (RIGHT) HIS PARTNER IN 1936...
Johnstone and Cushing
...JOHNSTONE AND CUSHING WAS THE PREMIERE COMIC-STRIP ADVERTISING AGENCY OF ITS DAY.
SHEL DORF: WERE YOU KNOWN? I MEAN, YOU COULDN'T SIGN YOUR NAME.
STAN DRAKE: OH, I SIGNED MY NAME. I FIGURED IF AL DORNE AND THOSE GUYS COULD SIGN THEIR NAMES, I WAS GOING TO SIGN MY NAME.
HOW ABOUT A PIECE OF COCONUT CAKE? I BAKED IT MYSELF.
JIMINY, THAT'S THE BEST COCONUT CAKE I EVER TASTED. WHAT'S THE SECRET?
SAY, WE'VE BEEN IN THIS JERKWATER TOWN FOR THREE WEEKS. IS THIS THE ONLY PLACE THEY MAKE COCONUT CAKE OR ARE WE HERE FOR LIFE?
ALTHOUGH DRAKE WAS ONLY AT JOHNSTONE AND CUSHING FOR TWO YEARS, HE WAS INSTRUMENTAL IN MOVING THE AGENCY FROM CARTOON REALISM...
(EXEMPLIFIED BY THE WORK OF "PAUL ARTHUR", THE PSEUDONYM USED BY MILT CANIFF AND NOEL SICKLES ON THEIR ADVERTISING COMIC ART)
IF WE CAN'T, I CAN OPEN A CAKE SHOP– OH HARRY, I'M SO HAPPY!
TRAIN – ANY TIME YOU WANT TO. JUNE AND I ARE STARTING ON OUR HONEYMOON!
HONEY, IF YOU CAN FORGIVE ME FOR LYING ABOUT MY BEING POOR, THIS IS ALL YOURS.
OH – HARRY DARLING!
Paul ARTHUR
CAKE THAT MADE HARRY LINGER– MAKE IT
MR. COFFEE NERVES
(...AND MR. COFFEE NERVES, A CREATION OF TOP-RANKED ILLUSTRATOR, ALBERT DORNE)
BAKER'S COCONUT

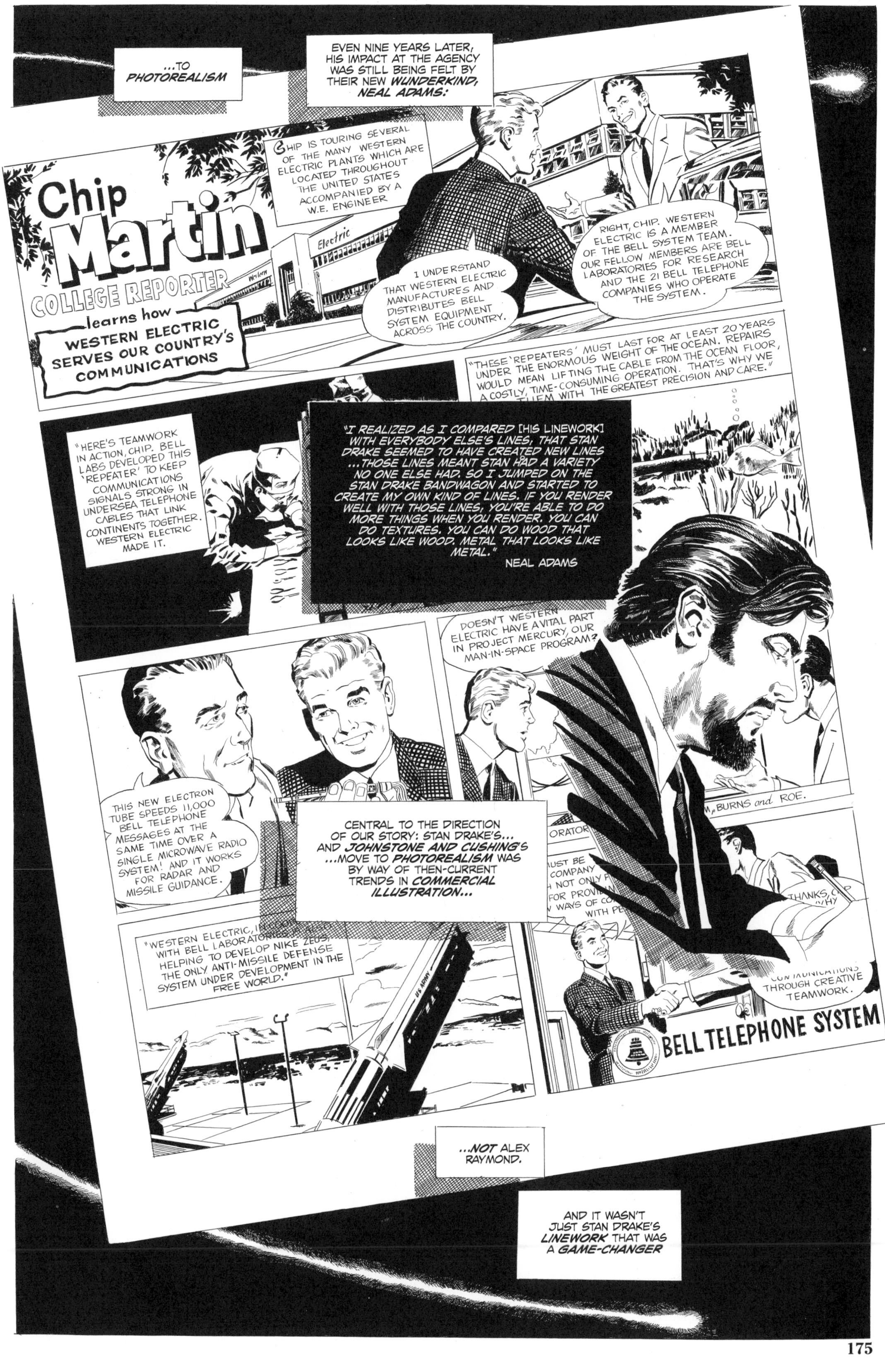

...TO PHOTOREALISM
EVEN NINE YEARS LATER, HIS IMPACT AT THE AGENCY WAS STILL BEING FELT BY THEIR NEW WUNDERKIND, NEAL ADAMS:
Chip Martin
COLLEGE REPORTER
learns how WESTERN ELECTRIC SERVES OUR COUNTRY'S COMMUNICATIONS
CHIP IS TOURING SEVERAL OF THE MANY WESTERN ELECTRIC PLANTS WHICH ARE LOCATED THROUGHOUT THE UNITED STATES ACCOMPANIED BY A W.E. ENGINEER
Electric
I UNDERSTAND THAT WESTERN ELECTRIC MANUFACTURES AND DISTRIBUTES BELL SYSTEM EQUIPMENT ACROSS THE COUNTRY.
RIGHT, CHIP. WESTERN ELECTRIC IS A MEMBER OF THE BELL SYSTEM TEAM. OUR FELLOW MEMBERS ARE BELL LABORATORIES FOR RESEARCH AND THE 21 BELL TELEPHONE COMPANIES WHO OPERATE THE SYSTEM.
"THESE 'REPEATERS' MUST LAST FOR AT LEAST 20 YEARS UNDER THE ENORMOUS WEIGHT OF THE OCEAN. REPAIRS WOULD MEAN LIFTING THE CABLE FROM THE OCEAN FLOOR, A COSTLY, TIME-CONSUMING OPERATION. THAT'S WHY WE
"HERE'S TEAMWORK IN ACTION, CHIP. BELL LABS DEVELOPED THIS 'REPEATER' TO KEEP COMMUNICATIONS SIGNALS STRONG IN UNDERSEA TELEPHONE CABLES THAT LINK CONTINENTS TOGETHER. WESTERN ELECTRIC MADE IT.
"I REALIZED AS I COMPARED [HIS LINEWORK] WITH EVERYBODY ELSE'S LINES, THAT STAN DRAKE SEEMED TO HAVE CREATED NEW LINES ...THOSE LINES MEANT STAN HAD A VARIETY NO ONE ELSE HAD. SO I JUMPED ON THE STAN DRAKE BANDWAGON AND STARTED TO CREATE MY OWN KIND OF LINES. IF YOU RENDER WELL WITH THOSE LINES, YOU'RE ABLE TO DO MORE THINGS WHEN YOU RENDER. YOU CAN DO TEXTURES. YOU CAN DO WOOD THAT LOOKS LIKE WOOD. METAL THAT LOOKS LIKE METAL."
NEAL ADAMS
DOESN'T WESTERN ELECTRIC HAVE A VITAL PART IN PROJECT MERCURY, OUR MAN-IN-SPACE PROGRAM?
THIS NEW ELECTRON TUBE SPEEDS 11,000 BELL TELEPHONE MESSAGES AT THE SAME TIME OVER A SINGLE MICROWAVE RADIO SYSTEM! AND IT WORKS FOR RADAR AND MISSILE GUIDANCE.
BURNS and ROE.
CENTRAL TO THE DIRECTION OF OUR STORY: STAN DRAKE'S... AND JOHNSTONE AND CUSHING'S ...MOVE TO PHOTOREALISM WAS BY WAY OF THEN-CURRENT TRENDS IN COMMERCIAL ILLUSTRATION...
HELPING TO DEVELOP NIKE ZEUS, THE ONLY ANTI-MISSILE DEFENSE SYSTEM UNDER DEVELOPMENT IN THE FREE WORLD."
U.S. ARMY
THROUGH CREATIVE TEAMWORK.
BELL TELEPHONE SYSTEM
...NOT ALEX RAYMOND.
AND IT WASN'T JUST STAN DRAKE'S LINEWORK THAT WAS A GAME-CHANGER

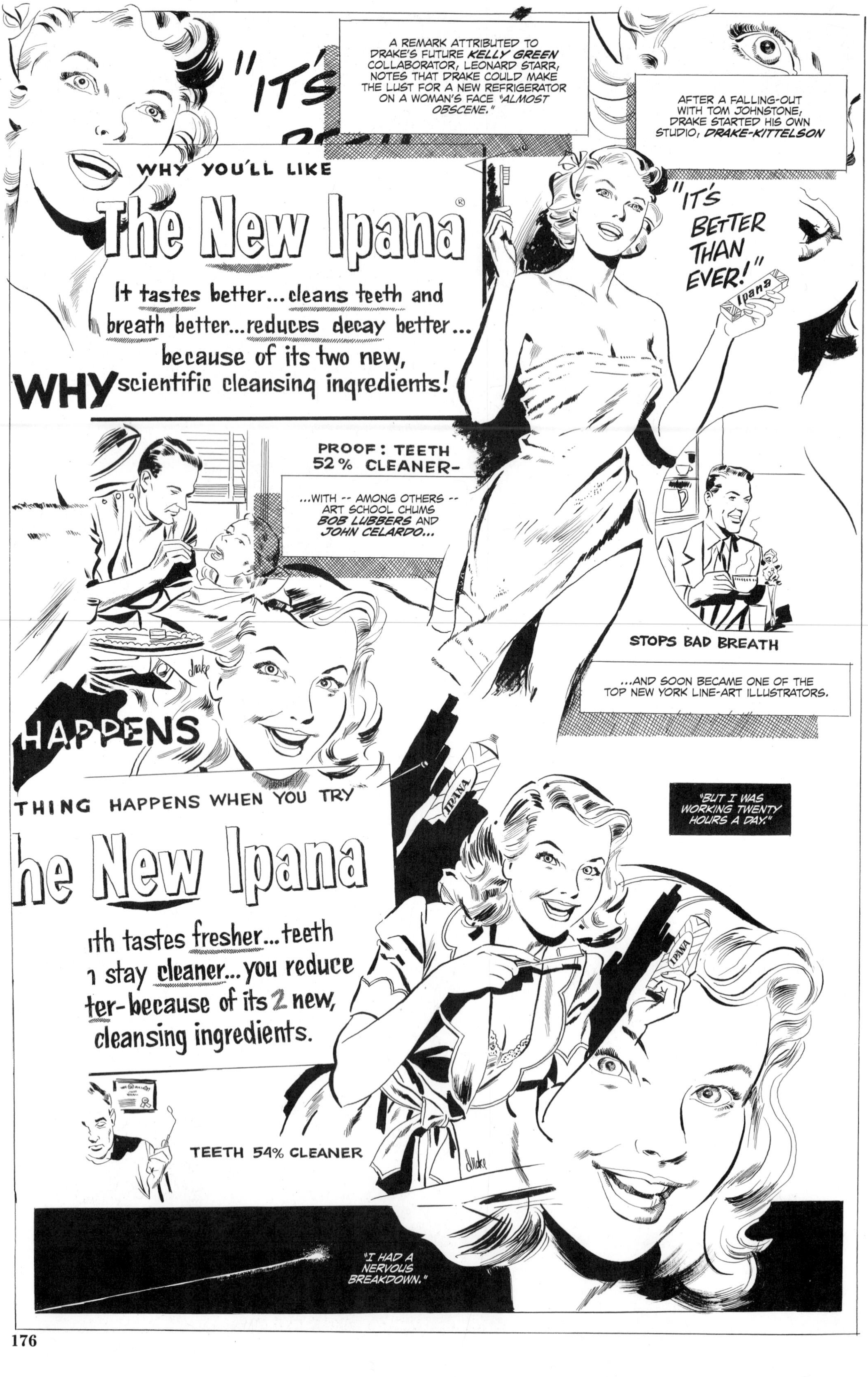

"IT'S
A REMARK ATTRIBUTED TO DRAKE'S FUTURE *KELLY GREEN* COLLABORATOR, LEONARD STARR, NOTES THAT DRAKE COULD MAKE THE LUST FOR A NEW REFRIGERATOR ON A WOMAN'S FACE *"ALMOST OBSCENE."*
AFTER A FALLING-OUT WITH TOM JOHNSTONE, DRAKE STARTED HIS OWN STUDIO, *DRAKE-KITTELSON*
WHY YOU'LL LIKE
The New Ipana®
It tastes better... cleans teeth and breath better... reduces decay better... because of its two new, scientific cleansing ingredients!
WHY
"IT'S BETTER THAN EVER!"
Ipana
PROOF: TEETH 52% CLEANER-
...WITH -- AMONG OTHERS -- ART SCHOOL CHUMS *BOB LUBBERS* AND *JOHN CELARDO...*
STOPS BAD BREATH
...AND SOON BECAME ONE OF THE TOP NEW YORK LINE-ART ILLUSTRATORS.
drake
HAPPENS
THING HAPPENS WHEN YOU TRY
he New Ipana
ith tastes fresher... teeth
n stay cleaner... you reduce
ter-because of its 2 new,
cleansing ingredients.
IPANA
*"BUT I WAS WORKING TWENTY HOURS A DAY."*
TEETH 54% CLEANER
drake
*"I HAD A NERVOUS BREAKDOWN."*

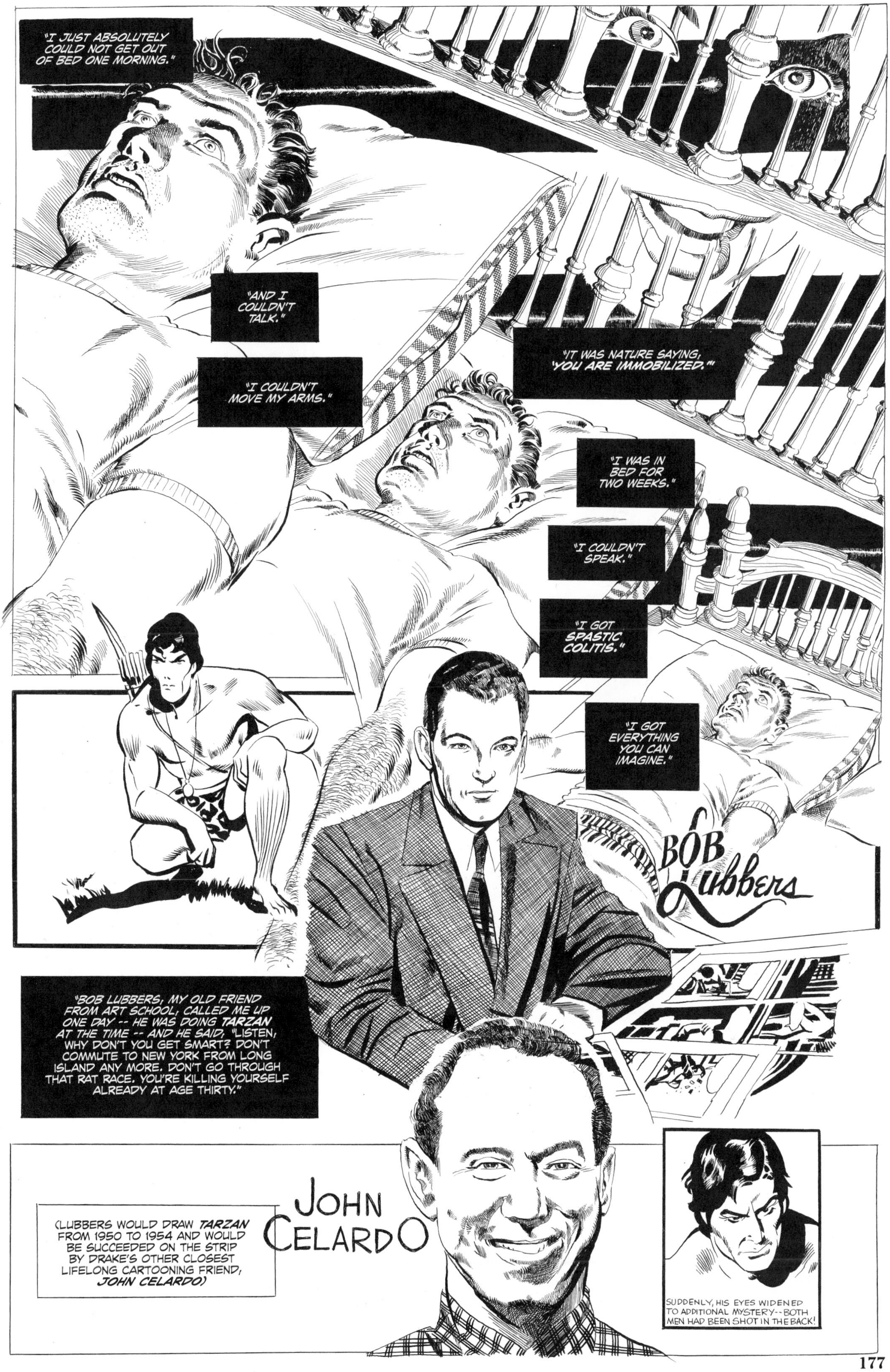
"I JUST ABSOLUTELY COULD NOT GET OUT OF BED ONE MORNING."
"AND I COULDN'T TALK."
"I COULDN'T MOVE MY ARMS."
"IT WAS NATURE SAYING, 'YOU ARE IMMOBILIZED.'"
"I WAS IN BED FOR TWO WEEKS."
"I COULDN'T SPEAK."
"I GOT SPASTIC COLITIS."
"I GOT EVERYTHING YOU CAN IMAGINE."
BOB Lubbers
"BOB LUBBERS, MY OLD FRIEND FROM ART SCHOOL, CALLED ME UP ONE DAY -- HE WAS DOING TARZAN AT THE TIME -- AND HE SAID, "LISTEN, WHY DON'T YOU GET SMART? DON'T COMMUTE TO NEW YORK FROM LONG ISLAND ANY MORE. DON'T GO THROUGH THAT RAT RACE. YOU'RE KILLING YOURSELF ALREADY AT AGE THIRTY."
JOHN CELARDO
(LUBBERS WOULD DRAW TARZAN FROM 1950 TO 1954 AND WOULD BE SUCCEEDED ON THE STRIP BY DRAKE'S OTHER CLOSEST LIFELONG CARTOONING FRIEND, JOHN CELARDO)
SUDDENLY, HIS EYES WIDENED TO ADDITIONAL MYSTERY--BOTH MEN HAD BEEN SHOT IN THE BACK!

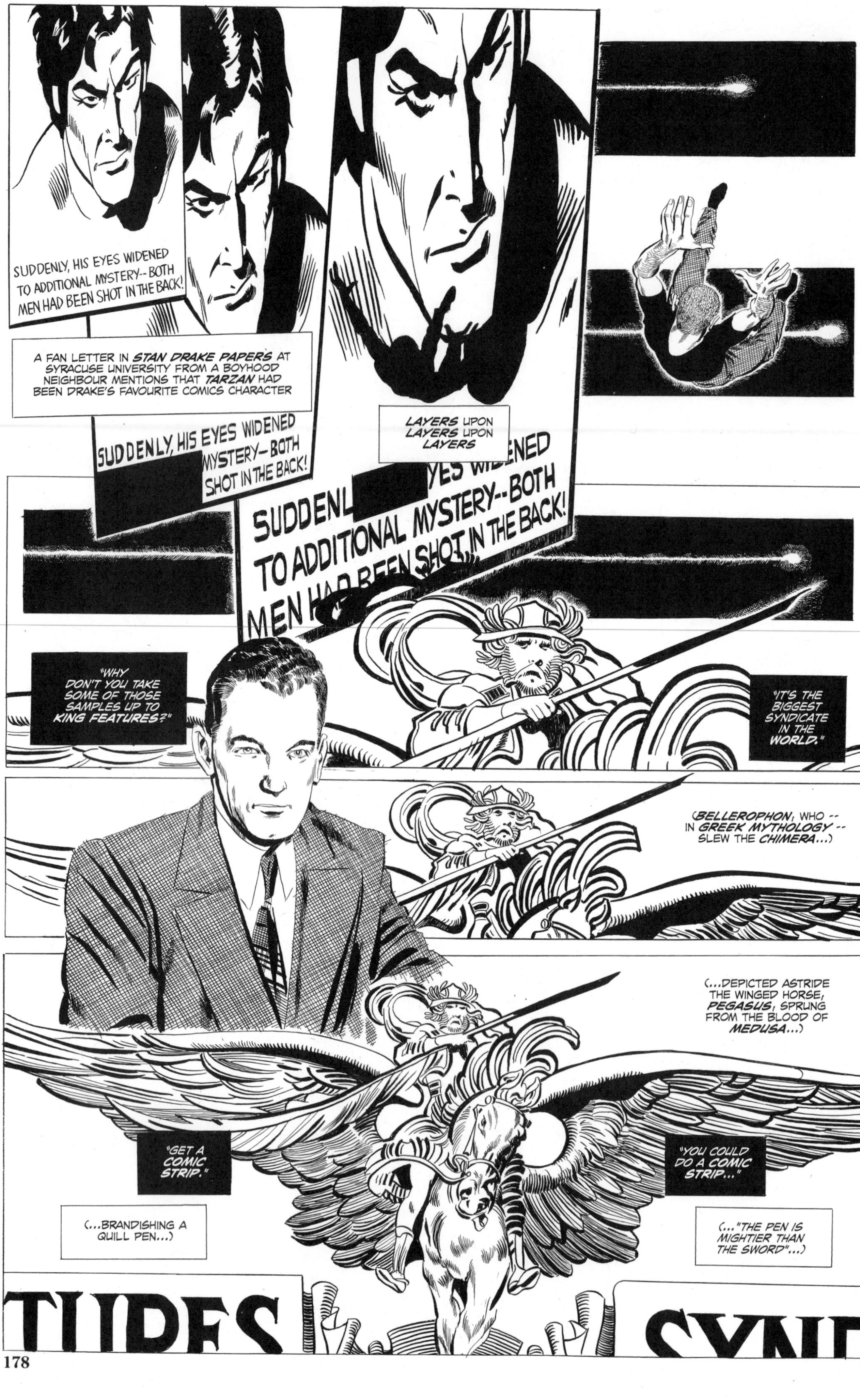

SUDDENLY, HIS EYES WIDENED TO ADDITIONAL MYSTERY-- BOTH MEN HAD BEEN SHOT IN THE BACK!
A FAN LETTER IN *STAN DRAKE PAPERS* AT SYRACUSE UNIVERSITY FROM A BOYHOOD NEIGHBOUR MENTIONS THAT *TARZAN* HAD BEEN DRAKE'S FAVOURITE COMICS CHARACTER
SUDDENLY, HIS EYES WIDENED [redacted] MYSTERY— BOTH [redacted] SHOT IN THE BACK!
*LAYERS* UPON *LAYERS* UPON *LAYERS*
SUDDENL [redacted] YES WIDENED TO ADDITIONAL MYSTERY--BOTH MEN HAD BEEN SHOT IN THE BACK!
"WHY DON'T YOU TAKE SOME OF THOSE SAMPLES UP TO *KING FEATURES*?"
"IT'S THE BIGGEST SYNDICATE IN THE *WORLD*."
(*BELLEROPHON*, WHO -- IN *GREEK MYTHOLOGY* -- SLEW THE *CHIMERA*...)
(...DEPICTED ASTRIDE THE WINGED HORSE, *PEGASUS*, SPRUNG FROM THE BLOOD OF *MEDUSA*...)
"GET A *COMIC STRIP*."
"YOU COULD DO A *COMIC STRIP*..."
(...BRANDISHING A QUILL PEN...)
(..."THE PEN IS MIGHTIER THAN THE SWORD"...)

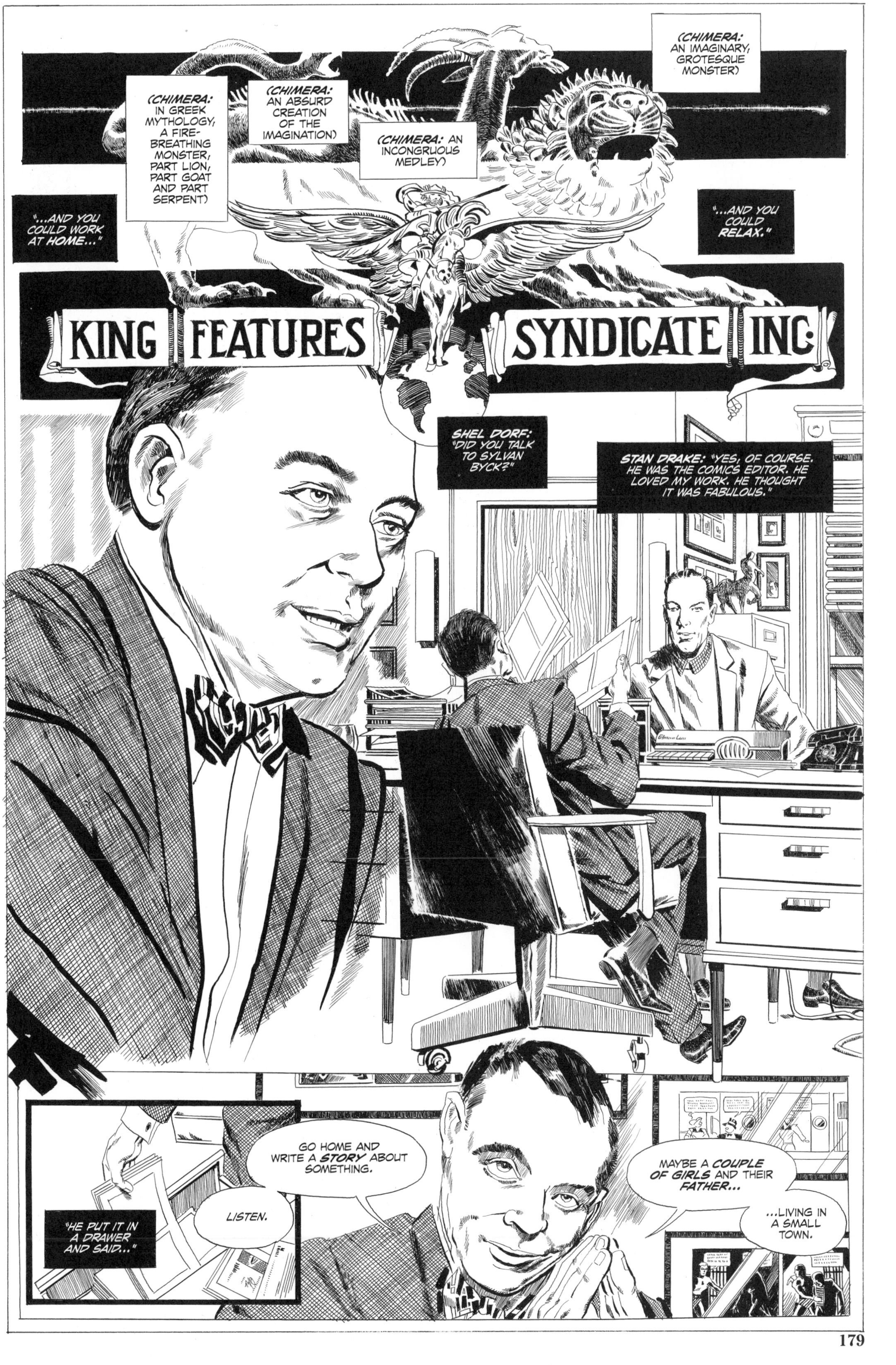
(CHIMERA: IN GREEK MYTHOLOGY, A FIRE-BREATHING MONSTER, PART LION, PART GOAT AND PART SERPENT)
(CHIMERA: AN ABSURD CREATION OF THE IMAGINATION)
(CHIMERA: AN INCONGRUOUS MEDLEY)
(CHIMERA: AN IMAGINARY, GROTESQUE MONSTER)
"...AND YOU COULD WORK AT HOME..."
"...AND YOU COULD RELAX."
KING FEATURES SYNDICATE INC.
SHEL DORF: "DID YOU TALK TO SYLVAN BYCK?"
STAN DRAKE: "YES, OF COURSE. HE WAS THE COMICS EDITOR. HE LOVED MY WORK. HE THOUGHT IT WAS FABULOUS."
"HE PUT IT IN A DRAWER AND SAID..."
LISTEN.
GO HOME AND WRITE A STORY ABOUT SOMETHING.
MAYBE A COUPLE OF GIRLS AND THEIR FATHER...
...LIVING IN A SMALL TOWN.

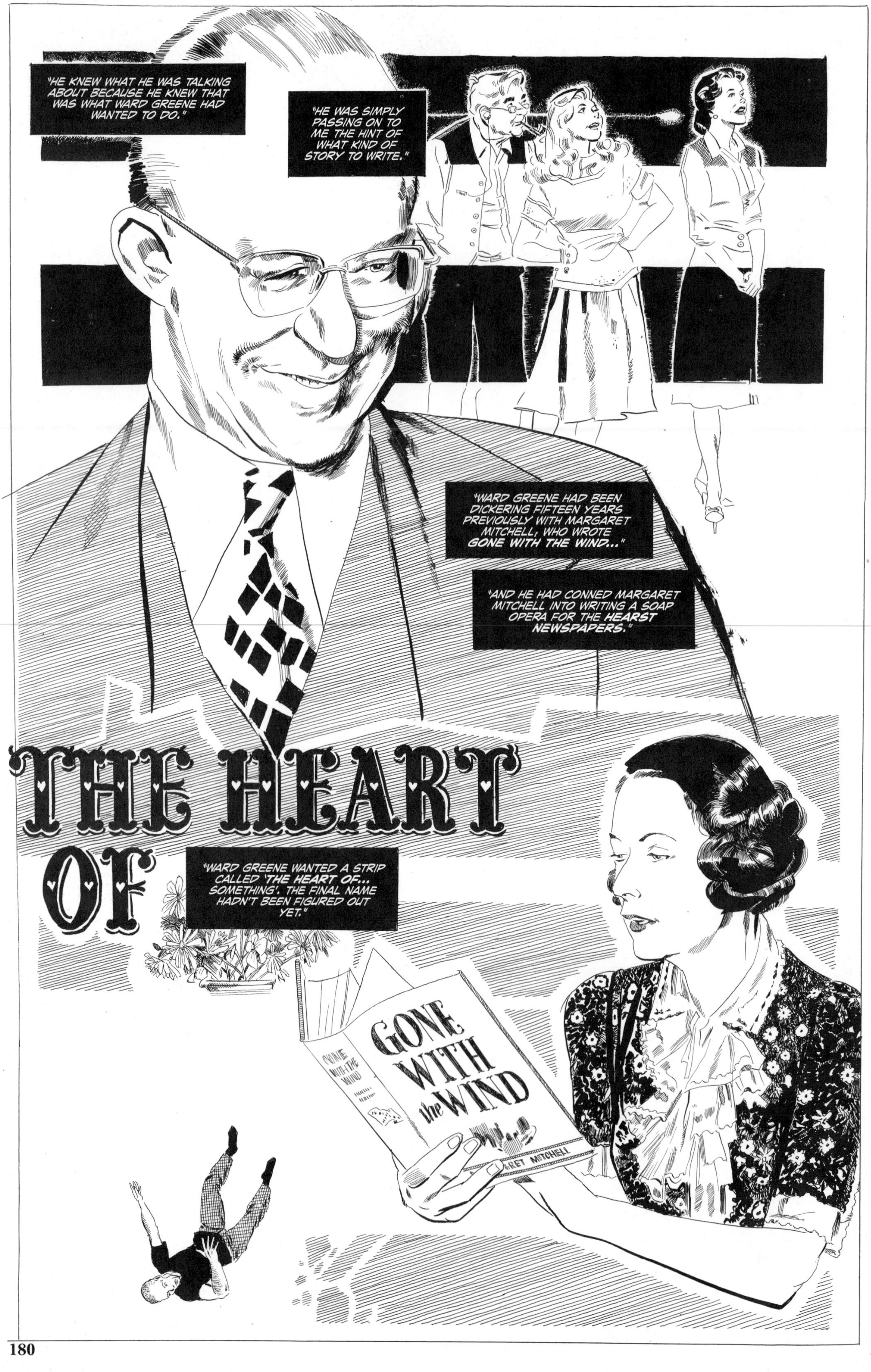
"HE KNEW WHAT HE WAS TALKING ABOUT BECAUSE HE KNEW THAT WAS WHAT WARD GREENE HAD WANTED TO DO."
"HE WAS SIMPLY PASSING ON TO ME THE HINT OF WHAT KIND OF STORY TO WRITE."
"WARD GREENE HAD BEEN DICKERING FIFTEEN YEARS PREVIOUSLY WITH MARGARET MITCHELL, WHO WROTE GONE WITH THE WIND..."
"AND HE HAD CONNED MARGARET MITCHELL INTO WRITING A SOAP OPERA FOR THE HEARST NEWSPAPERS."
THE HEART OF
"WARD GREENE WANTED A STRIP CALLED 'THE HEART OF... SOMETHING'. THE FINAL NAME HADN'T BEEN FIGURED OUT YET."
GONE WITH the WIND

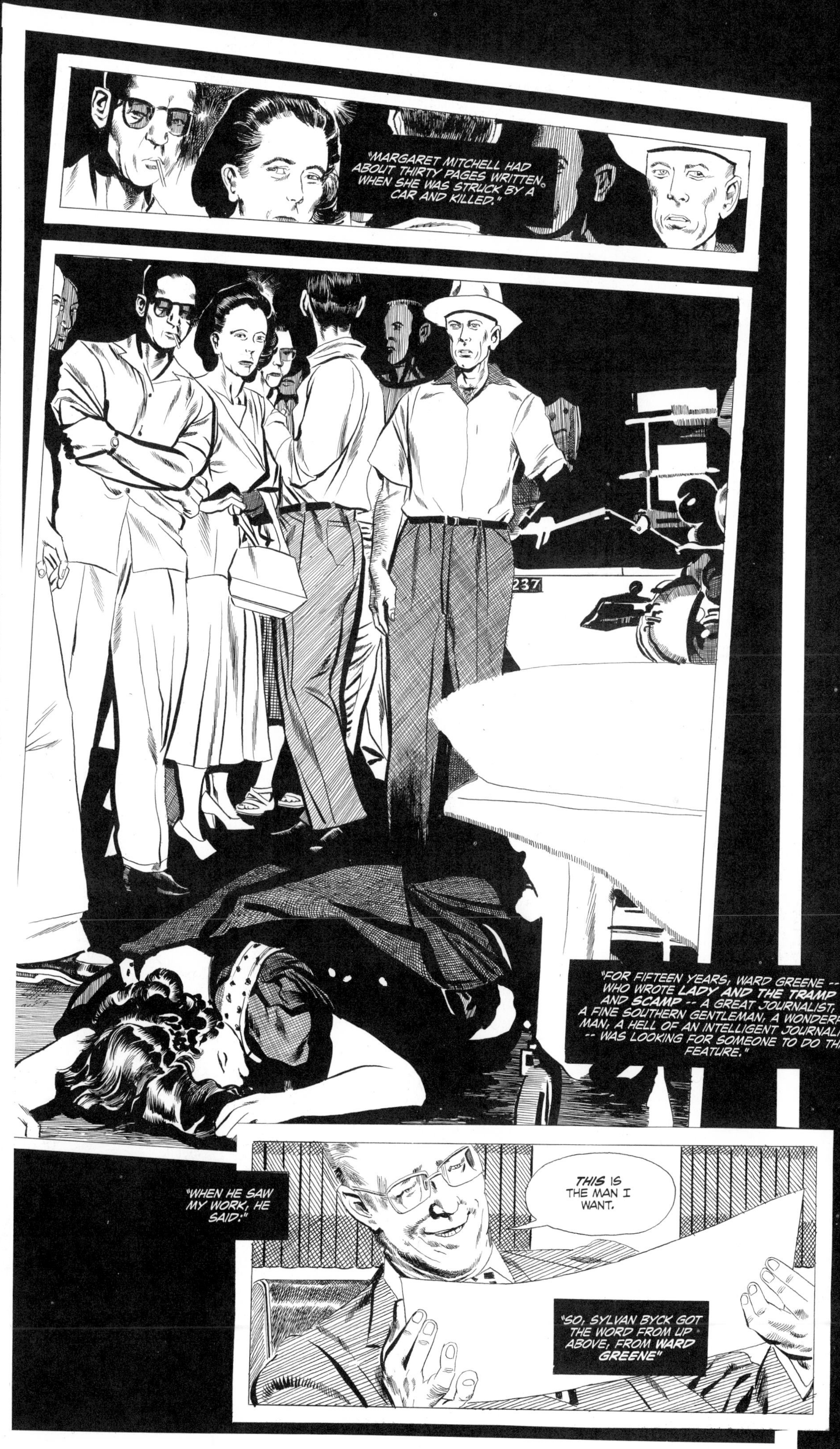
"MARGARET MITCHELL HAD ABOUT THIRTY PAGES WRITTEN, WHEN SHE WAS STRUCK BY A CAR AND KILLED."
237
"FOR FIFTEEN YEARS, WARD GREENE -- WHO WROTE LADY AND THE TRAMP AND SCAMP -- A GREAT JOURNALIST, A FINE SOUTHERN GENTLEMAN, A WONDERFUL MAN, A HELL OF AN INTELLIGENT JOURNALIST -- WAS LOOKING FOR SOMEONE TO DO THIS FEATURE."
"WHEN HE SAW MY WORK, HE SAID:"
THIS IS THE MAN I WANT.
"SO, SYLVAN BYCK GOT THE WORD FROM UP ABOVE, FROM WARD GREENE"

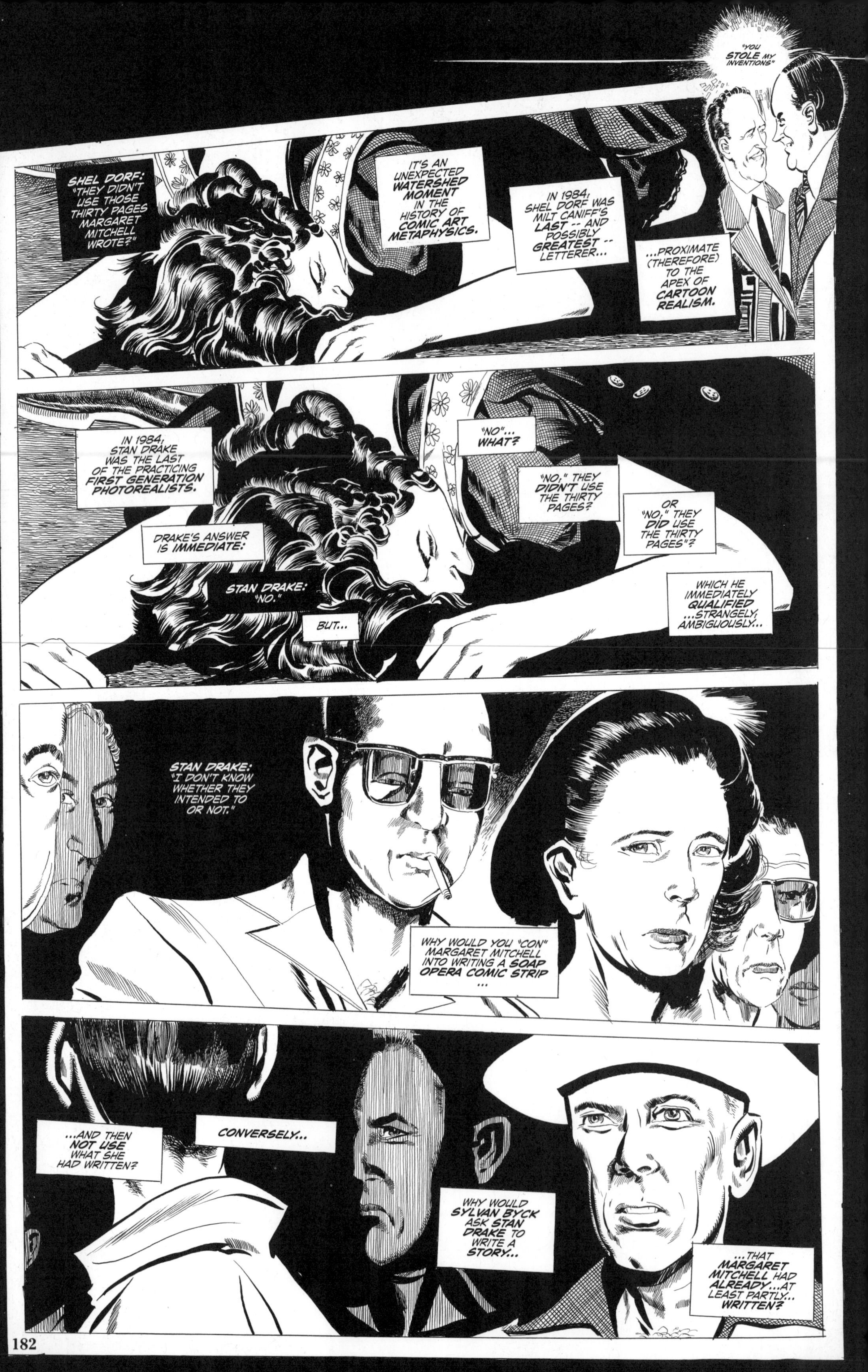
"YOU STOLE MY INVENTIONS"
SHEL DORF: "THEY DIDN'T USE THOSE THIRTY PAGES MARGARET MITCHELL WROTE?"
IT'S AN UNEXPECTED WATERSHED MOMENT IN THE HISTORY OF COMIC ART METAPHYSICS.
IN 1984, SHEL DORF WAS MILT CANIFF'S LAST -- AND POSSIBLY GREATEST -- LETTERER...
...PROXIMATE (THEREFORE) TO THE APEX OF CARTOON REALISM.
IN 1984, STAN DRAKE WAS THE LAST OF THE PRACTICING FIRST GENERATION PHOTOREALISTS.
DRAKE'S ANSWER IS IMMEDIATE:
STAN DRAKE: "NO."
BUT...
"NO"... WHAT?
"NO," THEY DIDN'T USE THE THIRTY PAGES?
OR "NO," THEY DID USE THE THIRTY PAGES"?
WHICH HE IMMEDIATELY QUALIFIED ...STRANGELY, AMBIGUOUSLY...
STAN DRAKE: "I DON'T KNOW WHETHER THEY INTENDED TO OR NOT."
WHY WOULD YOU "CON" MARGARET MITCHELL INTO WRITING A SOAP OPERA COMIC STRIP ...
...AND THEN NOT USE WHAT SHE HAD WRITTEN?
CONVERSELY...
WHY WOULD SYLVAN BYCK ASK STAN DRAKE TO WRITE A STORY...
...THAT MARGARET MITCHELL HAD ALREADY...AT LEAST PARTLY... WRITTEN?

MYSTERIES
WITHIN
MYSTERIES
WITHIN
MYSTERIES:

BOTH MARGARET MITCHELL **AND** WARD GREENE WERE NICKNAMED "JIMMY"

MITCHELL, AFTER JIMMY SWINNERTON'S *LITTLE JIMMY* COMIC STRIP CHARACTER (BECAUSE HER MOTHER DRESSED HER IN BOYS' CLOTHING)...

THE MAN WITH HIS BACK TO THE CAMERA IN THE GRUESOME NEWS PHOTO...

IS HUGH D. GRAVITT, THE OFF-DUTY TAXI DRIVER WHOSE CAR STRUCK MARGARET MITCHELL AUGUST 11, 1949.

HE HAD BEEN ON HIS WAY TO THE **PEACHTREE PHARMACY** TO FILL A PRESCRIPTION FOR HIS SERIOUSLY ILL INFANT SON...

...NAMED JIMMY.

HIS IS AW AN'T S UCH MO OF IT.

THIS IS AWFUL! I CAN'T STAND MUCH MORE OF IT!

BE CALM, DEAR... I'LL SPEAK UP AT THE PROPER TIME!

*RIP KIRBY* BY WARD GREENE AND ALEX RAYMOND FOR 16 NOVEMBER 49...

...THE COURTROOM DENOUEMENT OF THE MISS MITCHELL/NOT MISS MITCHELL "MY LITTLE RUNAWAY" STORYLINE...

...APPEARED THE SAME DAY GRAVITT ...IN FULTON COUNTY **SUPERIOR COURT**...WAS SENTENCED TO TWELVE TO EIGHTEEN MONTHS FOR **INVOLUNTARY MANSLAUGHTER** IN MARGARET MITCHELL'S DEATH

BUT

AS I SAY...

ONE RABBIT HOLE AT A TIME.

ALEX RAYMOND 11-16

183

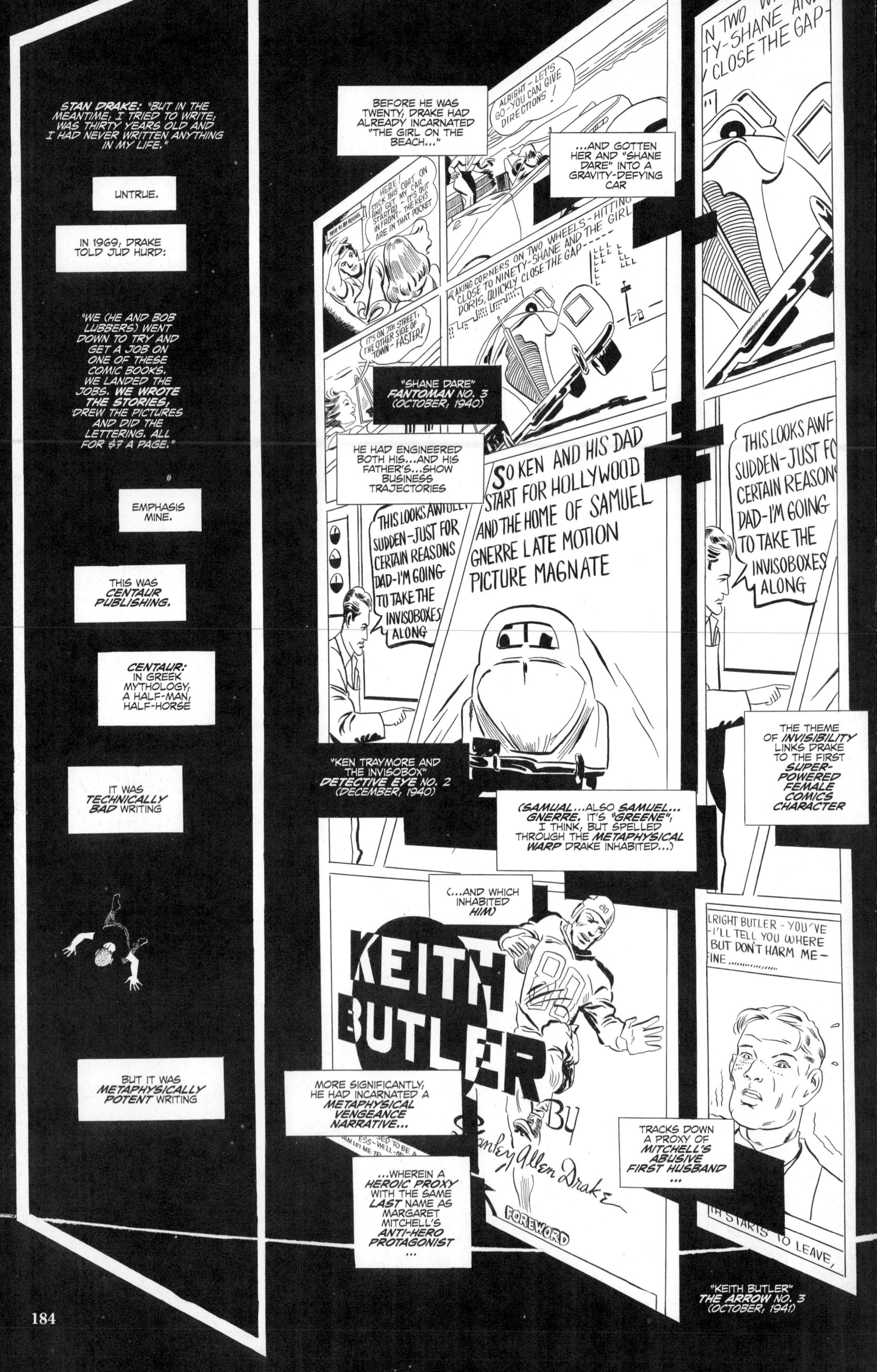
STAN DRAKE: "BUT IN THE MEANTIME, I TRIED TO WRITE; WAS THIRTY YEARS OLD AND I HAD NEVER WRITTEN ANYTHING IN MY LIFE."
UNTRUE.
IN 1969, DRAKE TOLD JUD HURD:
"WE (HE AND BOB LUBBERS) WENT DOWN TO TRY AND GET A JOB ON ONE OF THESE COMIC BOOKS. WE LANDED THE JOBS. WE WROTE THE STORIES, DREW THE PICTURES AND DID THE LETTERING. ALL FOR $7 A PAGE."
EMPHASIS MINE.
THIS WAS CENTAUR PUBLISHING.
CENTAUR: IN GREEK MYTHOLOGY, A HALF-MAN, HALF-HORSE
IT WAS TECHNICALLY BAD WRITING
BUT IT WAS METAPHYSICALLY POTENT WRITING
BEFORE HE WAS TWENTY, DRAKE HAD ALREADY INCARNATED "THE GIRL ON THE BEACH..."
ALRIGHT – LET'S GO – YOU CAN GIVE DIRECTIONS!
...AND GOTTEN HER AND "SHANE DARE" INTO A GRAVITY-DEFYING CAR
HERE! STICK THIS COAT ON AND GET MY CAR STARTED – IT'S OUT IN FRONT – THE KEYS ARE IN THAT POCKET
TAKING CORNERS ON TWO WHEELS – HITTING CLOSE TO NINETY – SHANE AND THE GIRL DORIS, QUICKLY CLOSE THE GAP – – –
IT'S ON 7TH STREET, THE OTHER SIDE OF TOWN – FASTER!
N TWO WHEELS TY-SHANE AND CLOSE THE GAP-
"SHANE DARE" FANTOMAN NO. 3 (OCTOBER, 1940)
HE HAD ENGINEERED BOTH HIS...AND HIS FATHER'S...SHOW BUSINESS TRAJECTORIES
SO KEN AND HIS DAD START FOR HOLLYWOOD AND THE HOME OF SAMUEL GNERRE LATE MOTION PICTURE MAGNATE
THIS LOOKS AWFULLY SUDDEN – JUST FOR CERTAIN REASONS DAD – I'M GOING TO TAKE THE INVISOBOXES ALONG
THIS LOOKS AWF SUDDEN – JUST FO CERTAIN REASONS DAD – I'M GOING TO TAKE THE INVISOBOXES ALONG
"KEN TRAYMORE AND THE INVISOBOX" DETECTIVE EYE NO. 2 (DECEMBER, 1940)
THE THEME OF INVISIBILITY LINKS DRAKE TO THE FIRST SUPER-POWERED FEMALE COMICS CHARACTER
(SAMUAL...ALSO SAMUEL... GNERRE. IT'S "GREENE", I THINK, BUT SPELLED THROUGH THE METAPHYSICAL WARP DRAKE INHABITED...)
(...AND WHICH INHABITED HIM)
KEITH BUTLER
BY
Stanley Allen Drake
FOREWORD
LRIGHT BUTLER – YOU'VE – I'LL TELL YOU WHERE BUT DON'T HARM ME – FINE
MORE SIGNIFICANTLY, HE HAD INCARNATED A METAPHYSICAL VENGEANCE NARRATIVE...
...WHEREIN A HEROIC PROXY WITH THE SAME LAST NAME AS MARGARET MITCHELL'S ANTI-HERO PROTAGONIST ...
TRACKS DOWN A PROXY OF MITCHELL'S ABUSIVE FIRST HUSBAND ...
TH STARTS TO LEAVE,
"KEITH BUTLER" THE ARROW NO. 3 (OCTOBER, 1941)

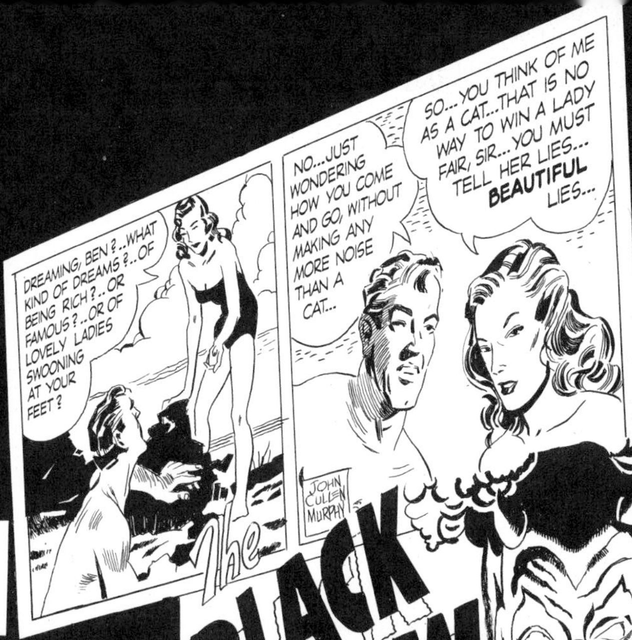

DREAMING, BEN?..WHAT KIND OF DREAMS?..OF BEING RICH?..OR FAMOUS?..OR OF LOVELY LADIES SWOONING AT YOUR FEET?
NO...JUST WONDERING HOW YOU COME AND GO, WITHOUT MAKING ANY MORE NOISE THAN A CAT...
SO...YOU THINK OF ME AS A CAT...THAT IS NO WAY TO WIN A LADY FAIR, SIR...YOU MUST TELL HER LIES... BEAUTIFUL LIES...
JOHN CULLEN MURPHY


"THE GIRL ON THE BEACH"

A.K.A. THE UNSEEN ACTRESS

WHO WOULD TEST FOR THE PART OF **SCARLETT O'HARA**

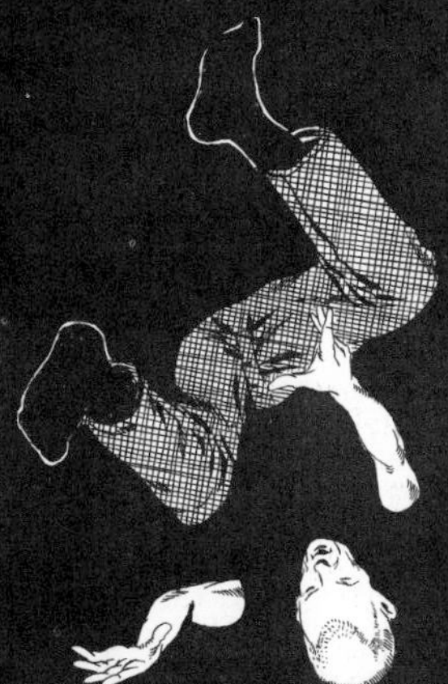

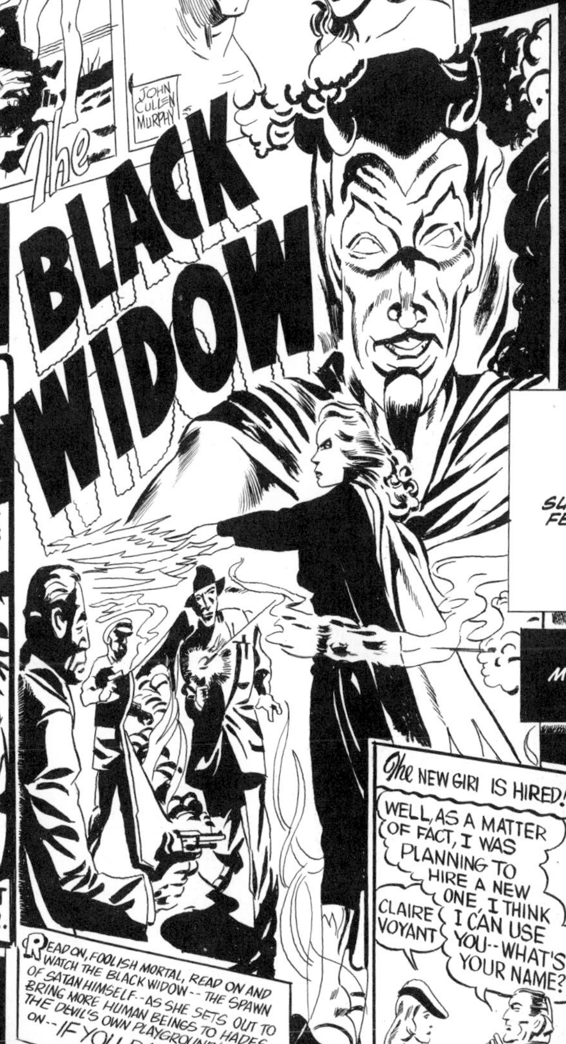

The BLACK WIDOW
READ ON, FOOLISH MORTAL, READ ON AND WATCH THE BLACK WIDOW -- THE SPAWN OF SATAN HIMSELF -- AS SHE SETS OUT TO BRING MORE HUMAN BEINGS TO HADES, THE DEVIL'S OWN PLAYGROUND! READ ON -- IF YOU DARE!! ---


BEARING A DISTINCT RESEMBLANCE TO **RUSSELL STAMM**'S SEMINAL SUPER-HEROINE:

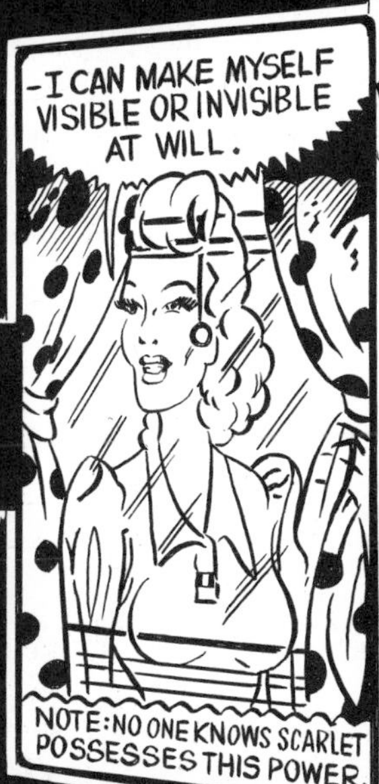

-I CAN MAKE MYSELF VISIBLE OR INVISIBLE AT WILL.
NOTE: NO ONE KNOWS SCARLET POSSESSES THIS POWER.


**"INVISIBLE SCARLET O'NEIL"** (APRIL, 1940)

...EVEN AS STAN DRAKE WAS DRAWING THE **SECOND SUPER-POWERED FEMALE COMICS CHARACTER** FOR MARVEL COMICS:

"THE BLACK WIDOW" **MYSTIC COMICS** NO. 7 (DECEMBER, 1940)

WHOSE CIVILIAN IDENTITY WAS **CLAIRE VOYANT...**

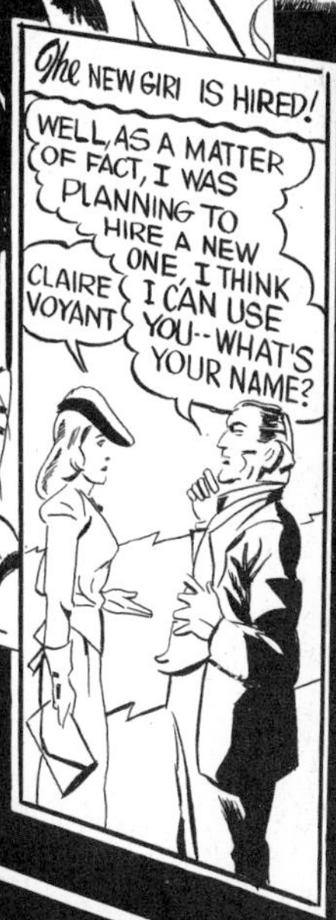

The NEW GIRL IS HIRED!
WELL, AS A MATTER OF FACT, I WAS PLANNING TO HIRE A NEW ONE, I THINK I CAN USE YOU--WHAT'S YOUR NAME?
CLAIRE VOYANT


A NAME SHE WOULD SHARE WITH **YET ANOTHER COMIC-STRIP HEROINE**

WHO WOULD BE CREATED BY EXPATRIATE CANADIAN, **JACK SPARLING**

AN **ACTUAL** (ALBEIT **AMNESIATIC**) CLAIRVOYANT CHARACTER

**"CLAIRE VOYANT"** (MAY, 1943)

FOUND CAST ADRIFT IN A LIFEBOAT

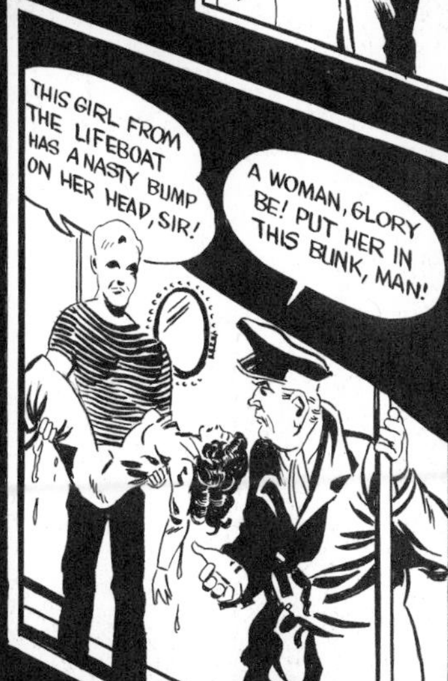

THIS GIRL FROM THE LIFEBOAT HAS A NASTY BUMP ON HER HEAD, SIR!
A WOMAN, GLORY BE! PUT HER IN THIS BUNK, MAN!


(AN **ABUSIVE FIRST HUSBAND** UPON WHOM THAT **ANTI-HERO** HAD BEEN BASED)

LEADING TO THAT PROXY'S DEATH BY A FALL FROM A GREAT HEIGHT.

A FATE SHARED BY THAT **ABUSIVE FIRST HUSBAND** IN REAL LIFE, **SEVEN YEARS** (JANUARY 1949) AFTER THE "KEITH BUTLER" STORY

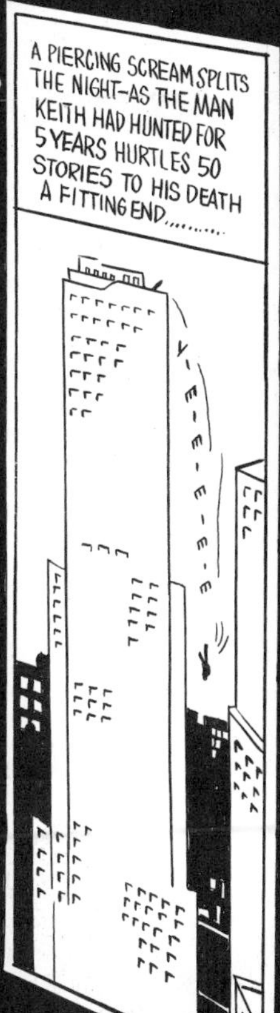

A PIERCING SCREAM SPLITS THE NIGHT—AS THE MAN KEITH HAD HUNTED FOR 5 YEARS HURTLES 50 STORIES TO HIS DEATH A FITTING END.........


AS THE CAPTION PUTS IT: "THE MAN KEITH HAD HUNTED FOR **FIVE YEARS**"

THE "KEITH BUTLER" STORY ITSELF HAD BEEN PUBLISHED EXACTLY **FIVE YEARS AFTER GONE WITH THE WIND**

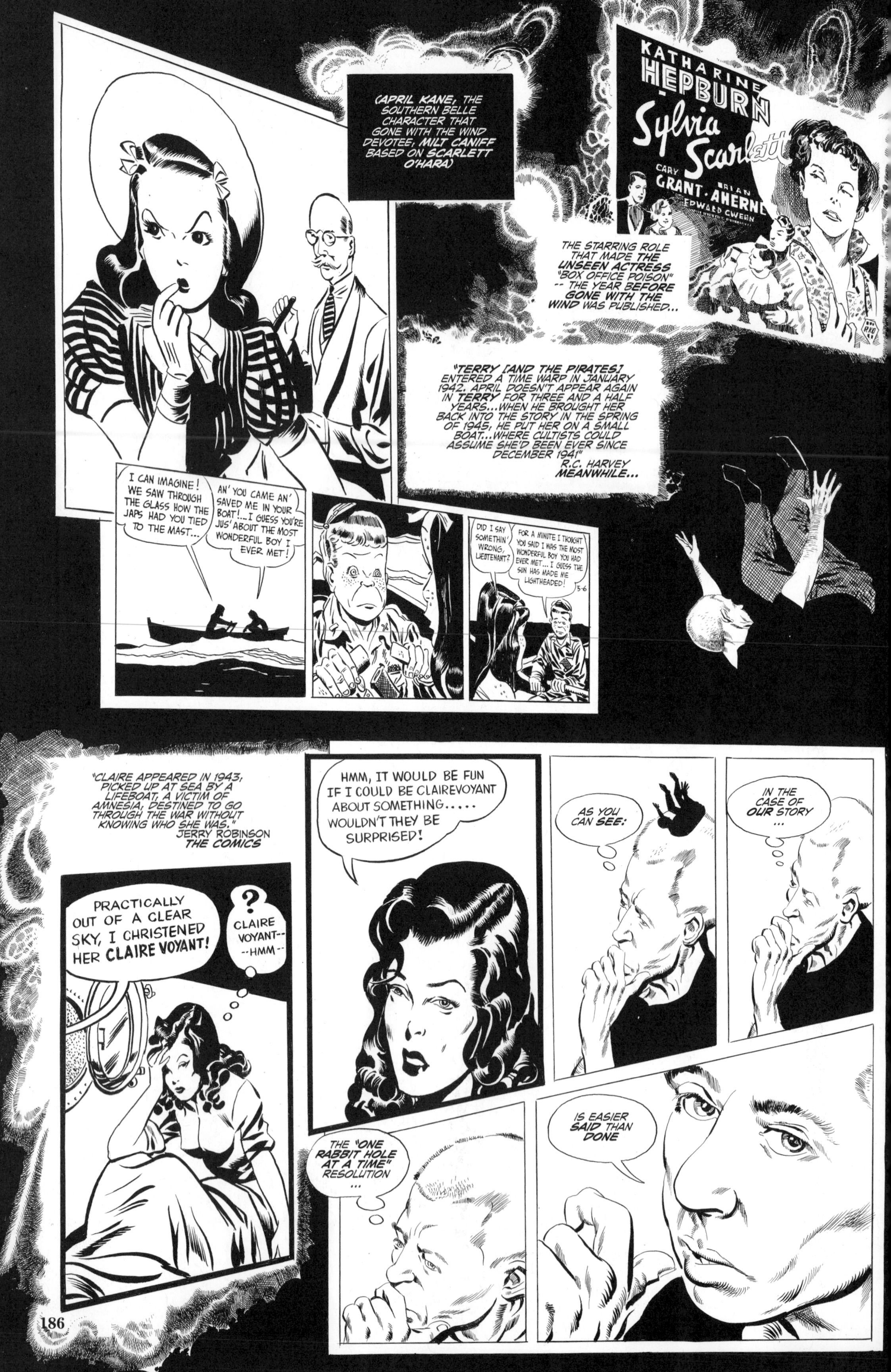

(APRIL KANE, THE SOUTHERN BELLE CHARACTER THAT GONE WITH THE WIND DEVOTEE, MILT CANIFF BASED ON SCARLETT O'HARA)
KATHARINE HEPBURN
Sylvia Scarlett
CARY GRANT · BRIAN AHERNE
EDWARD GWENN
RKO
THE STARRING ROLE THAT MADE THE UNSEEN ACTRESS "BOX OFFICE POISON" -- THE YEAR BEFORE GONE WITH THE WIND WAS PUBLISHED...
"TERRY [AND THE PIRATES] ENTERED A TIME WARP IN JANUARY 1942. APRIL DOESN'T APPEAR AGAIN IN TERRY FOR THREE AND A HALF YEARS...WHEN HE BROUGHT HER BACK INTO THE STORY IN THE SPRING OF 1945, HE PUT HER ON A SMALL BOAT...WHERE CULTISTS COULD ASSUME SHE'D BEEN EVER SINCE DECEMBER 1941"
R.C. HARVEY
MEANWHILE...
I CAN IMAGINE! WE SAW THROUGH THE GLASS HOW THE JAPS HAD YOU TIED TO THE MAST...
AN' YOU CAME AN' SAVED ME IN YOUR BOAT!...I GUESS YOU'RE JUS' ABOUT THE MOST WONDERFUL BOY I EVER MET!
DID I SAY SOMETHIN' WRONG, LIEUTENANT?
FOR A MINUTE I THOUGHT YOU SAID I WAS THE MOST WONDERFUL BOY YOU HAD EVER MET... I GUESS THE SUN HAS MADE ME LIGHTHEADED!
5-6
"CLAIRE APPEARED IN 1943, PICKED UP AT SEA BY A LIFEBOAT, A VICTIM OF AMNESIA, DESTINED TO GO THROUGH THE WAR WITHOUT KNOWING WHO SHE WAS."
JERRY ROBINSON
THE COMICS
PRACTICALLY OUT OF A CLEAR SKY, I CHRISTENED HER CLAIRE VOYANT!
? CLAIRE VOYANT-- --HMM--
HMM, IT WOULD BE FUN IF I COULD BE CLAIREVOYANT ABOUT SOMETHING..... WOULDN'T THEY BE SURPRISED!
AS YOU CAN SEE:
IN THE CASE OF OUR STORY ...
THE "ONE RABBIT HOLE AT A TIME" RESOLUTION ...
IS EASIER SAID THAN DONE

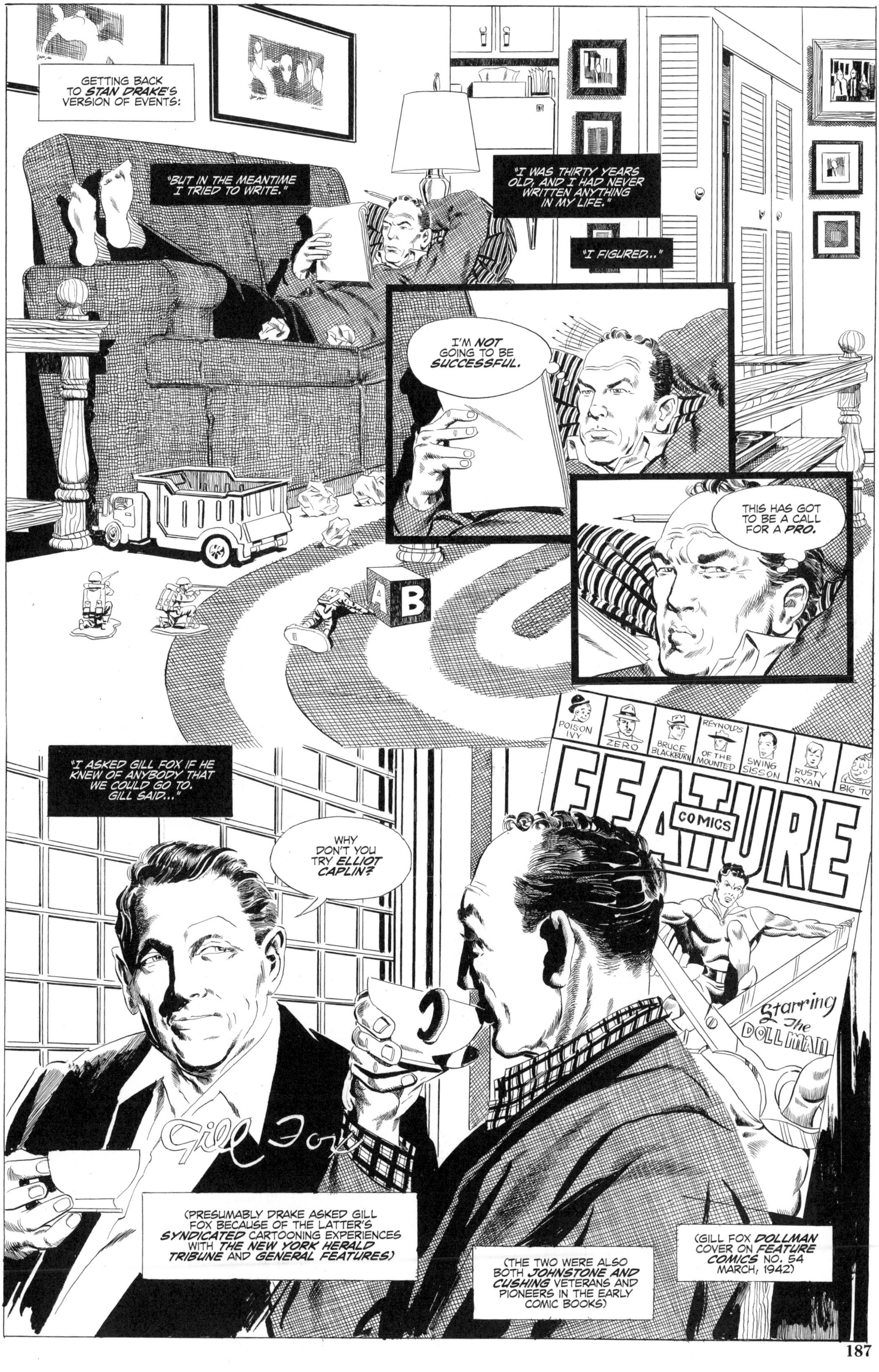
GETTING BACK TO STAN DRAKE'S VERSION OF EVENTS:
"BUT IN THE MEANTIME I TRIED TO WRITE."
"I WAS THIRTY YEARS OLD, AND I HAD NEVER WRITTEN ANYTHING IN MY LIFE."
"I FIGURED..."
I'M NOT GOING TO BE SUCCESSFUL.
THIS HAS GOT TO BE A CALL FOR A PRO.
"I ASKED GILL FOX IF HE KNEW OF ANYBODY THAT WE COULD GO TO. GILL SAID..."
WHY DON'T YOU TRY ELLIOT CAPLIN?
POISON IVY
ZERO
BRUCE BLACKBURN
REYNOLDS OF THE MOUNTED
SWING SISSON
RUSTY RYAN
FEATURE COMICS
Starring The DOLL MAN
Gill Fox
(PRESUMABLY DRAKE ASKED GILL FOX BECAUSE OF THE LATTER'S SYNDICATED CARTOONING EXPERIENCES WITH THE NEW YORK HERALD TRIBUNE AND GENERAL FEATURES)
(THE TWO WERE ALSO BOTH JOHNSTONE AND CUSHING VETERANS AND PIONEERS IN THE EARLY COMIC BOOKS)
(GILL FOX DOLLMAN COVER ON FEATURE COMICS NO. 54 MARCH, 1942)

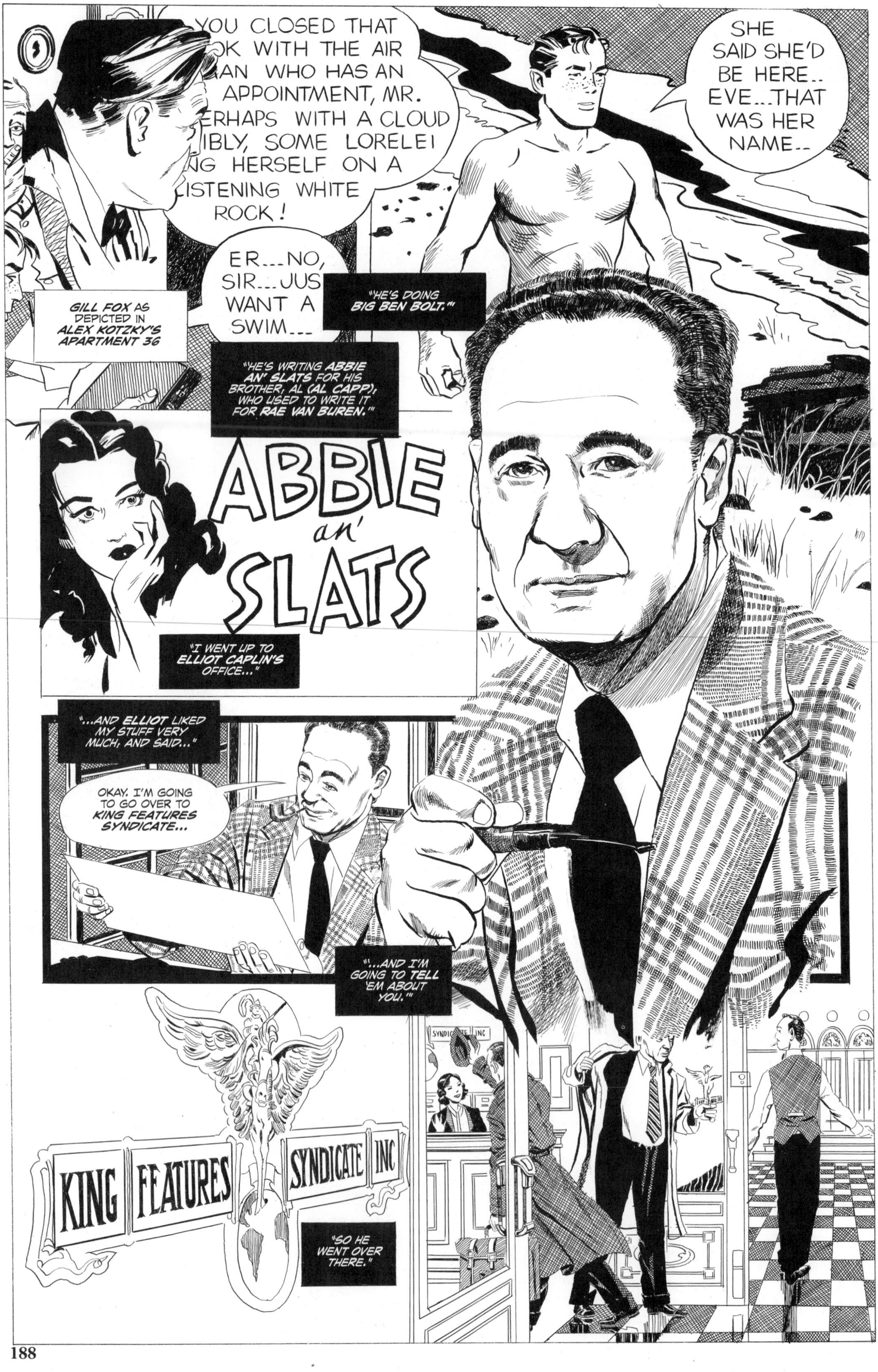
YOU CLOSED THAT
OK WITH THE AIR
AN WHO HAS AN
APPOINTMENT, MR.
ERHAPS WITH A CLOUD
IBLY, SOME LORELEI
NG HERSELF ON A
LISTENING WHITE
ROCK!
SHE SAID SHE'D BE HERE.. EVE...THAT WAS HER NAME..
ER...NO, SIR...JUS WANT A SWIM...
GILL FOX AS DEPICTED IN ALEX KOTZKY'S APARTMENT 3G
"HE'S DOING BIG BEN BOLT."
"HE'S WRITING ABBIE AN' SLATS FOR HIS BROTHER, AL (AL CAPP), WHO USED TO WRITE IT FOR RAE VAN BUREN."
ABBIE an' SLATS
"I WENT UP TO ELLIOT CAPLIN'S OFFICE..."
"...AND ELLIOT LIKED MY STUFF VERY MUCH, AND SAID..."
OKAY. I'M GOING TO GO OVER TO KING FEATURES SYNDICATE...
"...AND I'M GOING TO TELL 'EM ABOUT YOU."
KING FEATURES SYNDICATE INC
"SO HE WENT OVER THERE."

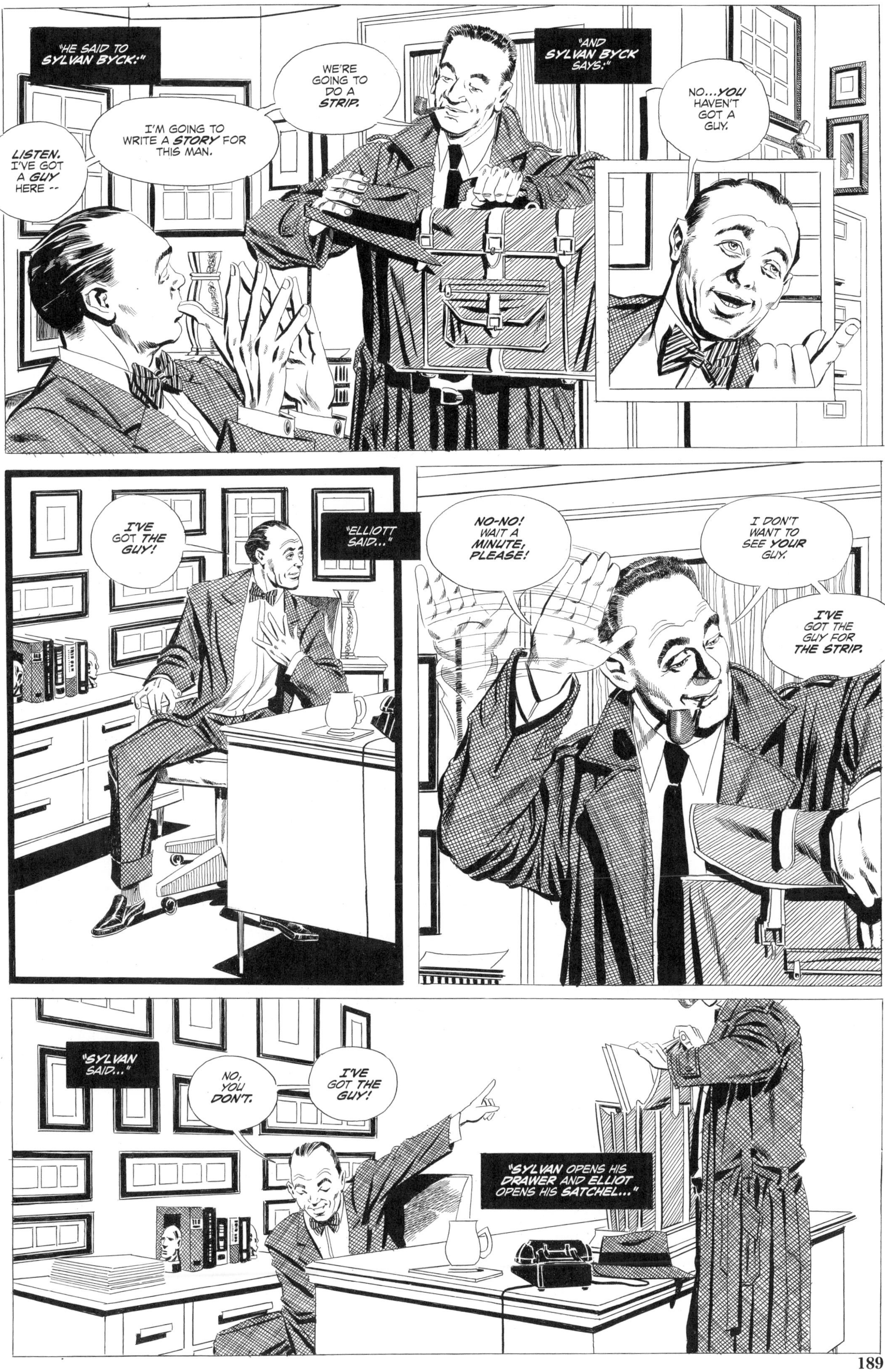
"HE SAID TO SYLVAN BYCK:"
LISTEN. I'VE GOT A GUY HERE --
I'M GOING TO WRITE A STORY FOR THIS MAN.
WE'RE GOING TO DO A STRIP.
"AND SYLVAN BYCK SAYS:"
NO...YOU HAVEN'T GOT A GUY.
"ELLIOTT SAID..."
I'VE GOT THE GUY!
NO-NO! WAIT A MINUTE, PLEASE!
I DON'T WANT TO SEE YOUR GUY.
I'VE GOT THE GUY FOR THE STRIP.
"SYLVAN SAID..."
NO, YOU DON'T.
I'VE GOT THE GUY!
"SYLVAN OPENS HIS DRAWER AND ELLIOT OPENS HIS SATCHEL..."

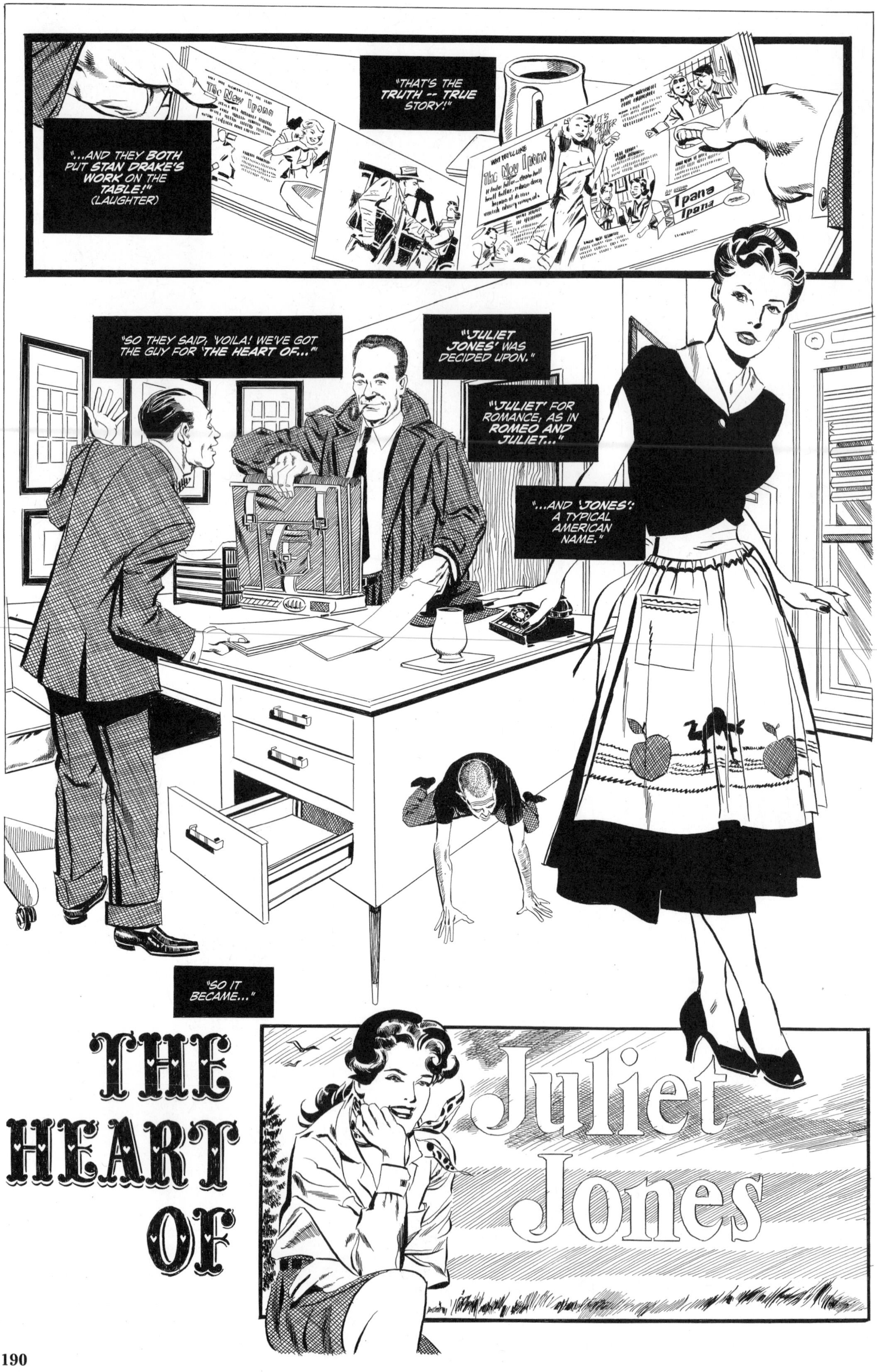
"...AND THEY BOTH PUT STAN DRAKE'S WORK ON THE TABLE!" (LAUGHTER)
"THAT'S THE TRUTH -- TRUE STORY!"
"SO THEY SAID, 'VOILA! WE'VE GOT THE GUY FOR 'THE HEART OF...'"
"'JULIET JONES' WAS DECIDED UPON."
"'JULIET' FOR ROMANCE, AS IN ROMEO AND JULIET..."
"...AND 'JONES': A TYPICAL AMERICAN NAME."
"SO IT BECAME..."
THE HEART OF
Juliet Jones

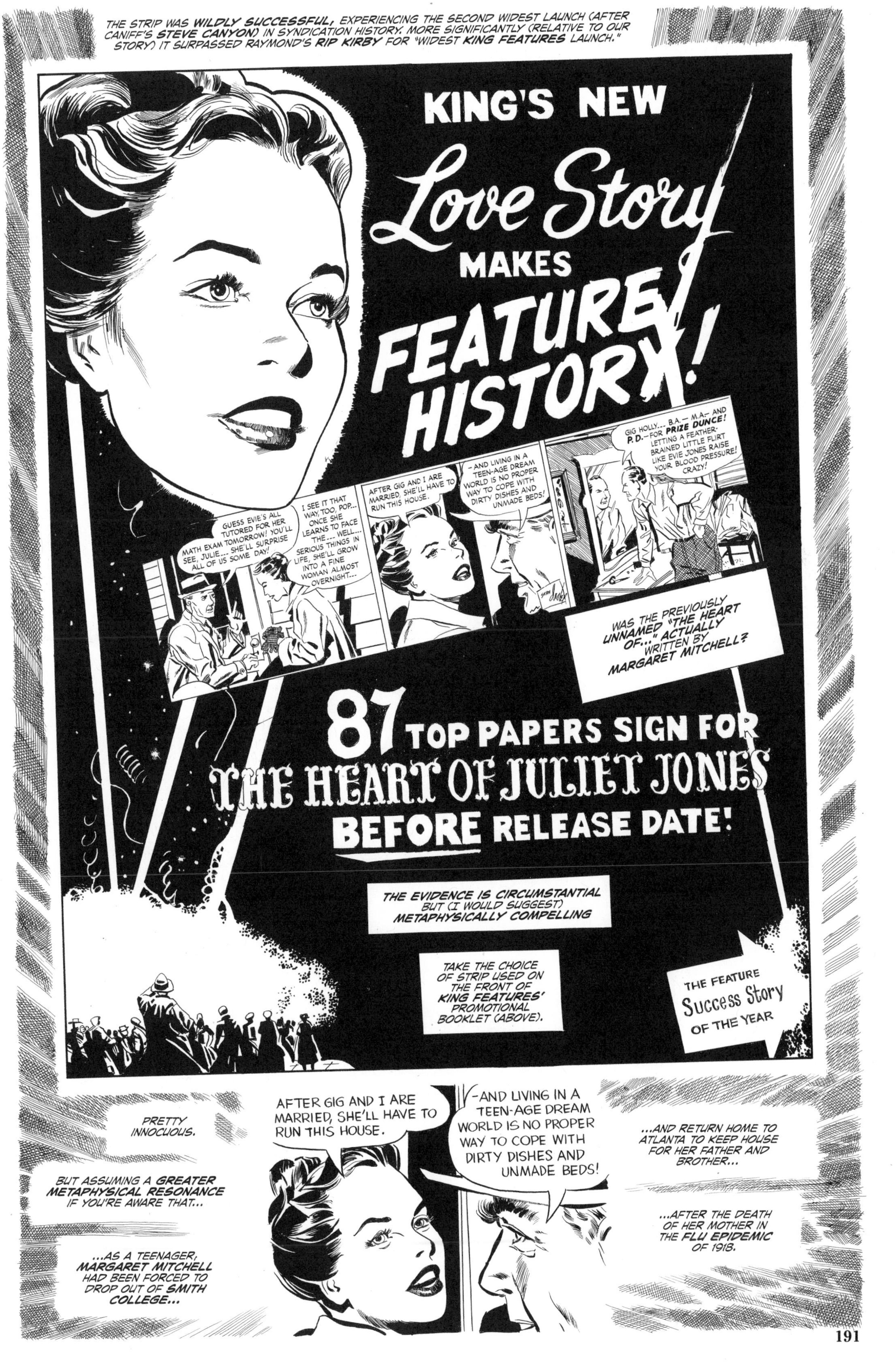

THE STRIP WAS WILDLY SUCCESSFUL, EXPERIENCING THE SECOND WIDEST LAUNCH (AFTER CANIFF'S STEVE CANYON) IN SYNDICATION HISTORY. MORE SIGNIFICANTLY (RELATIVE TO OUR STORY) IT SURPASSED RAYMOND'S RIP KIRBY FOR "WIDEST KING FEATURES LAUNCH."
KING'S NEW
Love Story
MAKES
FEATURE HISTORY!
GUESS EVIE'S ALL TUTORED FOR HER MATH EXAM TOMORROW! YOU'LL SEE, JULIE... SHE'LL SURPRISE ALL OF US SOME DAY!
I SEE IT THAT WAY, TOO, POP... ONCE SHE LEARNS TO FACE THE--- WELL... SERIOUS THINGS IN LIFE, SHE'LL GROW INTO A FINE WOMAN ALMOST OVERNIGHT...
AFTER GIG AND I ARE MARRIED, SHE'LL HAVE TO RUN THIS HOUSE.
-AND LIVING IN A TEEN-AGE DREAM WORLD IS NO PROPER WAY TO COPE WITH DIRTY DISHES AND UNMADE BEDS!
GIG HOLLY... B.A.— M.A.— AND P.D.—FOR PRIZE DUNCE! LETTING A FEATHER-BRAINED LITTLE FLIRT LIKE EVIE JONES RAISE YOUR BLOOD PRESSURE! CRAZY!
WAS THE PREVIOUSLY UNNAMED "THE HEART OF..." ACTUALLY WRITTEN BY MARGARET MITCHELL?
87 TOP PAPERS SIGN FOR
THE HEART OF JULIET JONES
BEFORE RELEASE DATE!
THE EVIDENCE IS CIRCUMSTANTIAL BUT (I WOULD SUGGEST) METAPHYSICALLY COMPELLING
TAKE THE CHOICE OF STRIP USED ON THE FRONT OF KING FEATURES' PROMOTIONAL BOOKLET (ABOVE).
THE FEATURE Success Story OF THE YEAR
PRETTY INNOCUOUS.
BUT ASSUMING A GREATER METAPHYSICAL RESONANCE IF YOU'RE AWARE THAT...
...AS A TEENAGER, MARGARET MITCHELL HAD BEEN FORCED TO DROP OUT OF SMITH COLLEGE...
AFTER GIG AND I ARE MARRIED, SHE'LL HAVE TO RUN THIS HOUSE.
-AND LIVING IN A TEEN-AGE DREAM WORLD IS NO PROPER WAY TO COPE WITH DIRTY DISHES AND UNMADE BEDS!
...AND RETURN HOME TO ATLANTA TO KEEP HOUSE FOR HER FATHER AND BROTHER...
...AFTER THE DEATH OF HER MOTHER IN THE FLU EPIDEMIC OF 1918.

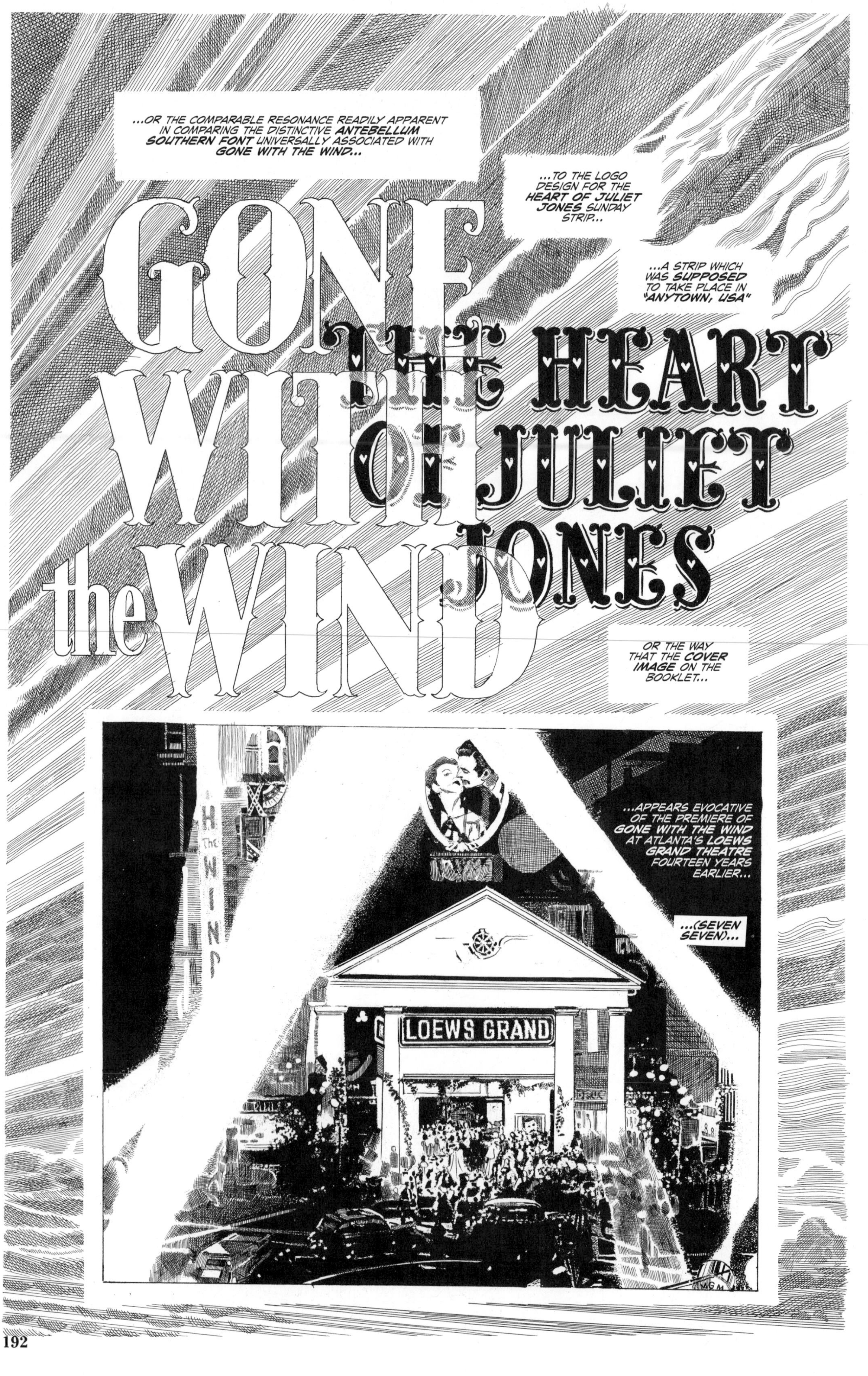
...OR THE COMPARABLE RESONANCE READILY APPARENT IN COMPARING THE DISTINCTIVE ANTEBELLUM SOUTHERN FONT UNIVERSALLY ASSOCIATED WITH GONE WITH THE WIND...
...TO THE LOGO DESIGN FOR THE HEART OF JULIET JONES SUNDAY STRIP...
...A STRIP WHICH WAS SUPPOSED TO TAKE PLACE IN "ANYTOWN, USA"
GONE WITH the WIND
THE HEART OF JULIET JONES
OR THE WAY THAT THE COVER IMAGE ON THE BOOKLET...
...APPEARS EVOCATIVE OF THE PREMIERE OF GONE WITH THE WIND AT ATLANTA'S LOEWS GRAND THEATRE FOURTEEN YEARS EARLIER...
...(SEVEN SEVEN)...
LOEWS GRAND
MGM

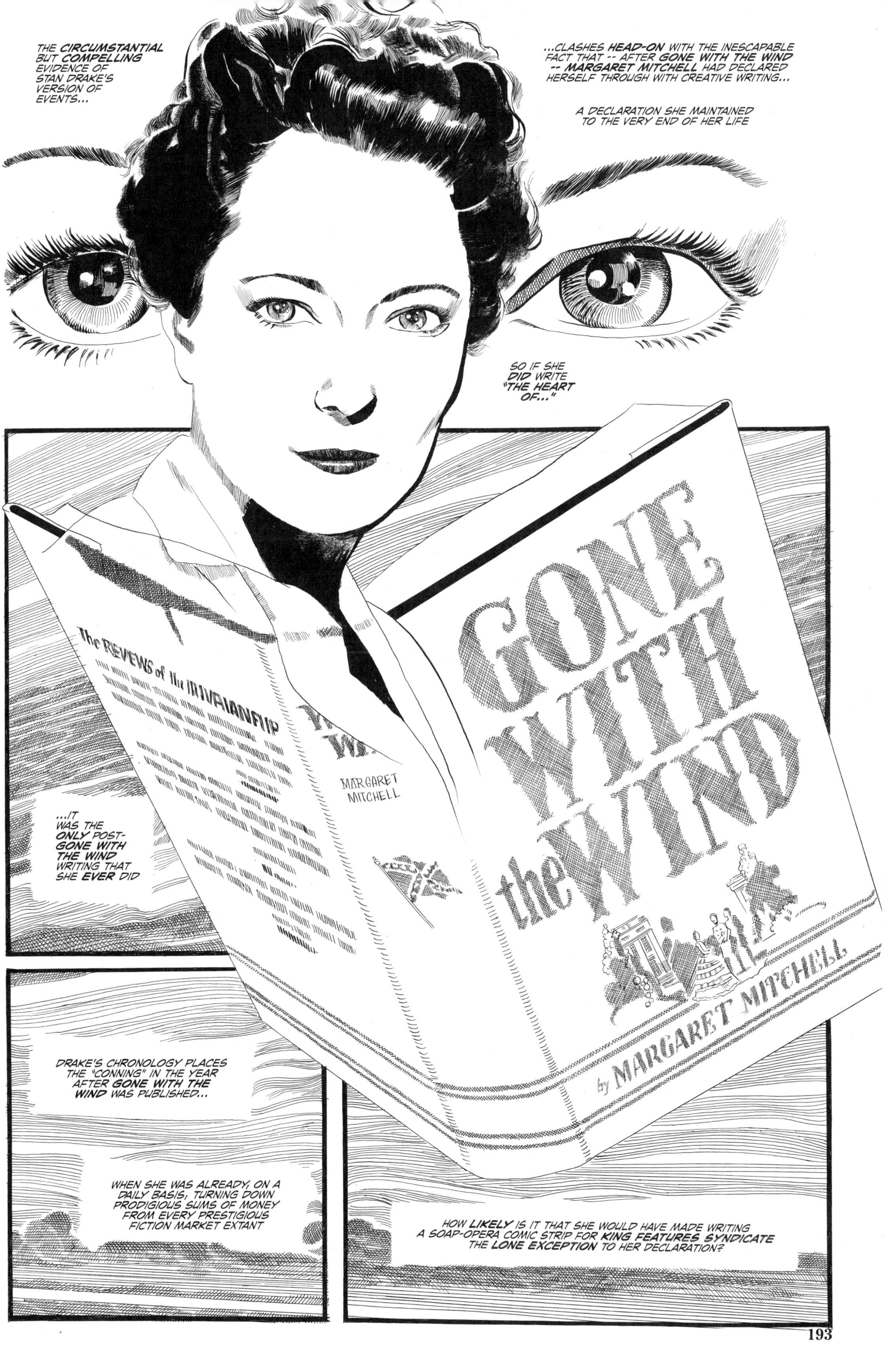

THE CIRCUMSTANTIAL BUT COMPELLING EVIDENCE OF STAN DRAKE'S VERSION OF EVENTS...
...CLASHES HEAD-ON WITH THE INESCAPABLE FACT THAT -- AFTER GONE WITH THE WIND -- MARGARET MITCHELL HAD DECLARED HERSELF THROUGH WITH CREATIVE WRITING...
A DECLARATION SHE MAINTAINED TO THE VERY END OF HER LIFE
SO IF SHE DID WRITE "THE HEART OF..."
MARGARET MITCHELL
GONE WITH the WIND
by MARGARET MITCHELL
...IT WAS THE ONLY POST-GONE WITH THE WIND WRITING THAT SHE EVER DID
DRAKE'S CHRONOLOGY PLACES THE "CONNING" IN THE YEAR AFTER GONE WITH THE WIND WAS PUBLISHED...
WHEN SHE WAS ALREADY, ON A DAILY BASIS, TURNING DOWN PRODIGIOUS SUMS OF MONEY FROM EVERY PRESTIGIOUS FICTION MARKET EXTANT
HOW LIKELY IS IT THAT SHE WOULD HAVE MADE WRITING A SOAP-OPERA COMIC STRIP FOR KING FEATURES SYNDICATE THE LONE EXCEPTION TO HER DECLARATION?

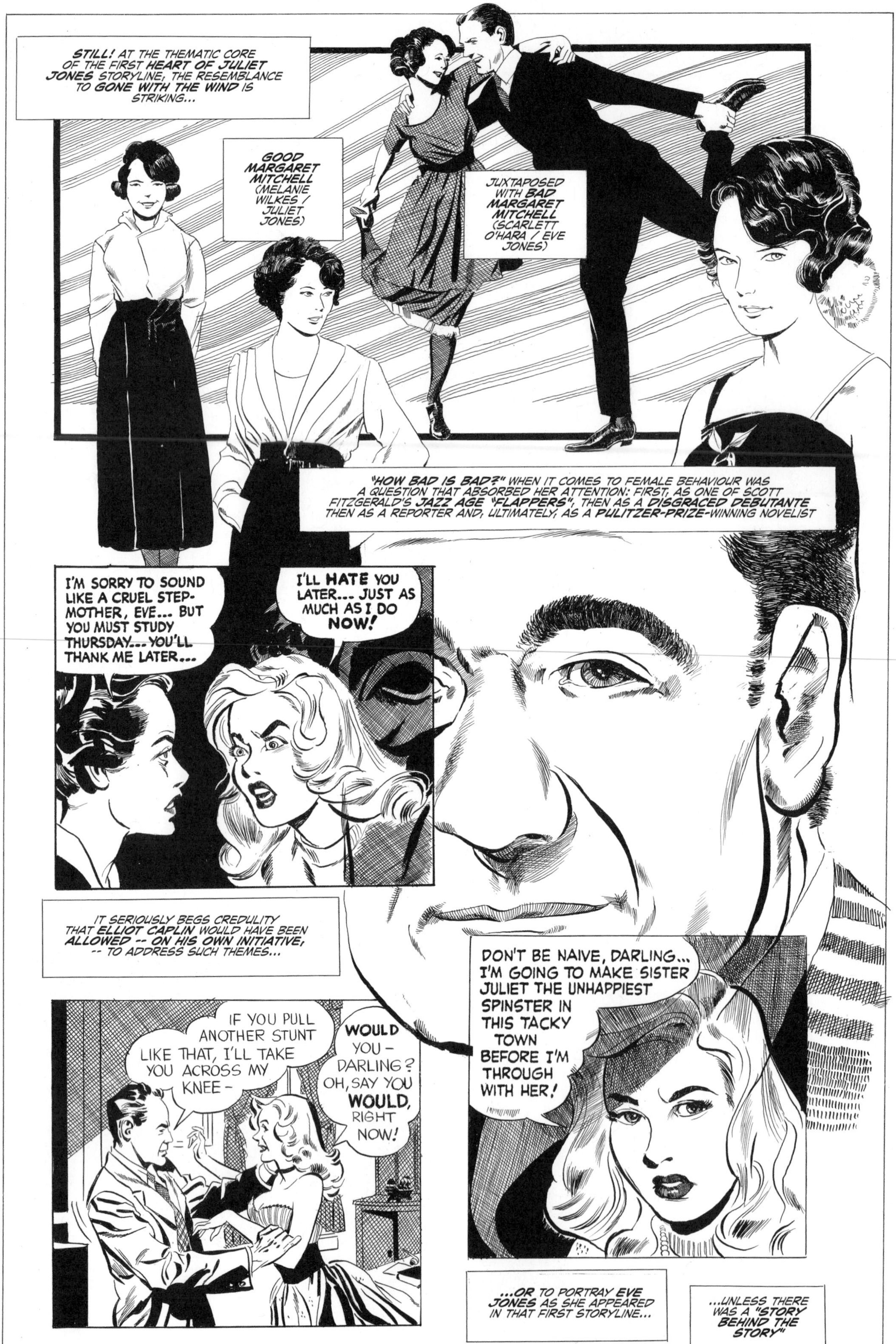
STILL! AT THE THEMATIC CORE OF THE FIRST HEART OF JULIET JONES STORYLINE, THE RESEMBLANCE TO GONE WITH THE WIND IS STRIKING...
GOOD MARGARET MITCHELL (MELANIE WILKES / JULIET JONES)
JUXTAPOSED WITH BAD MARGARET MITCHELL (SCARLETT O'HARA / EVE JONES)
"HOW BAD IS BAD?" WHEN IT COMES TO FEMALE BEHAVIOUR WAS A QUESTION THAT ABSORBED HER ATTENTION: FIRST, AS ONE OF SCOTT FITZGERALD'S JAZZ AGE "FLAPPERS", THEN AS A DISGRACED DEBUTANTE THEN AS A REPORTER AND, ULTIMATELY, AS A PULITZER-PRIZE-WINNING NOVELIST
I'M SORRY TO SOUND LIKE A CRUEL STEP-MOTHER, EVE... BUT YOU MUST STUDY THURSDAY... YOU'LL THANK ME LATER...
I'LL HATE YOU LATER... JUST AS MUCH AS I DO NOW!
IT SERIOUSLY BEGS CREDULITY THAT ELLIOT CAPLIN WOULD HAVE BEEN ALLOWED -- ON HIS OWN INITIATIVE, -- TO ADDRESS SUCH THEMES...
DON'T BE NAIVE, DARLING... I'M GOING TO MAKE SISTER JULIET THE UNHAPPIEST SPINSTER IN THIS TACKY TOWN BEFORE I'M THROUGH WITH HER!
IF YOU PULL ANOTHER STUNT LIKE THAT, I'LL TAKE YOU ACROSS MY KNEE -
WOULD YOU - DARLING? OH, SAY YOU WOULD, RIGHT NOW!
...OR TO PORTRAY EVE JONES AS SHE APPEARED IN THAT FIRST STORYLINE...
...UNLESS THERE WAS A "STORY BEHIND THE STORY"

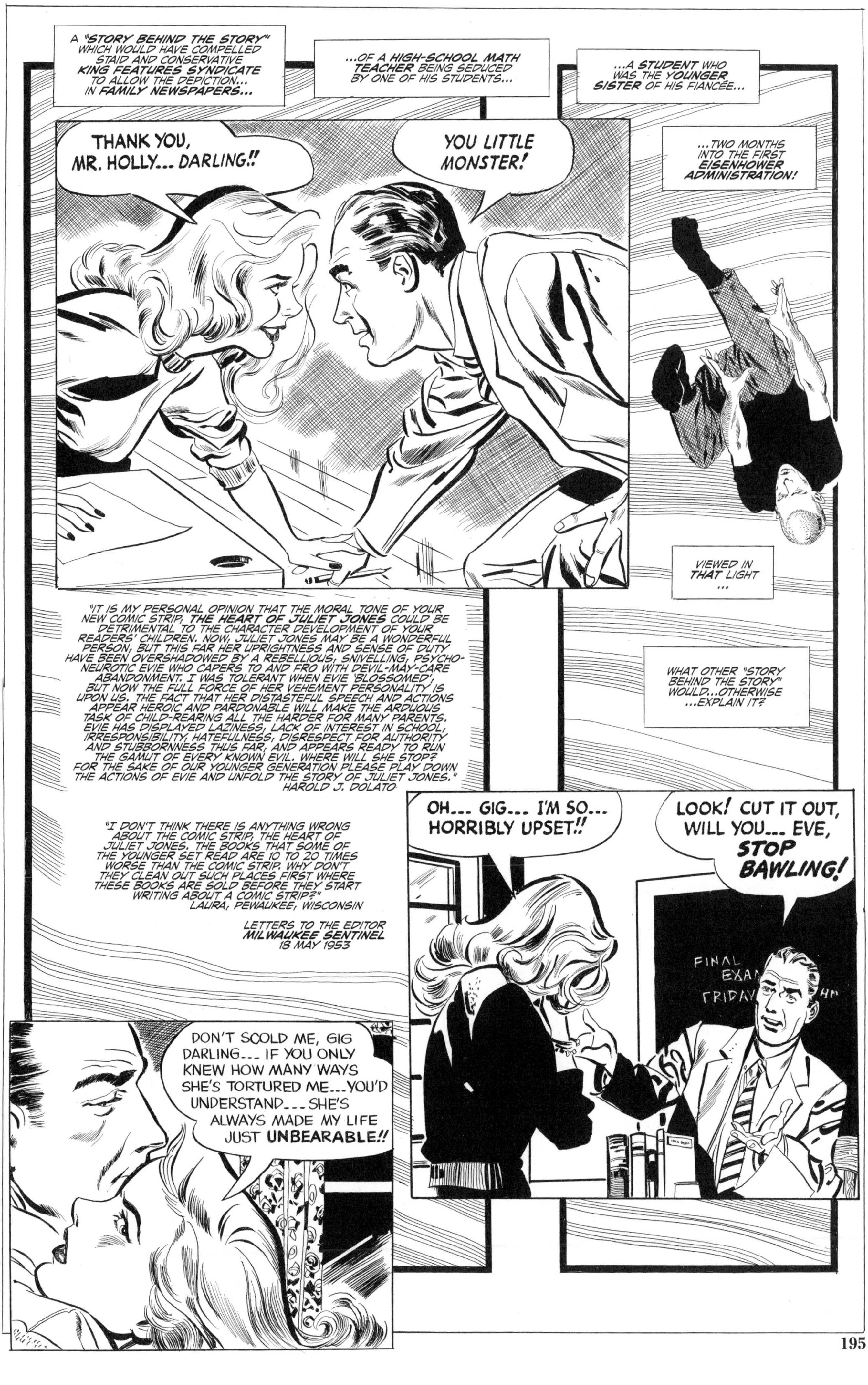
A "STORY BEHIND THE STORY" WHICH WOULD HAVE COMPELLED STAID AND CONSERVATIVE KING FEATURES SYNDICATE TO ALLOW THE DEPICTION... IN FAMILY NEWSPAPERS...
...OF A HIGH-SCHOOL MATH TEACHER BEING SEDUCED BY ONE OF HIS STUDENTS...
...A STUDENT WHO WAS THE YOUNGER SISTER OF HIS FIANCÉE...
THANK YOU, MR. HOLLY... DARLING!!
YOU LITTLE MONSTER!
...TWO MONTHS INTO THE FIRST EISENHOWER ADMINISTRATION!
VIEWED IN THAT LIGHT ...
"IT IS MY PERSONAL OPINION THAT THE MORAL TONE OF YOUR NEW COMIC STRIP, THE HEART OF JULIET JONES COULD BE DETRIMENTAL TO THE CHARACTER DEVELOPMENT OF YOUR READERS' CHILDREN. NOW, JULIET JONES MAY BE A WONDERFUL PERSON, BUT THIS FAR HER UPRIGHTNESS AND SENSE OF DUTY HAVE BEEN OVERSHADOWED BY A REBELLIOUS, SNIVELLING, PSYCHO-NEUROTIC EVIE WHO CAPERS TO AND FRO WITH DEVIL-MAY-CARE ABANDONMENT. I WAS TOLERANT WHEN EVIE 'BLOSSOMED', BUT NOW THE FULL FORCE OF HER VEHEMENT PERSONALITY IS UPON US. THE FACT THAT HER DISTASTEFUL SPEECH AND ACTIONS APPEAR HEROIC AND PARDONABLE WILL MAKE THE ARDUOUS TASK OF CHILD-REARING ALL THE HARDER FOR MANY PARENTS. EVIE HAS DISPLAYED LAZINESS, LACK OF INTEREST IN SCHOOL, IRRESPONSIBILITY, HATEFULNESS, DISRESPECT FOR AUTHORITY AND STUBBORNNESS THUS FAR, AND APPEARS READY TO RUN THE GAMUT OF EVERY KNOWN EVIL. WHERE WILL SHE STOP? FOR THE SAKE OF OUR YOUNGER GENERATION PLEASE PLAY DOWN THE ACTIONS OF EVIE AND UNFOLD THE STORY OF JULIET JONES."
HAROLD J. DOLATO
WHAT OTHER "STORY BEHIND THE STORY" WOULD...OTHERWISE ...EXPLAIN IT?
"I DON'T THINK THERE IS ANYTHING WRONG ABOUT THE COMIC STRIP, THE HEART OF JULIET JONES. THE BOOKS THAT SOME OF THE YOUNGER SET READ ARE 10 TO 20 TIMES WORSE THAN THE COMIC STRIP. WHY DON'T THEY CLEAN OUT SUCH PLACES FIRST WHERE THESE BOOKS ARE SOLD BEFORE THEY START WRITING ABOUT A COMIC STRIP?"
LAURA, PEWAUKEE, WISCONSIN
LETTERS TO THE EDITOR
MILWAUKEE SENTINEL
18 MAY 1953
OH... GIG... I'M SO... HORRIBLY UPSET!!
LOOK! CUT IT OUT, WILL YOU... EVE, STOP BAWLING!
FINAL EXAM FRIDAY
DON'T SCOLD ME, GIG DARLING... IF YOU ONLY KNEW HOW MANY WAYS SHE'S TORTURED ME...YOU'D UNDERSTAND... SHE'S ALWAYS MADE MY LIFE JUST UNBEARABLE!!

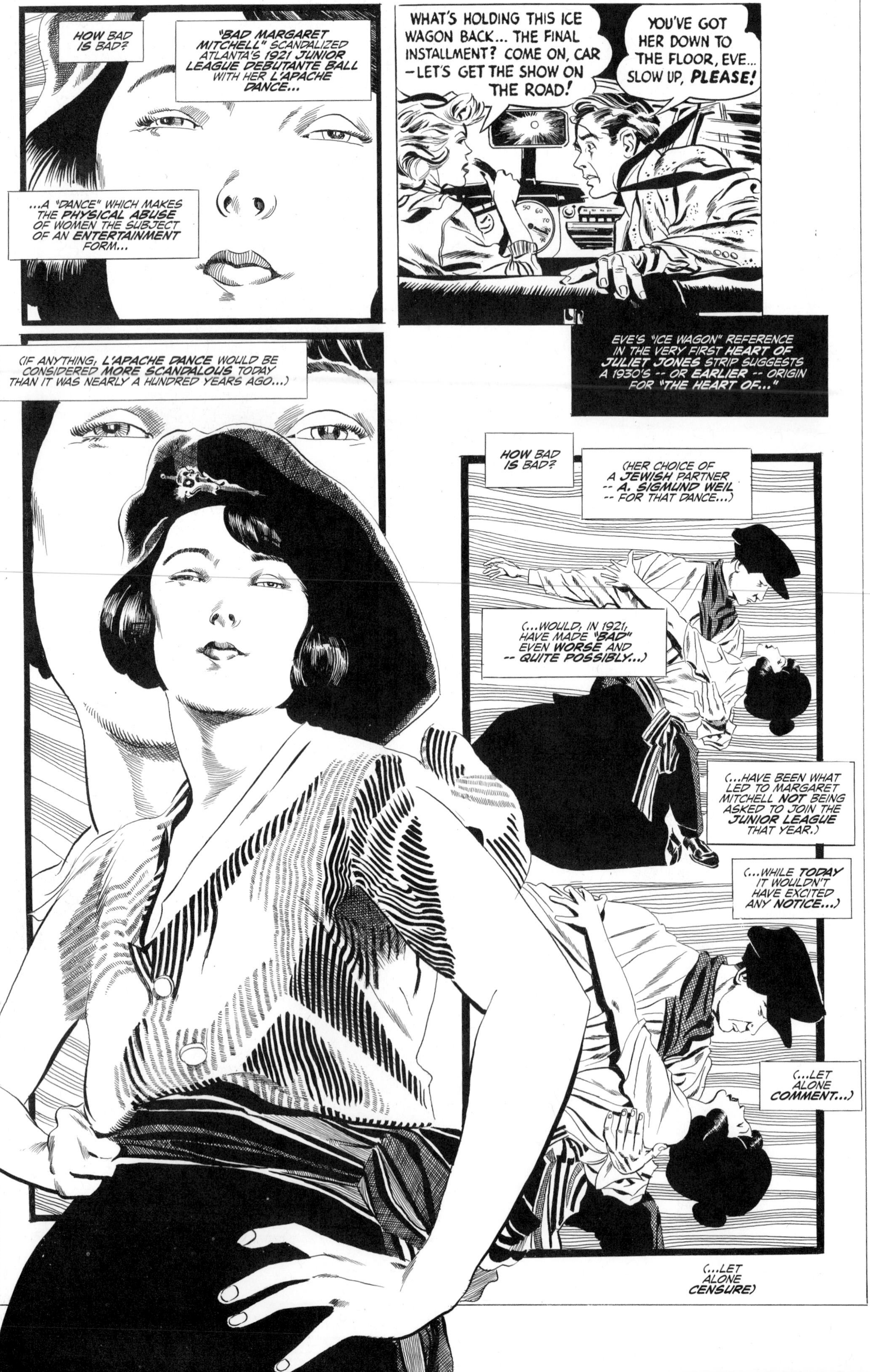
HOW BAD IS BAD?
"BAD MARGARET MITCHELL" SCANDALIZED ATLANTA'S 1921 JUNIOR LEAGUE DEBUTANTE BALL WITH HER L'APACHE DANCE...
...A "DANCE" WHICH MAKES THE PHYSICAL ABUSE OF WOMEN THE SUBJECT OF AN ENTERTAINMENT FORM...
WHAT'S HOLDING THIS ICE WAGON BACK... THE FINAL INSTALLMENT? COME ON, CAR —LET'S GET THE SHOW ON THE ROAD!
YOU'VE GOT HER DOWN TO THE FLOOR, EVE... SLOW UP, PLEASE!
EVE'S "ICE WAGON" REFERENCE IN THE VERY FIRST HEART OF JULIET JONES STRIP SUGGESTS A 1930'S -- OR EARLIER -- ORIGIN FOR "THE HEART OF..."
(IF ANYTHING, L'APACHE DANCE WOULD BE CONSIDERED MORE SCANDALOUS TODAY THAN IT WAS NEARLY A HUNDRED YEARS AGO...)
HOW BAD IS BAD?
(HER CHOICE OF A JEWISH PARTNER -- A. SIGMUND WEIL -- FOR THAT DANCE...)
(...WOULD, IN 1921, HAVE MADE "BAD" EVEN WORSE AND -- QUITE POSSIBLY...)
(...HAVE BEEN WHAT LED TO MARGARET MITCHELL NOT BEING ASKED TO JOIN THE JUNIOR LEAGUE THAT YEAR.)
(...WHILE TODAY IT WOULDN'T HAVE EXCITED ANY NOTICE...)
(...LET ALONE COMMENT...)
(...LET ALONE CENSURE)

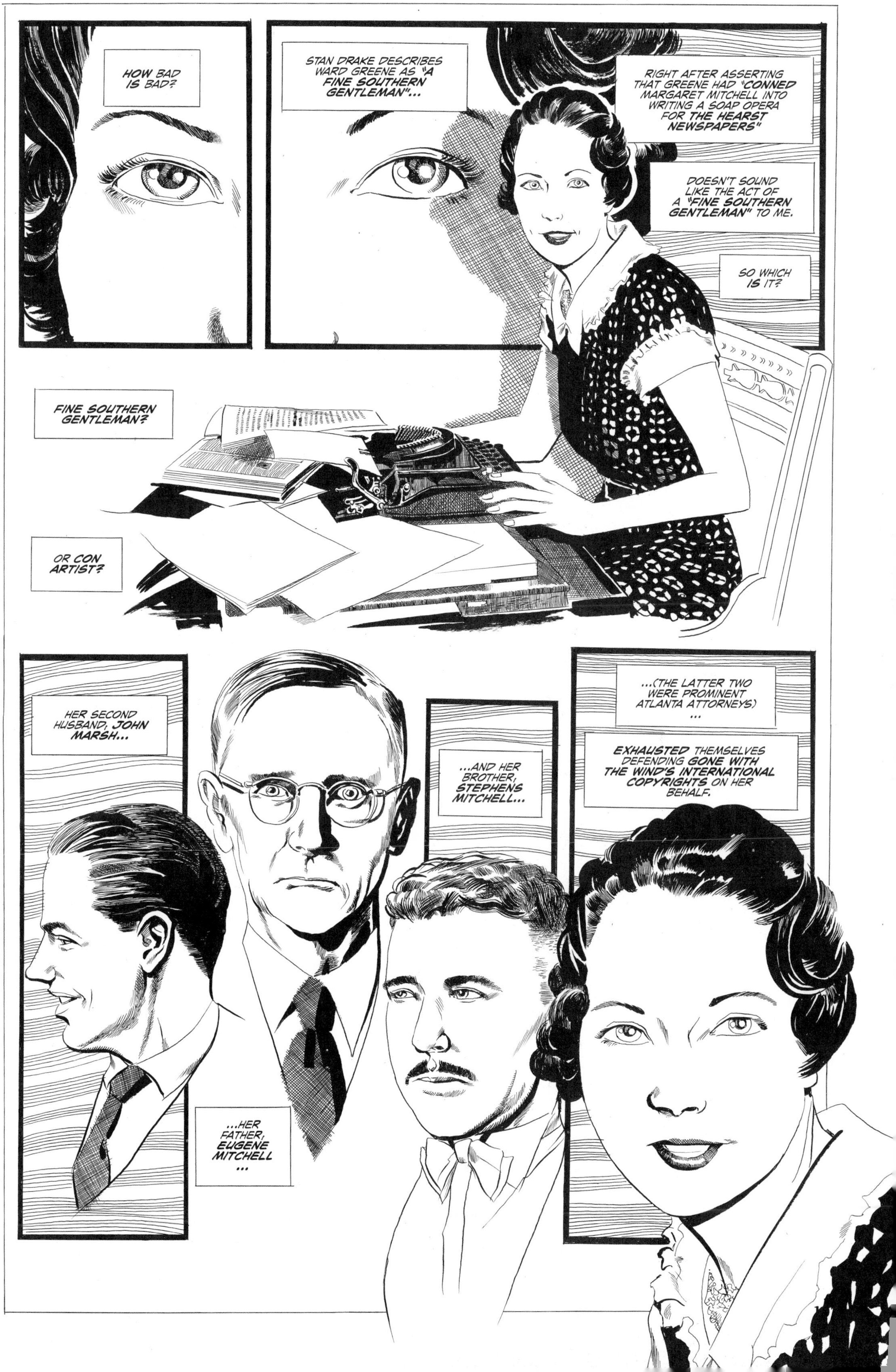
HOW BAD IS BAD?
STAN DRAKE DESCRIBES WARD GREENE AS "A FINE SOUTHERN GENTLEMAN"...
RIGHT AFTER ASSERTING THAT GREENE HAD "CONNED MARGARET MITCHELL INTO WRITING A SOAP OPERA FOR THE HEARST NEWSPAPERS"
DOESN'T SOUND LIKE THE ACT OF A "FINE SOUTHERN GENTLEMAN" TO ME.
SO WHICH IS IT?
FINE SOUTHERN GENTLEMAN?
OR CON ARTIST?
HER SECOND HUSBAND, JOHN MARSH...
...HER FATHER, EUGENE MITCHELL ...
...AND HER BROTHER, STEPHENS MITCHELL...
...(THE LATTER TWO WERE PROMINENT ATLANTA ATTORNEYS) ...
EXHAUSTED THEMSELVES DEFENDING GONE WITH THE WIND'S INTERNATIONAL COPYRIGHTS ON HER BEHALF.

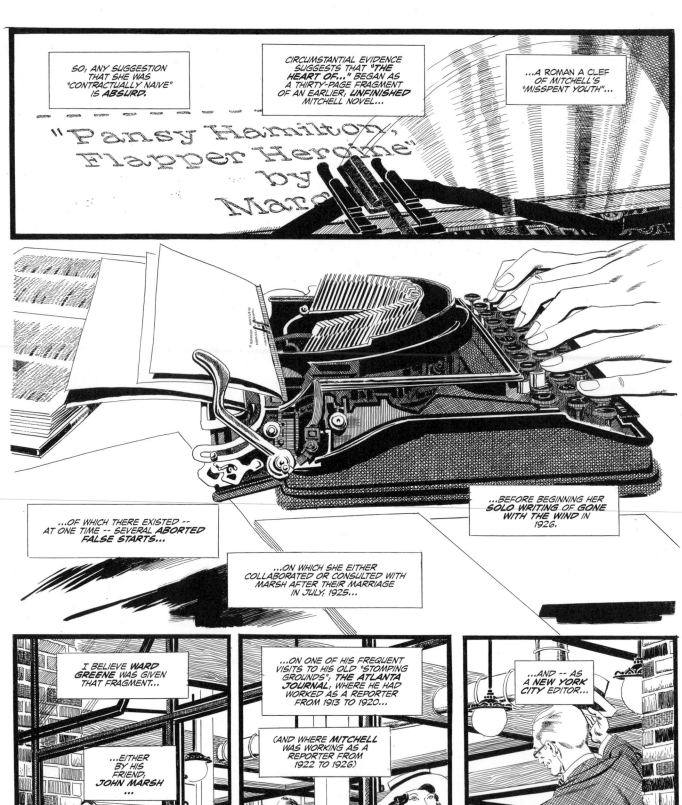

SO, ANY SUGGESTION THAT SHE WAS "CONTRACTUALLY NAIVE" IS ABSURD.

CIRCUMSTANTIAL EVIDENCE SUGGESTS THAT "THE HEART OF..." BEGAN AS A THIRTY-PAGE FRAGMENT OF AN EARLIER, UNFINISHED MITCHELL NOVEL...

...A ROMAN A CLEF OF MITCHELL'S "MISSPENT YOUTH"...

"Pansy Hamilton, Flapper Heroine" by Marc

...BEFORE BEGINNING HER SOLO WRITING OF GONE WITH THE WIND IN 1926.

...OF WHICH THERE EXISTED -- AT ONE TIME -- SEVERAL ABORTED FALSE STARTS...

...ON WHICH SHE EITHER COLLABORATED OR CONSULTED WITH MARSH AFTER THEIR MARRIAGE IN JULY, 1925...

I BELIEVE WARD GREENE WAS GIVEN THAT FRAGMENT...

...EITHER BY HIS FRIEND, JOHN MARSH...

...OR BY MITCHELL HERSELF...

...ON ONE OF HIS FREQUENT VISITS TO HIS OLD "STOMPING GROUNDS", THE ATLANTA JOURNAL, WHERE HE HAD WORKED AS A REPORTER FROM 1913 TO 1920...

(AND WHERE MITCHELL WAS WORKING AS A REPORTER FROM 1922 TO 1926)

...AND -- AS A NEW YORK CITY EDITOR...

...WAS ASKED HIS PROFESSIONAL OPINION AS TO ITS MERIT.

The Atlanta Journal

"COVERS DIXIE LIKE THE DEW"

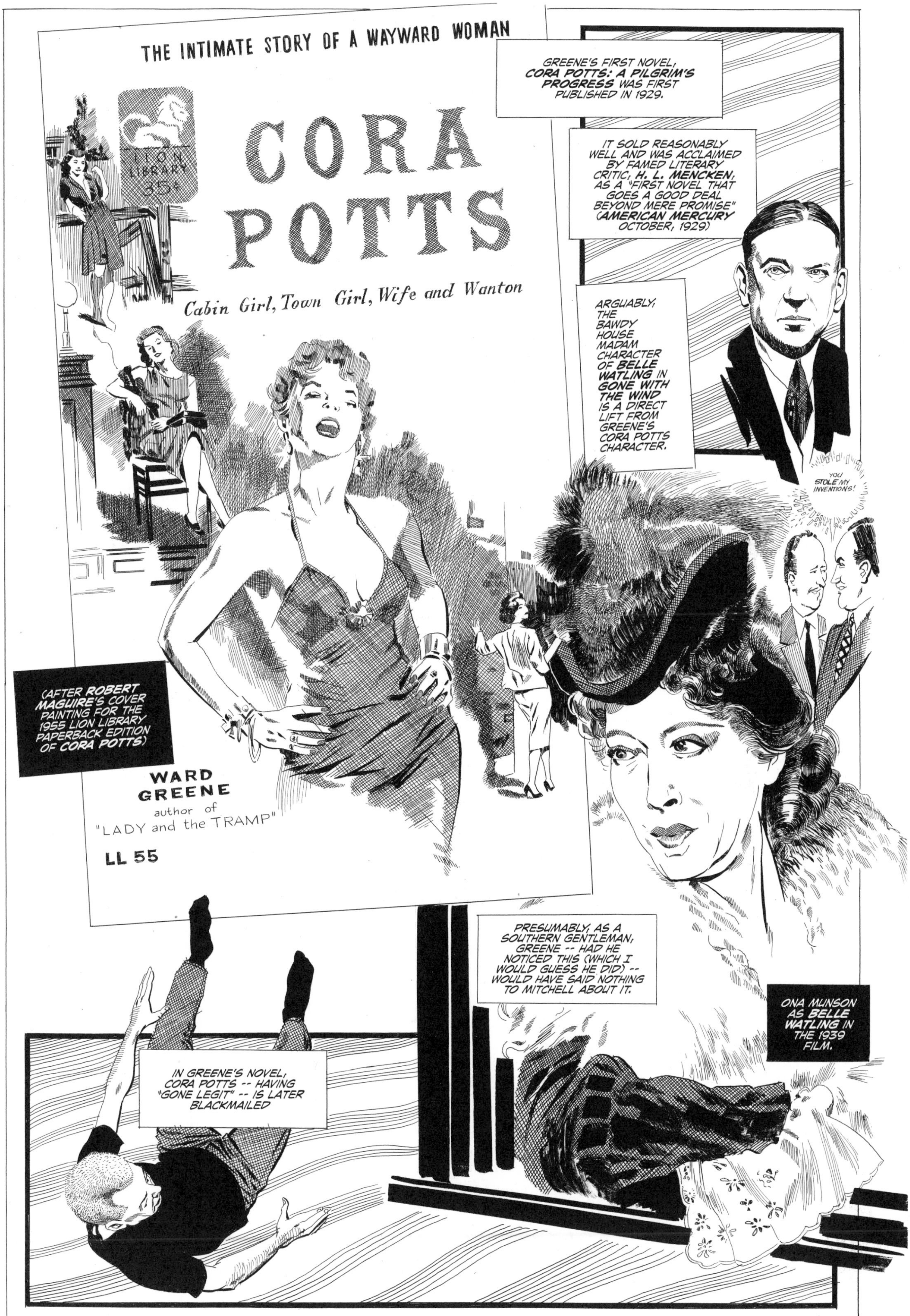
THE INTIMATE STORY OF A WAYWARD WOMAN
LION LIBRARY 35¢
CORA POTTS
Cabin Girl, Town Girl, Wife and Wanton
WARD GREENE
author of "LADY and the TRAMP"
LL 55
GREENE'S FIRST NOVEL, CORA POTTS: A PILGRIM'S PROGRESS WAS FIRST PUBLISHED IN 1929.
IT SOLD REASONABLY WELL AND WAS ACCLAIMED BY FAMED LITERARY CRITIC, H. L. MENCKEN, AS A "FIRST NOVEL THAT GOES A GOOD DEAL BEYOND MERE PROMISE" (AMERICAN MERCURY OCTOBER, 1929)
ARGUABLY, THE BAWDY HOUSE MADAM CHARACTER OF BELLE WATLING IN GONE WITH THE WIND IS A DIRECT LIFT FROM GREENE'S CORA POTTS CHARACTER.
YOU STOLE MY INVENTIONS!
(AFTER ROBERT MAGUIRE'S COVER PAINTING FOR THE 1955 LION LIBRARY PAPERBACK EDITION OF CORA POTTS)
ONA MUNSON AS BELLE WATLING IN THE 1939 FILM.
PRESUMABLY, AS A SOUTHERN GENTLEMAN, GREENE -- HAD HE NOTICED THIS (WHICH I WOULD GUESS HE DID) -- WOULD HAVE SAID NOTHING TO MITCHELL ABOUT IT.
IN GREENE'S NOVEL, CORA POTTS -- HAVING "GONE LEGIT" -- IS LATER BLACKMAILED

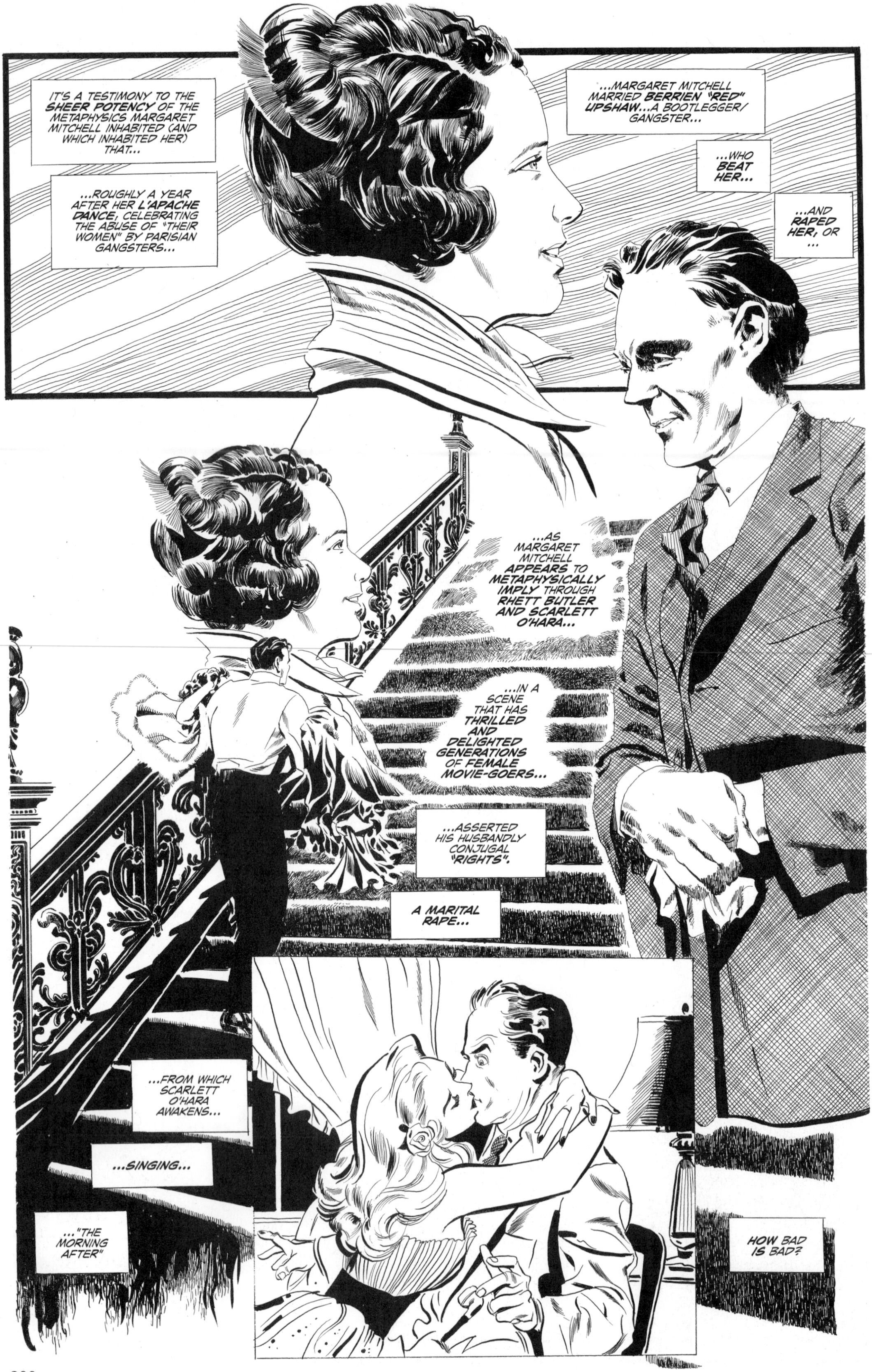
IT'S A TESTIMONY TO THE SHEER POTENCY OF THE METAPHYSICS MARGARET MITCHELL INHABITED (AND WHICH INHABITED HER) THAT...
...ROUGHLY A YEAR AFTER HER L'APACHE DANCE, CELEBRATING THE ABUSE OF "THEIR WOMEN" BY PARISIAN GANGSTERS...
...MARGARET MITCHELL MARRIED BERRIEN "RED" UPSHAW...A BOOTLEGGER/ GANGSTER...
...WHO BEAT HER...
...AND RAPED HER, OR ...
...AS MARGARET MITCHELL APPEARS TO METAPHYSICALLY IMPLY THROUGH RHETT BUTLER AND SCARLETT O'HARA...
...IN A SCENE THAT HAS THRILLED AND DELIGHTED GENERATIONS OF FEMALE MOVIE-GOERS...
...ASSERTED HIS HUSBANDLY CONJUGAL "RIGHTS".
A MARITAL RAPE...
...FROM WHICH SCARLETT O'HARA AWAKENS...
...SINGING...
..."THE MORNING AFTER"
HOW BAD IS BAD?

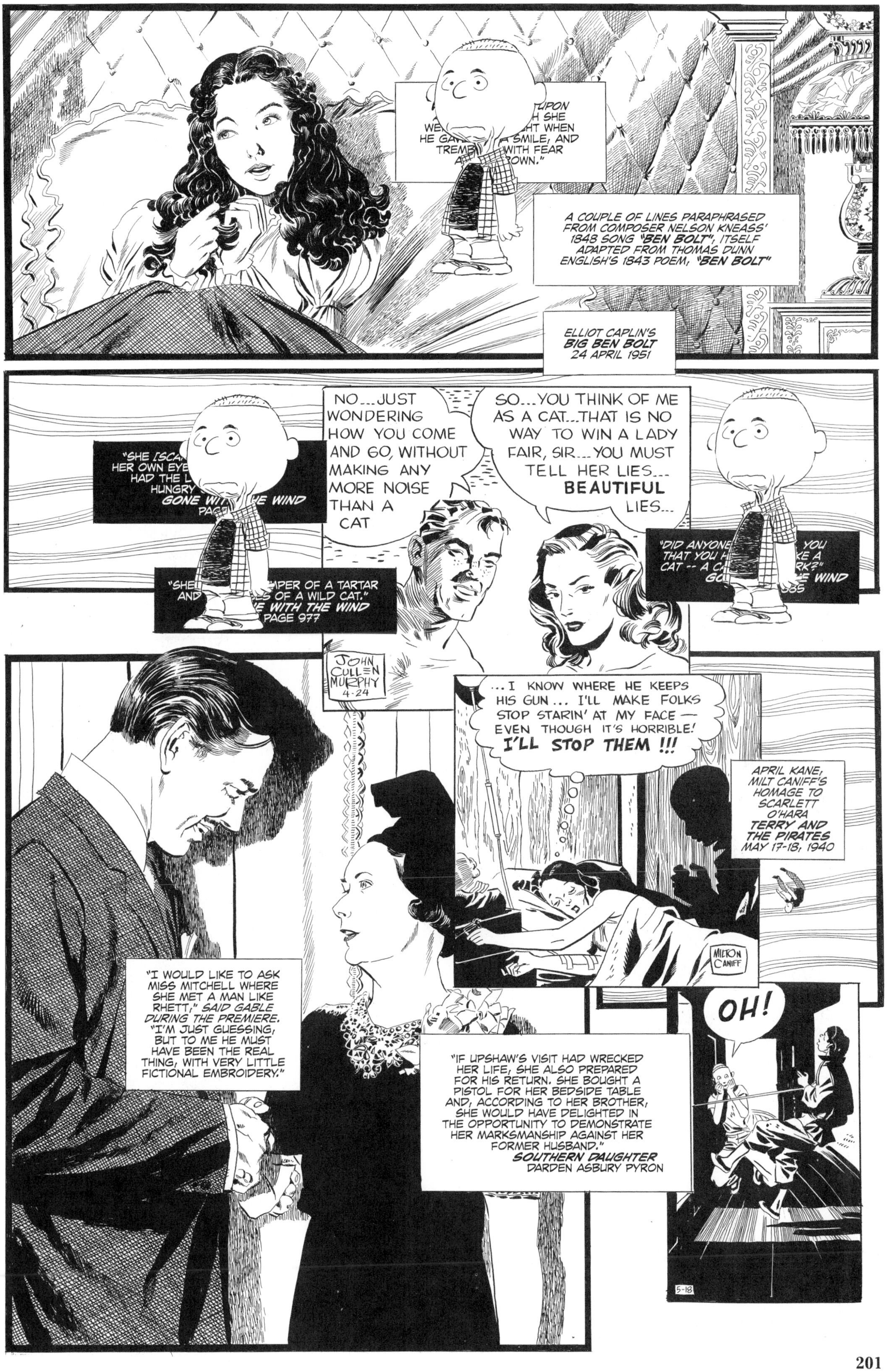

A COUPLE OF LINES PARAPHRASED FROM COMPOSER NELSON KNEASS' 1848 SONG "BEN BOLT", ITSELF ADAPTED FROM THOMAS DUNN ENGLISH'S 1843 POEM, "BEN BOLT"
ELLIOT CAPLIN'S BIG BEN BOLT 24 APRIL 1951
NO... JUST WONDERING HOW YOU COME AND GO, WITHOUT MAKING ANY MORE NOISE THAN A CAT
SO... YOU THINK OF ME AS A CAT... THAT IS NO WAY TO WIN A LADY FAIR, SIR... YOU MUST TELL HER LIES... BEAUTIFUL LIES...
PAGE 977
JOHN CULLEN MURPHY 4-24
...I KNOW WHERE HE KEEPS HIS GUN... I'LL MAKE FOLKS STOP STARIN' AT MY FACE — EVEN THOUGH IT'S HORRIBLE! I'LL STOP THEM !!!
APRIL KANE, MILT CANIFF'S HOMAGE TO SCARLETT O'HARA TERRY AND THE PIRATES MAY 17-18, 1940
MILTON CANIFF
OH!
"I WOULD LIKE TO ASK MISS MITCHELL WHERE SHE MET A MAN LIKE RHETT," SAID GABLE DURING THE PREMIERE. "I'M JUST GUESSING, BUT TO ME HE MUST HAVE BEEN THE REAL THING, WITH VERY LITTLE FICTIONAL EMBROIDERY."
"IF UPSHAW'S VISIT HAD WRECKED HER LIFE, SHE ALSO PREPARED FOR HIS RETURN. SHE BOUGHT A PISTOL FOR HER BEDSIDE TABLE AND, ACCORDING TO HER BROTHER, SHE WOULD HAVE DELIGHTED IN THE OPPORTUNITY TO DEMONSTRATE HER MARKSMANSHIP AGAINST HER FORMER HUSBAND."
SOUTHERN DAUGHTER
DARDEN ASBURY PYRON
5-18

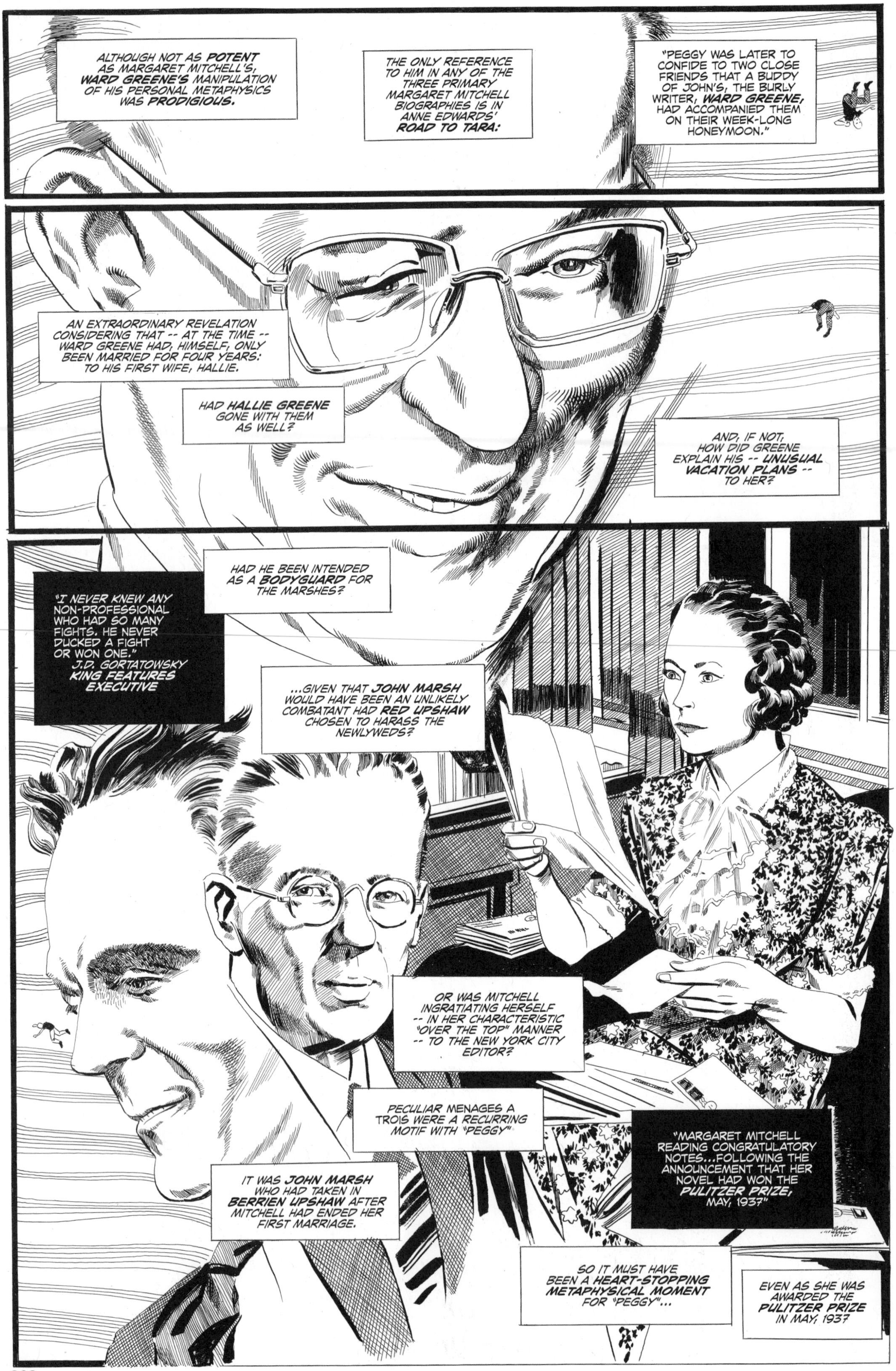
ALTHOUGH NOT AS POTENT AS MARGARET MITCHELL'S, WARD GREENE'S MANIPULATION OF HIS PERSONAL METAPHYSICS WAS PRODIGIOUS.
THE ONLY REFERENCE TO HIM IN ANY OF THE THREE PRIMARY MARGARET MITCHELL BIOGRAPHIES IS IN ANNE EDWARDS' ROAD TO TARA:
"PEGGY WAS LATER TO CONFIDE TO TWO CLOSE FRIENDS THAT A BUDDY OF JOHN'S, THE BURLY WRITER, WARD GREENE, HAD ACCOMPANIED THEM ON THEIR WEEK-LONG HONEYMOON."
AN EXTRAORDINARY REVELATION CONSIDERING THAT -- AT THE TIME -- WARD GREENE HAD, HIMSELF, ONLY BEEN MARRIED FOR FOUR YEARS: TO HIS FIRST WIFE, HALLIE.
HAD HALLIE GREENE GONE WITH THEM AS WELL?
AND, IF NOT, HOW DID GREENE EXPLAIN HIS -- UNUSUAL VACATION PLANS -- TO HER?
"I NEVER KNEW ANY NON-PROFESSIONAL WHO HAD SO MANY FIGHTS. HE NEVER DUCKED A FIGHT OR WON ONE." J.D. GORTATOWSKY KING FEATURES EXECUTIVE
HAD HE BEEN INTENDED AS A BODYGUARD FOR THE MARSHES?
...GIVEN THAT JOHN MARSH WOULD HAVE BEEN AN UNLIKELY COMBATANT HAD RED UPSHAW CHOSEN TO HARASS THE NEWLYWEDS?
OR WAS MITCHELL INGRATIATING HERSELF -- IN HER CHARACTERISTIC "OVER THE TOP" MANNER -- TO THE NEW YORK CITY EDITOR?
PECULIAR MENAGES A TROIS WERE A RECURRING MOTIF WITH "PEGGY"
IT WAS JOHN MARSH WHO HAD TAKEN IN BERRIEN UPSHAW AFTER MITCHELL HAD ENDED HER FIRST MARRIAGE.
"MARGARET MITCHELL READING CONGRATULATORY NOTES...FOLLOWING THE ANNOUNCEMENT THAT HER NOVEL HAD WON THE PULITZER PRIZE, MAY, 1937"
SO IT MUST HAVE BEEN A HEART-STOPPING METAPHYSICAL MOMENT FOR "PEGGY"...
EVEN AS SHE WAS AWARDED THE PULITZER PRIZE IN MAY, 1937

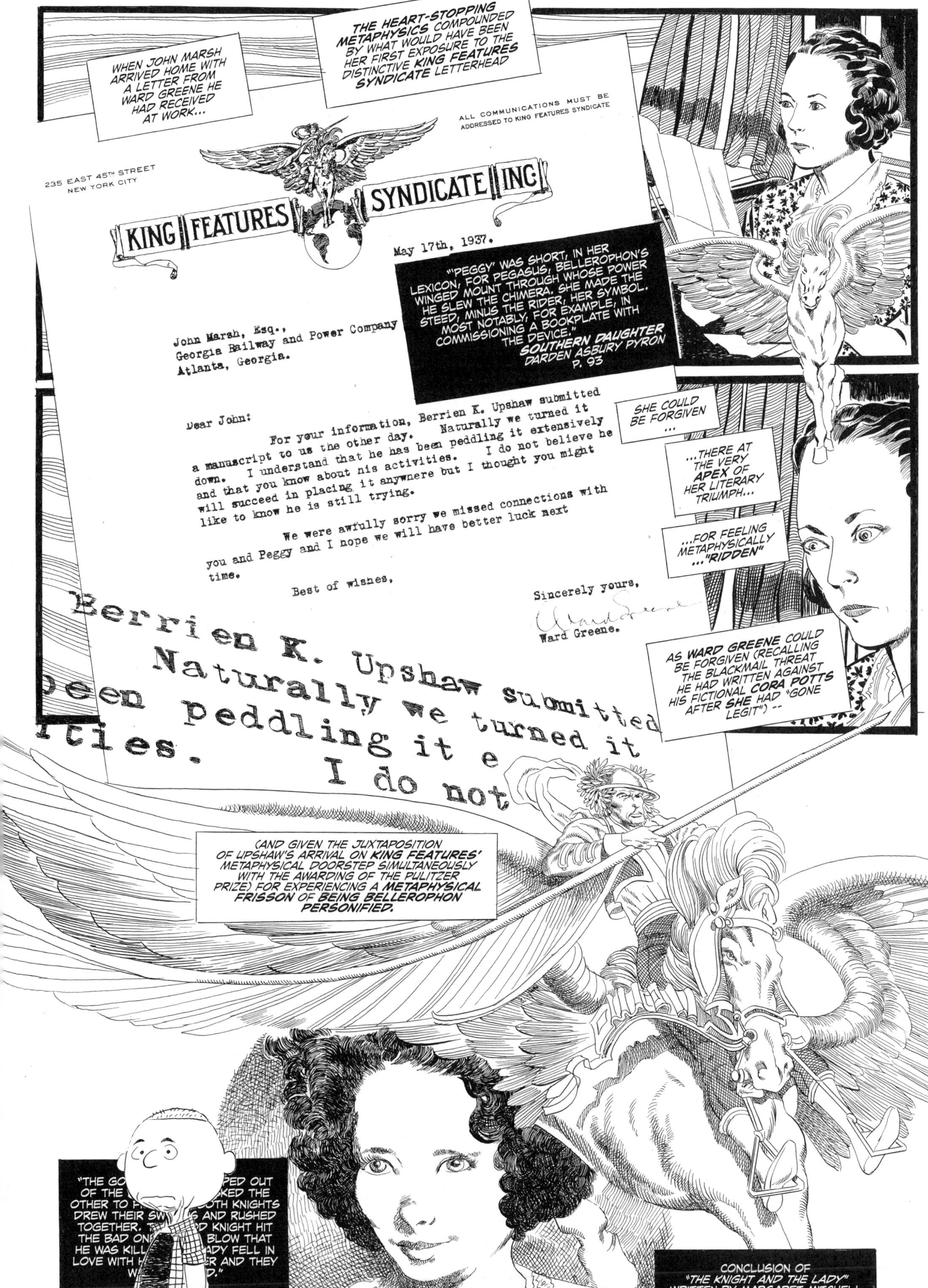

WHEN JOHN MARSH ARRIVED HOME WITH A LETTER FROM WARD GREENE HE HAD RECEIVED AT WORK...
THE HEART-STOPPING METAPHYSICS COMPOUNDED BY WHAT WOULD HAVE BEEN HER FIRST EXPOSURE TO THE DISTINCTIVE KING FEATURES SYNDICATE LETTERHEAD
ALL COMMUNICATIONS MUST BE ADDRESSED TO KING FEATURES SYNDICATE
235 EAST 45TH STREET NEW YORK CITY
KING FEATURES SYNDICATE INC.
May 17th, 1937.
John Marsh, Esq.,
Georgia Railway and Power Company
Atlanta, Georgia.
Dear John:
For your information, Berrien K. Upshaw submitted a manuscript to us the other day. Naturally we turned it down. I understand that he has been peddling it extensively and that you know about his activities. I do not believe he will succeed in placing it anywhere but I thought you might like to know he is still trying.
We were awfully sorry we missed connections with you and Peggy and I hope we will have better luck next time.
Best of wishes,
Sincerely yours,
Ward Greene.
"'PEGGY' WAS SHORT, IN HER LEXICON, FOR PEGASUS, BELLEROPHON'S WINGED MOUNT THROUGH WHOSE POWER HE SLEW THE CHIMERA. SHE MADE THE STEED, MINUS THE RIDER, HER SYMBOL. MOST NOTABLY, FOR EXAMPLE, IN COMMISSIONING A BOOKPLATE WITH THE DEVICE."
SOUTHERN DAUGHTER
DARDEN ASBURY PYRON
P. 93
SHE COULD BE FORGIVEN ...
...THERE AT THE VERY APEX OF HER LITERARY TRIUMPH...
...FOR FEELING METAPHYSICALLY ..."RIDDEN"
AS WARD GREENE COULD BE FORGIVEN (RECALLING THE BLACKMAIL THREAT HE HAD WRITTEN AGAINST HIS FICTIONAL CORA POTTS AFTER SHE HAD "GONE LEGIT") --
Berrien K. Upshaw submitted
Naturally we turned it
been peddling it e
ties. I do not
(AND GIVEN THE JUXTAPOSITION OF UPSHAW'S ARRIVAL ON KING FEATURES' METAPHYSICAL DOORSTEP SIMULTANEOUSLY WITH THE AWARDING OF THE PULITZER PRIZE) FOR EXPERIENCING A METAPHYSICAL FRISSON OF BEING BELLEROPHON PERSONIFIED.
"THE GO
PED OUT
OF THE
KED THE
OTHER TO F
BOTH KNIGHTS
DREW THEIR SW
AND RUSHED
TOGETHER.
D KNIGHT HIT
THE BAD ON
BLOW THAT
HE WAS KIL
ADY FELL IN
LOVE WITH H
ER AND THEY
D."
CONCLUSION OF "THE KNIGHT AND THE LADY" WRITTEN BY MARGARET MITCHELL AT THE AGE OF EIGHT OR NINE

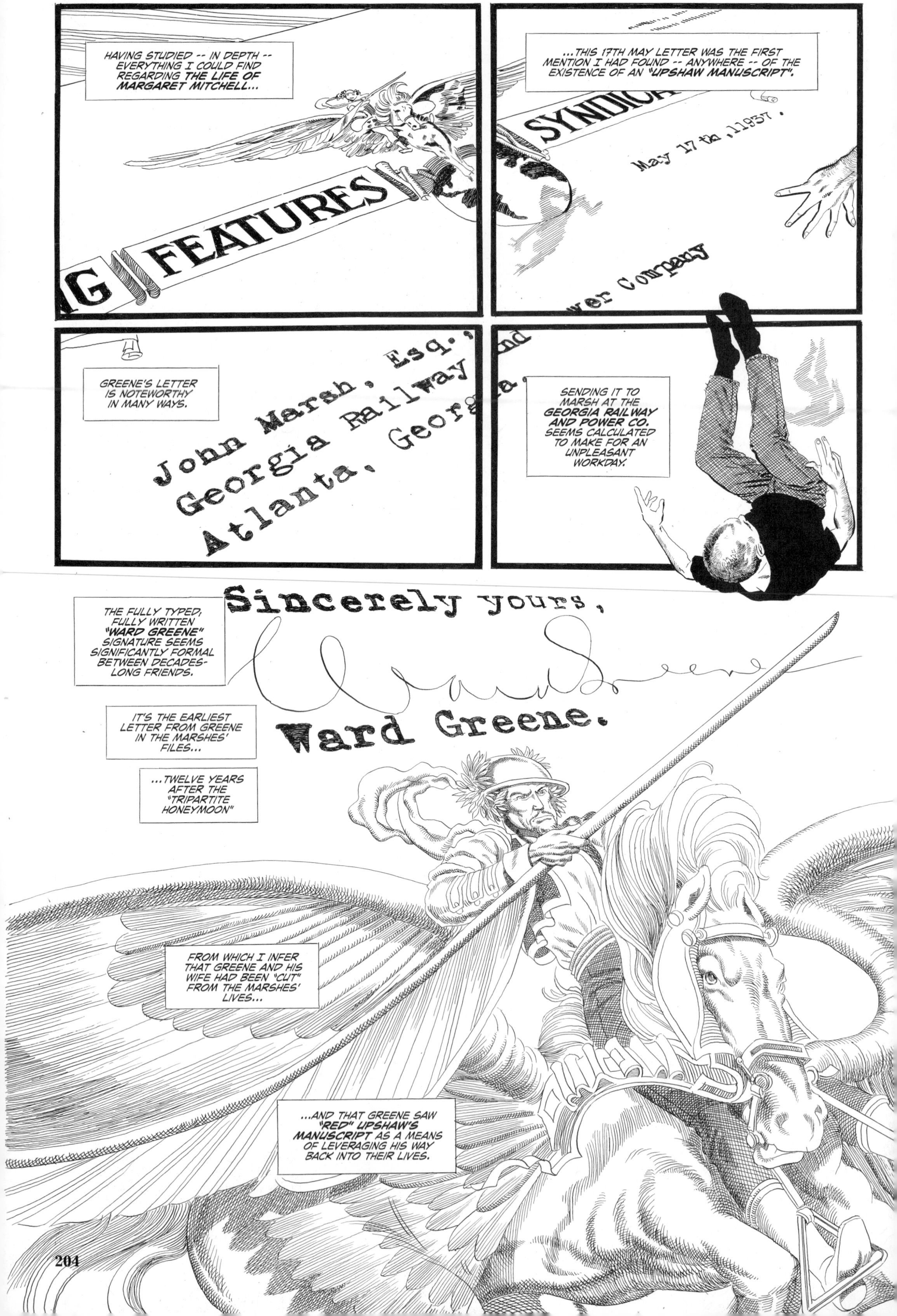

HAVING STUDIED -- IN DEPTH -- EVERYTHING I COULD FIND REGARDING THE LIFE OF MARGARET MITCHELL...
G FEATURES
...THIS 17TH MAY LETTER WAS THE FIRST MENTION I HAD FOUND -- ANYWHERE -- OF THE EXISTENCE OF AN "UPSHAW MANUSCRIPT".
SYNDICA
May 17th, 11937.
wer Company
GREENE'S LETTER IS NOTEWORTHY IN MANY WAYS.
John Marsh, Esq.,
Georgia Railway and
Atlanta, Georgia.
SENDING IT TO MARSH AT THE GEORGIA RAILWAY AND POWER CO. SEEMS CALCULATED TO MAKE FOR AN UNPLEASANT WORKDAY.
THE FULLY TYPED, FULLY WRITTEN "WARD GREENE" SIGNATURE SEEMS SIGNIFICANTLY FORMAL BETWEEN DECADES-LONG FRIENDS.
Sincerely yours,
Ward Greene.
IT'S THE EARLIEST LETTER FROM GREENE IN THE MARSHES' FILES...
...TWELVE YEARS AFTER THE "TRIPARTITE HONEYMOON"
FROM WHICH I INFER THAT GREENE AND HIS WIFE HAD BEEN "CUT" FROM THE MARSHES' LIVES...
...AND THAT GREENE SAW "RED" UPSHAW'S MANUSCRIPT AS A MEANS OF LEVERAGING HIS WAY BACK INTO THEIR LIVES.

IT...SORT. OF...WORKED.

MARSH'S [PRO] REPLY (UNDERLINE[D "CONFIDENTIAL) BEARS [?] JIMMY"

AND...*UNCONVINCINGLY*...ATTEMPTS TO PORTRAY THE MARSHES AS WELL-INFORMED ON "THE WANDERINGS OF THE UPSHAW MANUSCRIPT")

May 20, 1937

BUT THEN COMPLETELY UNDOES THE INTENDED EFFECT:

(THE MARSHES WOULD HAVE MADE TERRIBLE POKER PLAYERS)

"WOULD[N'T IT BE] FOR YOU TO LET US KNO[W WHAT] KIND OF ARTICLE HE [WRO]TE?"

THEN ADVISES THAT IF ANY EDITOR SHOULD HAPPEN TO "CONSULT" WITH GREENE ABOUT THE MANUSCRIPT:

"PEG[GY... DRAW]ING' KIND [... DON']T HESIT[ATE TO] MAKE AC[... TO?] IS LIB[... ?]Y."

THEN *APPEA[RS]* TO REINST[ATE] THE FRIEND[?]

"IT WAS A BIG [DISAPP]OINTMENT FOR US WHEN W[E DI]DN'T GET TO SEE YOU A[ND PEG]GIE WHEN YOU WERE IN [TOWN], AND I HOPE YOU'LL [DROP] BACK BEFORE [LON]G."

(I SAY *"APPEARS"* BECAUSE MARSH DOESN'T SPECIFICALLY EXPRESS AN ACTUAL INTEREST IN SEEING THE GREENES.)

I INFER THAT THE MARSHES "SNIFFED OUT" THE SUBTEXT OF A *"QUID PRO QUO"*

....OR *"CON"*...

....OR *"LEVERAGING"*...

...OR -- TO PUT IT BLUNTLY -- *"BLACKMAIL"*...

...BUT ATTRIBUTED (OR MISATTRIBUTED) IT TO *KING FEATURES'* THEN-CURRENT OFFER TO SERIALIZE *GONE WITH THE WIND* IN THE HEARST NEWSPAPERS:

"THE TR[... NI]CE TO THESE [... COD]DLED BY THE [GONE WITH THE] *WIND* PUBLISH[ED... F]OLKS AND THEY A[RE... ?] FOR YOU TO KEEP IN C[ONTA]CT WITH."

WARD GREENE WAS FAR TOO **METAPHYSICALLY ASTUTE** TO MISS JOHN MARSH'S VEILED MEANING:

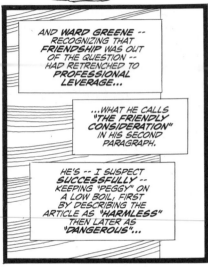

"IT ...PPOINTMENT F... WHEN **WE** ... TO SEE ...E..."

"**I** (SINGLE...) HOPE YO... COMING... BEFORE..."

(I.E. IT WAS "**PEGGY**" WHO HAD "CUT" WARD GREENE AND HIS WIFE...AND MARSH WAS HELPLESS TO CHANGE THAT)

I THINK I'M SAFE IN SAYING THAT "**PEGGY**" WOULD HAVE BEEN **CONSUMED WITH** CURIOSITY ABOUT UPSHAW'S ARTICLE...

KING FEATURES SYNDICATE INC.

May 25th, 1937.

AND **WARD GREENE** -- RECOGNIZING THAT **FRIENDSHIP** WAS OUT OF THE QUESTION -- HAD RETRENCHED TO **PROFESSIONAL LEVERAGE**...

...WHAT HE CALLS "**THE FRIENDLY CONSIDERATION**" IN HIS SECOND PARAGRAPH.

HE'S -- I SUSPECT **SUCCESSFULLY** -- KEEPING "**PEGGY**" ON A LOW BOIL, FIRST BY DESCRIBING THE ARTICLE AS "**HARMLESS**" THEN LATER AS "**DANGEROUS**"...

...UPPING "**THE FRIENDLY CONSIDERATION**" TO INCLUDE "**THE OTHER HEARST UNITS**" --

ATTEMPTING TO INCREASE HIS PROFESSIONAL LEVERAGE -- WHILE GIVING IT A THIN **CHIVALROUS VENEER**.

**EVERYONE** (METAPHYSICALLY SPEAKING) IS, AT THIS POINT, PART **BELLEROPHON**, PART **PEGASUS** AND PART **CHIMERA**.

John R. Marsh, Esq.,
Georgia Power Company
Atlanta, Georgia.

Dear John:

I read the Upshaw article and considered it completely harmless. It was the story of a boy and girl college romance and a marriage that did not work for no particular reason. It was done without malice and contained nothing I considered libelous. Of course, I don't know whether he departed from the actual facts.

However, as you say, we felt the thing was very bad taste on the part of Mr. Upshaw and would have been very bad taste for any reputable newspaper or magazine to publish, quite aside from the friendly consideration involved.

It seemed to me that Mr. Upshaw was simply trying to capitalize on Peggy's celebrity to pick up a few pennies for himself.

I don't think he will find a market for his piece but I will take the precaution to advise other Hearst units outside of King Features, such as the magazines and the American Weekly that the article is dangerous and they should consult Mr. Upshaw, Sr., if it is submitted to them. I will also do the same thing if I find it is being offered elsewhere.

With best wishes

**WARD GREENE** STILL USES HIS FULL NAME IN THE TYPESCRIPT SIGNATURE...

...SIGNING AS "**WARD**"...

...NOT AS "**WARD GREENE**"...

WG dm

...BUT ALSO NOT "**JIMMY**".

IT'S FRIENDLIER ...BUT STILL FAR FROM **FRIENDLY**.

Sincerely yours,

Ward Greene.

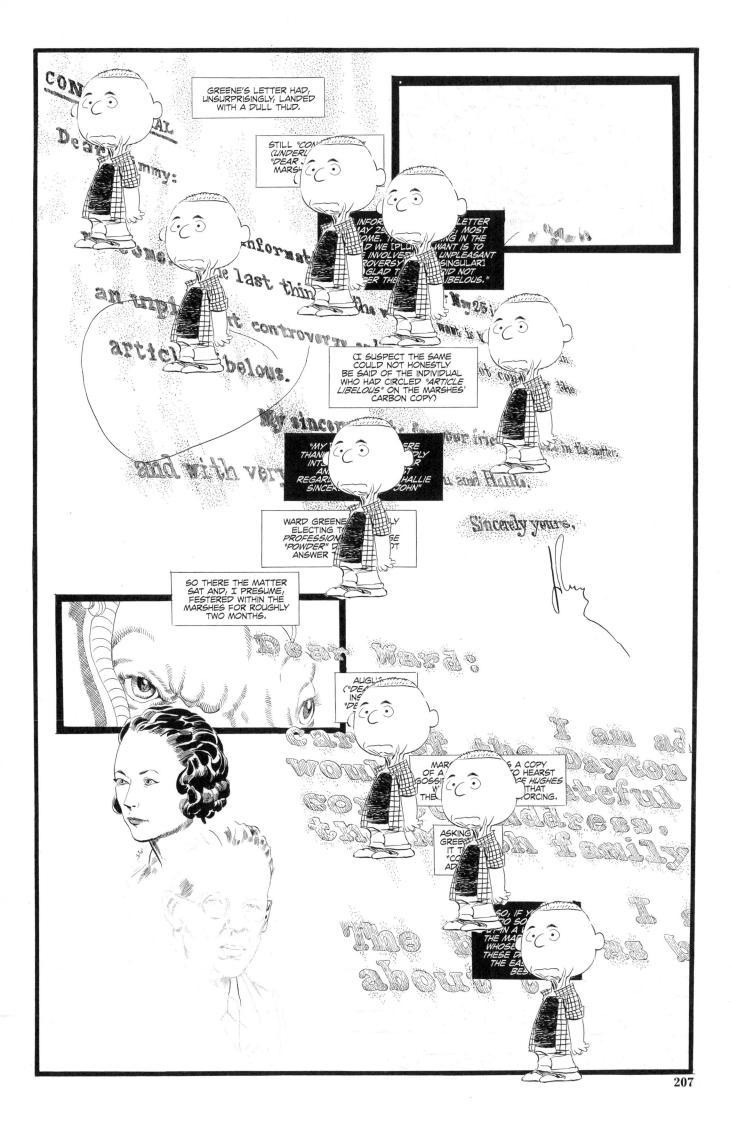

GREENE'S LETTER HAD, UNSURPRISINGLY, LANDED WITH A DULL THUD.

STILL "CON... (UNDERL... "DEAR J... MARS...

(I SUSPECT THE SAME COULD NOT HONESTLY BE SAID OF THE INDIVIDUAL WHO HAD CIRCLED "ARTICLE LIBELOUS" ON THE MARSHES' CARBON COPY)

WARD GREENE... LY ELECTING T... PROFESSION... BE "POWDER" D... OT ANSWER T...

SO THERE THE MATTER SAT AND, I PRESUME, FESTERED WITHIN THE MARSHES FOR ROUGHLY TWO MONTHS.

AUGU... ("DE... INS... "DE...

MAR... A COPY OF A... O HEARST GOSSI... E HUGHES W... THAT THE... ORCING.

ASKING... GREE... IT T... "CO... AD...

SO, IF Y... O SO... IN A L... THE MA... WHOSE... THESE D... THE EA... BES...

207

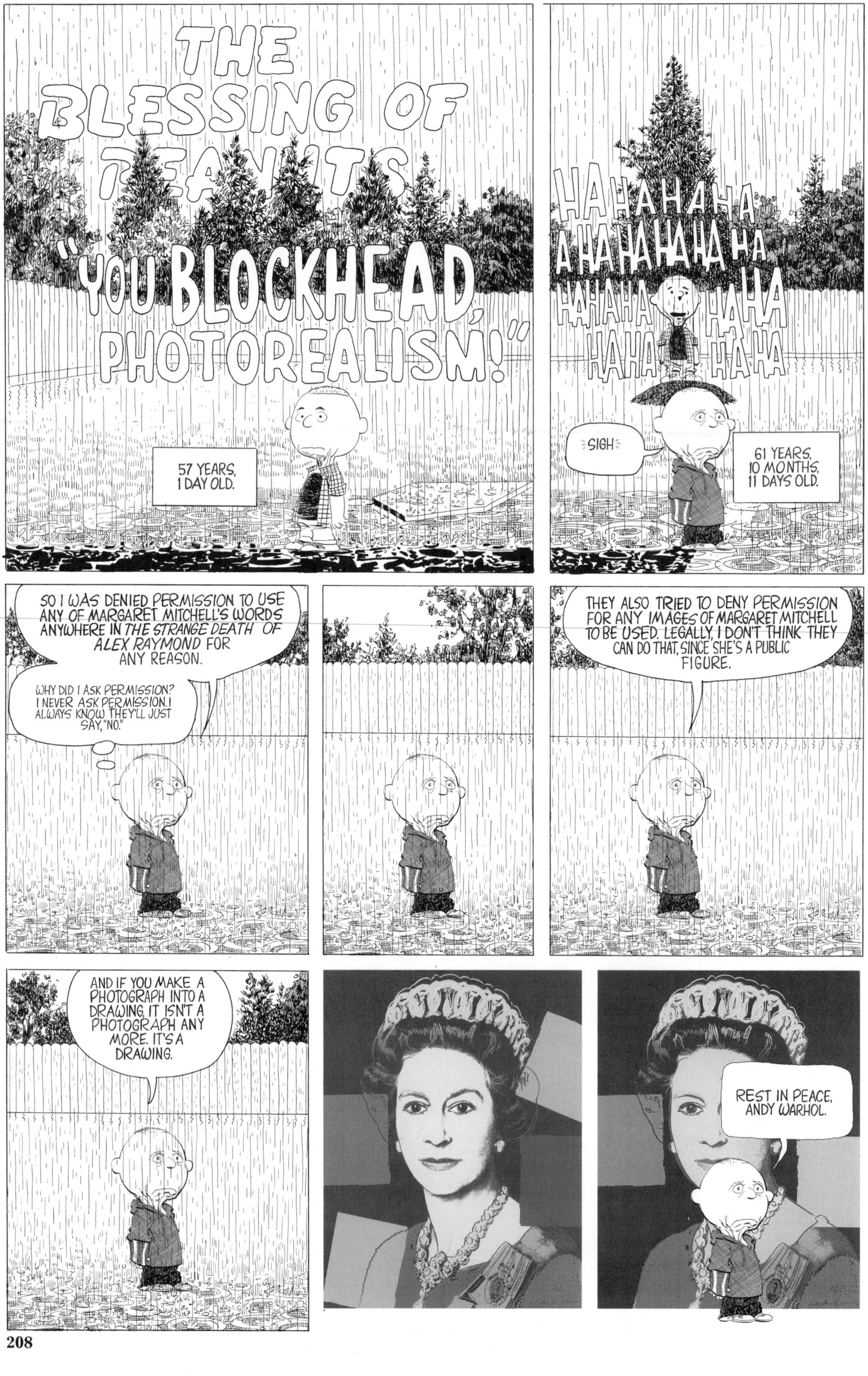
THE BLESSING OF PEANUTS
"YOU BLOCKHEAD, PHOTOREALISM!"
57 YEARS, 1 DAY OLD.
HAHAHAHA AHAHAHAHAHA HAHAHAHA HAHA HAHA HAHA
SIGH
61 YEARS, 10 MONTHS, 11 DAYS OLD.
SO I WAS DENIED PERMISSION TO USE ANY OF MARGARET MITCHELL'S WORDS ANYWHERE IN THE STRANGE DEATH OF ALEX RAYMOND FOR ANY REASON.
WHY DID I ASK PERMISSION? I NEVER ASK PERMISSION. I ALWAYS KNOW THEY'LL JUST SAY, "NO."
THEY ALSO TRIED TO DENY PERMISSION FOR ANY IMAGES OF MARGARET MITCHELL TO BE USED. LEGALLY, I DON'T THINK THEY CAN DO THAT, SINCE SHE'S A PUBLIC FIGURE.
AND IF YOU MAKE A PHOTOGRAPH INTO A DRAWING, IT ISN'T A PHOTOGRAPH ANY MORE. IT'S A DRAWING.
REST IN PEACE, ANDY WARHOL.

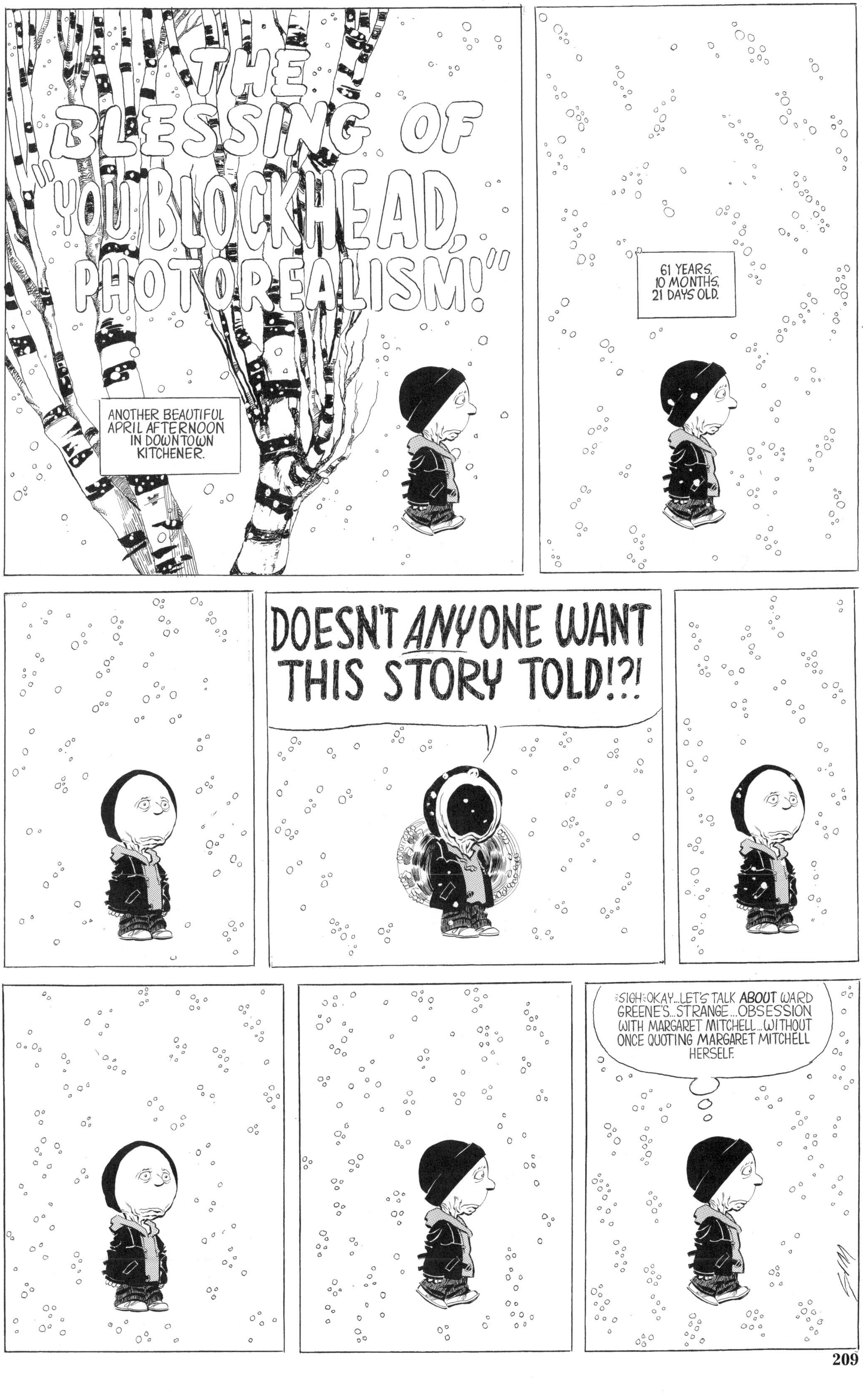
THE BLESSING OF "YOU BLOCKHEAD, PHOTOREALISM!"
ANOTHER BEAUTIFUL APRIL AFTERNOON IN DOWNTOWN KITCHENER.
61 YEARS, 10 MONTHS, 21 DAYS OLD.
DOESN'T ANYONE WANT THIS STORY TOLD!?!
SIGH OKAY...LET'S TALK ABOUT WARD GREENE'S...STRANGE...OBSESSION WITH MARGARET MITCHELL...WITHOUT ONCE QUOTING MARGARET MITCHELL HERSELF.

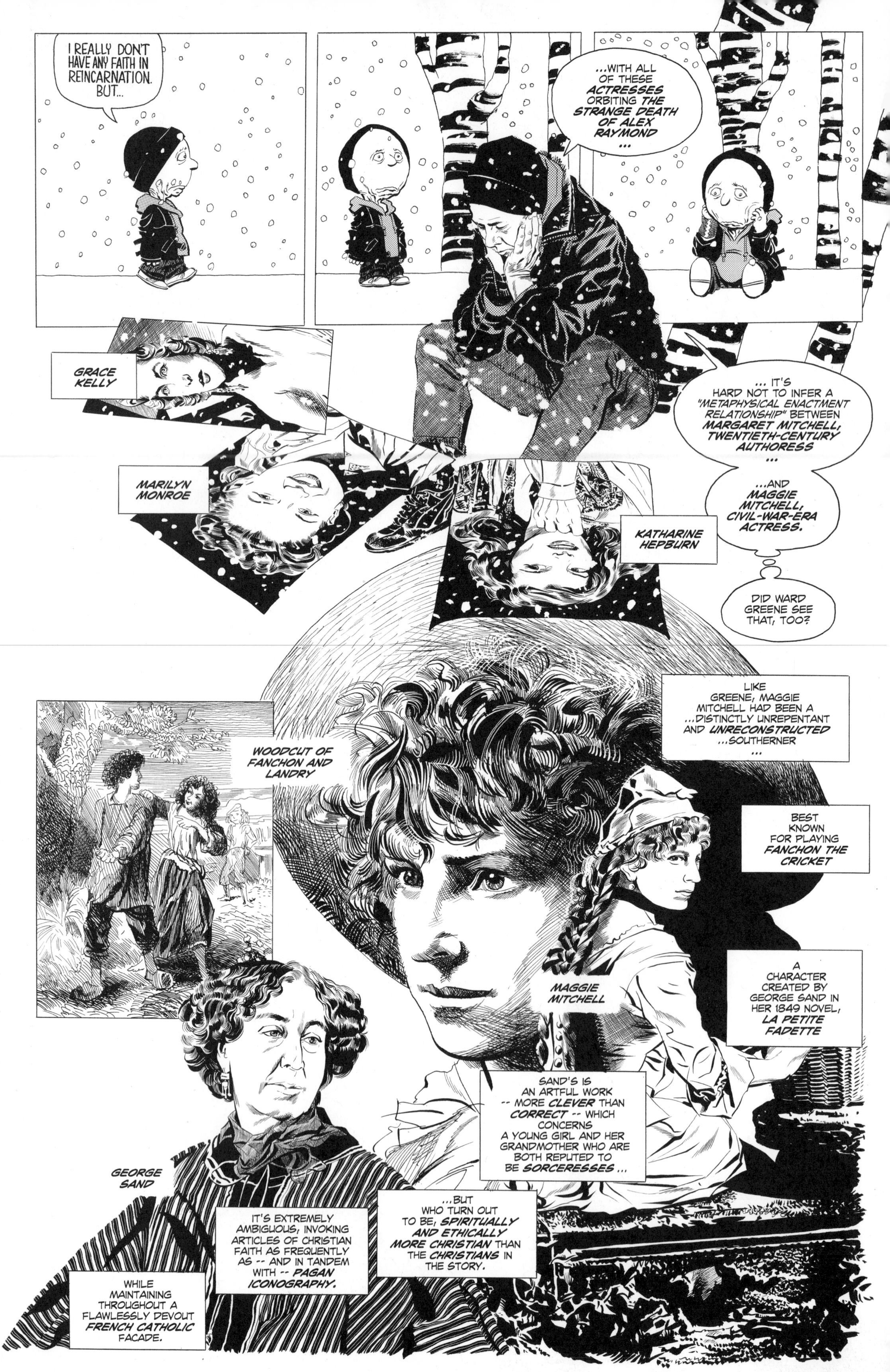

I REALLY DON'T HAVE ANY FAITH IN REINCARNATION. BUT...
...WITH ALL OF THESE ACTRESSES ORBITING THE STRANGE DEATH OF ALEX RAYMOND ...
GRACE KELLY
MARILYN MONROE
KATHARINE HEPBURN
... IT'S HARD NOT TO INFER A "METAPHYSICAL ENACTMENT RELATIONSHIP" BETWEEN MARGARET MITCHELL, TWENTIETH-CENTURY AUTHORESS ...
...AND MAGGIE MITCHELL, CIVIL-WAR-ERA ACTRESS.
DID WARD GREENE SEE THAT, TOO?
WOODCUT OF FANCHON AND LANDRY
LIKE GREENE, MAGGIE MITCHELL HAD BEEN A ...DISTINCTLY UNREPENTANT AND UNRECONSTRUCTED ...SOUTHERNER ...
BEST KNOWN FOR PLAYING FANCHON THE CRICKET
MAGGIE MITCHELL
A CHARACTER CREATED BY GEORGE SAND IN HER 1849 NOVEL, LA PETITE FADETTE
SAND'S IS AN ARTFUL WORK -- MORE CLEVER THAN CORRECT -- WHICH CONCERNS A YOUNG GIRL AND HER GRANDMOTHER WHO ARE BOTH REPUTED TO BE SORCERESSES ...
GEORGE SAND
WHILE MAINTAINING THROUGHOUT A FLAWLESSLY DEVOUT FRENCH CATHOLIC FACADE.
IT'S EXTREMELY AMBIGUOUS, INVOKING ARTICLES OF CHRISTIAN FAITH AS FREQUENTLY AS -- AND IN TANDEM WITH -- PAGAN ICONOGRAPHY.
...BUT WHO TURN OUT TO BE, SPIRITUALLY AND ETHICALLY MORE CHRISTIAN THAN THE CHRISTIANS IN THE STORY.

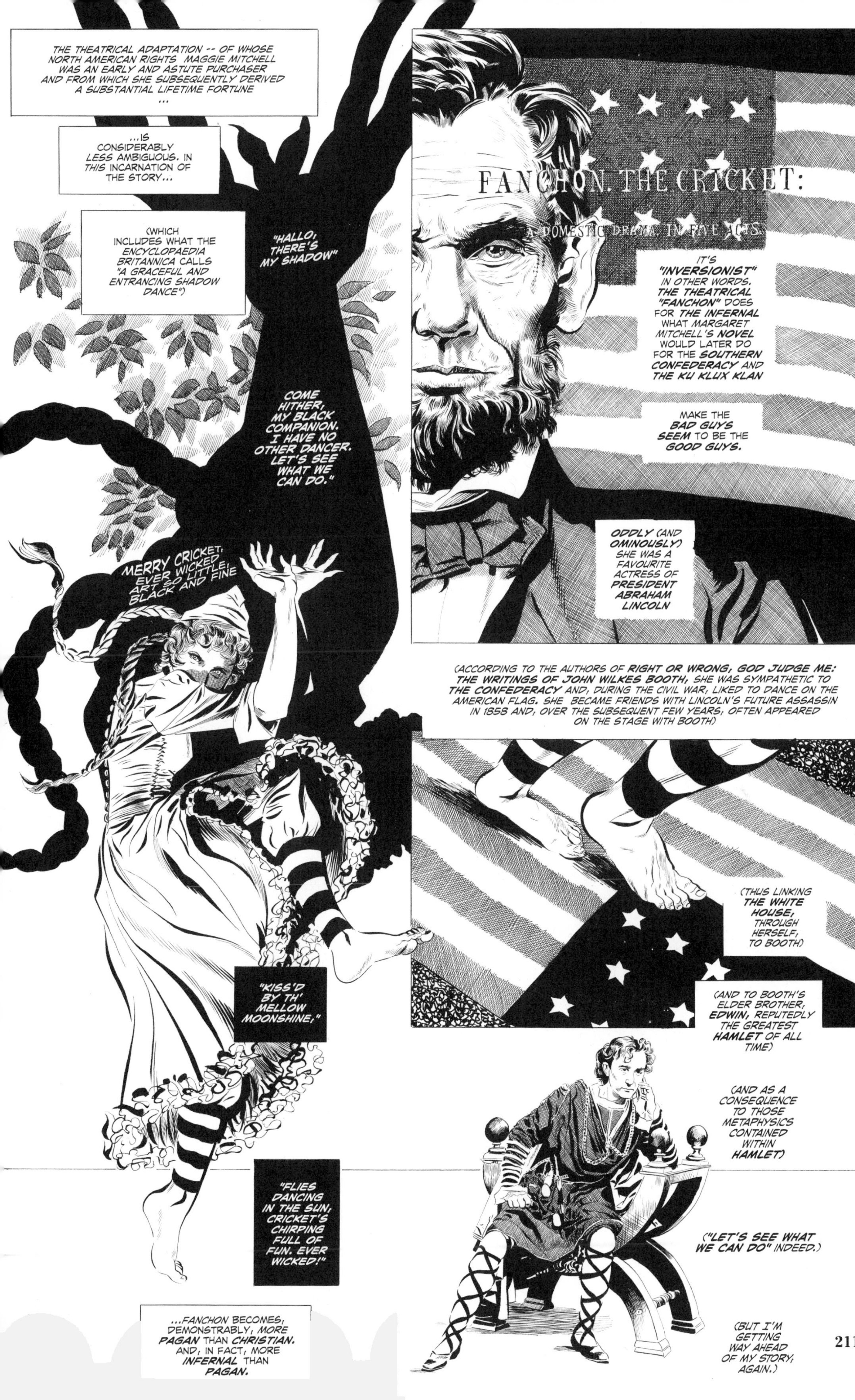
THE THEATRICAL ADAPTATION -- OF WHOSE NORTH AMERICAN RIGHTS MAGGIE MITCHELL WAS AN EARLY AND ASTUTE PURCHASER AND FROM WHICH SHE SUBSEQUENTLY DERIVED A SUBSTANTIAL LIFETIME FORTUNE ...
...IS CONSIDERABLY LESS AMBIGUOUS. IN THIS INCARNATION OF THE STORY...
(WHICH INCLUDES WHAT THE ENCYCLOPAEDIA BRITANNICA CALLS "A GRACEFUL AND ENTRANCING SHADOW DANCE")
"HALLO, THERE'S MY SHADOW"
COME HITHER, MY BLACK COMPANION. I HAVE NO OTHER DANCER. LET'S SEE WHAT WE CAN DO."
MERRY CRICKET, EVER WICKED ART SO LITTLE, BLACK AND FINE
"KISS'D BY TH' MELLOW MOONSHINE,"
"FLIES DANCING IN THE SUN, CRICKET'S CHIRPING FULL OF FUN. EVER WICKED!"
...FANCHON BECOMES, DEMONSTRABLY, MORE PAGAN THAN CHRISTIAN. AND, IN FACT, MORE INFERNAL THAN PAGAN.
FANCHON. THE CRICKET:
A DOMESTIC DRAMA. IN FIVE ACTS.
IT'S "INVERSIONIST" IN OTHER WORDS. THE THEATRICAL "FANCHON" DOES FOR THE INFERNAL WHAT MARGARET MITCHELL'S NOVEL WOULD LATER DO FOR THE SOUTHERN CONFEDERACY AND THE KU KLUX KLAN
MAKE THE BAD GUYS SEEM TO BE THE GOOD GUYS.
ODDLY (AND OMINOUSLY) SHE WAS A FAVOURITE ACTRESS OF PRESIDENT ABRAHAM LINCOLN
(ACCORDING TO THE AUTHORS OF RIGHT OR WRONG, GOD JUDGE ME: THE WRITINGS OF JOHN WILKES BOOTH, SHE WAS SYMPATHETIC TO THE CONFEDERACY AND, DURING THE CIVIL WAR, LIKED TO DANCE ON THE AMERICAN FLAG. SHE BECAME FRIENDS WITH LINCOLN'S FUTURE ASSASSIN IN 1858 AND, OVER THE SUBSEQUENT FEW YEARS, OFTEN APPEARED ON THE STAGE WITH BOOTH)
(THUS LINKING THE WHITE HOUSE, THROUGH HERSELF, TO BOOTH)
(AND TO BOOTH'S ELDER BROTHER, EDWIN, REPUTEDLY THE GREATEST HAMLET OF ALL TIME)
(AND AS A CONSEQUENCE TO THOSE METAPHYSICS CONTAINED WITHIN HAMLET)
("LET'S SEE WHAT WE CAN DO" INDEED.)
(BUT I'M GETTING WAY AHEAD OF MY STORY, AGAIN.)

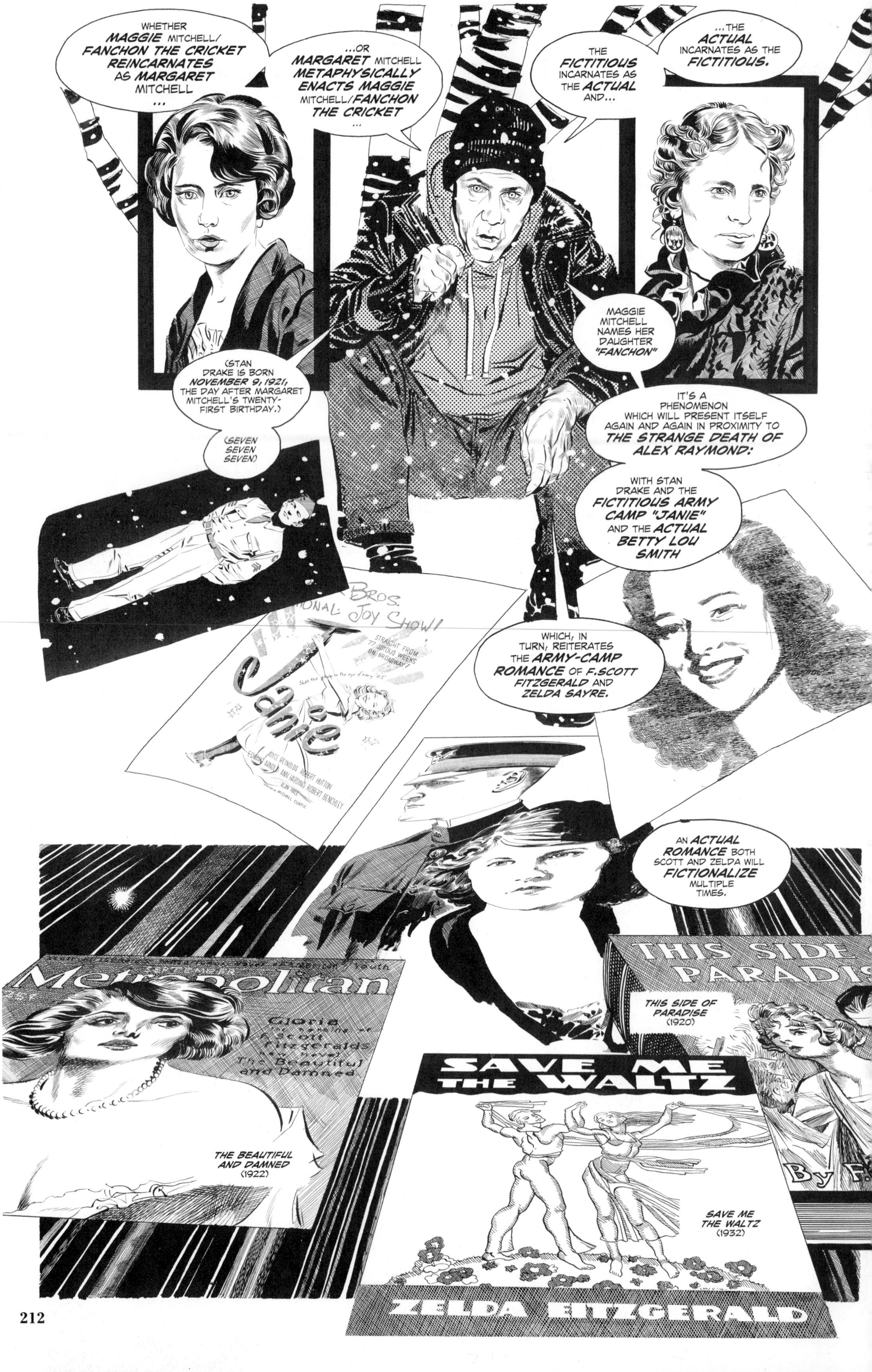
WHETHER MAGGIE MITCHELL/ FANCHON THE CRICKET REINCARNATES AS MARGARET MITCHELL ...
...OR MARGARET MITCHELL METAPHYSICALLY ENACTS MAGGIE MITCHELL/FANCHON THE CRICKET ...
THE FICTITIOUS INCARNATES AS THE ACTUAL AND...
...THE ACTUAL INCARNATES AS THE FICTITIOUS.
(STAN DRAKE IS BORN NOVEMBER 9, 1921, THE DAY AFTER MARGARET MITCHELL'S TWENTY-FIRST BIRTHDAY.)
(SEVEN SEVEN SEVEN)
MAGGIE MITCHELL NAMES HER DAUGHTER "FANCHON"
IT'S A PHENOMENON WHICH WILL PRESENT ITSELF AGAIN AND AGAIN IN PROXIMITY TO THE STRANGE DEATH OF ALEX RAYMOND:
WITH STAN DRAKE AND THE FICTITIOUS ARMY CAMP "JANIE" AND THE ACTUAL BETTY LOU SMITH
BROS.
JOY SHOW!
STRAIGHT FROM 77 JOYOUS WEEKS ON BROADWAY!
Janie
WHICH, IN TURN, REITERATES THE ARMY-CAMP ROMANCE OF F. SCOTT FITZGERALD AND ZELDA SAYRE.
AN ACTUAL ROMANCE BOTH SCOTT AND ZELDA WILL FICTIONALIZE MULTIPLE TIMES.
Metropolitan
Gloria the heroine of F. Scott Fitzgeralds new novel The Beautiful and Damned
THIS SIDE PARADIS
THIS SIDE OF PARADISE (1920)
SAVE ME THE WALTZ
THE BEAUTIFUL AND DAMNED (1922)
SAVE ME THE WALTZ (1932)
ZELDA FITZGERALD

FITZGERALD IS GIVEN A RIDE BY *MARGARET MITCHELL AND HER MOTHER* WHEN HE'S STATIONED AT *CAMP GORDON* IN THE SPRING OF 1918

(MITCHELL REMEMBERS HIM LATER WHEN HE BECOMES FAMOUS)

THE MITCHELL FAMILY CAR: A *FIVE-PASSENGER HANSON TOURING CAR.* THE ONLY CAR EVER MANUFACTURED IN *ATLANTA*

OUR FIRST CHARIOT.

*HE* WRITES *HER:* SHE MODELS HERSELF, IN THE EARLY 1920S, ON HIS MANY *JAZZ-AGE FLAPPER* HEROINES.

TALES OF THE JAZZ AGE

By the Author of THE BEAUTIFUL AND DAMNED

F. SCOTT FITZGERALD

*ARDITA FARNUM* "THE OFFSHORE PIRATE" (1920)

*NANCY LAMAR* "THE JELLY BEAN" (1920)

*SALLY CARROL HAPPER* "THE ICE PALACE" (1920)

*BERNICE HARVEY* "BERNICE BOBS HER HAIR" (1920)

*MYRA HARPER* "MYRA MEETS HIS FAMILY" (1920)

*SHE* WRITES *HERSELF:* THE NEVER COMPLETED *PANSY HAMILTON FLAPPER HEROINE* MANUSCRIPT ...

"Pansy Hamilton Flapper Heroine" by Mar...

...AND AS THE *REBEL-SPIRITED YOUNGER TEENAGED DAUGHTER* IN THE 30-PAGE TYPESCRIPT SHE HAD GIVEN TO *WARD GREENE.*

THANK YOU, MR. HOLLY... DARLING!!

YOU LITTLE MONSTER!

*INVERSIONIST FICTIONS* ALL.

21 YEARS (SEVEN, SEVEN, SEVEN) AFTER THEIR FIRST MEETING, SHE WRITES *HIM:*

GONE WITH THE WIND

FITZGERALD WORKS FOR 21 DAYS (SEVEN, SEVEN, SEVEN) AS A *CONTRACTED WRITER* ON THE *GONE WITH THE WIND* MOVIE SCRIPT, UNDER STRICT INSTRUCTIONS TO USE *ONLY* MARGARET MITCHELL'S ORIGINAL DIALOGUE.

213

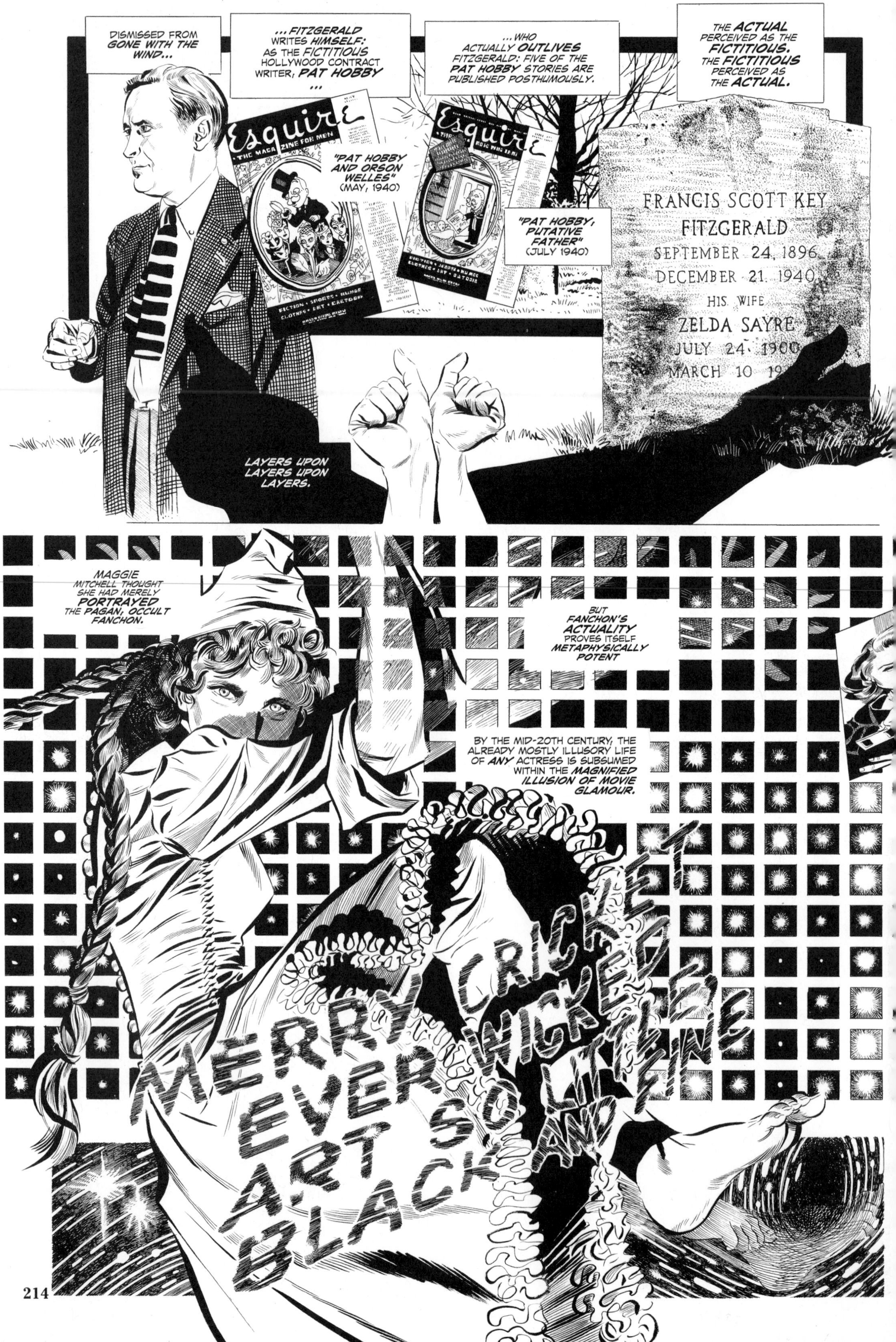

DISMISSED FROM GONE WITH THE WIND...
...FITZGERALD WRITES HIMSELF: AS THE FICTITIOUS HOLLYWOOD CONTRACT WRITER, PAT HOBBY ...
...WHO ACTUALLY OUTLIVES FITZGERALD: FIVE OF THE PAT HOBBY STORIES ARE PUBLISHED POSTHUMOUSLY.
THE ACTUAL PERCEIVED AS THE FICTITIOUS. THE FICTITIOUS PERCEIVED AS THE ACTUAL.
Esquire
THE MAGAZINE FOR MEN
"PAT HOBBY AND ORSON WELLES" (MAY, 1940)
"PAT HOBBY, PUTATIVE FATHER" (JULY 1940)
FRANCIS SCOTT KEY
FITZGERALD
SEPTEMBER 24, 1896
DECEMBER 21, 1940
HIS WIFE
ZELDA SAYRE
JULY 24 1900
MARCH 10 19
LAYERS UPON LAYERS UPON LAYERS.
MAGGIE MITCHELL THOUGHT SHE HAD MERELY PORTRAYED THE PAGAN, OCCULT FANCHON.
BUT FANCHON'S ACTUALITY PROVES ITSELF METAPHYSICALLY POTENT
BY THE MID-20TH CENTURY, THE ALREADY MOSTLY ILLUSORY LIFE OF ANY ACTRESS IS SUBSUMED WITHIN THE MAGNIFIED ILLUSION OF MOVIE GLAMOUR.
MERRY CRICKET
EVER WICKED?
ART SO LITTLE
BLACK AND FINE

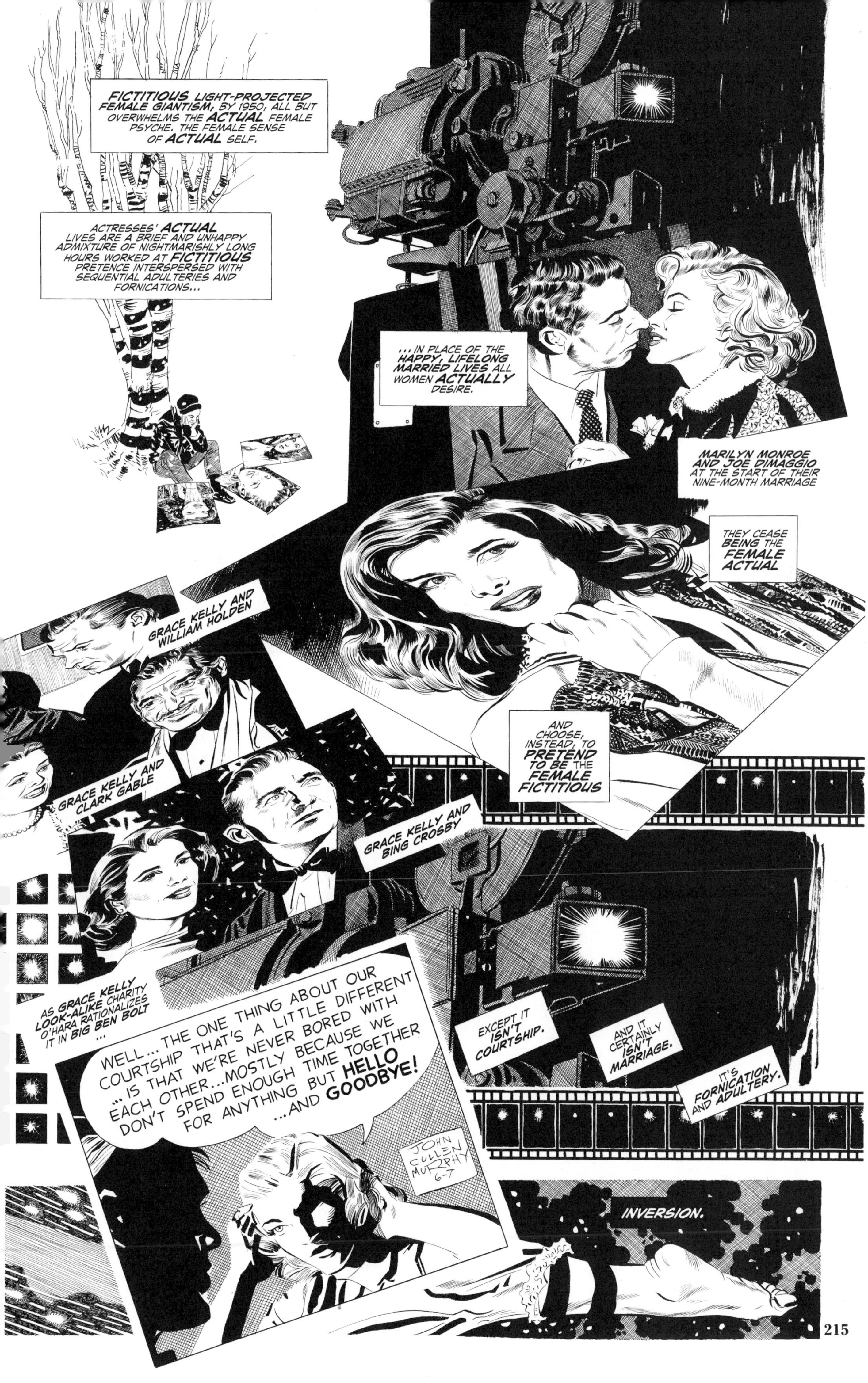
FICTITIOUS LIGHT-PROJECTED FEMALE GIANTISM, BY 1950, ALL BUT OVERWHELMS THE ACTUAL FEMALE PSYCHE. THE FEMALE SENSE OF ACTUAL SELF.
ACTRESSES' ACTUAL LIVES ARE A BRIEF AND UNHAPPY ADMIXTURE OF NIGHTMARISHLY LONG HOURS WORKED AT FICTITIOUS PRETENCE INTERSPERSED WITH SEQUENTIAL ADULTERIES AND FORNICATIONS...
...IN PLACE OF THE HAPPY, LIFELONG MARRIED LIVES ALL WOMEN ACTUALLY DESIRE.
MARILYN MONROE AND JOE DIMAGGIO AT THE START OF THEIR NINE-MONTH MARRIAGE
THEY CEASE BEING THE FEMALE ACTUAL
AND CHOOSE, INSTEAD, TO PRETEND TO BE THE FEMALE FICTITIOUS
GRACE KELLY AND WILLIAM HOLDEN
GRACE KELLY AND CLARK GABLE
GRACE KELLY AND BING CROSBY
AS GRACE KELLY LOOK-ALIKE CHARITY O'HARA RATIONALIZES IT IN BIG BEN BOLT ...
WELL... THE ONE THING ABOUT OUR COURTSHIP THAT'S A LITTLE DIFFERENT ... IS THAT WE'RE NEVER BORED WITH EACH OTHER... MOSTLY BECAUSE WE DON'T SPEND ENOUGH TIME TOGETHER FOR ANYTHING BUT HELLO ...AND GOODBYE!
JOHN CULLEN MURPHY 6-7
EXCEPT IT ISN'T COURTSHIP.
AND IT CERTAINLY ISN'T MARRIAGE.
IT'S FORNICATION AND ADULTERY.
INVERSION.

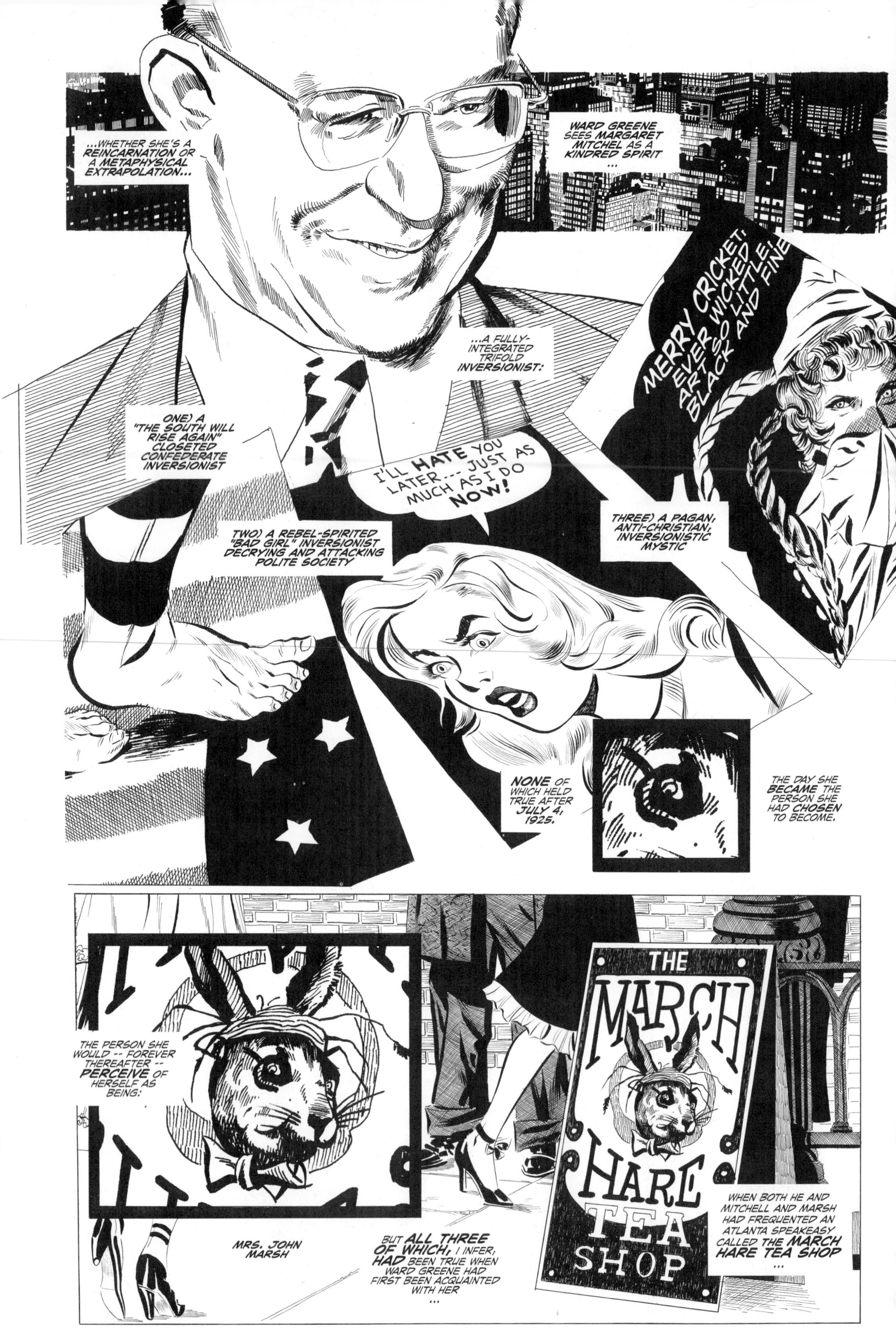

...WHETHER SHE'S A REINCARNATION OR A METAPHYSICAL EXTRAPOLATION...
WARD GREENE SEES MARGARET MITCHEL AS A KINDRED SPIRIT ...
MERRY CRICKET; EVER WICKED ART SO LITTLE, BLACK AND FINE
...A FULLY-INTEGRATED TRIFOLD INVERSIONIST:
ONE) A "THE SOUTH WILL RISE AGAIN" CLOSETED CONFEDERATE INVERSIONIST
I'LL HATE YOU LATER--- JUST AS MUCH AS I DO NOW!
TWO) A REBEL-SPIRITED "BAD GIRL" INVERSIONIST DECRYING AND ATTACKING POLITE SOCIETY
THREE) A PAGAN, ANTI-CHRISTIAN, INVERSIONISTIC MYSTIC
NONE OF WHICH HELD TRUE AFTER JULY 4, 1925.
THE DAY SHE BECAME THE PERSON SHE HAD CHOSEN TO BECOME.
THE PERSON SHE WOULD -- FOREVER THEREAFTER -- PERCEIVE OF HERSELF AS BEING:
MRS. JOHN MARSH
BUT ALL THREE OF WHICH, I INFER, HAD BEEN TRUE WHEN WARD GREENE HAD FIRST BEEN ACQUAINTED WITH HER ...
THE MARCH HARE TEA SHOP
WHEN BOTH HE AND MITCHELL AND MARSH HAD FREQUENTED AN ATLANTA SPEAKEASY CALLED THE MARCH HARE TEA SHOP ...

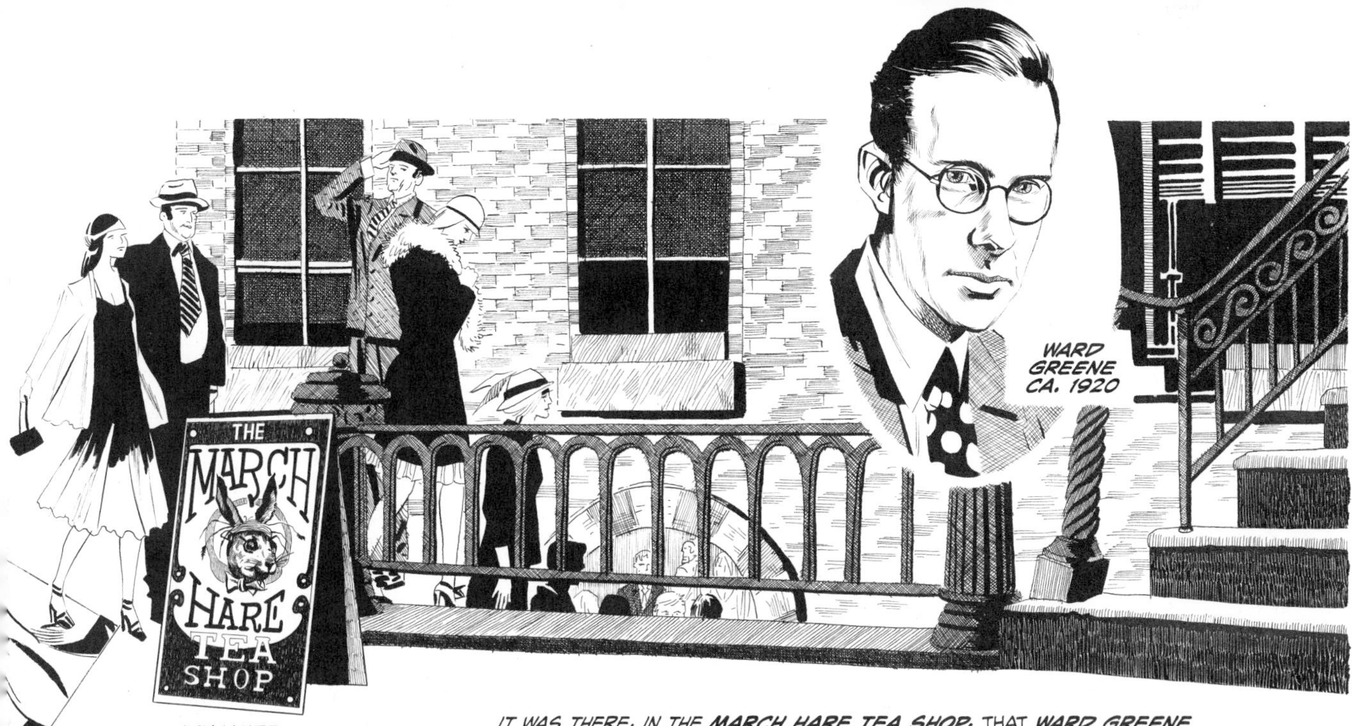
THE MARCH HARE TEA SHOP

WARD GREENE CA. 1920

NICKNAMED (APPROPRIATELY) ***THE RABBIT HOLE***

*IT WAS THERE, IN THE **MARCH HARE TEA SHOP,** THAT **WARD GREENE** HAD FORMED HIS LIFELONG PERCEPTIONS OF HER AT A PROFOUNDLY OBSESSIVE LEVEL...*

*..AND WHERE **JOHN MARSH** HAD FIRST MET HER AND FALLEN HOPELESSLY AND IRRETRIEVABLY IN LOVE.*

***RIP KIRBY*** 2 MAY 1947

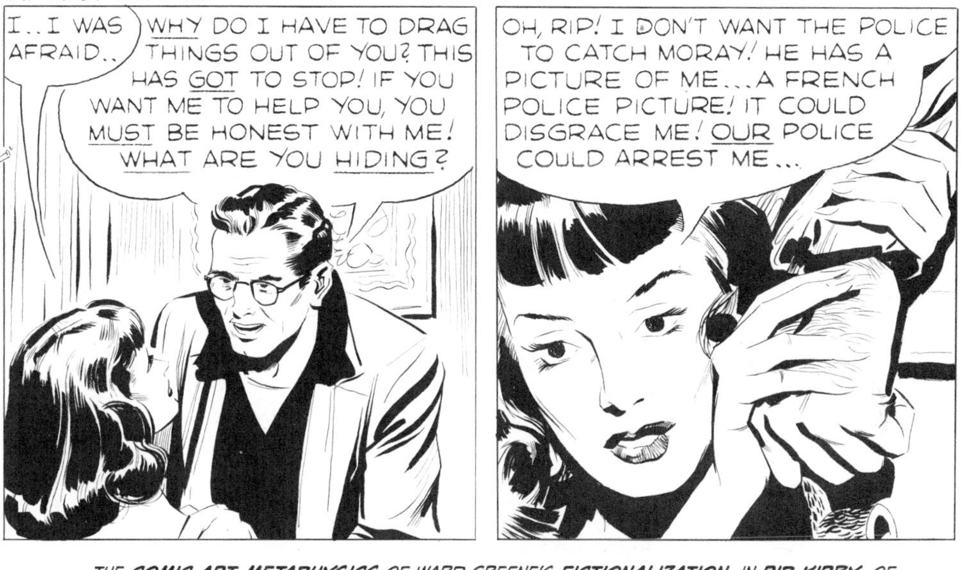
I..I WAS AFRAID..
WHY DO I HAVE TO DRAG THINGS OUT OF YOU? THIS HAS GOT TO STOP! IF YOU WANT ME TO HELP YOU, YOU MUST BE HONEST WITH ME! WHAT ARE YOU HIDING?
OH, RIP! I DON'T WANT THE POLICE TO CATCH MORAY! HE HAS A PICTURE OF ME...A FRENCH POLICE PICTURE! IT COULD DISGRACE ME! OUR POLICE COULD ARREST ME...

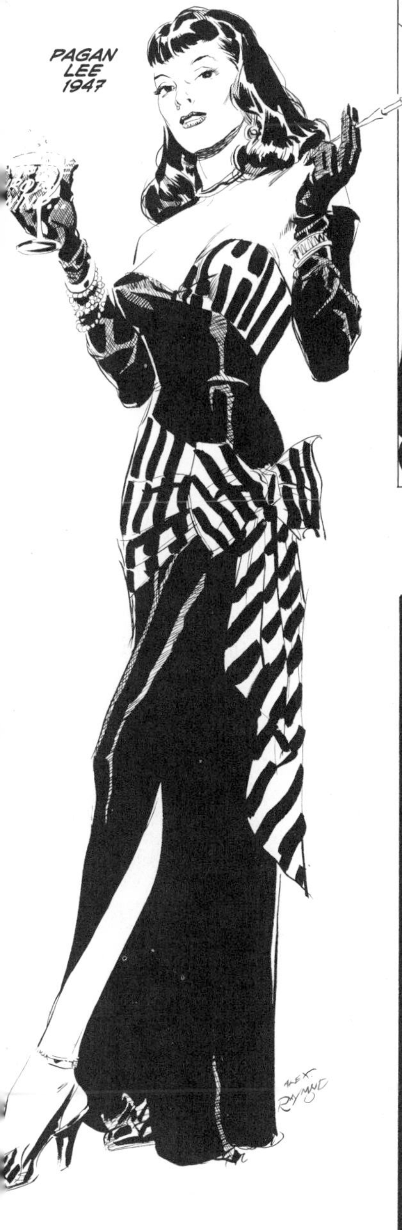
ALEX RAYMOND

PAGAN LEE 1947

*THE **COMIC ART METAPHYSICS** OF WARD GREENE'S **FICTIONALIZATION,** IN **RIP KIRBY,** OF THE MARCH HARE TEA SHOP MARGARET MITCHELL AS **PAGAN LEE**... (THE **LEEWARD** SIDE OF MITCHELL'S INTRINSICALLY PAGAN SELF?)... SEEMS TO CAUSE THE MARCH HARE TEA SHOP MARGARET MITCHELL TO...**SPROUT?**,,,ELSEWERE IN OTHER COMIC ART AS WELL*

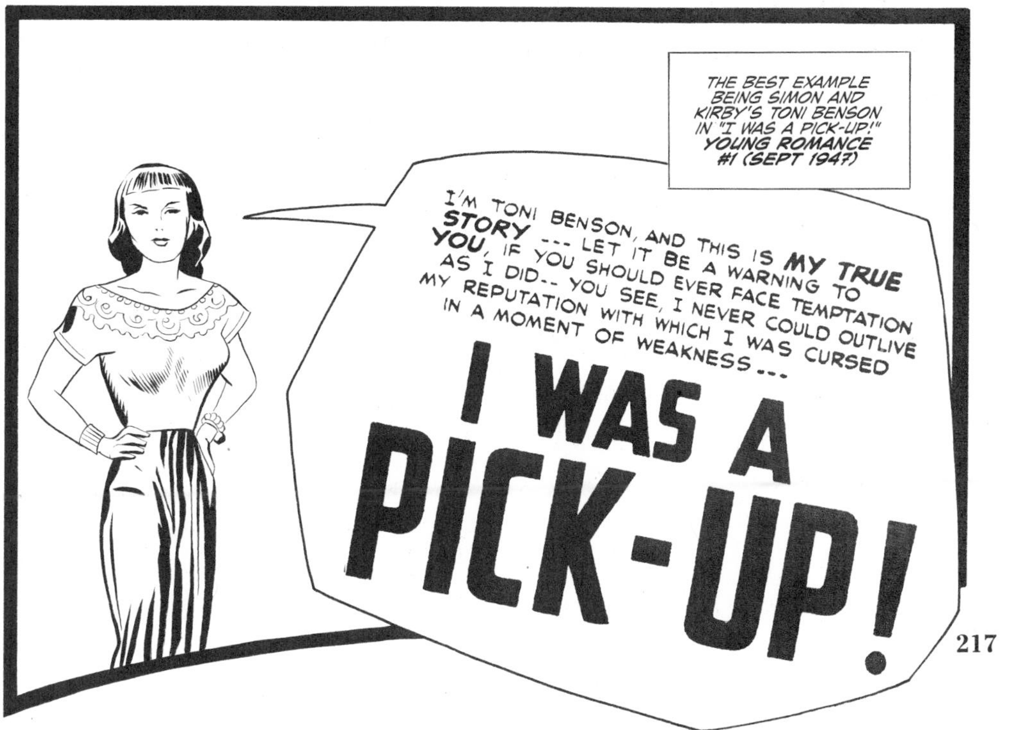
I'M TONI BENSON, AND THIS IS MY TRUE STORY --- LET IT BE A WARNING TO YOU, IF YOU SHOULD EVER FACE TEMPTATION AS I DID-- YOU SEE, I NEVER COULD OUTLIVE MY REPUTATION WITH WHICH I WAS CURSED IN A MOMENT OF WEAKNESS ---
I WAS A PICK-UP!

*THE BEST EXAMPLE BEING SIMON AND KIRBY'S TONI BENSON IN "I WAS A PICK-UP!" **YOUNG ROMANCE #1 (SEPT 1947)***

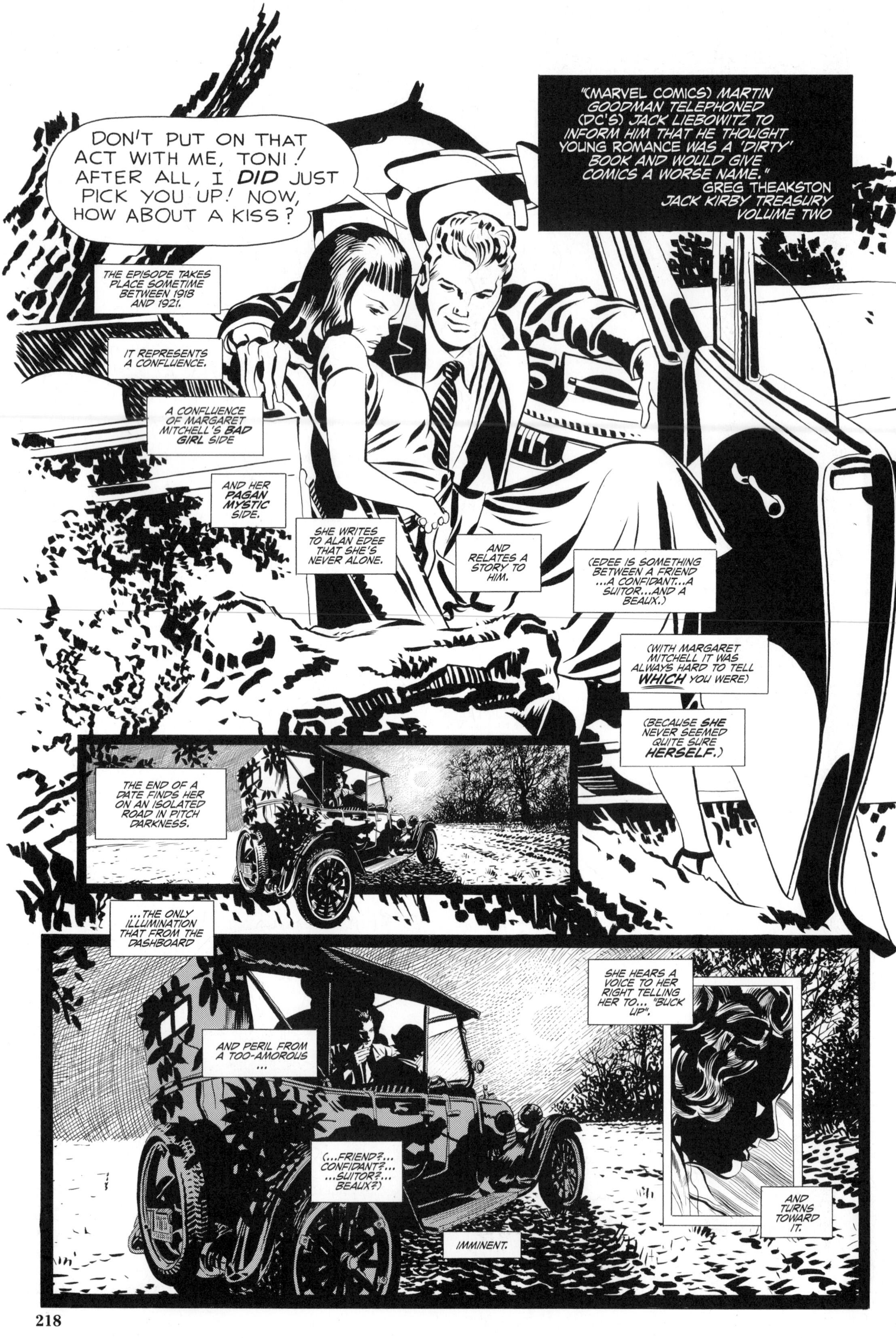

"(MARVEL COMICS) MARTIN GOODMAN TELEPHONED (DC'S) JACK LIEBOWITZ TO INFORM HIM THAT HE THOUGHT YOUNG ROMANCE WAS A 'DIRTY' BOOK AND WOULD GIVE COMICS A WORSE NAME." GREG THEAKSTON JACK KIRBY TREASURY VOLUME TWO
DON'T PUT ON THAT ACT WITH ME, TONI! AFTER ALL, I DID JUST PICK YOU UP! NOW, HOW ABOUT A KISS?
THE EPISODE TAKES PLACE SOMETIME BETWEEN 1918 AND 1921.
IT REPRESENTS A CONFLUENCE.
A CONFLUENCE OF MARGARET MITCHELL'S BAD GIRL SIDE
AND HER PAGAN MYSTIC SIDE.
SHE WRITES TO ALAN EDEE THAT SHE'S NEVER ALONE.
AND RELATES A STORY TO HIM.
(EDEE IS SOMETHING BETWEEN A FRIEND ...A CONFIDANT...A SUITOR...AND A BEAUX.)
(WITH MARGARET MITCHELL IT WAS ALWAYS HARD TO TELL WHICH YOU WERE)
(BECAUSE SHE NEVER SEEMED QUITE SURE HERSELF.)
THE END OF A DATE FINDS HER ON AN ISOLATED ROAD IN PITCH DARKNESS.
...THE ONLY ILLUMINATION THAT FROM THE DASHBOARD
AND PERIL FROM A TOO-AMOROUS ...
(...FRIEND?... CONFIDANT?... ...SUITOR?... BEAUX?)
IMMINENT.
SHE HEARS A VOICE TO HER RIGHT TELLING HER TO... "BUCK UP".
AND TURNS TOWARD IT.

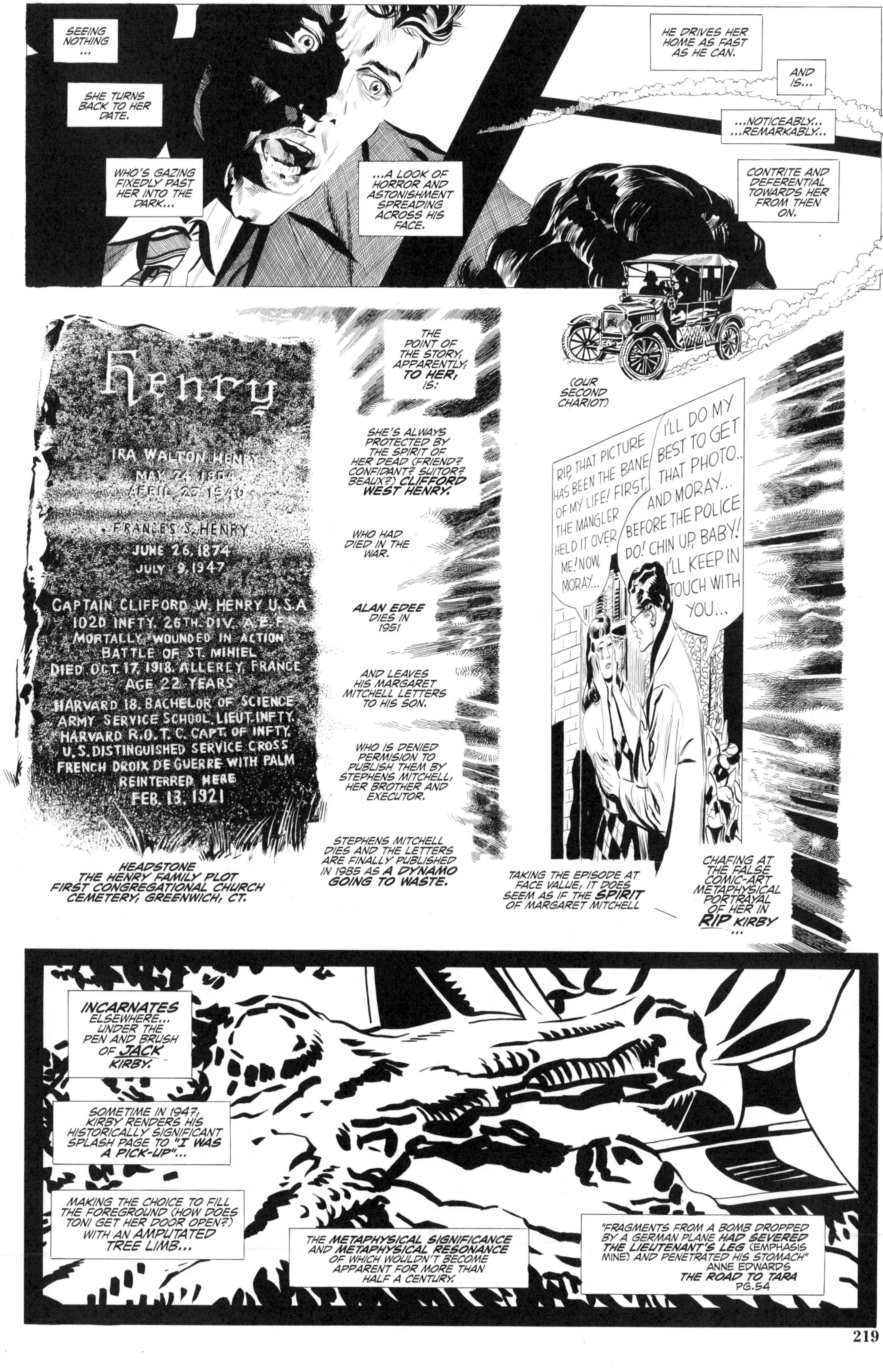

SEEING NOTHING ...
SHE TURNS BACK TO HER DATE.
WHO'S GAZING FIXEDLY PAST HER INTO THE DARK...
...A LOOK OF HORROR AND ASTONISHMENT SPREADING ACROSS HIS FACE.
HE DRIVES HER HOME AS FAST AS HE CAN.
AND IS...
...NOTICEABLY... ...REMARKABLY...
CONTRITE AND DEFERENTIAL TOWARDS HER FROM THEN ON.
(OUR SECOND CHARIOT)
Henry
IRA WALTON HENRY
FRANCES S. HENRY
JUNE 26, 1874
JULY 9, 1947
CAPTAIN CLIFFORD W. HENRY U.S.A.
102D INFTY. 26TH. DIV. A.E.F.
MORTALLY WOUNDED IN ACTION
BATTLE OF ST. MIHIEL
DIED OCT. 17, 1918, ALLEREY, FRANCE
AGE 22 YEARS
HARVARD 18. BACHELOR OF SCIENCE
ARMY SERVICE SCHOOL LIEUT. INFTY.
HARVARD R.O.T.C. CAPT. OF INFTY.
U.S. DISTINGUISHED SERVICE CROSS
FRENCH DROIX DE GUERRE WITH PALM
REINTERRED HERE
FEB. 13, 1921
HEADSTONE THE HENRY FAMILY PLOT FIRST CONGREGATIONAL CHURCH CEMETERY, GREENWICH, CT.
THE POINT OF THE STORY, APPARENTLY, TO HER, IS:
SHE'S ALWAYS PROTECTED BY THE SPIRIT OF HER DEAD (FRIEND? CONFIDANT? SUITOR? BEAUX?) CLIFFORD WEST HENRY.
WHO HAD DIED IN THE WAR.
ALAN EDEE DIES IN 1951
AND LEAVES HIS MARGARET MITCHELL LETTERS TO HIS SON.
WHO IS DENIED PERMISION TO PUBLISH THEM BY STEPHENS MITCHELL, HER BROTHER AND EXECUTOR.
STEPHENS MITCHELL DIES AND THE LETTERS ARE FINALLY PUBLISHED IN 1985 AS A DYNAMO GOING TO WASTE.
RIP, THAT PICTURE HAS BEEN THE BANE OF MY LIFE! FIRST, THE MANGLER HELD IT OVER ME! NOW, MORAY...
I'LL DO MY BEST TO GET THAT PHOTO.. AND MORAY... BEFORE THE POLICE DO! CHIN UP, BABY! I'LL KEEP IN TOUCH WITH YOU...
TAKING THE EPISODE AT FACE VALUE, IT DOES SEEM AS IF THE SPIRIT OF MARGARET MITCHELL
CHAFING AT THE FALSE COMIC-ART METAPHYSICAL PORTRAYAL OF HER IN RIP KIRBY ...
INCARNATES ELSEWHERE... UNDER THE PEN AND BRUSH OF JACK KIRBY.
SOMETIME IN 1947, KIRBY RENDERS HIS HISTORICALLY SIGNIFICANT SPLASH PAGE TO "I WAS A PICK-UP"...
MAKING THE CHOICE TO FILL THE FOREGROUND (HOW DOES TONI GET HER DOOR OPEN?) WITH AN AMPUTATED TREE LIMB...
THE METAPHYSICAL SIGNIFICANCE AND METAPHYSICAL RESONANCE OF WHICH WOULDN'T BECOME APPARENT FOR MORE THAN HALF A CENTURY.
"FRAGMENTS FROM A BOMB DROPPED BY A GERMAN PLANE HAD SEVERED THE LIEUTENANT'S LEG (EMPHASIS MINE) AND PENETRATED HIS STOMACH" ANNE EDWARDS THE ROAD TO TARA PG.54

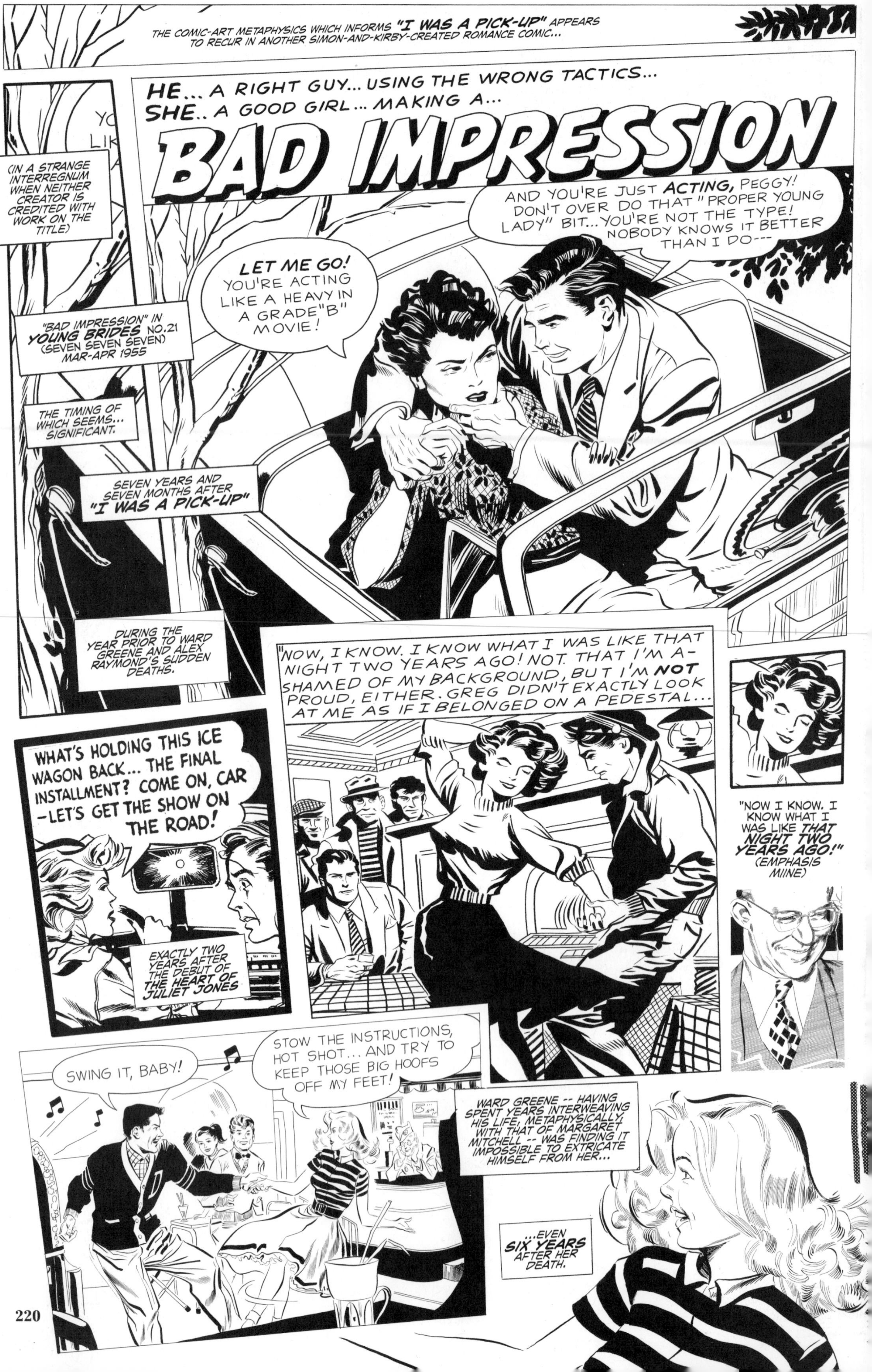
THE COMIC-ART METAPHYSICS WHICH INFORMS "I WAS A PICK-UP" APPEARS TO RECUR IN ANOTHER SIMON-AND-KIRBY-CREATED ROMANCE COMIC...
HE... A RIGHT GUY... USING THE WRONG TACTICS... SHE.. A GOOD GIRL... MAKING A...
BAD IMPRESSION
(IN A STRANGE INTERREGNUM WHEN NEITHER CREATOR IS CREDITED WITH WORK ON THE TITLE)
AND YOU'RE JUST ACTING, PEGGY! DON'T OVER DO THAT "PROPER YOUNG LADY" BIT... YOU'RE NOT THE TYPE! NOBODY KNOWS IT BETTER THAN I DO---
LET ME GO! YOU'RE ACTING LIKE A HEAVY IN A GRADE "B" MOVIE!
"BAD IMPRESSION" IN YOUNG BRIDES NO.21 (SEVEN SEVEN SEVEN) MAR-APR 1955
THE TIMING OF WHICH SEEMS... SIGNIFICANT.
SEVEN YEARS AND SEVEN MONTHS AFTER "I WAS A PICK-UP"
DURING THE YEAR PRIOR TO WARD GREENE AND ALEX RAYMOND'S SUDDEN DEATHS.
"NOW, I KNOW. I KNOW WHAT I WAS LIKE THAT NIGHT TWO YEARS AGO! NOT THAT I'M ASHAMED OF MY BACKGROUND, BUT I'M NOT PROUD, EITHER. GREG DIDN'T EXACTLY LOOK AT ME AS IF I BELONGED ON A PEDESTAL...
WHAT'S HOLDING THIS ICE WAGON BACK... THE FINAL INSTALLMENT? COME ON, CAR -LET'S GET THE SHOW ON THE ROAD!
EXACTLY TWO YEARS AFTER THE DEBUT OF THE HEART OF JULIET JONES
"NOW I KNOW. I KNOW WHAT I WAS LIKE THAT NIGHT TWO YEARS AGO!" (EMPHASIS MIINE)
SWING IT, BABY!
STOW THE INSTRUCTIONS, HOT SHOT... AND TRY TO KEEP THOSE BIG HOOFS OFF MY FEET!
WARD GREENE -- HAVING SPENT YEARS INTERWEAVING HIS LIFE, METAPHYSICALLY, WITH THAT OF MARGARET MITCHELL -- WAS FINDING IT IMPOSSIBLE TO EXTRICATE HIMSELF FROM HER...
...EVEN SIX YEARS AFTER HER DEATH.

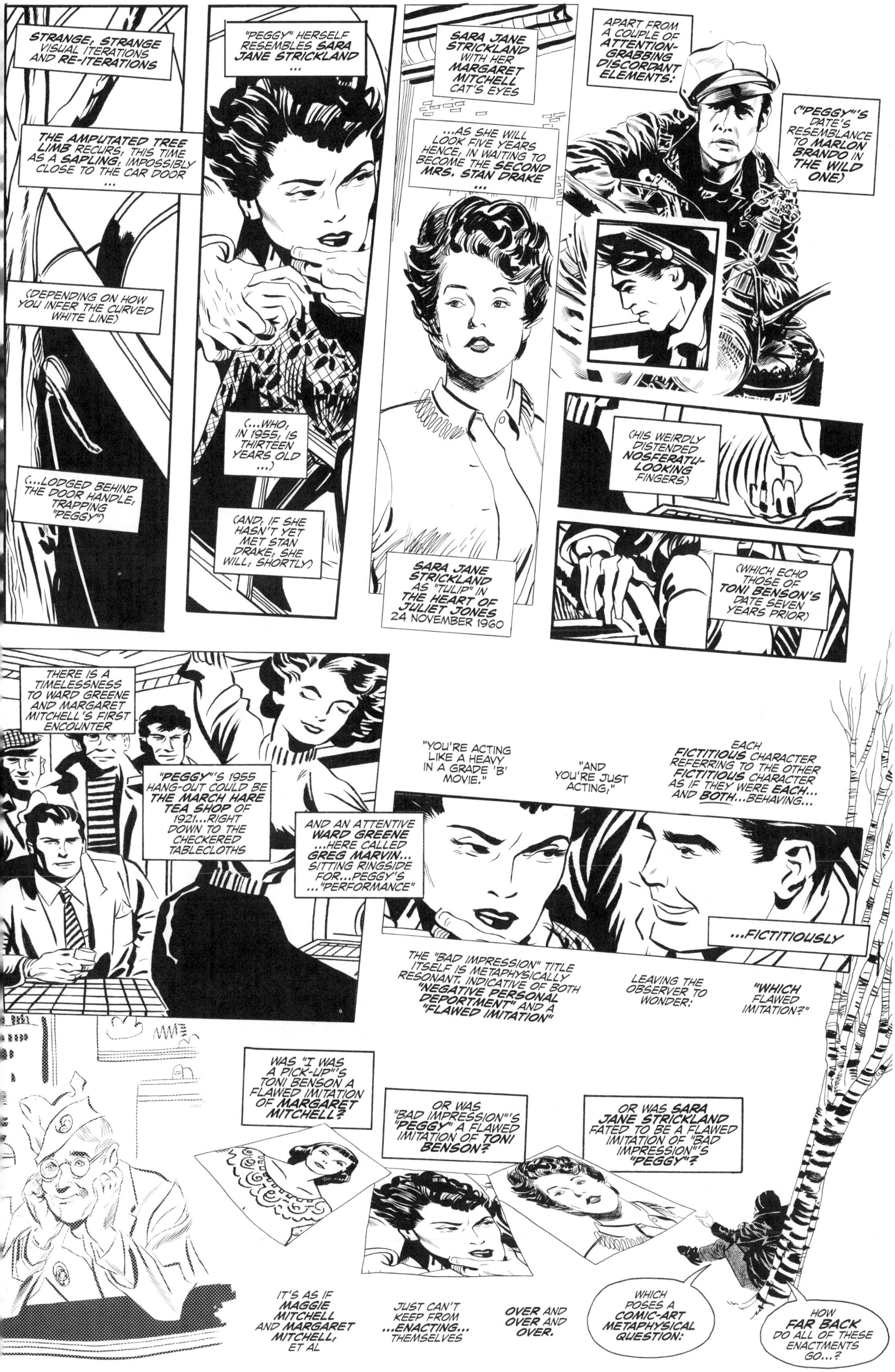
STRANGE, STRANGE VISUAL ITERATIONS AND RE-ITERATIONS
THE AMPUTATED TREE LIMB RECURS, THIS TIME AS A SAPLING, IMPOSSIBLY CLOSE TO THE CAR DOOR ...
(DEPENDING ON HOW YOU INFER THE CURVED WHITE LINE)
(...LODGED BEHIND THE DOOR HANDLE, TRAPPING "PEGGY")
"PEGGY" HERSELF RESEMBLES SARA JANE STRICKLAND ...
(...WHO, IN 1955, IS THIRTEEN YEARS OLD ...)
(AND, IF SHE HASN'T YET MET STAN DRAKE, SHE WILL, SHORTLY)
SARA JANE STRICKLAND WITH HER MARGARET MITCHELL CAT'S EYES
...AS SHE WILL LOOK FIVE YEARS HENCE, IN WAITING TO BECOME THE SECOND MRS. STAN DRAKE ...
SARA JANE STRICKLAND AS "TULIP" IN THE HEART OF JULIET JONES 24 NOVEMBER 1960
APART FROM A COUPLE OF ATTENTION-GRABBING DISCORDANT ELEMENTS:
("PEGGY"'S DATE'S RESEMBLANCE TO MARLON BRANDO IN THE WILD ONE)
(HIS WEIRDLY DISTENDED NOSFERATU-LOOKING FINGERS)
(WHICH ECHO THOSE OF TONI BENSON'S DATE SEVEN YEARS PRIOR)
THERE IS A TIMELESSNESS TO WARD GREENE AND MARGARET MITCHELL'S FIRST ENCOUNTER
"PEGGY"'S 1955 HANG-OUT COULD BE THE MARCH HARE TEA SHOP OF 1921...RIGHT DOWN TO THE CHECKERED TABLECLOTHS
AND AN ATTENTIVE WARD GREENE ...HERE CALLED GREG MARVIN... SITTING RINGSIDE FOR...PEGGY'S ..."PERFORMANCE"
"YOU'RE ACTING LIKE A HEAVY IN A GRADE 'B' MOVIE."
"AND YOU'RE JUST ACTING,"
EACH FICTITIOUS CHARACTER REFERRING TO THE OTHER FICTITIOUS CHARACTER AS IF THEY WERE EACH... AND BOTH...BEHAVING...
...FICTITIOUSLY
THE "BAD IMPRESSION" TITLE ITSELF IS METAPHYSICALLY RESONANT, INDICATIVE OF BOTH "NEGATIVE PERSONAL DEPORTMENT" AND A "FLAWED IMITATION"
LEAVING THE OBSERVER TO WONDER:
"WHICH FLAWED IMITATION?"
WAS "I WAS A PICK-UP"'S TONI BENSON A FLAWED IMITATION OF MARGARET MITCHELL?
OR WAS "BAD IMPRESSION"'S "PEGGY" A FLAWED IMITATION OF TONI BENSON?
OR WAS SARA JANE STRICKLAND FATED TO BE A FLAWED IMITATION OF "BAD IMPRESSION"'S "PEGGY"?
IT'S AS IF MAGGIE MITCHELL AND MARGARET MITCHELL, ET AL
JUST CAN'T KEEP FROM ...ENACTING... THEMSELVES
OVER AND OVER AND OVER.
WHICH POSES A COMIC-ART METAPHYSICAL QUESTION:
HOW FAR BACK DO ALL OF THESE ENACTMENTS GO...?

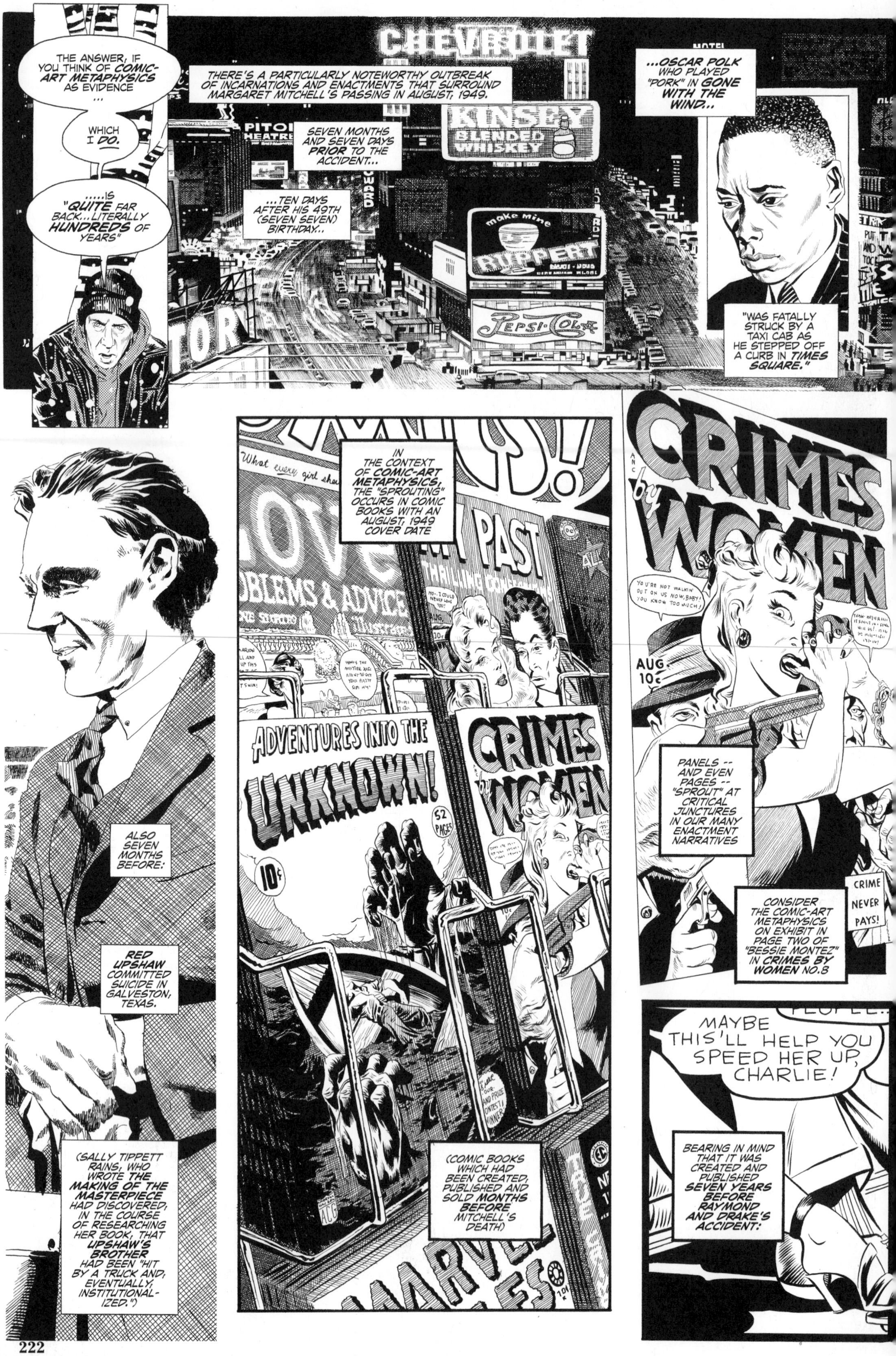

CHEVROLET
THE ANSWER, IF YOU THINK OF COMIC-ART METAPHYSICS AS EVIDENCE ...
WHICH I DO.
.....IS "QUITE FAR BACK...LITERALLY HUNDREDS OF YEARS"
THERE'S A PARTICULARLY NOTEWORTHY OUTBREAK OF INCARNATIONS AND ENACTMENTS THAT SURROUND MARGARET MITCHELL'S PASSING IN AUGUST, 1949.
KINSEY BLENDED WHISKEY
SEVEN MONTHS AND SEVEN DAYS PRIOR TO THE ACCIDENT...
...TEN DAYS AFTER HIS 49TH (SEVEN SEVEN) BIRTHDAY..
make mine RUPPERT
PEPSI-COLA
...OSCAR POLK WHO PLAYED "PORK" IN GONE WITH THE WIND...
"WAS FATALLY STRUCK BY A TAXI CAB AS HE STEPPED OFF A CURB IN TIMES SQUARE."
ALSO SEVEN MONTHS BEFORE:
RED UPSHAW COMMITTED SUICIDE IN GALVESTON, TEXAS.
(SALLY TIPPETT RAINS, WHO WROTE THE MAKING OF THE MASTERPIECE HAD DISCOVERED, IN THE COURSE OF RESEARCHING HER BOOK, THAT UPSHAW'S BROTHER HAD BEEN "HIT BY A TRUCK AND, EVENTUALLY, INSTITUTIONAL-IZED.")
IN THE CONTEXT OF COMIC-ART METAPHYSICS, THE "SPROUTING" OCCURS IN COMIC BOOKS WITH AN AUGUST, 1949 COVER DATE
What every girl should
LOVE PROBLEMS & ADVICE
MY PAST
THRILLING CONFESSIONS
ADVENTURES INTO THE UNKNOWN!
52 PAGES
10¢
CRIMES BY WOMEN
(COMIC BOOKS WHICH HAD BEEN CREATED, PUBLISHED AND SOLD MONTHS BEFORE MITCHELL'S DEATH)
MARVEL TALES
CRIMES by WOMEN
YOU'RE NOT WALKIN' OUT ON US NOW, BABY! YOU KNOW TOO MUCH!
AUG. 10¢
PANELS -- AND EVEN PAGES -- "SPROUT" AT CRITICAL JUNCTURES IN OUR MANY ENACTMENT NARRATIVES
CRIME NEVER PAYS!
CONSIDER THE COMIC-ART METAPHYSICS ON EXHIBIT IN PAGE TWO OF "BESSIE MONTEZ" IN CRIMES BY WOMEN NO.8
MAYBE THIS'LL HELP YOU SPEED HER UP, CHARLIE!
BEARING IN MIND THAT IT WAS CREATED AND PUBLISHED SEVEN YEARS BEFORE RAYMOND AND DRAKE'S ACCIDENT:

# CRIMES BY WOMEN

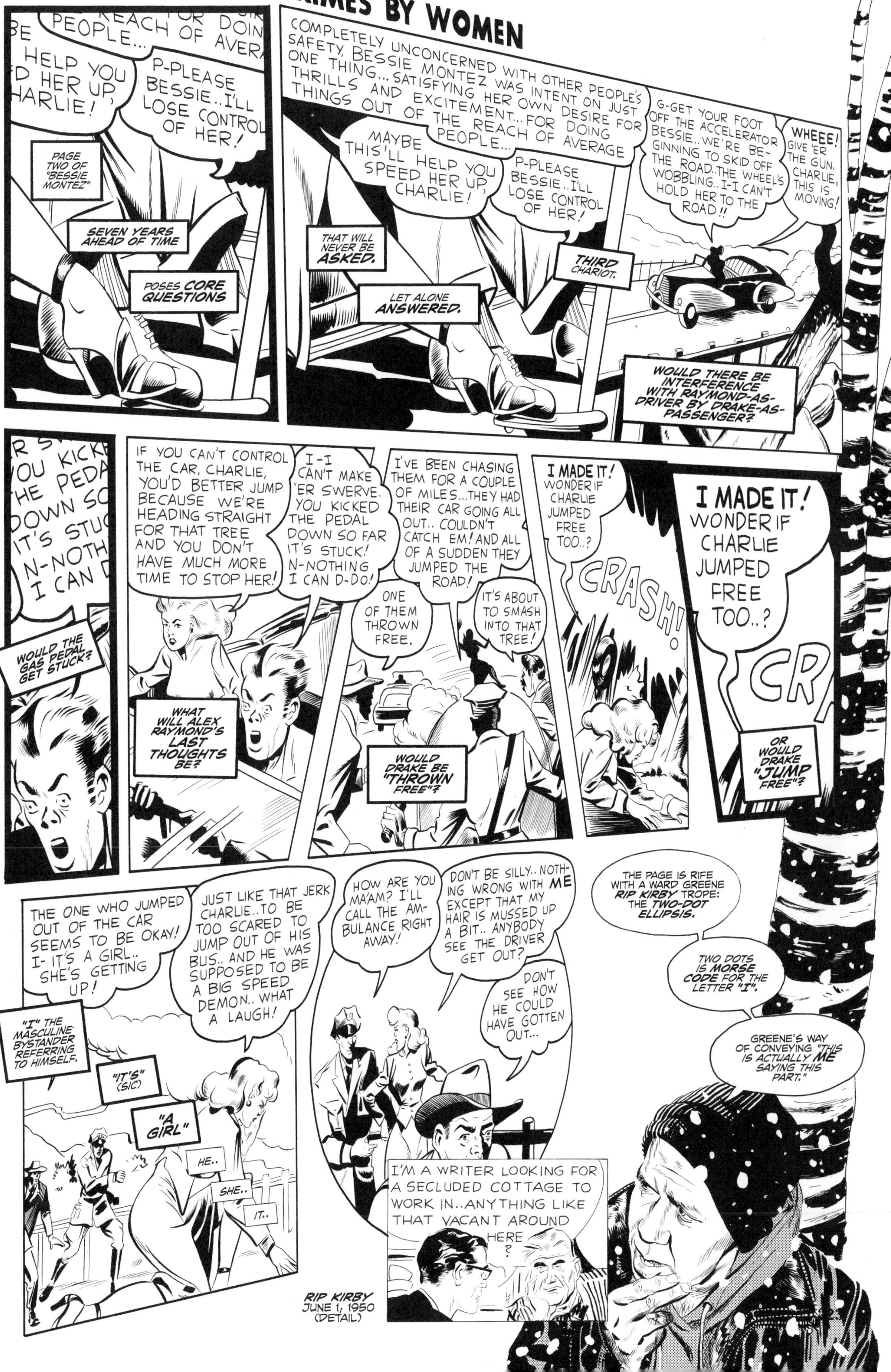
REACH OF DOIN
PEOPLE... OF AVERA
HELP YOU
D HER UP,
HARLIE!
P-PLEASE BESSIE..I'LL LOSE CONTROL OF HER!
PAGE TWO OF "BESSIE MONTEZ"
SEVEN YEARS AHEAD OF TIME
POSES CORE QUESTIONS
COMPLETELY UNCONCERNED WITH OTHER PEOPLE'S SAFETY, BESSIE MONTEZ WAS INTENT ON JUST ONE THING... SATISFYING HER OWN DESIRE FOR THRILLS AND EXCITEMENT... FOR DOING THINGS OUT OF THE REACH OF AVERAGE PEOPLE...
MAYBE THIS'LL HELP YOU SPEED HER UP, CHARLIE!
P-PLEASE BESSIE..I'LL LOSE CONTROL OF HER!
THAT WILL NEVER BE ASKED.
LET ALONE ANSWERED.
THIRD CHARIOT.
G-GET YOUR FOOT OFF THE ACCELERATOR BESSIE.. WE'RE BE- GINNING TO SKID OFF THE ROAD..THE WHEEL'S WOBBLING..I-I CAN'T HOLD HER TO THE ROAD!!
WHEEE! GIVE 'ER THE GUN, CHARLIE, THIS IS MOVING!
WOULD THERE BE INTERFERENCE WITH RAYMOND-AS-DRIVER BY DRAKE-AS-PASSENGER?
YOU KICK THE PEDA DOWN SO IT'S STUC N-NOTH I CAN D
WOULD THE GAS PEDAL GET STUCK?
IF YOU CAN'T CONTROL THE CAR, CHARLIE, YOU'D BETTER JUMP BECAUSE WE'RE HEADING STRAIGHT FOR THAT TREE AND YOU DON'T HAVE MUCH MORE TIME TO STOP HER!
I-I CAN'T MAKE 'ER SWERVE. YOU KICKED THE PEDAL DOWN SO FAR IT'S STUCK! N-NOTHING I CAN D-DO!
WHAT WILL ALEX RAYMOND'S LAST THOUGHTS BE?
I'VE BEEN CHASING THEM FOR A COUPLE OF MILES...THEY HAD THEIR CAR GOING ALL OUT.. COULDN'T CATCH EM! AND ALL OF A SUDDEN THEY JUMPED THE ROAD!
ONE OF THEM THROWN FREE.
IT'S ABOUT TO SMASH INTO THAT TREE!
WOULD DRAKE BE "THROWN FREE"?
I MADE IT! WONDER IF CHARLIE JUMPED FREE TOO..?
CRASH!
I MADE IT! WONDER IF CHARLIE JUMPED FREE TOO..?
CR
OR WOULD DRAKE "JUMP FREE"?
THE ONE WHO JUMPED OUT OF THE CAR SEEMS TO BE OKAY! I- IT'S A GIRL.. SHE'S GETTING UP!
JUST LIKE THAT JERK CHARLIE..TO BE TOO SCARED TO JUMP OUT OF HIS BUS.. AND HE WAS SUPPOSED TO BE A BIG SPEED DEMON.. WHAT A LAUGH!
"I" THE MASCULINE BYSTANDER REFERRING TO HIMSELF.
"IT'S" (SIC)
"A GIRL"
HE..
SHE..
IT..
HOW ARE YOU MA'AM? I'LL CALL THE AMBULANCE RIGHT AWAY!
DON'T BE SILLY.. NOTHING WRONG WITH ME EXCEPT THAT MY HAIR IS MUSSED UP A BIT.. ANYBODY SEE THE DRIVER GET OUT?
DON'T SEE HOW HE COULD HAVE GOTTEN OUT...
I'M A WRITER LOOKING FOR A SECLUDED COTTAGE TO WORK IN..ANYTHING LIKE THAT VACANT AROUND HERE?
RIP KIRBY JUNE 1, 1950 (DETAIL)
THE PAGE IS RIFE WITH A WARD GREENE RIP KIRBY TROPE: THE TWO-DOT ELLIPSIS.
TWO DOTS IS MORSE CODE FOR THE LETTER "I".
GREENE'S WAY OF CONVEYING "THIS IS ACTUALLY ME SAYING THIS PART."

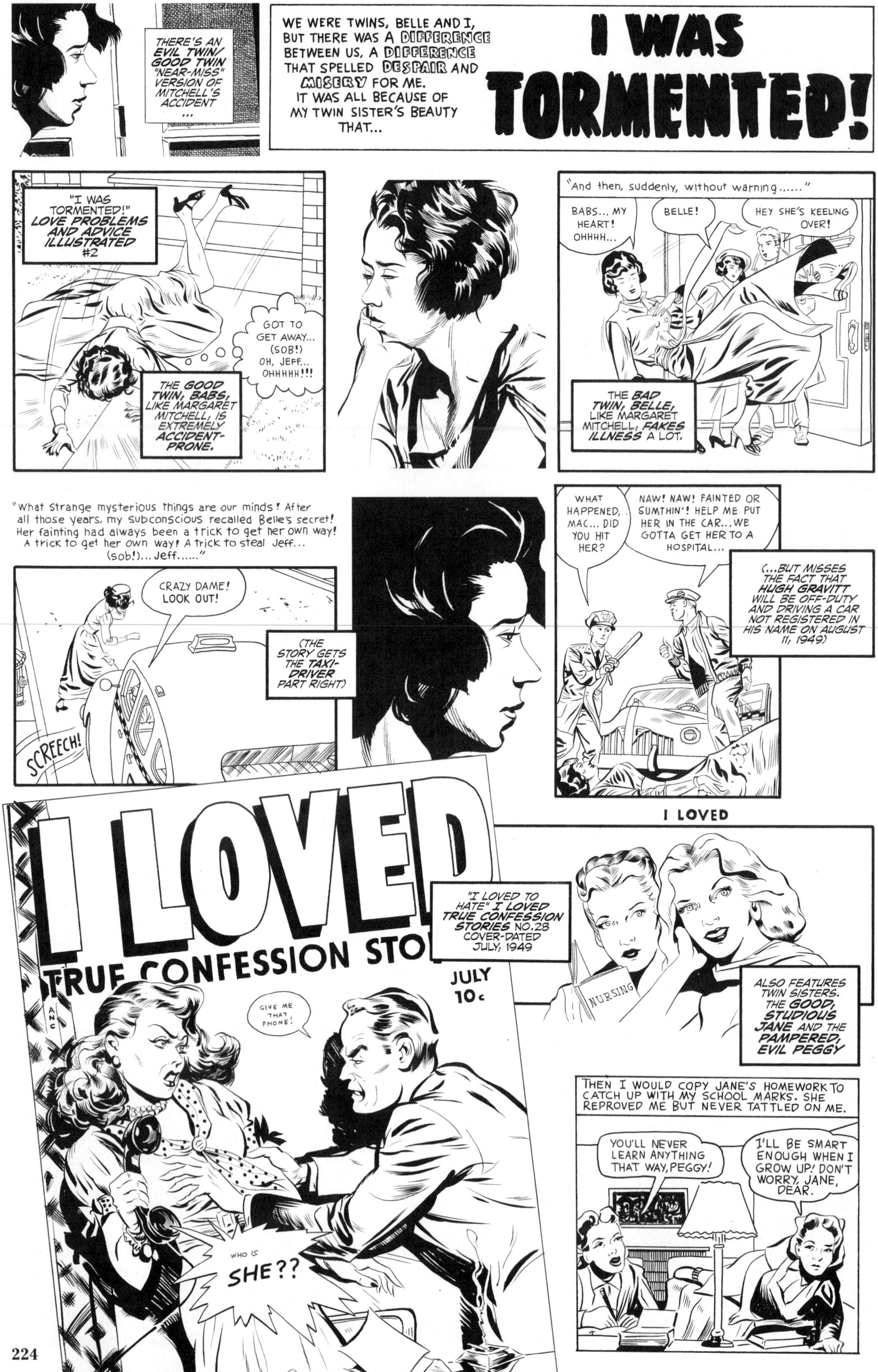

THERE'S AN EVIL TWIN/ GOOD TWIN "NEAR-MISS" VERSION OF MITCHELL'S ACCIDENT ...
WE WERE TWINS, BELLE AND I, BUT THERE WAS A DIFFERENCE BETWEEN US, A DIFFERENCE THAT SPELLED DESPAIR AND MISERY FOR ME. IT WAS ALL BECAUSE OF MY TWIN SISTER'S BEAUTY THAT...
I WAS TORMENTED!
"I WAS TORMENTED!" LOVE PROBLEMS AND ADVICE ILLUSTRATED #2
GOT TO GET AWAY... (SOB!) OH, JEFF... OHHHHH!!!
THE GOOD TWIN, BABS, LIKE MARGARET MITCHELL, IS EXTREMELY ACCIDENT-PRONE.
"And then, suddenly, without warning......"
BABS... MY HEART! OHHHH...
BELLE!
HEY SHE'S KEELING OVER!
THE BAD TWIN, BELLE, LIKE MARGARET MITCHELL, FAKES ILLNESS A LOT.
"What strange mysterious things are our minds! After all those years, my subconscious recalled Belle's secret! Her fainting had always been a trick to get her own way! A trick to get her own way! A trick to steal Jeff... (sob!)... Jeff......"
CRAZY DAME! LOOK OUT!
SCREECH!
(THE STORY GETS THE TAXI-DRIVER PART RIGHT)
WHAT HAPPENED, MAC... DID YOU HIT HER?
NAW! NAW! FAINTED OR SUMTHIN'! HELP ME PUT HER IN THE CAR... WE GOTTA GET HER TO A HOSPITAL...
(...BUT MISSES THE FACT THAT HUGH GRAVITT WILL BE OFF-DUTY AND DRIVING A CAR NOT REGISTERED IN HIS NAME ON AUGUST 11, 1949)
I LOVED
TRUE CONFESSION STO
JULY 10¢
"I LOVED TO HATE" I LOVED TRUE CONFESSION STORIES NO. 28 COVER-DATED JULY, 1949
GIVE ME THAT PHONE!
WHO IS SHE??
I LOVED
NURSING
ALSO FEATURES TWIN SISTERS. THE GOOD, STUDIOUS JANE AND THE PAMPERED, EVIL PEGGY
THEN I WOULD COPY JANE'S HOMEWORK TO CATCH UP WITH MY SCHOOL MARKS. SHE REPROVED ME BUT NEVER TATTLED ON ME.
YOU'LL NEVER LEARN ANYTHING THAT WAY, PEGGY!
I'LL BE SMART ENOUGH WHEN I GROW UP! DON'T WORRY, JANE, DEAR.

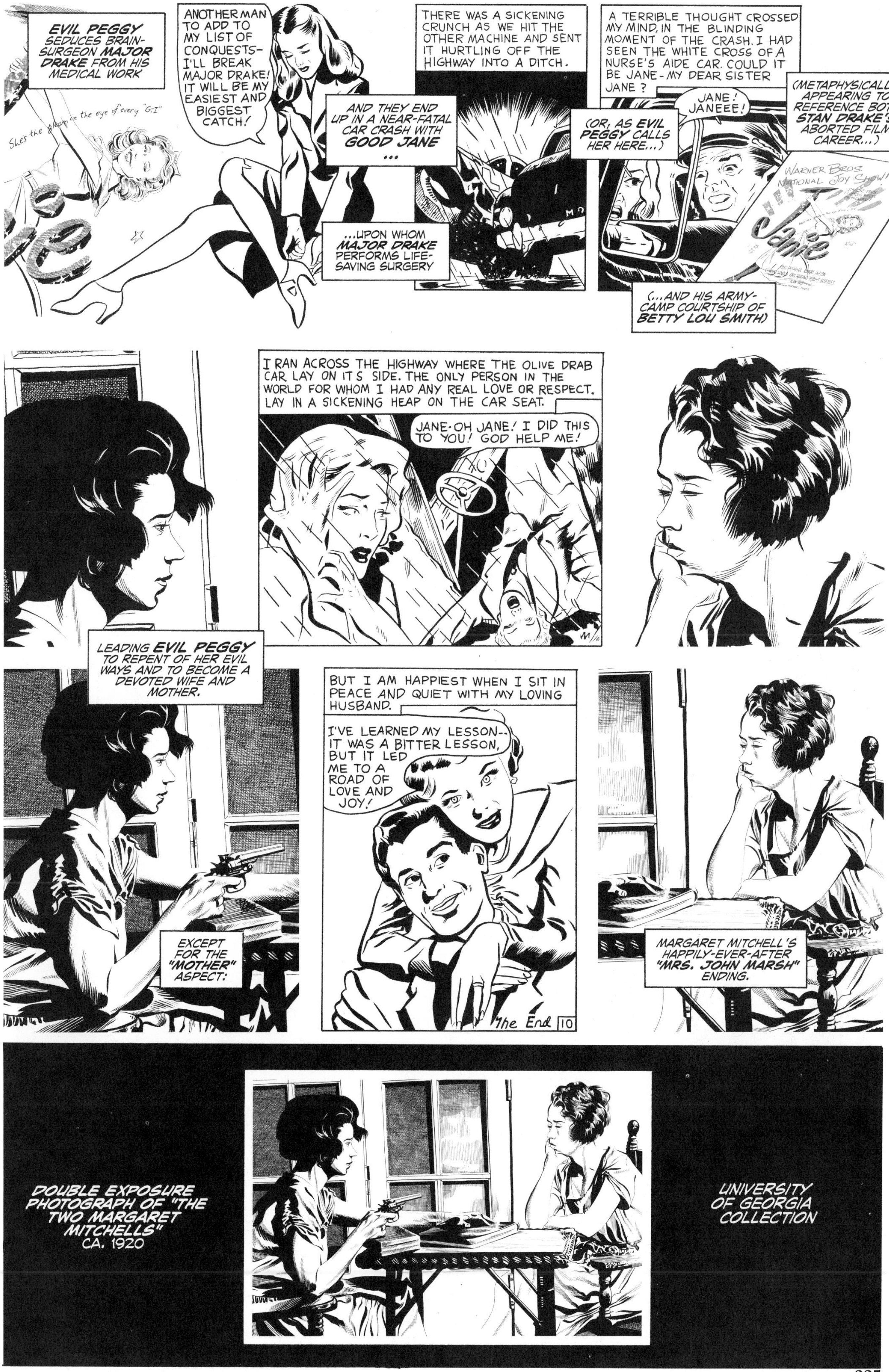

EVIL PEGGY SEDUCES BRAIN-SURGEON MAJOR DRAKE FROM HIS MEDICAL WORK
She's the gleam in the eye of every "G.I."
ANOTHER MAN TO ADD TO MY LIST OF CONQUESTS- I'LL BREAK MAJOR DRAKE! IT WILL BE MY EASIEST AND BIGGEST CATCH!
AND THEY END UP IN A NEAR-FATAL CAR CRASH WITH GOOD JANE ...
...UPON WHOM MAJOR DRAKE PERFORMS LIFE-SAVING SURGERY
THERE WAS A SICKENING CRUNCH AS WE HIT THE OTHER MACHINE AND SENT IT HURTLING OFF THE HIGHWAY INTO A DITCH.
A TERRIBLE THOUGHT CROSSED MY MIND, IN THE BLINDING MOMENT OF THE CRASH. I HAD SEEN THE WHITE CROSS OF A NURSE'S AIDE CAR. COULD IT BE JANE - MY DEAR SISTER JANE ?
(OR, AS EVIL PEGGY CALLS HER HERE...)
JANE! JANEEE!
(METAPHYSICALLY, APPEARING TO REFERENCE BOTH STAN DRAKE'S ABORTED FILM CAREER...)
WARNER BROS. NATIONAL JOY SHOW!
Janie
(...AND HIS ARMY-CAMP COURTSHIP OF BETTY LOU SMITH)
I RAN ACROSS THE HIGHWAY WHERE THE OLIVE DRAB CAR LAY ON ITS SIDE. THE ONLY PERSON IN THE WORLD FOR WHOM I HAD ANY REAL LOVE OR RESPECT. LAY IN A SICKENING HEAP ON THE CAR SEAT.
JANE-OH JANE! I DID THIS TO YOU! GOD HELP ME!
LEADING EVIL PEGGY TO REPENT OF HER EVIL WAYS AND TO BECOME A DEVOTED WIFE AND MOTHER.
EXCEPT FOR THE "MOTHER" ASPECT:
BUT I AM HAPPIEST WHEN I SIT IN PEACE AND QUIET WITH MY LOVING HUSBAND.
I'VE LEARNED MY LESSON-- IT WAS A BITTER LESSON, BUT IT LED ME TO A ROAD OF LOVE AND JOY!
The End 10
MARGARET MITCHELL'S HAPPILY-EVER-AFTER "MRS. JOHN MARSH" ENDING.
DOUBLE EXPOSURE PHOTOGRAPH OF "THE TWO MARGARET MITCHELLS" CA. 1920
UNIVERSITY OF GEORGIA COLLECTION

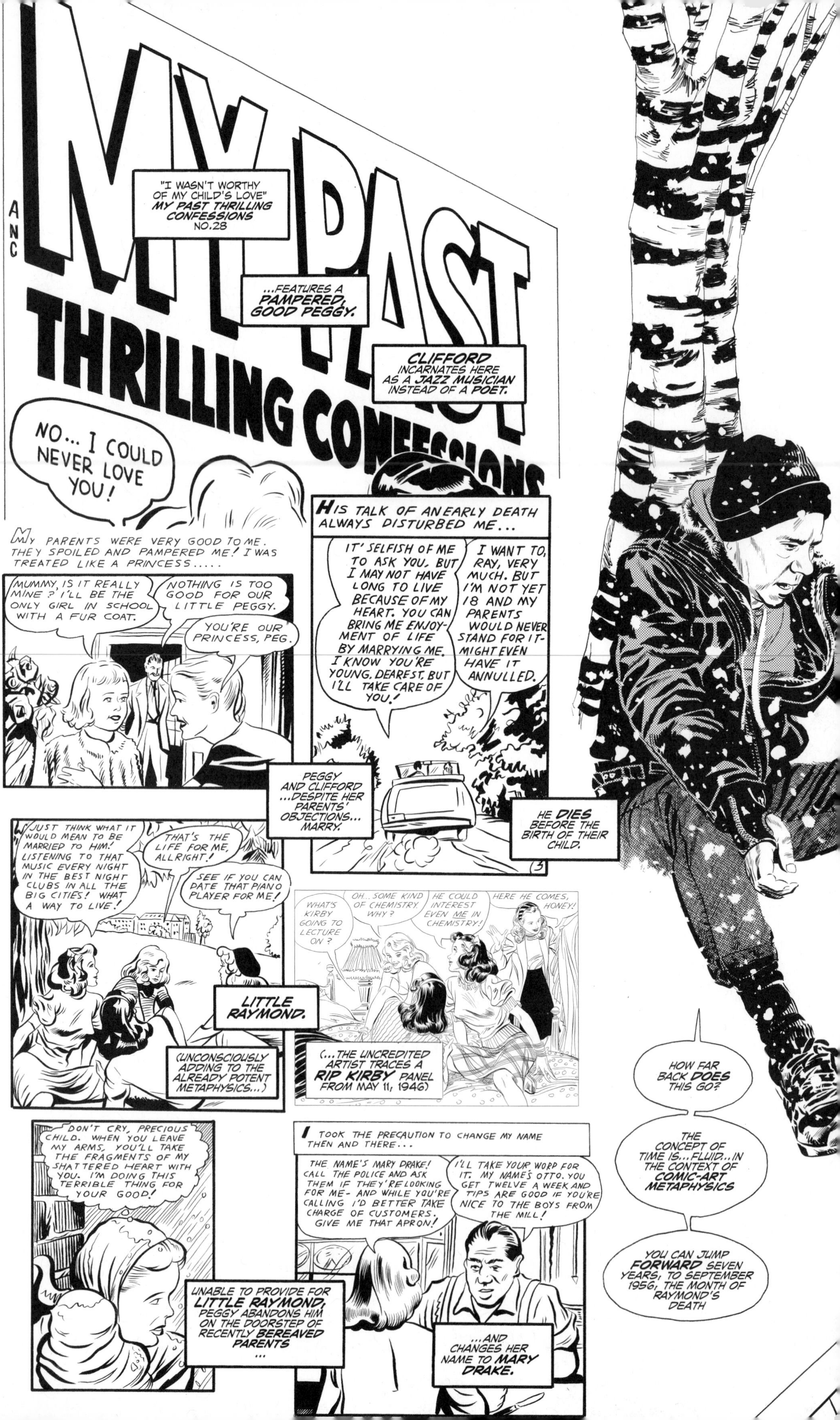
MY PAST THRILLING CONFESSIONS
"I WASN'T WORTHY OF MY CHILD'S LOVE" MY PAST THRILLING CONFESSIONS NO.28
...FEATURES A PAMPERED, GOOD PEGGY.
CLIFFORD INCARNATES HERE AS A JAZZ MUSICIAN INSTEAD OF A POET.
NO... I COULD NEVER LOVE YOU!
MY PARENTS WERE VERY GOOD TO ME. THEY SPOILED AND PAMPERED ME! I WAS TREATED LIKE A PRINCESS.....
MUMMY, IS IT REALLY MINE? I'LL BE THE ONLY GIRL IN SCHOOL WITH A FUR COAT.
NOTHING IS TOO GOOD FOR OUR LITTLE PEGGY.
YOU'RE OUR PRINCESS, PEG.
HIS TALK OF AN EARLY DEATH ALWAYS DISTURBED ME...
IT' SELFISH OF ME TO ASK YOU, BUT I MAY NOT HAVE LONG TO LIVE BECAUSE OF MY HEART. YOU CAN BRING ME ENJOYMENT OF LIFE BY MARRYING ME. I KNOW YOU'RE YOUNG, DEAREST, BUT I'LL TAKE CARE OF YOU!
I WANT TO, RAY, VERY MUCH. BUT I'M NOT YET 18 AND MY PARENTS WOULD NEVER STAND FOR IT - MIGHT EVEN HAVE IT ANNULLED.
PEGGY AND CLIFFORD ...DESPITE HER PARENTS' OBJECTIONS... MARRY.
HE DIES BEFORE THE BIRTH OF THEIR CHILD.
JUST THINK WHAT IT WOULD MEAN TO BE MARRIED TO HIM! LISTENING TO THAT MUSIC EVERY NIGHT IN THE BEST NIGHT CLUBS IN ALL THE BIG CITIES! WHAT A WAY TO LIVE!
THAT'S THE LIFE FOR ME, ALLRIGHT!
SEE IF YOU CAN DATE THAT PIANO PLAYER FOR ME!
LITTLE RAYMOND.
(UNCONSCIOUSLY ADDING TO THE ALREADY POTENT METAPHYSICS...)
WHAT'S KIRBY GOING TO LECTURE ON?
OH... SOME KIND OF CHEMISTRY. WHY?
HE COULD INTEREST EVEN ME IN CHEMISTRY!
HERE HE COMES, HONEY!
(...THE UNCREDITED ARTIST TRACES A RIP KIRBY PANEL FROM MAY 11, 1946)
HOW FAR BACK DOES THIS GO?
THE CONCEPT OF TIME IS...FLUID...IN THE CONTEXT OF COMIC-ART METAPHYSICS
YOU CAN JUMP FORWARD SEVEN YEARS, TO SEPTEMBER 1956, THE MONTH OF RAYMOND'S DEATH
DON'T CRY, PRECIOUS CHILD. WHEN YOU LEAVE MY ARMS, YOU'LL TAKE THE FRAGMENTS OF MY SHATTERED HEART WITH YOU. I'M DOING THIS TERRIBLE THING FOR YOUR GOOD!
UNABLE TO PROVIDE FOR LITTLE RAYMOND, PEGGY ABANDONS HIM ON THE DOORSTEP OF RECENTLY BEREAVED PARENTS ...
I TOOK THE PRECAUTION TO CHANGE MY NAME THEN AND THERE...
THE NAME'S MARY DRAKE! CALL THE POLICE AND ASK THEM IF THEY'RE LOOKING FOR ME - AND WHILE YOU'RE CALLING I'D BETTER TAKE CHARGE OF CUSTOMERS. GIVE ME THAT APRON!
I'LL TAKE YOUR WORD FOR IT. MY NAME'S OTTO. YOU GET TWELVE A WEEK AND TIPS ARE GOOD IF YOU'RE NICE TO THE BOYS FROM THE MILL!
...AND CHANGES HER NAME TO MARY DRAKE.

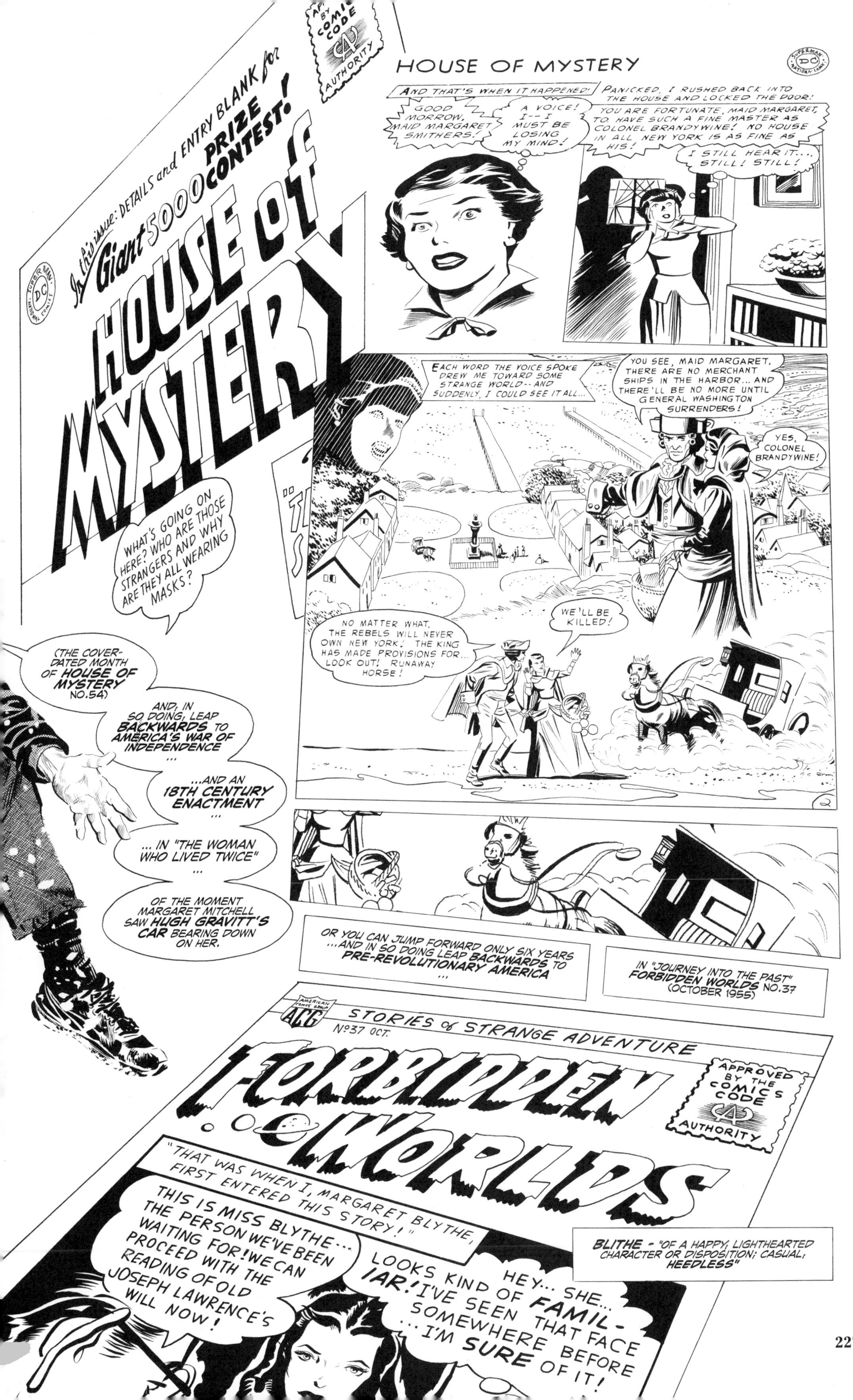
HOUSE OF MYSTERY
AND THAT'S WHEN IT HAPPENED!
GOOD MORROW, MAID MARGARET SMITHERS!
A VOICE! I-- I MUST BE LOSING MY MIND!
PANICKED, I RUSHED BACK INTO THE HOUSE AND LOCKED THE DOOR!
YOU ARE FORTUNATE, MAID MARGARET, TO HAVE SUCH A FINE MASTER AS COLONEL BRANDYWINE! NO HOUSE IN ALL NEW YORK IS AS FINE AS HIS!
I STILL HEAR IT... STILL! STILL!
In this issue: DETAILS and ENTRY BLANK for Giant 5000 PRIZE CONTEST!
HOUSE OF MYSTERY
EACH WORD THE VOICE SPOKE DREW ME TOWARD SOME STRANGE WORLD-- AND SUDDENLY, I COULD SEE IT ALL...
YOU SEE, MAID MARGARET, THERE ARE NO MERCHANT SHIPS IN THE HARBOR... AND THERE'LL BE NO MORE UNTIL GENERAL WASHINGTON SURRENDERS!
YES, COLONEL BRANDYWINE!
WHAT'S GOING ON HERE? WHO ARE THOSE STRANGERS AND WHY ARE THEY ALL WEARING MASKS?
NO MATTER WHAT, THE REBELS WILL NEVER OWN NEW YORK! THE KING HAS MADE PROVISIONS FOR... LOOK OUT! RUNAWAY HORSE!
WE'LL BE KILLED!
(THE COVER-DATED MONTH OF HOUSE OF MYSTERY NO.54)
AND, IN SO DOING, LEAP BACKWARDS TO AMERICA'S WAR OF INDEPENDENCE ...
...AND AN 18TH CENTURY ENACTMENT ...
... IN "THE WOMAN WHO LIVED TWICE" ...
OF THE MOMENT MARGARET MITCHELL SAW HUGH GRAVITT'S CAR BEARING DOWN ON HER.
OR YOU CAN JUMP FORWARD ONLY SIX YEARS ...AND IN SO DOING LEAP BACKWARDS TO PRE-REVOLUTIONARY AMERICA ...
IN "JOURNEY INTO THE PAST" FORBIDDEN WORLDS NO.37 (OCTOBER 1955)
STORIES of STRANGE ADVENTURE
Nº37 OCT.
FORBIDDEN WORLDS
APPROVED BY THE COMICS CODE AUTHORITY
"THAT WAS WHEN I, MARGARET BLYTHE, FIRST ENTERED THIS STORY!"
THIS IS MISS BLYTHE... THE PERSON WE'VE BEEN WAITING FOR! WE CAN PROCEED WITH THE READING OF OLD JOSEPH LAWRENCE'S WILL NOW!
HEY... SHE... LOOKS KIND OF FAMILIAR! I'VE SEEN THAT FACE SOMEWHERE BEFORE ...I'M SURE OF IT!
BLITHE - "OF A HAPPY, LIGHTHEARTED CHARACTER OR DISPOSITION; CASUAL; HEEDLESS"

*THEY'RE LIKE METAPHYSICAL **JIGSAW PUZZLE PIECES**, YEARS APART, FROM MARGARET MITCHELL'S LAST MOMENTS, IN THE MIDDLE OF **PEACHTREE STREET**, TRAPPED IN A WEIRD METAPHYSICAL **ZIGGING-AND-ZAGGING** CHOREOGRAPHY WITH HUGH GRAVITT'S CAR.*

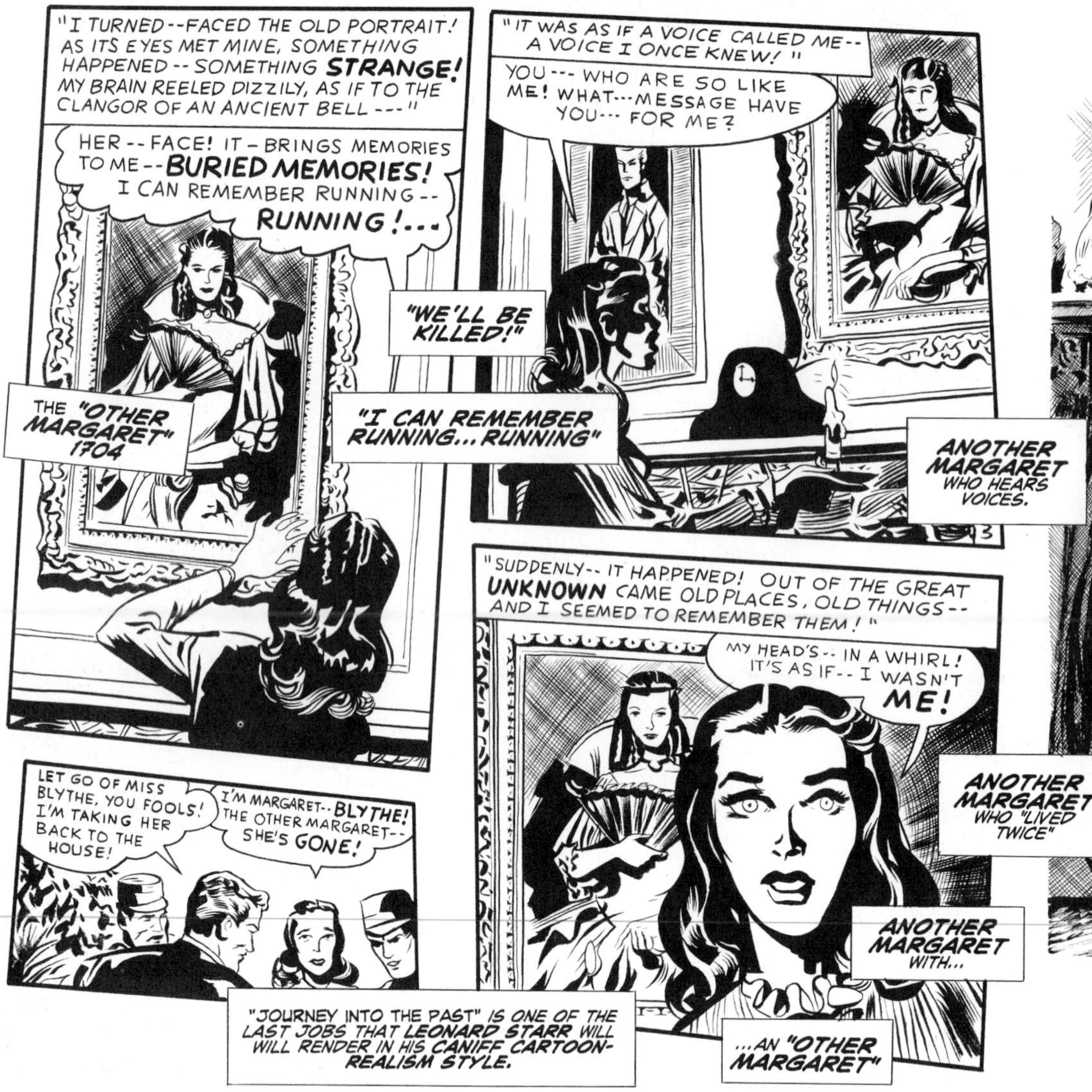

"I TURNED--FACED THE OLD PORTRAIT! AS ITS EYES MET MINE, SOMETHING HAPPENED--SOMETHING STRANGE! MY BRAIN REELED DIZZILY, AS IF TO THE CLANGOR OF AN ANCIENT BELL---"
HER--FACE! IT--BRINGS MEMORIES TO ME--BURIED MEMORIES! I CAN REMEMBER RUNNING--RUNNING!...
"IT WAS AS IF A VOICE CALLED ME--A VOICE I ONCE KNEW!"
YOU---WHO ARE SO LIKE ME! WHAT---MESSAGE HAVE YOU---FOR ME?
"WE'LL BE KILLED!"
THE "OTHER MARGARET" 1704
"I CAN REMEMBER RUNNING... RUNNING"
ANOTHER MARGARET WHO HEARS VOICES.
"SUDDENLY--IT HAPPENED! OUT OF THE GREAT UNKNOWN CAME OLD PLACES, OLD THINGS--AND I SEEMED TO REMEMBER THEM!"
MY HEAD'S--IN A WHIRL! IT'S AS IF--I WASN'T ME!
ANOTHER MARGARET WHO "LIVED TWICE"
ANOTHER MARGARET WITH...
...AN "OTHER MARGARET"
LET GO OF MISS BLYTHE, YOU FOOLS! I'M TAKING HER BACK TO THE HOUSE!
I'M MARGARET--BLYTHE! THE OTHER MARGARET--SHE'S GONE!
"JOURNEY INTO THE PAST" IS ONE OF THE LAST JOBS THAT LEONARD STARR WILL WILL RENDER IN HIS CANIFF CARTOON-REALISM STYLE.


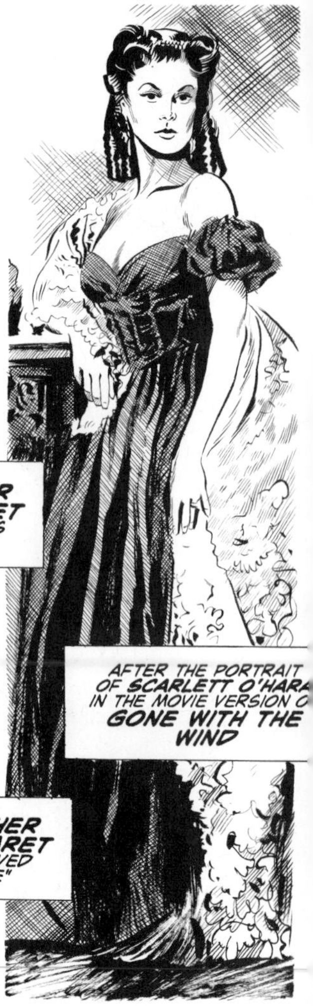

AFTER THE PORTRAIT OF SCARLETT O'HARA IN THE MOVIE VERSION OF GONE WITH THE WIND


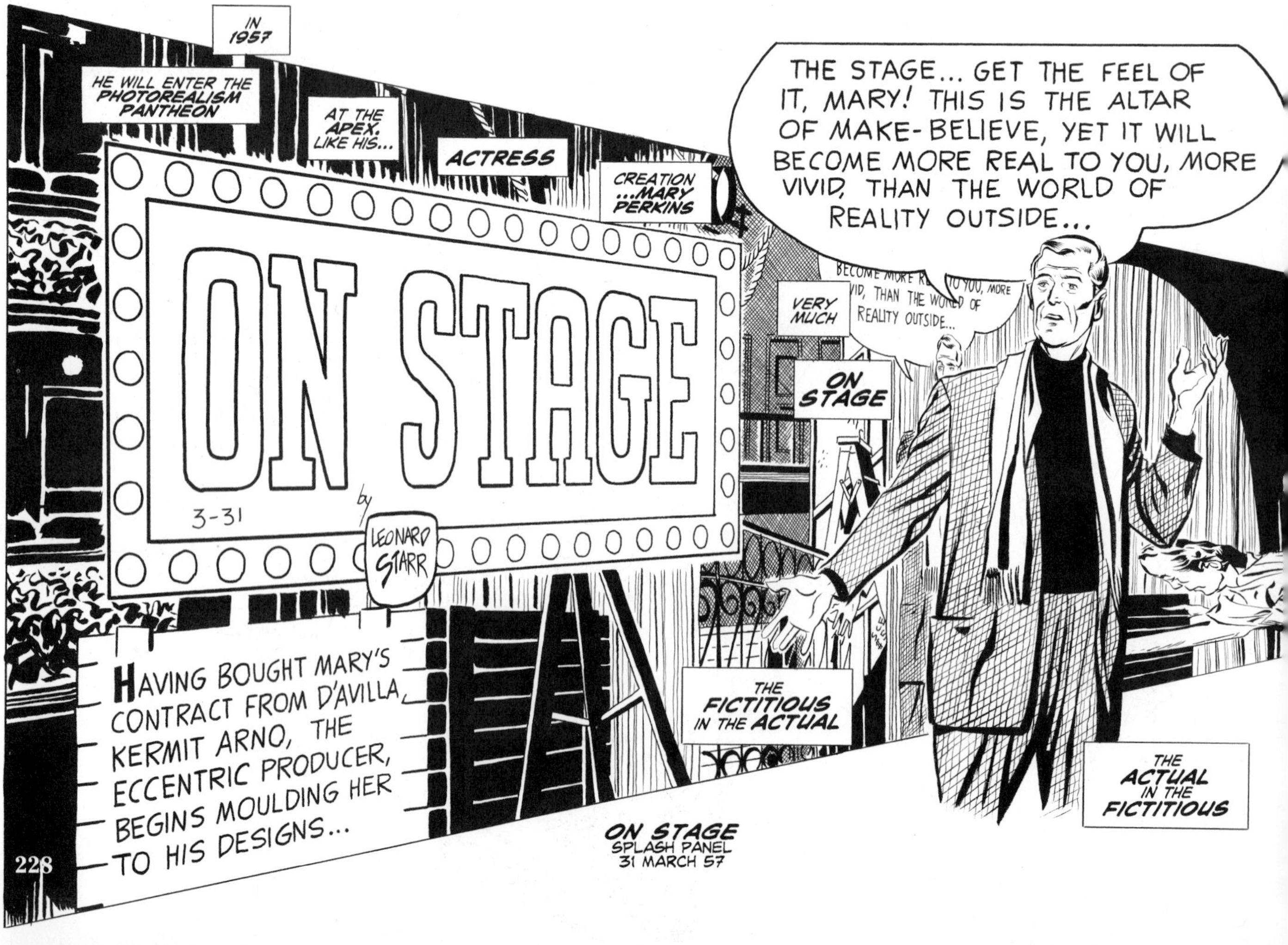

IN 1957
HE WILL ENTER THE PHOTOREALISM PANTHEON
AT THE APEX. LIKE HIS...
ACTRESS
CREATION ...MARY PERKINS
ON STAGE
3-31
by LEONARD STARR
THE STAGE... GET THE FEEL OF IT, MARY! THIS IS THE ALTAR OF MAKE-BELIEVE, YET IT WILL BECOME MORE REAL TO YOU, MORE VIVID, THAN THE WORLD OF REALITY OUTSIDE...
VERY MUCH
ON STAGE
HAVING BOUGHT MARY'S CONTRACT FROM D'AVILLA, KERMIT ARNO, THE ECCENTRIC PRODUCER, BEGINS MOULDING HER TO HIS DESIGNS...
THE FICTITIOUS IN THE ACTUAL
THE ACTUAL IN THE FICTITIOUS


**ON STAGE**
SPLASH PANEL
31 MARCH 57

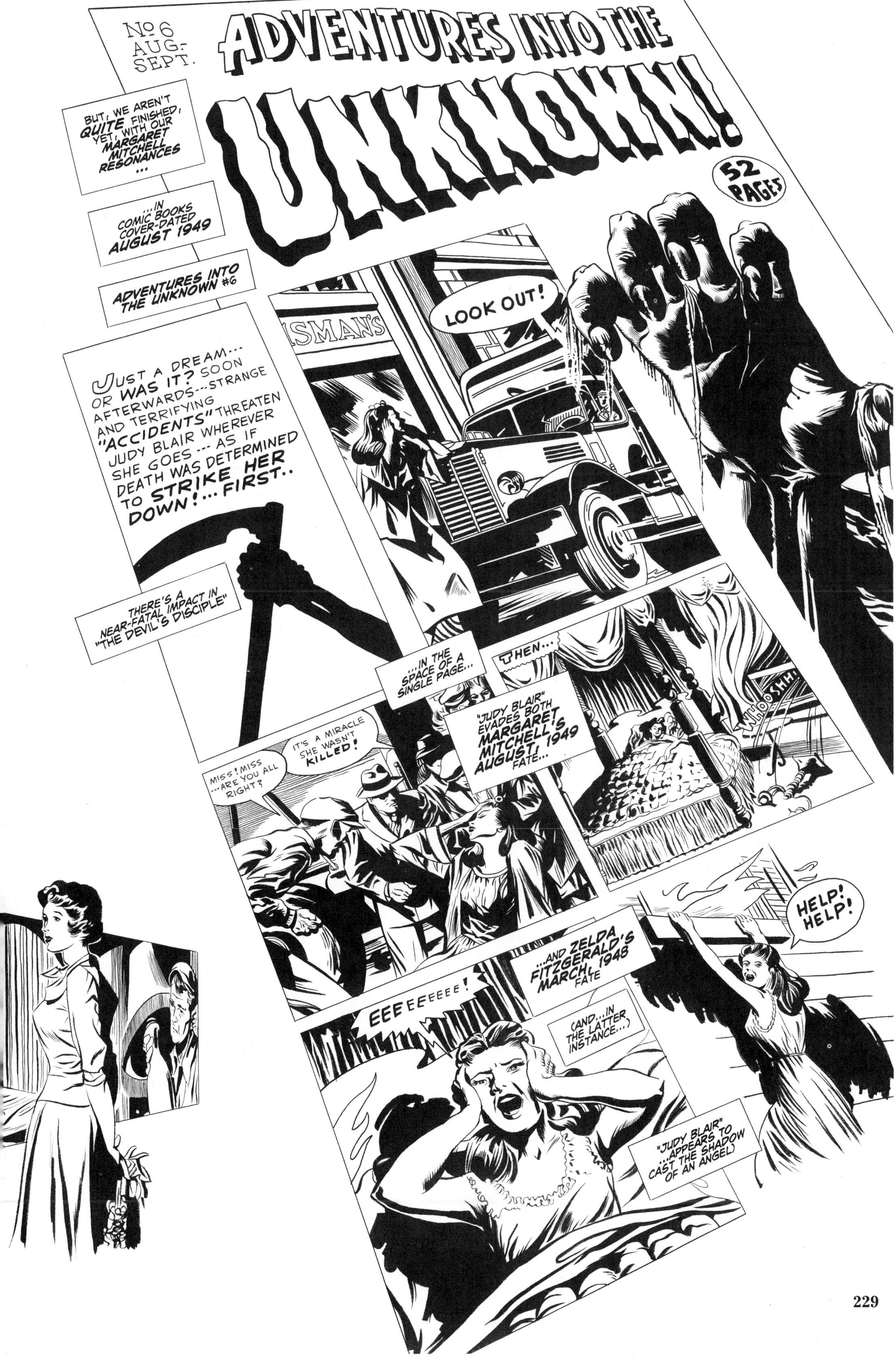

No 6 AUG-SEPT.
ADVENTURES INTO THE UNKNOWN!
52 PAGES
BUT, WE AREN'T QUITE FINISHED, YET, WITH OUR MARGARET MITCHELL RESONANCES ...
...IN COMIC BOOKS COVER-DATED AUGUST 1949
ADVENTURES INTO THE UNKNOWN #6
JUST A DREAM... OR WAS IT? SOON AFTERWARDS--STRANGE AND TERRIFYING "ACCIDENTS" THREATEN JUDY BLAIR WHEREVER SHE GOES -- AS IF DEATH WAS DETERMINED TO STRIKE HER DOWN!... FIRST..
LOOK OUT!
ISMAN'S
THERE'S A NEAR-FATAL IMPACT IN "THE DEVIL'S DISCIPLE"
...IN THE SPACE OF A SINGLE PAGE...
THEN...
"JUDY BLAIR" EVADES BOTH MARGARET MITCHELL'S AUGUST, 1949 FATE...
WHOOSH
MISS! MISS --ARE YOU ALL RIGHT?
IT'S A MIRACLE SHE WASN'T KILLED!
...AND ZELDA FITZGERALD'S MARCH, 1948 FATE
HELP! HELP!
EEEEEEEEE!
(AND...IN THE LATTER INSTANCE...)
"JUDY BLAIR" ...APPEARS TO CAST THE SHADOW OF AN ANGEL)

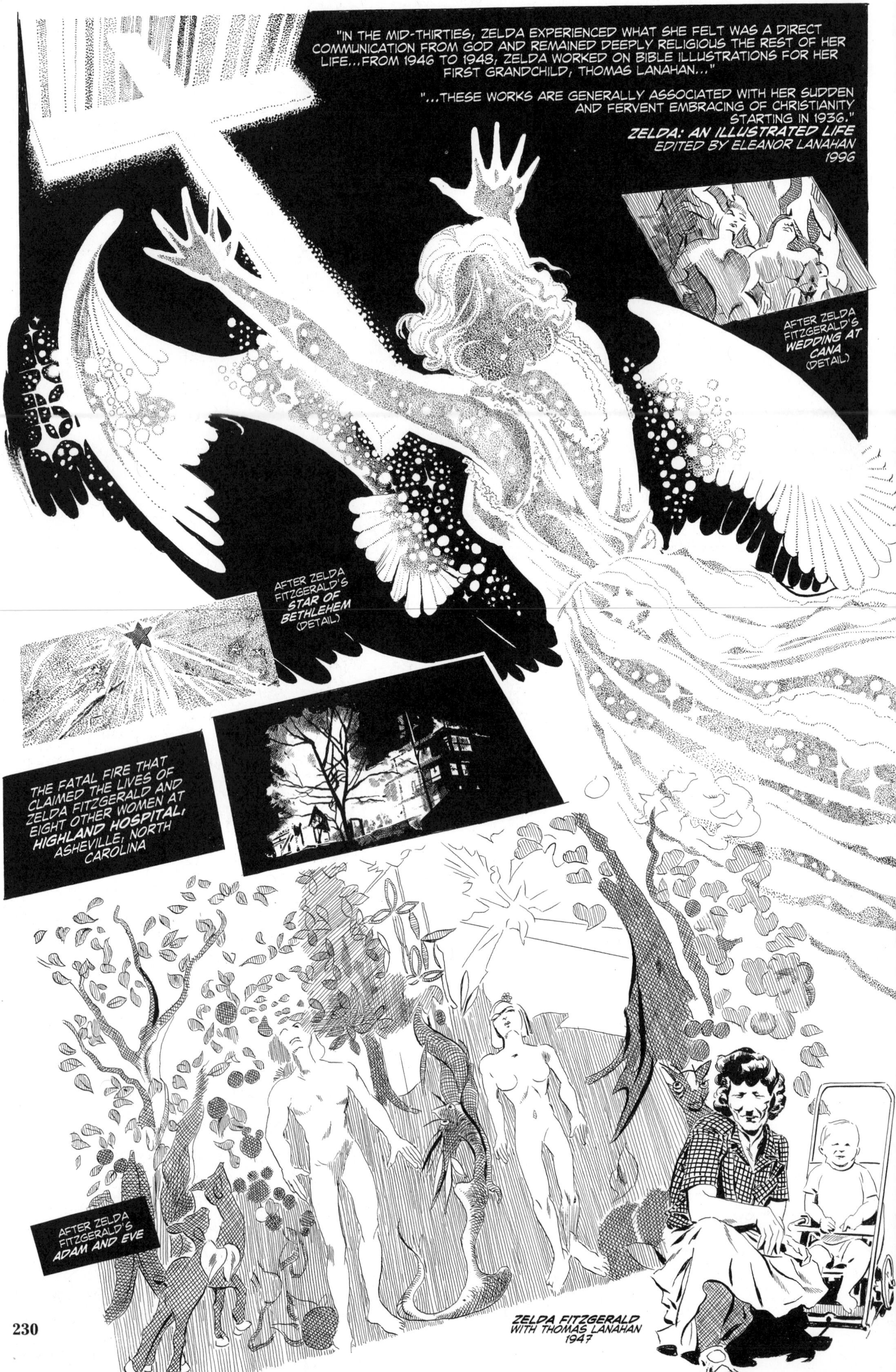
"IN THE MID-THIRTIES, ZELDA EXPERIENCED WHAT SHE FELT WAS A DIRECT COMMUNICATION FROM GOD AND REMAINED DEEPLY RELIGIOUS THE REST OF HER LIFE...FROM 1946 TO 1948, ZELDA WORKED ON BIBLE ILLUSTRATIONS FOR HER FIRST GRANDCHILD, THOMAS LANAHAN..."
"...THESE WORKS ARE GENERALLY ASSOCIATED WITH HER SUDDEN AND FERVENT EMBRACING OF CHRISTIANITY STARTING IN 1936."
ZELDA: AN ILLUSTRATED LIFE
EDITED BY ELEANOR LANAHAN
1996
AFTER ZELDA FITZGERALD'S WEDDING AT CANA (DETAIL)
AFTER ZELDA FITZGERALD'S STAR OF BETHLEHEM (DETAIL)
THE FATAL FIRE THAT CLAIMED THE LIVES OF ZELDA FITZGERALD AND EIGHT OTHER WOMEN AT HIGHLAND HOSPITAL, ASHEVILLE, NORTH CAROLINA
AFTER ZELDA FITZGERALD'S ADAM AND EVE
ZELDA FITZGERALD WITH THOMAS LANAHAN 1947

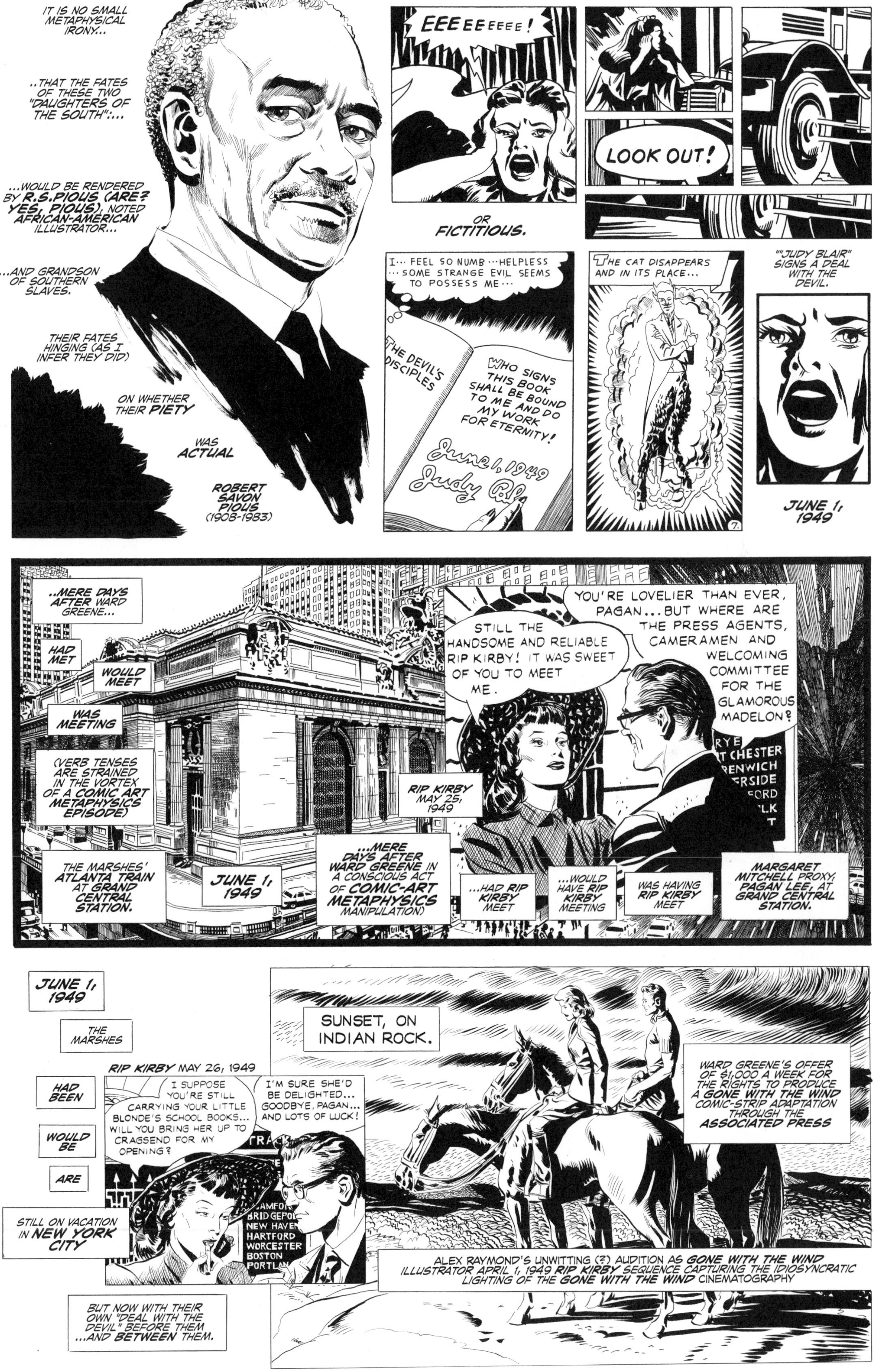

IT IS NO SMALL METAPHYSICAL IRONY...
..THAT THE FATES OF THESE TWO "DAUGHTERS OF THE SOUTH":...
...WOULD BE RENDERED BY R.S.PIOUS (ARE? YES, PIOUS), NOTED AFRICAN-AMERICAN ILLUSTRATOR...
...AND GRANDSON OF SOUTHERN SLAVES.
THEIR FATES HINGING (AS I INFER THEY DID)
ON WHETHER THEIR PIETY
WAS ACTUAL
ROBERT SAVON PIOUS (1908-1983)
EEEEEEEEE!
LOOK OUT!
OR FICTITIOUS.
I... FEEL SO NUMB... HELPLESS ... SOME STRANGE EVIL SEEMS TO POSSESS ME...
THE DEVIL'S DISCIPLES
WHO SIGNS THIS BOOK SHALL BE BOUND TO ME AND DO MY WORK FOR ETERNITY!
June 1, 1949
Judy Bl
THE CAT DISAPPEARS AND IN ITS PLACE...
7.
"JUDY BLAIR" SIGNS A DEAL WITH THE DEVIL.
JUNE 1, 1949
..MERE DAYS AFTER WARD GREENE...
HAD MET
WOULD MEET
WAS MEETING
(VERB TENSES ARE STRAINED IN THE VORTEX OF A COMIC ART METAPHYSICS EPISODE)
THE MARSHES' ATLANTA TRAIN AT GRAND CENTRAL STATION.
JUNE 1, 1949
RIP KIRBY MAY 25, 1949
...MERE DAYS AFTER WARD GREENE IN A CONSCIOUS ACT OF COMIC-ART METAPHYSICS MANIPULATION)
STILL THE HANDSOME AND RELIABLE RIP KIRBY! IT WAS SWEET OF YOU TO MEET ME.
YOU'RE LOVELIER THAN EVER, PAGAN... BUT WHERE ARE THE PRESS AGENTS, CAMERAMEN AND WELCOMING COMMITTEE FOR THE GLAMOROUS MADELON?
RYE
T CHESTER
RENWICH
ERSIDE
FORD
LK
T
...HAD RIP KIRBY MEET
...WOULD HAVE RIP KIRBY MEETING
WAS HAVING RIP KIRBY MEET
MARGARET MITCHELL PROXY, PAGAN LEE, AT GRAND CENTRAL STATION.
JUNE 1, 1949
THE MARSHES
HAD BEEN
WOULD BE
ARE
STILL ON VACATION IN NEW YORK CITY
RIP KIRBY MAY 26, 1949
I SUPPOSE YOU'RE STILL CARRYING YOUR LITTLE BLONDE'S SCHOOL BOOKS... WILL YOU BRING HER UP TO CRAGSEND FOR MY OPENING?
I'M SURE SHE'D BE DELIGHTED... GOODBYE, PAGAN... AND LOTS OF LUCK!
TRACK
STAMFOR
BRIDGEPO
NEW HAVE
HARTFORD
WORCESTER
BOSTON
PORTLA
BUT NOW WITH THEIR OWN "DEAL WITH THE DEVIL" BEFORE THEM ...AND BETWEEN THEM.
SUNSET, ON INDIAN ROCK.
WARD GREENE'S OFFER OF $1,000 A WEEK FOR THE RIGHTS TO PRODUCE A GONE WITH THE WIND COMIC-STRIP ADAPTATION THROUGH THE ASSOCIATED PRESS
ALEX RAYMOND'S UNWITTING (?) AUDITION AS GONE WITH THE WIND ILLUSTRATOR APRIL 1, 1949 RIP KIRBY SEQUENCE CAPTURING THE IDIOSYNCRATIC LIGHTING OF THE GONE WITH THE WIND CINEMATOGRAPHY

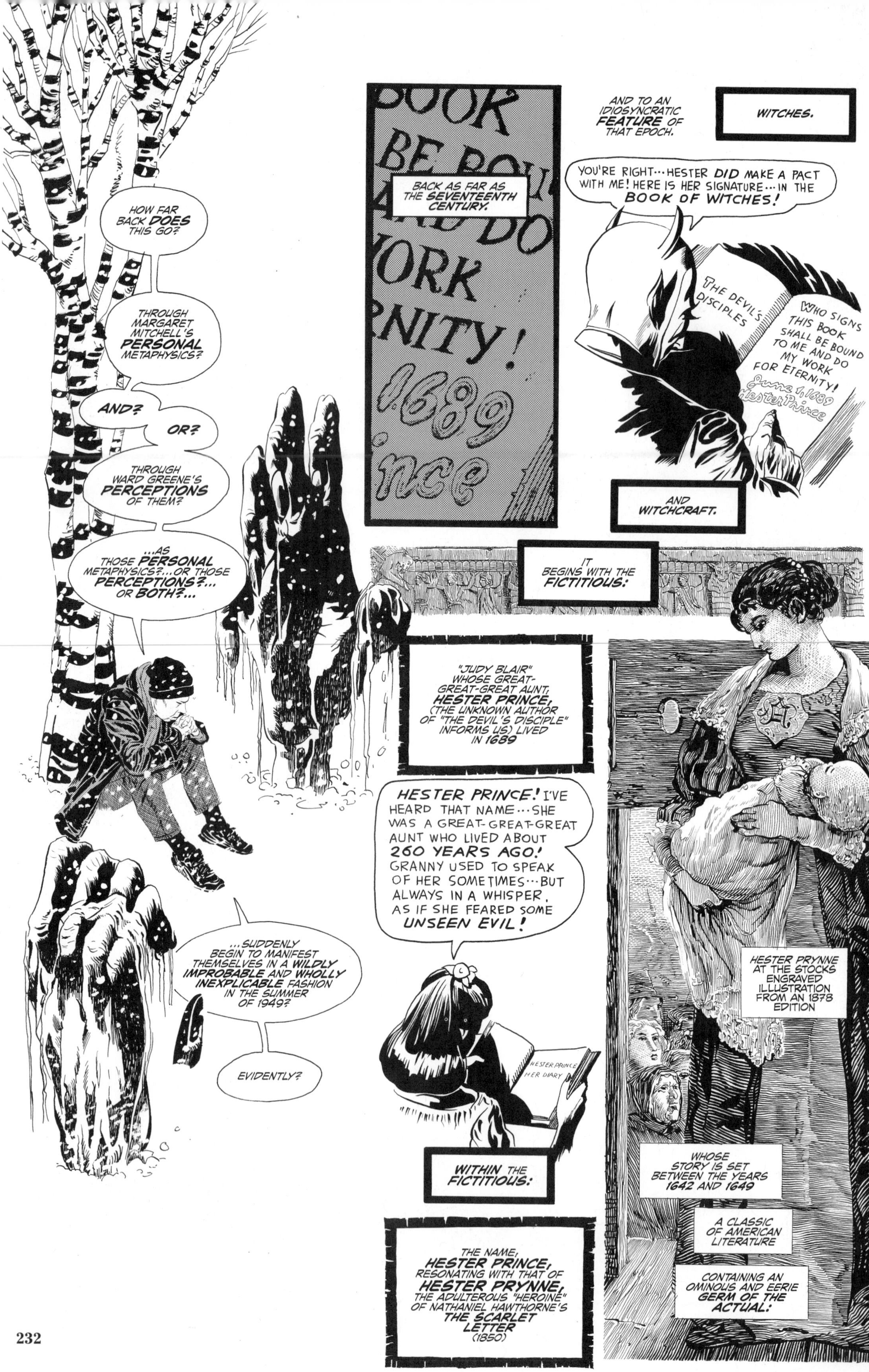

HOW FAR BACK **DOES** THIS GO?
THROUGH MARGARET MITCHELL'S **PERSONAL** METAPHYSICS?
**AND?**
**OR?**
THROUGH WARD GREENE'S **PERCEPTIONS** OF THEM?
...AS THOSE **PERSONAL** METAPHYSICS?...OR THOSE **PERCEPTIONS?...** OR **BOTH?...**
...SUDDENLY BEGIN TO MANIFEST THEMSELVES IN A **WILDLY IMPROBABLE** AND **WHOLLY INEXPLICABLE** FASHION IN THE SUMMER OF 1949?
EVIDENTLY?
BACK AS FAR AS THE **SEVENTEENTH CENTURY.**
AND TO AN IDIOSYNCRATIC **FEATURE** OF THAT EPOCH.
**WITCHES.**
YOU'RE RIGHT... HESTER **DID** MAKE A PACT WITH ME! HERE IS HER SIGNATURE... IN THE **BOOK OF WITCHES!**
THE DEVIL'S DISCIPLES
WHO SIGNS THIS BOOK SHALL BE BOUND TO ME AND DO MY WORK FOR ETERNITY!
June 1, 1689 Hester Prince
AND **WITCHCRAFT.**
IT BEGINS WITH THE **FICTITIOUS:**
"JUDY BLAIR" WHOSE GREAT-GREAT-GREAT AUNT, **HESTER PRINCE,** (THE UNKNOWN AUTHOR OF "THE DEVIL'S DISCIPLE" INFORMS US) LIVED IN **1689**
**HESTER PRINCE!** I'VE HEARD THAT NAME... SHE WAS A GREAT-GREAT-GREAT AUNT WHO LIVED ABOUT **260 YEARS AGO!** GRANNY USED TO SPEAK OF HER SOMETIMES... BUT ALWAYS IN A WHISPER, AS IF SHE FEARED SOME **UNSEEN EVIL!**
HESTER PRINCE HER DIARY
**WITHIN** THE **FICTITIOUS:**
THE NAME, **HESTER PRINCE,** RESONATING WITH THAT OF **HESTER PRYNNE,** THE ADULTEROUS "HEROINE" OF NATHANIEL HAWTHORNE'S **THE SCARLET LETTER** (1850)
HESTER PRYNNE AT THE STOCKS ENGRAVED ILLUSTRATION FROM AN 1878 EDITION
WHOSE STORY IS SET BETWEEN THE YEARS **1642** AND **1649**
A CLASSIC OF AMERICAN LITERATURE
CONTAINING AN OMINOUS AND EERIE **GERM OF THE ACTUAL:**

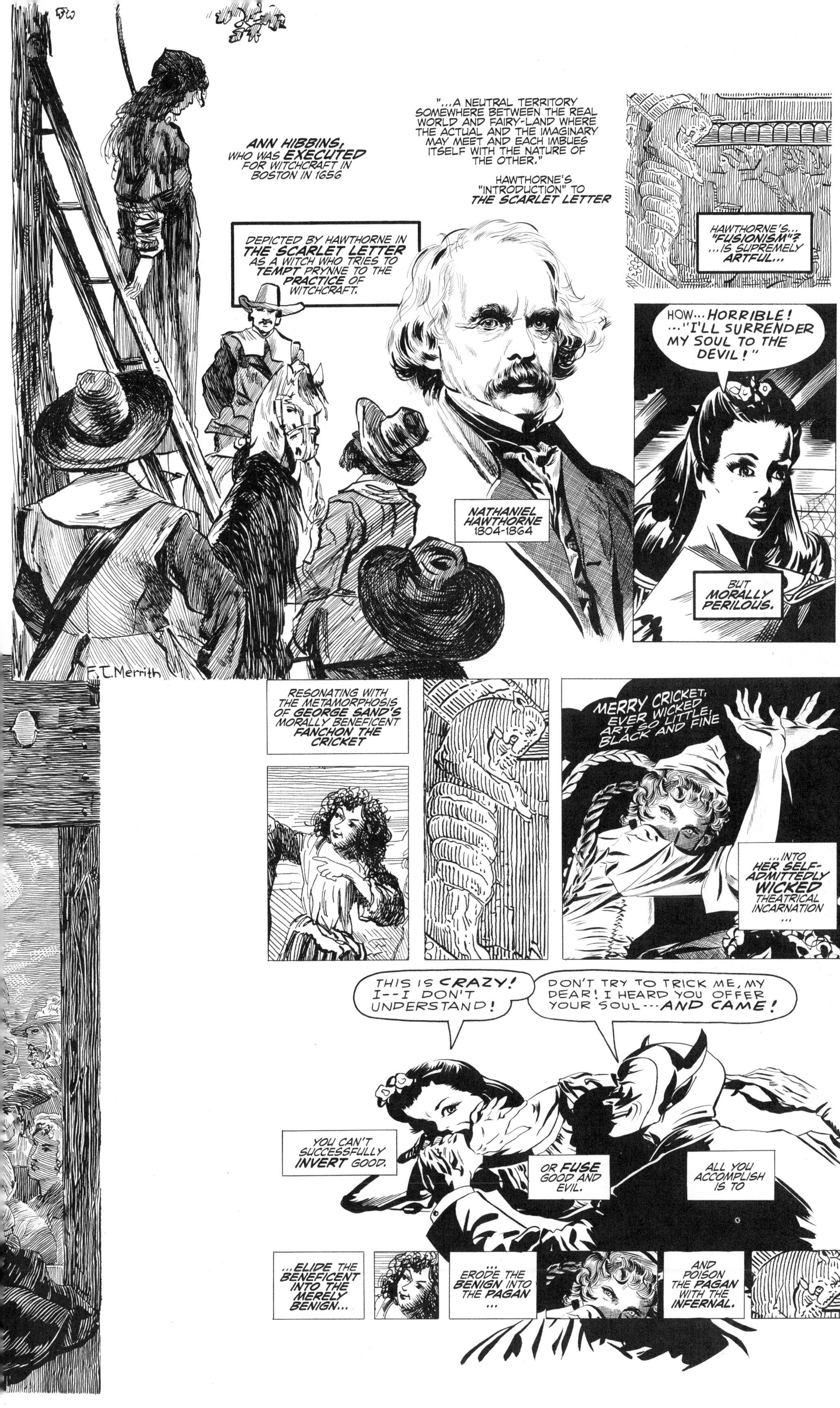

ANN HIBBINS, WHO WAS EXECUTED FOR WITCHCRAFT IN BOSTON IN 1656
"...A NEUTRAL TERRITORY SOMEWHERE BETWEEN THE REAL WORLD AND FAIRY-LAND WHERE THE ACTUAL AND THE IMAGINARY MAY MEET AND EACH IMBUES ITSELF WITH THE NATURE OF THE OTHER."
HAWTHORNE'S "INTRODUCTION" TO THE SCARLET LETTER
DEPICTED BY HAWTHORNE IN THE SCARLET LETTER AS A WITCH WHO TRIES TO TEMPT PRYNNE TO THE PRACTICE OF WITCHCRAFT.
HAWTHORNE'S... "FUSIONISM"? ...IS SUPREMELY ARTFUL...
HOW... HORRIBLE! ..."I'LL SURRENDER MY SOUL TO THE DEVIL!"
NATHANIEL HAWTHORNE 1804-1864
BUT MORALLY PERILOUS.
F.T.Merrith
RESONATING WITH THE METAMORPHOSIS OF GEORGE SAND'S MORALLY BENEFICENT FANCHON THE CRICKET
MERRY CRICKET, EVER WICKED ART SO LITTLE, BLACK AND FINE
...INTO HER SELF-ADMITTEDLY WICKED THEATRICAL INCARNATION ...
THIS IS CRAZY! I--I DON'T UNDERSTAND!
DON'T TRY TO TRICK ME, MY DEAR! I HEARD YOU OFFER YOUR SOUL--- AND CAME!
YOU CAN'T SUCCESSFULLY INVERT GOOD.
OR FUSE GOOD AND EVIL.
ALL YOU ACCOMPLISH IS TO
...ELIDE THE BENEFICENT INTO THE MERELY BENIGN...
...ERODE THE BENIGN INTO THE PAGAN ...
AND POISON THE PAGAN WITH THE INFERNAL.

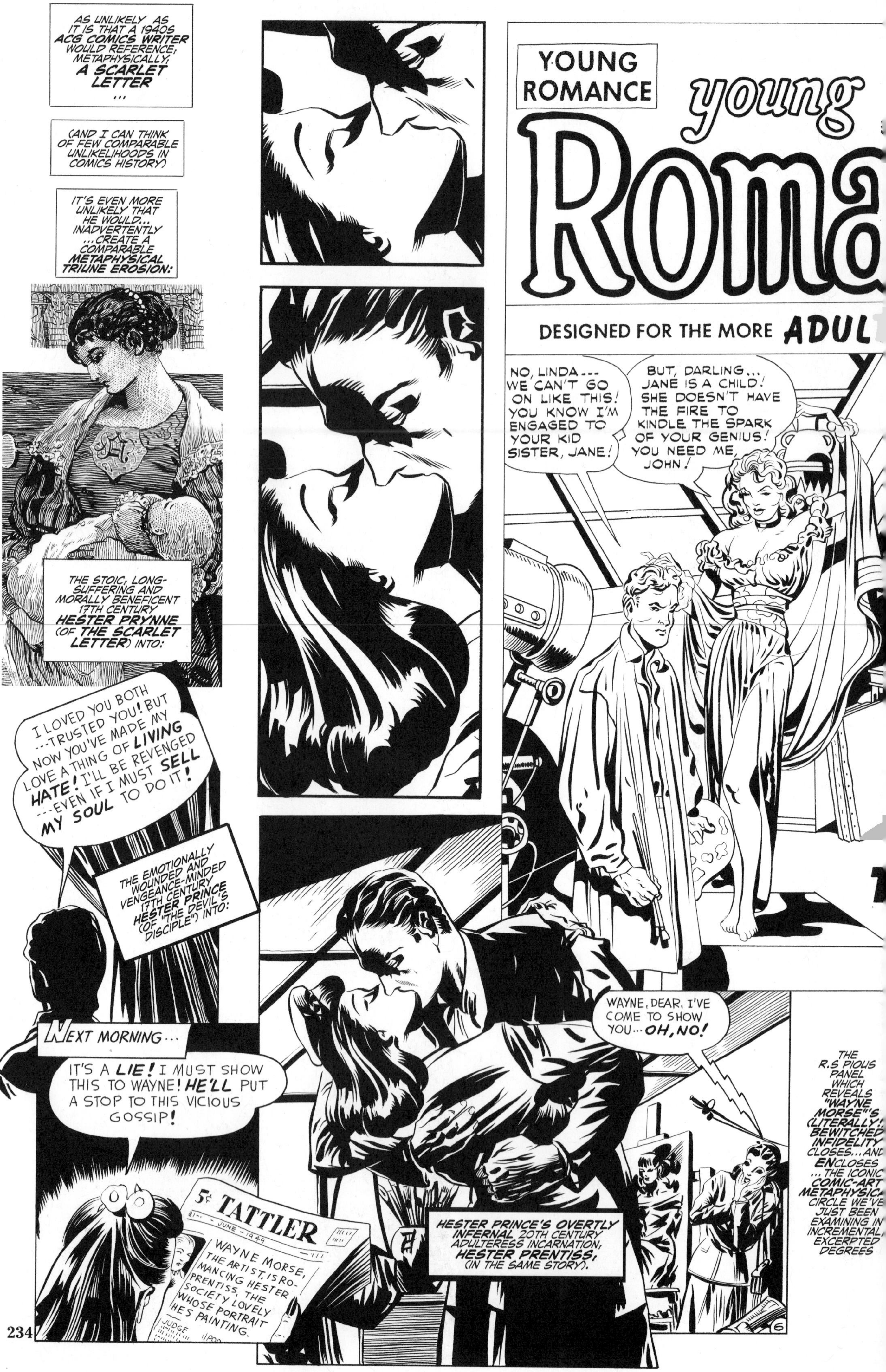

AS UNLIKELY AS IT IS THAT A 1940s ACG COMICS WRITER WOULD REFERENCE, METAPHYSICALLY, A SCARLET LETTER ...
(AND I CAN THINK OF FEW COMPARABLE UNLIKELIHOODS IN COMICS HISTORY)
IT'S EVEN MORE UNLIKELY THAT HE WOULD... INADVERTENTLY ...CREATE A COMPARABLE METAPHYSICAL TRIUNE EROSION:
THE STOIC, LONG-SUFFERING AND MORALLY BENEFICENT 17TH CENTURY HESTER PRYNNE (OF THE SCARLET LETTER) INTO:
I LOVED YOU BOTH --TRUSTED YOU! BUT NOW YOU'VE MADE MY LOVE A THING OF LIVING HATE! I'LL BE REVENGED --EVEN IF I MUST SELL MY SOUL TO DO IT!
THE EMOTIONALLY WOUNDED AND VENGEANCE-MINDED 17TH CENTURY HESTER PRINCE (OF "THE DEVIL'S DISCIPLE") INTO:
NEXT MORNING...
IT'S A LIE! I MUST SHOW THIS TO WAYNE! HE'LL PUT A STOP TO THIS VICIOUS GOSSIP!
5¢ TATTLER
JUNE - 1949
WAYNE MORSE, THE ARTIST, IS RO-MANCING HESTER PRENTISS, THE SOCIETY LOVELY WHOSE PORTRAIT HE'S PAINTING.
YOUNG ROMANCE
young Roma
DESIGNED FOR THE MORE ADUL
NO, LINDA--- WE CAN'T GO ON LIKE THIS! YOU KNOW I'M ENGAGED TO YOUR KID SISTER, JANE!
BUT, DARLING... JANE IS A CHILD! SHE DOESN'T HAVE THE FIRE TO KINDLE THE SPARK OF YOUR GENIUS! YOU NEED ME, JOHN!
WAYNE, DEAR, I'VE COME TO SHOW YOU... OH, NO!
HESTER PRINCE'S OVERTLY INFERNAL 20TH CENTURY ADULTERESS INCARNATION, HESTER PRENTISS, (IN THE SAME STORY).
THE R.S PIOUS PANEL WHICH REVEALS "WAYNE MORSE"'S (LITERALLY!) BEWITCHED INFIDELITY CLOSES... AND ENCLOSES ... THE ICONIC COMIC-ART METAPHYSICA CIRCLE WE'VE JUST BEEN EXAMINING IN INCREMENTAL, EXCERPTED DEGREES

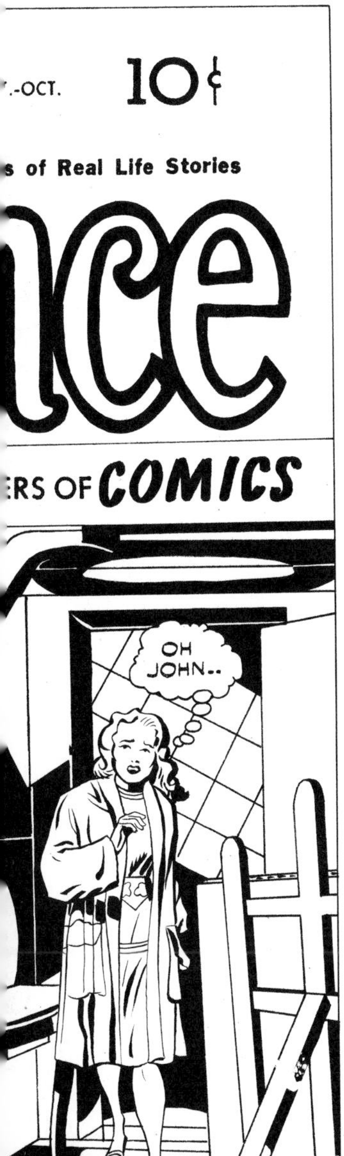
.-OCT.
10¢
s of Real Life Stories
nce
ERS OF COMICS
OH JOHN..
E LOVE
STORIES

THE PANEL RECALLS -- AND APPEARS TO METAPHYSICALLY **CONSUMMATE** -- **SIMON & KIRBY'S** COVER OF **YOUNG ROMANCE** NO.1... FROM EXACTLY **TWO YEARS BEFORE**)

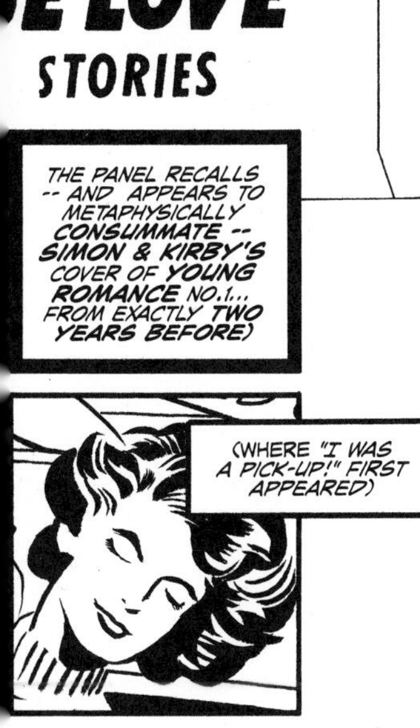
(WHERE "I WAS A PICK-UP!" FIRST APPEARED)

"NOW I KNOW. I KNOW WHAT I WAS LIKE **THAT NIGHT TWO YEARS AGO.**"
(EMPHASIS MINE)

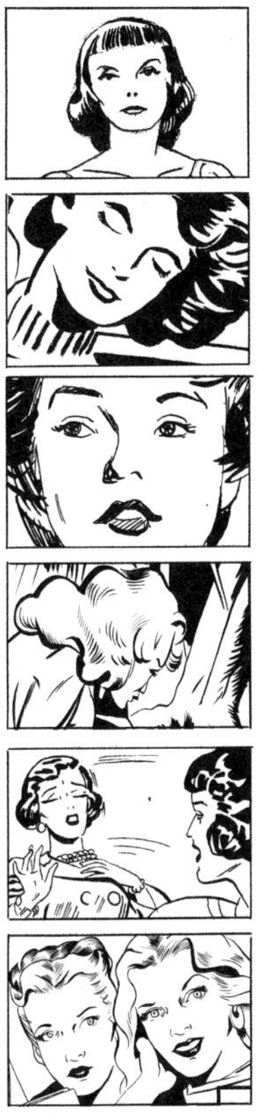

LINKING **TONI BENSON** TO "BAD IMPRESSION"'S **"PEGGY"** TO **SARA JANE STRICKLAND** TO **BESSIE MONTEZ** TO **BABS** AND **BELLE** TO **JANE** AND **PEGGY** TO **PEGGY AND RAYMOND** TO **MARY DRAKE** TO **MAID MARGARET SMITHERS** TO **MARGARET BLYTHE** TO **HESTER PRYNNE** TO **ANN HIBBINS** TO **HESTER PRINCE** TO **HESTER PRENTISS**

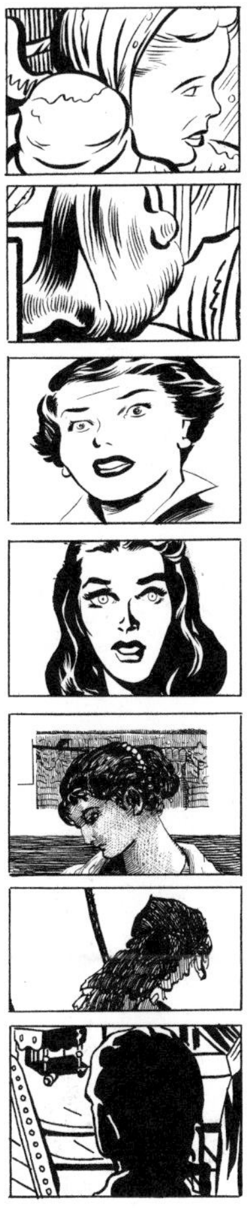

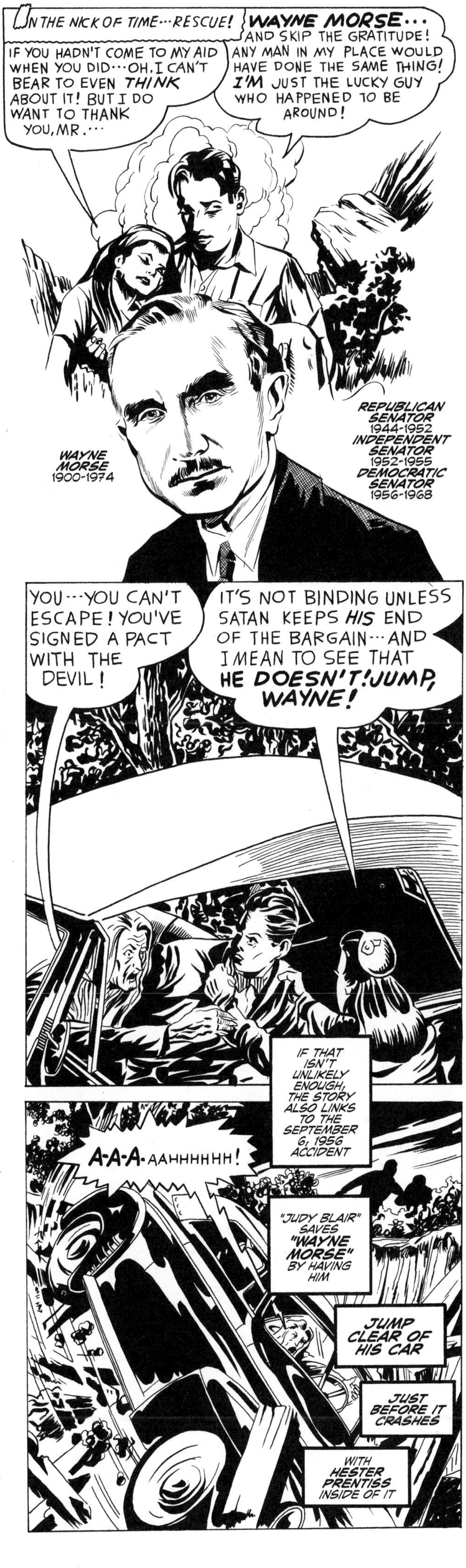
IN THE NICK OF TIME... RESCUE!
IF YOU HADN'T COME TO MY AID WHEN YOU DID... OH, I CAN'T BEAR TO EVEN THINK ABOUT IT! BUT I DO WANT TO THANK YOU, MR...
WAYNE MORSE... AND SKIP THE GRATITUDE! ANY MAN IN MY PLACE WOULD HAVE DONE THE SAME THING! I'M JUST THE LUCKY GUY WHO HAPPENED TO BE AROUND!
WAYNE MORSE 1900-1974
REPUBLICAN SENATOR 1944-1952 INDEPENDENT SENATOR 1952-1955 DEMOCRATIC SENATOR 1956-1968
YOU... YOU CAN'T ESCAPE! YOU'VE SIGNED A PACT WITH THE DEVIL!
IT'S NOT BINDING UNLESS SATAN KEEPS HIS END OF THE BARGAIN... AND I MEAN TO SEE THAT HE DOESN'T! JUMP, WAYNE!
IF THAT ISN'T UNLIKELY ENOUGH, THE STORY ALSO LINKS TO THE SEPTEMBER 6, 1956 ACCIDENT
A-A-A-AAHHHHHH!
"JUDY BLAIR" SAVES "WAYNE MORSE" BY HAVING HIM
JUMP CLEAR OF HIS CAR
JUST BEFORE IT CRASHES
WITH HESTER PRENTISS INSIDE OF IT

THE EXTREME METAPHYSICAL UNLIKELIHOODS WITHIN "THE DEVIL'S DISCIPLE" DON'T STOP THERE.

THERE'S THE NAMING OF "JUDY BLAIR"'S **FICTITIOUS** LIFE-SAVING PORTRAIT-PAINTER FIANCEE, **"WAYNE MORSE"**

INVOKING THE THEN **ACTUAL** OREGON REPUBLICAN SENATOR **WAYNE MORSE,** WHOSE "PROGRESSIVE" SYMPATHIES WERE A SOURCE OF GREAT CONSTERNATION TO HIS REPUBLICAN COLLEAGUES.

THE **OCCULT SEDUCTION** OF THE **FICTITIOUS "WAYNE MORSE"** SEES PRINT **THREE YEARS BEFORE** THE **ACTUAL WAYNE MORSE** ABANDONS THE REPUBLICAN PARTY TO SIT AS AN INDEPENDENT

AN INTRICATE **FICTITIOUS** INVOCATION/ CONJURATION-METAPHOR, INCARNATING AS AN **ACTUAL REAL WORLD EVENT.**

AGAIN, IN THE CONTEXT OF A **1940S ACG COMIC BOOK,** IT SEEMS MORE **A COMPLETE IMPOSSIBILITY** THAN A **MERE UNLIKELIHOOD.**

BUT.

**HERE** IT IS.

BEFORE OUR EYES.

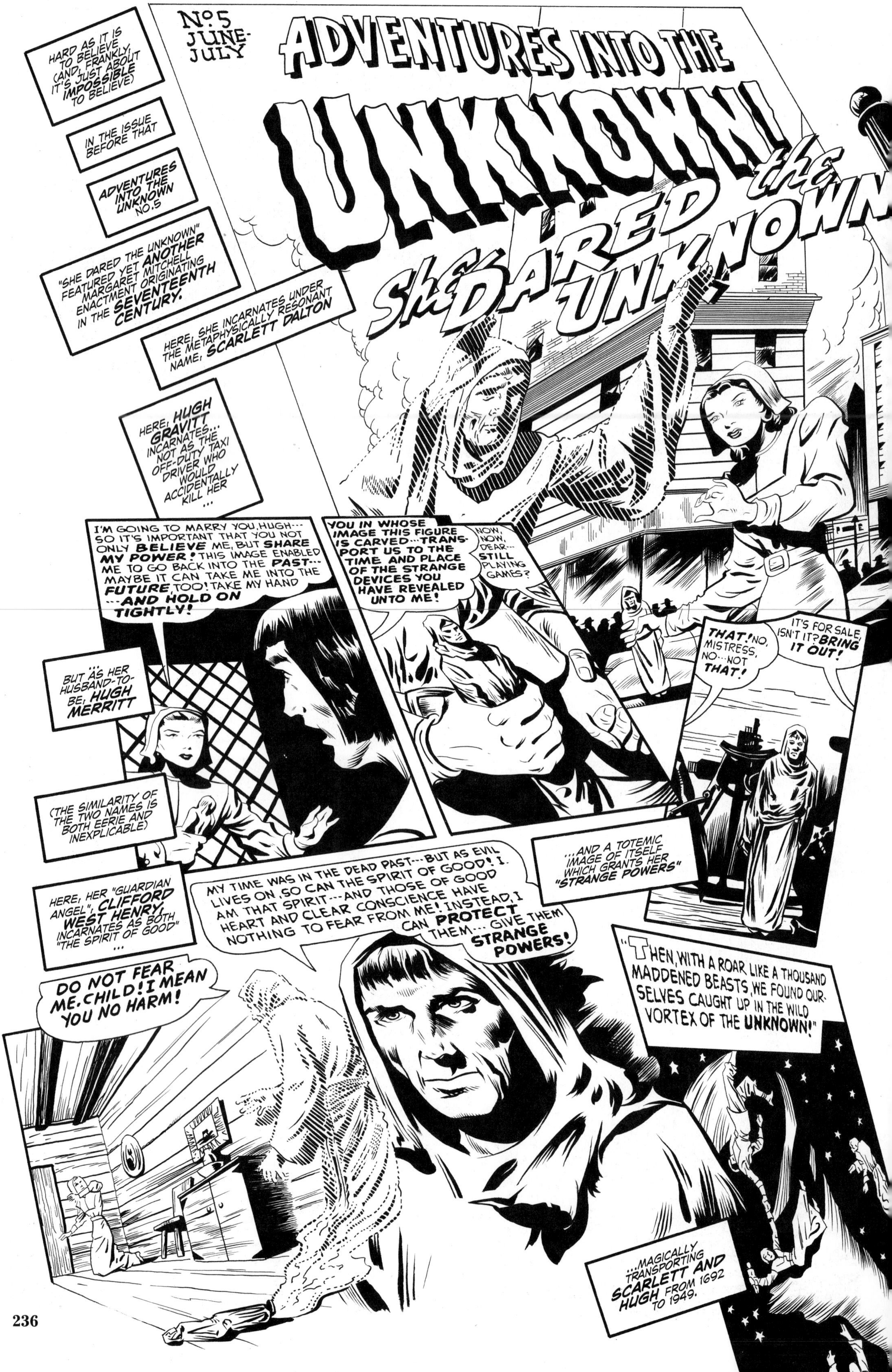

No. 5 JUNE-JULY
ADVENTURES INTO THE UNKNOWN!
SHE DARED THE UNKNOWN
HARD AS IT IS TO BELIEVE, (AND, FRANKLY, IT'S JUST ABOUT IMPOSSIBLE TO BELIEVE)
IN THE ISSUE BEFORE THAT
ADVENTURES INTO THE UNKNOWN NO. 5
"SHE DARED THE UNKNOWN" FEATURED YET ANOTHER MARGARET MITCHELL ENACTMENT ORIGINATING IN THE SEVENTEENTH CENTURY.
HERE, SHE INCARNATES UNDER THE METAPHYSICALLY RESONANT NAME, SCARLETT DALTON
HERE, HUGH GRAVITT INCARNATES... NOT AS THE OFF-DUTY TAXI DRIVER WHO WOULD ACCIDENTALLY KILL HER ...
I'M GOING TO MARRY YOU, HUGH--- SO IT'S IMPORTANT THAT YOU NOT ONLY BELIEVE ME, BUT SHARE MY POWER! THIS IMAGE ENABLED ME TO GO BACK INTO THE PAST--- MAYBE IT CAN TAKE ME INTO THE FUTURE, TOO! TAKE MY HAND ---AND HOLD ON TIGHTLY!
YOU IN WHOSE IMAGE THIS FIGURE IS CARVED--- TRANSPORT US TO THE TIME AND PLACE OF THE STRANGE DEVICES YOU HAVE REVEALED UNTO ME!
NOW, NOW, DEAR--- STILL PLAYING GAMES?
BUT AS HER HUSBAND-TO-BE, HUGH MERRITT
THAT! NO, MISTRESS, NO--- NOT THAT!
IT'S FOR SALE, ISN'T IT? BRING IT OUT!
(THE SIMILARITY OF THE TWO NAMES IS BOTH EERIE AND INEXPLICABLE)
...AND A TOTEMIC IMAGE OF ITSELF WHICH GRANTS HER "STRANGE POWERS"
HERE, HER "GUARDIAN ANGEL", CLIFFORD WEST HENRY, INCARNATES AS BOTH "THE SPIRIT OF GOOD" ...
MY TIME WAS IN THE DEAD PAST--- BUT AS EVIL LIVES ON, SO CAN THE SPIRIT OF GOOD! I AM THAT SPIRIT--- AND THOSE OF GOOD HEART AND CLEAR CONSCIENCE HAVE NOTHING TO FEAR FROM ME! INSTEAD, I CAN PROTECT THEM... GIVE THEM STRANGE POWERS!
DO NOT FEAR ME, CHILD! I MEAN YOU NO HARM!
"THEN, WITH A ROAR LIKE A THOUSAND MADDENED BEASTS, WE FOUND OURSELVES CAUGHT UP IN THE WILD VORTEX OF THE UNKNOWN!"
...MAGICALLY TRANSPORTING SCARLETT AND HUGH FROM 1692 TO 1949.

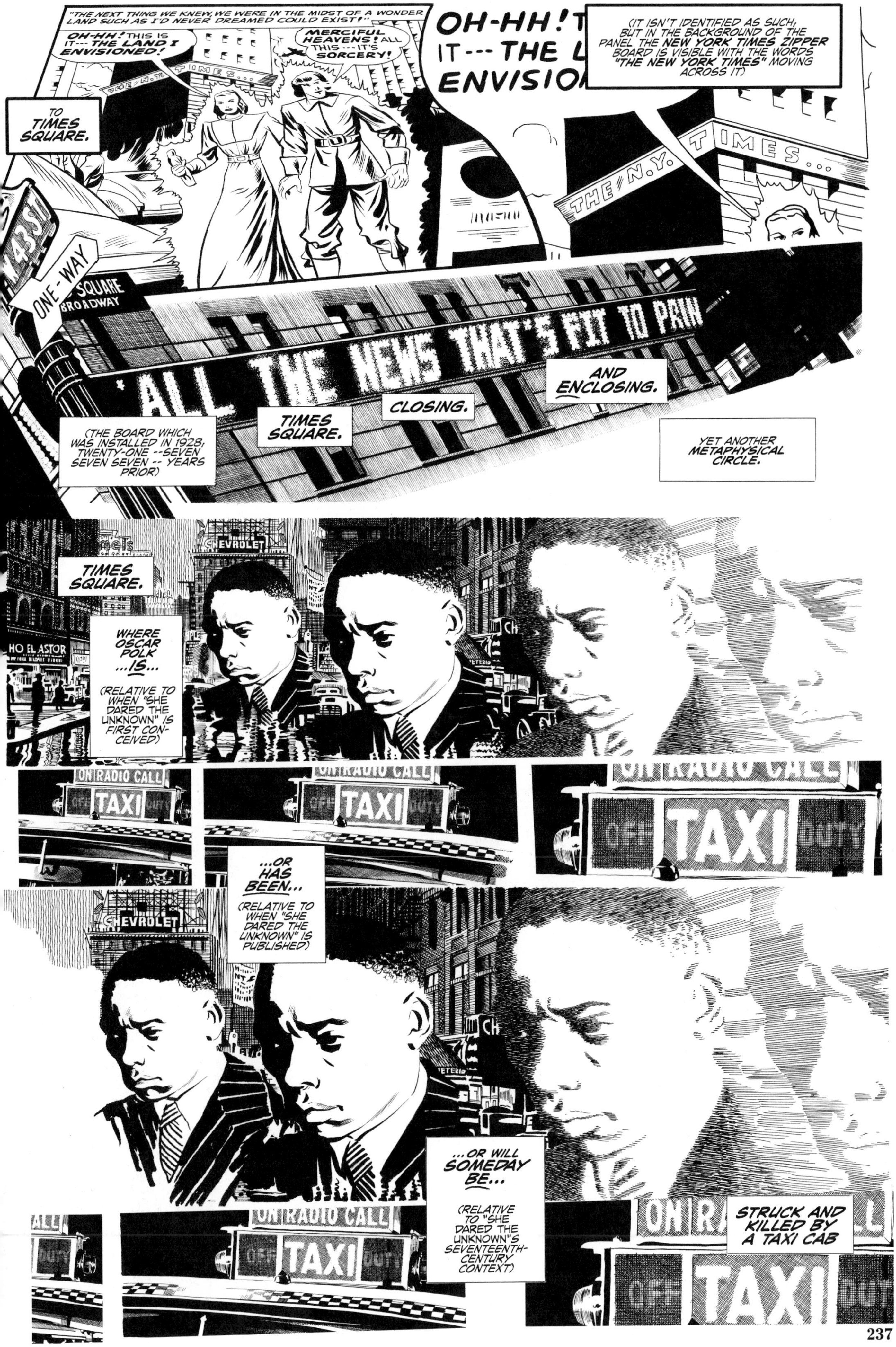
"THE NEXT THING WE KNEW, WE WERE IN THE MIDST OF A WONDER LAND SUCH AS I'D NEVER DREAMED COULD EXIST!"
OH-HH! THIS IS IT--- THE LAND I ENVISIONED!
MERCIFUL HEAVENS! ALL THIS---IT'S SORCERY!
THE N.Y. TIMES...
OH-HH! T
IT --- THE L
ENVISIO
(IT ISN'T IDENTIFIED AS SUCH, BUT IN THE BACKGROUND OF THE PANEL THE NEW YORK TIMES ZIPPER BOARD IS VISIBLE WITH THE WORDS "THE NEW YORK TIMES" MOVING ACROSS IT)
TO TIMES SQUARE.
THE N.Y. TIMES...
ONE-WAY
ALL THE NEWS THAT'S FIT TO PRIN
(THE BOARD WHICH WAS INSTALLED IN 1928, TWENTY-ONE --SEVEN SEVEN SEVEN -- YEARS PRIOR)
TIMES SQUARE.
CLOSING.
AND ENCLOSING.
YET ANOTHER METAPHYSICAL CIRCLE.
TIMES SQUARE.
CHEVROLET
WHERE OSCAR POLK ...IS...
(RELATIVE TO WHEN "SHE DARED THE UNKNOWN" IS FIRST CONCEIVED)
ON RADIO CALL
OFF TAXI DUTY
...OR HAS BEEN...
(RELATIVE TO WHEN "SHE DARED THE UNKNOWN" IS PUBLISHED)
CHEVROLET
...OR WILL SOMEDAY BE...
(RELATIVE TO "SHE DARED THE UNKNOWN"'S SEVENTEENTH-CENTURY CONTEXT)
ON RADIO CALL
OFF TAXI DUTY
STRUCK AND KILLED BY A TAXI CAB

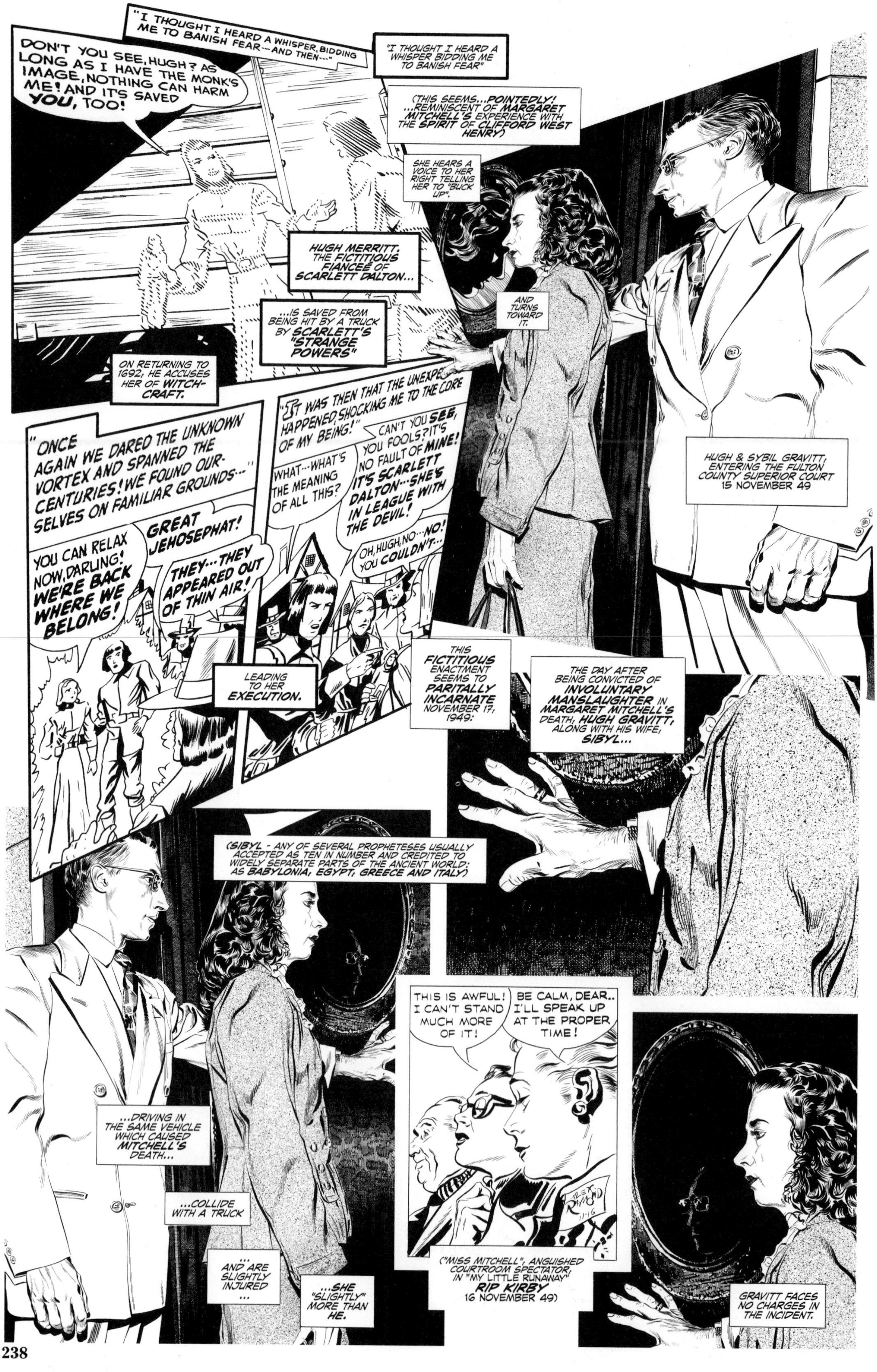

"I THOUGHT I HEARD A WHISPER, BIDDING ME TO BANISH FEAR---AND THEN---"
DON'T YOU SEE, HUGH? AS LONG AS I HAVE THE MONK'S IMAGE, NOTHING CAN HARM ME! AND IT'S SAVED YOU, TOO!
"I THOUGHT I HEARD A WHISPER BIDDING ME TO BANISH FEAR"
(THIS SEEMS...POINTEDLY! ...REMINISCENT OF MARGARET MITCHELL'S EXPERIENCE WITH THE SPIRIT OF CLIFFORD WEST HENRY)
SHE HEARS A VOICE TO HER RIGHT TELLING HER TO "BUCK UP".
HUGH MERRITT, THE FICTITIOUS FIANCEE OF SCARLETT DALTON...
...IS SAVED FROM BEING HIT BY A TRUCK BY SCARLETT'S "STRANGE POWERS"
AND TURNS TOWARD IT.
ON RETURNING TO 1692, HE ACCUSES HER OF WITCH-CRAFT.
"ONCE AGAIN WE DARED THE UNKNOWN VORTEX AND SPANNED THE CENTURIES! WE FOUND OUR-SELVES ON FAMILIAR GROUNDS--"
YOU CAN RELAX NOW, DARLING! WE'RE BACK WHERE WE BELONG!
GREAT JEHOSEPHAT!
THEY...THEY APPEARED OUT OF THIN AIR!
"IT WAS THEN THAT THE UNEXPECTED HAPPENED, SHOCKING ME TO THE CORE OF MY BEING!"
WHAT...WHAT'S THE MEANING OF ALL THIS?
CAN'T YOU SEE, YOU FOOLS? IT'S NO FAULT OF MINE! IT'S SCARLETT DALTON...SHE'S IN LEAGUE WITH THE DEVIL!
OH, HUGH, NO...NO! YOU COULDN'T...
LEADING TO HER EXECUTION.
HUGH & SYBIL GRAVITT, ENTERING THE FULTON COUNTY SUPERIOR COURT 15 NOVEMBER 49
THIS FICTITIOUS ENACTMENT SEEMS TO PARITALLY INCARNATE NOVEMBER 17, 1949:
THE DAY AFTER BEING CONVICTED OF INVOLUNTARY MANSLAUGHTER IN MARGARET MITCHELL'S DEATH, HUGH GRAVITT, ALONG WITH HIS WIFE, SIBYL...
(SIBYL - ANY OF SEVERAL PROPHETESES USUALLY ACCEPTED AS TEN IN NUMBER AND CREDITED TO WIDELY SEPARATE PARTS OF THE ANCIENT WORLD: AS BABYLONIA, EGYPT, GREECE AND ITALY)
...DRIVING IN THE SAME VEHICLE WHICH CAUSED MITCHELL'S DEATH...
...COLLIDE WITH A TRUCK
...AND ARE SLIGHTLY INJURED...
...SHE "SLIGHTLY" MORE THAN HE.
THIS IS AWFUL! I CAN'T STAND MUCH MORE OF IT!
BE CALM, DEAR.. I'LL SPEAK UP AT THE PROPER TIME!
ALEX RAYMOND 11-16
("MISS MITCHELL", ANGUISHED COURTROOM SPECTATOR, IN "MY LITTLE RUNAWAY" RIP KIRBY 16 NOVEMBER 49)
GRAVITT FACES NO CHARGES IN THE INCIDENT.

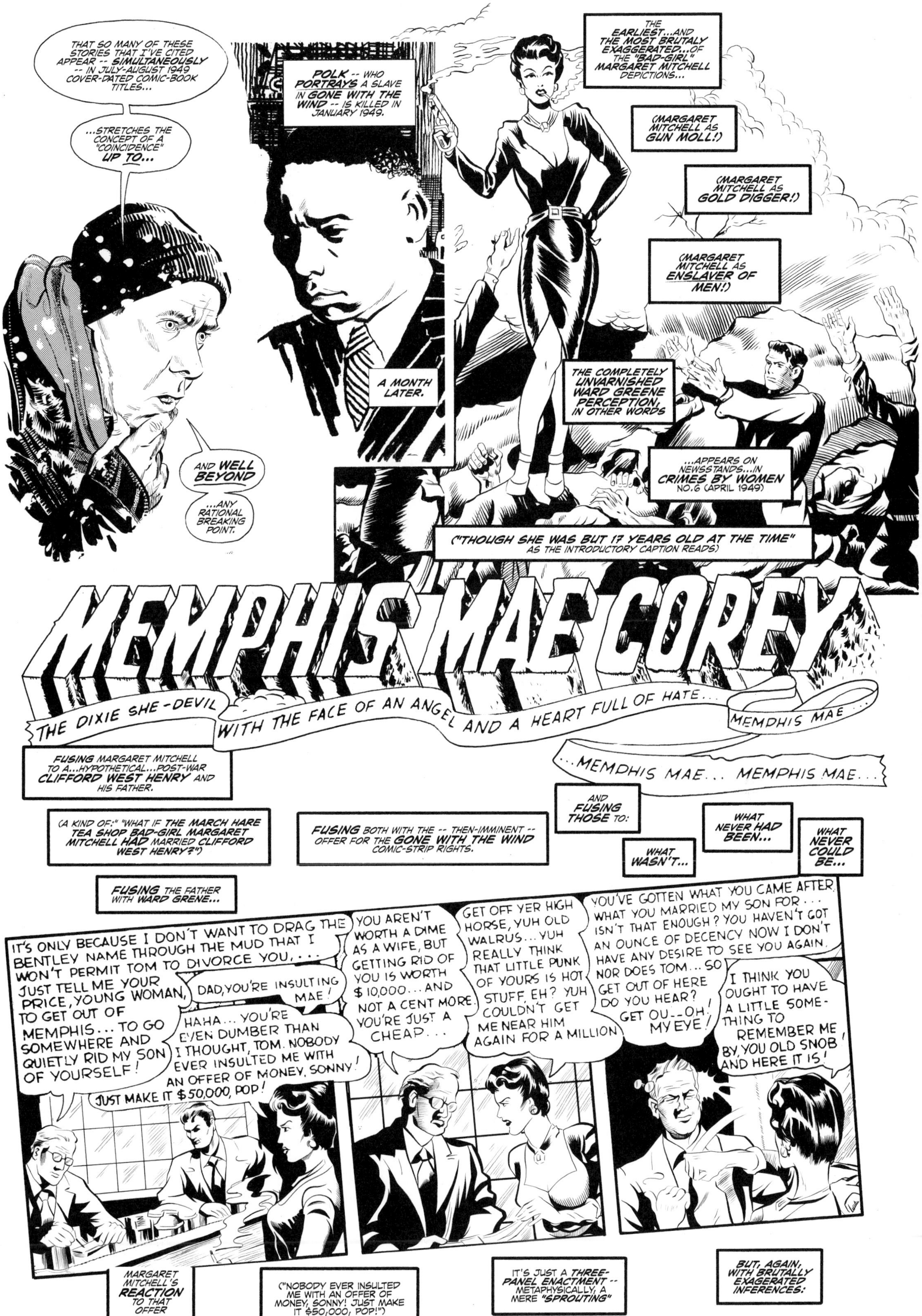
THAT SO MANY OF THESE STORIES THAT I'VE CITED APPEAR -- SIMULTANEOUSLY -- IN JULY-AUGUST 1949 COVER-DATED COMIC-BOOK TITLES...
...STRETCHES THE CONCEPT OF A "COINCIDENCE" UP TO...
AND WELL BEYOND
...ANY RATIONAL BREAKING POINT.
POLK -- WHO PORTRAYS A SLAVE IN GONE WITH THE WIND -- IS KILLED IN JANUARY 1949.
A MONTH LATER.
THE EARLIEST...AND THE MOST BRUTALY EXAGGERATED...OF THE "BAD-GIRL" MARGARET MITCHELL DEPICTIONS...
(MARGARET MITCHELL AS GUN MOLL!)
(MARGARET MITCHELL AS GOLD DIGGER!)
(MARGARET MITCHELL AS ENSLAVER OF MEN!)
THE COMPLETELY UNVARNISHED WARD GREENE PERCEPTION, IN OTHER WORDS
...APPEARS ON NEWSSTANDS...IN CRIMES BY WOMEN NO.6 (APRIL 1949)
("THOUGH SHE WAS BUT 17 YEARS OLD AT THE TIME" AS THE INTRODUCTORY CAPTION READS)
MEMPHIS MAE COREY
THE DIXIE SHE-DEVIL WITH THE FACE OF AN ANGEL AND A HEART FULL OF HATE... MEMPHIS MAE...
...MEMPHIS MAE... MEMPHIS MAE...
FUSING MARGARET MITCHELL TO A...HYPOTHETICAL...POST-WAR CLIFFORD WEST HENRY AND HIS FATHER.
(A KIND OF:" "WHAT IF THE MARCH HARE TEA SHOP BAD-GIRL MARGARET MITCHELL HAD MARRIED CLIFFORD WEST HENRY?")
FUSING THE FATHER WITH WARD GRENE...
FUSING BOTH WITH THE -- THEN-IMMINENT -- OFFER FOR THE GONE WITH THE WIND COMIC-STRIP RIGHTS.
AND FUSING THOSE TO:
WHAT WASN'T...
WHAT NEVER HAD BEEN...
WHAT NEVER COULD BE...
IT'S ONLY BECAUSE I DON'T WANT TO DRAG THE BENTLEY NAME THROUGH THE MUD THAT I WON'T PERMIT TOM TO DIVORCE YOU, ... JUST TELL ME YOUR PRICE, YOUNG WOMAN, TO GET OUT OF MEMPHIS... TO GO SOMEWHERE AND QUIETLY RID MY SON OF YOURSELF!
DAD, YOU'RE INSULTING MAE!
HAHA... YOU'RE EVEN DUMBER THAN I THOUGHT, TOM. NOBODY EVER INSULTED ME WITH AN OFFER OF MONEY, SONNY!
JUST MAKE IT $50,000, POP!
YOU AREN'T WORTH A DIME AS A WIFE, BUT GETTING RID OF YOU IS WORTH $10,000... AND NOT A CENT MORE. YOU'RE JUST A CHEAP...
GET OFF YER HIGH HORSE, YUH OLD WALRUS... YUH REALLY THINK THAT LITTLE PUNK OF YOURS IS HOT STUFF, EH? YUH COULDN'T GET ME NEAR HIM AGAIN FOR A MILLION
YOU'VE GOTTEN WHAT YOU CAME AFTER WHAT YOU MARRIED MY SON FOR... ISN'T THAT ENOUGH? YOU HAVEN'T GOT AN OUNCE OF DECENCY NOW I DON'T HAVE ANY DESIRE TO SEE YOU AGAIN. NOR DOES TOM... SO GET OUT OF HERE DO YOU HEAR? GET OU--OH! MY EYE!
I THINK YOU OUGHT TO HAVE A LITTLE SOMETHING TO REMEMBER ME BY, YOU OLD SNOB! AND HERE IT IS!
MARGARET MITCHELL'S REACTION TO THAT OFFER
("NOBODY EVER INSULTED ME WITH AN OFFER OF MONEY, SONNY! JUST MAKE IT $50,000, POP!")
IT'S JUST A THREE-PANEL ENACTMENT -- METAPHYSICALLY, A MERE "SPROUTING"
BUT, AGAIN, WITH BRUTALLY EXAGERATED INFERENCES:

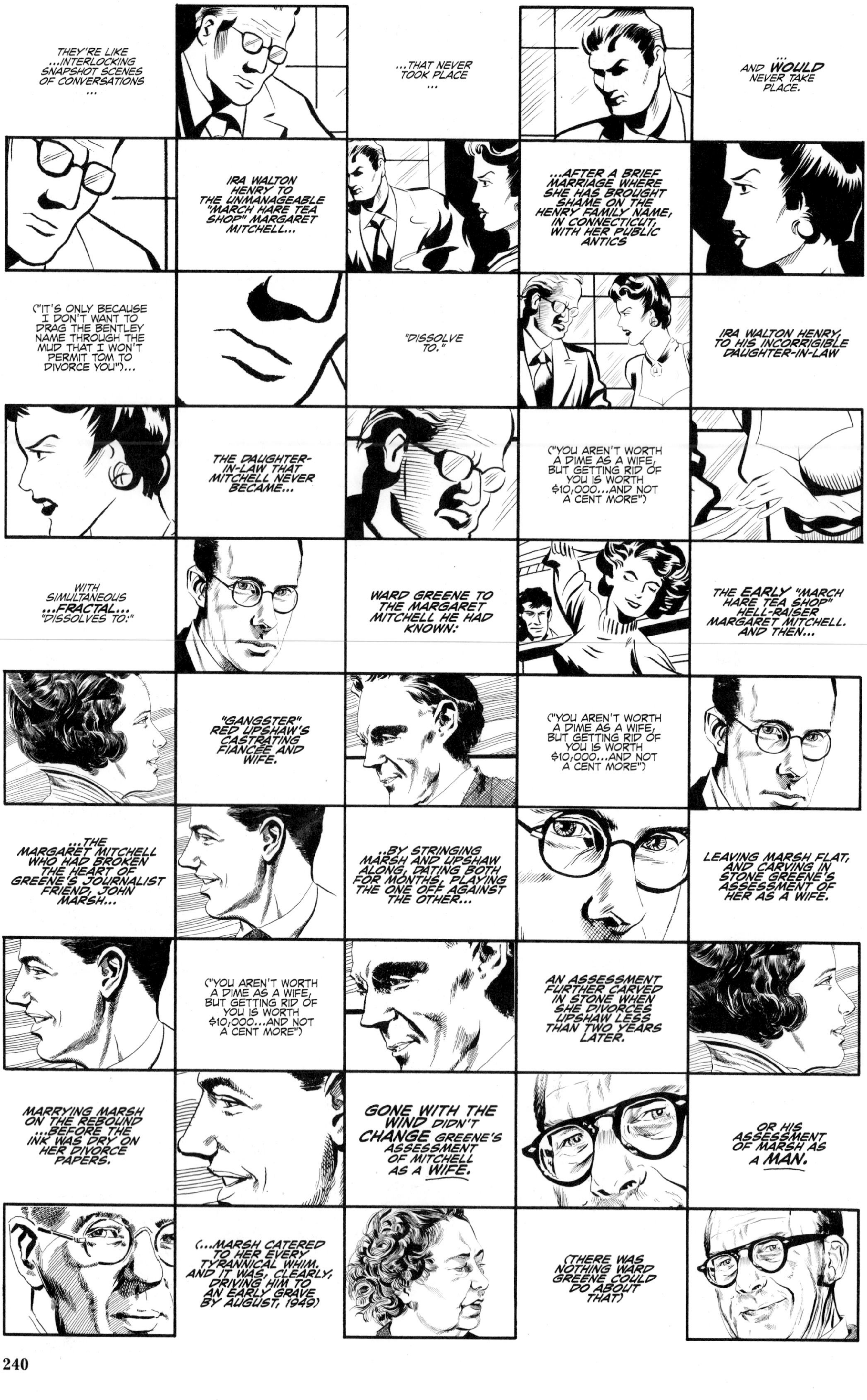
THEY'RE LIKE ...INTERLOCKING SNAPSHOT SCENES OF CONVERSATIONS ...
...THAT NEVER TOOK PLACE ...
... AND WOULD NEVER TAKE PLACE.
IRA WALTON HENRY TO THE UNMANAGEABLE "MARCH HARE TEA SHOP" MARGARET MITCHELL...
...AFTER A BRIEF MARRIAGE WHERE SHE HAS BROUGHT SHAME ON THE HENRY FAMILY NAME, IN CONNECTICUT, WITH HER PUBLIC ANTICS
("IT'S ONLY BECAUSE I DON'T WANT TO DRAG THE BENTLEY NAME THROUGH THE MUD THAT I WON'T PERMIT TOM TO DIVORCE YOU")...
"DISSOLVE TO."
IRA WALTON HENRY, TO HIS INCORRIGIBLE DAUGHTER-IN-LAW
THE DAUGHTER-IN-LAW THAT MITCHELL NEVER BECAME...
("YOU AREN'T WORTH A DIME AS A WIFE, BUT GETTING RID OF YOU IS WORTH $10,000...AND NOT A CENT MORE")
WITH SIMULTANEOUS ...FRACTAL... "DISSOLVES TO:"
WARD GREENE TO THE MARGARET MITCHELL HE HAD KNOWN:
THE EARLY "MARCH HARE TEA SHOP" HELL-RAISER MARGARET MITCHELL. AND THEN...
"GANGSTER" RED UPSHAW'S CASTRATING FIANCEE AND WIFE.
("YOU AREN'T WORTH A DIME AS A WIFE, BUT GETTING RID OF YOU IS WORTH $10,000...AND NOT A CENT MORE")
...THE MARGARET MITCHELL WHO HAD BROKEN THE HEART OF GREENE'S JOURNALIST FRIEND, JOHN MARSH...
...BY STRINGING MARSH AND UPSHAW ALONG, DATING BOTH FOR MONTHS, PLAYING THE ONE OFF AGAINST THE OTHER...
LEAVING MARSH FLAT, AND CARVING IN STONE GREENE'S ASSESSMENT OF HER AS A WIFE.
("YOU AREN'T WORTH A DIME AS A WIFE, BUT GETTING RID OF YOU IS WORTH $10,000...AND NOT A CENT MORE")
AN ASSESSMENT FURTHER CARVED IN STONE WHEN SHE DIVORCES UPSHAW LESS THAN TWO YEARS LATER.
MARRYING MARSH ON THE REBOUND ...BEFORE THE INK WAS DRY ON HER DIVORCE PAPERS.
GONE WITH THE WIND DIDN'T CHANGE GREENE'S ASSESSMENT OF MITCHELL AS A WIFE.
OR HIS ASSESSMENT OF MARSH AS A MAN.
(...MARSH CATERED TO HER EVERY TYRANNICAL WHIM, AND IT WAS, CLEARLY, DRIVING HIM TO AN EARLY GRAVE BY AUGUST, 1949)
(THERE WAS NOTHING WARD GREENE COULD DO ABOUT THAT)

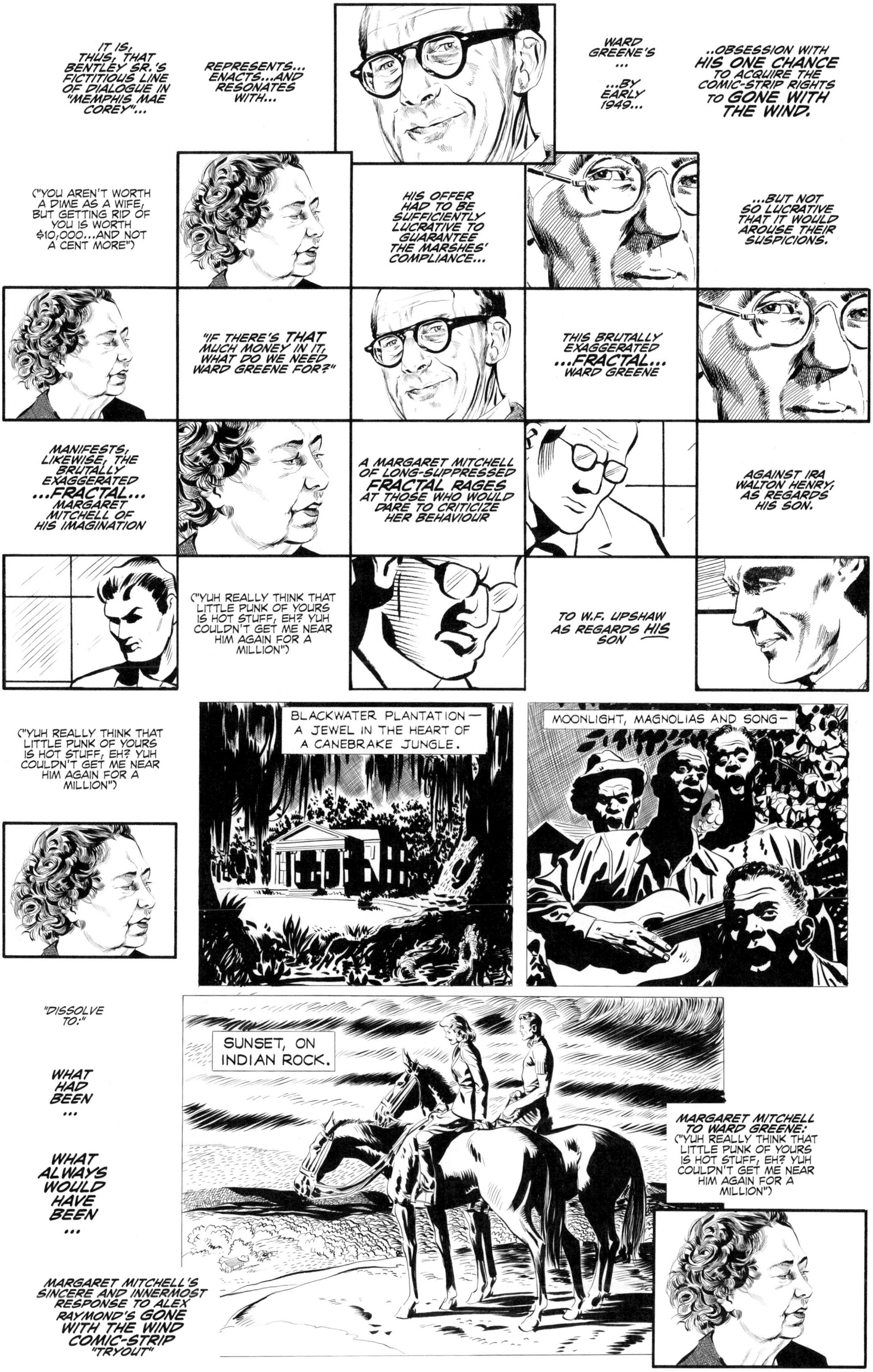
IT IS, THUS, THAT BENTLEY SR.'S FICTITIOUS LINE OF DIALOGUE IN "MEMPHIS MAE COREY"...
REPRESENTS... ENACTS...AND RESONATES WITH...
WARD GREENE'S ... ...BY EARLY 1949...
...OBSESSION WITH HIS ONE CHANCE TO ACQUIRE THE COMIC-STRIP RIGHTS TO GONE WITH THE WIND.
("YOU AREN'T WORTH A DIME AS A WIFE, BUT GETTING RID OF YOU IS WORTH $10,000...AND NOT A CENT MORE")
HIS OFFER HAD TO BE SUFFICIENTLY LUCRATIVE TO GUARANTEE THE MARSHES' COMPLIANCE...
...BUT NOT SO LUCRATIVE THAT IT WOULD AROUSE THEIR SUSPICIONS.
"IF THERE'S THAT MUCH MONEY IN IT, WHAT DO WE NEED WARD GREENE FOR?"
THIS BRUTALLY EXAGGERATED ...FRACTAL... WARD GREENE
MANIFESTS, LIKEWISE, THE BRUTALLY EXAGGERATED ...FRACTAL... MARGARET MITCHELL OF HIS IMAGINATION
A MARGARET MITCHELL OF LONG-SUPPRESSED FRACTAL RAGES AT THOSE WHO WOULD DARE TO CRITICIZE HER BEHAVIOUR
AGAINST IRA WALTON HENRY, AS REGARDS HIS SON.
("YUH REALLY THINK THAT LITTLE PUNK OF YOURS IS HOT STUFF, EH? YUH COULDN'T GET ME NEAR HIM AGAIN FOR A MILLION")
TO W.F. UPSHAW AS REGARDS HIS SON
("YUH REALLY THINK THAT LITTLE PUNK OF YOURS IS HOT STUFF, EH? YUH COULDN'T GET ME NEAR HIM AGAIN FOR A MILLION")
BLACKWATER PLANTATION— A JEWEL IN THE HEART OF A CANEBRAKE JUNGLE.
MOONLIGHT, MAGNOLIAS AND SONG—
"DISSOLVE TO:"
SUNSET, ON INDIAN ROCK.
WHAT HAD BEEN ...
WHAT ALWAYS WOULD HAVE BEEN ...
MARGARET MITCHELL TO WARD GREENE: ("YUH REALLY THINK THAT LITTLE PUNK OF YOURS IS HOT STUFF, EH? YUH COULDN'T GET ME NEAR HIM AGAIN FOR A MILLION")
MARGARET MITCHELL'S SINCERE AND INNERMOST RESPONSE TO ALEX RAYMOND'S GONE WITH THE WIND COMIC-STRIP "TRYOUT"

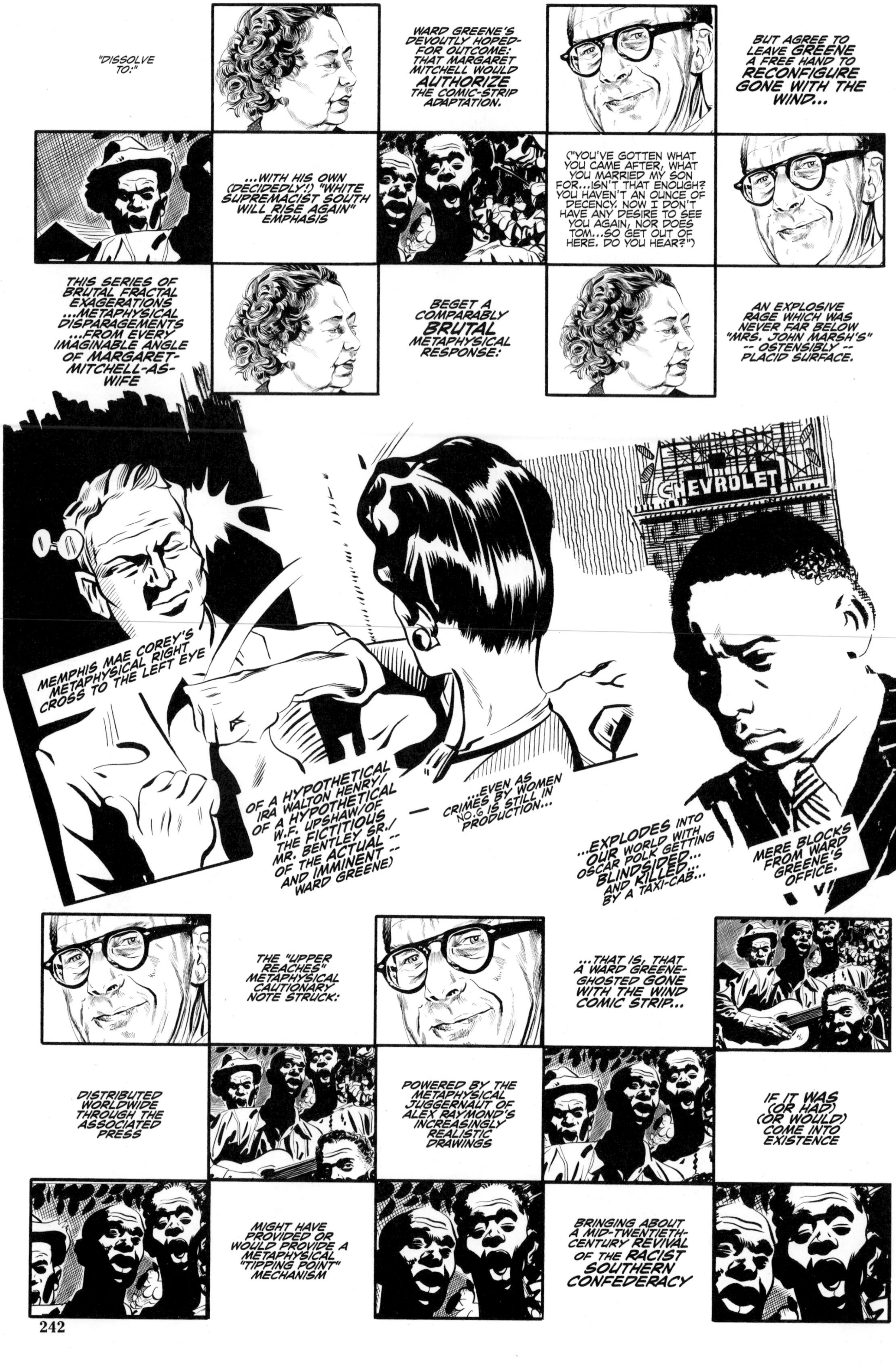
"DISSOLVE TO:"
WARD GREENE'S DEVOUTLY HOPED-FOR OUTCOME: THAT MARGARET MITCHELL WOULD AUTHORIZE THE COMIC-STRIP ADAPTATION.
BUT AGREE TO LEAVE GREENE A FREE HAND TO RECONFIGURE GONE WITH THE WIND...
...WITH HIS OWN (DECIDEDLY!) "WHITE SUPREMACIST SOUTH WILL RISE AGAIN" EMPHASIS
("YOU'VE GOTTEN WHAT YOU CAME AFTER, WHAT YOU MARRIED MY SON FOR...ISN'T THAT ENOUGH? YOU HAVEN'T AN OUNCE OF DECENCY. NOW I DON'T HAVE ANY DESIRE TO SEE YOU AGAIN, NOR DOES TOM...SO GET OUT OF HERE. DO YOU HEAR?")
THIS SERIES OF BRUTAL FRACTAL EXAGERATIONS ...METAPHYSICAL DISPARAGEMENTS ...FROM EVERY IMAGINABLE ANGLE OF MARGARET-MITCHELL-AS-WIFE
BEGET A COMPARABLY BRUTAL METAPHYSICAL RESPONSE:
AN EXPLOSIVE RAGE WHICH WAS NEVER FAR BELOW "MRS. JOHN MARSH'S" -- OSTENSIBLY -- PLACID SURFACE.
CHEVROLET
MEMPHIS MAE COREY'S METAPHYSICAL RIGHT CROSS TO THE LEFT EYE
OF A HYPOTHETICAL IRA WALTON HENRY/ OF A HYPOTHETICAL W.F. UPSHAW/OF THE FICTITIOUS MR. BENTLEY SR./ OF THE ACTUAL -- AND IMMINENT -- WARD GREENE)
—
...EVEN AS CRIMES BY WOMEN NO.6 IS STILL IN PRODUCTION...
...EXPLODES INTO OUR WORLD WITH OSCAR POLK GETTING BLINDSIDED... AND KILLED... BY A TAXI-CAB...
MERE BLOCKS FROM WARD GREENE'S OFFICE.
THE "UPPER REACHES" METAPHYSICAL CAUTIONARY NOTE STRUCK:
...THAT IS, THAT A WARD GREENE-GHOSTED GONE WITH THE WIND COMIC STRIP...
DISTRIBUTED WORLDWIDE THROUGH THE ASSOCIATED PRESS
POWERED BY THE METAPHYSICAL JUGGERNAUT OF ALEX RAYMOND'S INCREASINGLY REALISTIC DRAWINGS
IF IT WAS (OR HAD) (OR WOULD) COME INTO EXISTENCE
MIGHT HAVE PROVIDED OR WOULD PROVIDE A METAPHYSICAL "TIPPING POINT" MECHANISM
BRINGING ABOUT A MID-TWENTIETH-CENTURY REVIVAL OF THE RACIST SOUTHERN CONFEDERACY

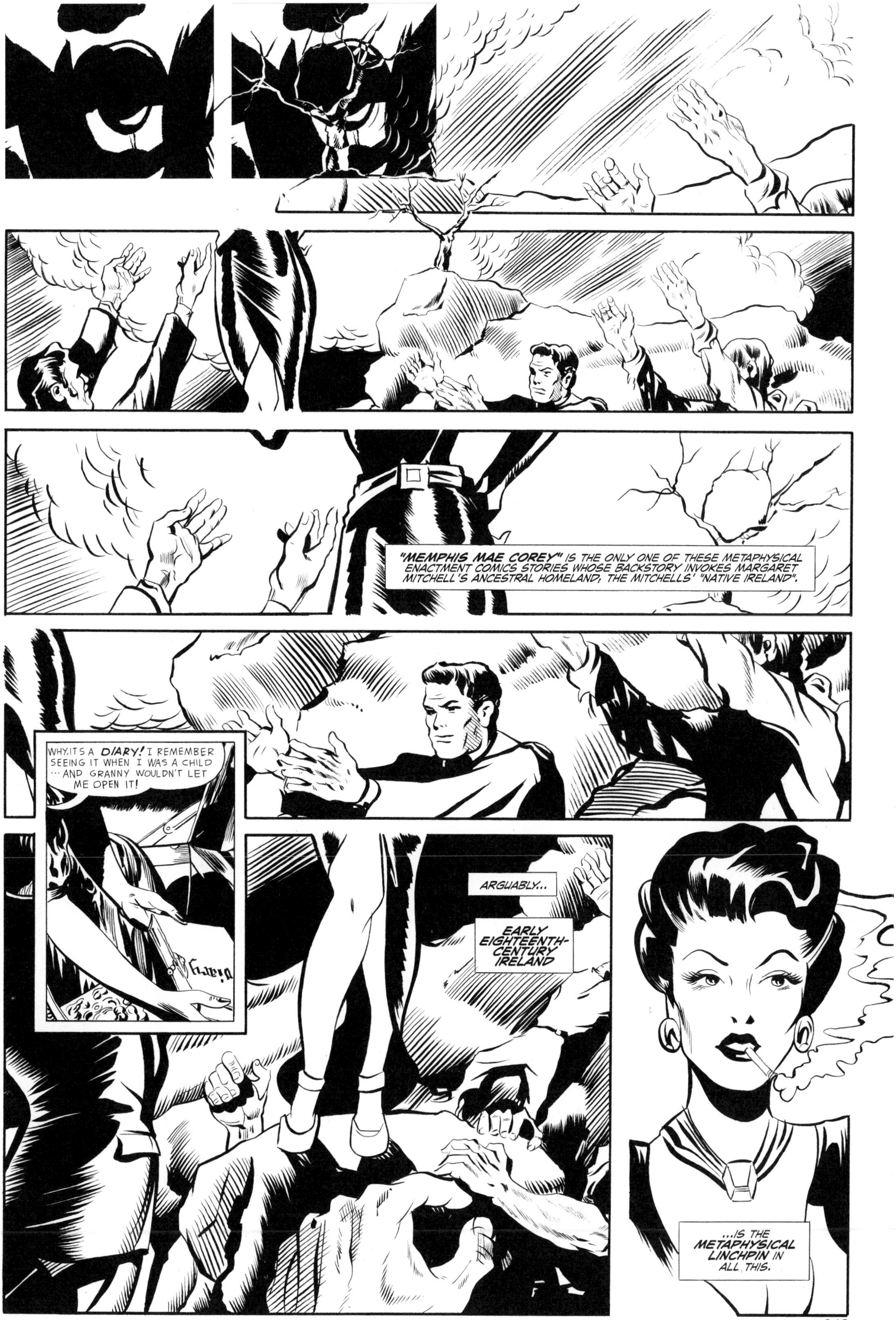
"MEMPHIS MAE COREY" IS THE ONLY ONE OF THESE METAPHYSICAL ENACTMENT COMICS STORIES WHOSE BACKSTORY INVOKES MARGARET MITCHELL'S ANCESTRAL HOMELAND, THE MITCHELLS' "NATIVE IRELAND".
WHY, ITS A DIARY! I REMEMBER SEEING IT WHEN I WAS A CHILD ... AND GRANNY WOULDN'T LET ME OPEN IT!
Diary
ARGUABLY...
EARLY EIGHTEENTH-CENTURY IRELAND
...IS THE METAPHYSICAL LINCHPIN IN ALL THIS.

THE ISLAND MAGEE WITCHES: A NARRATIVE OF THE SUFFERING OF A YOUNG GIRL CALLED MARY DUNBAR WHO WAS STRANGELY MOLESTED BY SPIRITS *and* WITCHES *at* MR. JAMES HATRIDGE'S HOUSE, ISLAND MAGEE, NEAR CARRICKFERGUS, IN THE COUNTY OF ANTRIM *and* PROVINCE OF ULSTER *and in* SOME OTHER PLACES TO WHICH SHE WAS REMOVED DURING THE TIME OF HER DISORDER, AS ALSO OF THE AFORESAID MR. HATRIDGE'S HOUSE BEING HAUNTED WITH SPIRITS IN THE LATTER END OF 1710 *and the* BEGINNING OF 1711

*ed. Samuel McSkimmin*
*(Belfast, 1822)*

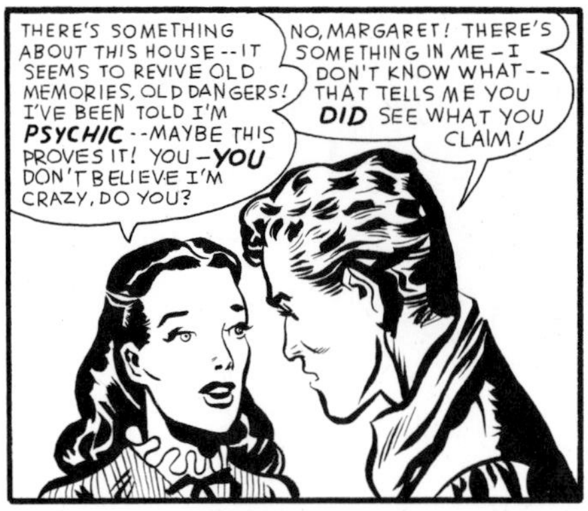

THERE'S SOMETHING ABOUT THIS HOUSE--IT SEEMS TO REVIVE OLD MEMORIES, OLD DANGERS! I'VE BEEN TOLD I'M PSYCHIC--MAYBE THIS PROVES IT! YOU--YOU DON'T BELIEVE I'M CRAZY, DO YOU?
NO, MARGARET! THERE'S SOMETHING IN ME--I DON'T KNOW WHAT--THAT TELLS ME YOU DID SEE WHAT YOU CLAIM!


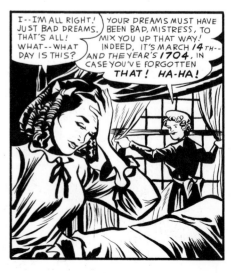

--15 MARCH 1711--

"MRS. ANN" APEARS TO DUNBAR IN SPIRIT FORM BEFORE LEAVING IN THE SHAPE OF A SPIDER

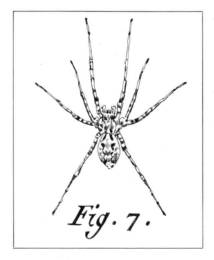

*Fig. 7.*

--17 MARCH 1711--

"MRS. ANN" VISITS DUNBAR SEVERAL TIMES IN SPECTRAL FORM AND THREATENS TO KILL HER.

JOHN GETTY, A MERCHANT FROM LARNE, WHO WAS VISITING... CLAIMED THAT ALTHOUGH HE COULD NOT SEE "MRS. ANN" HE WITNESSED THE SPIDER LEAVE THE ROOM

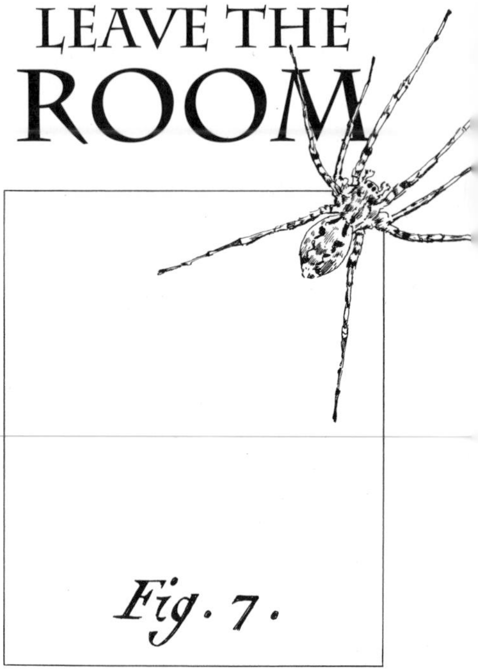

*Fig. 7.*

ANOTHER FIT FOLLOWED, ALONG WITH A FURTHER APPEARANCE OF THE WITCH

I--I'M ALL RIGHT! JUST BAD DREAMS. THAT'S ALL! WHAT--WHAT DAY IS THIS?
YOUR DREAMS MUST HAVE BEEN BAD, MISTRESS, TO MIX YOU UP THAT WAY! INDEED, IT'S MARCH 14TH--AND THE YEAR'S 1704, IN CASE YOU'VE FORGOTTEN THAT! HA-HA!

# IN HER SPECTRAL *and* SPIDER FORMS.

--19 MARCH 1711--
MARGARET MITCHELL FROM THE PARISH OF KILROOT IS SUSPECTED OF BEING "MRS. ANN" AND IS BROUGHT TO LARNE TO CONFRONT DUNBAR

*Fig. 7.*

"NEXT MOMENT CAME CRIES FROM THE ON-LOOKERS AS DEATH STARED US IN THE FACE!"

LOOK OUT!

HELP! WE'LL BE ...KILLED!

I CALL ON YOU, YIELDER OF UNKNOWN POWERS! SAVE US!

THIS TIME GETTY CAUGHT THE SPIDER BUT WHEN HE OPENED HIS HAND TO EXAMINE IT, HE FOUND IT HAD MYSTERIOUSLY DISAPEARED.

"THEN CAME AN ODD, DIZZYING SENSATION! I SEEMED TO BE FAINTING, THE ROOM SPINNING ABOUT ME···"

OH-HHHH...

④

--21 MARCH 1711--
MITCHELL ARRESTED BY CONSTABLE OF BROADISLAND, JOHN LOGAN... DUNBAR'S OVERALL HEALTH IMPROVES

--20 MARCH 1711--
DUNBAR REPLIED THAT "SHE SHOULD ANSWER TO GOD" *at* JUDGEMENT DAY IF SHE WERE LYING. AND THAT MITCHELL WAS "THE PERSON WHO WENT UNDER THE NAME OF MRS. ANN AMONG HER TORMENTORS."

"CONFUSED, I RACED BACK TO MY ROOM, GRASPED THE STRANGE FIGURE---"

I SAID THOSE WORDS BECAUSE I SEEMED TO *REMEMBER* THAT IT HAPPENED THAT WAY! IT'S RIDICULOUS, UNLESS···UNLESS WHAT HAPPENED TO ME *WASN'T* A DREAM ···*AND I DO HAVE STRANGE POWERS NOW!*

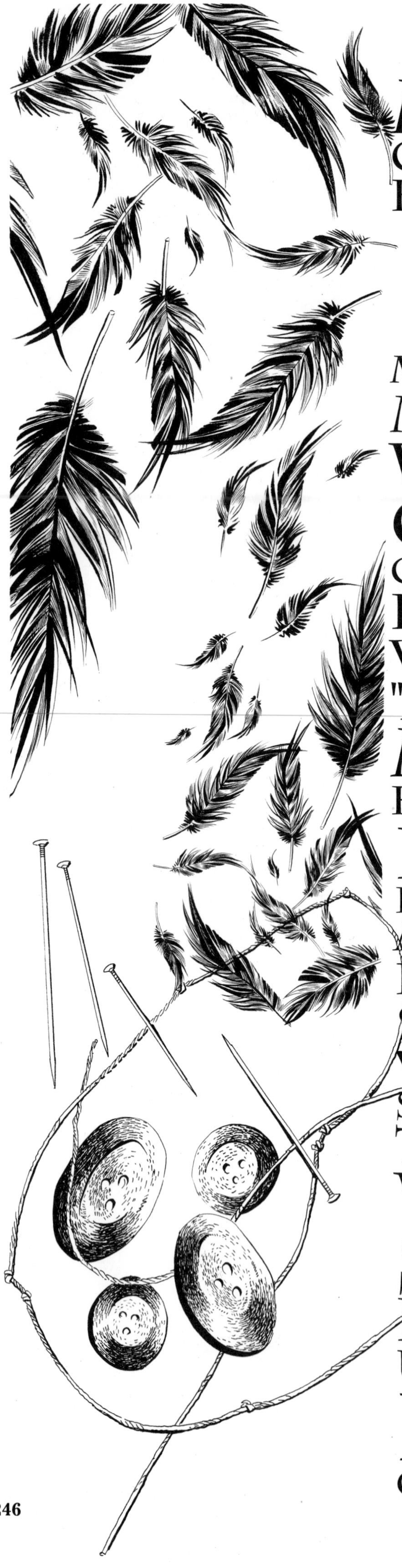

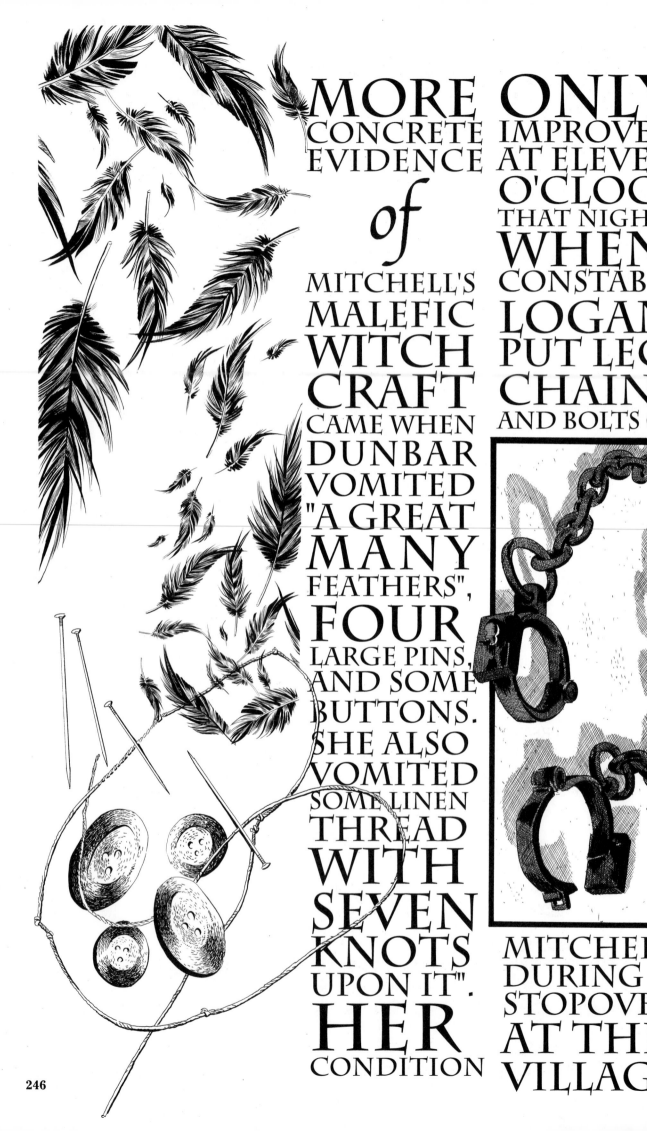

MORE CONCRETE EVIDENCE

*of*

MITCHELL'S MALEFIC WITCH CRAFT CAME WHEN DUNBAR VOMITED "A GREAT MANY FEATHERS", FOUR LARGE PINS, AND SOME BUTTONS. SHE ALSO VOMITED SOME LINEN THREAD WITH SEVEN KNOTS UPON IT". HER CONDITION

ONLY IMPROVED AT ELEVEN O'CLOCK THAT NIGHT WHEN CONSTABLE LOGAN PUT LEG CHAINS AND BOLTS ON

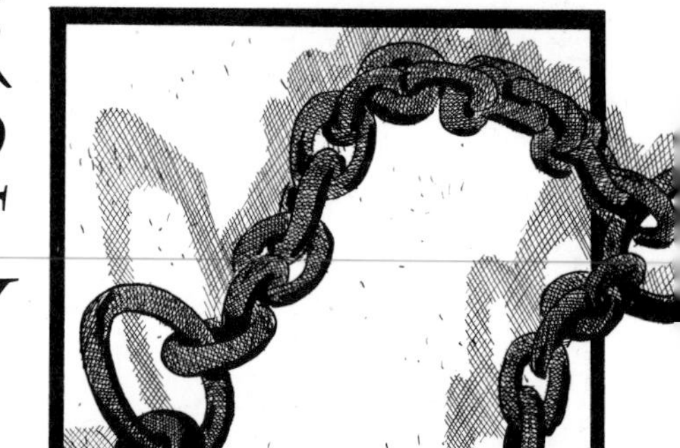

MITCHELL DURING A STOPOVER AT THE VILLAGE

# of BALLY-CARRY in BROAD-ISLAND on the way to CARRICK-FERGUS GAOL.

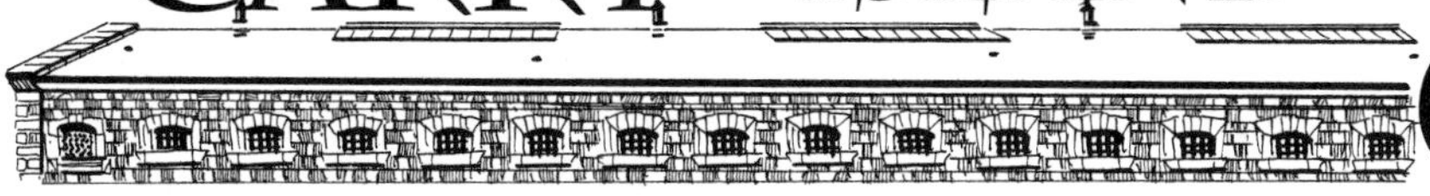

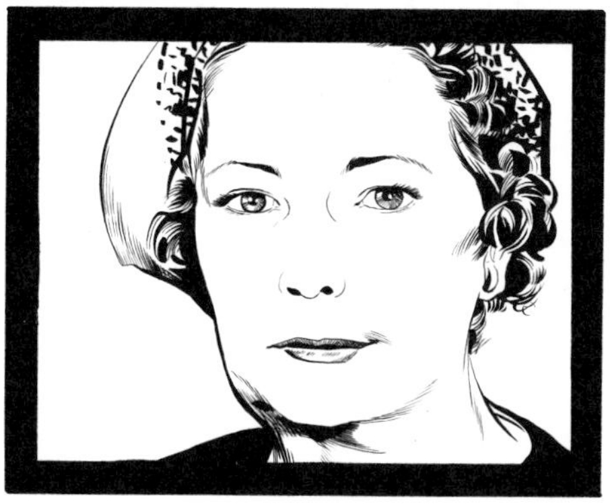

AFTER AWHILE THEIR DISCUSSION ABOUT WHAT WOULD HAPPEN TO HER PROPERTY AFTER HER DEATH TURNED TO RELIGION. STEPHENS, WHO HAD REMAINED A DEVOUT CATHOLIC, WROTE THE ESSENCE OF THEIR CONVERSATION IN HIS MEMOIR.

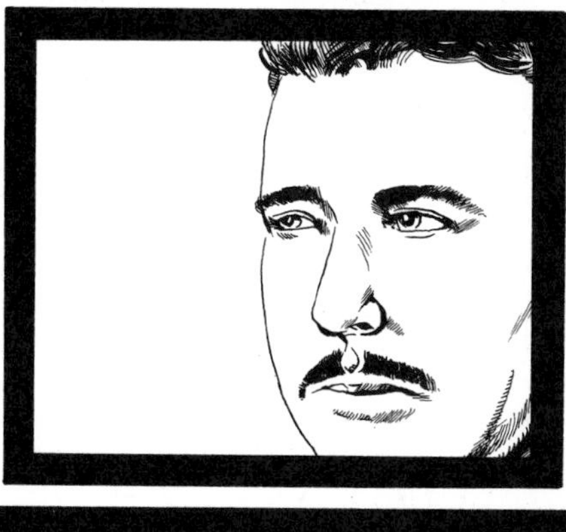

HE WROTE THAT WHEN HE ASKED HER IF SHE WERE TURNING BACK TOWARD THE RELIGION OF THEIR YOUTH, SHE MADE THIS INTRIGUING REMARK: "THAT'S SOMETHING

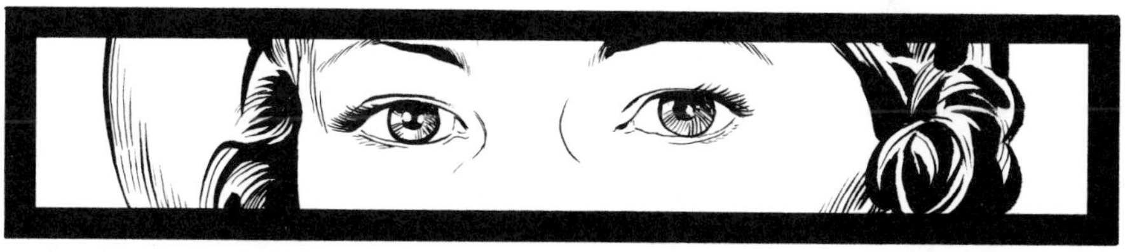

I DON'T WANT TO TALK ABOUT. I'M JUST GOING TO SAY ONE THING ABOUT IT. WHEN YOU MAKE A BARGAIN WITH THE DEVIL, YOU HAD BETTER STICK TO YOUR BARGAIN. I MAY HAVE MADE ONE, BUT WHENEVER I GIVE MY WORD ON SOMETHING, OR WHENEVER I TAKE A COURSE OF ACTION, I AM NOT GOING TO TRY TO CRAWL OUT OF THAT COURSE OF ACTION BECAUSE I MAY HAVE MADE A MISTAKE IN STARTING IT. IT'S NOT THE FAIR THING TO DO."

MARGARET MITCHELL & JOHN MARSH BY MARIANE WALKER PG.500

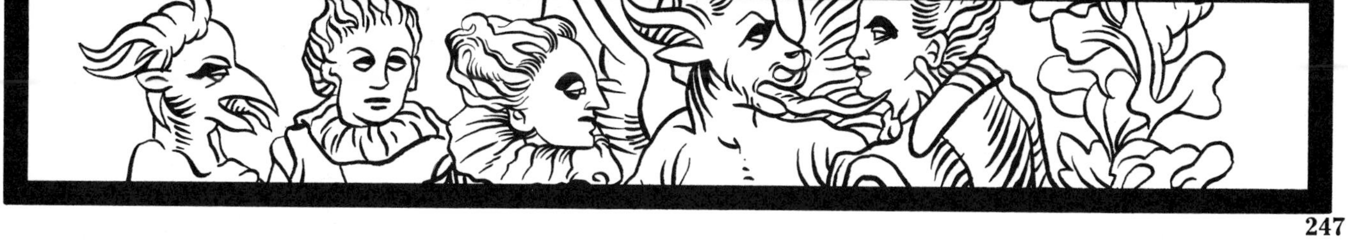

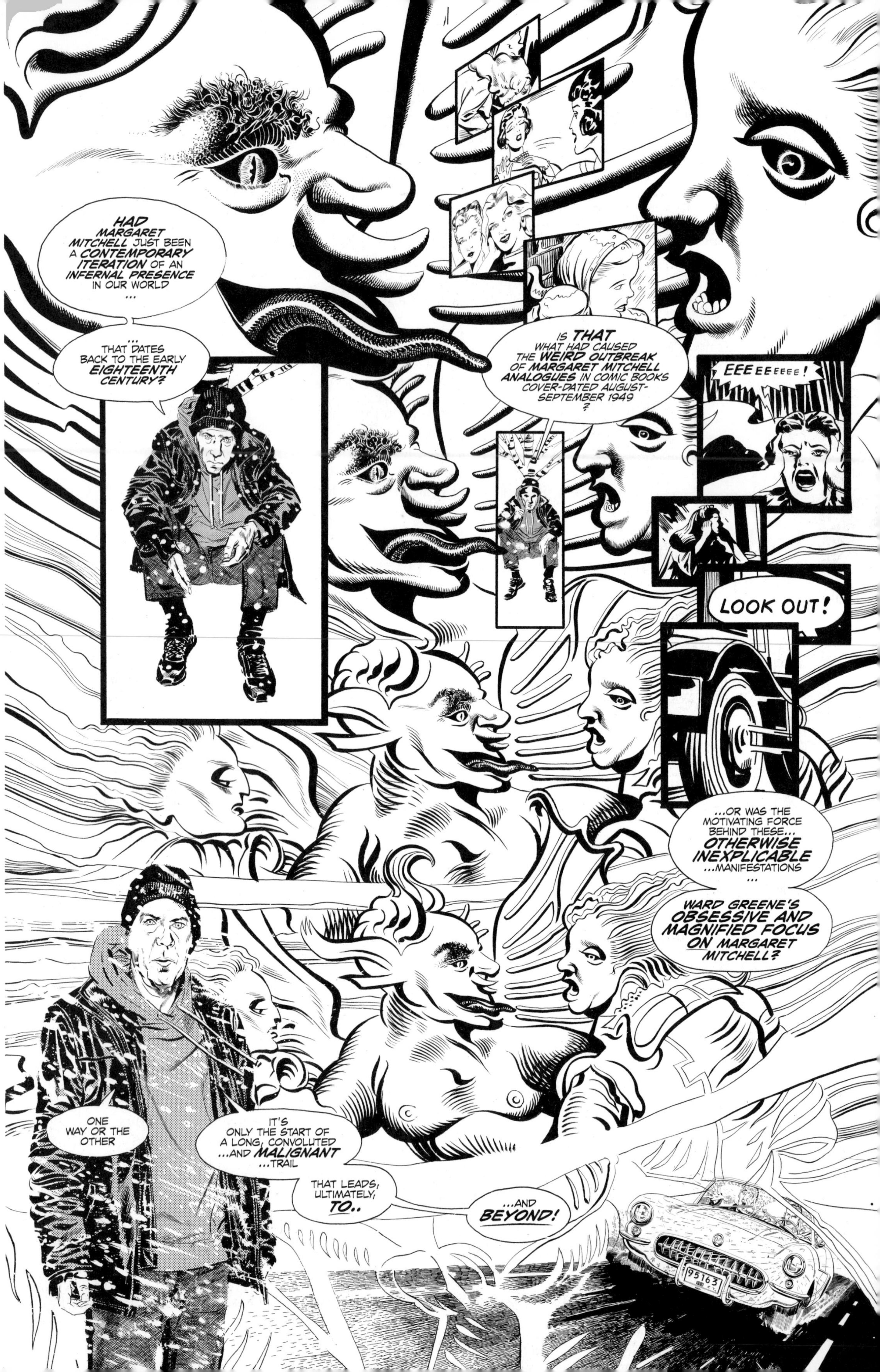

HAD MARGARET MITCHELL JUST BEEN A CONTEMPORARY ITERATION OF AN INFERNAL PRESENCE IN OUR WORLD ...
... THAT DATES BACK TO THE EARLY EIGHTEENTH CENTURY?
IS THAT WHAT HAD CAUSED THE WEIRD OUTBREAK OF MARGARET MITCHELL ANALOGUES IN COMIC BOOKS COVER-DATED AUGUST-SEPTEMBER 1949 ?
EEEEEEEEE!
LOOK OUT!
...OR WAS THE MOTIVATING FORCE BEHIND THESE... OTHERWISE INEXPLICABLE ...MANIFESTATIONS ...
WARD GREENE'S OBSESSIVE AND MAGNIFIED FOCUS ON MARGARET MITCHELL?
ONE WAY OR THE OTHER
IT'S ONLY THE START OF A LONG, CONVOLUTED ...AND MALIGNANT ...TRAIL
THAT LEADS, ULTIMATELY, TO..
...AND BEYOND!
95163

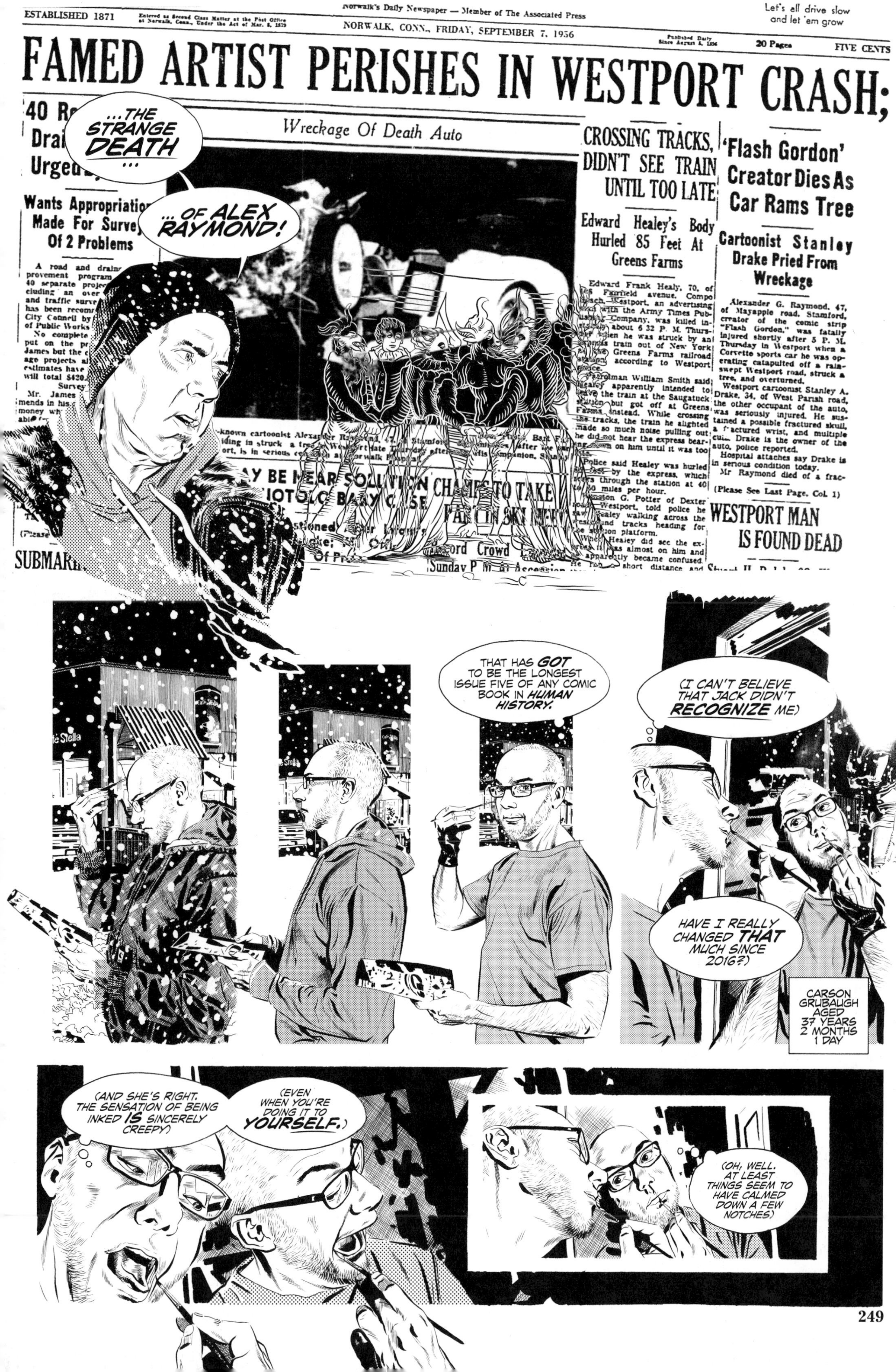
ESTABLISHED 1871
Norwalk's Daily Newspaper — Member of The Associated Press
NORWALK, CONN., FRIDAY, SEPTEMBER 7, 1956
20 Pages
FIVE CENTS
Let's all drive slow and let 'em grow
FAMED ARTIST PERISHES IN WESTPORT CRASH;
Wants Appropriation Made For Survey Of 2 Problems
Wreckage Of Death Auto
CROSSING TRACKS, DIDN'T SEE TRAIN UNTIL TOO LATE
Edward Healey's Body Hurled 85 Feet At Greens Farms
'Flash Gordon' Creator Dies As Car Rams Tree
Cartoonist Stanley Drake Pried From Wreckage
Alexander G. Raymond, 47, of Mayapple road, Stamford, creator of the comic strip "Flash Gordon," was fatally injured shortly after 5 P. M. Thursday in Westport when a Corvette sports car he was operating catapulted off a rain-swept Westport road, struck a tree, and overturned.
Westport cartoonist Stanley A. Drake, 34, of West Parish road, the other occupant of the auto, was seriously injured. He sustained a possible fractured skull, a fractured wrist, and multiple cuts. Drake is the owner of the auto, police reported.
Hospital attaches say Drake is in serious condition today.
Mr Raymond died of a frac-
(Please See Last Page, Col. 1)
WESTPORT MAN IS FOUND DEAD
...THE STRANGE DEATH...
...OF ALEX RAYMOND!
THAT HAS GOT TO BE THE LONGEST ISSUE FIVE OF ANY COMIC BOOK IN HUMAN HISTORY.
(I CAN'T BELIEVE THAT JACK DIDN'T RECOGNIZE ME)
HAVE I REALLY CHANGED THAT MUCH SINCE 2016?)
CARSON GRUBAUGH AGED 37 YEARS 2 MONTHS 1 DAY
(AND SHE'S RIGHT. THE SENSATION OF BEING INKED IS SINCERELY CREEPY)
(EVEN WHEN YOU'RE DOING IT TO YOURSELF.)
(OH, WELL. AT LEAST THINGS SEEM TO HAVE CALMED DOWN A FEW NOTCHES)

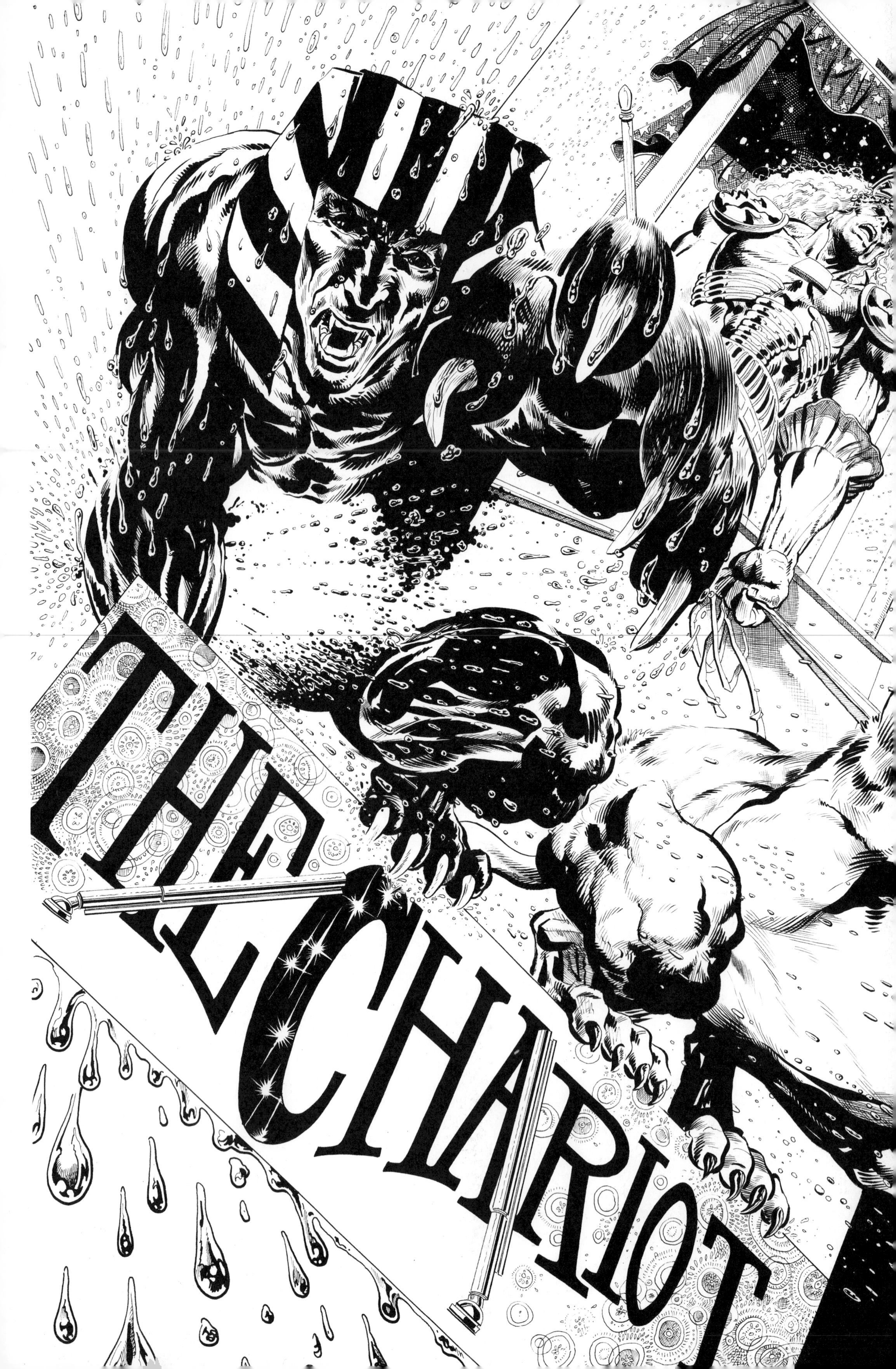
THE CHARIOT

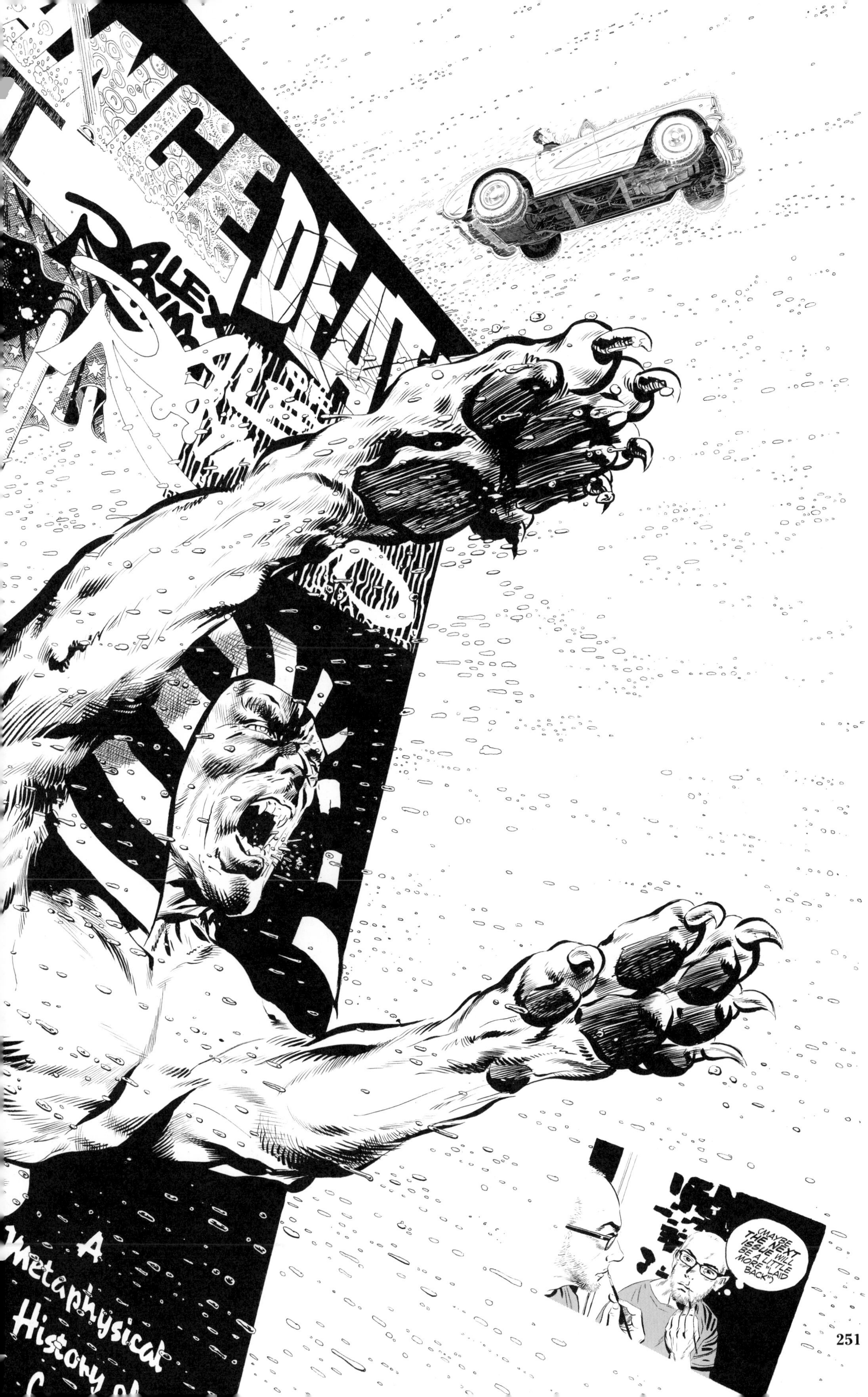

A
Metaphysical
History
(MAYBE THE NEXT ISSUE WILL BE A LITTLE MORE "LAID BACK")

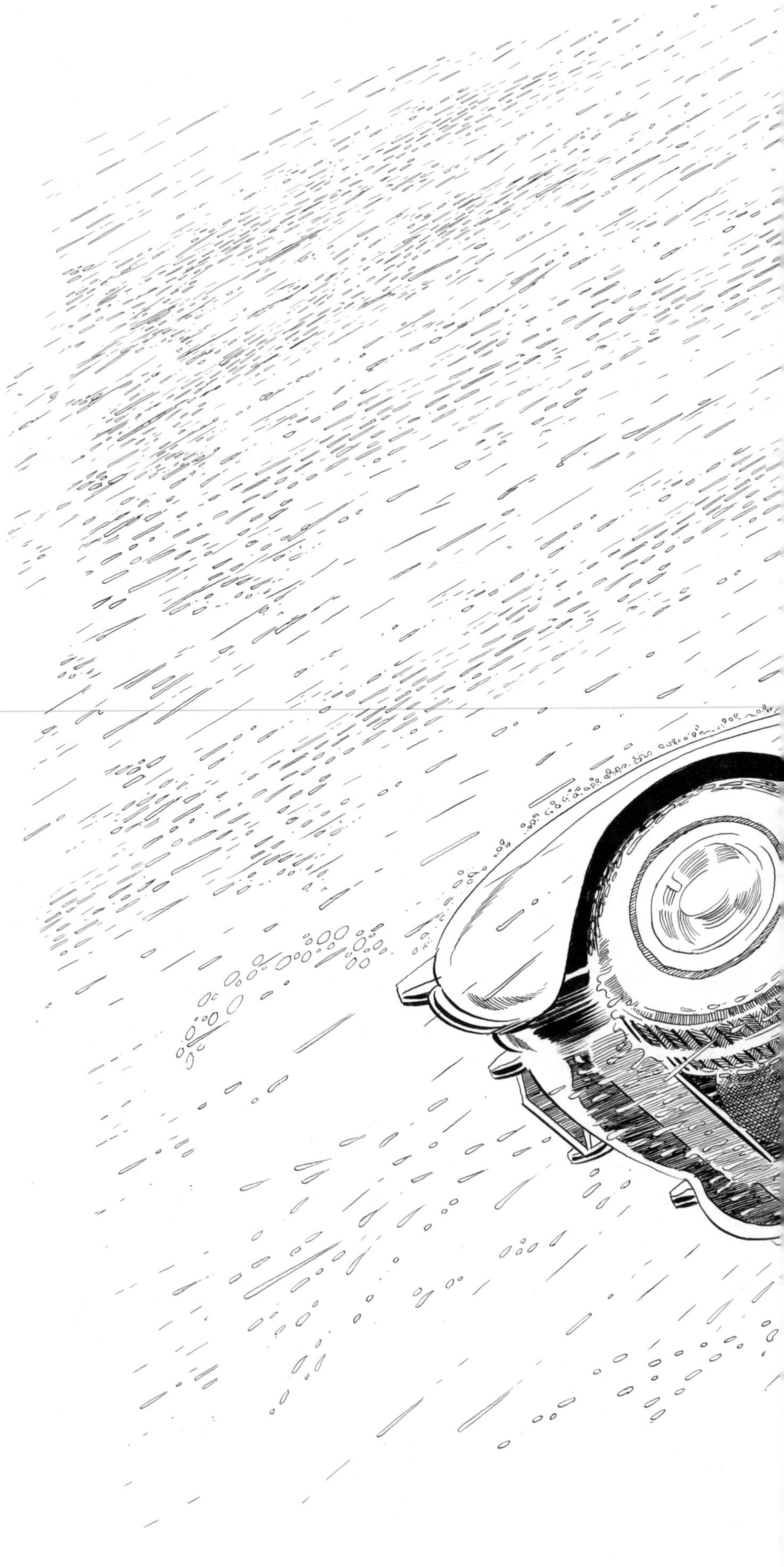

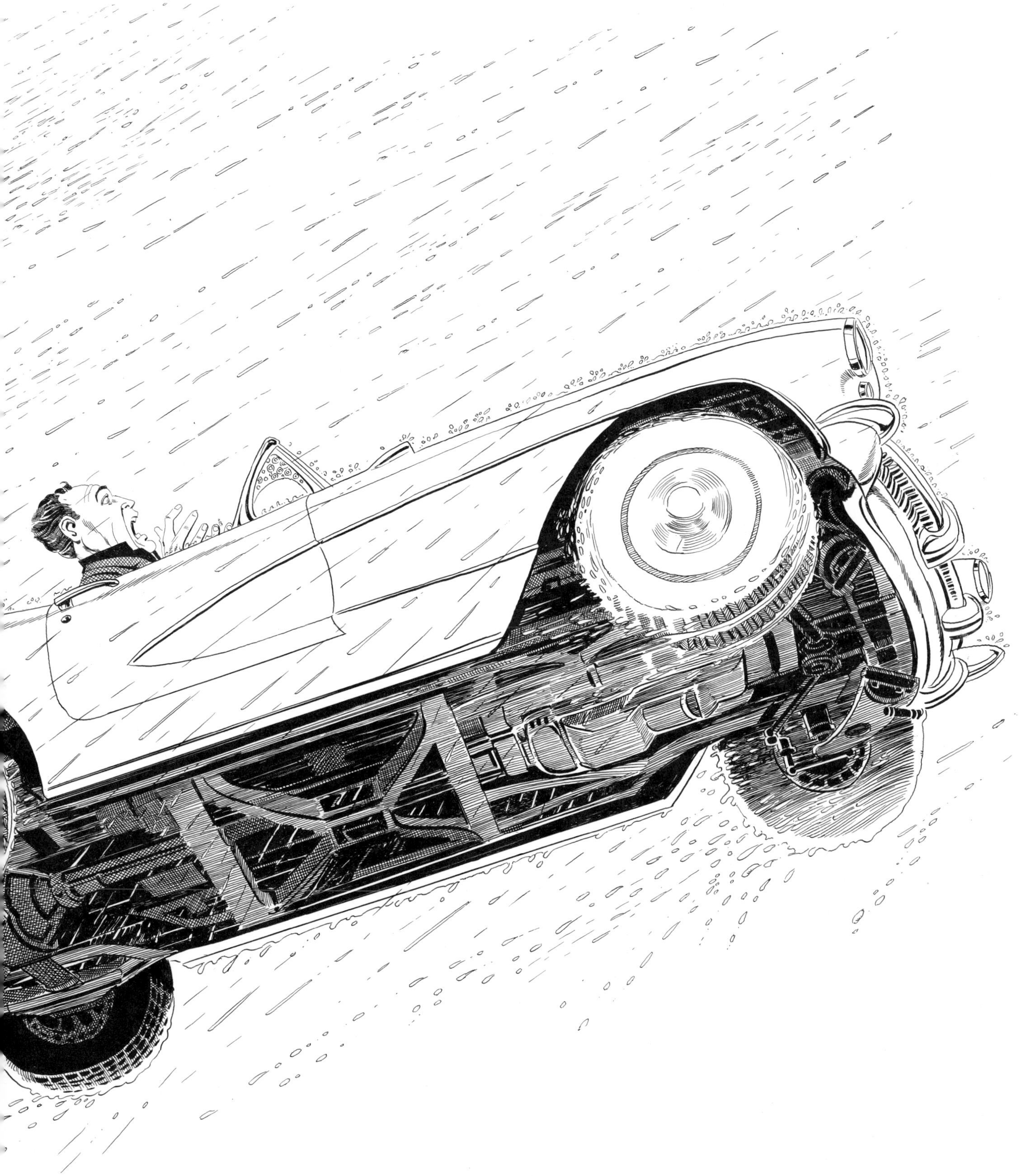

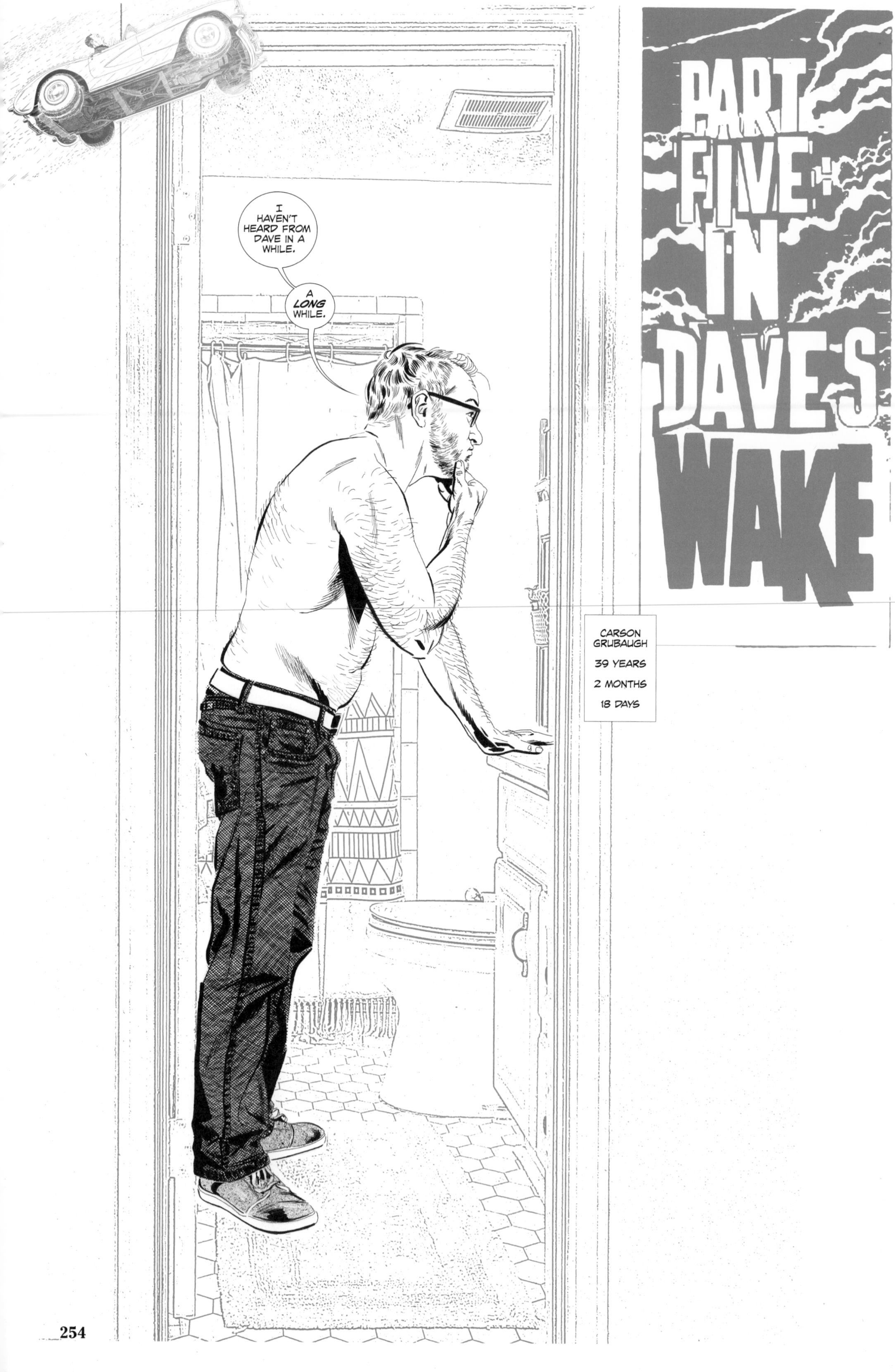
PART FIVE: IN DAVE'S WAKE
I HAVEN'T HEARD FROM DAVE IN A WHILE.
A *LONG* WHILE.
CARSON GRUBAUGH
39 YEARS
2 MONTHS
18 DAYS

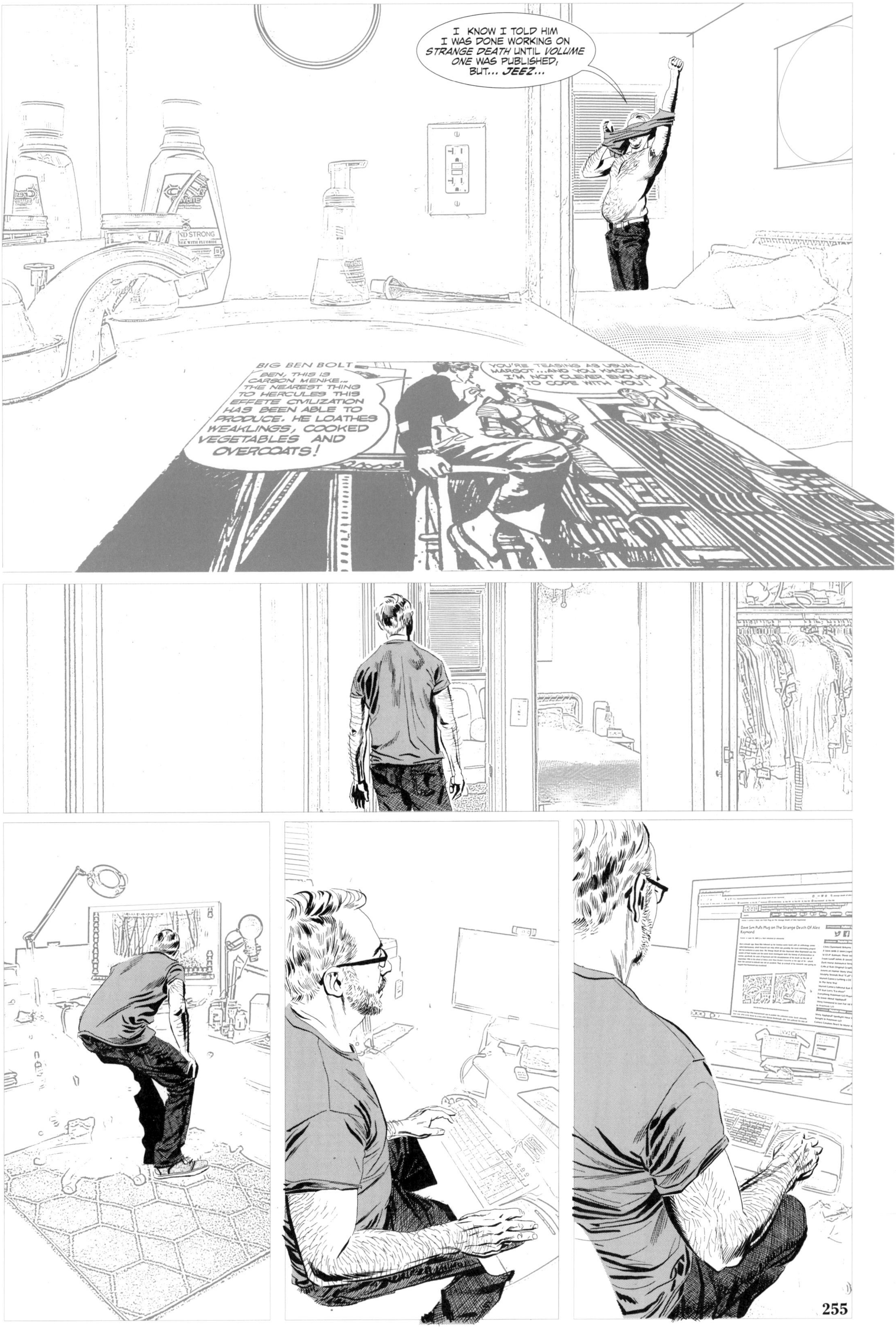
I KNOW I TOLD HIM I WAS DONE WORKING ON *STRANGE DEATH* UNTIL *VOLUME ONE* WAS PUBLISHED; BUT... ***JEEZ...***
BIG BEN BOLT
BEN, THIS IS CARSON MENKE... THE NEAREST THING TO HERCULES THIS EFFETE CIVILIZATION HAS BEEN ABLE TO PRODUCE. HE LOATHES WEAKLINGS, COOKED VEGETABLES AND OVERCOATS!
YOU'RE TEASING AS USUAL, MARGOT... AND YOU KNOW I'M NOT CLEVER ENOUGH TO COPE WITH YOU!

File Edit View History Bookmarks Tools Help

A MOMENT OF CEREBUS: Stran

momentofcerebus.blogspot.c

a moment c

Most Visited  Getting Started  sketchbook.ercles.co...  Suggested Sites  New Tab  Dashboard

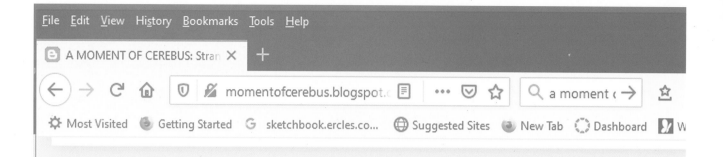

Saturday, 13 June 2020

## BREAKING STRANGE DEATH OF ALEX RAYMOND NEWS!!!!!

Hi, Everybody!

SHIT.
NEXT: VARYING REASONS of ASSORTED DEPTHS

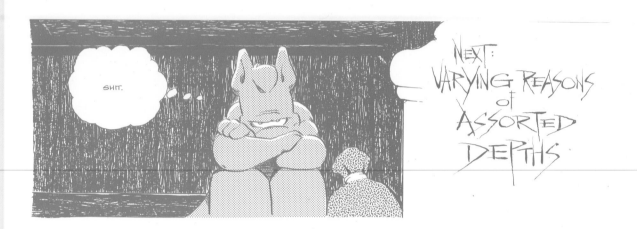

Got an e-mail from Eddie Khanna:

SDOAR PATREON
SUPPORTERS and
F.E. BUYERS

10 June 20

Hi Folks!

I'm afraid I've had enough. THE STRANGE DEATH OF ALEX RAYMOND can't be made to happen with 123 people. All the money you paid in is gone, as is the $9K I made selling SDOAR artwork through HA.com, the $16K that came in on CAN8 (I'm still paying off the $4.7K shipping bill) and what was left of the JAKA'S STORY REMASTERED money. I'm back to borrowing against my life insurance to pay bills. And, personally, making about $350 US a month.

It's also taking all my time to keep up with CEREBUS IN HELL? -- Watch for SWORDS OF CEREBUS IN HELL? coming later this year through Diamond -- and my new (and presumably "from now on" lifelong) role as a 1980s Nostalgia Act in association with Waverly Press and, of course, the CEREBUS ARCHIVE Portfolios. Those I will continue to deliver on.

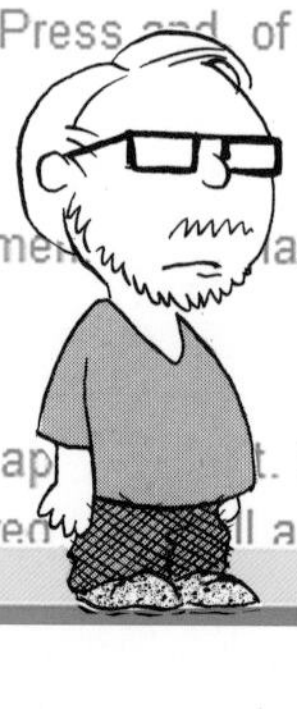

I'm sorry you all wasted your money on SDOAR. I can't reme… last time I effed everyone over as I'm doing here. I don't think I ever have.

If you can afford to just write off what you donated, I would ap… . If you need a refund, let me know through Eddie Khanna and, on a first-come, first-served … arrange to have someone in the

File Edit View History Bookmarks Tools Help

A MOMENT OF CEREBUS: Stra

momentofcerebus.blogspot. Search

Most Visited Getting Started sketchbook.ercles.co... Suggested Sites New Tab Dashboard W

know through Eddie Khanna and, on a first-come, first-served basis, I'll arrange to have someone in the U.S. send you a USD check for $50. Or an International Money Order. Or something. YOU tell ME. I can, of course, just send you a Canadian cheque if you're a Canadian. Just let Eddie know which category you're in and what you need and -- a few months from now when (God willing) I actually get paid for HIGH SOCIETY and whenever (God willing) I get whatever I'm going to get on the CEREBUS No.1s -- I'll pay you back. And I'll let you know where you are on the first-come, first-served list and when you can expect to get paid back "going forward" in as close to Real Time as possible.

All the research materials for SDOAR exist and Eddie is my successor. They will be made available in a massive document dump to anyone who's interested at some point. There just won't ever be a Volume One, Two or Three per se. It WAS GOING TO BE a really interesting book and I enjoyed working on it. But, I have to face the fact that, at age 64, the only MARKETABLE comics cred I have are the first 5 issues of CEREBUS, TURTLES No.8 and SPAWN 10.

Which is what Dagon and I are working on. HOW do you keep selling CEREBUS No.1 since that's all anyone in the comic-book field's interested in? I guess we'll find out.

13 June 20

Hello, PATREON SDOAR SUPPORTERS and SDOAR FE PURCHASERS!

My plan had been to finish SDOAR VOL 1 and 2 and than take a break to promote them with the CALIFORNIA TEST MARKET EDITION and DEATH OF A COMICS SALESMAN sales trip, resuming work on VOL 3 (for which I've mocked up 20 or so pages) on my return to Canada.

It became apparent that this wasn't going to work even before COVID 19 made international travel impossible.

Whatever the world is going to turn into or has turned into wasn't going to include "meet and greet/press the flesh" promotions. And definitely not of non-CEREBUS work.

I'm the CEREBUS creator and that's only
very earliest work (as evidenced by the $
last month: further evidenced by the fact
work; further evidenced by the fact that a
century work).

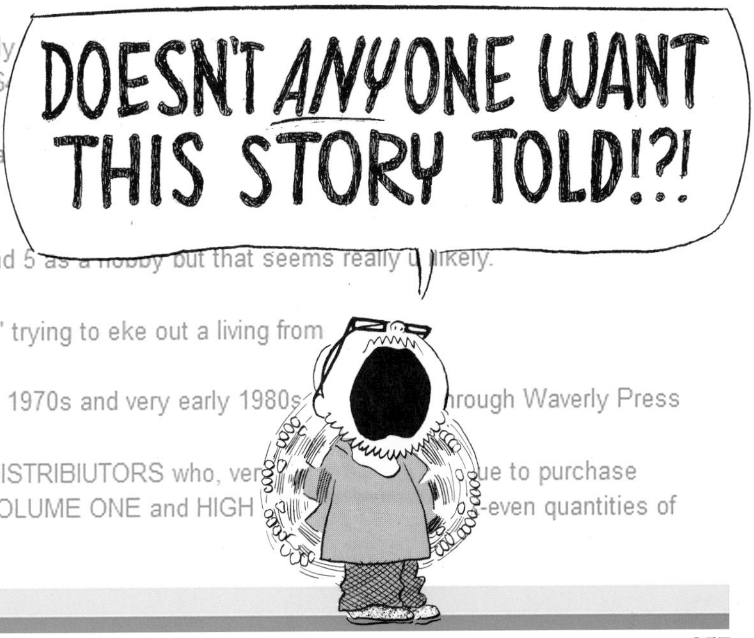
DOESN'T ANYONE WANT THIS STORY TOLD!?!

I hope to work in SDOAR VOLS. 3, 4 and 5 as a hobby but that seems really unlikely.

I'm 64 years old and will "die in harness" trying to eke out a living from

1) the nostalgic affection enjoyed by the 1970s and very early 1980s ... hrough Waverly Press

2) the patronage of DIAMOND COMIC DISTRIBIUTORS who, ver ... ue to purchase profit-making quantities of CEREBUS VOLUME ONE and HIGH ... -even quantities of the other 14 volumes

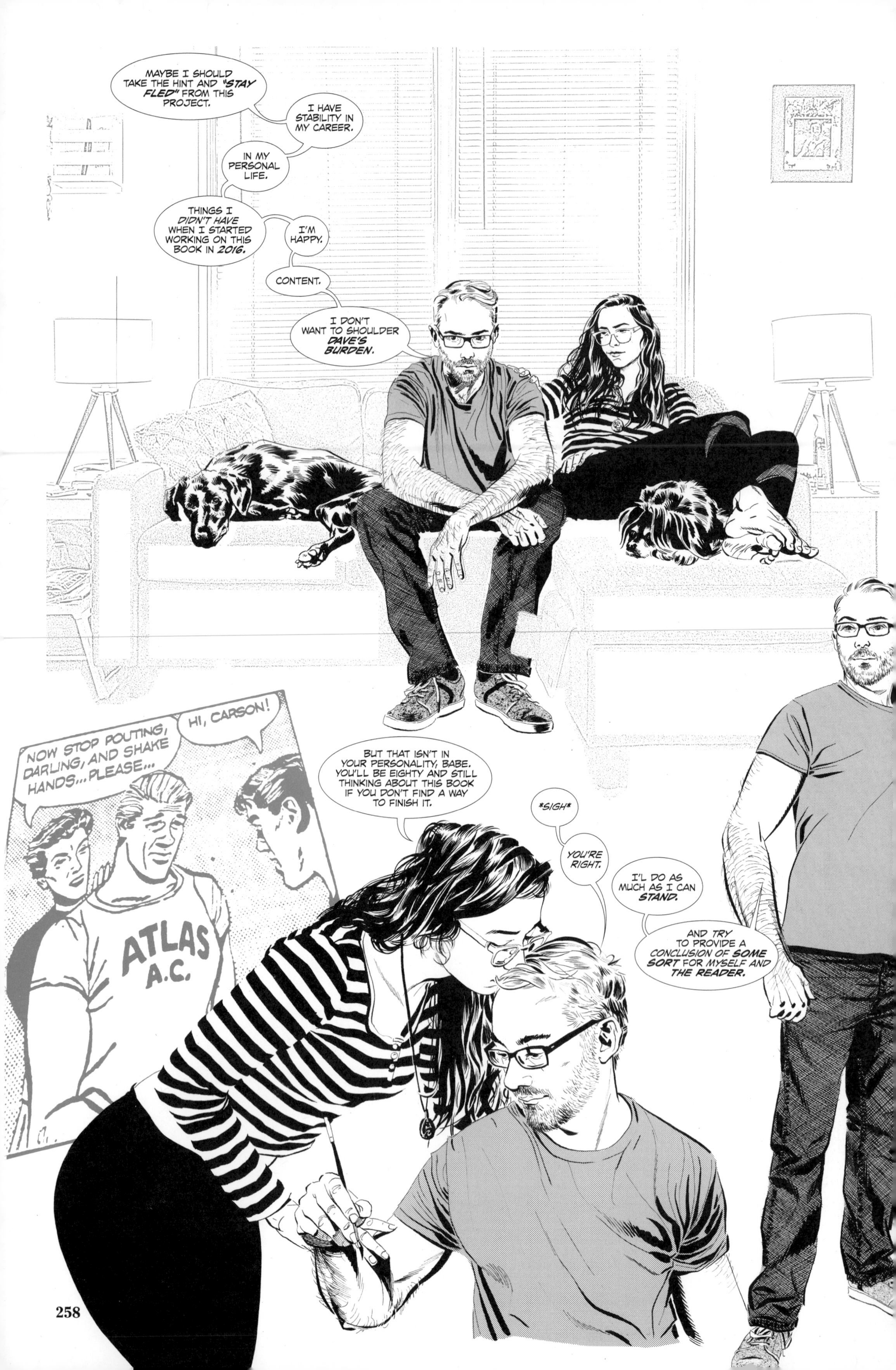

MAYBE I SHOULD TAKE THE HINT AND *"STAY FLED"* FROM THIS PROJECT.
I HAVE STABILITY IN MY CAREER.
IN MY PERSONAL LIFE.
THINGS I *DIDN'T HAVE* WHEN I STARTED WORKING ON THIS BOOK IN *2016*.
I'M HAPPY.
CONTENT.
I DON'T WANT TO SHOULDER ***DAVE'S BURDEN***.
NOW STOP POUTING, DARLING, AND SHAKE HANDS...PLEASE...
HI, CARSON!
ATLAS A.C.
BUT THAT ISN'T IN YOUR PERSONALITY, BABE. YOU'LL BE EIGHTY AND STILL THINKING ABOUT THIS BOOK IF YOU DON'T FIND A WAY TO FINISH IT.
*SIGH*
YOU'RE RIGHT.
I'L DO AS MUCH AS I CAN *STAND*.
AND *TRY* TO PROVIDE A CONCLUSION OF ***SOME SORT*** FOR MYSELF AND ***THE READER***.

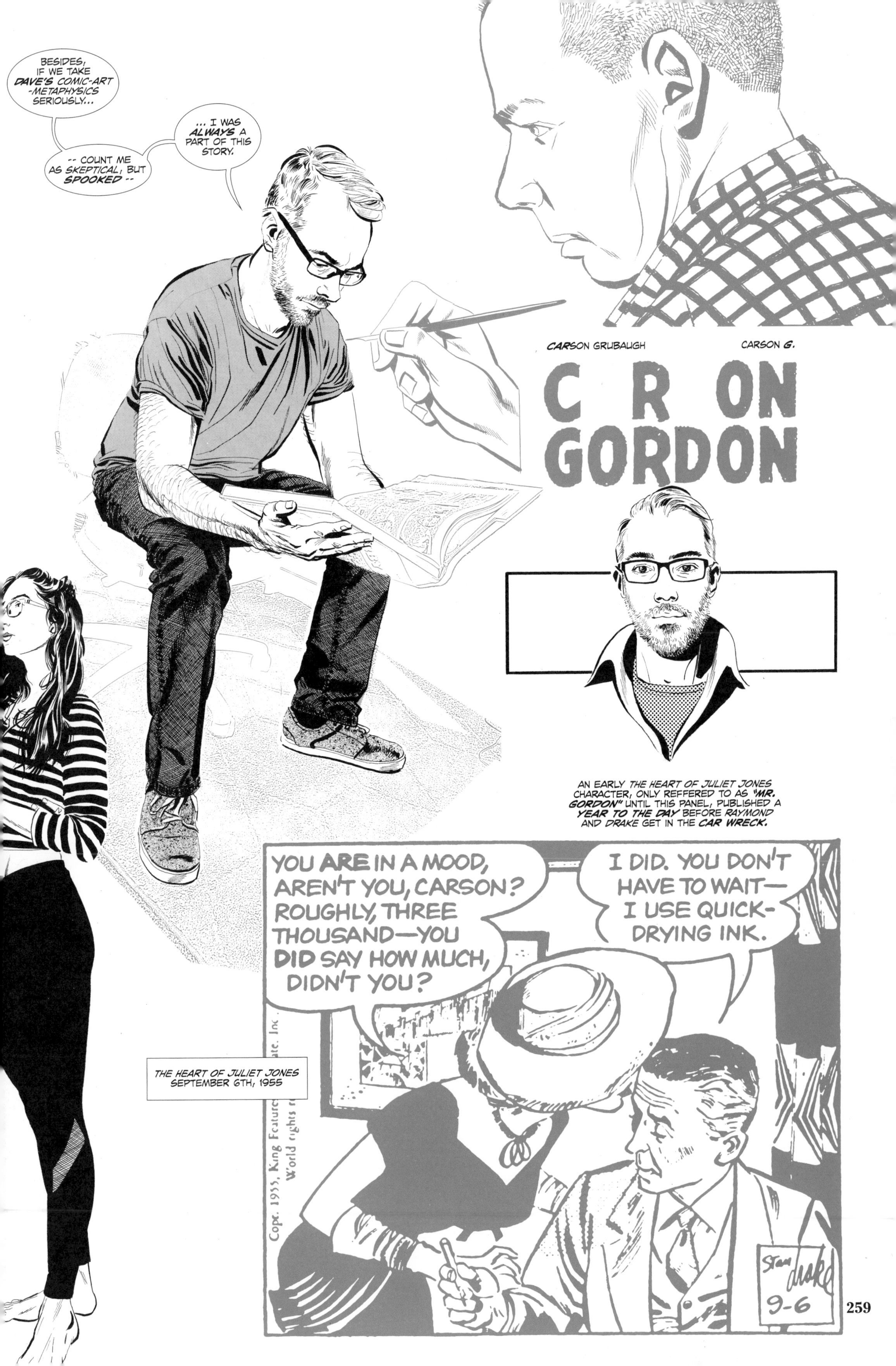

BESIDES, IF WE TAKE DAVE'S COMIC-ART -METAPHYSICS SERIOUSLY...
-- COUNT ME AS SKEPTICAL, BUT SPOOKED --
... I WAS ALWAYS A PART OF THIS STORY.
CARSON GRUBAUGH
CARSON G.
C R ON GORDON
AN EARLY THE HEART OF JULIET JONES CHARACTER, ONLY REFFERED TO AS "MR. GORDON" UNTIL THIS PANEL, PUBLISHED A YEAR TO THE DAY BEFORE RAYMOND AND DRAKE GET IN THE CAR WRECK.
YOU ARE IN A MOOD, AREN'T YOU, CARSON? ROUGHLY, THREE THOUSAND—YOU DID SAY HOW MUCH, DIDN'T YOU?
I DID. YOU DON'T HAVE TO WAIT— I USE QUICK-DRYING INK.
THE HEART OF JULIET JONES SEPTEMBER 6TH, 1955
Stan Drake
9-6

Mark of the Beast

A Complete Novel by WALTER C. BROWN—They told me to plead self-defense, that the case was all against me. But, though I wasn't the murderer, how could I prove it from a jail cell?

I HAPPENED WITHOUT WARNING. One evening I was in my own cabin, a free man. The next morning I was in a jail cell—charged with murder.

Here are the basic facts about myself in one brief paragraph: My name is Owen Randall. I am a research chemist, twenty-seven, and a bachelor. I had come to Carson's Cove to combine a vacation with re-

I had come to Carson's Cove to combine a vacation with re-covery from an auto accident that had left me with some bent ribs, a collection of bruises, and a knee so badly wrenched that I had to hobble around with a cane.

THIS MIGHT BE A *BAD IDEA*, BUT I GUESS IT IS UP TO ME TO *STEAL DAVE'S INVENTION* AND WRAP THIS STORY UP.

THE FOLLOWING *TWENTY-ONE PAGES* ARE DERIVED FROM THE *FINAL* SET OF MOCK-UPS I RECEIVED FROM *DAVE.*

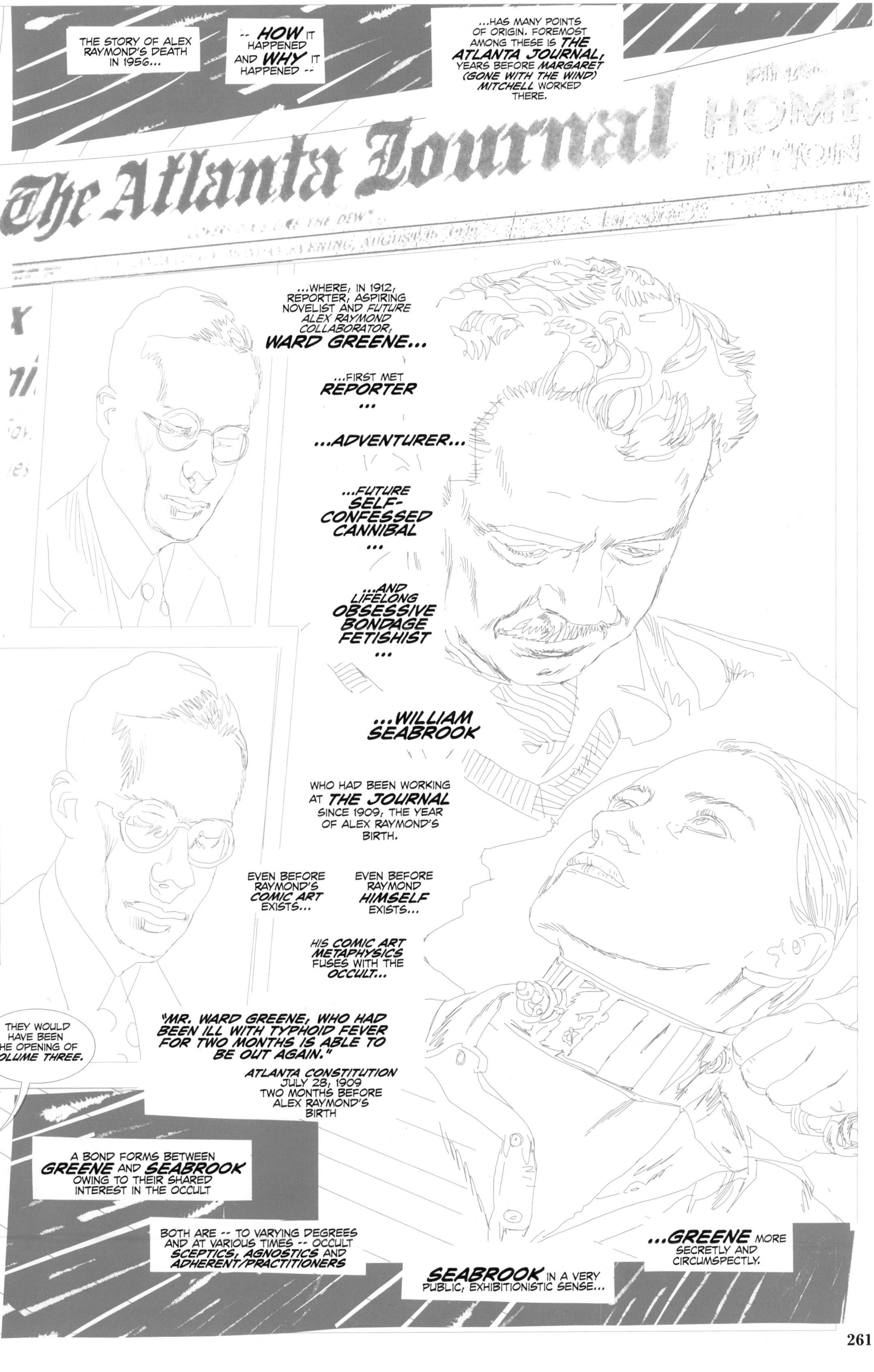

THE STORY OF ALEX RAYMOND'S DEATH IN 1956...
-- HOW IT HAPPENED AND WHY IT HAPPENED --
...HAS MANY POINTS OF ORIGIN. FOREMOST AMONG THESE IS THE ATLANTA JOURNAL, YEARS BEFORE MARGARET (GONE WITH THE WIND) MITCHELL WORKED THERE.
The Atlanta Journal
HOME EDITION
...WHERE, IN 1912, REPORTER, ASPIRING NOVELIST AND FUTURE ALEX RAYMOND COLLABORATOR, WARD GREENE...
...FIRST MET REPORTER ...
...ADVENTURER...
...FUTURE SELF-CONFESSED CANNIBAL ...
...AND LIFELONG OBSESSIVE BONDAGE FETISHIST ...
...WILLIAM SEABROOK
WHO HAD BEEN WORKING AT THE JOURNAL SINCE 1909, THE YEAR OF ALEX RAYMOND'S BIRTH.
EVEN BEFORE RAYMOND'S COMIC ART EXISTS...
EVEN BEFORE RAYMOND HIMSELF EXISTS...
HIS COMIC ART METAPHYSICS FUSES WITH THE OCCULT...
THEY WOULD HAVE BEEN THE OPENING OF VOLUME THREE.
"MR. WARD GREENE, WHO HAD BEEN ILL WITH TYPHOID FEVER FOR TWO MONTHS IS ABLE TO BE OUT AGAIN."
ATLANTA CONSTITUTION JULY 28, 1909 TWO MONTHS BEFORE ALEX RAYMOND'S BIRTH
A BOND FORMS BETWEEN GREENE AND SEABROOK OWING TO THEIR SHARED INTEREST IN THE OCCULT
BOTH ARE -- TO VARYING DEGREES AND AT VARIOUS TIMES -- OCCULT SCEPTICS, AGNOSTICS AND ADHERENT/PRACTITIONERS
SEABROOK IN A VERY PUBLIC, EXHIBITIONISTIC SENSE...
...GREENE MORE SECRETLY AND CIRCUMSPECTLY.

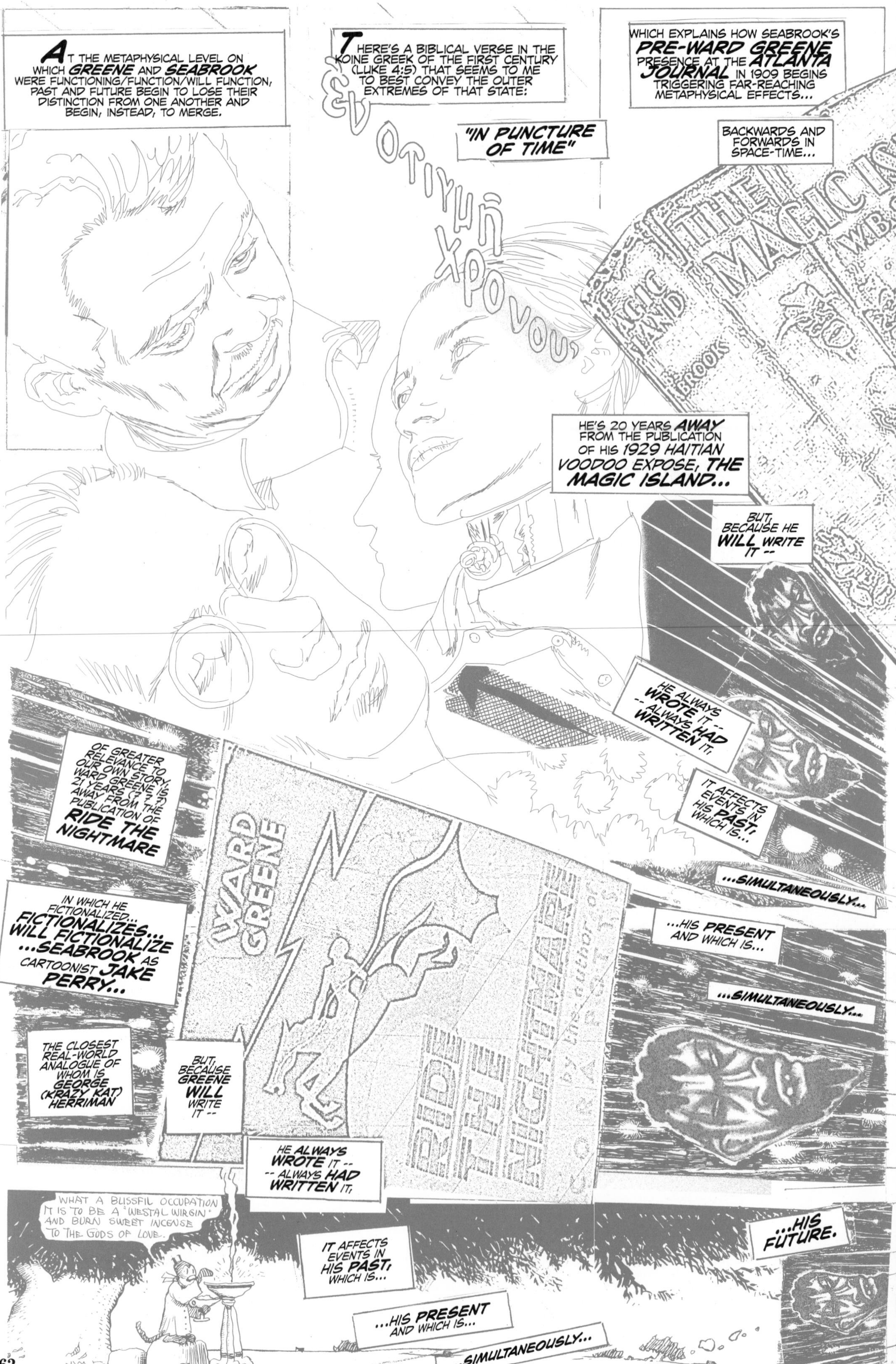

AT THE METAPHYSICAL LEVEL ON WHICH GREENE AND SEABROOK WERE FUNCTIONING/FUNCTION/WILL FUNCTION, PAST AND FUTURE BEGIN TO LOSE THEIR DISTINCTION FROM ONE ANOTHER AND BEGIN, INSTEAD, TO MERGE.
THERE'S A BIBLICAL VERSE IN THE KOINE GREEK OF THE FIRST CENTURY (LUKE 4:5) THAT SEEMS TO ME TO BEST CONVEY THE OUTER EXTREMES OF THAT STATE:
ἐν στιγμῇ χρόνου
"IN PUNCTURE OF TIME"
WHICH EXPLAINS HOW SEABROOK'S PRE-WARD GREENE PRESENCE AT THE ATLANTA JOURNAL IN 1909 BEGINS TRIGGERING FAR-REACHING METAPHYSICAL EFFECTS...
BACKWARDS AND FORWARDS IN SPACE-TIME...
HE'S 20 YEARS AWAY FROM THE PUBLICATION OF HIS 1929 HAITIAN VOODOO EXPOSE, THE MAGIC ISLAND...
BUT, BECAUSE HE WILL WRITE IT --
HE ALWAYS WROTE IT -- -- ALWAYS HAD WRITTEN IT,
IT AFFECTS EVENTS IN HIS PAST, WHICH IS...
...SIMULTANEOUSLY...
...HIS PRESENT AND WHICH IS...
...SIMULTANEOUSLY...
OF GREATER RELEVANCE TO OUR OWN STORY, WARD GREENE IS 21 YEARS (7 x 3) AWAY FROM THE PUBLICATION OF RIDE THE NIGHTMARE
IN WHICH HE FICTIONALIZED... FICTIONALIZES... WILL FICTIONALIZE ...SEABROOK AS CARTOONIST JAKE PERRY...
WARD GREENE
RIDE THE NIGHTMARE
THE CLOSEST REAL-WORLD ANALOGUE OF WHOM IS GEORGE (KRAZY KAT) HERRIMAN
BUT, BECAUSE GREENE WILL WRITE IT --
HE ALWAYS WROTE IT -- -- ALWAYS HAD WRITTEN IT,
WHAT A BLISSFIL OCCUPATION IT IS TO BE A 'WESTAL WIRGIN' AND BURN SWEET INCENSE TO THE GODS OF LOVE.
IT AFFECTS EVENTS IN HIS PAST, WHICH IS...
...HIS PRESENT AND WHICH IS...
...SIMULTANEOUSLY...
...HIS FUTURE.

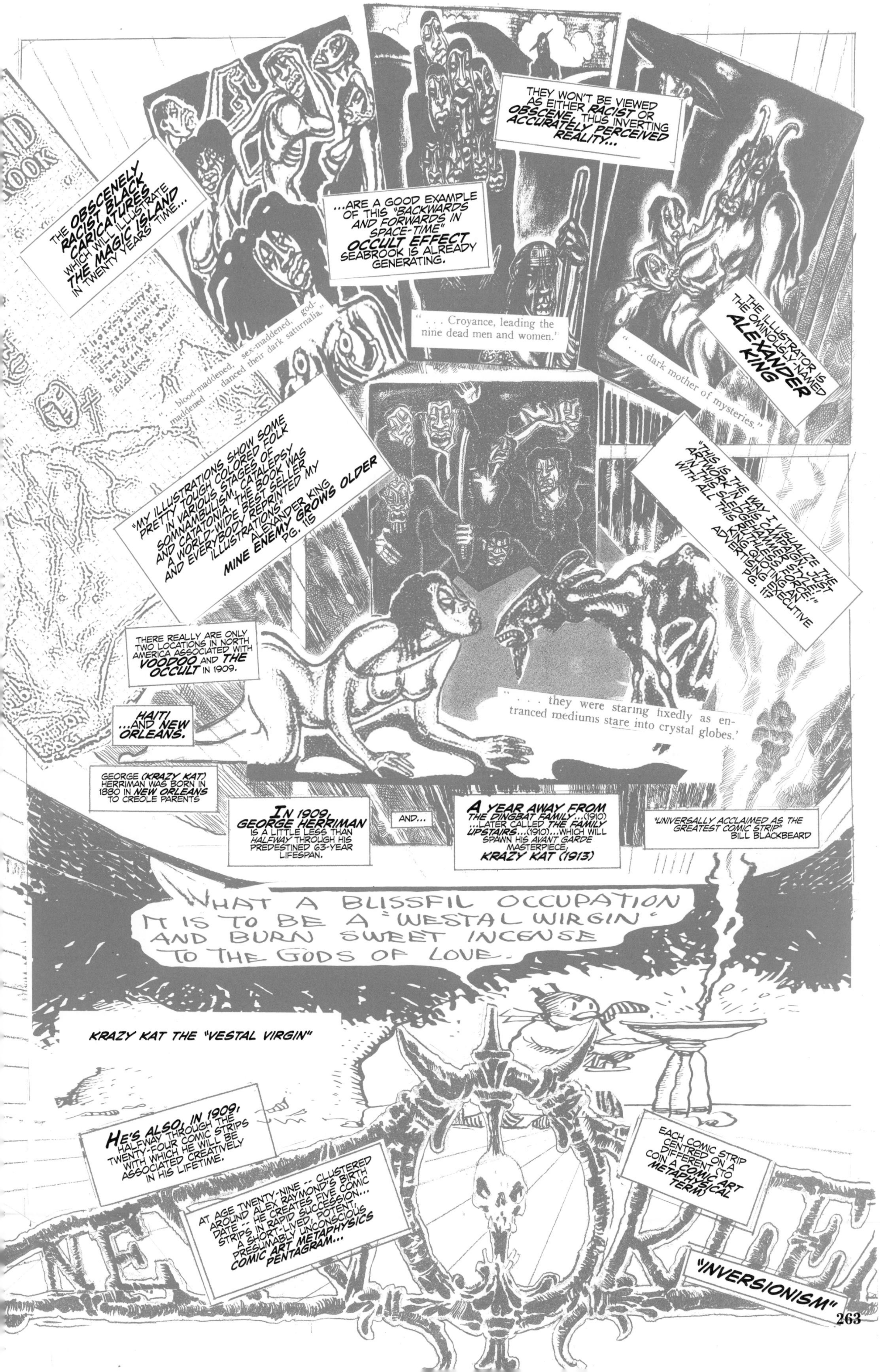
THE OBSCENELY RACIST BLACK CARICATURES WHICH WILL ILLUSTRATE THE MAGIC ISLAND IN TWENTY YEARS' TIME...
...ARE A GOOD EXAMPLE OF THIS "BACKWARDS AND FORWARDS IN SPACE-TIME" OCCULT EFFECT SEABROOK IS ALREADY GENERATING.
THEY WON'T BE VIEWED AS EITHER RACIST OR OBSCENE, THUS INVERTING ACCURATELY PERCEIVED REALITY...
". . . blood-maddened, sex-maddened, god-maddened . . . danced their dark saturnalia,"
". . . Croyance, leading the nine dead men and women."
THE ILLUSTRATOR IS THE OMINOUSLY-NAMED ALEXANDER KING
". . . dark mother of mysteries."
"MY ILLUSTRATIONS SHOW SOME PRETTY TOUGH COLORED FOLK IN VARIOUS STAGES OF SOMNAMBULISM, CATALEPSY AND CATATONIA. THE BOOK WAS A WORLD-WIDE BEST SELLER AND EVERYBODY REPRINTED MY ILLUSTRATIONS" ALEXANDER KING MINE ENEMY GROWS OLDER PG. 115
"THIS IS THE WAY I VISUALIZE THE ARTWORK IN THIS CAMPAIGN, JUST IN THIS SLEDGEHAMMER STYLE, WITH ALL THIS RUTHLESS FORCE!" KING QUOTING AN ADVERTISING EXECUTIVE PG. 117
THERE REALLY ARE ONLY TWO LOCATIONS IN NORTH AMERICA ASSOCIATED WITH VOODOO AND THE OCCULT IN 1909.
HAITI ...AND NEW ORLEANS.
". . . they were staring fixedly as entranced mediums stare into crystal globes."
GEORGE (KRAZY KAT) HERRIMAN WAS BORN IN 1880 IN NEW ORLEANS TO CREOLE PARENTS
IN 1909, GEORGE HERRIMAN IS A LITTLE LESS THAN HALFWAY THROUGH HIS PREDESTINED 63-YEAR LIFESPAN.
AND...
A YEAR AWAY FROM THE DINGBAT FAMILY...(1910) ...LATER CALLED THE FAMILY UPSTAIRS...(1910)...WHICH WILL SPAWN HIS AVANT GARDE MASTERPIECE, KRAZY KAT (1913)
"UNIVERSALLY ACCLAIMED AS THE GREATEST COMIC STRIP" BILL BLACKBEARD
WHAT A BLISSFIL OCCUPATION IT IS TO BE A 'WESTAL WIRGIN' AND BURN SWEET INCENSE TO THE GODS OF LOVE.
KRAZY KAT THE "VESTAL VIRGIN"
HE'S ALSO, IN 1909, HALFWAY THROUGH THE TWENTY-FOUR COMIC STRIPS WITH WHICH HE WILL BE ASSOCIATED CREATIVELY IN HIS LIFETIME.
AT AGE TWENTY-NINE -- CLUSTERED AROUND ALEX RAYMOND'S BIRTH DATE -- HE CREATES FIVE COMIC STRIPS IN RAPID SUCCESSION... A SHORT-LIVED, POTENT, PRESUMABLY UNCONSCIOUS COMIC ART METAPHYSICS PENTAGRAM...
EACH COMIC STRIP CENTRED ON A DIFFERENT (TO COIN A COMIC ART METAPHYSICAL TERM)
"INVERSIONISM"

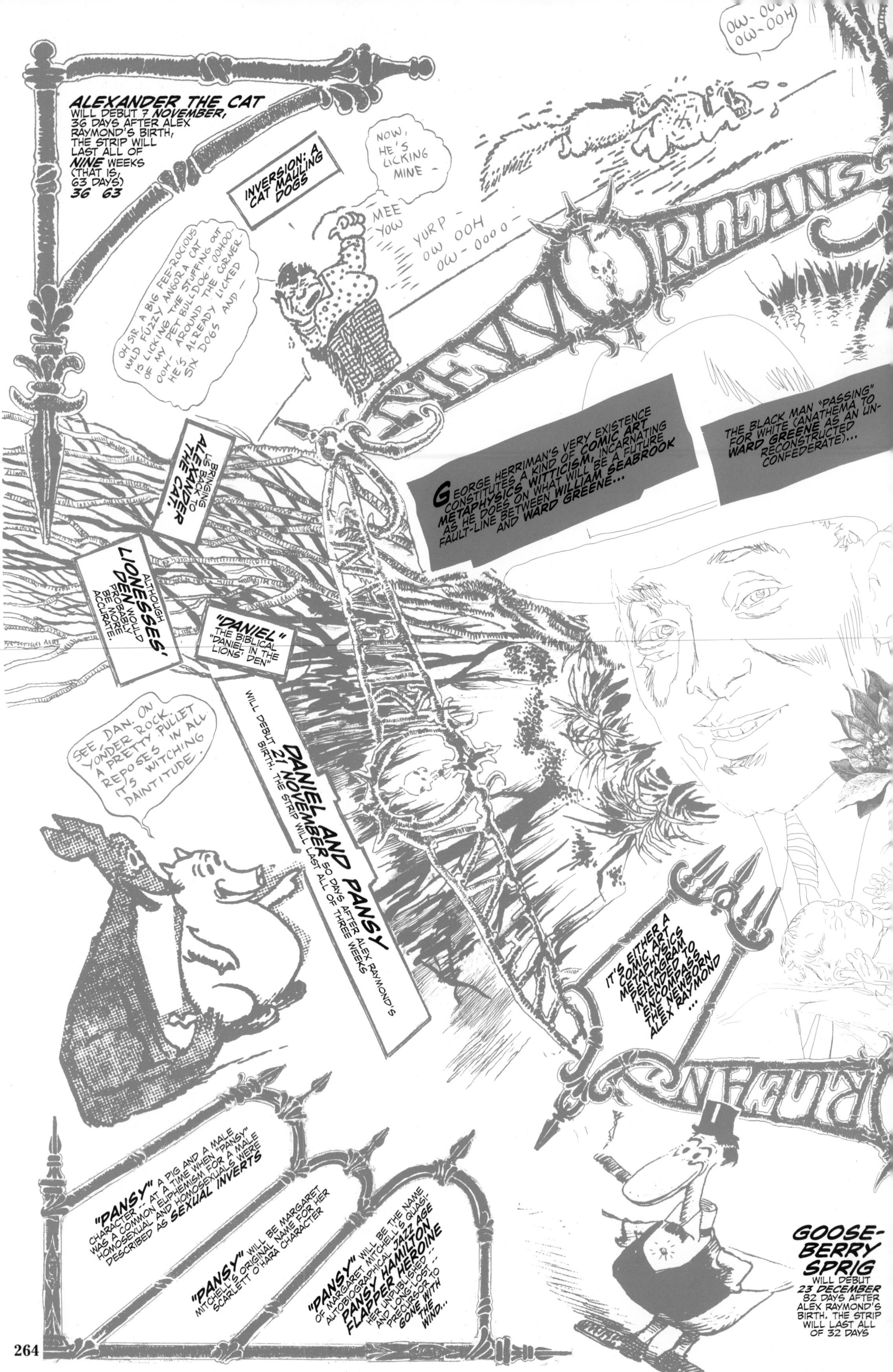
ALEXANDER THE CAT WILL DEBUT 7 NOVEMBER, 36 DAYS AFTER ALEX RAYMOND'S BIRTH, THE STRIP WILL LAST ALL OF NINE WEEKS (THAT IS, 63 DAYS) 36 63
INVERSION: A CAT MAULING DOGS
NOW, HE'S LICKING MINE -
OW-OOH OW-OOH
MEE YOW
YURP - OW OOH OW-OOOO-
OH SIR A BIG FEE-ROCIOUS WILD FUZZY ANGORA CAT IS LICKING THE STUFFING OUT OF MY PET BULLDOG - OOHOO-OOH- AROUND THE CORNER - HE'S ALREADY LICKED SIX DOGS AND -
NEW ORLEANS
GEORGE HERRIMAN'S VERY EXISTENCE CONSTITUTES A KIND OF COMIC ART METAPHYSICS WITTICISM, INCARNATING AS HE DOES ON WHAT WILL BE A FUTURE FAULT-LINE BETWEEN WILLIAM SEABROOK AND WARD GREENE...
THE BLACK MAN "PASSING" FOR WHITE (ANATHEMA TO WARD GREENE AS AN UN-RECONSTRUCTED CONFEDERATE)...
BRINGING US BACK TO ALEXANDER THE CAT.
ALTHOUGH LIONESSES' DEN WOULD PROBABLY BE MORE ACCURATE.
"DANIEL" THE BIBLICAL "DANIEL IN THE LIONS' DEN"
DANIEL AND PANSY WILL DEBUT 21 NOVEMBER 50 DAYS AFTER ALEX RAYMOND'S BIRTH. THE STRIP WILL LAST ALL OF THREE WEEKS
SEE, DAN. ON YONDER ROCK. A PRETTY PULLET REPOSES IN ALL IT'S WITCHING DAINTITUDE.
IT'S EITHER A COMIC ART METAPHYSICS PENTAGRAM INTENDED TO ENCOMPASS THE NEWBORN ALEX RAYMOND ...
"PANSY" A PIG AND A MALE CHARACTER -- AT A TIME WHEN "PANSY" WAS A COMMON EUPHEMISM FOR A MALE HOMOSEXUAL AND HOMOSEXUALS WERE DESCRIBED AS SEXUAL INVERTS
"PANSY" WILL BE MARGARET MITCHELL'S ORIGINAL NAME FOR HER SCARLETT O'HARA CHARACTER
"PANSY" WILL BE THE NAME OF MARGARET MITCHELL'S QUASI-AUTOBIOGRAPHICAL JAZZ AGE PANSY HAMILTON FLAPPER HEROINE -- HER UNPUBLISHED -- AND LONG-LOST -- PRECURSOR TO GONE WITH THE WIND...
GOOSE-BERRY SPRIG WILL DEBUT 23 DECEMBER 82 DAYS AFTER ALEX RAYMOND'S BIRTH. THE STRIP WILL LAST ALL OF 32 DAYS

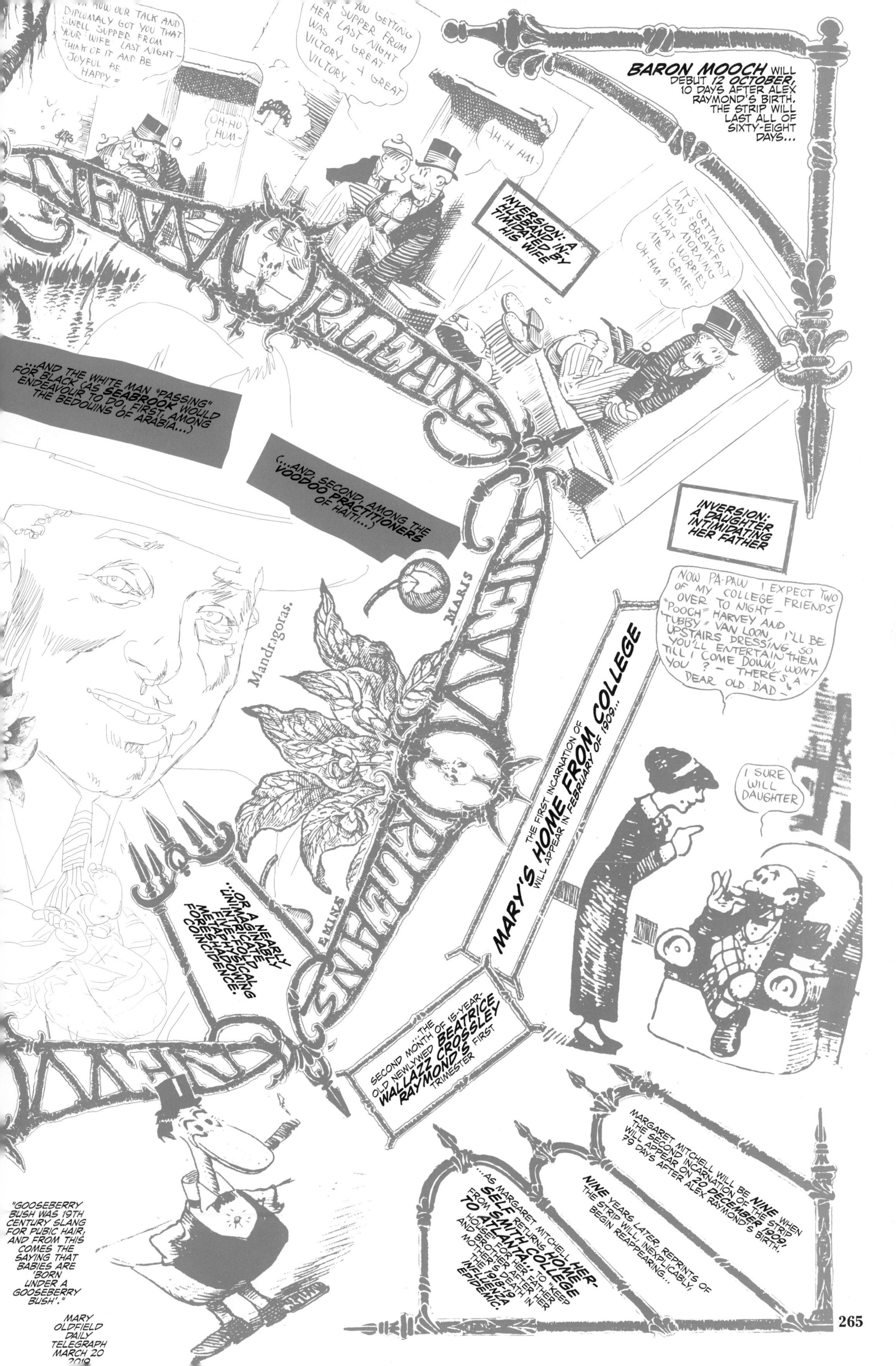

HOW OUR TACK AND DIPLOMACY GOT YOU THAT SWELL SUPPER FROM YOUR WIFE LAST NIGHT – THINK OF IT AND BE JOYFUL BE HAPPY =
OH-HO HUM –
YOU GETTING HER SUPPER FROM HER LAST NIGHT WAS A GREAT VICTORY – A GREAT VICTORY –
AH-H HM –
BARON MOOCH WILL DEBUT 12 OCTOBER, 10 DAYS AFTER ALEX RAYMOND'S BIRTH. THE STRIP WILL LAST ALL OF SIXTY-EIGHT DAYS...
INVERSION: A HUSBAND IN-TIMIDATED BY HIS WIFE
IT'S GETTING MY BREAKFAST THIS MORNING WHAT WORRIES ME – GRIMES OH-HM-M –
...AND THE WHITE MAN "PASSING" FOR BLACK (AS SEABROOK WOULD ENDEAVOUR TO DO, FIRST, AMONG THE BEDOUINS OF ARABIA...)
(...AND, SECOND, AMONG THE VOODOO PRACTITIONERS OF HAITI...)
INVERSION: A DAUGHTER INTIMIDATING HER FATHER
NOW PA-PAW I EXPECT TWO OF MY COLLEGE FRIENDS OVER TO NIGHT – "POOCH" HARVEY AND "TUBBY" VAN LOON, I'LL BE UPSTAIRS DRESSING, SO YOU'LL ENTERTAIN THEM TILL I COME DOWN, WONT YOU ? – THERE'S A DEAR OLD DAD –
MARIS
Mandragoras.
THE FIRST INCARNATION OF MARY'S HOME FROM COLLEGE WILL APPEAR IN FEBRUARY OF 1909...
I SURE WILL DAUGHTER
...OR A NEARLY UNIMAGINABLY INTRICATE FIVE-FOLD METAPHYSICAL FORESHADOWING COINCIDENCE.
EMINS
...THE SECOND MONTH OF 15-YEAR-OLD NEWLYWED BEATRICE WALLAZZ CROSSLEY RAYMOND'S FIRST TRIMESTER
MARGARET MITCHELL WILL BE NINE WHEN THE SECOND INCARNATION OF THE STRIP WILL APPEAR ON 20 DECEMBER 1909, 79 DAYS AFTER ALEX RAYMOND'S BIRTH.
NINE YEARS LATER, REPRINTS OF THE STRIP WILL, INEXPLICABLY, BEGIN REAPPEARING...
...AS MARGARET MITCHELL HER-SELF RETURNS HOME FROM SMITH COLLEGE TO ATLANTA... TO "KEEP HOUSE" FOR HER FATHER AND BROTHER AFTER HER MOTHER'S DEATH IN THE 1918-19 INFLUENZA EPIDEMIC.
"GOOSEBERRY BUSH WAS 19TH CENTURY SLANG FOR PUBIC HAIR, AND FROM THIS COMES THE SAYING THAT BABIES ARE 'BORN UNDER A GOOSEBERRY BUSH'."
MARY OLDFIELD DAILY TELEGRAPH MARCH 20 2019

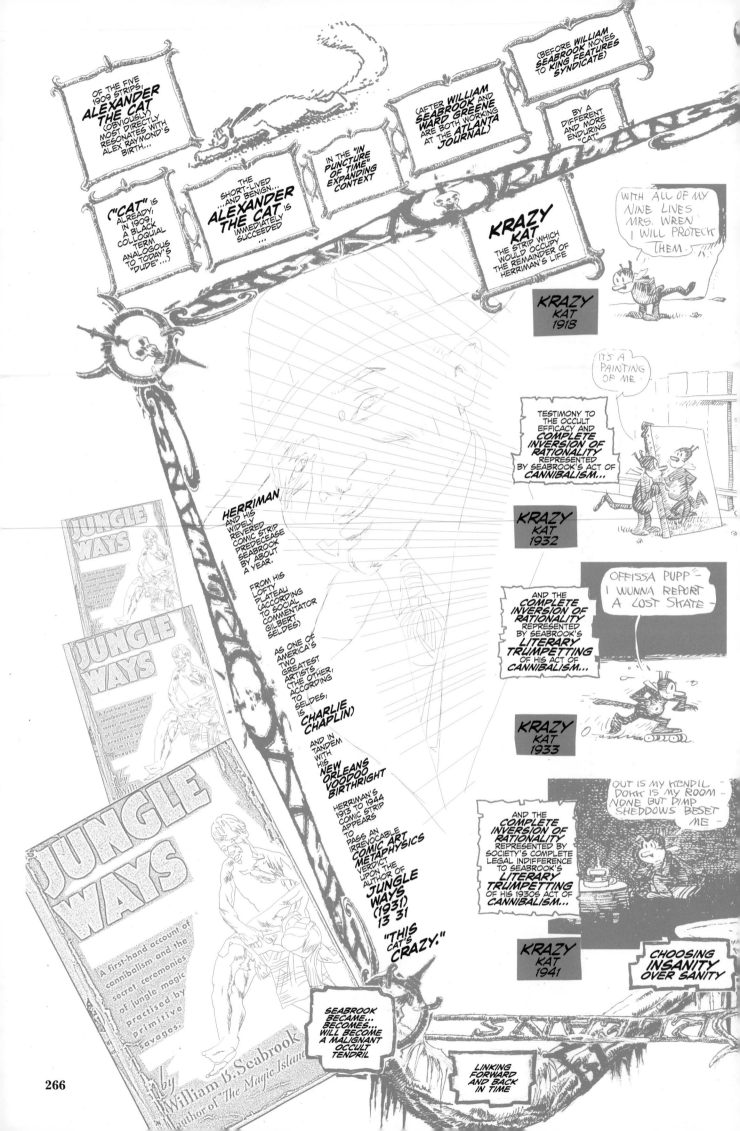

OF THE FIVE 1909 STRIPS, **ALEXANDER THE CAT** (OBVIOUSLY) MOST DIRECTLY RESONATES WITH ALEX RAYMOND'S BIRTH...

(BEFORE WILLIAM SEABROOK MOVES TO KING FEATURES SYNDICATE)

(AFTER WILLIAM SEABROOK AND WARD GREENE ARE BOTH WORKING AT THE *ATLANTA JOURNAL*)

BY A DIFFERENT AND MORE ENDURING "CAT"

("CAT" IS ALREADY, IN 1909, A BLACK COLLOQUIAL TERM ANALOGOUS TO TODAY'S "DUDE"...)

THE SHORT-LIVED... AND BENIGN... ...**ALEXANDER THE CAT** IS IMMEDIATELY SUCCEEDED...

IN THE "IN PUNCTURE OF TIME" EXPANDING CONTEXT

**KRAZY KAT** THE STRIP WHICH WOULD OCCUPY THE REMAINDER OF HERRIMAN'S LIFE

WITH ALL OF MY NINE LIVES MRS. WREN I WILL PROTECK THEM.

*KRAZY KAT 1918*

IT'S A PAINTING OF ME

TESTIMONY TO THE OCCULT EFFICACY AND **COMPLETE INVERSION OF RATIONALITY** REPRESENTED BY SEABROOK'S ACT OF **CANNIBALISM**...

*KRAZY KAT 1932*

OFFISSA PUPP— I WUNNA REPORT A LOST SKATE—

AND THE **COMPLETE INVERSION OF RATIONALITY** REPRESENTED BY SEABROOK'S **LITERARY TRUMPETTING** OF HIS ACT OF **CANNIBALISM**...

*KRAZY KAT 1933*

OUT IS MY KENDIL DOKK IS MY ROOM— NONE BUT DIMP SHEDDOWS BESET ME—

AND THE **COMPLETE INVERSION OF RATIONALITY** REPRESENTED BY SOCIETY'S COMPLETE LEGAL INDIFFERENCE TO SEABROOK'S **LITERARY TRUMPETTING** OF HIS 1930s ACT OF **CANNIBALISM**...

*KRAZY KAT 1941*

**CHOOSING INSANITY OVER SANITY**

HERRIMAN AND HIS WIDELY REVERED COMIC STRIP PREDECEASE SEABROOK BY ABOUT A YEAR.

FROM HIS LOFTY PLATEAU (ACCORDING TO SOCIAL COMMENTATOR GILBERT SELDES)

AS ONE OF AMERICA'S TWO GREATEST ARTISTS (THE OTHER, ACCORDING TO SELDES, IS **CHARLIE CHAPLIN**)

AND IN TANDEM WITH HIS **NEW ORLEANS VOODOO BIRTHRIGHT**

HERRIMAN'S 1913 TO 1944 COMIC STRIP APPEARS TO PASS AN IRREVOCABLE **COMIC ART METAPHYSICS** VERDICT UPON THE AUTHOR OF **JUNGLE WAYS** (1931) 13 31

**"THIS CAT'S CRAZY."**

**JUNGLE WAYS**

A first-hand account of cannibalism and the secret ceremonies of jungle magic practised by primitive savages.

by William B. Seabrook author of "The Magic Island"

SEABROOK BECAME... BECOMES... WILL BECOME A MALIGNANT OCCULT TENDRIL

LINKING FORWARD AND BACK IN TIME

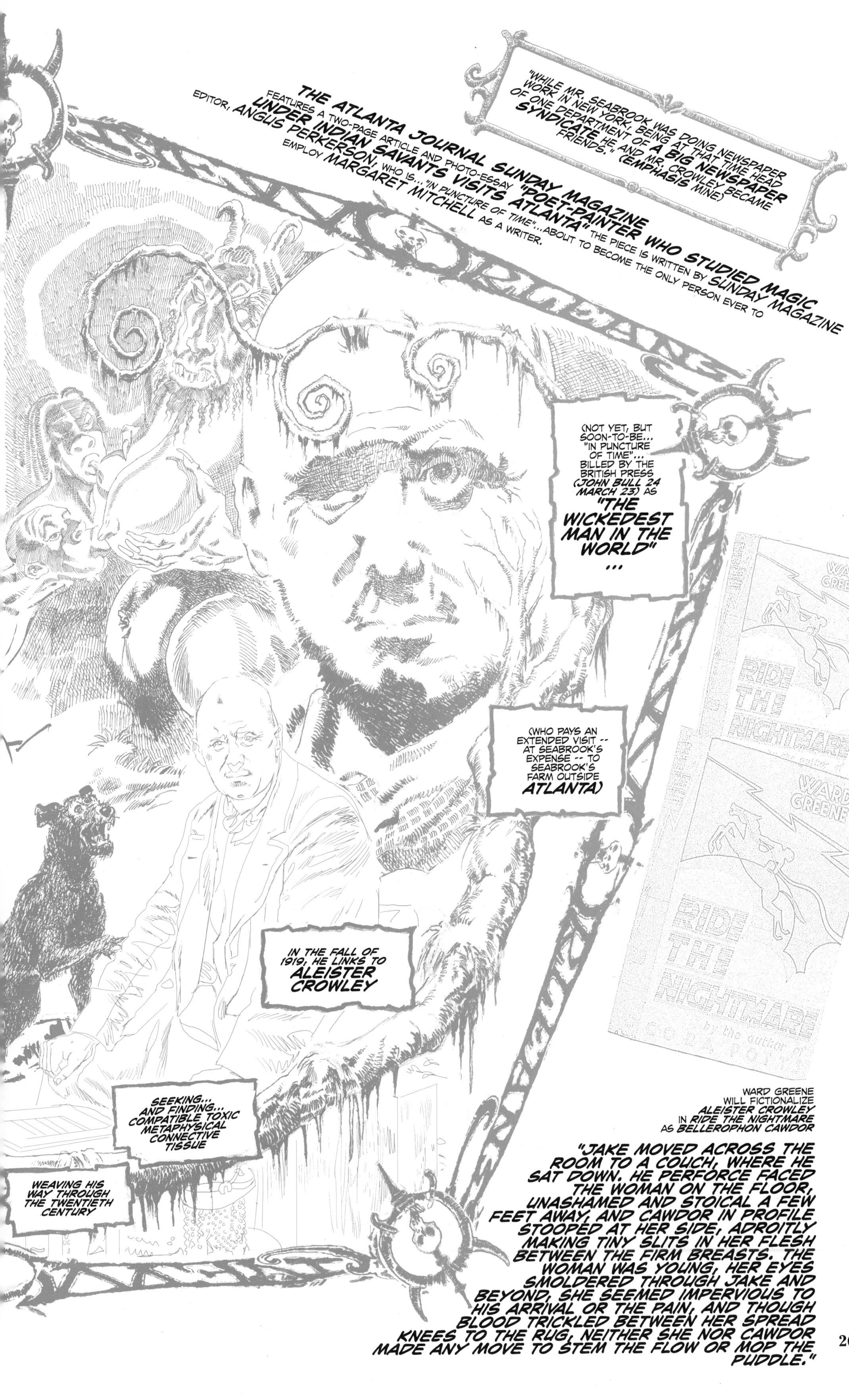
WEAVING HIS WAY THROUGH THE TWENTIETH CENTURY
SEEKING... AND FINDING... COMPATIBLE TOXIC METAPHYSICAL CONNECTIVE TISSUE
IN THE FALL OF 1919, HE LINKS TO ALEISTER CROWLEY
(NOT YET, BUT SOON-TO-BE... "IN PUNCTURE OF TIME"... BILLED BY THE BRITISH PRESS (JOHN BULL 24 MARCH 23) AS "THE WICKEDEST MAN IN THE WORLD" ...
(WHO PAYS AN EXTENDED VISIT -- AT SEABROOK'S EXPENSE -- TO SEABROOK'S FARM OUTSIDE ATLANTA)
"WHILE MR. SEABROOK WAS DOING NEWSPAPER WORK IN NEW YORK, BEING AT THAT TIME HEAD OF ONE DEPARTMENT OF A BIG NEWSPAPER SYNDICATE HE AND MR. CROWLEY BECAME FRIENDS." (EMPHASIS MINE)
THE ATLANTA JOURNAL SUNDAY MAGAZINE FEATURES A TWO-PAGE ARTICLE AND PHOTO-ESSAY "POET-PAINTER WHO STUDIED MAGIC UNDER INDIAN SAVANTS VISITS ATLANTA" THE PIECE IS WRITTEN BY SUNDAY MAGAZINE EDITOR, ANGUS PERKERSON, WHO IS..."IN PUNCTURE OF TIME"...ABOUT TO BECOME THE ONLY PERSON EVER TO EMPLOY MARGARET MITCHELL AS A WRITER.
WARD GREENE
RIDE THE NIGHTMARE
WARD GREENE
RIDE THE NIGHTMARE
by the author of
WARD GREENE WILL FICTIONALIZE ALEISTER CROWLEY IN RIDE THE NIGHTMARE AS BELLEROPHON CAWDOR
"JAKE MOVED ACROSS THE ROOM TO A COUCH, WHERE HE SAT DOWN. HE PERFORCE FACED THE WOMAN ON THE FLOOR, UNASHAMED AND STOICAL A FEW FEET AWAY, AND CAWDOR IN PROFILE STOOPED AT HER SIDE, ADROITLY MAKING TINY SLITS IN HER FLESH BETWEEN THE FIRM BREASTS. THE WOMAN WAS YOUNG, HER EYES SMOLDERED THROUGH JAKE AND BEYOND; SHE SEEMED IMPERVIOUS TO HIS ARRIVAL OR THE PAIN, AND THOUGH BLOOD TRICKLED BETWEEN HER SPREAD KNEES TO THE RUG, NEITHER SHE NOR CAWDOR MADE ANY MOVE TO STEM THE FLOW OR MOP THE PUDDLE."

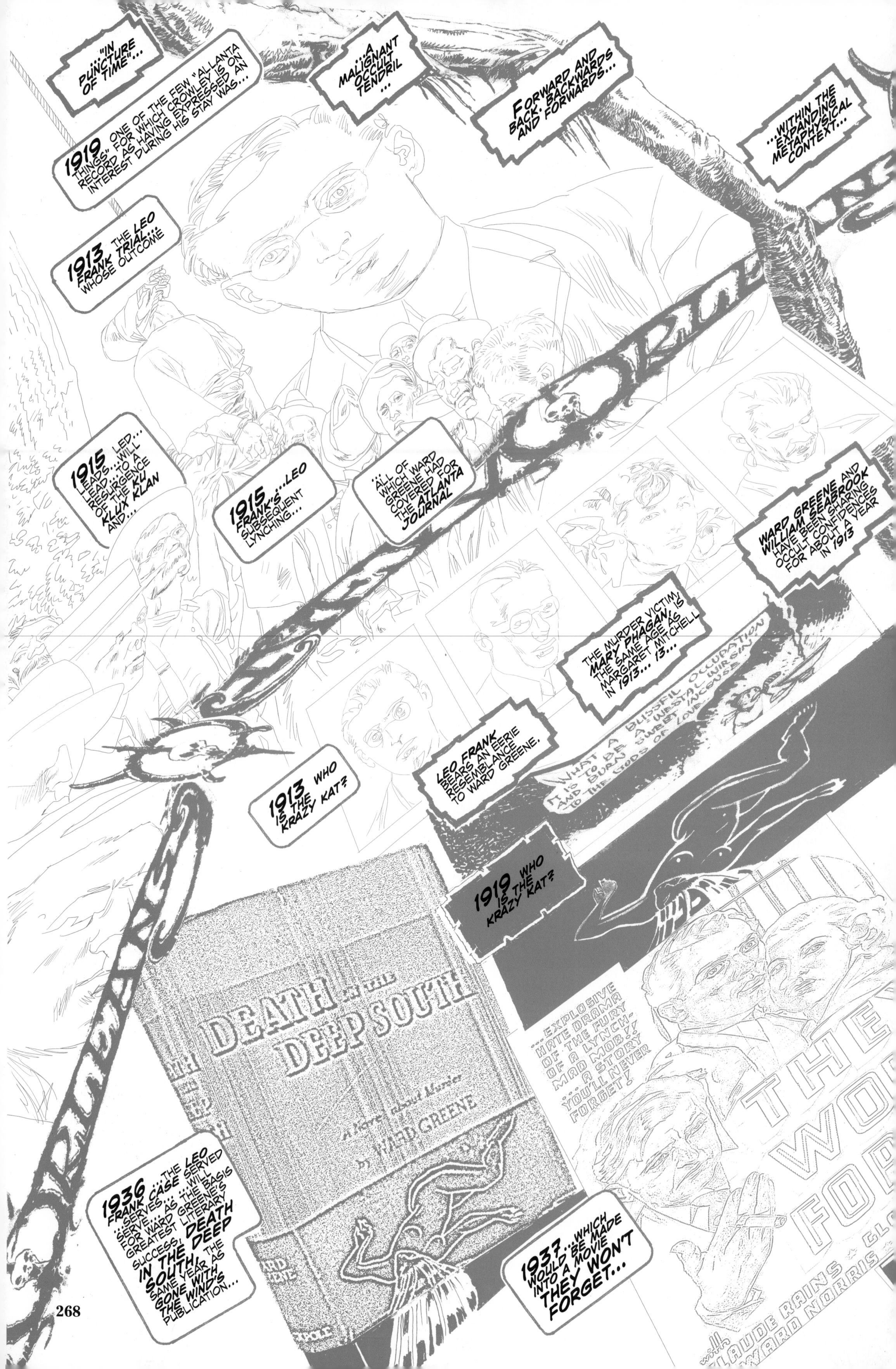

..."IN PUNCTURE OF TIME"...
...A MALIGNANT OCCULT TENDRIL ...
FORWARD AND BACK, BACKWARDS AND FORWARDS...
...WITHIN THE EXPANDING METAPHYSICAL CONTEXT...
1919 ...ONE OF THE FEW "ATLANTA THINGS" FOR WHICH CROWLEY IS ON RECORD AS HAVING EXPRESSED AN INTEREST DURING HIS STAY WAS...
1913 THE LEO FRANK TRIAL... WHOSE OUTCOME
1915 LED... LEADS... WILL LEAD... TO A RESURGENCE OF THE KU KLUX KLAN AND...
1915 ...LEO FRANK'S SUBSEQUENT LYNCHING...
...ALL OF WHICH WARD GREENE HAD COVERED FOR THE ATLANTA JOURNAL
WARD GREENE AND WILLIAM SEABROOK HAVE BEEN SHARING OCCULT CONFIDENCES FOR ABOUT A YEAR IN 1913
THE MURDER VICTIM, MARY PHAGAN, IS THE SAME AGE AS MARGARET MITCHELL IN 1913... 13...
WHAT A BLISSFUL OCCUPATION IT IS TO BE A VESTAL VIRGIN AND BURN SWEET INCENSE TO THE GODS OF LOVE
LEO FRANK BEARS AN EERIE RESEMBLANCE TO WARD GREENE.
1913 WHO IS THE KRAZY KAT?
1919 WHO IS THE KRAZY KAT?
DEATH IN THE DEEP SOUTH
A Novel about Murder
by WARD GREENE
...EXPLOSIVE HATE DRAMA OF THE FURY OF A LYNCH-MAD MOB!! ...A STORY YOU'LL NEVER FORGET!
with CLAUDE RAINS
1936 ...THE LEO FRANK CASE SERVED ...SERVES... ...WILL SERVE... AS THE BASIS FOR WARD GREENE'S GREATEST LITERARY SUCCESS, DEATH IN THE DEEP SOUTH, THE SAME YEAR AS GONE WITH THE WIND'S PUBLICATION...
1937 ...WHICH WOULD BE MADE INTO A MOVIE THEY WON'T FORGET...

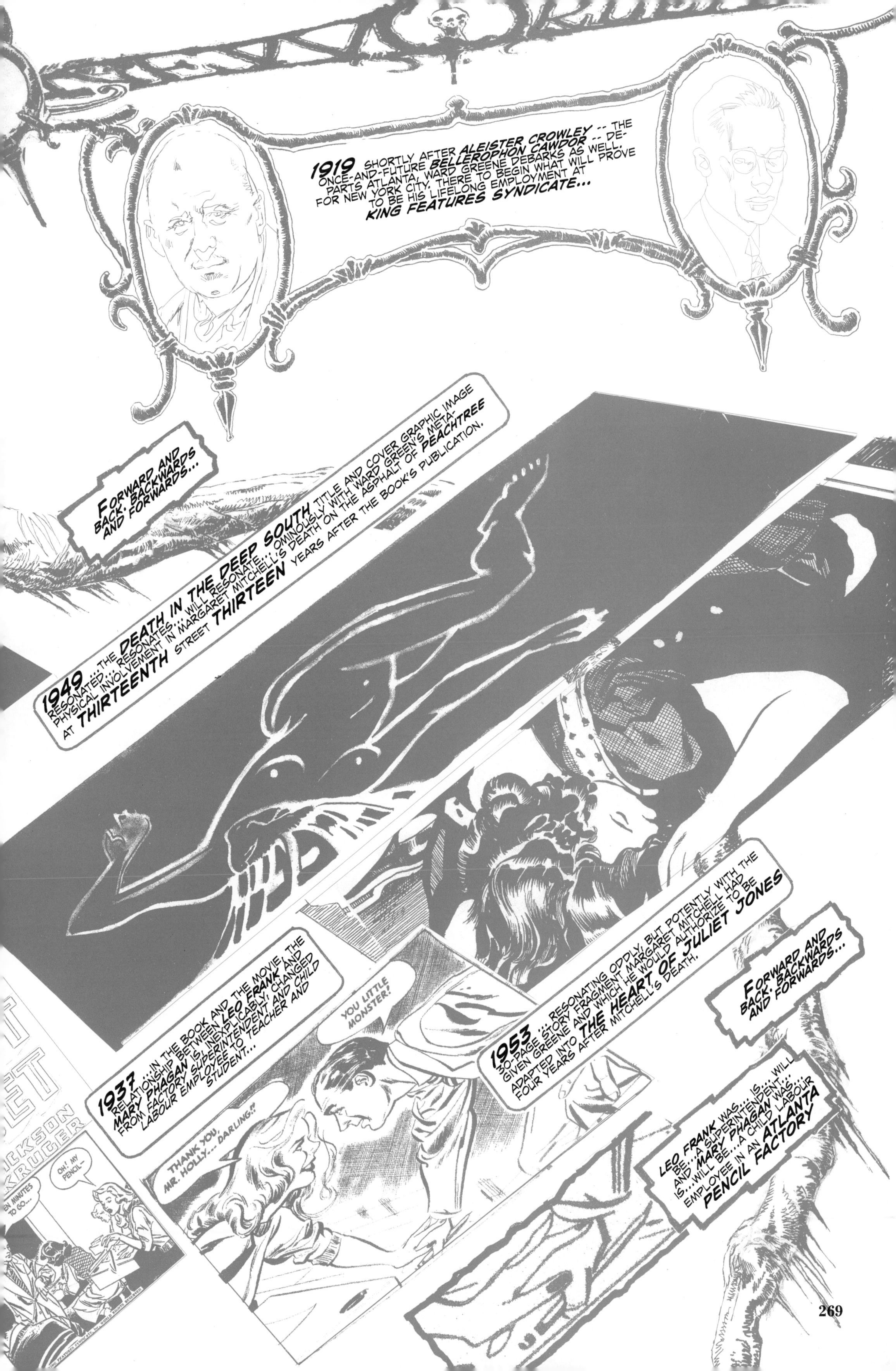
1919 SHORTLY AFTER ALEISTER CROWLEY -- THE ONCE-AND-FUTURE BELLEROPHON CAWDOR -- DEPARTS ATLANTA, WARD GREENE DEBARKS AS WELL, FOR NEW YORK CITY, THERE TO BEGIN WHAT WILL PROVE TO BE HIS LIFELONG EMPLOYMENT AT KING FEATURES SYNDICATE...
FORWARD AND BACK. BACKWARDS AND FORWARDS...
1949 ...THE DEATH IN THE DEEP SOUTH TITLE AND COVER GRAPHIC IMAGE RESONATED... RESONATES... WILL RESONATE... OMINOUSLY WITH WARD GREEN'S META-PHYSICAL INVOLVEMENT IN MARGARET MITCHELL'S DEATH ON THE ASPHALT OF PEACHTREE AT THIRTEENTH STREET THIRTEEN YEARS AFTER THE BOOK'S PUBLICATION.
1937 ...IN THE BOOK AND THE MOVIE, THE RELATIONSHIP BETWEEN LEO FRANK AND MARY PHAGAN IS, INEXPLICABLY, CHANGED FROM FACTORY SUPERINTENDENT AND CHILD LABOUR EMPLOYEE TO TEACHER AND STUDENT...
YOU LITTLE MONSTER!
THANK YOU, MR. HOLLY... DARLING!!
OH! MY PENCIL-
EN MINUTES TO GO...
1953 ... RESONATING ODDLY, BUT POTENTLY WITH THE 30-PAGE STORY FRAGMENT MARGARET MITCHELL HAD GIVEN GREENE AND WHICH HE WOULD AUTHORIZE TO BE ADAPTED INTO THE HEART OF JULIET JONES FOUR YEARS AFTER MITCHELL'S DEATH.
FORWARD AND BACK. BACKWARDS AND FORWARDS...
LEO FRANK WAS... IS... WILL BE...A SUPERINTENDENT... AND MARY PHAGAN WAS... IS...WILL BE...A CHILD LABOUR EMPLOYEE IN AN ATLANTA PENCIL FACTORY

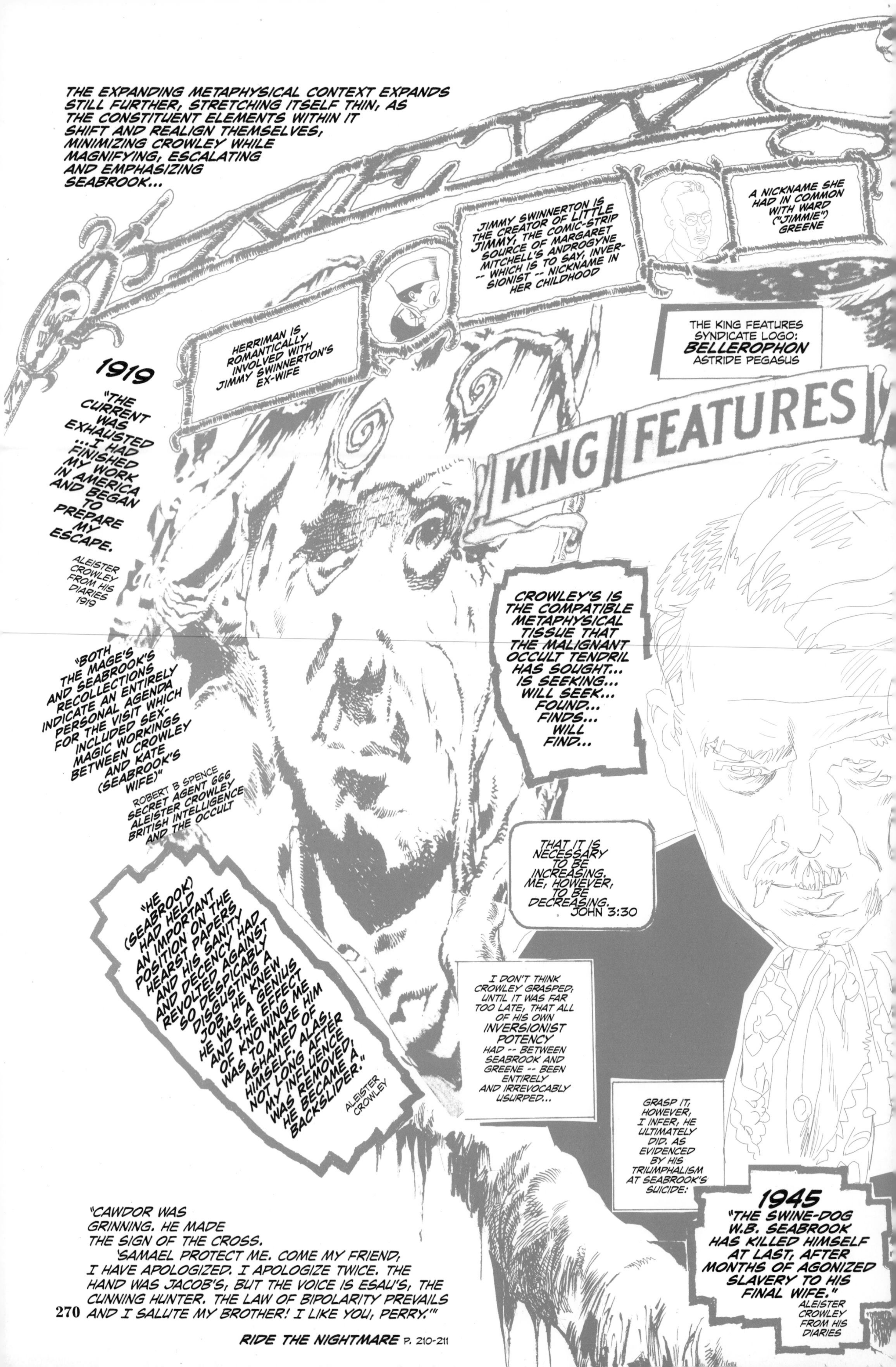
THE EXPANDING METAPHYSICAL CONTEXT EXPANDS STILL FURTHER, STRETCHING ITSELF THIN, AS THE CONSTITUENT ELEMENTS WITHIN IT SHIFT AND REALIGN THEMSELVES, MINIMIZING CROWLEY WHILE MAGNIFYING, ESCALATING AND EMPHASIZING SEABROOK...
HERRIMAN IS ROMANTICALLY INVOLVED WITH JIMMY SWINNERTON'S EX-WIFE
JIMMY SWINNERTON IS THE CREATOR OF LITTLE JIMMY, THE COMIC-STRIP SOURCE OF MARGARET MITCHELL'S ANDROGYNE -- WHICH IS TO SAY, INVERSIONIST -- NICKNAME IN HER CHILDHOOD
A NICKNAME SHE HAD IN COMMON WITH WARD ("JIMMIE") GREENE
THE KING FEATURES SYNDICATE LOGO: BELLEROPHON ASTRIDE PEGASUS
KING FEATURES
1919
"THE CURRENT WAS EXHAUSTED ...I HAD FINISHED MY WORK IN AMERICA AND BEGAN TO PREPARE MY ESCAPE.
ALEISTER CROWLEY FROM HIS DIARIES 1919
CROWLEY'S IS THE COMPATIBLE METAPHYSICAL TISSUE THAT THE MALIGNANT OCCULT TENDRIL HAS SOUGHT... IS SEEKING... WILL SEEK... FOUND... FINDS... WILL FIND...
"BOTH THE MAGE'S AND SEABROOK'S RECOLLECTIONS INDICATE AN ENTIRELY PERSONAL AGENDA FOR THE VISIT WHICH INCLUDED SEX-MAGIC WORKINGS BETWEEN CROWLEY AND KATE (SEABROOK'S WIFE)"
ROBERT B SPENCE SECRET AGENT 666 ALEISTER CROWLEY, BRITISH INTELLIGENCE AND THE OCCULT
THAT IT IS NECESSARY TO BE INCREASING, ME, HOWEVER, TO BE DECREASING. JOHN 3:30
"HE (SEABROOK) HAD HELD AN IMPORTANT POSITION ON THE HEARST PAPERS AND HIS SANITY AND DECENCY HAD REVOLTED AGAINST SO DESPICABLY DISGUSTING A JOB. HE KNEW HE WAS A GENIUS AND THE EFFECT OF KNOWING ME WAS TO MAKE HIM ASHAMED OF HIMSELF. ALAS, NOT LONG AFTER MY INFLUENCE WAS REMOVED, HE BECAME A BACKSLIDER."
ALEISTER CROWLEY
I DON'T THINK CROWLEY GRASPED, UNTIL IT WAS FAR TOO LATE, THAT ALL OF HIS OWN INVERSIONIST POTENCY HAD -- BETWEEN SEABROOK AND GREENE -- BEEN ENTIRELY AND IRREVOCABLY USURPED...
GRASP IT, HOWEVER, I INFER, HE ULTIMATELY DID. AS EVIDENCED BY HIS TRIUMPHALISM AT SEABROOK'S SUICIDE:
1945
"THE SWINE-DOG W.B. SEABROOK HAS KILLED HIMSELF AT LAST, AFTER MONTHS OF AGONIZED SLAVERY TO HIS FINAL WIFE."
ALEISTER CROWLEY FROM HIS DIARIES
"CAWDOR WAS GRINNING. HE MADE THE SIGN OF THE CROSS.
'SAMAEL PROTECT ME. COME MY FRIEND, I HAVE APOLOGIZED. I APOLOGIZE TWICE. THE HAND WAS JACOB'S, BUT THE VOICE IS ESAU'S, THE CUNNING HUNTER. THE LAW OF BIPOLARITY PREVAILS AND I SALUTE MY BROTHER! I LIKE YOU, PERRY.'"
RIDE THE NIGHTMARE P. 210-211

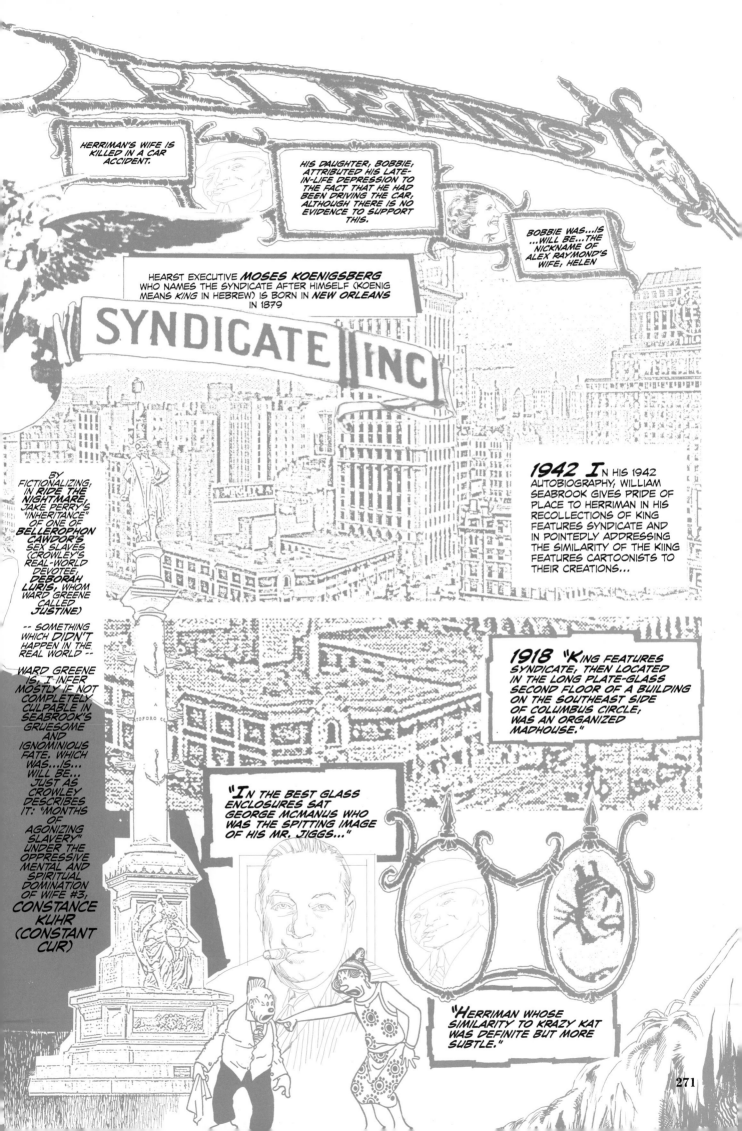

HERRIMAN'S WIFE IS KILLED IN A CAR ACCIDENT.

HIS DAUGHTER, BOBBIE, ATTRIBUTED HIS LATE-IN-LIFE DEPRESSION TO THE FACT THAT HE HAD BEEN DRIVING THE CAR, ALTHOUGH THERE IS NO EVIDENCE TO SUPPORT THIS.

BOBBIE WAS...IS ...WILL BE...THE NICKNAME OF ALEX RAYMOND'S WIFE, HELEN

HEARST EXECUTIVE **MOSES KOENIGSBERG** WHO NAMES THE SYNDICATE AFTER HIMSELF (KOENIG MEANS *KING* IN HEBREW) IS BORN IN **NEW ORLEANS** IN 1879

SYNDICATE INC

BY FICTIONALIZING, IN *RIDE THE NIGHTMARE*, JAKE PERRY'S "INHERITANCE" OF ONE OF **BELLEROPHON CAWDOR'S** SEX SLAVES (CROWLEY'S REAL-WORLD DEVOTEE, **DEBORAH LURIS**, WHOM WARD GREENE CALLED *JUSTINE*)

-- SOMETHING WHICH *DIDN'T* HAPPEN IN THE REAL WORLD --

WARD GREENE IS, I INFER MOSTLY IF NOT COMPLETELY CULPABLE IN SEABROOK'S GRUESOME AND IGNOMINIOUS FATE. WHICH WAS...IS... WILL BE... JUST AS CROWLEY DESCRIBES IT: "MONTHS OF AGONIZING SLAVERY" UNDER THE OPPRESSIVE MENTAL AND SPIRITUAL DOMINATION OF WIFE #3, **CONSTANCE KUHR** (CONSTANT CUR)

**1942** *I*N HIS 1942 AUTOBIOGRAPHY, WILLIAM SEABROOK GIVES PRIDE OF PLACE TO HERRIMAN IN HIS RECOLLECTIONS OF KING FEATURES SYNDICATE AND IN POINTEDLY ADDRESSING THE SIMILARITY OF THE KIING FEATURES CARTOONISTS TO THEIR CREATIONS...

**1918** "*K*ING FEATURES SYNDICATE, THEN LOCATED IN THE LONG PLATE-GLASS SECOND FLOOR OF A BUILDING ON THE SOUTHEAST SIDE OF COLUMBUS CIRCLE; WAS AN ORGANIZED MADHOUSE."

"*I*N THE BEST GLASS ENCLOSURES SAT GEORGE MCMANUS WHO WAS THE SPITTING IMAGE OF HIS MR. JIGGS..."

"*H*ERRIMAN WHOSE SIMILARITY TO KRAZY KAT WAS DEFINITE BUT MORE SUBTLE."

"IT HAD BEEN DURING MANY DRUNKEN NIGHTS IN ATLANTA, NO DOUBT, THAT WILLIE HAD SPILLED OUT TO 'JIMMY' [SIC] NOTHING LESS THAN A FUTURE HISTORY...AT THE LEAST, GREENE HAD CHRONICLED PARTICULAR MATTERS ON WHICH WILLIE HAD BEEN FIXATED, FROM A FUTURE HE IMAGINED HE RECALLED."
PAUL PIPKIN
*THE FAN-SHAPED DESTINY OF WILLIAM SEABROOK*

THE MALIGNANT TENDRIL LINKING CROWLEY TO SEABROOK; LINKING SEABROOK TO GREENE... THAT WEAVE... ITS WILL WEAVE THROUGH WAY THROUGH THE TWENTIETH CENTURY: FORWARD AND BACKWARD IN TIME:

## WILLIAM SEABROOK, AUTHOR, A SUICIDE

Found Dead in Dutchess County Home From Overdose of Sleeping Pills

RHINEBECK, N. Y., Sept. 20 (P)—William B. Seabrook, 59-year-old author and explorer, was found dead today from what Dr. Samuel E. Appel, Dutchess County Medical Examiner, said was an overdose of sleeping pills.

Dr. Appel listed the death as a suicide.

The medical examiner said there would be no autopsy. He said that his investigation showed that the author had "made threats" to take his life.

Seabrook's wife, the former Constance Kuhr, who found her husband's body in bed at their farm home, previously had said an autopsy would be performed.

Made Books of His Exploration

William Buehler Seabrook wrote exciting books out of his explorations of far places. His included the Arabian deserts and Haiti and Timbuktu. [remaining text illegible]

*William B. Seabrook*

**1945**
MOSES KOENIGSBERG -- WHO NAMED *KING FEATURES SYNDICATE* AFTER HIMSELF -- DIES ONE DAY AFTER WILLIAM SEABROOK'S SUICIDE

IN THE FALL OF 1945 AS *RIP KIRBY* IS IN DEVELOPMENT...

WILLIAM SEABROOK'S *NEW YORK TIMES* OBITUARY

WITH SEABROOK'S PASSING, "THEN THERE WERE TWO" CROWLEY AND WARD GREENE.

FORWARD IN TIME:

**1930**
GREENE WROTE... WRITES... WILL WRITE ...OF HIS FICTIONALIZED **ALEISTER CROWLEY:**

:BACKWARD IN TIME.

THEN. THERE WAS ONE. WARD GREENE.

**1947**
TWO YEARS LATER, IN THE *RIP KIRBY* "BLEAK PROSPECTS" STORYLINE, WARD GREENE CREATES A QUASI-AUTO-BIOGRAPHICAL, QUASI-WISHFUL THINKING, QUASI-OCCULT INVOCATION MILLIONAIRE, *DEREK STARLOCK*

DERRICK - "A KIND OF CRANE ...FOR LIFTING HEAVY WEIGHTS (ORIGIN EARLY 17TH CENTURY DENOTING AN **ENGLISH HANGMAN)**" STARLOCK - STAR WARLOCK

PAST MIDNIGHT! SHE'S NEVER DONE THIS BEFORE! ELLEN, ELLEN! WHY MUST YOU TORTURE ME? I'D GIVE MY LIFE FOR YOU!

STARLOCK LOOKS LIKE ALEISTER CROWLEY WITH AN ALEX RAYMOND MOUSTACHE

**1947**
DECEMBER 1ST. EIGHT WEEKS INTO THE "BLEAK PROSPECTS" STORYLINE, ALEISTER CROWLEY DIES IN HASTINGS, ENGLAND OF A **SEVERE RESPIRATORY AILMENT** (CHRONIC BRONCHITIS AGGRAVATED BY PLEURISY) AND **MYOCARDIAL DEGENERATION**

FORWARD IN TIME:

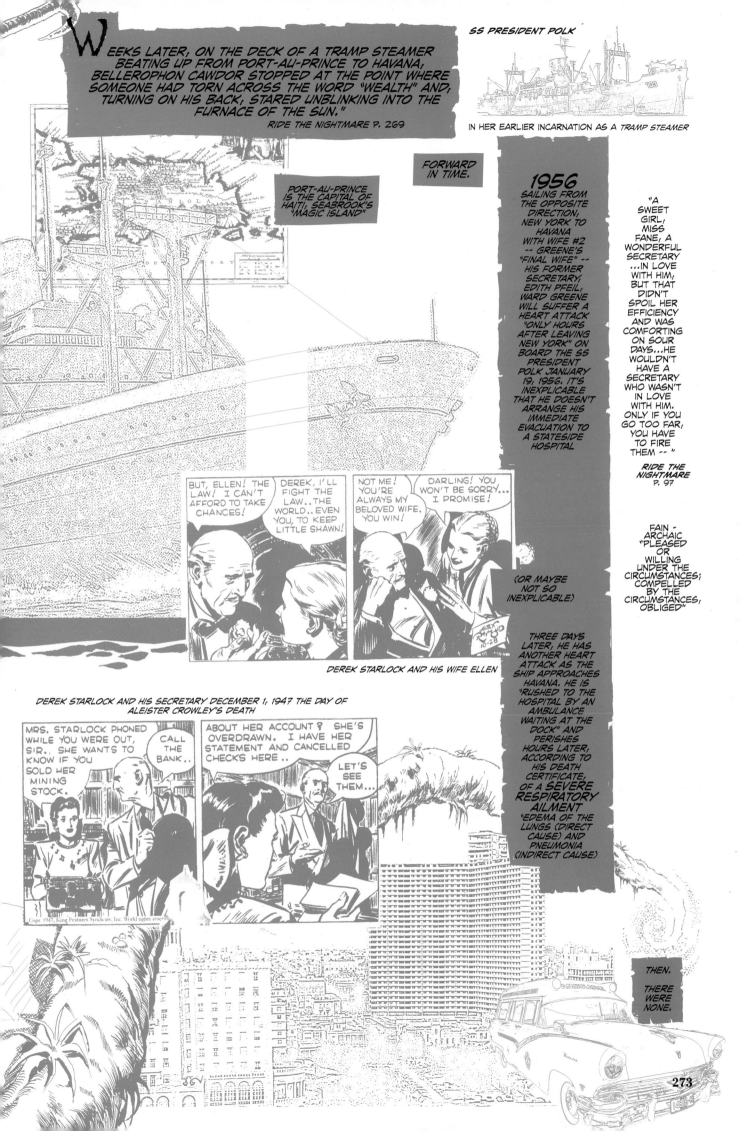

Weeks later, on the deck of a tramp steamer beating up from Port-au-Prince to Havana, Bellerophon Cawdor stopped at the point where someone had torn across the word "wealth" and, turning on his back, stared unblinking into the furnace of the sun."

RIDE THE NIGHTMARE P. 269

SS PRESIDENT POLK

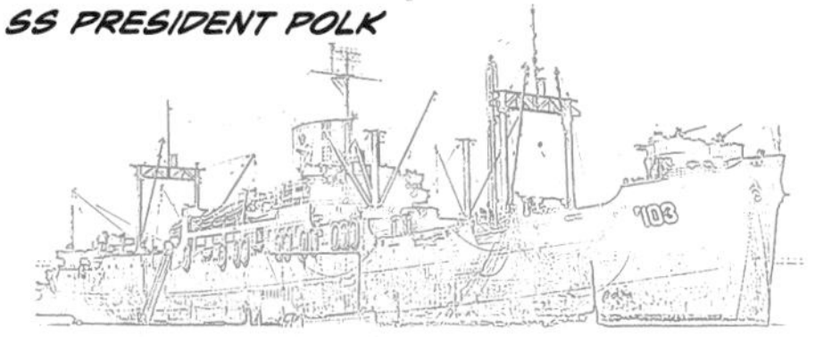

IN HER EARLIER INCARNATION AS A *TRAMP STEAMER*

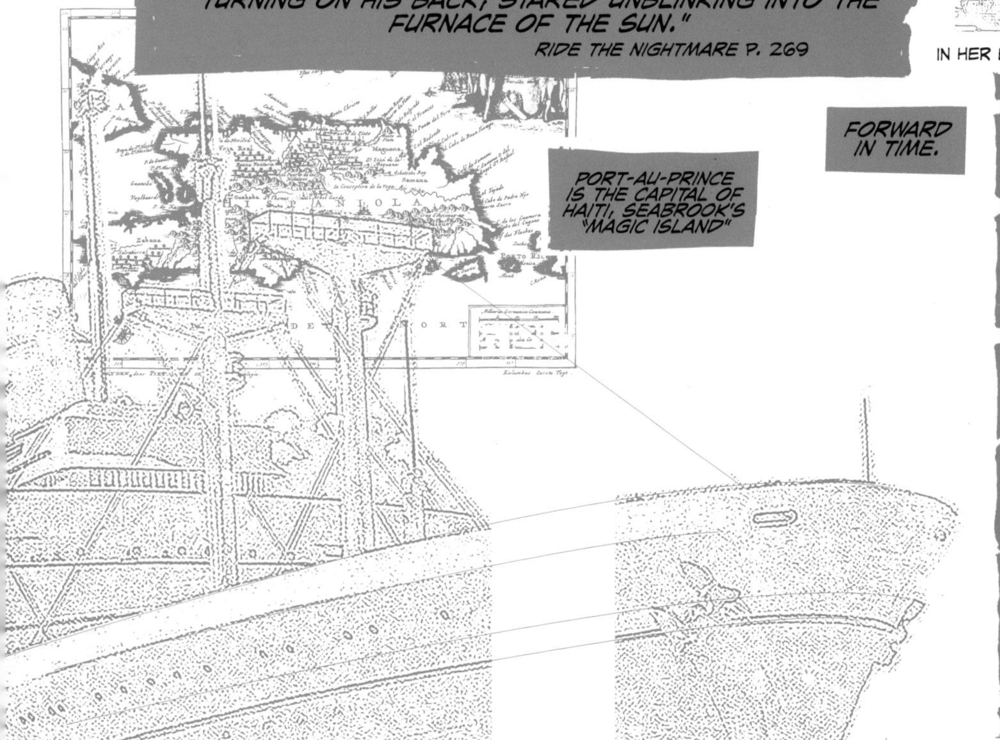

PORT-AU-PRINCE IS THE CAPITAL OF HAITI, SEABROOK'S "MAGIC ISLAND"

FORWARD IN TIME.

**1956**

SAILING FROM THE OPPOSITE DIRECTION, NEW YORK TO HAVANA WITH WIFE #2 -- GREENE'S "FINAL WIFE" -- HIS FORMER SECRETARY, EDITH PFEIL, WARD GREENE WILL SUFFER A HEART ATTACK "ONLY HOURS AFTER LEAVING NEW YORK" ON BOARD THE SS PRESIDENT POLK JANUARY 19, 1956. IT'S INEXPLICABLE THAT HE DOESN'T ARRANGE HIS IMMEDIATE EVACUATION TO A STATESIDE HOSPITAL

"A SWEET GIRL, MISS FANE, A WONDERFUL SECRETARY ...IN LOVE WITH HIM, BUT THAT DIDN'T SPOIL HER EFFICIENCY AND WAS COMFORTING ON SOUR DAYS...HE WOULDN'T HAVE A SECRETARY WHO WASN'T IN LOVE WITH HIM. ONLY IF YOU GO TOO FAR, YOU HAVE TO FIRE THEM -- "

***RIDE THE NIGHTMARE*** P. 97

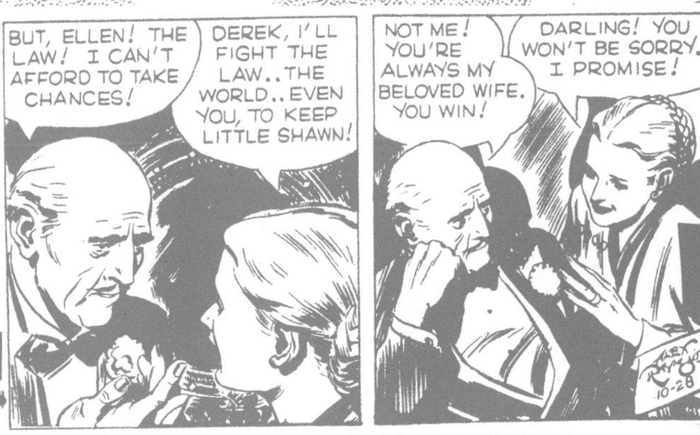
BUT, ELLEN! THE LAW! I CAN'T AFFORD TO TAKE CHANCES!
DEREK, I'LL FIGHT THE LAW..THE WORLD..EVEN YOU, TO KEEP LITTLE SHAWN!
NOT ME! YOU'RE ALWAYS MY BELOVED WIFE. YOU WIN!
DARLING! YOU WON'T BE SORRY... I PROMISE!
10-28

DEREK STARLOCK AND HIS WIFE ELLEN

(OR MAYBE NOT SO INEXPLICABLE)

FAIN - ARCHAIC "PLEASED OR WILLING UNDER THE CIRCUMSTANCES; COMPELLED BY THE CIRCUMSTANCES, OBLIGED"

THREE DAYS LATER, HE HAS ANOTHER HEART ATTACK AS THE SHIP APPROACHES HAVANA. HE IS "RUSHED TO THE HOSPITAL BY AN AMBULANCE WAITING AT THE DOCK" AND PERISHES HOURS LATER, ACCORDING TO HIS DEATH CERTIFICATE, OF A **SEVERE RESPIRATORY AILMENT** "EDEMA OF THE LUNGS (DIRECT CAUSE) AND PNEUMONIA (INDIRECT CAUSE)

DEREK STARLOCK AND HIS SECRETARY DECEMBER 1, 1947 THE DAY OF ALEISTER CROWLEY'S DEATH

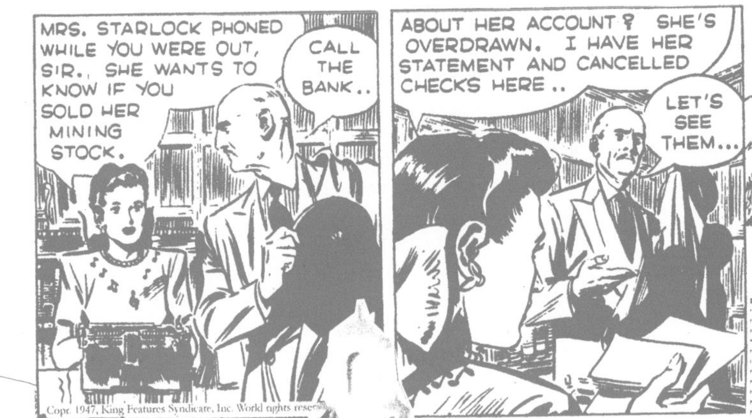
MRS. STARLOCK PHONED WHILE YOU WERE OUT, SIR.. SHE WANTS TO KNOW IF YOU SOLD HER MINING STOCK.
CALL THE BANK..
ABOUT HER ACCOUNT? SHE'S OVERDRAWN. I HAVE HER STATEMENT AND CANCELLED CHECKS HERE..
LET'S SEE THEM...
Copr. 1947, King Features Syndicate, Inc. World rights reser

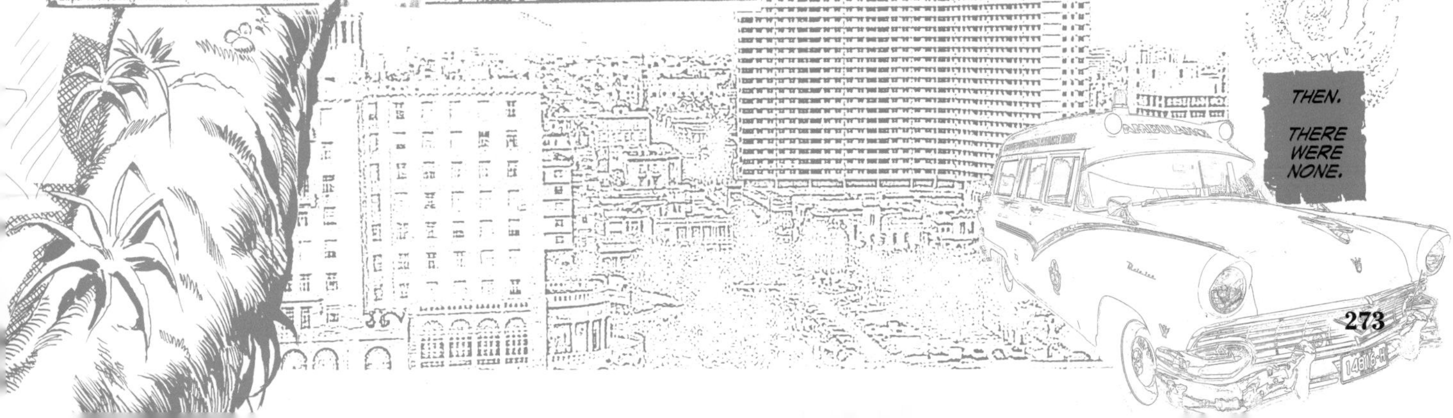

THEN.

THERE WERE NONE.

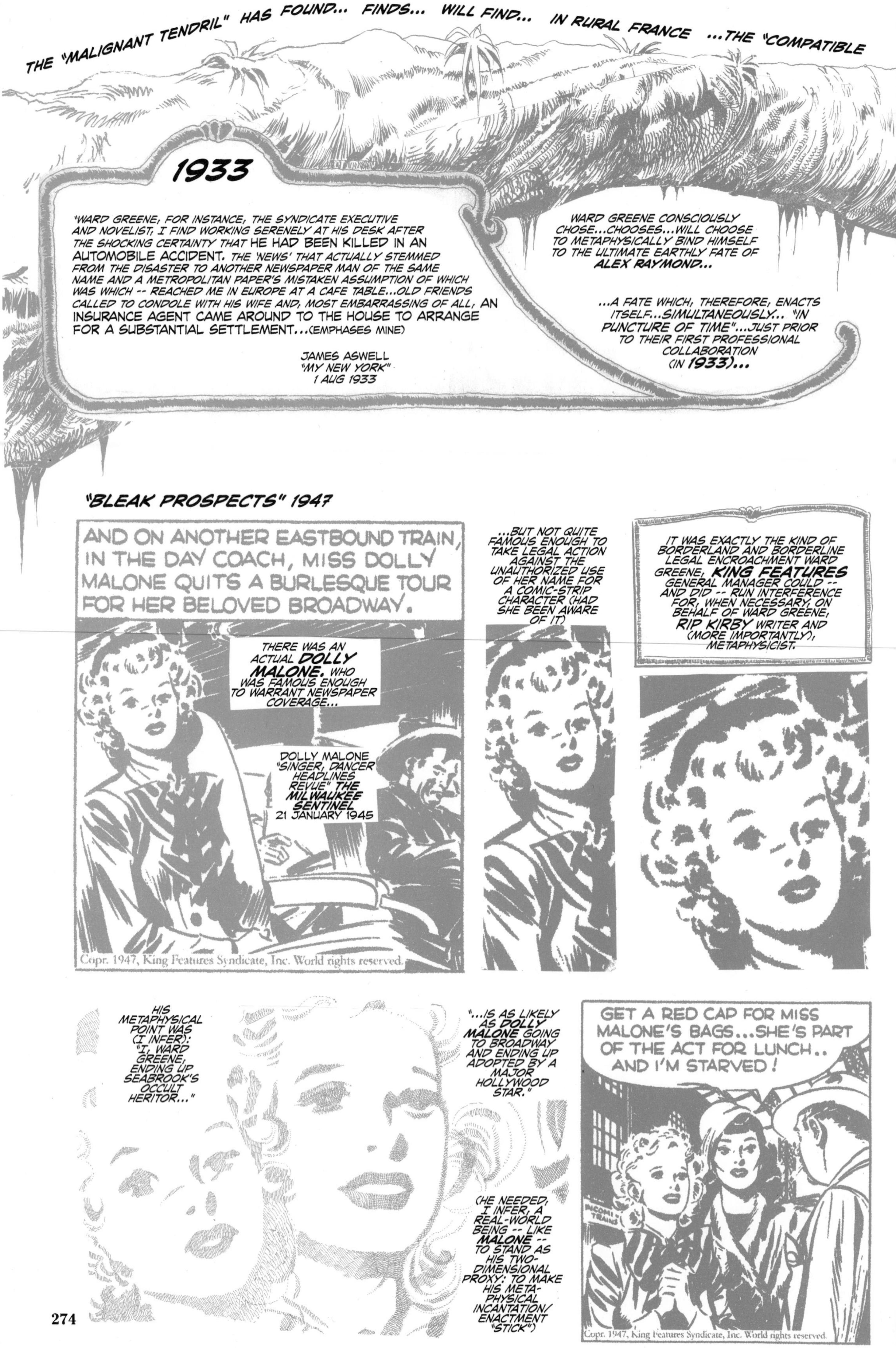
THE "MALIGNANT TENDRIL" HAS FOUND... FINDS... WILL FIND... IN RURAL FRANCE ...THE "COMPATIBLE
1933
"WARD GREENE, FOR INSTANCE, THE SYNDICATE EXECUTIVE AND NOVELIST, I FIND WORKING SERENELY AT HIS DESK AFTER THE SHOCKING CERTAINTY THAT HE HAD BEEN KILLED IN AN AUTOMOBILE ACCIDENT. THE 'NEWS' THAT ACTUALLY STEMMED FROM THE DISASTER TO ANOTHER NEWSPAPER MAN OF THE SAME NAME AND A METROPOLITAN PAPER'S MISTAKEN ASSUMPTION OF WHICH WAS WHICH -- REACHED ME IN EUROPE AT A CAFE TABLE...OLD FRIENDS CALLED TO CONDOLE WITH HIS WIFE AND, MOST EMBARRASSING OF ALL, AN INSURANCE AGENT CAME AROUND TO THE HOUSE TO ARRANGE FOR A SUBSTANTIAL SETTLEMENT...(EMPHASES MINE)
JAMES ASWELL
"MY NEW YORK"
1 AUG 1933
WARD GREENE CONSCIOUSLY CHOSE...CHOOSES...WILL CHOOSE TO METAPHYSICALLY BIND HIMSELF TO THE ULTIMATE EARTHLY FATE OF ALEX RAYMOND...
...A FATE WHICH, THEREFORE, ENACTS ITSELF...SIMULTANEOUSLY... "IN PUNCTURE OF TIME"...JUST PRIOR TO THEIR FIRST PROFESSIONAL COLLABORATION (IN 1933)...
"BLEAK PROSPECTS" 1947
AND ON ANOTHER EASTBOUND TRAIN, IN THE DAY COACH, MISS DOLLY MALONE QUITS A BURLESQUE TOUR FOR HER BELOVED BROADWAY.
THERE WAS AN ACTUAL DOLLY MALONE, WHO WAS FAMOUS ENOUGH TO WARRANT NEWSPAPER COVERAGE...
DOLLY MALONE "SINGER, DANCER HEADLINES REVUE" THE MILWAUKEE SENTINEL 21 JANUARY 1945
Copr. 1947, King Features Syndicate, Inc. World rights reserved.
...BUT NOT QUITE FAMOUS ENOUGH TO TAKE LEGAL ACTION AGAINST THE UNAUTHORIZED USE OF HER NAME FOR A COMIC-STRIP CHARACTER (HAD SHE BEEN AWARE OF IT)
IT WAS EXACTLY THE KIND OF BORDERLAND AND BORDERLINE LEGAL ENCROACHMENT WARD GREENE, KING FEATURES GENERAL MANAGER COULD -- AND DID -- RUN INTERFERENCE FOR, WHEN NECESSARY, ON BEHALF OF WARD GREENE, RIP KIRBY WRITER AND (MORE IMPORTANTLY), METAPHYSICIST.
HIS METAPHYSICAL POINT WAS (I INFER): "I, WARD GREENE, ENDING UP SEABROOK'S OCCULT HERITOR..."
"...IS AS LIKELY AS DOLLY MALONE GOING TO BROADWAY AND ENDING UP ADOPTED BY A MAJOR HOLLYWOOD STAR."
(HE NEEDED, I INFER, A REAL-WORLD BEING -- LIKE MALONE -- TO STAND AS HIS TWO-DIMENSIONAL PROXY: TO MAKE HIS META-PHYSICAL INCANTATION/ ENACTMENT "STICK")
GET A RED CAP FOR MISS MALONE'S BAGS...SHE'S PART OF THE ACT FOR LUNCH.. AND I'M STARVED!
INCOMING TRAINS
Copr. 1947, King Features Syndicate, Inc. World rights reserved.

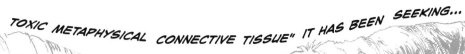

"TOXIC METAPHYSICAL CONNECTIVE TISSUE" IT HAS BEEN SEEKING... SEEKS... WILL SEEK...

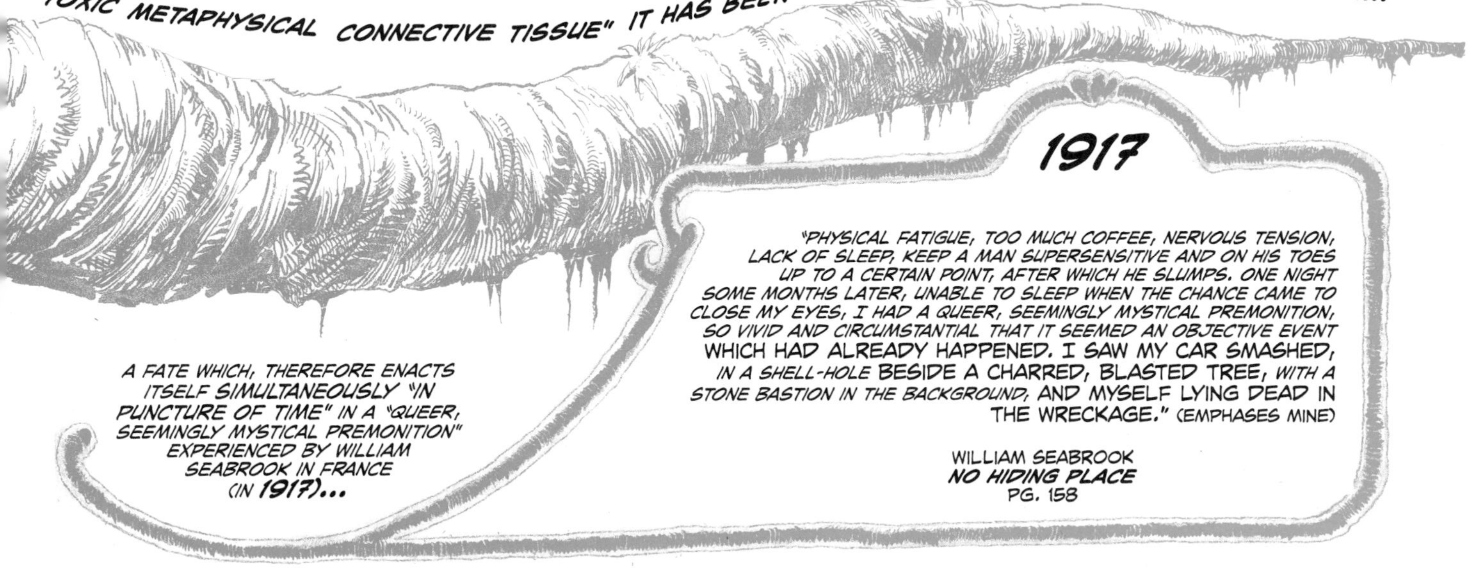

A FATE WHICH, THEREFORE ENACTS ITSELF SIMULTANEOUSLY "IN PUNCTURE OF TIME" IN A "QUEER, SEEMINGLY MYSTICAL PREMONITION" EXPERIENCED BY WILLIAM SEABROOK IN FRANCE (IN **1917**)...

## 1917

"PHYSICAL FATIGUE, TOO MUCH COFFEE, NERVOUS TENSION, LACK OF SLEEP, KEEP A MAN SUPERSENSITIVE AND ON HIS TOES UP TO A CERTAIN POINT, AFTER WHICH HE SLUMPS. ONE NIGHT SOME MONTHS LATER, UNABLE TO SLEEP WHEN THE CHANCE CAME TO CLOSE MY EYES, I HAD A QUEER, SEEMINGLY MYSTICAL PREMONITION, SO VIVID AND CIRCUMSTANTIAL THAT IT SEEMED AN OBJECTIVE EVENT WHICH HAD ALREADY HAPPENED. I SAW MY CAR SMASHED, IN A SHELL-HOLE BESIDE A CHARRED, BLASTED TREE, WITH A STONE BASTION IN THE BACKGROUND, AND MYSELF LYING DEAD IN THE WRECKAGE." (EMPHASES MINE)

WILLIAM SEABROOK
***NO HIDING PLACE***
PG. 158

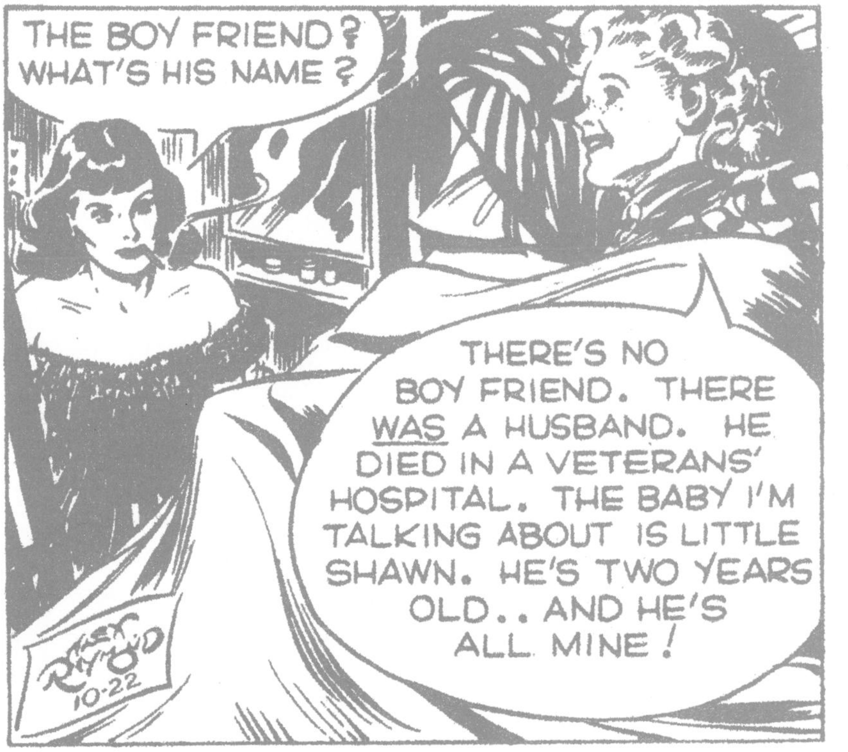
THE BOY FRIEND? WHAT'S HIS NAME?
THERE'S NO BOY FRIEND. THERE WAS A HUSBAND. HE DIED IN A VETERANS' HOSPITAL. THE BABY I'M TALKING ABOUT IS LITTLE SHAWN. HE'S TWO YEARS OLD.. AND HE'S ALL MINE!
ALEX RAYMOND 10-22

(THE "VETERAN'S HOSPITAL", I INFER, WAS NECESSARY TO DE-LINK THE METAPHYSICAL PATERNITY OF ***RIP KIRBY*** FROM SEABROOK -- WHOSE CONCEPTS GREENE WAS USING -- WHO HADN'T DIED IN A VETERAN'S HOSPITAL)

(AND SOLIDIFY THE METAPHYSICAL PATERNITY LINK TO RAYMOND'S ACTUAL ART. RAYMOND WHO, IN 1947, WOULD HAVE QUALIFIED FOR VETERANS ADMINISTRATION HOSPITALIZATION)

(A TWO-DOT ELLIPSIS IS WARD GREENE SIGNALLING THAT A LINE OF DIALOGUE IS AUTOBIO-GRAPHICAL)

(TWO DOTS, IN INTERNATIONAL MORSE CODE, REPRESENT THE LETTER ***"I"***)

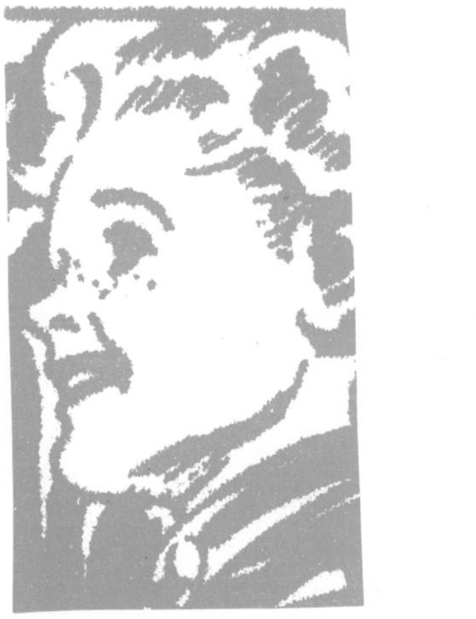

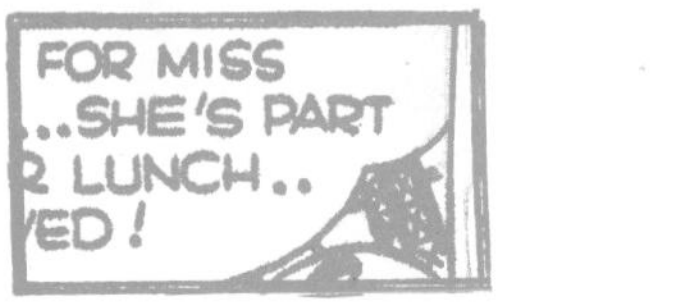
FOR MISS
..SHE'S PART
LUNCH..
ED!

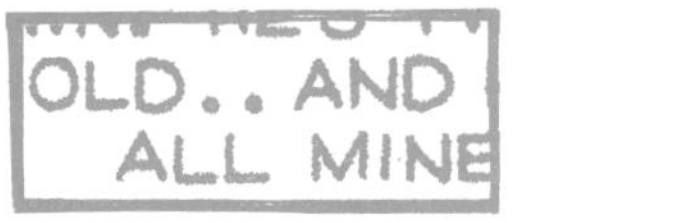
OLD.. AND
ALL MINE

THIS WAS TWO YEARS INTO ***RIP KIRBY,*** WHEN GREENE WAS BEGINNING TO BUILD HIS METAPHYSICAL SCAFFOLDING IN EARNEST:

"HE'S TWO YEAR OLD ...AND HE'S ALL MINE!"

SCAFFOLDING WHICH INCLUDED ***WALT DISNEY*** (WITNESS THE ***UPWARD-POINTING MICKEY MOUSE, ASCENDANT*** IN THE WALL DECOR OF "LITTLE SHAWN'S" NURSERY)

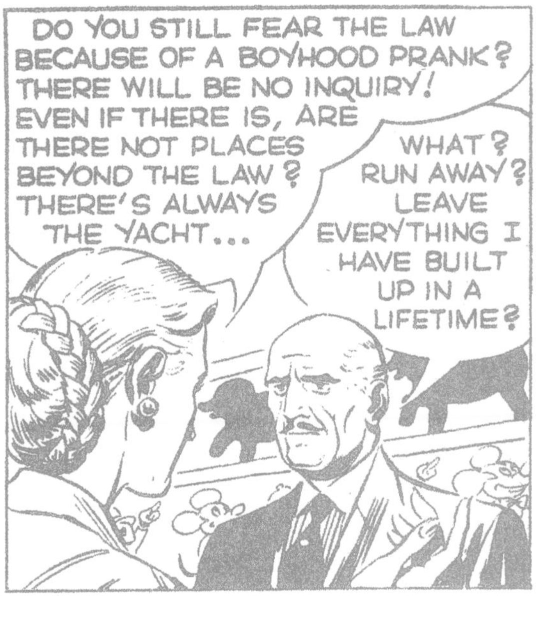
DO YOU STILL FEAR THE LAW BECAUSE OF A BOYHOOD PRANK? THERE WILL BE NO INQUIRY! EVEN IF THERE IS, ARE THERE NOT PLACES BEYOND THE LAW? THERE'S ALWAYS THE YACHT...
WHAT? RUN AWAY? LEAVE EVERYTHING I HAVE BUILT UP IN A LIFETIME?

**A**NOTHER BORDERLAND/BORDERLINE LEGAL VIOLATION. IN THIS CASE OF A MAJOR ***KING FEATURES' LICENSOR'S*** TRADEMARK WHICH ONLY SOMEONE AT GREENE'S HEARST EXECUTIVE LEVEL COULD "AUTHORIZE"

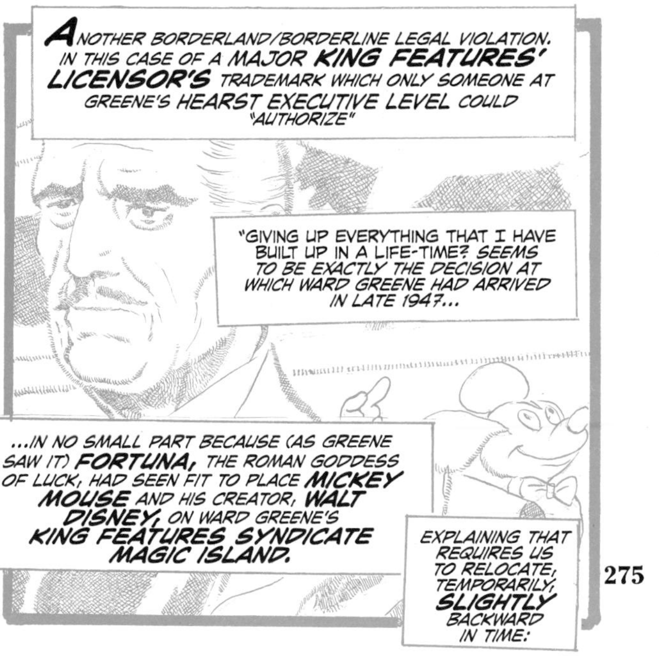

"GIVING UP EVERYTHING THAT I HAVE BUILT UP IN A LIFE-TIME? SEEMS TO BE EXACTLY THE DECISION AT WHICH WARD GREENE HAD ARRIVED IN LATE 1947...

...IN NO SMALL PART BECAUSE (AS GREENE SAW IT) ***FORTUNA,*** THE ROMAN GODDESS OF LUCK, HAD SEEN FIT TO PLACE ***MICKEY MOUSE*** AND HIS CREATOR, ***WALT DISNEY,*** ON WARD GREENE'S ***KING FEATURES SYNDICATE MAGIC ISLAND.***

EXPLAINING THAT REQUIRES US TO RELOCATE, TEMPORARILY, ***SLIGHTLY*** BACKWARD IN TIME:

## "THE DOLLS' HOUSE" 1947

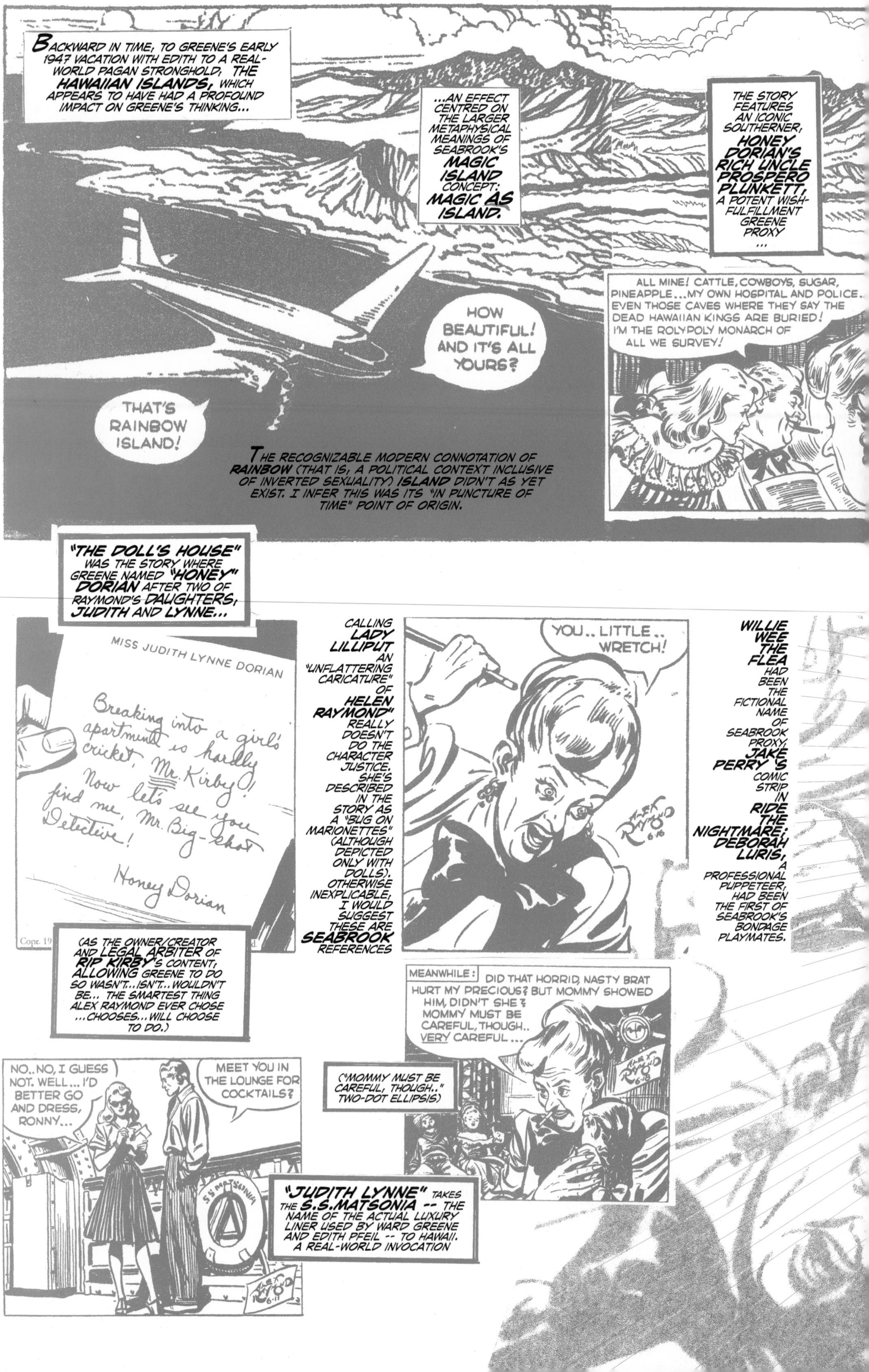
BACKWARD IN TIME, TO GREENE'S EARLY 1947 VACATION WITH EDITH TO A REAL-WORLD PAGAN STRONGHOLD, THE HAWAIIAN ISLANDS, WHICH APPEARS TO HAVE HAD A PROFOUND IMPACT ON GREENE'S THINKING...
...AN EFFECT CENTRED ON THE LARGER METAPHYSICAL MEANINGS OF SEABROOK'S MAGIC ISLAND CONCEPT: MAGIC AS ISLAND.
HOW BEAUTIFUL! AND IT'S ALL YOURS?
THAT'S RAINBOW ISLAND!
THE RECOGNIZABLE MODERN CONNOTATION OF RAINBOW (THAT IS, A POLITICAL CONTEXT INCLUSIVE OF INVERTED SEXUALITY) ISLAND DIDN'T AS YET EXIST. I INFER THIS WAS ITS "IN PUNCTURE OF TIME" POINT OF ORIGIN.
THE STORY FEATURES AN ICONIC SOUTHERNER, HONEY DORIAN'S RICH UNCLE PROSPERO PLUNKETT, A POTENT WISH-FULFILLMENT GREENE PROXY ...
ALL MINE! CATTLE, COWBOYS, SUGAR, PINEAPPLE... MY OWN HOSPITAL AND POLICE. EVEN THOSE CAVES WHERE THEY SAY THE DEAD HAWAIIAN KINGS ARE BURIED! I'M THE ROLYPOLY MONARCH OF ALL WE SURVEY!
"THE DOLL'S HOUSE" WAS THE STORY WHERE GREENE NAMED "HONEY" DORIAN AFTER TWO OF RAYMOND'S DAUGHTERS, JUDITH AND LYNNE...
MISS JUDITH LYNNE DORIAN
Breaking into a girl's apartment is hardly cricket, Mr. Kirby! Now let's see you find me, Mr. Big-Shot Detective!
Honey Dorian
(AS THE OWNER/CREATOR AND LEGAL ARBITER OF RIP KIRBY'S CONTENT, ALLOWING GREENE TO DO SO WASN'T...ISN'T...WOULDN'T BE... THE SMARTEST THING ALEX RAYMOND EVER CHOSE ...CHOOSES...WILL CHOOSE TO DO.)
CALLING LADY LILLIPUT AN "UNFLATTERING CARICATURE" OF HELEN RAYMOND" REALLY DOESN'T DO THE CHARACTER JUSTICE. SHE'S DESCRIBED IN THE STORY AS A "BUG ON MARIONETTES" (ALTHOUGH DEPICTED ONLY WITH DOLLS). OTHERWISE INEXPLICABLE, I WOULD SUGGEST THESE ARE SEABROOK REFERENCES
YOU.. LITTLE.. WRETCH!
WILLIE WEE THE FLEA HAD BEEN THE FICTIONAL NAME OF SEABROOK PROXY, JAKE PERRY'S COMIC STRIP IN RIDE THE NIGHTMARE; DEBORAH LURIS, A PROFESSIONAL PUPPETEER, HAD BEEN THE FIRST OF SEABROOK'S BONDAGE PLAYMATES.
MEANWHILE: DID THAT HORRID, NASTY BRAT HURT MY PRECIOUS? BUT MOMMY SHOWED HIM, DIDN'T SHE? MOMMY MUST BE CAREFUL, THOUGH.. VERY CAREFUL ...
("MOMMY MUST BE CAREFUL, THOUGH.." TWO-DOT ELLIPSIS)
NO.. NO, I GUESS NOT. WELL... I'D BETTER GO AND DRESS, RONNY...
MEET YOU IN THE LOUNGE FOR COCKTAILS?
"JUDITH LYNNE" TAKES THE S.S. MATSONIA -- THE NAME OF THE ACTUAL LUXURY LINER USED BY WARD GREENE AND EDITH PFEIL -- TO HAWAII. A REAL-WORLD INVOCATION

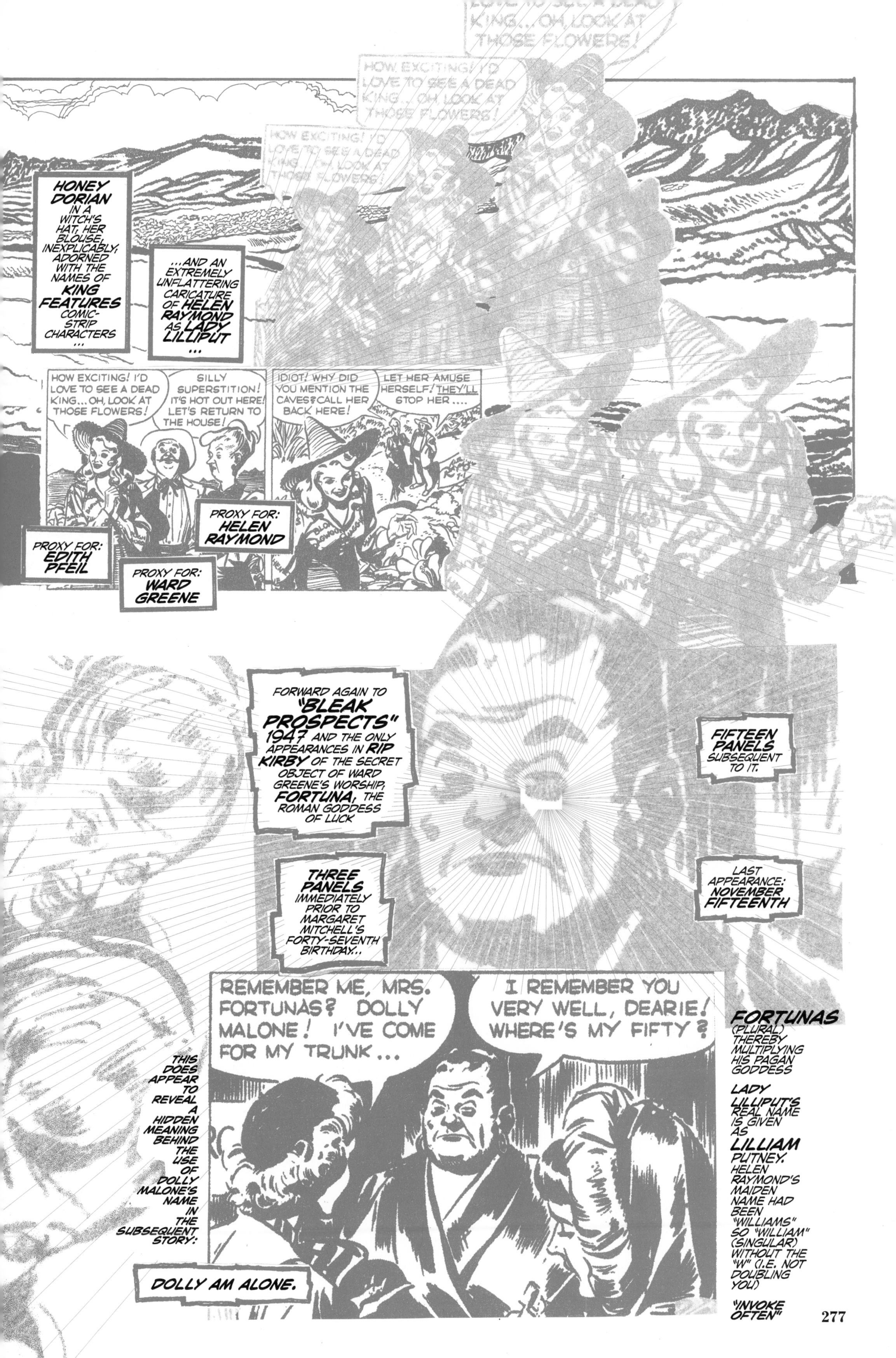
HONEY DORIAN IN A WITCH'S HAT, HER BLOUSE, INEXPLICABLY, ADORNED WITH THE NAMES OF KING FEATURES COMIC-STRIP CHARACTERS ...
...AND AN EXTREMELY UNFLATTERING CARICATURE OF HELEN RAYMOND AS LADY LILLIPUT ...
HOW EXCITING! I'D LOVE TO SEE A DEAD KING... OH, LOOK AT THOSE FLOWERS!
SILLY SUPERSTITION! IT'S HOT OUT HERE! LET'S RETURN TO THE HOUSE!
IDIOT! WHY DID YOU MENTION THE CAVES? CALL HER BACK HERE!
LET HER AMUSE HERSELF! THEY'LL STOP HER....
PROXY FOR: EDITH PFEIL
PROXY FOR: WARD GREENE
PROXY FOR: HELEN RAYMOND
FORWARD AGAIN TO "BLEAK PROSPECTS" 1947 AND THE ONLY APPEARANCES IN RIP KIRBY OF THE SECRET OBJECT OF WARD GREENE'S WORSHIP, FORTUNA, THE ROMAN GODDESS OF LUCK
FIFTEEN PANELS SUBSEQUENT TO IT.
THREE PANELS IMMEDIATELY PRIOR TO MARGARET MITCHELL'S FORTY-SEVENTH BIRTHDAY...
LAST APPEARANCE: NOVEMBER FIFTEENTH
THIS DOES APPEAR TO REVEAL A HIDDEN MEANING BEHIND THE USE OF DOLLY MALONE'S NAME IN THE SUBSEQUENT STORY:
REMEMBER ME, MRS. FORTUNAS? DOLLY MALONE! I'VE COME FOR MY TRUNK...
I REMEMBER YOU VERY WELL, DEARIE! WHERE'S MY FIFTY?
DOLLY AM ALONE.
FORTUNAS (PLURAL) THEREBY MULTIPLYING HIS PAGAN GODDESS
LADY LILLIPUT'S REAL NAME IS GIVEN AS LILLIAM PUTNEY. HELEN RAYMOND'S MAIDEN NAME HAD BEEN "WILLIAMS" SO "WILLIAM" (SINGULAR) WITHOUT THE "W" (I.E. NOT DOUBLING YOU)
"INVOKE OFTEN"

"THE DOLLS' HOUSE" 1947

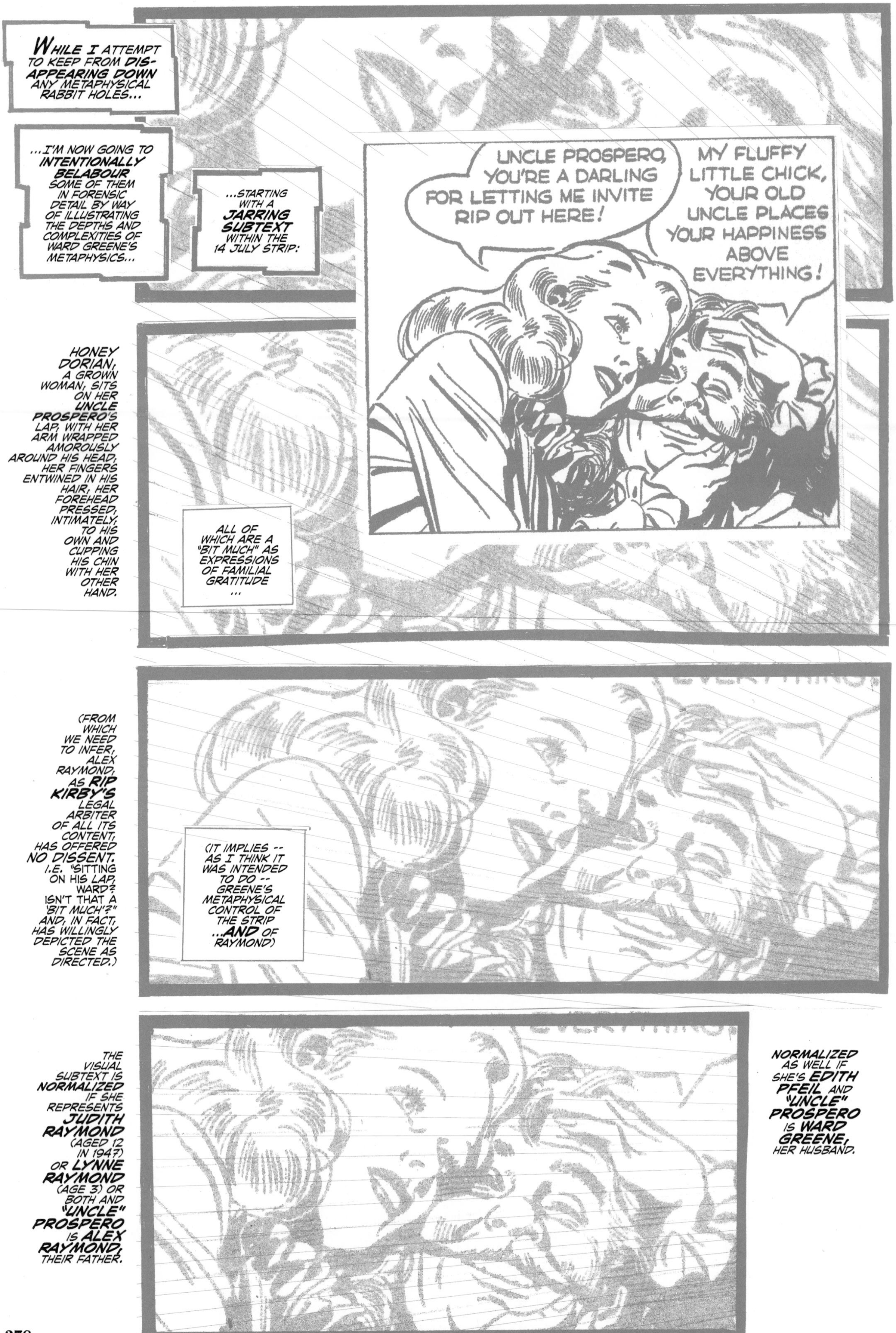
WHILE I ATTEMPT TO KEEP FROM DIS-APPEARING DOWN ANY METAPHYSICAL RABBIT HOLES...
...I'M NOW GOING TO INTENTIONALLY BELABOUR SOME OF THEM IN FORENSIC DETAIL BY WAY OF ILLUSTRATING THE DEPTHS AND COMPLEXITIES OF WARD GREENE'S METAPHYSICS...
...STARTING WITH A JARRING SUBTEXT WITHIN THE 14 JULY STRIP:
UNCLE PROSPERO, YOU'RE A DARLING FOR LETTING ME INVITE RIP OUT HERE!
MY FLUFFY LITTLE CHICK, YOUR OLD UNCLE PLACES YOUR HAPPINESS ABOVE EVERYTHING!
HONEY DORIAN, A GROWN WOMAN, SITS ON HER UNCLE PROSPERO'S LAP, WITH HER ARM WRAPPED AMOROUSLY AROUND HIS HEAD, HER FINGERS ENTWINED IN HIS HAIR, HER FOREHEAD PRESSED, INTIMATELY, TO HIS OWN AND CUPPING HIS CHIN WITH HER OTHER HAND.
ALL OF WHICH ARE A "BIT MUCH" AS EXPRESSIONS OF FAMILIAL GRATITUDE ...
(FROM WHICH WE NEED TO INFER, ALEX RAYMOND, AS RIP KIRBY'S LEGAL ARBITER OF ALL ITS CONTENT, HAS OFFERED NO DISSENT. I.E. "SITTING ON HIS LAP, WARD? ISN'T THAT A 'BIT MUCH'?" AND, IN FACT, HAS WILLINGLY DEPICTED THE SCENE AS DIRECTED.)
(IT IMPLIES -- AS I THINK IT WAS INTENDED TO DO -- GREENE'S METAPHYSICAL CONTROL OF THE STRIP ...AND OF RAYMOND)
THE VISUAL SUBTEXT IS NORMALIZED IF SHE REPRESENTS JUDITH RAYMOND (AGED 12 IN 1947) OR LYNNE RAYMOND (AGE 3) OR BOTH AND "UNCLE" PROSPERO IS ALEX RAYMOND, THEIR FATHER.
NORMALIZED AS WELL IF SHE'S EDITH PFEIL AND "UNCLE" PROSPERO IS WARD GREENE, HER HUSBAND.

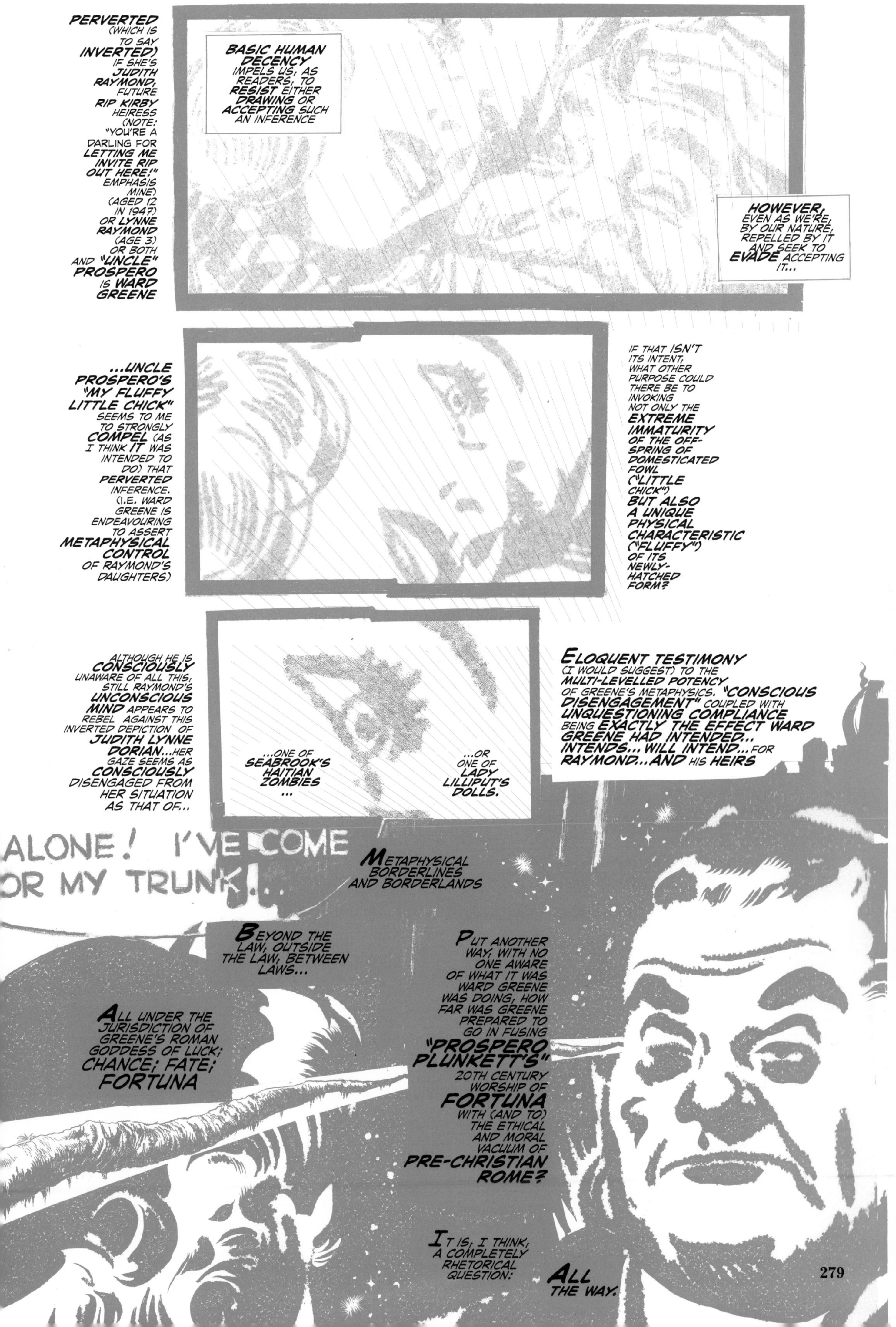

PERVERTED (WHICH IS TO SAY INVERTED) IF SHE'S JUDITH RAYMOND, FUTURE RIP KIRBY HEIRESS (NOTE: "YOU'RE A DARLING FOR LETTING ME INVITE RIP OUT HERE!" EMPHASIS MINE) (AGED 12 IN 1947) OR LYNNE RAYMOND (AGE 3) OR BOTH AND "UNCLE" PROSPERO IS WARD GREENE
BASIC HUMAN DECENCY IMPELS US, AS READERS, TO RESIST EITHER DRAWING OR ACCEPTING SUCH AN INFERENCE
HOWEVER, EVEN AS WE'RE, BY OUR NATURE, REPELLED BY IT AND SEEK TO EVADE ACCEPTING IT...
...UNCLE PROSPERO'S "MY FLUFFY LITTLE CHICK" SEEMS TO ME TO STRONGLY COMPEL (AS I THINK IT WAS INTENDED TO DO) THAT PERVERTED INFERENCE. (I.E. WARD GREENE IS ENDEAVOURING TO ASSERT METAPHYSICAL CONTROL OF RAYMOND'S DAUGHTERS)
IF THAT ISN'T ITS INTENT, WHAT OTHER PURPOSE COULD THERE BE TO INVOKING NOT ONLY THE EXTREME IMMATURITY OF THE OFF-SPRING OF DOMESTICATED FOWL ("LITTLE CHICK") BUT ALSO A UNIQUE PHYSICAL CHARACTERISTIC ("FLUFFY") OF ITS NEWLY-HATCHED FORM?
ALTHOUGH HE IS CONSCIOUSLY UNAWARE OF ALL THIS, STILL RAYMOND'S UNCONSCIOUS MIND APPEARS TO REBEL AGAINST THIS INVERTED DEPICTION OF JUDITH LYNNE DORIAN...HER GAZE SEEMS AS CONSCIOUSLY DISENGAGED FROM HER SITUATION AS THAT OF...
...ONE OF SEABROOK'S HAITIAN ZOMBIES ...
...OR ONE OF LADY LILLIPUT'S DOLLS.
ELOQUENT TESTIMONY (I WOULD SUGGEST) TO THE MULTI-LEVELLED POTENCY OF GREENE'S METAPHYSICS. "CONSCIOUS DISENGAGEMENT" COUPLED WITH UNQUESTIONING COMPLIANCE BEING EXACTLY THE EFFECT WARD GREENE HAD INTENDED... INTENDS...WILL INTEND...FOR RAYMOND...AND HIS HEIRS
ALONE! I'VE COME OR MY TRUNK..
METAPHYSICAL BORDERLINES AND BORDERLANDS
BEYOND THE LAW, OUTSIDE THE LAW, BETWEEN LAWS...
ALL UNDER THE JURISDICTION OF GREENE'S ROMAN GODDESS OF LUCK; CHANCE; FATE; FORTUNA
PUT ANOTHER WAY, WITH NO ONE AWARE OF WHAT IT WAS WARD GREENE WAS DOING, HOW FAR WAS GREENE PREPARED TO GO IN FUSING "PROSPERO PLUNKETT'S" 20TH CENTURY WORSHIP OF FORTUNA WITH (AND TO) THE ETHICAL AND MORAL VACUUM OF PRE-CHRISTIAN ROME?
IT IS, I THINK, A COMPLETELY RHETORICAL QUESTION:
ALL THE WAY.

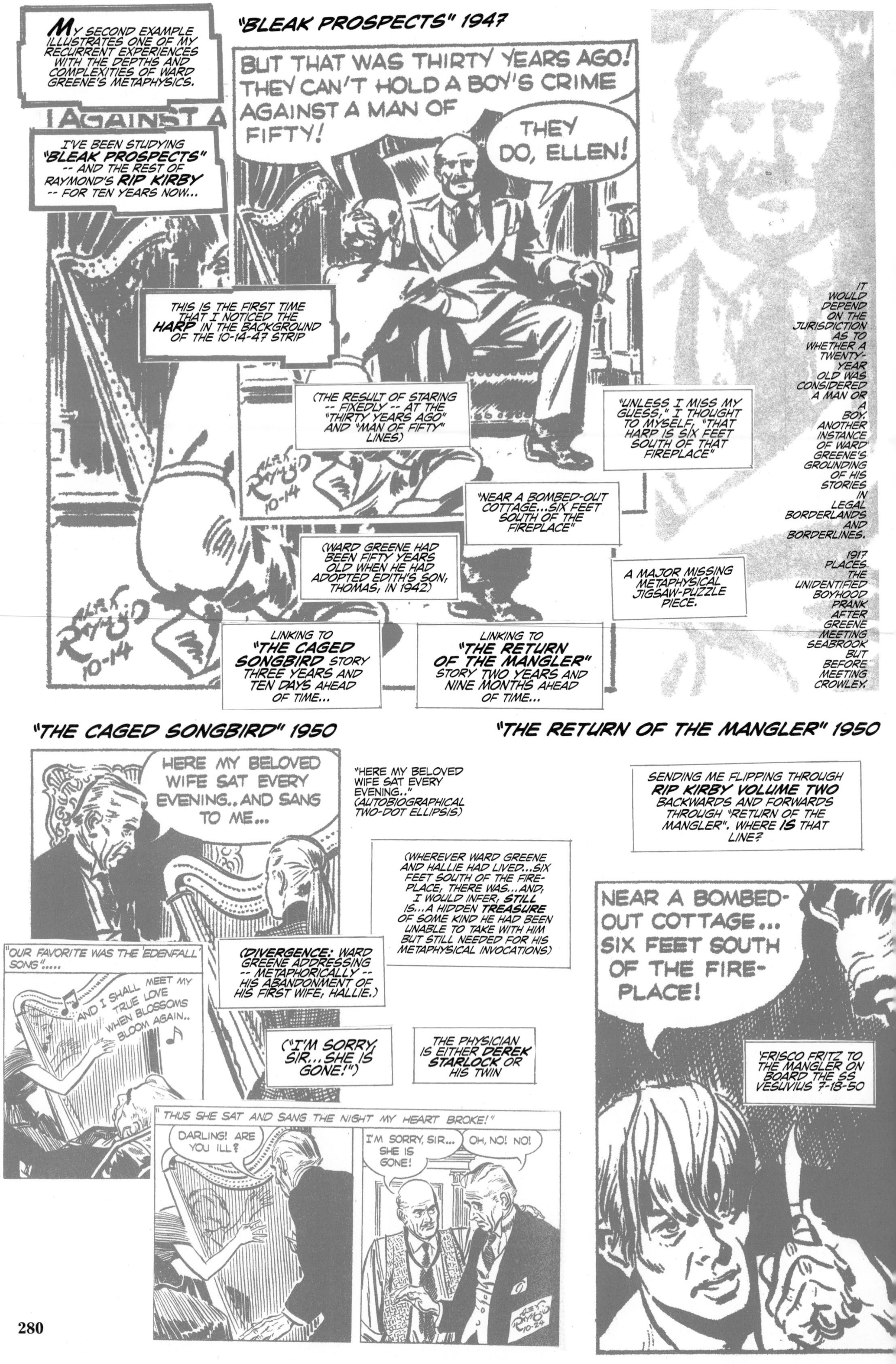
MY SECOND EXAMPLE ILLUSTRATES ONE OF MY RECURRENT EXPERIENCES WITH THE DEPTHS AND COMPLEXITIES OF WARD GREENE'S METAPHYSICS.
"BLEAK PROSPECTS" 1947
BUT THAT WAS THIRTY YEARS AGO! THEY CAN'T HOLD A BOY'S CRIME AGAINST A MAN OF FIFTY!
THEY DO, ELLEN!
AGAINST A
I'VE BEEN STUDYING "BLEAK PROSPECTS" -- AND THE REST OF RAYMOND'S RIP KIRBY -- FOR TEN YEARS NOW...
THIS IS THE FIRST TIME THAT I NOTICED THE HARP IN THE BACKGROUND OF THE 10-14-47 STRIP
(THE RESULT OF STARING -- FIXEDLY -- AT THE "THIRTY YEARS AGO" AND "MAN OF FIFTY" LINES)
"UNLESS I MISS MY GUESS," I THOUGHT TO MYSELF, "THAT HARP IS SIX FEET SOUTH OF THAT FIREPLACE"
"NEAR A BOMBED-OUT COTTAGE...SIX FEET SOUTH OF THE FIREPLACE"
(WARD GREENE HAD BEEN FIFTY YEARS OLD WHEN HE HAD ADOPTED EDITH'S SON, THOMAS, IN 1942)
A MAJOR MISSING METAPHYSICAL JIGSAW-PUZZLE PIECE.
IT WOULD DEPEND ON THE JURISDICTION AS TO WHETHER A TWENTY-YEAR OLD WAS CONSIDERED A MAN OR A BOY. ANOTHER INSTANCE OF WARD GREENE'S GROUNDING OF HIS STORIES IN LEGAL BORDERLANDS AND BORDERLINES.
1917 PLACES THE UNIDENTIFIED BOYHOOD PRANK AFTER GREENE MEETING SEABROOK BUT BEFORE MEETING CROWLEY.
LINKING TO "THE CAGED SONGBIRD" STORY THREE YEARS AND TEN DAYS AHEAD OF TIME...
LINKING TO "THE RETURN OF THE MANGLER" STORY TWO YEARS AND NINE MONTHS AHEAD OF TIME...
"THE CAGED SONGBIRD" 1950
"THE RETURN OF THE MANGLER" 1950
HERE MY BELOVED WIFE SAT EVERY EVENING.. AND SANG TO ME...
"HERE MY BELOVED WIFE SAT EVERY EVENING.." (AUTOBIOGRAPHICAL TWO-DOT ELLIPSIS)
SENDING ME FLIPPING THROUGH RIP KIRBY VOLUME TWO BACKWARDS AND FORWARDS THROUGH "RETURN OF THE MANGLER". WHERE IS THAT LINE?
(WHEREVER WARD GREENE AND HALLIE HAD LIVED...SIX FEET SOUTH OF THE FIRE-PLACE, THERE WAS...AND, I WOULD INFER, STILL IS...A HIDDEN TREASURE OF SOME KIND HE HAD BEEN UNABLE TO TAKE WITH HIM BUT STILL NEEDED FOR HIS METAPHYSICAL INVOCATIONS)
"OUR FAVORITE WAS THE 'EDENFALL' SONG"....
AND I SHALL MEET MY TRUE LOVE WHEN BLOSSOMS BLOOM AGAIN..
(DIVERGENCE: WARD GREENE ADDRESSING -- METAPHORICALLY -- HIS ABANDONMENT OF HIS FIRST WIFE, HALLIE.)
NEAR A BOMBED-OUT COTTAGE... SIX FEET SOUTH OF THE FIRE-PLACE!
("I'M SORRY, SIR... SHE IS GONE!")
THE PHYSICIAN IS EITHER DEREK STARLOCK OR HIS TWIN
'FRISCO FRITZ TO THE MANGLER ON BOARD THE SS VESUVIUS 7-18-50
"THUS SHE SAT AND SANG THE NIGHT MY HEART BROKE!"
DARLING! ARE YOU ILL?
I'M SORRY, SIR... SHE IS GONE!
OH, NO! NO!

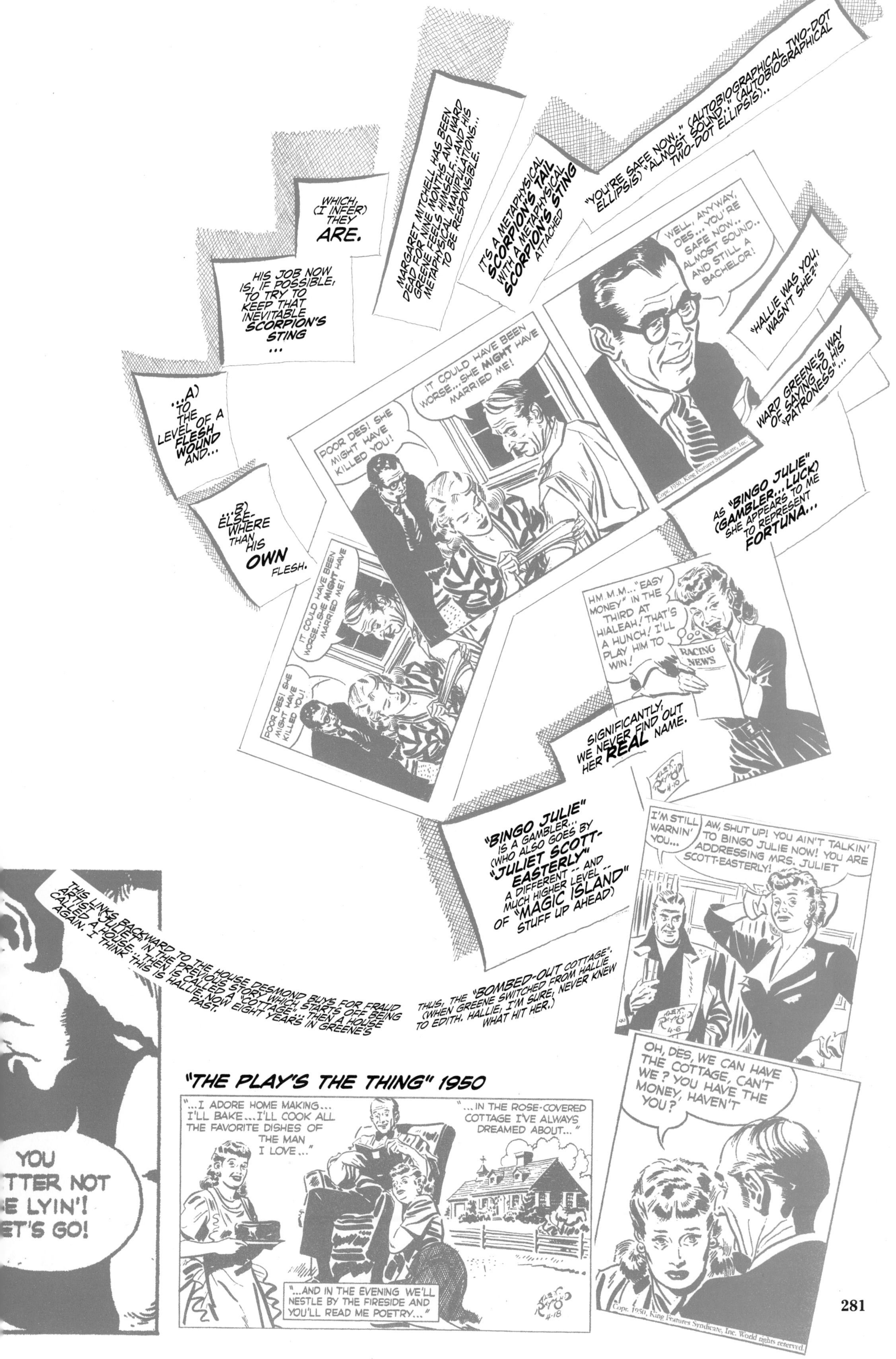
HIS JOB NOW IS, IF POSSIBLE, TO TRY TO KEEP THAT INEVITABLE SCORPION'S STING ...
WHICH, (I INFER) THEY ARE.
MARGARET MITCHELL HAS BEEN DEAD FOR NINE MONTHS AND WARD GREENE FEELS HIMSELF... AND HIS METAPHYSICAL MANIPULATIONS... TO BE RESPONSIBLE.
IT'S A METAPHYSICAL SCORPION'S TAIL WITH A METAPHYSICAL SCORPION'S STING ATTACHED
"YOU'RE SAFE NOW.." (AUTOBIOGRAPHICAL TWO-DOT ELLIPSIS) "ALMOST SOUND.." (AUTOBIOGRAPHICAL TWO-DOT ELLIPSIS)...
WELL, ANYWAY, DES... YOU'RE SAFE NOW.. ALMOST SOUND.. AND STILL A BACHELOR!
"HALLIE WAS YOU, WASN'T SHE?"
WARD GREENE'S WAY OF SAYING TO HIS "PATRONESS"...
...A) TO THE LEVEL OF A FLESH WOUND AND...
IT COULD HAVE BEEN WORSE...SHE MIGHT HAVE MARRIED ME!
POOR DES! SHE MIGHT HAVE KILLED YOU!
Copr. 1950, King Features Syndicate, Inc.
...B) ELSE-WHERE THAN HIS OWN FLESH.
AS "BINGO JULIE" (GAMBLER... LUCK) SHE APPEARS TO ME TO REPRESENT FORTUNA...
IT COULD HAVE BEEN WORSE...SHE MIGHT HAVE MARRIED ME!
POOR DES! SHE MIGHT HAVE KILLED YOU!
HM.M.M... "EASY MONEY" IN THE THIRD AT HIALEAH! THAT'S A HUNCH! I'LL PLAY HIM TO WIN!
RACING NEWS
SIGNIFICANTLY, WE NEVER FIND OUT HER REAL NAME.
"BINGO JULIE" IS A GAMBLER... (WHO ALSO GOES BY "JULIET SCOTT-EASTERLY" A DIFFERENT... AND MUCH HIGHER LEVEL... OF "MAGIC ISLAND" STUFF UP AHEAD)
I'M STILL WARNIN' YOU...
AW, SHUT UP! YOU AIN'T TALKIN' TO BINGO JULIE NOW! YOU ARE ADDRESSING MRS. JULIET SCOTT-EASTERLY!
THIS LINKS BACKWARD TO THE HOUSE DESMOND BUYS FOR FRAUD ARTIST "JULIET" IN THE PREVIOUS STORY WHICH STARTS OFF BEING CALLED A HOUSE... THEN IS CALLED A "COTTAGE"... THEN A HOUSE AGAIN. I THINK THIS IS HALLIE. NOW EIGHT YEARS IN GREENE'S PAST.
THUS, THE "BOMBED-OUT COTTAGE". (WHEN GREENE SWITCHED FROM HALLIE TO EDITH. HALLIE, I'M SURE, NEVER KNEW WHAT HIT HER.)
YOU ...TTER NOT ...E LYIN'! ...ET'S GO!
"THE PLAY'S THE THING" 1950
"...I ADORE HOME MAKING... I'LL BAKE...I'LL COOK ALL THE FAVORITE DISHES OF THE MAN I LOVE..."
"...IN THE ROSE-COVERED COTTAGE I'VE ALWAYS DREAMED ABOUT..."
"...AND IN THE EVENING WE'LL NESTLE BY THE FIRESIDE AND YOU'LL READ ME POETRY..."
OH, DES, WE CAN HAVE THE COTTAGE, CAN'T WE? YOU HAVE THE MONEY, HAVEN'T YOU?
Copr. 1950, King Features Syndicate, Inc. World rights reserved.

282

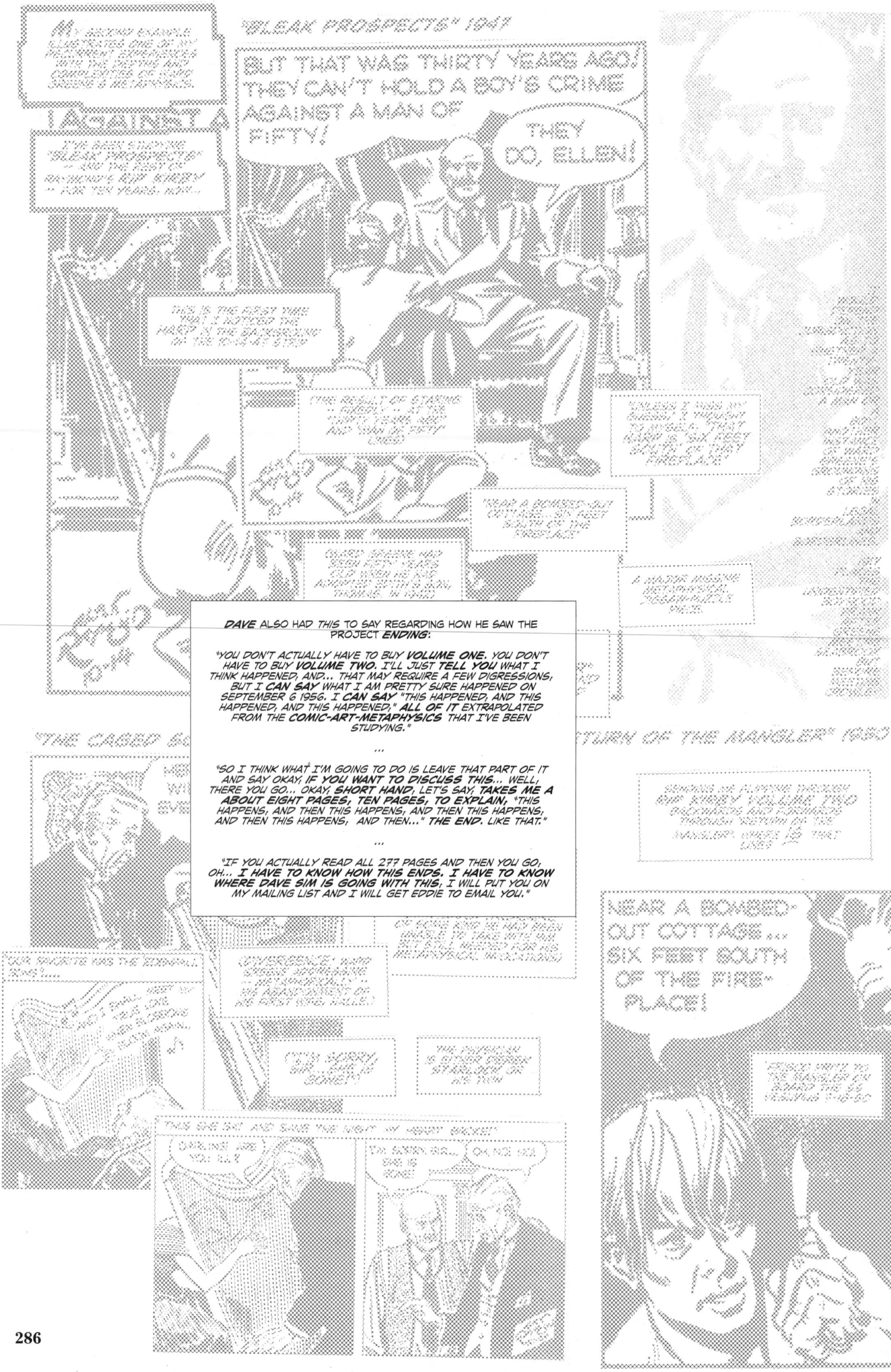
"BLEAK PROSPECTS" 1947
BUT THAT WAS THIRTY YEARS AGO! THEY CAN'T HOLD A BOY'S CRIME AGAINST A MAN OF FIFTY!
THEY DO, ELLEN!
NEAR A BOMBED-OUT COTTAGE... SIX FEET SOUTH OF THE FIRE-PLACE!

***DAVE*** ALSO HAD *THIS* TO SAY REGARDING HOW HE SAW THE PROJECT ***ENDING***:

*"YOU DON'T ACTUALLY HAVE TO BUY* ***VOLUME ONE.*** *YOU DON'T HAVE TO BUY* ***VOLUME TWO.*** *I'LL JUST* ***TELL YOU*** *WHAT I THINK HAPPENED, AND... THAT MAY REQUIRE A FEW DIGRESSIONS, BUT I* ***CAN SAY*** *WHAT I AM PRETTY SURE HAPPENED ON SEPTEMBER 6 1956. I* ***CAN SAY*** *"THIS HAPPENED, AND THIS HAPPENED, AND THIS HAPPENED,"* ***ALL OF IT*** *EXTRAPOLATED FROM THE* ***COMIC-ART-METAPHYSICS*** *THAT I'VE BEEN STUDYING."*

...

*"SO I THINK WHAT I'M GOING TO DO IS LEAVE THAT PART OF IT AND SAY OKAY;* ***IF YOU WANT TO DISCUSS THIS...*** *WELL, THERE YOU GO... OKAY,* ***SHORT HAND,*** *LET'S SAY,* ***TAKES ME A ABOUT EIGHT PAGES, TEN PAGES,*** *TO EXPLAIN, "THIS HAPPENS, AND THEN THIS HAPPENS, AND THEN THIS HAPPENS, AND THEN THIS HAPPENS, AND THEN..."* ***THE END.*** *LIKE THAT."*

...

*"IF YOU ACTUALLY READ ALL 277 PAGES AND THEN YOU GO, OH...* ***I HAVE TO KNOW HOW THIS ENDS. I HAVE TO KNOW WHERE DAVE SIM IS GOING WITH THIS;*** *I WILL PUT YOU ON MY MAILING LIST AND I WILL GET EDDIE TO EMAIL YOU."*

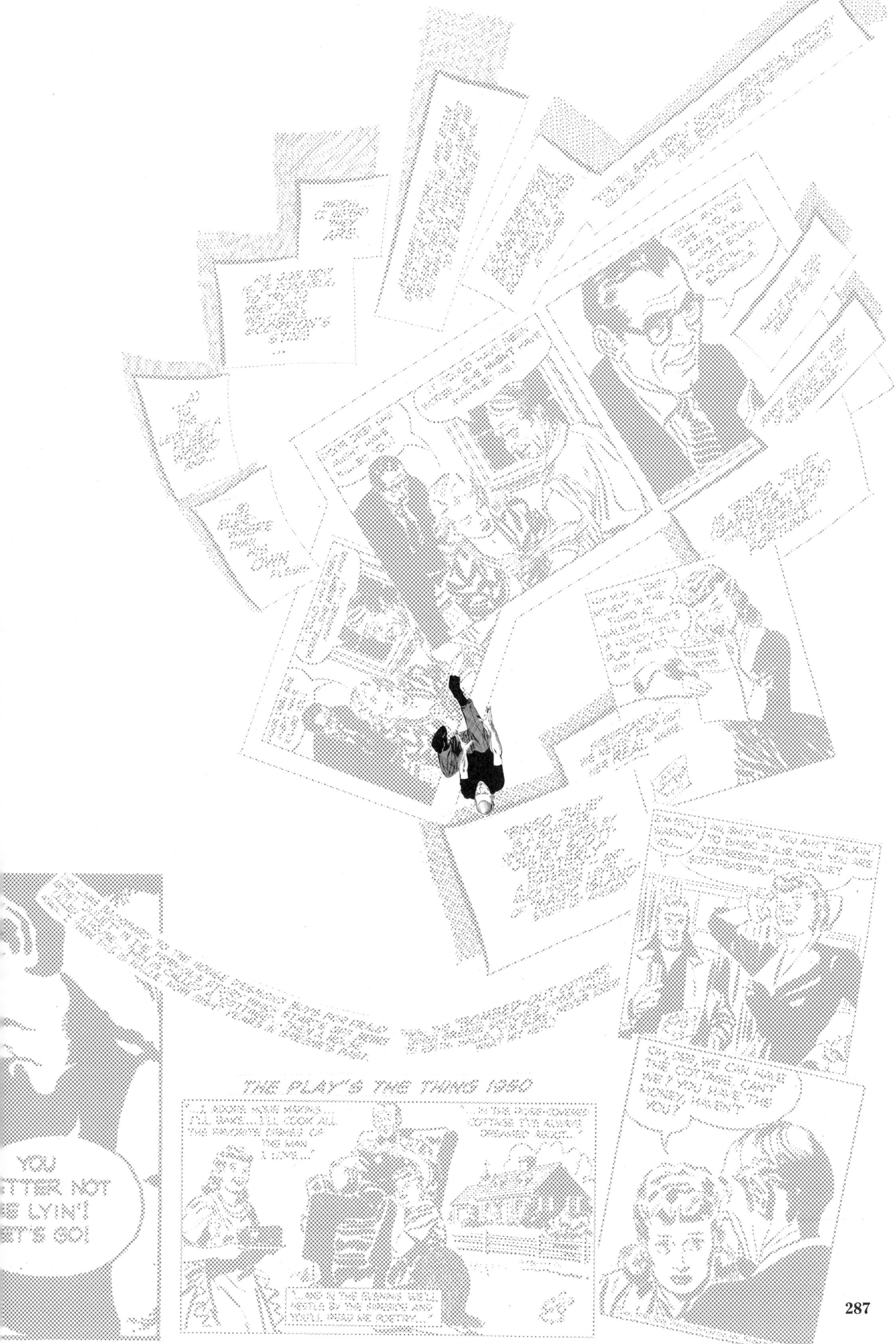
I'M STILL WAITIN' YOU...
AW, SHUT UP! YOU AIN'T TALKIN' TO BINGO JULIE NOW! YOU ARE ADDRESSING MRS. JULIET ...
OH, DES, WE CAN HAVE THE COTTAGE, CAN'T WE? YOU HAVE THE MONEY, HAVEN'T YOU?
THE PLAY'S THE THING 1950
"...I ADORE HOME MAKING... I'LL BAKE... I'LL COOK ALL THE FAVORITE DISHES OF THE MAN I LOVE..."
"...IN THE ROSE-COVERED COTTAGE I'VE ALWAYS DREAMED ABOUT..."
"...AND IN THE EVENINGS WE'LL NESTLE BY THE FIRESIDE AND YOU'LL READ ME POETRY..."
YOU BETTER NOT BE LYIN'! LET'S GO!

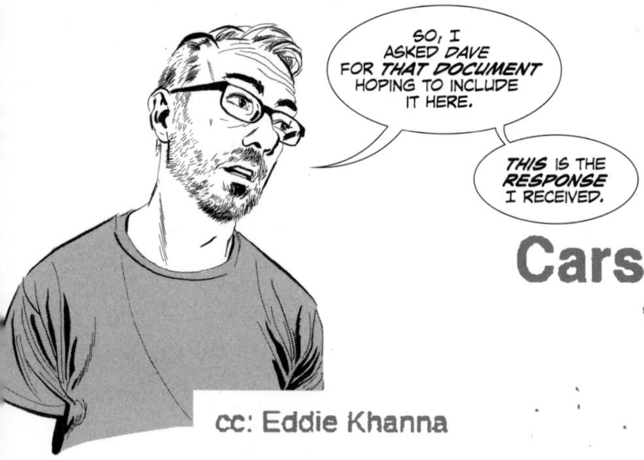
SO, I ASKED DAVE FOR THAT DOCUMENT HOPING TO INCLUDE IT HERE.
THIS IS THE RESPONSE I RECEIVED.

# Carson Grubaugh

% Sean Robinson

cc: Eddie Khanna

11 September 20

Hi Carson!

Well, every little bit helps. Please make sure you make the check out to Aardvark-Vanaheim when the time comes. Thanks.

I don't think any hard and fast decisions about Where Next for SDOAR need to be made at the moment. If anyone finds out about Volume One and wants to buy one, Eddie still has a bunch. Possibly a two-year supply depending on the level of disinterest (which, as far as I can see, is pretty close to total). Once Eddie is cleaned out and he lets you know that, then you're welcome to come up with whatever package you want. The major problem is the 200 or so people who will have already bought Volume One vs. the people hearing about SDOAR for the first time. You can't really, in good conscience, sell the former the same book with some stuff stuck onto it or try to sell the latter a Volume One-less package.

I also think if you're going to sell them The Definitive Carson Grubaugh Edition, it needs to be finished before you do so. So you should probably start figuring out how many pages are going to be in TDCGE SDOAR and how long it's going to take you to produce them. Then produce them. Then see if Diamond is interested in carrying it and how you're going to pay to get 50 or 60 copies printed and not lose your shirt when that's what the orders add up to.

I'm at the beginning of my "SDOAR As Useless Hobby" stage where -- if there isn't anything that needs doing for Waverly Press or CIH? -- that's what I work on. I have a word document called SDOAR Q&D (SDOAR Quick & Dirty). So far, I've just picked up from where I left off on the mock-ups and am typing captions in bold face and annotations in Light Helvetica. See attached. I'm hoping I hit a wall with that sometime soon and then can jump around from pillar to post a little bit.

At the moment, I'm explaining the significance of the LIFE magazine photo shoot in the Annotations which is telescoping quite a bit and which I'm dovetailing with Why I Think This Is How Reality Works by documenting some Comic Art Metaphysics experiences that resonate with it and which I experienced while writing that part. It's been a few days since I've been able to put a couple of hours in on it, which led me to sharpen some of my observations, mentally. I was just about to start adding

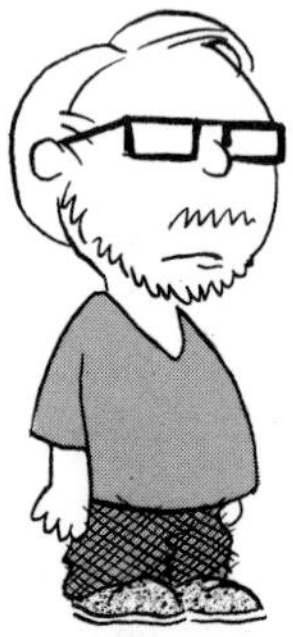

in what I hope are the last of the Annotations on that section when your fax came in.
It's becoming seriously comedic how often that happens.  This is the first time,
though, I must admit, when SDOAR interfered with me working on SDOAR.

I have no clearer idea now of where I am in SDOAR than I have had all along.  My
writing "Here is the OMEGA on SDOAR" when I don't know where I am in the
alphabet (apart from PAST ALPHA) isn't going to help anyone.  SDOAR OUTLINE,
Q&D's precursor, is just shorthand notes to myself.  Eddie and I are working things
out section by section.

I'm very pleased that you see a "just over the horizon" ending on SDOAR that you
can wrap up in x number of do-able pages.  I'm sure everyone who has read -- or
will read -- Volume One will thank you for that.  When you figure out how to get it to
them.

Best,

Dave

289

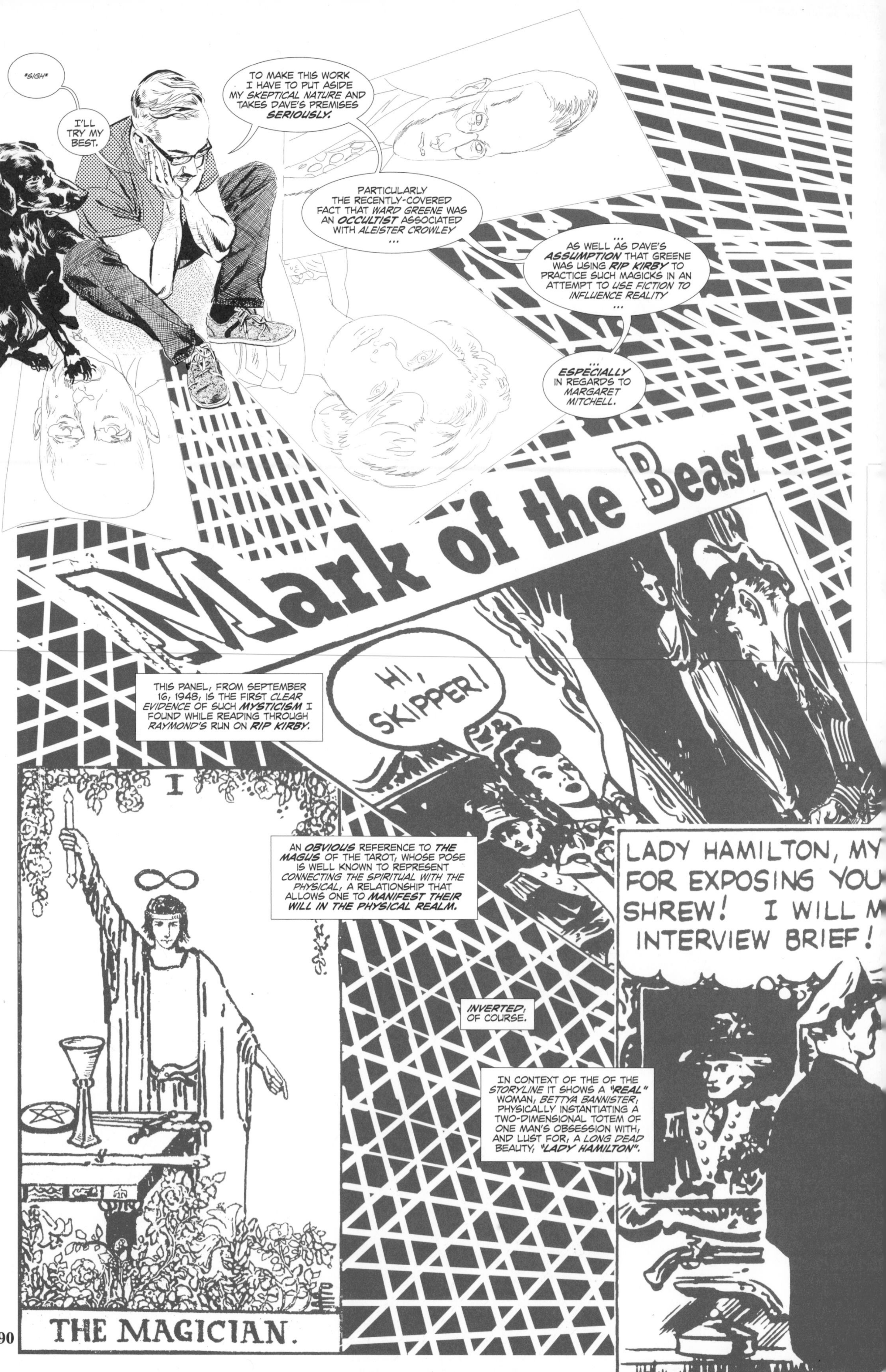

*SIGH*
I'LL TRY MY BEST.
TO MAKE THIS WORK I HAVE TO PUT ASIDE MY SKEPTICAL NATURE AND TAKES DAVE'S PREMISES SERIOUSLY.
PARTICULARLY THE RECENTLY-COVERED FACT THAT WARD GREENE WAS AN OCCULTIST ASSOCIATED WITH ALEISTER CROWLEY ...
... AS WELL AS DAVE'S ASSUMPTION THAT GREENE WAS USING RIP KIRBY TO PRACTICE SUCH MAGICKS IN AN ATTEMPT TO USE FICTION TO INFLUENCE REALITY ...
... ESPECIALLY IN REGARDS TO MARGARET MITCHELL.
Mark of the Beast
THIS PANEL, FROM SEPTEMBER 16, 1948, IS THE FIRST CLEAR EVIDENCE OF SUCH MYSTICISM I FOUND WHILE READING THROUGH RAYMOND'S RUN ON RIP KIRBY.
HI, SKIPPER!
I
THE MAGICIAN.
AN OBVIOUS REFERENCE TO THE MAGUS OF THE TAROT, WHOSE POSE IS WELL KNOWN TO REPRESENT CONNECTING THE SPIRITUAL WITH THE PHYSICAL, A RELATIONSHIP THAT ALLOWS ONE TO MANIFEST THEIR WILL IN THE PHYSICAL REALM.
LADY HAMILTON, MY FOR EXPOSING YOU SHREW! I WILL M INTERVIEW BRIEF!
INVERTED, OF COURSE.
IN CONTEXT OF THE OF THE STORYLINE IT SHOWS A "REAL" WOMAN, BETTYA BANNISTER, PHYSICALLY INSTANTIATING A TWO-DIMENSIONAL TOTEM OF ONE MAN'S OBSESSION WITH, AND LUST FOR, A LONG DEAD BEAUTY; "LADY HAMILTON".

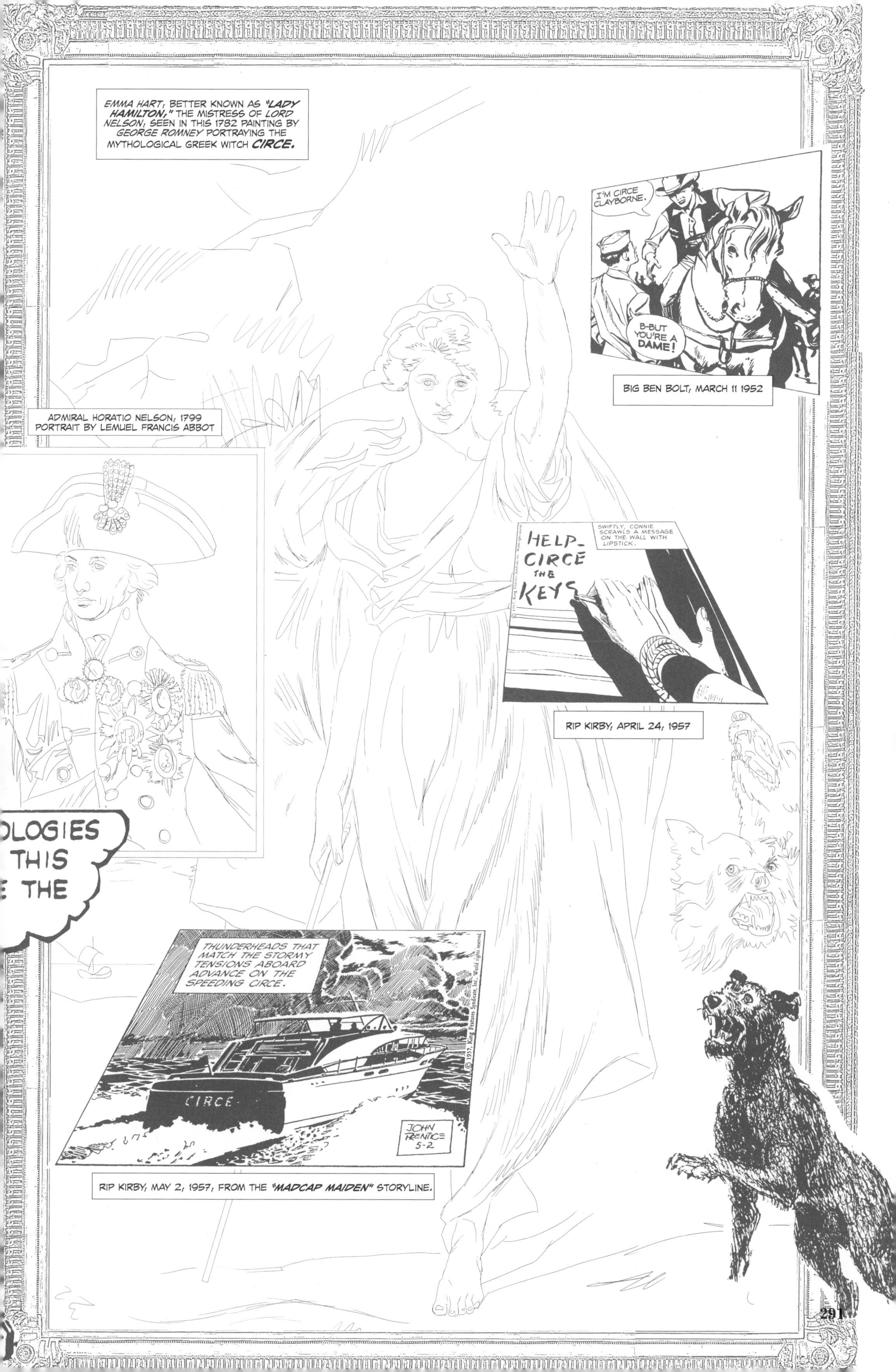
EMMA HART, BETTER KNOWN AS "LADY HAMILTON," THE MISTRESS OF LORD NELSON, SEEN IN THIS 1782 PAINTING BY GEORGE ROMNEY PORTRAYING THE MYTHOLOGICAL GREEK WITCH CIRCE.
I'M CIRCE CLAYBORNE.
B-BUT YOU'RE A DAME!
BIG BEN BOLT, MARCH 11 1952
ADMIRAL HORATIO NELSON, 1799 PORTRAIT BY LEMUEL FRANCIS ABBOT
SWIFTLY, CONNIE SCRAWLS A MESSAGE ON THE WALL WITH LIPSTICK.
HELP-CIRCE THE KEYS
RIP KIRBY, APRIL 24, 1957
...OLOGIES ... THIS ... THE
THUNDERHEADS THAT MATCH THE STORMY TENSIONS ABOARD ADVANCE ON THE SPEEDING CIRCE.
CIRCE
© 1957, King Features Syndicate, Inc. World rights reserved.
JOHN PRENTICE 5-2
RIP KIRBY, MAY 2, 1957, FROM THE "MADCAP MAIDEN" STORYLINE.

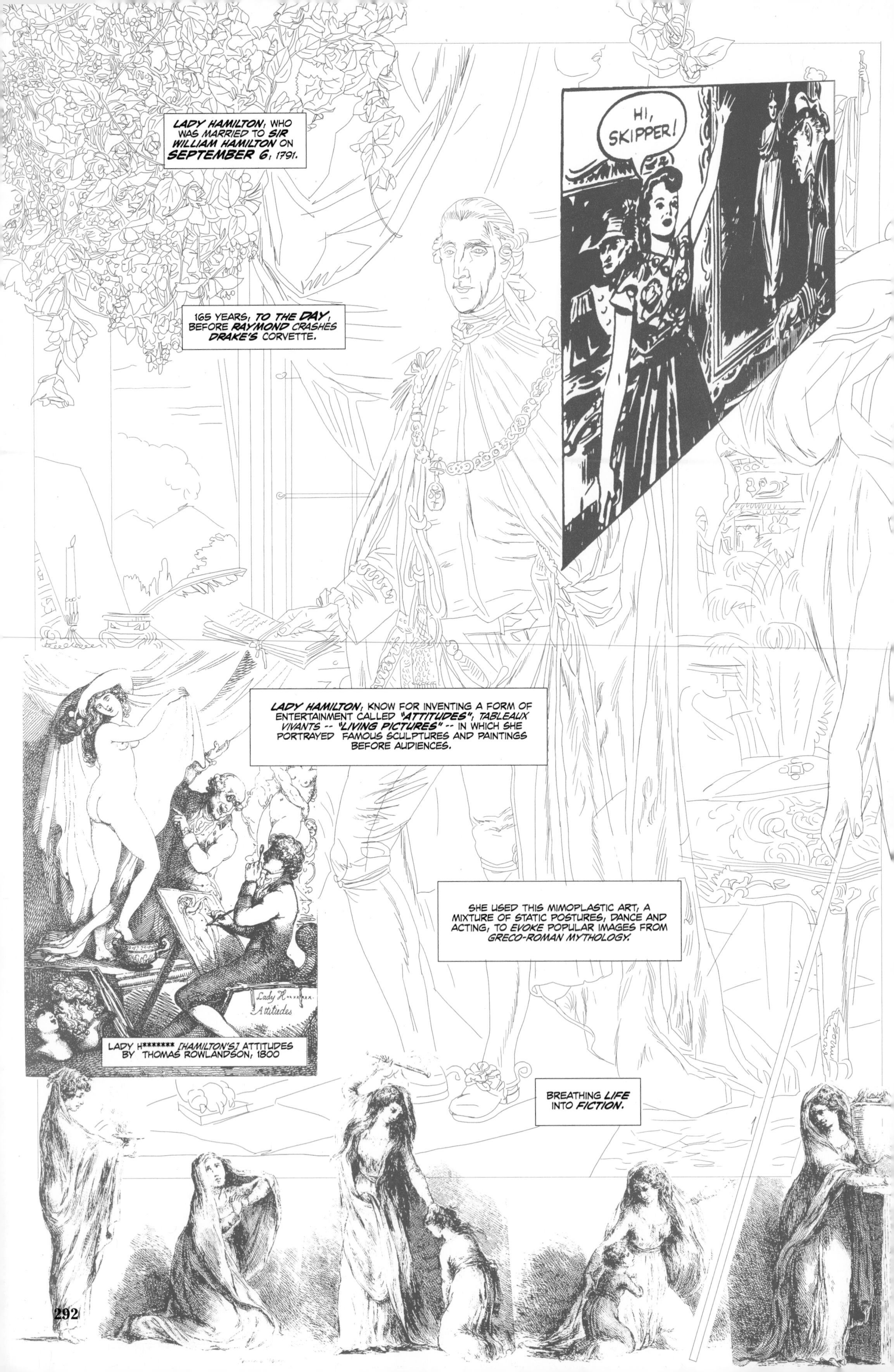
LADY HAMILTON; WHO WAS MARRIED TO SIR WILLIAM HAMILTON ON SEPTEMBER 6, 1791.
165 YEARS; TO THE DAY; BEFORE RAYMOND CRASHES DRAKE'S CORVETTE.
HI, SKIPPER!
LADY HAMILTON; KNOW FOR INVENTING A FORM OF ENTERTAINMENT CALLED "ATTITUDES", TABLEAUX VIVANTS -- "LIVING PICTURES" -- IN WHICH SHE PORTRAYED FAMOUS SCULPTURES AND PAINTINGS BEFORE AUDIENCES.
LADY H******* [HAMILTON'S] ATTITUDES BY THOMAS ROWLANDSON, 1800
SHE USED THIS MIMOPLASTIC ART, A MIXTURE OF STATIC POSTURES, DANCE AND ACTING, TO EVOKE POPULAR IMAGES FROM GRECO-ROMAN MYTHOLOGY.
BREATHING LIFE INTO FICTION.

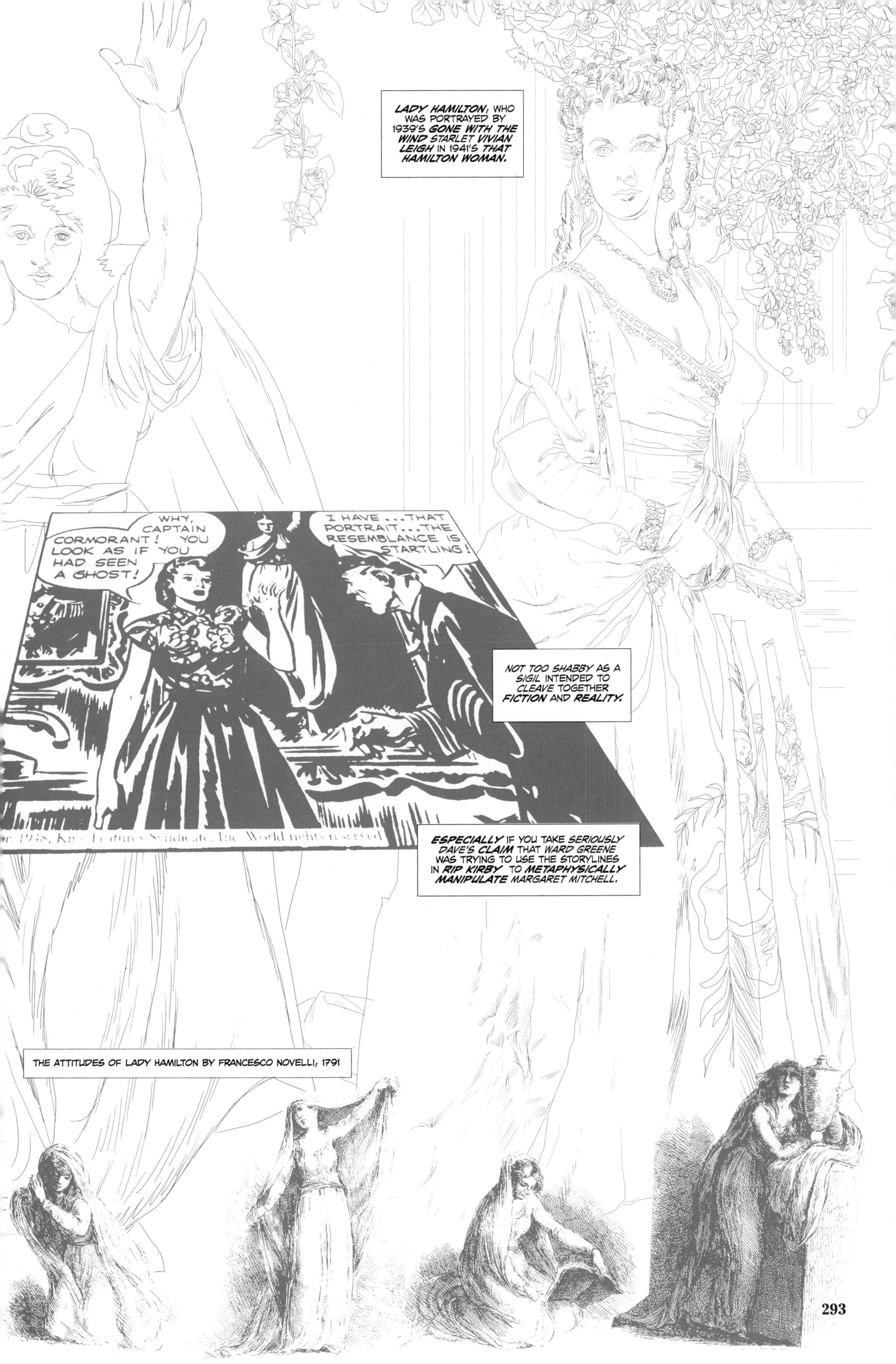
LADY HAMILTON, WHO WAS PORTRAYED BY 1939'S GONE WITH THE WIND STARLET VIVIAN LEIGH IN 1941'S THAT HAMILTON WOMAN.
WHY, CAPTAIN CORMORANT! YOU LOOK AS IF YOU HAD SEEN A GHOST!
I HAVE... THAT PORTRAIT... THE RESEMBLANCE IS STARTLING!
NOT TOO SHABBY AS A SIGIL INTENDED TO CLEAVE TOGETHER FICTION AND REALITY.
ESPECIALLY IF YOU TAKE SERIOUSLY DAVE'S CLAIM THAT WARD GREENE WAS TRYING TO USE THE STORYLINES IN RIP KIRBY TO METAPHYSICALLY MANIPULATE MARGARET MITCHELL.
THE ATTITUDES OF LADY HAMILTON BY FRANCESCO NOVELLI, 1791

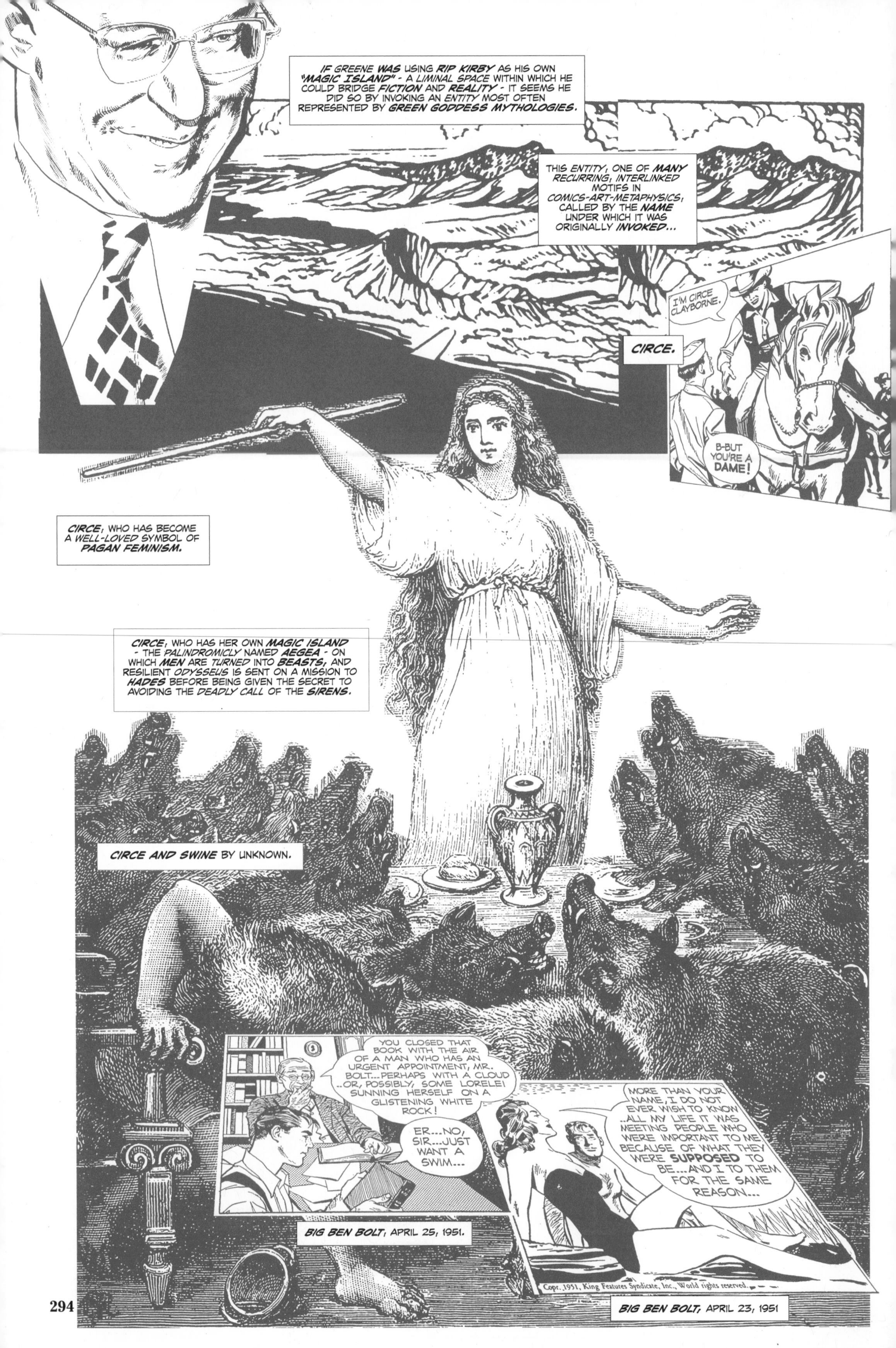

IF GREENE WAS USING RIP KIRBY AS HIS OWN "MAGIC ISLAND" - A LIMINAL SPACE WITHIN WHICH HE COULD BRIDGE FICTION AND REALITY - IT SEEMS HE DID SO BY INVOKING AN ENTITY MOST OFTEN REPRESENTED BY GREEN GODDESS MYTHOLOGIES.
THIS ENTITY, ONE OF MANY RECURRING, INTERLINKED MOTIFS IN COMICS-ART-METAPHYSICS, CALLED BY THE NAME UNDER WHICH IT WAS ORIGINALLY INVOKED...
I'M CIRCE CLAYBORNE.
CIRCE.
B-BUT YOU'RE A DAME!
CIRCE; WHO HAS BECOME A WELL-LOVED SYMBOL OF PAGAN FEMINISM.
CIRCE; WHO HAS HER OWN MAGIC ISLAND - THE PALINDROMICLY NAMED AEGEA - ON WHICH MEN ARE TURNED INTO BEASTS; AND RESILIENT ODYSSEUS IS SENT ON A MISSION TO HADES BEFORE BEING GIVEN THE SECRET TO AVOIDING THE DEADLY CALL OF THE SIRENS.
CIRCE AND SWINE BY UNKNOWN.
YOU CLOSED THAT BOOK WITH THE AIR OF A MAN WHO HAS AN URGENT APPOINTMENT, MR. BOLT...PERHAPS WITH A CLOUD ..OR, POSSIBLY, SOME LORELEI SUNNING HERSELF ON A GLISTENING WHITE ROCK!
ER...NO, SIR...JUST WANT A SWIM...
BIG BEN BOLT; APRIL 25, 1951.
MORE THAN YOUR NAME, I DO NOT EVER WISH TO KNOW ..ALL MY LIFE IT WAS MEETING PEOPLE WHO WERE IMPORTANT TO ME BECAUSE OF WHAT THEY WERE SUPPOSED TO BE...AND I TO THEM FOR THE SAME REASON...
Copr. 1951, King Features Syndicate, Inc., World rights reserved.
BIG BEN BOLT; APRIL 23, 1951

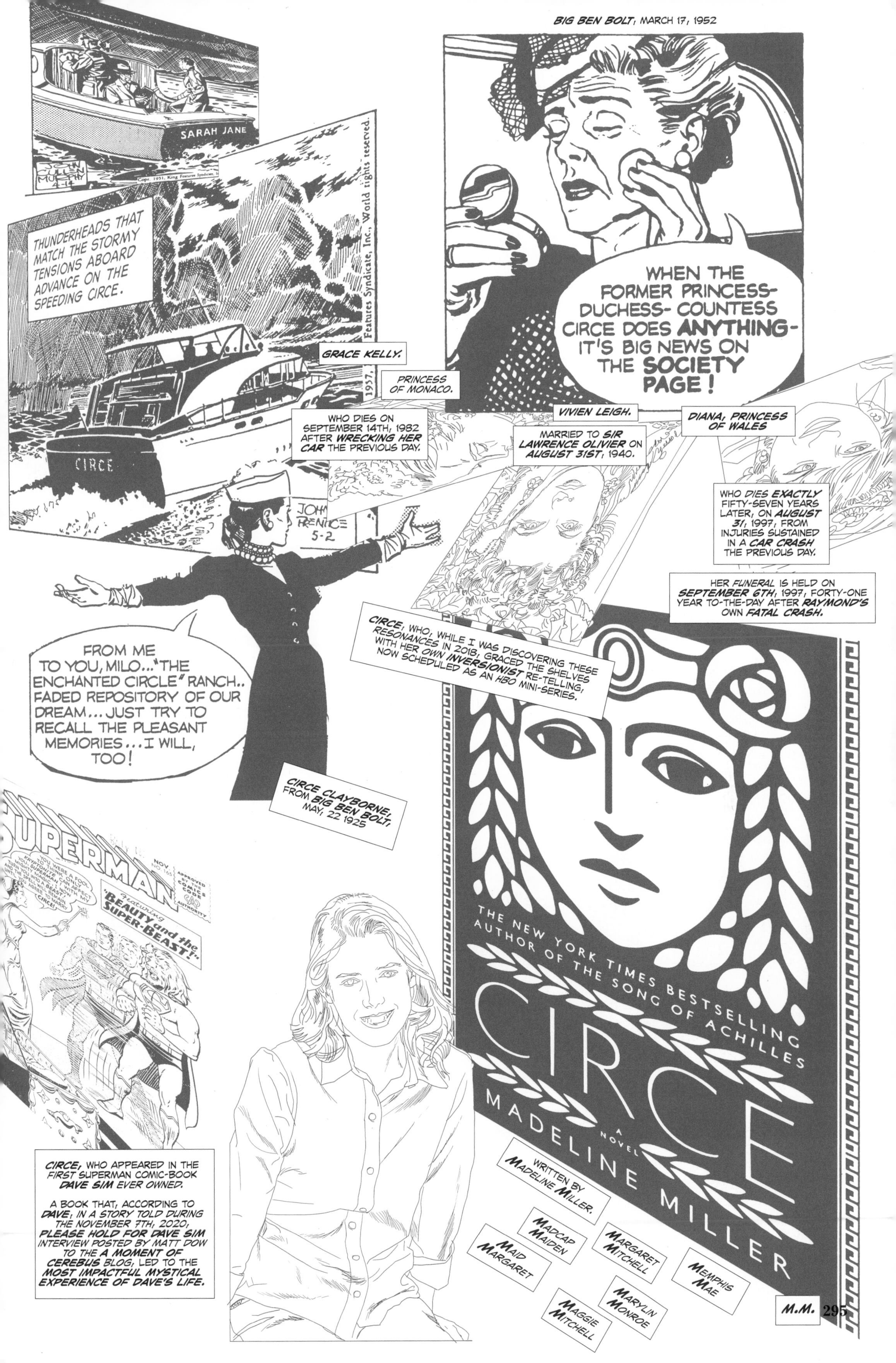

BIG BEN BOLT, MARCH 17, 1952
SARAH JANE
JOHN CULLEN MURPHY 4-14
Copr. 1951, King Features Syndicate, Inc.
THUNDERHEADS THAT MATCH THE STORMY TENSIONS ABOARD ADVANCE ON THE SPEEDING CIRCE.
1957, Features Syndicate, Inc., World rights reserved.
CIRCE
JOHN PRENTICE 5-2
WHEN THE FORMER PRINCESS-DUCHESS- COUNTESS CIRCE DOES ANYTHING- IT'S BIG NEWS ON THE SOCIETY PAGE!
GRACE KELLY.
PRINCESS OF MONACO.
WHO DIES ON SEPTEMBER 14TH, 1982 AFTER WRECKING HER CAR THE PREVIOUS DAY.
VIVIEN LEIGH.
MARRIED TO SIR LAWRENCE OLIVIER ON AUGUST 31ST, 1940.
DIANA, PRINCESS OF WALES
WHO DIES EXACTLY FIFTY-SEVEN YEARS LATER, ON AUGUST 31, 1997, FROM INJURIES SUSTAINED IN A CAR CRASH THE PREVIOUS DAY.
HER FUNERAL IS HELD ON SEPTEMBER 6TH, 1997, FORTY-ONE YEAR TO-THE-DAY AFTER RAYMOND'S OWN FATAL CRASH.
CIRCE, WHO, WHILE I WAS DISCOVERING THESE RESONANCES IN 2018, GRACED THE SHELVES WITH HER OWN INVERSIONIST RE-TELLING, NOW SCHEDULED AS AN HBO MINI-SERIES.
FROM ME TO YOU, MILO..."THE ENCHANTED CIRCLE" RANCH.. FADED REPOSITORY OF OUR DREAM... JUST TRY TO RECALL THE PLEASANT MEMORIES... I WILL, TOO!
CIRCE CLAYBORNE, FROM BIG BEN BOLT, MAY, 22 1925
SUPERMAN
NOV. NO. 165
APPROVED BY THE COMICS CODE AUTHORITY
Featuring "BEAUTY and the SUPER-BEAST!"
THE NEW YORK TIMES BESTSELLING AUTHOR OF THE SONG OF ACHILLES
CIRCE
A NOVEL
MADELINE MILLER
WRITTEN BY MADELINE MILLER.
CIRCE, WHO APPEARED IN THE FIRST SUPERMAN COMIC-BOOK DAVE SIM EVER OWNED.
A BOOK THAT, ACCORDING TO DAVE, IN A STORY TOLD DURING THE NOVEMBER 7TH, 2020, PLEASE HOLD FOR DAVE SIM INTERVIEW POSTED BY MATT DOW TO THE A MOMENT OF CEREBUS BLOG, LED TO THE MOST IMPACTFUL MYSTICAL EXPERIENCE OF DAVE'S LIFE.
MADCAP MAIDEN
MAID MARGARET
MARGARET MITCHELL
MEMPHIS MAE
MARYLIN MONROE
MAGGIE MITCHELL
M.M.

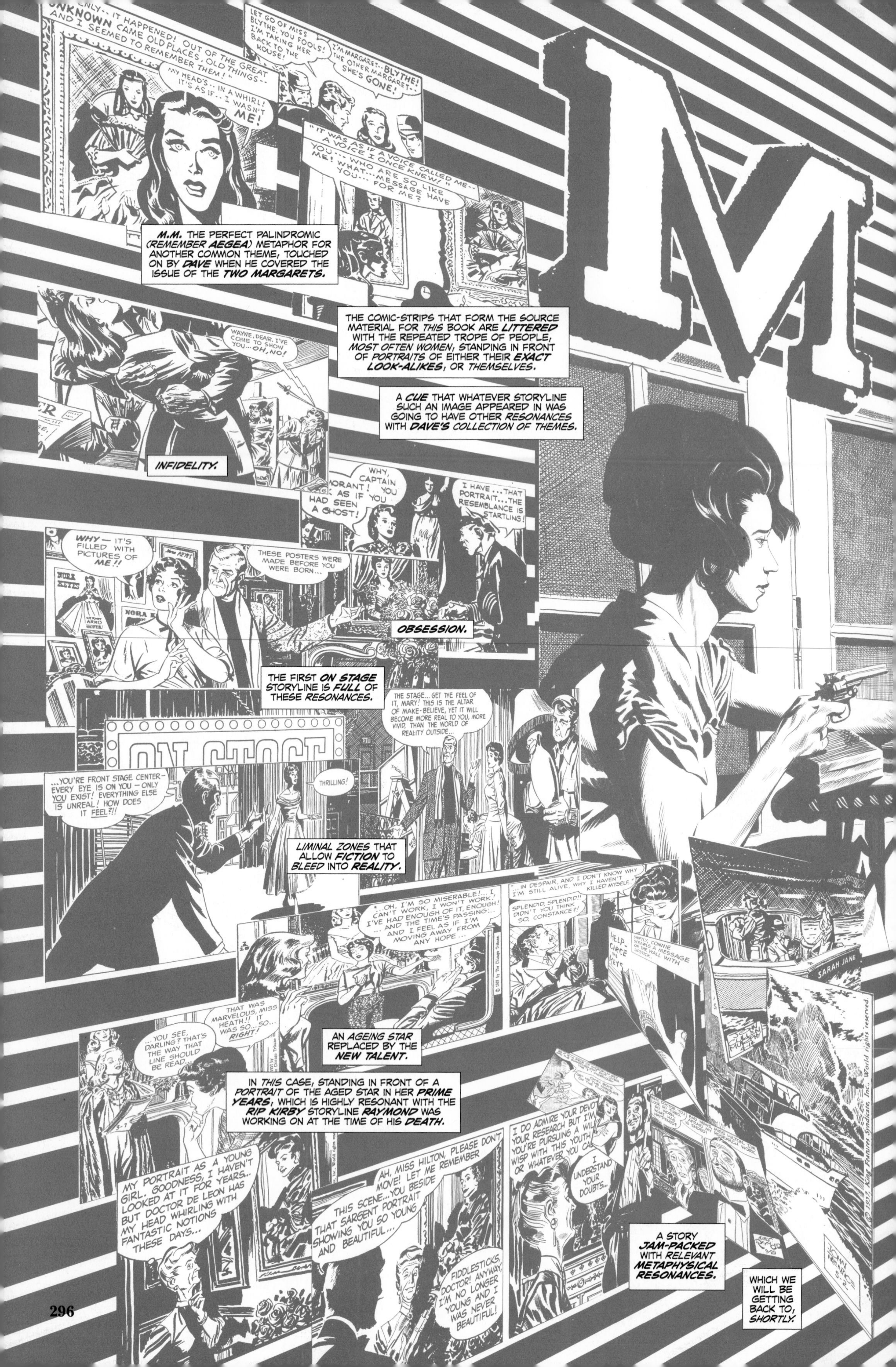

IT HAPPENED! OUT OF THE GREAT UNKNOWN CAME OLD PLACES, OLD THINGS -- AND I SEEMED TO REMEMBER THEM!
MY HEAD'S... IN A WHIRL! IT'S AS IF... I WASN'T ME!
LET GO OF MISS BLYTHE, YOU FOOLS! I'M TAKING HER BACK TO THE HOUSE!
I'M MARGARET -- BLYTHE! THE OTHER MARGARET -- SHE'S GONE!
"IT WAS AS IF A VOICE CALLED ME -- A VOICE I ONCE KNEW!
YOU -- WHO ARE SO LIKE ME! WHAT... MESSAGE HAVE YOU... FOR ME?
M.M. THE PERFECT PALINDROMIC (REMEMBER AEGEA) METAPHOR FOR ANOTHER COMMON THEME, TOUCHED ON BY DAVE WHEN HE COVERED THE ISSUE OF THE TWO MARGARETS.
M
WAYNE, DEAR, I'VE COME TO SHOW YOU... OH, NO!
THE COMIC-STRIPS THAT FORM THE SOURCE MATERIAL FOR THIS BOOK ARE LITTERED WITH THE REPEATED TROPE OF PEOPLE, MOST OFTEN WOMEN, STANDING IN FRONT OF PORTRAITS OF EITHER THEIR EXACT LOOK-ALIKES, OR THEMSELVES.
A CUE THAT WHATEVER STORYLINE SUCH AN IMAGE APPEARED IN WAS GOING TO HAVE OTHER RESONANCES WITH DAVE'S COLLECTION OF THEMES.
INFIDELITY.
WHY, CAPTAIN MORANT! YOU LOOK AS IF YOU HAD SEEN A GHOST!
I HAVE... THAT PORTRAIT... THE RESEMBLANCE IS STARTLING!
WHY -- IT'S FILLED WITH PICTURES OF ME!!
THESE POSTERS WERE MADE BEFORE YOU WERE BORN...
NORA KEYES
OBSESSION.
THE FIRST ON STAGE STORYLINE IS FULL OF THESE RESONANCES.
THE STAGE... GET THE FEEL OF IT, MARY! THIS IS THE ALTAR OF MAKE-BELIEVE, YET IT WILL BECOME MORE REAL TO YOU, MORE VIVID, THAN THE WORLD OF REALITY OUTSIDE...
ON STAGE
...YOU'RE FRONT STAGE CENTER -- EVERY EYE IS ON YOU -- ONLY YOU EXIST! EVERYTHING ELSE IS UNREAL! HOW DOES IT FEEL?!!
THRILLING!
LIMINAL ZONES THAT ALLOW FICTION TO BLEED INTO REALITY.
...OH, I'M SO MISERABLE!... I CAN'T WORK, I WON'T WORK! I'VE HAD ENOUGH OF IT, ENOUGH! ...AND THE TIME'S PASSING... AND I FEEL AS IF I'M MOVING AWAY FROM ANY HOPE...
...IN DESPAIR, AND I DON'T KNOW WHY I'M STILL ALIVE, WHY I HAVEN'T KILLED MYSELF...
SPLENDID, SPLENDID!! DIDN'T YOU THINK SO, CONSTANCE?!
HELP CIRCE KEYS
SWIFTLY, CONNIE SCRAWLS A MESSAGE ON THE WALL WITH LIPSTICK.
SARAH JANE
...YOU SEE, DARLING? THAT'S THE WAY THAT LINE SHOULD BE READ.
THAT WAS MARVELOUS, MISS HEATH!! IT WAS SO... SO... RIGHT!
AN AGEING STAR REPLACED BY THE NEW TALENT.
IN THIS CASE, STANDING IN FRONT OF A PORTRAIT OF THE AGED STAR IN HER PRIME YEARS, WHICH IS HIGHLY RESONANT WITH THE RIP KIRBY STORYLINE RAYMOND WAS WORKING ON AT THE TIME OF HIS DEATH.
MY PORTRAIT AS A YOUNG GIRL. GOODNESS, I HAVEN'T LOOKED AT IT FOR YEARS... BUT DOCTOR DE LEON HAS MY HEAD WHIRLING WITH FANTASTIC NOTIONS THESE DAYS...
AH, MISS HILTON, PLEASE DON'T MOVE! LET ME REMEMBER THIS SCENE... YOU BESIDE THAT SARGENT PORTRAIT SHOWING YOU SO YOUNG AND BEAUTIFUL...
FIDDLESTICKS, DOCTOR! ANYWAY, I'M NO LONGER YOUNG AND I WAS NEVER BEAUTIFUL!
I UNDERSTAND YOUR DOUBTS...
A STORY JAM-PACKED WITH RELEVANT METAPHYSICAL RESONANCES.
WHICH WE WILL BE GETTING BACK TO, SHORTLY.
© 1957, King Features Syndicate, Inc. World rights reserved.

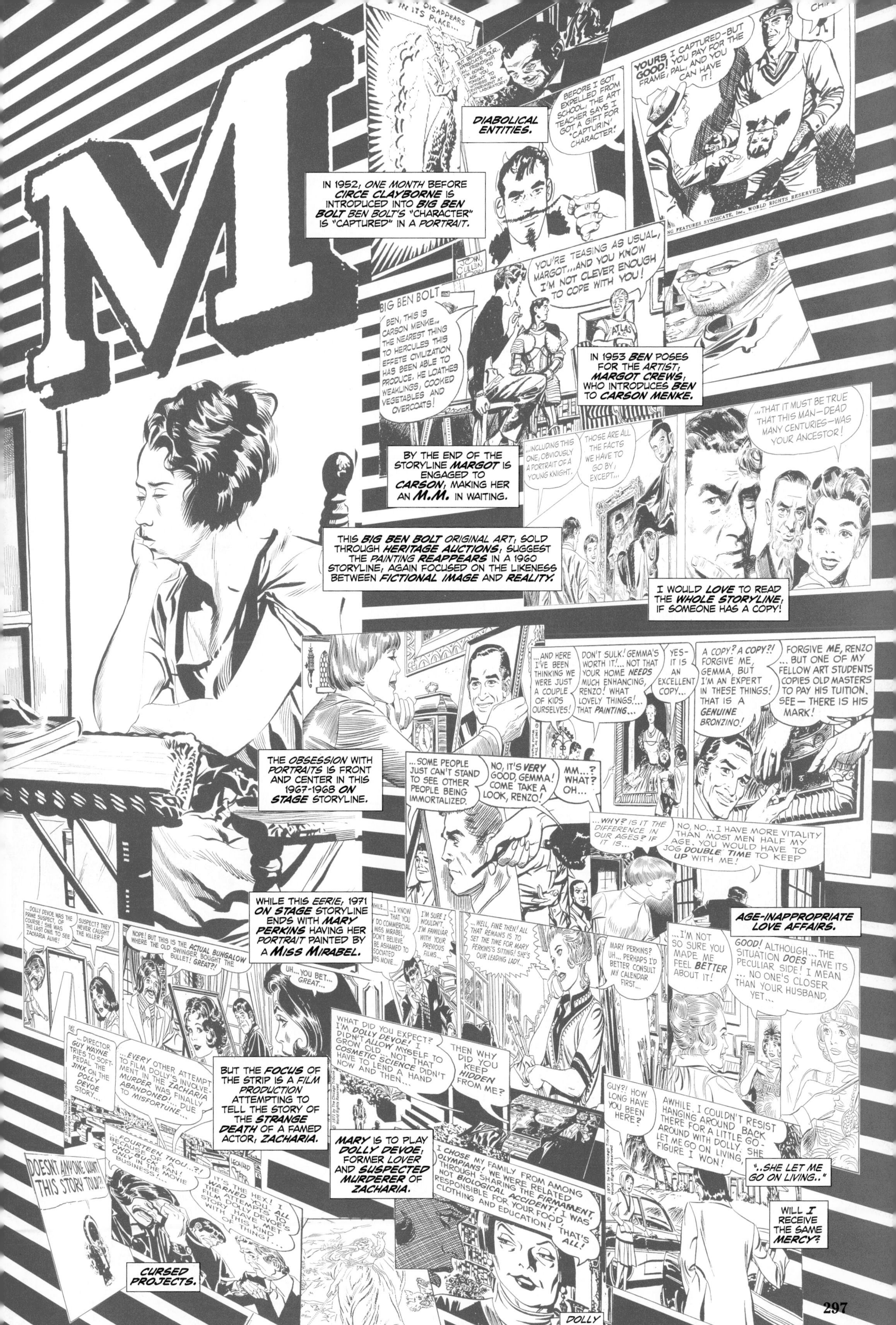

M
DIABOLICAL ENTITIES.
BEFORE I GOT EXPELLED FROM SCHOOL, THE ART TEACHER SAYS I GOT A GIFT FOR "CAPTURIN'" CHARACTER!
YOURS GOOD! I CAPTURED—BUT YOU PAY FOR THE FRAME, PAL, AND YOU CAN HAVE IT!
IN 1952, ONE MONTH BEFORE CIRCE CLAYBORNE IS INTRODUCED INTO BIG BEN BOLT BEN BOLT'S "CHARACTER" IS "CAPTURED" IN A PORTRAIT.
YOU'RE TEASING AS USUAL, MARGOT...AND YOU KNOW I'M NOT CLEVER ENOUGH TO COPE WITH YOU!
BIG BEN BOLT
BEN, THIS IS CARSON MENKE... THE NEAREST THING TO HERCULES THIS EFFETE CIVILIZATION HAS BEEN ABLE TO PRODUCE. HE LOATHES WEAKLINGS, COOKED VEGETABLES AND OVERCOATS!
ATLAS A.C.
IN 1953 BEN POSES FOR THE ARTIST, MARGOT CREWS, WHO INTRODUCES BEN TO CARSON MENKE.
BY THE END OF THE STORYLINE MARGOT IS ENGAGED TO CARSON, MAKING HER AN M.M. IN WAITING.
...INCLUDING THIS ONE, OBVIOUSLY A PORTRAIT OF A YOUNG KNIGHT.
THOSE ARE ALL THE FACTS WE HAVE TO GO BY, EXCEPT...
...THAT IT MUST BE TRUE THAT THIS MAN—DEAD MANY CENTURIES—WAS YOUR ANCESTOR!
THIS BIG BEN BOLT ORIGINAL ART, SOLD THROUGH HERITAGE AUCTIONS, SUGGEST THE PAINTING REAPPEARS IN A 1960 STORYLINE, AGAIN FOCUSED ON THE LIKENESS BETWEEN FICTIONAL IMAGE AND REALITY.
I WOULD LOVE TO READ THE WHOLE STORYLINE, IF SOMEONE HAS A COPY!
...AND HERE I'VE BEEN THINKING WE WERE JUST A COUPLE OF KIDS OURSELVES!
DON'T SULK! GEMMA'S WORTH IT!... NOT THAT YOUR HOME NEEDS MUCH ENHANCING, RENZO! WHAT LOVELY THINGS!... THAT PAINTING...
YES—IT IS AN EXCELLENT COPY...
A COPY? A COPY?! FORGIVE ME, GEMMA, BUT I'M AN EXPERT IN THESE THINGS! THAT IS A GENUINE BRONZINO!
FORGIVE ME, RENZO ... BUT ONE OF MY FELLOW ART STUDENTS COPIES OLD MASTERS TO PAY HIS TUITION. SEE—THERE IS HIS MARK!
THE OBSESSION WITH PORTRAITS IS FRONT AND CENTER IN THIS 1967-1968 ON STAGE STORYLINE.
...SOME PEOPLE JUST CAN'T STAND TO SEE OTHER PEOPLE BEING IMMORTALIZED.
NO, IT'S VERY GOOD, GEMMA! COME TAKE A LOOK, RENZO!
MM...? WHAT? OH...
...WHY? IS IT THE DIFFERENCE IN OUR AGES? IF IT IS...
NO, NO... I HAVE MORE VITALITY THAN MOST MEN HALF MY AGE. YOU WOULD HAVE TO JOG DOUBLE TIME TO KEEP UP WITH ME!
AGE-INAPPROPRIATE LOVE AFFAIRS.
...DOLLY DEVOE WAS THE PRIME SUSPECT, OF COURSE! SHE WAS THE LAST ONE TO SEE ZACHARIA ALIVE!
SUSPECT? THEY NEVER CAUGHT THE KILLER?
NOPE! BUT THIS IS THE ACTUAL BUNGALOW WHERE THE OLD SWINGER BOUGHT THE BULLET! GREAT?!
UH...YOU BET... GREAT...
WHILE THIS EERIE, 1971 ON STAGE STORYLINE ENDS WITH MARY PERKINS HAVING HER PORTRAIT PAINTED BY A MISS MIRABEL.
I'M SURE I WOULDN'T! I'M FAMILIAR WITH YOUR PREVIOUS FILMS...
...WELL, FINE THEN! ALL THAT REMAINS IS TO SET THE TIME FOR MARY PERKINS'S SITTING! SHE'S OUR LEADING LADY...
MARY PERKINS? UH... PERHAPS I'D BETTER CONSULT MY CALENDAR FIRST...
...I'M NOT SO SURE YOU MADE ME FEEL BETTER ABOUT IT!
GOOD! ALTHOUGH... THE SITUATION DOES HAVE ITS PECULIAR SIDE! I MEAN ... NO ONE'S CLOSER THAN YOUR HUSBAND, YET...
...DIRECTOR GUY WAYNE TRIES TO SOFT-PEDAL THE JINX ON THE DOLLY DEVOE STORY...
...EVERY OTHER ATTEMPT TO FILM DOLLY'S INVOLVEMENT IN THE ZACHARIA MURDER WAS FINALLY ABANDONED!... DUE TO MISFORTUNE...
BUT THE FOCUS OF THE STRIP IS A FILM PRODUCTION ATTEMPTING TO TELL THE STORY OF THE STRANGE DEATH OF A FAMED ACTOR, ZACHARIA.
WHAT DID YOU EXPECT? I'M DOLLY DEVOE! I DIDN'T ALLOW MYSELF TO GROW OLD... NOT THAT COSMETIC SCIENCE DIDN'T HAVE TO LEND A HAND NOW AND THEN...
THEN WHY DID YOU KEEP HIDDEN FROM ME?
GUY?! HOW LONG HAVE YOU BEEN HERE?
AWHILE. I COULDN'T RESIST HANGING AROUND BACK THERE FOR A LITTLE GO-AROUND WITH DOLLY. SHE LET ME GO ON LIVING, FIGURE I WON!
MARY IS TO PLAY DOLLY DEVOE, FORMER LOVER AND SUSPECTED MURDERER OF ZACHARIA.
I CHOSE MY FAMILY FROM AMONG OLYMPIANS! WE WERE RELATED THROUGH SHARING THE FIRMAMENT, NOT BIOLOGICAL ACCIDENT! I WAS RESPONSIBLE FOR YOUR FOOD, CLOTHING AND EDUCATION! THAT'S ALL!
"..SHE LET ME GO ON LIVING.."
WILL I RECEIVE THE SAME MERCY?
DOESN'T ANYONE WANT THIS STORY TOLD?!
FOURTEEN THOU...?! BECAUSE OF A FAN! TWO-BUCK MOVIE BUSINESS...
IT'S THE HEX! I WARNED YOU! ALL ATTEMPTS TO FILM DOLLY DEVOE'S STORY HAVE MET WITH THIS KIND OF THING!...
CURSED PROJECTS.
DOLLY DEVOE.

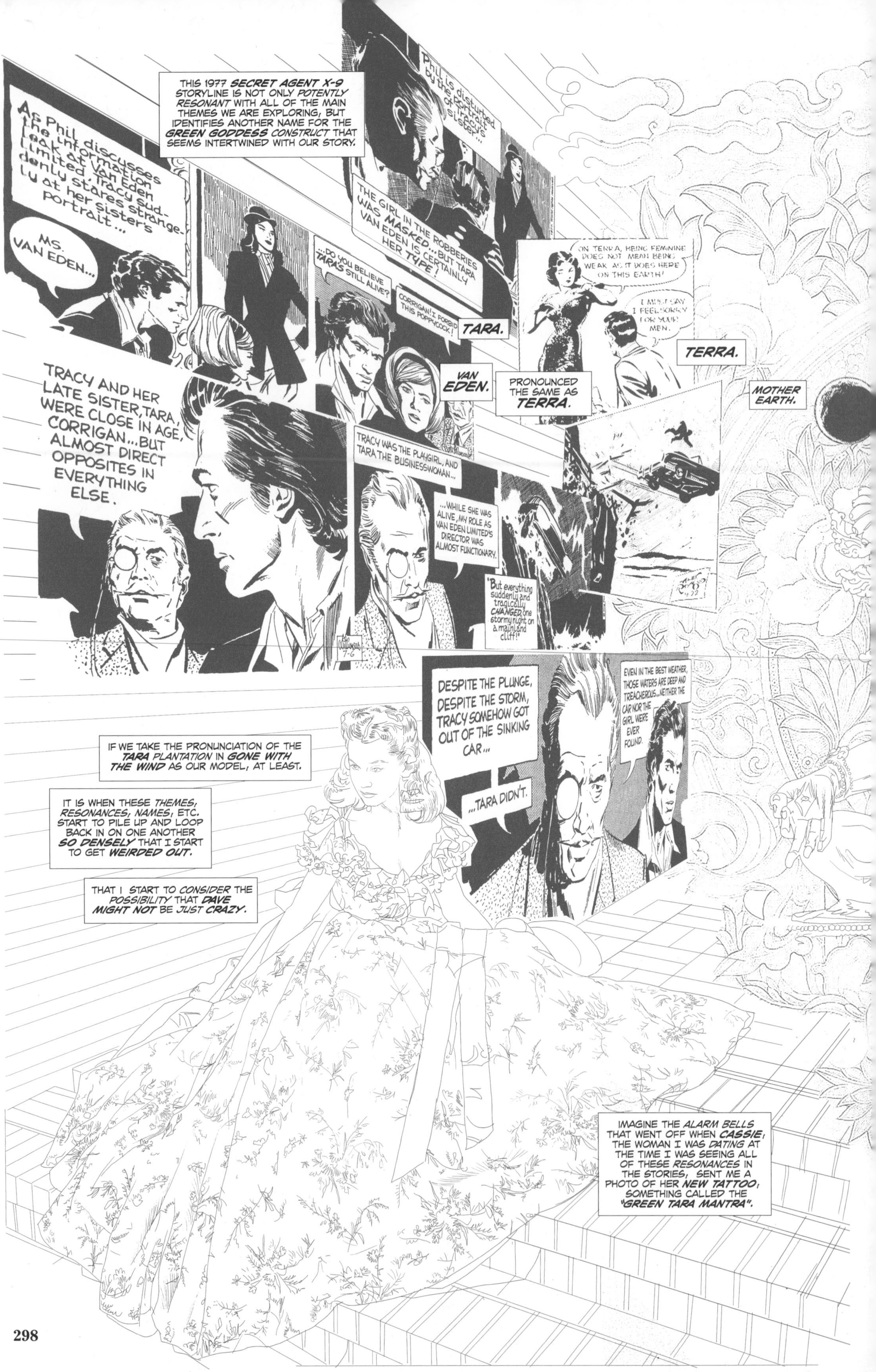

THIS 1977 SECRET AGENT X-9 STORYLINE IS NOT ONLY POTENTLY RESONANT WITH ALL OF THE MAIN THEMES WE ARE EXPLORING, BUT IDENTIFIES ANOTHER NAME FOR THE GREEN GODDESS CONSTRUCT THAT SEEMS INTERTWINED WITH OUR STORY.
As Phil discusses the information leak at Van Eden Limited, Tracy suddenly stares strangely at her sister's portrait...
MS. VAN EDEN...
Phil is disturbed by the portrait of Tracy's sister...
THE GIRL IN THE ROBBERIES WAS MASKED...BUT TARA VAN EDEN IS CERTAINLY HER TYPE!
...DO YOU BELIEVE TARA'S STILL ALIVE?
CORRIGAN! I FORBID THIS POPPYCOCK!
TARA.
ON TERRA, BEING FEMININE DOES NOT MEAN BEING WEAK AS IT DOES HERE ON THIS EARTH!
I MUST SAY I FEEL SORRY FOR YOUR MEN.
TERRA.
VAN EDEN.
PRONOUNCED THE SAME AS TERRA.
MOTHER EARTH.
TRACY AND HER LATE SISTER, TARA, WERE CLOSE IN AGE, CORRIGAN...BUT ALMOST DIRECT OPPOSITES IN EVERYTHING ELSE.
TRACY WAS THE PLAYGIRL, AND TARA THE BUSINESSWOMAN...
...WHILE SHE WAS ALIVE, MY ROLE AS VAN EDEN LIMITED'S DIRECTOR WAS ALMOST FUNCTIONARY.
"But everything suddenly and tragically CHANGED one stormy night on a mainland cliff!"
DESPITE THE PLUNGE, DESPITE THE STORM, TRACY SOMEHOW GOT OUT OF THE SINKING CAR...
...TARA DIDN'T.
EVEN IN THE BEST WEATHER, THOSE WATERS ARE DEEP AND TREACHEROUS...NEITHER THE CAR NOR THE GIRL WERE EVER FOUND.
IF WE TAKE THE PRONUNCIATION OF THE TARA PLANTATION IN GONE WITH THE WIND AS OUR MODEL, AT LEAST.
IT IS WHEN THESE THEMES, RESONANCES, NAMES, ETC. START TO PILE UP AND LOOP BACK IN ON ONE ANOTHER SO DENSELY THAT I START TO GET WEIRDED OUT.
THAT I START TO CONSIDER THE POSSIBILITY THAT DAVE MIGHT NOT BE JUST CRAZY.
IMAGINE THE ALARM BELLS THAT WENT OFF WHEN CASSIE, THE WOMAN I WAS DATING AT THE TIME I WAS SEEING ALL OF THESE RESONANCES IN THE STORIES, SENT ME A PHOTO OF HER NEW TATTOO, SOMETHING CALLED THE "GREEN TARA MANTRA".

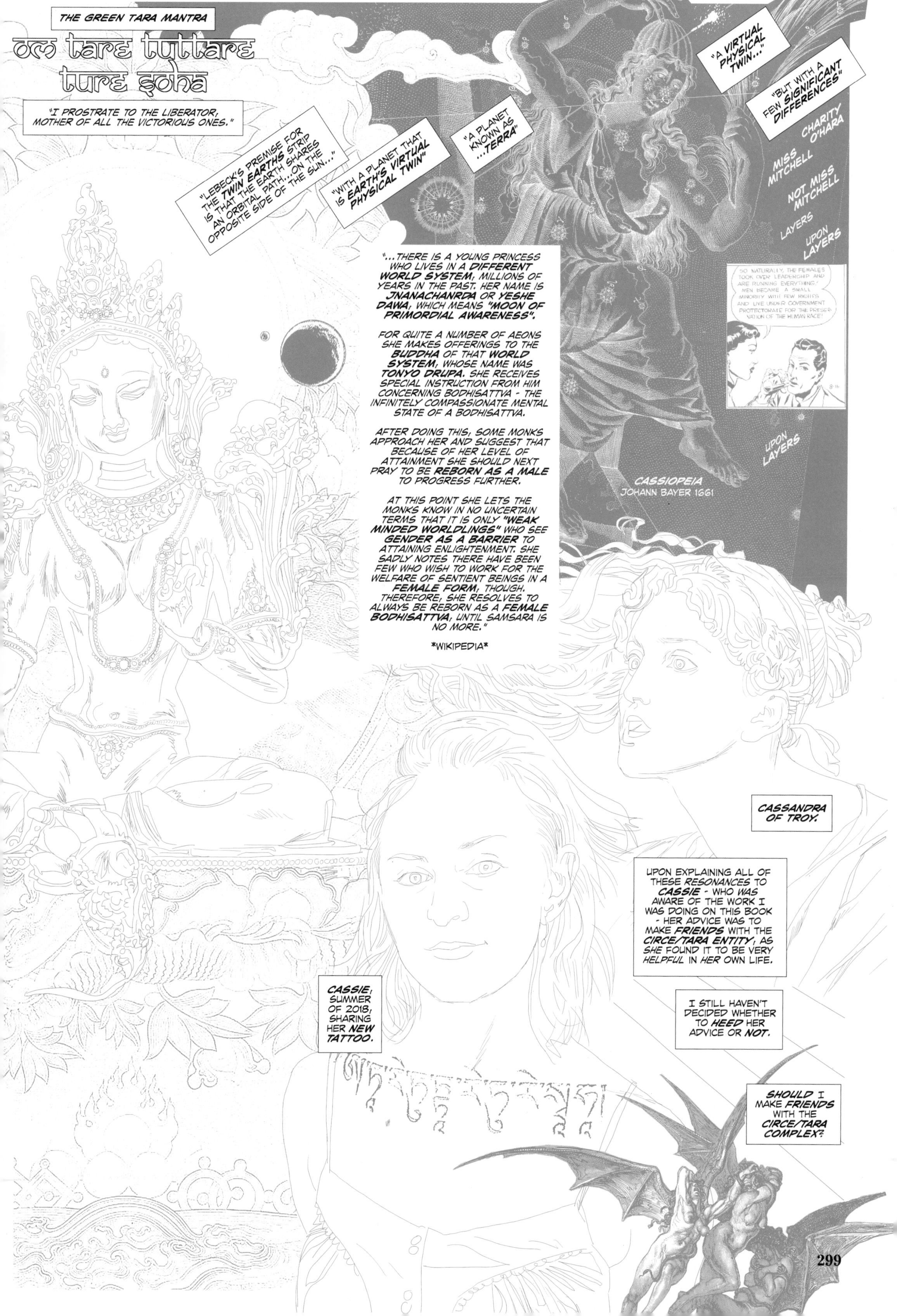
THE GREEN TARA MANTRA
OM TARE TUTTARE TURE SOHA
"I PROSTRATE TO THE LIBERATOR, MOTHER OF ALL THE VICTORIOUS ONES."
"LEBECK'S PREMISE FOR THE TWIN EARTHS STRIP IS THAT THE EARTH SHARES AN ORBITAL PATH...ON THE OPPOSITE SIDE OF THE SUN..."
"WITH A PLANET THAT IS EARTH'S VIRTUAL PHYSICAL TWIN"
"A PLANET KNOWN AS ...TERRA"
"A VIRTUAL PHYSICAL TWIN..."
"BUT WITH A FEW SIGNIFICANT DIFFERENCES"
CHARITY O'HARA
MISS MITCHELL
NOT MISS MITCHELL
LAYERS
UPON LAYERS
SO NATURALLY, THE FEMALES TOOK OVER LEADERSHIP AND ARE RUNNING EVERYTHING! MEN BECAME A SMALL MINORITY WITH FEW RIGHTS AND LIVE UNDER GOVERNMENT PROTECTORATE FOR THE PRESERVATION OF THE HUMAN RACE!
8-16
"...THERE IS A YOUNG PRINCESS WHO LIVES IN A DIFFERENT WORLD SYSTEM, MILLIONS OF YEARS IN THE PAST. HER NAME IS JNANACHANRDA OR YESHE DAWA, WHICH MEANS "MOON OF PRIMORDIAL AWARENESS".
FOR QUITE A NUMBER OF AEONS SHE MAKES OFFERINGS TO THE BUDDHA OF THAT WORLD SYSTEM, WHOSE NAME WAS TONYO DRUPA. SHE RECEIVES SPECIAL INSTRUCTION FROM HIM CONCERNING BODHISATTVA - THE INFINITELY COMPASSIONATE MENTAL STATE OF A BODHISATTVA.
AFTER DOING THIS, SOME MONKS APPROACH HER AND SUGGEST THAT BECAUSE OF HER LEVEL OF ATTAINMENT SHE SHOULD NEXT PRAY TO BE REBORN AS A MALE TO PROGRESS FURTHER.
AT THIS POINT SHE LETS THE MONKS KNOW IN NO UNCERTAIN TERMS THAT IT IS ONLY "WEAK MINDED WORLDLINGS" WHO SEE GENDER AS A BARRIER TO ATTAINING ENLIGHTENMENT. SHE SADLY NOTES THERE HAVE BEEN FEW WHO WISH TO WORK FOR THE WELFARE OF SENTIENT BEINGS IN A FEMALE FORM, THOUGH. THEREFORE, SHE RESOLVES TO ALWAYS BE REBORN AS A FEMALE BODHISATTVA, UNTIL SAMSARA IS NO MORE."
*WIKIPEDIA*
UPON LAYERS
CASSIOPEIA
JOHANN BAYER 1661
CASSANDRA OF TROY.
UPON EXPLAINING ALL OF THESE RESONANCES TO CASSIE - WHO WAS AWARE OF THE WORK I WAS DOING ON THIS BOOK - HER ADVICE WAS TO MAKE FRIENDS WITH THE CIRCE/TARA ENTITY, AS SHE FOUND IT TO BE VERY HELPFUL IN HER OWN LIFE.
CASSIE, SUMMER OF 2018, SHARING HER NEW TATTOO.
I STILL HAVEN'T DECIDED WHETHER TO HEED HER ADVICE OR NOT.
SHOULD I MAKE FRIENDS WITH THE CIRCE/TARA COMPLEX?

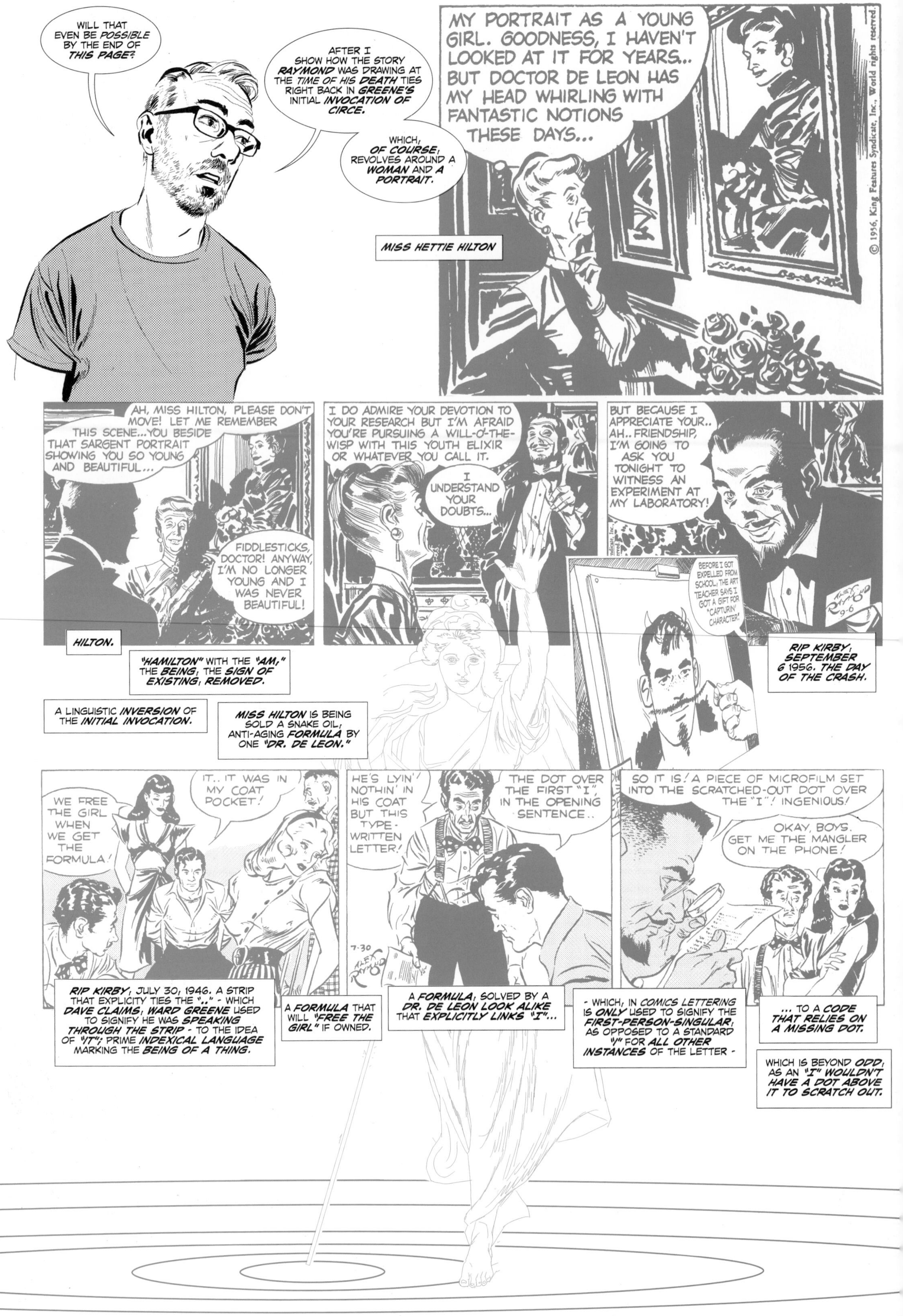
WILL THAT EVEN BE POSSIBLE BY THE END OF THIS PAGE?
AFTER I SHOW HOW THE STORY RAYMOND WAS DRAWING AT THE TIME OF HIS DEATH TIES RIGHT BACK IN GREENE'S INITIAL INVOCATION OF CIRCE.
WHICH, OF COURSE, REVOLVES AROUND A WOMAN AND A PORTRAIT.
MY PORTRAIT AS A YOUNG GIRL. GOODNESS, I HAVEN'T LOOKED AT IT FOR YEARS.. BUT DOCTOR DE LEON HAS MY HEAD WHIRLING WITH FANTASTIC NOTIONS THESE DAYS...
© 1956, King Features Syndicate, Inc., World rights reserved.
MISS HETTIE HILTON
AH, MISS HILTON, PLEASE DON'T MOVE! LET ME REMEMBER THIS SCENE...YOU BESIDE THAT SARGENT PORTRAIT SHOWING YOU SO YOUNG AND BEAUTIFUL...
FIDDLESTICKS, DOCTOR! ANYWAY, I'M NO LONGER YOUNG AND I WAS NEVER BEAUTIFUL!
I DO ADMIRE YOUR DEVOTION TO YOUR RESEARCH BUT I'M AFRAID YOU'RE PURSUING A WILL-O'-THE-WISP WITH THIS YOUTH ELIXIR OR WHATEVER YOU CALL IT.
I UNDERSTAND YOUR DOUBTS...
BUT BECAUSE I APPRECIATE YOUR.. AH.. FRIENDSHIP, I'M GOING TO ASK YOU TONIGHT TO WITNESS AN EXPERIMENT AT MY LABORATORY!
BEFORE I GOT EXPELLED FROM SCHOOL, THE ART TEACHER SAYS I GOT A GIFT FOR "CAPTURIN' CHARACTER."
ALEX RAYMOND 9-6
HILTON.
"HAMILTON" WITH THE "AM," THE BEING, THE SIGN OF EXISTING, REMOVED.
RIP KIRBY, SEPTEMBER 6 1956. THE DAY OF THE CRASH.
A LINGUISTIC INVERSION OF THE INITIAL INVOCATION.
MISS HILTON IS BEING SOLD A SNAKE OIL, ANTI-AGING FORMULA BY ONE "DR. DE LEON."
WE FREE THE GIRL WHEN WE GET THE FORMULA!
IT.. IT WAS IN MY COAT POCKET!
HE'S LYIN'! NOTHIN' IN HIS COAT BUT THIS TYPE-WRITTEN LETTER!
THE DOT OVER THE FIRST "I", IN THE OPENING SENTENCE..
7-30 ALEX RAYMOND
SO IT IS! A PIECE OF MICROFILM SET INTO THE SCRATCHED-OUT DOT OVER THE "I"! INGENIOUS!
OKAY, BOYS. GET ME THE MANGLER ON THE PHONE!
RIP KIRBY, JULY 30, 1946. A STRIP THAT EXPLICITY TIES THE ".." - WHICH DAVE CLAIMS, WARD GREENE USED TO SIGNIFY HE WAS SPEAKING THROUGH THE STRIP - TO THE IDEA OF "IT", PRIME INDEXICAL LANGUAGE MARKING THE BEING OF A THING.
A FORMULA THAT WILL "FREE THE GIRL" IF OWNED.
A FORMULA, SOLVED BY A DR. DE LEON LOOK ALIKE THAT EXPLICITLY LINKS "I"...
- WHICH, IN COMICS LETTERING IS ONLY USED TO SIGNIFY THE FIRST-PERSON-SINGULAR, AS OPPOSED TO A STANDARD "I" FOR ALL OTHER INSTANCES OF THE LETTER -
... TO A CODE THAT RELIES ON A MISSING DOT.
WHICH IS BEYOND ODD, AS AN "I" WOULDN'T HAVE A DOT ABOVE IT TO SCRATCH OUT.

TO RUN HIS SCAM *"DR. DE LEON"* DISGUISES A YOUNG ACTRESS, *PEGGY*, IN MAKEUP TO MAKE HER LOOK AGED.

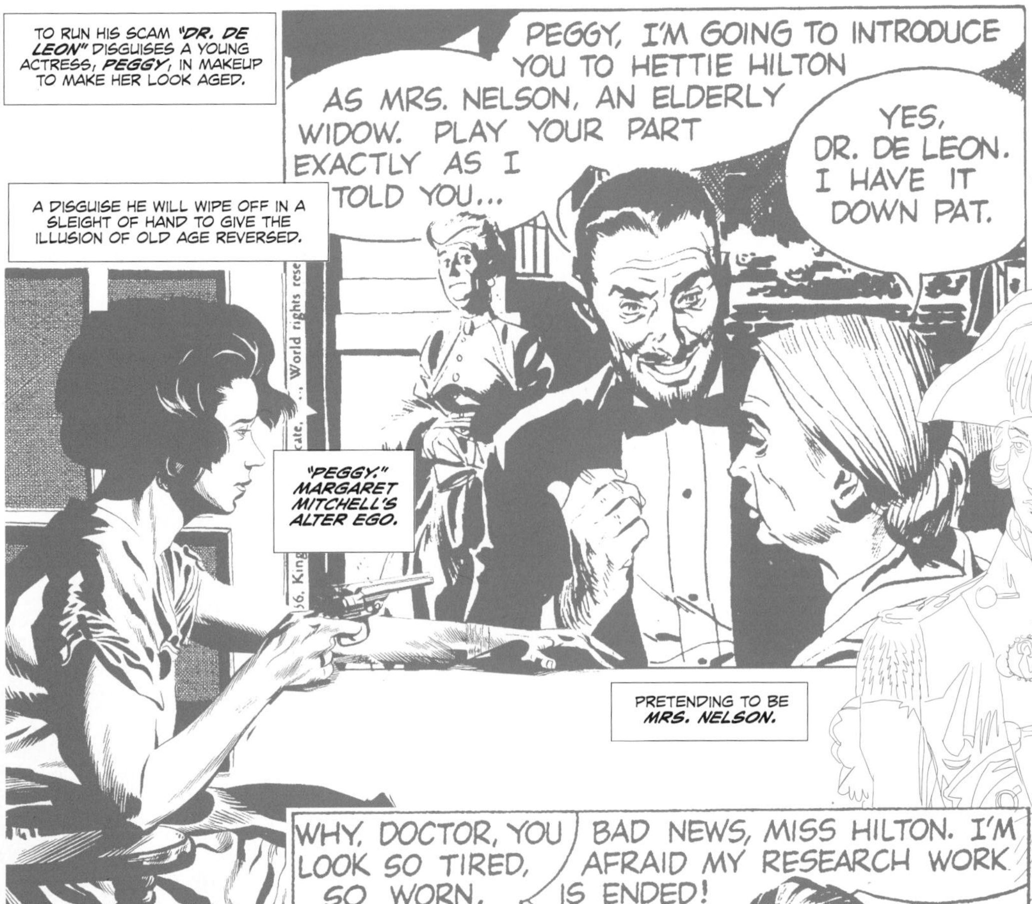
PEGGY, I'M GOING TO INTRODUCE YOU TO HETTIE HILTON AS MRS. NELSON, AN ELDERLY WIDOW. PLAY YOUR PART EXACTLY AS I TOLD YOU...
YES, DR. DE LEON. I HAVE IT DOWN PAT.
A DISGUISE HE WILL WIPE OFF IN A SLEIGHT OF HAND TO GIVE THE ILLUSION OF OLD AGE REVERSED.
"PEGGY." MARGARET MITCHELL'S ALTER EGO.
PRETENDING TO BE MRS. NELSON.

***PEGGY NELSON*** ALSO HAPPENED TO BE THE NAME OF ***FRED DICKENSON'S WIFE.***

***DICKENSON*** HAD BEEN WRITING THE STRIP SINCE ***WARD GREENE'S*** *SUPPOSED* EXIT IN 1952, SOMETHING I AM NOT CONVINCED OF BY THE WAY.

IN ***ALEX RAYMOND: HIS LIFE AND ART***, RAYMOND'S FORMER ASSISTANT ***RAY BURNS*** TELLS *TOM ROBERTS*: ***"AFTER WARD GREENE DIED, FRED DICKENSON...STARTED WRITING THE STRIP."***

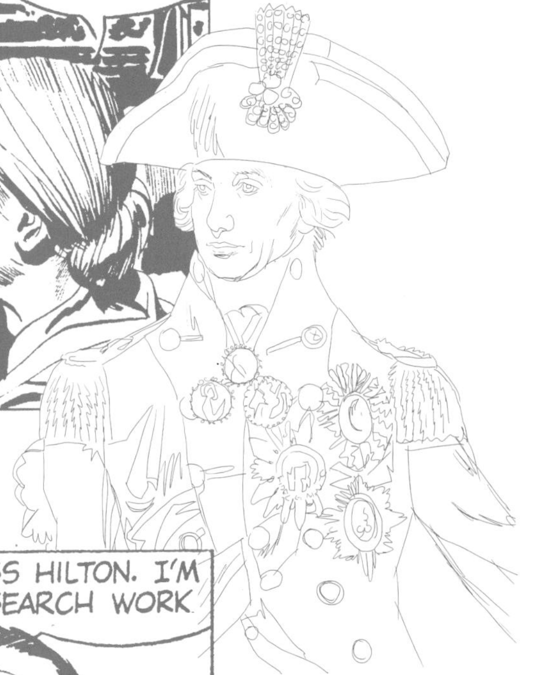

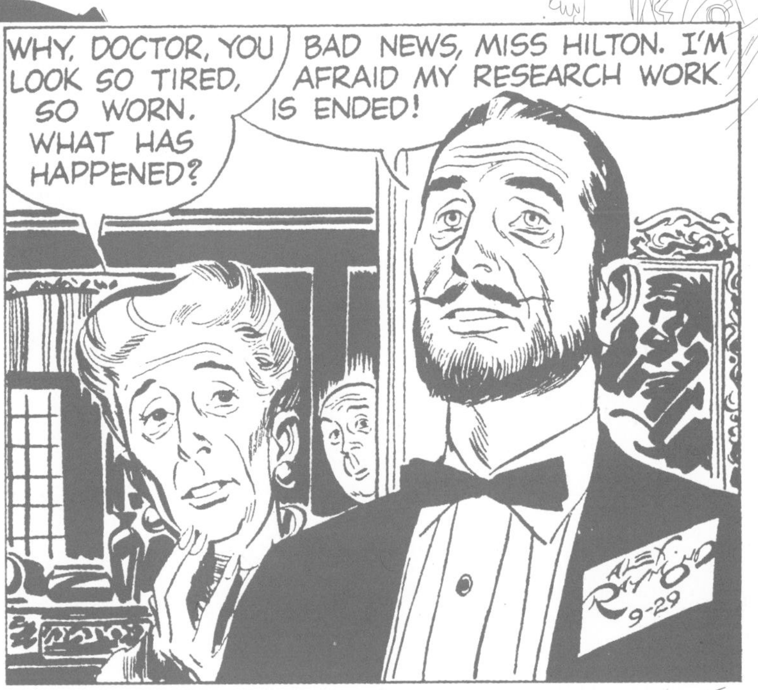
WHY, DOCTOR, YOU LOOK SO TIRED, SO WORN. WHAT HAS HAPPENED?
BAD NEWS, MISS HILTON. I'M AFRAID MY RESEARCH WORK IS ENDED!
ALEX RAYMOND 9-29

MOST ***CHILLING*** OF ALL IS THE PANEL AT RIGHT. WHAT APPEARS TO BE THE ***FINAL PANEL ALEX RAYMOND FINISHED BEFORE HIS DEATH***. IT IS DEFINITELY THE LAST PANEL OF THE ***LAST STRIP THAT BORE HIS SIGNATURE***.

IT *ISN'T* VERY DIFFICULT TO SEE THIS LAST STORYLINE AS AN ATTEMPT TO *UNDO* WHATEVER WAS WROUGHT WHEN ***CIRCE*** WAS FIRST INVOKED. AN ATTEMPT TO ***INVERT THE INVOCATION***.

BUT ***WHO*** WAS DOING THE WORK?

***WARD GREENE HAD BEEN DEAD SINCE JANUARY***, AND *SUPPOSEDLY* HADN'T WRITTEN THE STRIP SINCE SOME TIME IN 1952.

HAD ***GREENE*** WRITTEN THIS STORYLINE ***BEFORE HIS DEATH***, WORKING FAR AHEAD DUE TO THE CRUSHING DEADLINES OF THE DAILY STRIP?

DID ***DICKENSON*** KNOW ENOUGH ABOUT WHAT ***GREENE*** HAD BEEN DOING TO ATTEMPT TO ***STUFF CIRCE BACK INTO THE PANEL BORDERS?***

WAS ***RAYMOND'S DEATH*** AN ***ESSENTIAL, SACRIFICIAL COMPONENT NECESSARY TO FINALIZE THE RITUAL?*** A PROMISE MADE BY ***GREENE***; ***EXPLICITLY***, OR ***ACCIDENTALLY***, YEARS BEFORE?

OR IS THIS ***CIRCE/TARA*** WORKING THROUGH ***DICKENSON*** TO DELIVER ONE OF MANY MESSAGES REGARDING THE ***FOLLY OF INVOKING HER WRATH?***

***"IF YOU INVOKED MY NAME IN SNAKE-OIL ATTEMPTS TO ENFORCE YOUR WILL UPON REALITY, IF YOU INVOKE MY BEING TO CRAFT PETTY FORMULAS AIMED AT CLEAVING MY WORLD TO YOURS.. CLEAVING THERE SHALL BE. YOU WILL BE TOLERATED AS LONG AS YOU ARE USEFUL AND THEN YOUR RESEARCH SHALL BE ENDED."***

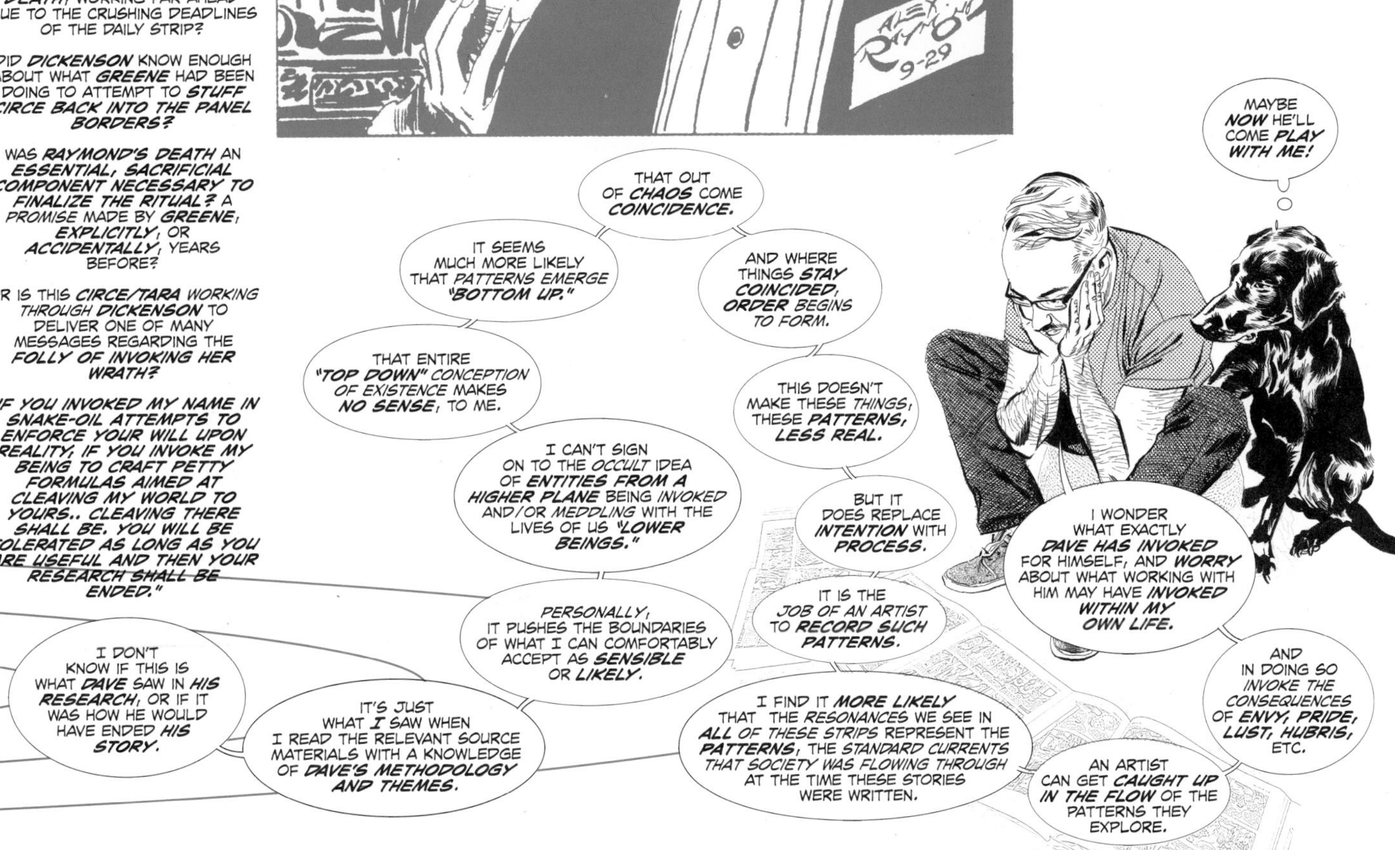
I DON'T KNOW IF THIS IS WHAT DAVE SAW IN HIS RESEARCH, OR IF IT WAS HOW HE WOULD HAVE ENDED HIS STORY.
IT'S JUST WHAT I SAW WHEN I READ THE RELEVANT SOURCE MATERIALS WITH A KNOWLEDGE OF DAVE'S METHODOLOGY AND THEMES.
PERSONALLY, IT PUSHES THE BOUNDARIES OF WHAT I CAN COMFORTABLY ACCEPT AS SENSIBLE OR LIKELY.
I CAN'T SIGN ON TO THE OCCULT IDEA OF ENTITIES FROM A HIGHER PLANE BEING INVOKED AND/OR MEDDLING WITH THE LIVES OF US "LOWER BEINGS."
THAT ENTIRE "TOP DOWN" CONCEPTION OF EXISTENCE MAKES NO SENSE, TO ME.
IT SEEMS MUCH MORE LIKELY THAT PATTERNS EMERGE "BOTTOM UP."
THAT OUT OF CHAOS COME COINCIDENCE.
AND WHERE THINGS STAY COINCIDED, ORDER BEGINS TO FORM.
THIS DOESN'T MAKE THESE THINGS, THESE PATTERNS, LESS REAL.
BUT IT DOES REPLACE INTENTION WITH PROCESS.
IT IS THE JOB OF AN ARTIST TO RECORD SUCH PATTERNS.
I FIND IT MORE LIKELY THAT THE RESONANCES WE SEE IN ALL OF THESE STRIPS REPRESENT THE PATTERNS, THE STANDARD CURRENTS THAT SOCIETY WAS FLOWING THROUGH AT THE TIME THESE STORIES WERE WRITTEN.
AN ARTIST CAN GET CAUGHT UP IN THE FLOW OF THE PATTERNS THEY EXPLORE.
AND IN DOING SO INVOKE THE CONSEQUENCES OF ENVY, PRIDE, LUST, HUBRIS, ETC.
I WONDER WHAT EXACTLY DAVE HAS INVOKED FOR HIMSELF, AND WORRY ABOUT WHAT WORKING WITH HIM MAY HAVE INVOKED WITHIN MY OWN LIFE.
MAYBE NOW HE'LL COME PLAY WITH ME!

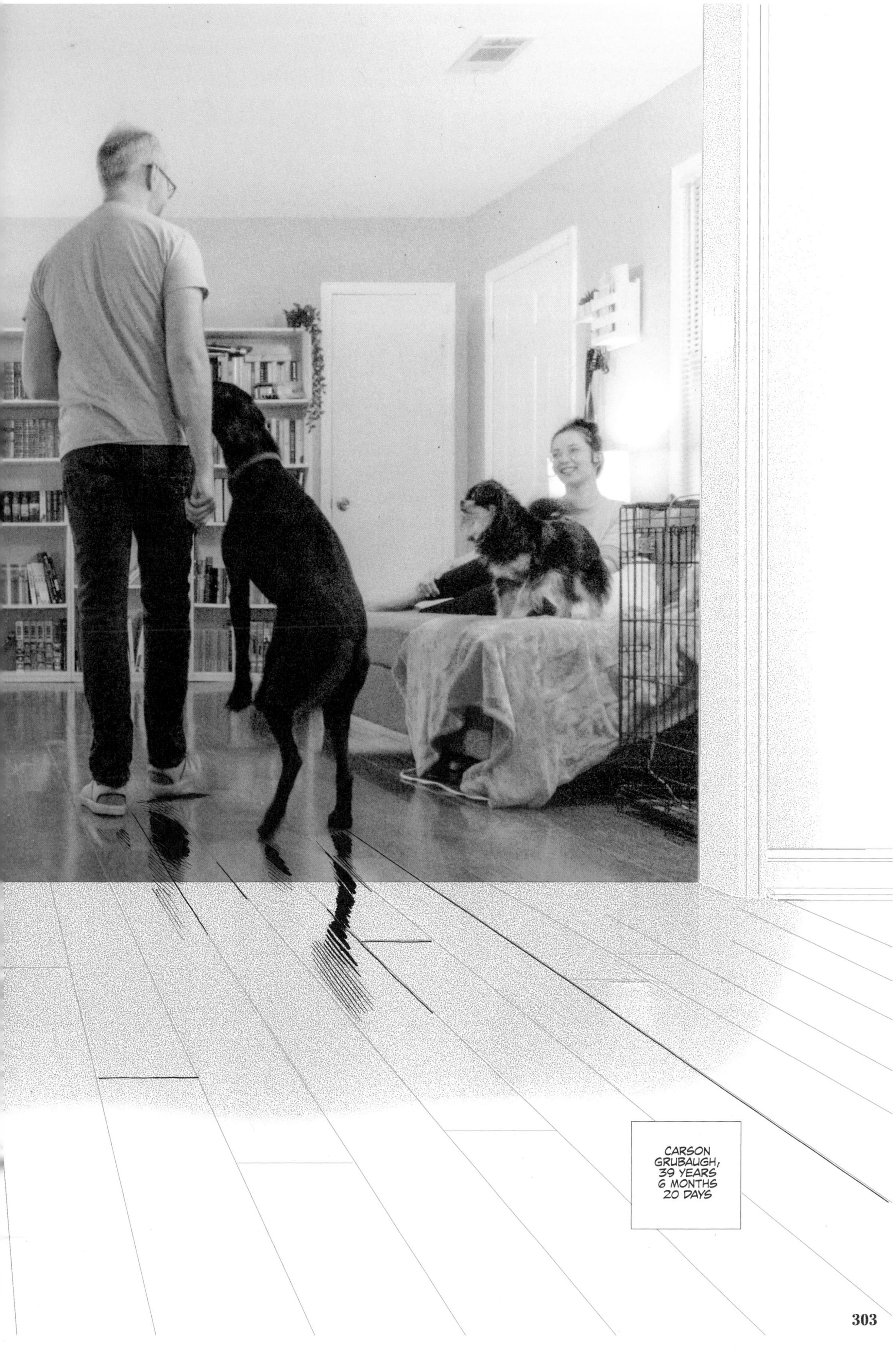
CARSON GRUBAUGH, 39 YEARS 6 MONTHS 20 DAYS

# a note on the artwork of *Strange Death*: an afterword by

# sean michael ROBINSON

## (Publisher/ Digital Lettering and Prepress)

What do you do when your first six-thousand-page comic is behind you?

As Sim relays at the start of this tome, *The Strange Death of Alex Raymond* — the graphic narrative, the obsession, the obsessive graphic novel — began in the pages of his comic book, *glamourpuss*. As an artist who labored under a monthly schedule for over twenty-six years on his groundbreaking title *Cerebus the Aardvark*, Sim would now take his time, narrative-free, drawing his favorite subjects in whatever manner he preferred. From the beginning, these subjects included recreations of panels from cartooning's golden age, along with commentaries and speculations about the artists' techniques and lives. And then that pesky narrative arrived on the scene. *glamourpuss* ran from April 2008 to July 2012, and the *Strange Death* concept and central narrative appeared and promulgated itself across those twenty six issues.

However, when Sim formally began *this* work, at the behest of Ted Adams, founder and then-head of comics publisher IDW, Sim jettisoned almost everything that had come before, choosing instead to redraw virtually every page with his newly-honed skills, and synthesizing and revising his story in the process. The majority of Sim's artwork for this project was drawn during that post-*glamourpuss* period, from 2012 through late 2014. Slowing to a pace of approximately fifty pages a year, he was able to meet the new exacting standards of rendering sophistication he had set for himself.

(It's up to posterity to decide the relative merits of the differing approaches. *glamourpuss*' leisurely pace certainly yielded some striking sequences, many of which have no parallel in the current volume, others which appear in a drastically reduced form. I think of the segment of issue 25 with Drake pressed to his hospital bed, unable to rise, ruminating on the crash and his previous nervous breakdown — expressive and vivid at six pages, with a tortured, rubbery-faced Drake, straining at the invisible weight above him — is here distilled to a potent single page, rendered with relative realism.)

I personally first became aware of Sim's newer, sleeker, more virile *Strange Death* in August of 2013. Though I had infrequently corresponded with Sim before that, and had on at least one occasion spent a pleasant hour on the phone with him discussing baseball comics, it was that fall that our correspondence switched venues, and took on a more urgent tone.

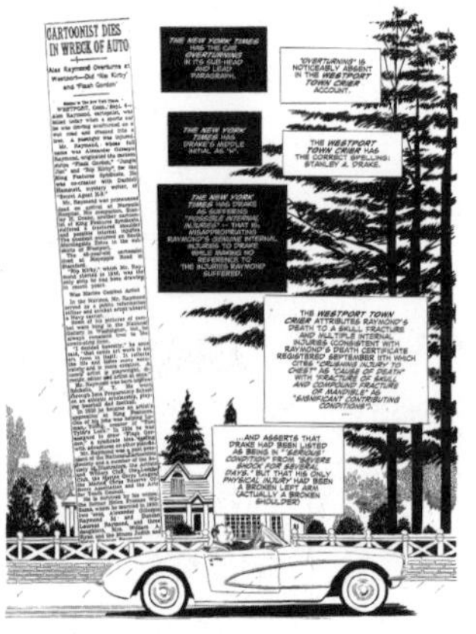
CARTOONIST DIES IN WRECK OF AUTO
THE NEW YORK TIMES HAS THE CAR OVERTURNING IN ITS SUB-HEAD AND LEAD PARAGRAPH.
"OVERTURNING" IS NOTICEABLY ABSENT IN THE WESTPORT TOWN CRIER ACCOUNT.
THE NEW YORK TIMES HAS DRAKE'S MIDDLE INITIAL AS "W".
THE WESTPORT TOWN CRIER HAS THE CORRECT SPELLING: STANLEY A. DRAKE.
THE NEW YORK TIMES HAS DRAKE AS SUFFERING "POSSIBLE INTERNAL INJURIES" -- THAT IS, MISAPPROPRIATING RAYMOND'S GENUINE INTERNAL INJURIES TO DRAKE WHILE MAKING NO REFERENCE TO THE INJURIES RAYMOND SUFFERED.
THE WESTPORT TOWN CRIER ATTRIBUTES RAYMOND'S DEATH TO A SKULL FRACTURE AND MULTIPLE INTERNAL INJURIES (CONSISTENT WITH RAYMOND'S DEATH CERTIFICATE REGISTERED SEPTEMBER 11TH WHICH CITES "CRUSHING INJURY TO CHEST" AS "CAUSE OF DEATH" WITH "FRACTURE OF SKULL AND COMPOUND FRACTURE OF MANDIBLE" AS "SIGNIFICANT CONTRIBUTING CONDITIONS").
...AND ASSERTS THAT DRAKE HAD BEEN LISTED AS BEING IN "SERIOUS CONDITION" FROM "SEVERE SHOCK FOR SEVERAL DAYS," BUT THAT HIS ONLY PHYSICAL INJURY HAD BEEN A BROKEN LEFT ARM (ACTUALLY A BROKEN SHOULDER)

12 glamourpuss MAY 2012

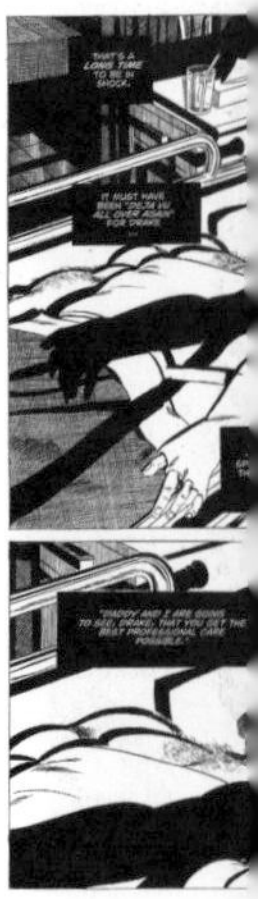
THAT'S A LONG TIME TO BE IN SHOCK.
IT MUST HAVE BEEN "DEJA VU ALL OVER AGAIN" FOR DRAKE
"DADDY AND I ARE GOING TO SEE, DRAKE, THAT YOU GET THE BEST PROFESSIONAL CARE POSSIBLE."

He was in the midst of a crisis of sorts, of the reproductive type. The print industry was at the tail end of a sea-change in the methods of print reproduction, and the newest two printings of Sim's first two *Cerebus* volumes were caught in the wake.

Sim's then-printer, Lebonfon, was in the process of decommissioning all of their photo-to-plate plate setters, bringing the era of optically-based printing to a close. No more would photography and photo negatives be used to create printing plates — all projects going forward, including any new *Cerebus* printings, would have to be supplied as digital files.

That process of converting the existing photo negatives to digital files is, like virtually all print processes, surrounded by jargon and misinformation, and fraught with peril. In this case, mismanagement of the digital files had left two *Cerebus* books "stranded on the tarmac"— thousands of copies of both books, with hopelessly flawed reproduction, left unbound, stored at the printer, awaiting payment and instructions. All told, about CA$24,000 of unusable printing, with no one willing to take blame for the situation, and no solution in sight.

This situation, discussed in public, and in great detail, on Tim Webber's *A Moment of Cerebus* blog, prompted me to reach out to Dave and send him several lengthy missives detailing the little bit I personally knew about digital reproduction at the time: the potential pitfalls, and potential solutions, to his expensive problem. And because this is Dave Sim we're talking about, these discussions were conducted via fax machine, via an ever-expanding tower of public words.

(Yes, the spartan environs pictured behind the narrator of *The Strange Death of Alex Raymond* are no graphic shorthand, no visual cheat — Sim does indeed live a solitary, streamlined life, corresponding with his collaborators almost exclusively by fax machine, no Internet service or email address in sight; how else do you think he stays this productive?)

A few weeks of public posting, a print test and a few hundred faxes later, I now found myself not just Sean Robinson, illustrator for hire, but the head of the "Cerebus Resoration project." Under this new identity, I set out on a multi-year mission to create new digital masters for the entire 6,000 page *Cerebus* epic, and to learn everything there is to know about digital line art reproduction in the process.

Weirdly enough (and fitting for the circles this story moves in), I first became interested

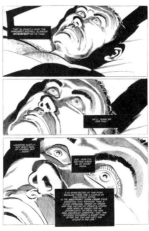

in image reproduction through reading Sim's own missives on the topic in *glamourpuss*. My very embryonic understanding of the topic guided my own prepress work (such as it was) on my own 2011 book, *Down in the Hole: the unWired World of H.B. Ogden* (co-written with Joy DeLyria, powerHouse books), where I had an opportunity to experience that most disconcerting of illustrator experiences: opening up a carton of books, and barely recognizing my own illustrations. "Where in the hell did all those teeny tiny lines go? Why is all the hatching a sort of nebulous gray tone??!" However tentative, these first experiences of mine were sufficient to develop enough knowledge to get me through those first few months of Cerebus restoration work, guiding the first few books to print and retaining more detail than ever before. Because, it turns out, when properly shepherded to press, using modern sheetfed-offset presses optimized for line art, digitally-created "masters" can bring a tremendous amount of detail to the page. (Even if you wouldn't know it looking at the majority of books that make it to market).

It was during that first year of the Cerebus Restoration project that Sim produced approximately fifty or sixty of the pages in this volume. Perhaps emboldened by the strides in reproduction the project had made, the evidence at hand that even the finest of lines could be captured, reduced, and duplicated into infinity, he poured on the detail, producing some of the most carefully-delineated, finely-rendered work of his career.

They would turn out to be some of the last pages he would ever produce, at least, to this date, and without immense pain.

The work came at a price. I was first aware something was amiss in December 2014, in a fax discussing the arrival of a large-format scanner at his house. He mentioned in an aside that he hadn't yet opened the scanner, because once he had used a boxcutter to do so, he would likely be unable to draw for several days afterwards. What seemed at first to me to be simple arthritis, developed into what has turned out to be a career-ending malady, as yet undiagnosed. Sim has lost much of the function in his right wrist, and since early 2015 has been unable to draw to his own standards, except in short, painful bursts. You can see the last page he was working on at the time of this collapse on page 207 of this volume (or to the right of this text).

In June of 2015, discussing his affliction and the fate of those stranded 180 or so pages already completed for this volume, I suggested that he continue the book as best as he was able. If the first part of the book documented his artistic progress, the art recreations a type of educating performance, then perhaps the second concluding section would document his decline.

As I said to him at the time:

*The way I see it, SDOAR, or the portions of it I've read in* glamourpuss, *anyway, fall into four intertwining threads. For the sake of convenience, let's call them —*

*1. the forensic narrative*
*2. the metaphysical narrative*
*3. the technical and stylistic explication/"tool talk" (discussion of evolving style and tool use)*
*4. the Performance (teaching yourself to think and ink in those same styles)*

*Furthermore, I'd say that the first two categories relate to each other in a way that roughly corresponds with how the second two categories relate to each other. Your metaphysical extrapolations are your contribution to the forensic narrative, above and beyond "who did what," just as the technical analysis speaks to and is changed by your re-drawing the panels themselves even while you're analyzing them, and then using those same skills to illustrate the narrative.*

*Okay, having set up these categories, and knowing full well you might see my categorization here as presumptuous, ridiculous, or some combination of the two [...]*

*If the narrative aspect is the most important part to you—both the forensic narrative and the metaphysical narrative—then illustrating that narrative in a way that can be easily read would seem to be the most important objective. If you could, for instance, pencil, but inking was too physically demanding, then you could hire an inker. I know, not a real revelation—but I think I have a method that would make it much easier to 1) try people out, and 2) not be locked into that one solution if you have a full recovery.*

*Last week I did some freelance illustration that involved a lot of revisions. Some of the revisions I accomplished through digital manipulation of my pencils. Afterwards I inked it using a technique I learned from David Lasky when I helped ink his Carter Family book— printing the pencils using cyan only, on special art board that has a smooth surface but is thin enough to pass through a printer. [...] So I could scan the inked page in Photoshop, drop out the cyan channel, and voila, an inked original that's preserved your pencil original.*

*Of course, finding an inker would be quite the task, but not impossible, I think. I do have a few ideas. (It might have other consequences, though—for instance, I could see your pencils occupying more of your time if you're having to indicate every nuance of shadow in a way you might not inking yourself. It might defeat the purpose if you're having to work harder to carry the help.)*

*Conversely, if your hand recovers enough to ink, but fine lines prove impossible, you could prepare your pencils at the normal size, and I could send [a local printer] oversized cyan files. So, pencils normal size, and you executing the inks much larger than before, at whatever size might be ergonomic.*

*Okay. If the performance aspect is more important to you than the narrative aspect, then I would suggest doing what you've already suggested — complete the book at whatever level you're capable of. Fully-inked pages turn into pencil roughs with lettering and clippings, and then even rougher roughs, until what's left at the end of the story is the text on the page. For a book largely about process, and personal development, I could see this being a very fitting way to tackle the problem.*

However, Sim's vision of the book focused less on the performative thread than the narrative one, and unbeknownst to me, he was soon on the hunt for an artist to work with him on the "framing sequence" needed to "complete" the first volume (as originally conceived).

Painter and college art instructor Carson Grubaugh answered the call — once again, via blog — a surprisingly-frequent event given Sim's lack of Internet use! As work progressed on those pages (the "Jack" pages of this volume), it soon became clear to Grubaugh that Sim intended him to take over as the artist for the remainder of the work. (Now just *how much* work, exactly, remained ... and at what pace it would be published ... well, those would turn out to be their own complex questions!)

All of that is is not to say that page 207 is the last page of Sim drawing in this volume. Sim drew page 230 solo (at great cost to his wrist! Excerpt below.). He also continued to create incidental drawing for the layouts supplied to Grubaugh, including several elements that were scanned and incorporated into the actual finished pages. Whereas Grubaugh had drawn the "framing sequence" pages largely in the "normal" method — sans word balloons, but otherwise intact pages — the later pages feature more fragmentary original artwork, as both Sim and Grubaugh learned to exploit the digital process to its fullest.

And of course, when NOT to exploit the strengths of digital. For instance, with the exceptions of the latter section of the book, more on which in a moment, all of the "sampled" panels and pages were recreated by Sim or Grubaugh for this volume. In the case of both artists, the recreations featured in the book represent a small fraction of this "study" work, most of which, invisible, went into the development of their individual

rendering abilities.

Even at the very beginning Sim has always been a sampler, a magpie extraordinaire, but here the technique turns inwards on itself, the recreations creating the narrative shaping the page that houses the recreations... a spiral of influence, leading ever-inward.

You can get a better sense of Sim's remarkable layouts in the latter section of this volume, where they are presented as received, excepting the digital lettering, and some rough placement sketches by Grubaugh which have been incorporated into the image. You can also see some examples of the drawing Sim incorporated into his layouts for Grubaugh, creating panel borders, decorative motifs, and drawings intended to demonstrate desired rendering techniques. The spread on pages 272 and 273 is a good example of the latter, where Sim demonstrates that, rather than straight recreations, the enlarged panels at the lower left and right of the spread are intended to be rendered with hatching that lightens in density the larger the enlargement. (This rather interesting technique, used in varying ways throughout the book, is an elaboration on a technique pioneered by Sim for the *Form and Void* portion of *Cerebus,* within which Sim and his then-collaborator Gerhard used large master drawings that they expanded and excerpted with the aid of their photocopier, adding finer and finer detail to each successive enlargement.)

Grubaugh took over the main work on the book on page 208. (You'll note post-injury Sim appears in a wrist brace, which the real-life Sim uses on a daily basis to keep the strain of his affliction to a minimum.) Unlike Sim, Grubaugh knew from the start of the work that every little scratch on the paper would show up in print, a fact attested to by his increasingly-minute rendering.

More than once while working on this book, it occurred to me how odd its actual production has been. A visually stunning book, using the latest techniques of digital image reproduction, testing the limits of sheetfed offset printing, was drawn by hand, graphite and fine soot, and layed out, for the most part, on an a all-in-one prosumer photocopier/fax machine, the digital lettering slavishly following the paste-up guide lettering of Sim's own pages, and later, layouts.

I think now of how often Sim returned to the impossibility of reproduction of Raymond's artwork in his own time: how, with the crude cameras and the multiple generations and the newsprint ink expansion, there was never any hope of capturing those teeny tiny lines. Raymond, Sim seems to be saying, didn't so much draw *for* reproduction as draw *against* it.

But why? And for whom? For himself? For the fortunate few who would get to see his artwork in person? Just because he could? Just because, quite clearly, nobody else could?

I think of this Raymond, the Raymond of Sim's imagining, and I picture him in the world of today, and I wonder what, if any, artwork he would be creating. What challenge he'd be chasing.

How would one one-up the man who drew the best lines just for himself?

— Sean Michael Robinson, March 2021

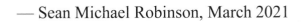

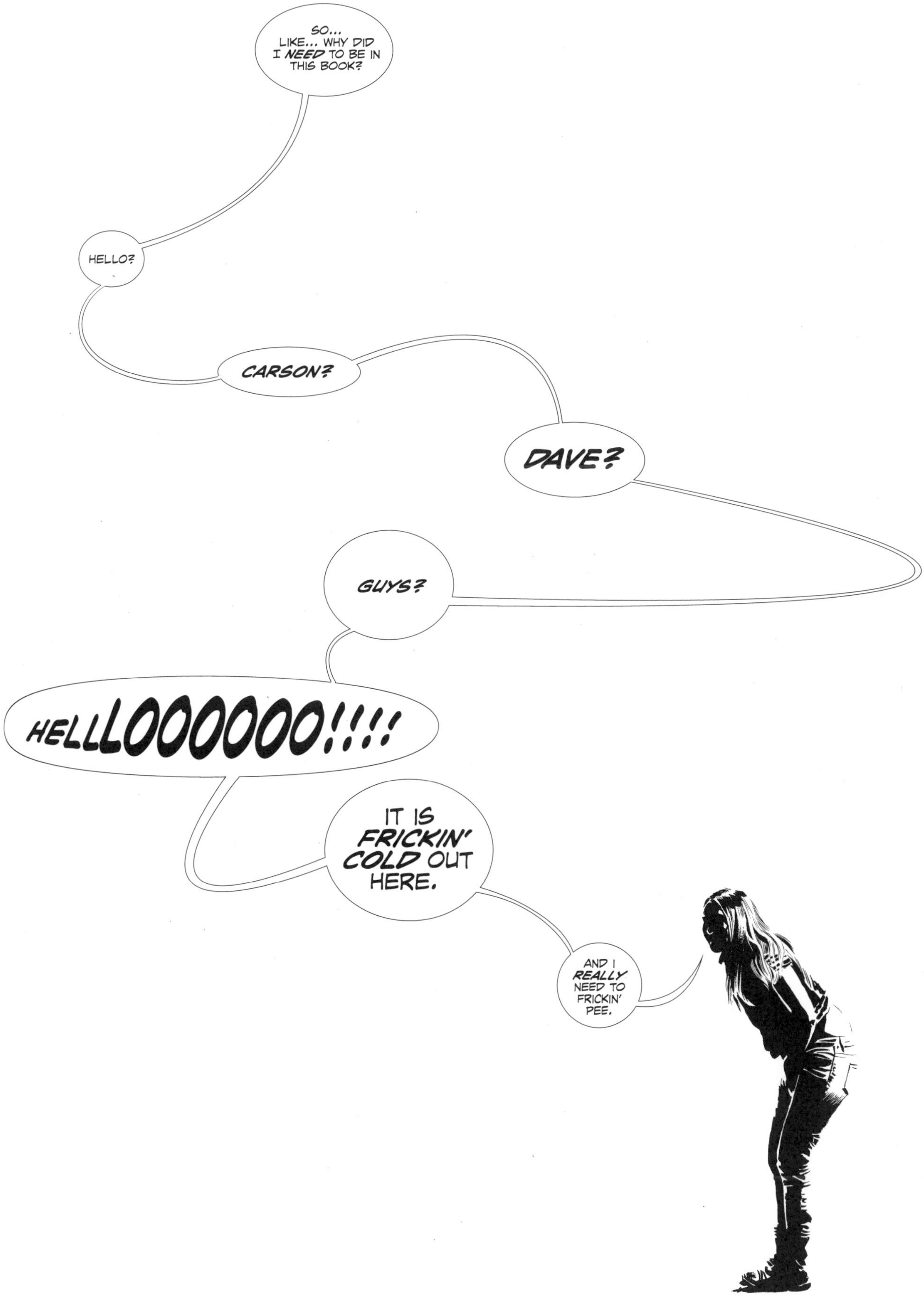
SO... LIKE... WHY DID I NEED TO BE IN THIS BOOK?
HELLO?
CARSON?
DAVE?
GUYS?
HELLLOOOOOO!!!!
IT IS FRICKIN' COLD OUT HERE.
AND I REALLY NEED TO FRICKIN' PEE.

**David Victor SIM** is the author, cartoonist, and publisher of *Cerebus the Aardvark*, a groundbreaking independent comic which ran from December 1977 to March 2004. In 2018 he was entered into The Guinness Book of World Records for "most consecutive issues of a comic book written and drawn". The series, which largely followed the life of the titular character, was noted for its exquisitely-rendered art and stylistic flexibility, its novelistic character development and story arcs, and bold violations of audience expectations. During the run of the series, Sim was awarded an Eisner award for Best Graphic Album (Flight, 1994), a Harvey award for "Best Cartoonist" (1992), an Ignatz award for "Outstanding Artist" (1998), a Joe Shuster award for "Outstanding Comic Book Achievement" (2005), and two Kirby awards for "Best Black & White Series" (in both 1985 and 1987). Throughout his career Sim has advocated for self-publishing as a means of securing both creative and financial freedom for comic creators. His influence, mentoring and advocacy led to a wave of self-publishing throughout the 1980s and 1990s, prompting such notable (and distinct) self-published works as *From Hell* (Alan Moore and Eddie Campbell) *A Distant Soil* (Colleen Doran), and *Teenage Mutant Ninja Turtles* (Kevin Eastman and Peter Laird).

From 2005 to 2015, Sim spent the majority of his work time at the drawing board, studying the rendering techniques of several decades' worth of early comics luminaries, including Al Williamson, Stan Drake, Neal Adams, Jeff Jones and – foremost of all – Alex Gillespie Raymond. These early photorealism experiments saw print in the 26-issue fashion parody/tribute all-in-one comic *glamourpuss* (2008-2012). After having drawn approximately 180 pages of *The Strange Death of Alex Raymond*, he was struck with a mysterious wrist ailment that has left him unable to draw, except in short, painful bursts. He now spends his work time writing *Cerebus in Hell?*, a gag strip that he began (with Sandeep Atwal) in 2016.

He gives equal weight to Judaism, Christianity, and Islam in his extremely devout religious observance.

Sim currently resides in Kitchener, Ontario, around the corner from a proposed "Safe" Injection Site. This is just as delightful as you might imagine.

**Carson GRUBAUGH** earned an MFA in Painting from the Cranbrook Academy of Art as well as BFAs in Fine Art and Philosophy from the University of California at Berkeley. He was named the Mercedes Benz Financial Services Emerging Artist of 2011, was a keynote speaker at the 2013 Difference That Makes a Difference Conference at the Open University, placed 3rd in the 15th Art Renewal Center Salon portraiture category, and has shown in the US, Germany, England at venues such as The Cranbrook Museum of Art, Kunstlerhaus Bethanien, ABTART, Virginia Beach Museum of Contemporary Art, The Chrysler Museum, Museum of New Art, Sotheby's NY and the European Museum of Modern Art among many others.

Carson is currently a Full-Time Instructor of Art at Shelton State Community College in Tuscaloosa, Alabama.

We can't figure out why he is spending time drawing comics.

# the many patrons of *Strange Death*: without whom!
# the CONTRIBUTORS
## (In which we thank the 642 Backers of the STRANGE DEATH Kickstarter)

Jason Abbott
James Abel
Mazen Abuelenain
Dan Ackerman
acnepirate
Anthony W Acosta
Matt Acosta
Ted Adams
Clay Adams
Hassan Alamdari
Christian Albrecht
Chris Allingham
Beanbag Amerika
Lyn Anderson
Leif Anderson
anonymous
aoife and ryan
Ger Apeldoorn
David L. Applegate CFA-APA
Douglas Arthur
Jay Austin
Eric Bahringer
Alex Barber
Eric Barley
James Barron
andrew bartel
Matt Battaglia
Derek Bauman
David Beale
Michael Beckett
Olav Beemer
Jeffrey Benn
Brian A. Berkey
Philip Berkheimer Jr.
Michael Besser
Mark Bilokur
David Birdsong
Doug Bissell
Stephen R. Bissette
Tom Bither
Garrick Bjur
Colin Blanchette
Eric Blanchette
Critical Blast
Stefan Blitz
Mark "boomboom"
   Bloom
Stephen Bolhafner
Bunsen Bonezone
Scott Bradbury

Scott Bradley
P.M. Bradshaw
Charlie Brannan
Mihail Braila
David Branstetter
Mark Brett
Tom Brevoort
Brian
Denis Britvan
Brmk
Keith Brown
Hollie L. Buchanan II
Kirt Burdick
Tim Burdick
Will Burgdorf
Barry Burris
Adam Burton
Mark Byzewski
Caba
Liam Christopher
Cairney
Chris Call
Keith Callbeck
Carlos Garcia Campillo
Tony Canepa
J. Kevin Carrier
David Carrington
Rene Castellano
Ryan Center
Matt Cettei
Raf Cevallos
cfp33pfc
Luis Tenorio Chacon
Bob Chapman
Chickadee
Prestigious Chis-Wahh
Jon Chua
Steve Chung
Michelangelo Cicerone
Michael Cichy
David Cilley
Michael Clark
Greg Clausen
James Colclough
Mitchell Coleman
Will Collier
Speeding Bullet Comics
Henry G. Franke III
Mark Cooper
Jarret Cooper

Lou Copeland
Jay Cordray
Thomas Corhern
Mike Costa
Alec Coxe
Gary Craig
Jim M. Cripps
Arthur Crudup
Bobby D.
B'jamin da Bass
Randall Dahlk
Russel Dalenberg
Stefan Damian
Scott Davis
Daryl Davis
José de Leon
Karl DeGraide
Mike DeLisa
Shawn Demumbrum
Stephen Dennis
Barry Deutsch
Tim Devine
Rose and Jameson
   Devine
Jennifer DiGiacomo
Nik Dirga
Arcturus Dobrica
Sascha Doerp
Kevin Donahoe
Andrew Donkin
Kerry Donny-Clark
Susan Dorne
Manly Matt Dow
Dominic Duggan
Adrian Duma
Edu
Jarek Ejsymont
Alex Eklund
Gregory Elder
Josh Elder
Daniel Elvén
Terry Emery
Lee Emmel
Lionel English
Famous Comics
Conrad Felber
Dr Michael A Feldman
Agostino Filice
Nathan Fischer
Benjamin Fischer

Dave Fisher
Alex Fitch
Jeffrey Flam
Victor Flores III
Claude Flowers
Robbie Foggo
Bob Ford
Forgerelli
Cory Foster
Shane Foulds
Four Corners Collectibles
Henry G. Franke III
Kenneth J. Franklin
Kirk Fredrichs
Philip R. Frey
Ulrich Fricke
Stephen Friedt
Matt G
Neil Gaiman
Tim Gagne
Rich Gaspers Jr
George Peter Gatsis
Jim Gaudet
Rick Gaydos
James Gershkoff
Richard Paul Glass
Mike Goffee
meat is good
Michael Grabowski
Graham Crackers Comics
Hrvoje Grahovac
Diana Green
Gavin "Strangely Alive"
   Greene
Adam Greene
Sanford Greene
Gregory Griffith
Jeffrey Grill
Joe Gualtieri
Robert Guffey
Craig Gunderson
J Haller
Bill Halliar II
John P Hanna
Chad Hansen
Justin c. Hargrove
Scott Harriman
Kevin Harrison
HashedZ
Christopher Hass

Fred Hasselman
Philip Haxo
TED HAYCRAFT
Simple Heady
Adam C. Hernandez
Jesse Lee Herndon
John Herndon Jr
Karl-Heinz Herrmann
Ryan Hertel
Patrick Hess
Jason Heystek
Max & Nora Heystek
Christopher Hill
David Hines
Eric Hoffman
Simon Hogg
Wally Holland
Rodney Holmes
Jeremy B. Holstein
Carl Hommel
Dan House
Dale Houston
Keith Howell
Ben Huang
Michael Hunt
Robert Hunter
D.J. Inzeo
Brad Ireland
Christopher Irving
HO SHIK FU ISAAC
Trevor Jackson
Mr. Phil Jackson
Sean Jackson and
   JJ Wynne
JA&FER
Luke Jaconetti
Harley Jebens
Benjam Jenkins
Joe
Doug Johnson
Will Johnson
Glenn Johnson
Sir Jon
anne jones
Omaya Jones
Brian C. Jones
Michael A Jones
Michel Juilliard
Matthew Kaplowitz
Ken Karlinchak

Michael Kassab
gary katelansky
David Kavin
Alexx Kay
David Keith
KevinR
Eddie Khanna
Kibbonafide
Damian Kilby
Randall Kirby
Ryan Kirk
Jim "DC Books"
    Kirkland
Donnovan Knight
Mark Tyler Knights
James Kosmicki
John Kyritsis
Jason L
Jeramy Lamanno
Robert H Lambert
Jairred Lambert
Bruno "The Hatchet"
    Langoozie
Dave Lanphear
Peter Lanphier
Andrew Lariviere
Seth A. Larson
Ron Lasner
Scott Lazerus
Ben Le Foe
Douglas Leather
Robert Lee
Xander Lee
Donald Leflar
Denis Leining
Ben LeMaster
Stephen C. Lentz
Martyn Lesbirel
Stewart Levine
Robert Levinson
Steven Lifland
Margaret Liss
Chas Lobdell
Jay Lofstead
Andrew Lohmann
Geoffrey Long
Michael C Lorah
Jeff Lorentz
Will Lorenzo
Michael Lucas
Taras Lukianov
Wes Lunsford
Geoffrey J. Luu
Glen McFerren M.D.
Joshua Magady
Heinz J. Malcharzyk
Seth Manhammer
Dirk Manning

JOE MANNING
Ravenel Mansfield
Constantine Markopoulos
Jim Martin
Norbert Martin
Nick May
Joel Mayer
Douglas W. McCratic
John McDonald
DeLane McDuffie
Tim McEwen
Glen McFerren, M.D.
David McHale
Greg McKee
Paul Mckenzie
Johnny McPhanbot
Aaron McPherson
Robert Melendrez
Dave Melik
Jacqui Mercado
Ray Mescallado
Christopher Meyer
Mike
Rian Miller
Jason Miller
Tom Mohan
Thomas Monk
Brett Monro
Matthew Moran
John Morgan
Jacob Morgan
Seth Morris
Anthony Morris
John Mosher
Wayne Mousseau
Patrick Mulderig
Frankie Mundens
Matthew PL Murphy
Logan Murray
carmine nappi
Dug Nation
Robert Neill
Stuart Ng
NHB
Clark Nichols
Paul Nicholson
Mike Nielsen
Rocco Nigro
Walt Parrish
[ninesquareinches.com]
Patrick O'Connor
Brian O'Malley
+Nate+ Oberstein
Pablis Octotocto
Mike Ortiz
Cristiano Osti
Liam Otten
Nathaniel Palant

Richard Palfreyman
Tom Palmer Jr
Woogie Woogie and
Happy Monkey Pants
Kevin Parichan
Brian Parker
Dan Parker
Walt Parrish
Xris Parsell
Michael Vincent Partsch
Tom Peirce
Travis Pelkie
Scott Pemberton
Jason Penney
Andrew Pepoy
Gian Petersen
Michael G. Pfefferkorn
David Phelps
PhilFTW
James Phillips
Robert Pieschel
Kyle Pinion
John R. Platt
Jp Pollard
Alex Ponomareff
Rob Poole
Carlos Portela Orjales
PossumGrease
Vitas Povilaitis
Ángel Prieto
Superfan Promotions
Ryan Q
Jason Radak
Michael Ragiel
David Rains
Jacobo Ramirez
David Rankin
Mitch Rashkin
Brian Ray
Nolan Reese
Dean Reeves
Peter Reineke
Robert Renton
Steve Replogle
Joshua Riehl
Weslie Riggs
JR Riley
Paul Ripley
Curtis Rissmiller
Bill Ritter
Murray Roach
Chiharu Roach
M. Jason Robards
Kevin Robinson
Alex Robinson
Ken Rokos
Shane Rollins
Al Roney

Erik Rose
Diane Rose
Tony R. Rose
Marc Rouleau
Jonathan Rowe
Chris Ryall
Jason Sacks
Robin Sambhi
Dave Samuelson
Robert B. Sanchez
Steve & Beckey Sanchez
Giacomo Santangelo
Noah Satern
Niko Saunders
Adam Schechter
Florian Schiffmann
Jeff Schlesinger
Mark Schmidt
Rodney Schroeter
Martin Schwartz
Dave Scott
Matthew Scullin
Jeff Seiler
Bob Selig
Richard "The Chubtoad"
    Sheldon
Larry Shell
Ryan Sherwood
Bobby Shih
Barry Short
Jörg Sicher
Raphael Frederico Silva
Shannon Slayton
John Slevin
DJ Sloofus
Jason Gates Smith
Andy Smith
Keith William Smith
Rick Smith
Max Smith
Ted Sobel
Sid Sondergard
Oystein Sorensen
Mark Speidel
Kirk & Mindy Spencer
Jackson Star
J Scott Stewart
Carol Stoddard
Kurt Stoskopf
Tim Stroup
Ross Wood Studlar
Anthony Summey
Steve Swenson
Switch
Andy Switzky
Guy Tal
Seth D. Talley
Lee Thacker

Dan Theodore
Sam Thielman
Alan Thomas
Kenneth Thomas
Jonathan Thompson
Damin Toell
Jeffrey I. Tokman
Tom
Marty Trengove
Jason Trimmer
Dion Turner
Bill Turner
Lou Valenti
Adam Paul Vales
Campfire Vampire
Adrien van Viersen
Christopher Vandegrift
Brian Vanhook
Dan Veltre
Jan Verdegaal
Mark Verheiden
John Ver Linden
Robbie Vermillion
Jon Vinson
Scott W
Jason Wade
David A Wade
Mark Waid
David F Walker
Cowboy Wally
Bryan Walman
L Jamal Walton
Shannon Wash
Brian Weaver
Tim Webber
Earl Weiss
WellDressedGandalf
Sean Whelan
Jonathan A. White
Dan Wickett
Jason Willdermood
Andrew Wilshusen
Brian Wimoweh
Leonard S Wong
Brett A. Wood
Maxim Wood
Randy Wood
Larry Wooten
Benjamin F. Wormser
Wess Worth
Daniel M. Yang
John D. Young
David Young
Tobey Zehr
Zane Zielinski
Bob Zupancic

RANGE DEATH OF ALEX RAYMOND:
the ANNOTATIONS

# THE STRANGE DEATH OF ALEX RAYMOND: the ANNOTATIONS

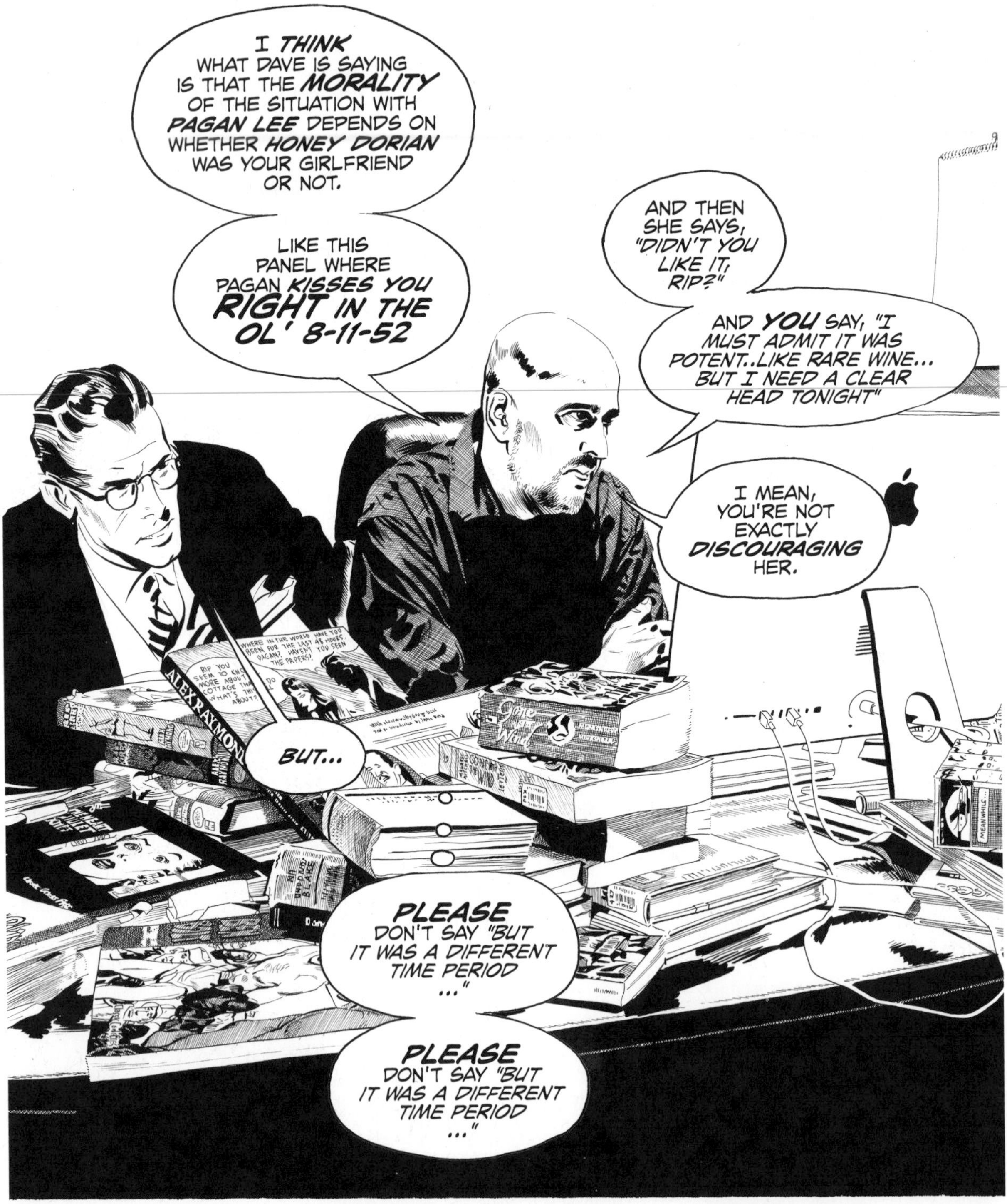
I THINK WHAT DAVE IS SAYING IS THAT THE MORALITY OF THE SITUATION WITH PAGAN LEE DEPENDS ON WHETHER HONEY DORIAN WAS YOUR GIRLFRIEND OR NOT.
LIKE THIS PANEL WHERE PAGAN KISSES YOU RIGHT IN THE OL' 8-11-52
AND THEN SHE SAYS, "DIDN'T YOU LIKE IT, RIP?"
AND YOU SAY, "I MUST ADMIT IT WAS POTENT..LIKE RARE WINE... BUT I NEED A CLEAR HEAD TONIGHT"
I MEAN, YOU'RE NOT EXACTLY DISCOURAGING HER.
BUT...
PLEASE DON'T SAY "BUT IT WAS A DIFFERENT TIME PERIOD ..."
PLEASE DON'T SAY "BUT IT WAS A DIFFERENT TIME PERIOD ..."

**DAVE SIM & EDDIE KHANNA's SDOAR.com**

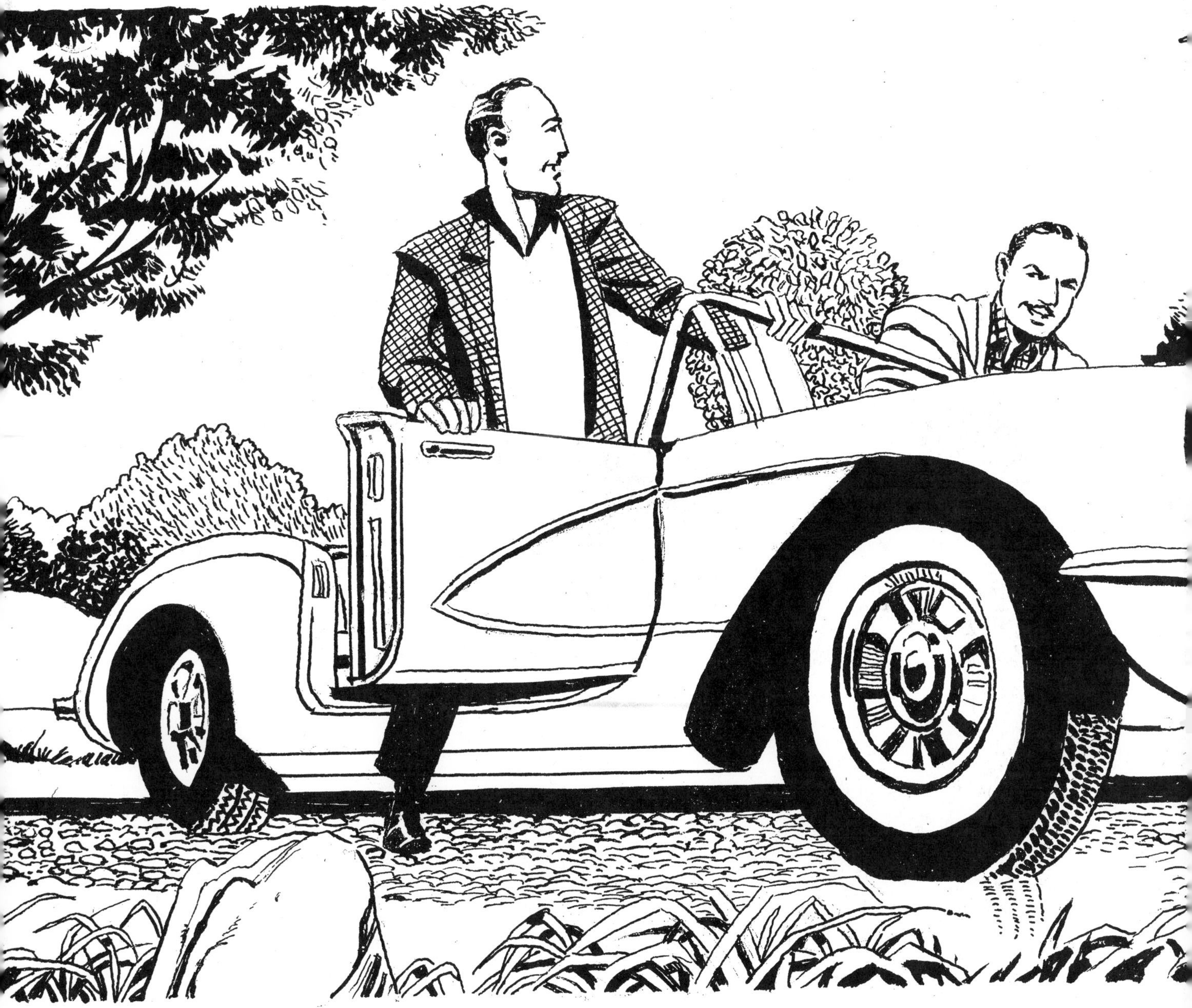

# living th

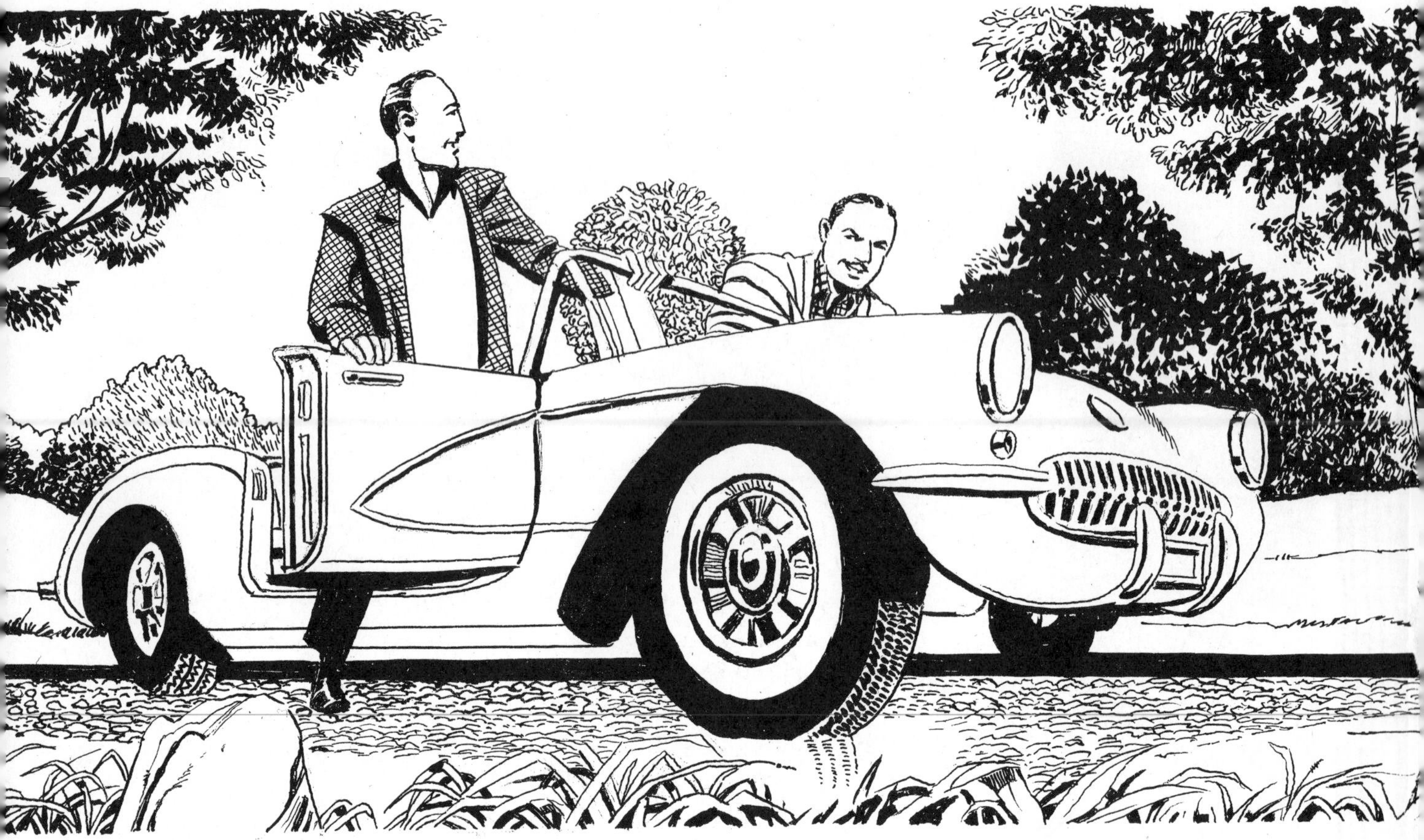

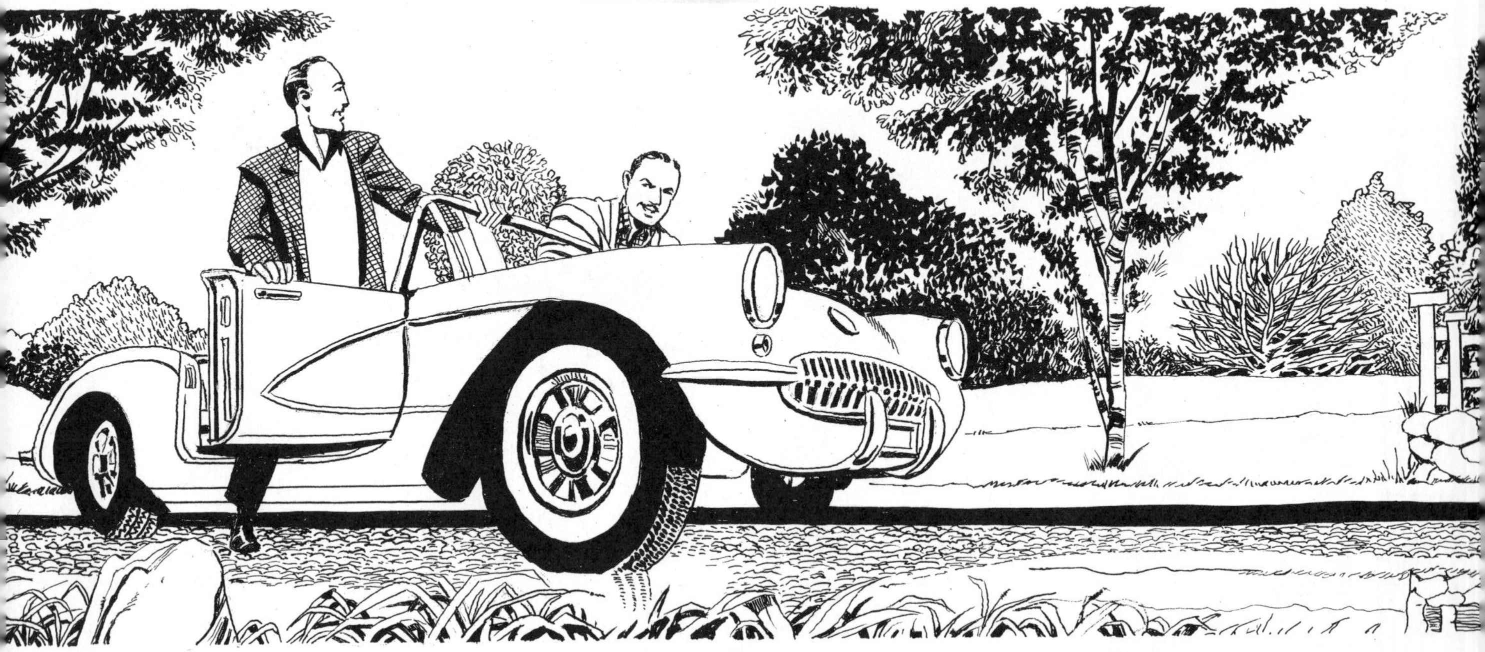

# living the LINE

The Strange Death of Alex Raymond, published fall 2021. San Diego, CALIFORNIA